Does Law Matter?

On Law and Economic Growth

Editors:
Michael Faure
Jan Smits

Does Law Matter?

On Law and Economic Growth

intersentia

METRO

Ius Commune Europaeum

Editors:
Michael Faure
Jan Smits

Does Law Matter?
On Law and Economic Growth

Intersentia Ltd
Trinity House | Cambridge Business Park | Cowley Road
Cambridge | CB4 0WZ | United Kingdom
mail@intersentia.co.uk

ISBN 978-94-000-0217-3
D/2011/7849/94

Michael Faure
Jan Smits

PREFACE

This book is the 100th volume of the Ius Commune Europaeum series. This jubilee issue calls for a special topic. The editorial board of the Ius Commune series therefore decided to devote this special volume to the question of 'Does law matter'? This title refers to one of the most discussed questions in social science of the last decade: to what extent can differences in economic development be explained by differing law and institutions in various countries? According to the 'legal origins'-thesis, the answer is clear: it claims that differences in economic performance are to a large extent dependent on whether a country belongs to the civil law or common law family. Others have severely criticised this thesis. This book takes stock of the debate and attempts to offer an integrated approach that not only takes into account the insights of economics, but also of comparative law and empirics. It thus captures what the Ius Commune Europaeum series is known for: to apply a comparative and interdisciplinary approach to real life-questions.

This book serves several purposes. Its main aim is of course to present contributions from a range of world class-authors on the important question of what is the relationship between law and economic growth and on which more details can be found in the Introduction. These contributions will be formally presented and discussed at a conference to be held at the Royal Netherlands Academy of Arts and Sciences (KNAW) on 21 October 2011. At the same time, this volume serves to celebrate not only the 100th volume of the Ius Commune Europaeum series, but also to mark two other events.

The first of these is the 20th anniversary of the Maastricht European Institute for Transnational Legal Research (METRO).[1] METRO started its activities on 1 September 1991. Its goal has been from the start to promote the European, comparative and international research undertaken within the Maastricht Faculty of Law. To further that aim it launched the Ius Commune Europaeum book series of which the first volume was published by Intersentia[2] in 1993. Furthermore, METRO has also been

1 See <www.maastrichtuniversity.nl/metro>.
2 See <www.intersentia.be>.

hosting the Ius Commune Research School[3] since its founding in 1995. The Research School is a collaboration between researchers from the Katholieke Universiteit Leuven (Belgium) and the law faculties of Maastricht, Amsterdam and Utrecht (the Netherlands) where academics do joint research on the role of law in integration processes. The question to what extent law matters to this integration process (and to achieve other goals) has been at the core of the research of both the Ius Commune Research School and the Maastricht Faculty of Law.

The second event is the founding of the Maastricht European Private Law Institute (M-EPLI), that started its activities on 1 January 2011.[4] M-EPLI does research in the field of integration processes with an emphasis on the role of private actors. It hosts researchers in the field of European private law in the broad sense (including European contract law, property law, tort law, procedural law and legal theory). M-EPLI is part of an effort of the Maastricht Faculty of Law to streamline its research in small institutes aimed at doing high-level and internationally relevant research in the field of law and related areas.

This book could not have been made without the enthusiastic collaboration of our authors. They were all willing to contribute on a relatively short notice, for which we are immensely grateful. We are also grateful to Marina Jodogne and Marjo Mullers, not only for their excellent editorial assistance in preparing this volume, but also for their quintessential superb role in the editing of the entire Ius Commune Europaeum series. This is also the place to thank the publisher on behalf of the entire editorial board (next to ourselves consisting of Ellen Vos, Jacques Du Plessis and Christian Joerges): we are grateful to Intersentia and in particular to Kris Moeremans as the responsible publisher for almost twenty years of commitment to our series. Finally, thanks are due to the Royal Netherlands Academy of Arts and Sciences (KNAW) for its willingness to support this project and for the grant it provided us with to organise the October conference.

The contribution co-authored by John Armour, Simon Deakin, Viviana Mollica and Mathias Siems is reproduced here with the kind permission of the authors and of Brigham Young University Law Review.

Maastricht, August 2011
The editors

3 See <www.iuscommune.eu>.

4 See <www.maastrichtuniversity.nl/mepli>.

TABLE OF CONTENTS

LIST OF CONTRIBUTORS

John Armour, Hogan Lovells Professor of Law and Finance at the University of Oxford

Robert D. Cooter, Herman F. Selvin Professor of Law at the UC Berkeley School of Law

Bertrand Crettez, Professor of Economics at the Université Pantheon-Assas (Paris II)

Giuseppe Dari-Mattiacci, Professor of Law and Economics at the Amsterdam Center for Law and Economics, University of Amsterdam

Simon Deakin, Robert Monks Professor of Corporate Governance at the University of Cambridge

Bruno Deffains, Professor of Economics at the Université Pantheon-Assas (Paris II)

Julan Du, Associate Professor of Economics at the Department of Economics, Chinese University of Hong Kong

Michael Faure, Professor of International and Comparative Environmental Law at Maastricht University, and Professor of Comparative Private Law and Economics at the Erasmus School of Law Rotterdam

Nuno Garoupa, Professor of Law, the H. Ross and Helen Workman Research Scholar and Co-Director of the Illinois Program in Law, Behaviour and Social Science at the University of Illinois at Urbana-Champaign

Carlos Gómez Ligüerre, Associate Professor of Private Law at the Universitat Pompeu Fabra

Carmine Guerriero, Assistant Professor Research Program: Foundations of Law and Economics at the Amsterdam Center for Law and Economics, University of Amsterdam

Eric Helland, Professor of Economics at the Claremont McKenna College

Jonathan Klick, Professor of Law at the University of Pennsylvania Law School

Guillaume Leyte, Professor of Legal History at the Université Pantheon-Assas (Paris II)

Ralf Michaels, Professor of Law at the Duke University School of Law

Viviana Mollica, Lecturer in Company Law at Queen Mary, University of London

Anthony Ogus, Emeritus Professor at the University of Manchester and Erasmus School of Law Rotterdam

Alessio M. Pacces, Associate Professor of Law and Economics at the Erasmus School of Law Rotterdam

Laurent Pfister, Professor of Legal History at the Université Pantheon-Assas (Paris II)

Mathias M. Siems, Professor of Commercial Law at Durham University

Hans-Bernd Schäfer, Affiliate Professor of Law and Economics at the Bucerius Law School, Hamburg

Jan Smits, Professor of European Private Law at Maastricht University

Tom Ulen, Swanlund Chair Emeritus at the University of Illinois at Urbana-Champaign, Professor Emeritus of Law at the University of Illinois College of Law, and Former Director of the Illinois Program in Law and Economics and the Illinois Program in Law, Behavioural, and Social Sciences

Guangdong Xu, Associate Professor of Law and Economics at the China University of Political Science, and Law, and Erasmus School of Law Rotterdam

Michael Faure
Jan Smits

INTRODUCTION*

1. Increasing Relevance

This book addresses the importance of institutions in economic development and in particular the role of law for economic growth. There are at least three different reasons why this topic is increasingly relevant from both an academic and a practical perspective.

First, we have seen in the last fifteen years the emergence of a strong economic scholarship pointing at the importance of law for economic development. This literature suggests not only that law is highly relevant in the development of countries, but also that particular legal systems do better than others. Thus, the so-called legal origins-thesis claims that the economic performance of a country is largely the result of that country's legal system and in particular of how this legal system has come about. Economic indicators would show that in particular common law countries are economically more developed, or at least better suited to the interests of business, than civil law countries.[1] According to this thesis, the main explanation for this phenomenon would lie in the fact that civil law countries are more geared towards State intervention whereas common law countries better facilitate the market economy.[2]

This legal origins-thesis was developed in a number of articles by economists Rafael La Porta, Andrei Shleifer and others.[3] Their original thesis was limited to the field of corporate governance, showing that if legal rules on protection of investors (shareholders) are measured, they show differences that correlate systematically with the legal traditions in which these rules find their origins, common law coun-

* The editors are grateful to Marina Jodogne and Marjo Mullers for excellent editorial assistance.

1 This claim as such is not entirely new. Already in the first edition (1972) of Posner 2011 the argument is made that many doctrines of the common law induce efficient behaviour, in particular because of the fact that the law is judge-made.

2 Cf. La Porta, Lopez-De Silanes & Shleifer 2008, p. 286.

3 La Porta *et al.* 1997; La Porta *et al.* 1998; Glaeser & Shleifer 2002; La Porta, Lopez-De Silanes & Shleifer 2008.

tries being more protective of shareholders than civil law countries.[4] In later studies, La Porta *et al.* broadened their thesis to other fields, claiming that legal origins could also explain differences among legal systems in the fields of e.g. banking, labour markets, ownership of the media and (mandatory) military service.[5] The core of their claim is that, compared to French civil law and the countries to which this was exported, the common law shows:[6]

> '(a) better investor protection, which in turn is associated with improved financial development, better access to finance, and higher ownership dispersion, (b) lighter government ownership and regulation, which are in turn associated with less corruption, better functioning labor markets, and smaller unofficial economies, and (c) less formalized and more independent judicial systems, which are in turn associated with more secure property rights and better contract enforcement'.

However, many scholars doubt the empirical claim of this literature and criticise its findings both on methodological grounds as on grounds of misconception of differences between the civil law and the common law. This led to a large literature in which not only the legal origins-thesis itself is attacked,[7] but in which the importance of legal origins is also discussed for other fields, such as procedural law,[8] labour law,[9] environmental law[10] and corporate law in general.[11]

Secondly, the question is increasingly asked whether legal institutions and the rule of law are also important in the process whereby poor nations develop their economy. For example Cooter, Schäfer and Ulen[12] have attempted to examine why some developing countries do relatively better than others and found that this is at least partly caused by different legal institutions. However, others point at the fact that legal rules may play some, but perhaps only a modest, role in economic development. A powerful example is in this respect China which, at least at first blush, does not seem to rely strongly on legal institutions (at least in the traditional sense)[13] and nevertheless has experienced a spectacular economic growth.[14] China has continued to have an annual growth rate of its GDP of 9 per cent for most of the past 30 years.[15] Also the recent economic success of civil law countries such as Brazil and Mexico remains puzzling in this debate. This discussion usually takes place

4 La Porta *et al.* 1997; cf. La Porta, Lopez-De Silanes & Shleifer 2008, p. 285.

5 Cf. La Porta, Lopez-De Silanes & Shleifer 2008, p. 286.

6 La Porta, Lopez-De Silanes & Shleifer 2008, p. 298.

7 Instead of many: Roe 2006 and Siems 2008a, p. 354; a reply to much of the criticism can be found in La Porta, Lopez-De Silanes & Shleifer 2008; also see the special volume of *Brigham Young University Law Review* 2009, p. 1413-1906.

8 Djankov *et al.* 2003.

9 Botero *et al.* 2004.

10 See the references in the contribution of Michael Faure to this volume.

11 See the references in the contribution of Alessio Pacces to this volume.

12 See e.g. Cooter 2006; Cooter & Schäfer 2011.

13 Although in China informal relations, so called 'Guanxi' seem to some extent to replace formal law. See Zhang & Jing 2007.

14 Cf. Ohnesorge 2007.

15 Ulen 2011.

under the heading of 'law and development'. Although this field became marginalized in the 1970's, the belief in the power of law reform received renewed impetus in the last decade,[16] possibly also as a result of the influence of the neoliberal Washington Consensus.[17]

Thirdly, there is an interesting aspect to this discussion from the viewpoint of comparative law. While comparative lawyers are prone to argue that existing jurisdictions differ from each other in many different ways,[18] they are not particularly good at finding explanations for these differences. While some seek to explain legal diversity from differences in culture[19] and others from varying preferences among citizens,[20] these explanations are not fully satisfactory.[21] The legal origins-thesis claims that differences among the civil law and the common law tradition go back to diverging roles of the administrative and judicial authorities in the very formation of France and England.[22] This has supposedly led to greater judicial independence in common law than in civil law, as well as to a better protection of private property and of enforcement of contracts in common law. The different ways of thinking about the role of the State that came about a long time ago would still prevail as part of separate mentalities in civil law and common law countries, leading to different ways of dealing with State abuse and market failure. They persist because[23]

> 'beliefs and ideologies become incorporated in legal rules, institutions, and education and, as such, are transmitted from one generation to the next. It is this incorporation of beliefs and ideologies into the legal and political infrastructure that enables legal origins to have such persistent consequences for rules, regulations, and economic outcomes'.

The 'toolkit' of civil law would more prominently feature nationalization and direct State control, whereas common law countries would favour litigation and a belief in the market. When a new problem arises, a civil law country will typically expand the scope of government control while a common law country is more likely to take measures to support the market.[24] However, this claim has not come to play an important role in comparative scholarship.[25] This is pitiful because it could shed new light on understanding differences among jurisdictions.

16 See Davies & Trebilcock 2008 and cf. the contribution of Ralf Michaels to this volume.
17 Also see the contribution of Julan Du to this volume.
18 Cf. Zweigert & Kötz 1998, p. 63.
19 Legrand 1996, p. 61.
20 Tiebout 1956; Wagner 2005, p. 5. Cf. Levmore 1986.
21 Also see Smits 2011.
22 Cf. Glaeser & Shleifer 2002.
23 La Porta, Lopez-De Silanes & Shleifer 2008, p. 308.
24 La Porta, Lopez-De Silanes & Shleifer 2008, p. 308.
25 The main textbooks remain silent: in the same vein Siems 2008b and Michaels 2009, p. 767. This is even more surprising in view of the fact that comparative lawyers are usually aware of the forceful argument made by Pierre Legrand that civil law and common law show 'unbridgeable' mentalities. Legrand 1996 does not cite La Porta *et al.* and La Porta *et al.* do not cite Legrand, even though both their positions could be made stronger if they did.

There is little doubt that these three aspects are all interesting in themselves. Despite their fairly recent publication, the original papers by La Porta, Shleifer and others even belong to the best-cited articles in the field of economics, in which they are broadly debated and criticized.[26] The idea probably found its best-known practical application in the annual Doing Business reports that are published by the World Bank since 2003.[27] The idea for these reports was developed under the leadership of Simeon Djankov, based on the article Djankov wrote together with La Porta, Lopez-de Silanes and Shleifer in 2002[28] and which heavily builds upon the legal origins thesis by claiming that countries with heavy regulation on starting a new business are more likely to have higher corruption and a bigger unofficial economy than countries with low regulation. The reports are famous for measuring the costs (in particular in so far as these are caused by regulations and government intervention) of doing business in 183 countries. In many developing countries, the annual reports are seen as an important benchmark and it is often part of the government policy to achieve a higher ranking in the next edition. The very publication of the reports thus promotes law reform from the inside out.

However, it is regrettable that the three mentioned aspects remain largely within their own domains. While the legal origins-thesis is mainly (though not exclusively) discussed by economists (primarily by those working in finance and institutional economics), the debate about law and development also remains mostly separate. In the same vein, the legal origins-thesis is not discussed in mainstream (comparative) law - as La Porta and Shleifer *et al.* in their seminal articles did not take much cognisance of what legal academics wrote about the differences between civil law and common law. It is a safe conclusion to say that the various streams of literature paying attention to the question to what extent legal origins matter for economic growth have not been strongly integrated.[29]

This book aims to overcome this deficiency of the present discussion and attempts to bring the various approaches together. It does so by presenting a wide range of views on how law and economic development are related. The book is loosely divided into three different parts. Part 1 is devoted to general questions and empirics, part 2 to the study of the separate legal traditions and China and part 3 to some specific areas of law. However, it is difficult to separate these three parts entirely: the questions discussed in the various contributions are all highly interrelated.

In the remainder of this Introduction, an attempt is made to summarize the findings of the individual contributions and to place these in the broader context of this book's main question: does law matter for economic growth?

26 Cf. Siems 2008.

27 The latest edition is World Bank Group 2010; also see <www.doingbusiness.org> (last visited 24 August 2011).

28 Djankov *et al.* 2002.

29 Also see the contribution of Ralf Michaels to this volume.

2. General Part

The legal origins-thesis and law and development studies are both based on the assumption that law matters for economic development. This implies the existence of some form of causality between a certain set of institutions or legal rules and economic development. The work on legal origins even claims that the present economic development of a country is largely dependent on how the history of that country is shaped. Law and development studies adopt a view of economic growth that is less based on historical accident, but here too it is emphasised that the law and the economy are closely linked. However, it is precisely this causal link that is often criticized in the literature. In brief, the main point of criticism is that legal origin is actually a proxy for something else, such as culture, history or politics. In reality, these factors are much more responsible for how a country develops economically than the formal legal institutions. This means that there is a problem of reverse causality: economic growth is not the result of better laws, but better laws come about in countries that have a better functioning economy anyway. It could for example very well be that shareholders are protected better in some countries because of the political pressure that investors can exercise on the lawmaker in these countries.[30]

In the General Part of this volume, several authors deal with this key question and with other points of methodology. The first is Ralf Michaels who, in an insightful contribution, discusses the interconnectedness of the legal origins-claim and functionalism as used in comparative law. Michaels clearly shows that the legal origins-thesis is largely dependent on the functionalist method. Glaeser and Shleifer[31] for example heavily rely on functionalism when they identify as a common problem of all legal systems the need to protect law enforcers against physical force and bribes. The French solution of centralizing the law is in their view thus functionally equivalent to the English solution of creating a jury-based legal system. The main point made by Michaels is that many of the objections that can be brought in against such (and other types of) functionalism can also be held against the legal origins-literature. It is surprising that while these critiques of functionalism have been lethal elsewhere (and in particular for the law and development-movement), they have not led to the demise of the legal origins-thesis. Michaels explains this 'strange lure of economics' by its ability to show results in the form of statistics and objective-looking data and rankings. The theoretical and empirical foundations of the legal origins-literature should therefore be revisited and thought through in a better way. One challenge presented by Michaels is the possibility to integrate the functionalist approach with culturalist comparative law. One way of doing this may be a combination of statistical analysis and case studies.

30 La Porta, Lopez-De Silanes & Shleifer 2008, p. 298 & 310.

31 Glaeser & Shleifer 2002.

The point made by Ralf Michaels is taken up in the contribution by John Armour, Simon Deakin, Viviana Mollica and Mathias Siems.[32] One way in which the existing work on legal origins can be ameliorated is by making use of alternative empirical testing. A major point of criticism is that the data used by La Porta *et al.* are largely based on cross-sectional datasets, only providing evidence on the state of the law at limited points in time. Armour *et al.* show what we can learn from so-called time-series evidence, which considers legal variations over time. Their contribution is important in criticizing one of the central points of the legal origins-literature: they show that, in a time-series analysis, an increase of shareholder rights does not foster economic development. More in general, they also cast doubt on the explanatory force of legal origins as an external factor explaining economic development and find it more plausible - in line with the general criticism on legal origins - that the legal system evolves in parallel with changes in national economic conditions and political structures.

An even more sceptical perspective is provided by Eric Helland and Jonathan Klick. In their contribution, they severely doubt the empirical credibility of the legal origins-thesis as such. The fundamental problem they see is one of statistical identification: although there is little doubt that there are correlations between various legal institutions and economic outcomes, one cannot claim with any certainty that these correlations provide evidence of causality. Helland and Klick convincingly show that the work of La Porta *et al.* is not robust, leading them to conclude that 'despite its tremendous influence in both academic and policy circles, the empirical estimates from the legal origins literature are simply not credible'. What is more, the authors also doubt whether present micro-economic tools can be used at all to establish a causal relationship between economic growth and legal institutions.[33] To draw policy conclusions about which legal rules should be adopted to promote economic growth is in any event premature.

This conclusion calls for a turning back to the very foundations of what it means 'to turn law into numbers'. Mathias Siems discusses this fundamental question. He makes clear that when economists measure legal rules and institutions, their approach is often a 'just do it' one, implicitly assuming that the complexity of the law does not prevent it from being turned into numbers. This is exactly the point that Ralf Michaels complained when he spoke about the 'strange lure of economics'. Legal academics, by contrast, typically have the attitude of 'just don't do it', often claiming that the law is not quantifiable. Siems explains and discusses six different ways of how law can be measured. For all methods, the measurement of law is not straightforward. This calls for more collaboration across disciplines and in particular for economists and other social scientists to benefit from lawyers' more sceptical attitude towards quantification.

This call for more collaboration and an interdisciplinary approach to the analysis of institutional change is shared by Giuseppe Dari-Mattiacci and Carmine

32 Previously published in *Brigham Young University Law Review* 2009, 1435-1500 and reprinted in this volume with the kind permission of the authors and the publisher. Also see Armour *et al.* 2009.

33 Also see Klick 2010.

Guerriero. In their contribution, they offer an account of how to understand the origins of formal and informal institutions of regulation and their impact on present day law. Their approach is also sceptical: it is impossible to establish causality between legal origins and a certain level of economic development. However, the important point made by them is that the civil law-common law-distinction is too simple to understand comparative variation: modern societies witness a wide variety of sources of law next to courts and legislatures. The analysis should therefore be broadened to include inter alia the internal functioning of lawmaking institutions and the complex interaction among different sources of law.

Robert D. Cooter and Hans-Bernd Schäfer discuss another point of methodology: what does economic growth exactly mean? While they recognize that law greatly matters for economic development, it is not so clear what criterion should be used to measure it. Cooter and Schäfer distinguish between wealth making and wealth taking and make a clear case for how influential the law can be in striking the balance between the makers and takers of wealth. They show with abundant examples how wealth can be taken from others in a criminal way (through theft and bribes), in a political way (through subsidies and regulations) and by the workings of the market (through cartels and monopolies) and how wealth can be made through the work of entrepreneurs, labourers, farmers, shopkeepers etc. The traditional Marxian labour theory of value and the micro-economic marginal productivity theory are not satisfactory in measuring how much wealth is created by this and they should be replaced by a novel theory on productivity of entrepreneurs who supply economic innovations.

Cooter and Schäfer thus share the basic insight of the legal origins-scholarship on the importance of law. However, the important point they make is that it depends entirely on one's definition of wealth (hence on the exact balance between taking and making of wealth) when exactly the law will promote economic welfare and when it will not. If people get their wealth by taking it from others, economic growth will be fostered by the abolition of capital markets. However, if wealth comes mostly from fostering innovation - as seems to be the case today as the world's richest people all collected their richness by some form of innovation - the law should primarily protect investors and secure (intellectual) property rights. Law can cause growth, but it depends on the source of growth which institutions and rules are best suited to guarantee this growth.

The question of how exactly different legal systems matter for economic development is also taken up in the contribution of Anthony Ogus on legal systems as networks. He shows how characteristics of networks apply to features within a legal system and to legal systems as a whole. This line of thinking emphasizes that the value to a single user of a product or a service depends on the number of other users, meaning that the social value of the network increases if more users adopt it. The great value of Ogus' contribution lies in the fact that he links the discussion about legal origins to the value of competition among legal networks. As Ogus states:

> 'A - perhaps the - key variable in evaluating the impact of legal systems on economic growth in developing countries is how well a legal network originally externally

imposed by colonialist regimes is adaptable to local conditions and pre-existing local legal networks'.

A dominant legal network – such as that of the former colonialist power – will only evolve efficiently if it is subject to competition, thwarting the ability of practitioners to capture rents by manipulating the law. Interestingly, this aspect does not feature in the work of La Porta *et al.* although it seems vital to understanding how successful a legal system is. It is in this respect also useful to refer to the work of Stefan Voigt who, in an article published in 2008,[34] expressed doubts about the superiority of the common law in view of the possibility of choice of law: if the legal origins-thesis is right, it would mean that rational actors would choose a common law jurisdiction as the applicable law – for which there is no conclusive evidence.

The final chapter in this part by Thomas Ulen argues powerfully that law may not be a necessary, but not even a sufficient condition for economic growth. One reason for a sceptical attitude towards the importance of law is that there may be important alternatives to law, such as social norms, which can largely fulfil the same role. To some extent social norms can hence fulfil the same societal functions as a well functioning modern legal system.[35] In addition the case of China, so Ulen argues, powerfully shows that even in the absence of formal legal institutions economic growth is still possible. China sustained a spectacular economic growth even though formal legal institutions were largely lacking. Ulen in addition argues that the case of China also demonstrates that democracy is not a precondition for economic growth.[36] In fact stability may be a crucial factor in promoting economic growth which may be easier to guarantee in more centrally controlled (not necessarily democratic) forms of government. Finally Ulen also points at the important role of political leaders and more particularly their political courage to engage in changes which can provide the necessary environment to foster economic growth.

In sum, the contributions to this first general part all take to some extent the legal origins literature as a starting point, but at the same time provide important nuances and criticisms. It is striking that criticisms, although of a different nature, are formulated both from an economic as well as from a legal perspective. From a legal perspective criticism is, for example, formulated on the 'strange lure of economics' to turn results in the form of statistics and objective looking data and rankings, thereby ignoring the fundamental question whether it is possible at all to 'turn law into numbers' (see Michaels and Siems). Criticism is equally formulated on the rather unbalanced way in which distinctions between the civil law and common law are presented, thereby largely ignoring the differences between the particular legal systems (see Dari Mattiacci and Guerriero).

More fundamentally the question is also asked whether it is at all possible to show a causal relationship between particular legal institutions and economic growth. If, in a time-series analysis the results of the legal origins literature are addressed in a more detailed manner the results are not sustained. This is, for

34 Voigt 2008.

35 This builds on the insights of Ellickson 1986, and Ellickson 1991.

36 Following the work of Lipset 1959.

example, what Armour *et al.* show with respect to the relationship between an increase of shareholder rights and economic growth. Helland and Klick also show that when the methodology of the legal origins literature is critically analysed the results are simply not robust. This leads them to doubt whether it is at all possible to prove a causal relationship between particular legal rules and economic growth.

Already these insights are important since at the policy level too easily normative conclusions were drawn from the legal origins literature e.g. on the importance of developing legal institutions in developing countries, but also on a preference for the common law. The chapters in this part show that to an important extent these policy advises may have been misguided also because (as Ulen powerfully argues) many other aspects than simply legal rules can be important in promoting economic growth.

Moreover, the chapters in this part are on the one hand doubting whether it is at all possible to show causal relationships between legal rules and economic growth, but on the other hand also provide indications for different approaches to the question how the quality of legal rules and the importance of legal institutions can be measured. Michaels and Siems both argue in favour of combining statistics with a more qualitative approach, using also the virtues of comparative law and, for example, combining statistics with a case studies approach. These approaches may provide more nuanced and therefore more valuable insights than a mere statistical approach, which seems to provide objective results, but which are not robust either and therefore even misleading.

3. Common Law, Civil Law and China

After the general and methodological insights provided in the first part, the second part of this volume considers the common law, civil law and China. For the purpose of this book, it is in particular important to look in detail at the suggested superiority of the common law compared to other jurisdictions. France (discussed by Bernard Crettez, Bruno Deffains, Guillaume Leyte and Laurent Pfister) and China are in this respect highly useful countries to consider. This does not need much explanation for France as this is the typical civil law country and also the jurisdiction that La Porta *et al.* consider as the main exporter of civil law. China is evidently interesting because of its spectacular economic development despite the absence of formal legal institutions as we know in the Western world.

Nuno Garoupa and Carlos Gómez go to the core of the legal origins-claim by reviewing the argument that the common law provides better incentives to induce efficient behaviour. They review the reasons why the common law may be more efficient, but conclude that these reasons are not satisfactory. And even if the common law would be evolving towards efficiency, this cannot explain persisting differences among common law jurisdictions: in each country where the common law found root, local circumstances made it depart from original English law. A more realistic account of the efficiency hypothesis of the common law is therefore that there is not one single efficient rule, but that different adequate rules exist dependent on the local circumstances. Their main conclusion is therefore that there is no conclusive evidence that French civil law is inferior because of a lack of efficiency. This conclusion is reinforced by the experience of mixed jurisdictions: if the stance of the legal origins-claim is that mixed legal families should give up the civil law aspect of their jurisdiction in search of efficiency, this is very unlikely to promote economic growth – if it were only because this would violate the prevailing local institutional arrangements in those jurisdictions.

The point that legal institutions (and the way in which they came about) do not have an overriding influence on economic development is also taken up by Bernard Crettez, Bruno Deffains, Guillaume Leyte and Laurent Pfister. In their contribution on the law and economics of the French Civil Code, they make clear that a legal system is not independent of the values of society and that therefore there is no reason why there would be one unique legal system (such as the common law) to favour economic growth. Their article builds upon the work by Arranuda and Andanova,[37] who have attempted to explain the formation of the French Civil Code from the behaviour of judges. Before the French Revolution, French judges were hostile to the market system: the courts were mostly populated with the nobility without much knowledge of (or sympathy for) merchants and their interests. In post-Revolutionary France, the only way to inhibit judges with a more market-friendly approach was to restrict their powers. This was done by making judges civil servants and by drafting a Code that took better account of commercial parties. This Commercial Code had, alongside the new Civil Code, to be interpreted strictly. In brief: the only way in which economic growth could be enhanced was by intervention of the legislature, forcing judges to make more market-oriented decisions. Also in the work of Lagarde,[38] the two Codes are presented as means to assure a desired order: next to the social order created by the Civil Code, the Commercial Code would foster risk-taking relationships. Despite the criticism of Crettez, Deffains, Leyte and Pfister on the views of both Arranuda and Andanova and Lagarde, they do acknowledge that they offer insightful explanations of why the French Civil Code came about. However, we should also submit that the historical account of Arranuda and Andanova is not too far apart from the legal origins-claim that French law is typically used as an instrument in the hands of the State. The question that remains unanswered is how this would affect the economic development compared to countries where the State plays a less important role.

Under the provocative title 'Does China need law for economic development?', Julan Du discusses the spectacular rise of China that does not seem to fit any of the predictions of the legal origins-literature. Despite the absence of formal legal institutions and a conception of the rule of law after the Western model, China has experienced an annual average growth rate of 9,5 per cent since 1978. China is now the second largest economy in the world, but ranks 79 in the 2011 World Business Report ranking on the ease of doing business.[39] Du asks how to explain this puzzle

37 Arranuda & Andonova 2005, and Arranuda & Andonova 2008.

38 E.g. Lagarde 2009.

39 World Bank Group 2010, p. 4.

of the coupling of economic success and weak legal institutions and provides a fascinating explanation. He argues that the Chinese government acts as a substitute for formal legal institutions in guaranteeing a stable business environment: in China, laws do not have the function of protecting entrepreneurs against governments and bureaucracy, but are instruments of the State to implement its policies. Du shows convincingly that this role of the State is pervasive and also extends to the role that courts traditionally have in Western countries. The examples he gives from commercial dispute resolution, corporate governance and regulation of financial markets show how authorities can take over the functions of courts and of the rule of law in helping entrepreneurs. Although this 'helping-hand regulatory State model' is now under pressure, its important role in the past does explain why China could develop its economy in the way it did. The important lesson for the legal origins-debate is clear: even though the judiciary in China is very weak in Western eyes, China does have a stabile economic growth thanks to the helping-hand regulatory state model that has largely filled the void left by the absence of formal legal institutions.

In sum, the chapters in this part to a large extent confirm the points made in the general part, by looking in a more detailed way at civil law, common law and the particular case of China. Like Dari Mattiacci and Guerriero already held in the previous part, Garoupa and Gómez also come to the conclusion that there is no inherent reason neither theoretically nor empirically to hold that the common law would be superior to the civil law in promoting economic growth. The findings of Du on China also confirm what was mentioned in the previous part by Ulen, being that China is apparently able to sustain economic growth without western style legal rules or a western style democracy. This puts the importance of legal rules in promoting economic growth into perspective since it shows that there may be alternatives to traditional legal rules which could replace its role. In the case of China it may be a strong central government, combined with social norms. This has, as Ulen also argued in the previous part, important normative implications. International institutions such as the World Bank strongly believe both in the importance of legal institutions to promote economic growth and in the superiority of the common law. This often led to policy advises to developing countries holding that the development of legal institutions would guarantee economic growth. Ulen argues in his chapter that this advice often seemed misguided as the expected economic growth did not follow. The chapters in this part show that this should to some extent not come as a surprise on the one hand since the legal transplants imposed upon developing countries may not always fit the receiving legal system (for example when common law rules would be imposed in a civil law jurisdiction) and the case of China underscores the fact developing countries may have alternatives which can fulfil the same role as legal rules in promoting economic growth.

4. Specific Fields of Law

The third and final part of this volume provides insights from some specific fields of law. As already mentioned in section 1, the debate about law and economic growth is not limited to corporate governance but was also taken up for other fields. In this part corporate law, property law and environmental law are discussed.

Corporate law is the field on which the first papers by La Porta *et al.* were written and it remains one of the most interesting fields to analyse to what extent law matters for economic growth, also because of the clearly distinctive models of corporate governance that have been adopted throughout the world. In his contribution, Alessio Pacces critically reviews the 'law and finance' literature that seeks to identify efficient corporate law by identifying the shareholders as the actors best suited to maximize the value of the firm. Pacces does not see convincing empirical arguments for the superiority of dispersed ownership. In his view, corporate law should be neutral to the ownership structure and enable both controlling shareholders and managers to be in control, as long as they are committed not to expropriate investors. On a more general note, Pacces notes what we saw before in part 1 of this volume: the problem with the 'law matters'-argument is that it is methodologically difficult to make. Legal protection of shareholders may not be the only institutional factor affecting the choice of corporate governance arrangements, let alone economic development. This makes the ambition of the law and finance scholarship to identify the 'best' system of corporate governance a failed one.

Guangdong Xu asks about the relationship between property rights and economic performance. It is common knowledge that effective property rights are vital to economic development: they create incentives for individuals to carry out productive activities such as investment, trade, and creation of wealth. In the context of this volume, however, the interesting question is whether one specific type of designing property rights is better for economic development than another. Xu's discussion of the available empirical evidence shows that this provides us with a puzzle: despite the advantages of formal ownership claimed by economists and lawyers, formal property rights and land titling fail in most developing countries. This is not surprising as mere formalization is not enough: good governance (including a consistent legal and institutional framework, access to information, and impartial agencies) is necessary for the functioning of formal property rights. In line with the lessons from China taught by Julan Du, Xu makes clear that the question how property rights matter is a complex one: its answer depends on how the local market in question works and how it interacts with the economy, polity, and society in general. Again, it is submitted that it is naïve to embrace property privatization and formalization as a means to create economic growth as this may work in some countries, but not in others.

Michael Faure has addressed the relationship between environmental law and economic growth from two separate angles. There is on the one hand an impressive literature addressing the question whether economic growth will lead to an increased environmental pollution. This literature is known as the Environmental Kuznets Curve which roughly shows that increasing income per capita first leads to increasing pollution levels, but later after reaching a turning point to decreasing pollution levels. Even though there has been substantial criticism on this EKC literature some empirical studies show that environmental quality did indeed increase with economic growth, but only when this was supported by decent environmental regulations, in other words institution. Again, the World Bank had originally supported economic growth arguing that this will automatically lead to better environmental quality, also for developing countries. Recent studies show that this is only the case when countries also enact effective environmental policies. There is hence no automatism in the relationship between per capita income and environmental quality; the quality of environmental law also matters. An other aspect is whether countries engage in a competition to attract industry with lenient environmental regulation, seducing industry to relocate to so-called pollution havens. The theoretical conditions for such a pollution haven hypothesis are highly debated. Some indeed argue that states will engage in a race to the bottom to attract industry with lax environmental regulations. Others argue that under different assumptions states could also benefit from strict environmental regulations (improving their competitive position trough technological innovations), hence leading to a race to the top. Empirical evidence for both hypothesis exists. Empirical evidence does confirm that even though industry may not necessarily relocate to pollution havens, pollution control costs do matter in the *ex ante* decision of industry on choosing an appropriate location.

In sum, the contributions in this part, addressing the relationship between particular fields of law and economic growth also come to nuanced conclusions in the sense that this relationship very much depends on particular circumstances. As far as corporate law is concerned Pacces showed that shareholder protection may not be the only institutional factor affecting the choice of corporate governance arrangements and Xu comes to a similar conclusion as far as property rights are concerned: the institution of property rights alone does not guarantee economic growth, since this depends on a number of other factors related to good governance. A similar nuanced conclusion was reached with respect to the relationship between economic growth and environmental policy: economic growth may lead to increased environmental quality, but again this may depend on the type of pollutants involved and also the institutional circumstances. The chapters show, in other words, that the truth is again in the detail and that the particular relationship between the fields of law and economic growth very much depends upon particular circumstances.

5. Conclusions

We argued above that there were several reasons to produce a multi-disciplinary volume addressing the relationship between legal rules and economic growth from both a legal and an economic perspective. One reason was the apparent contradiction between on the one hand the large attention attached to the legal origins literature by economists and on the other hand the large criticism that is equally formulated on this literature both by economists and by lawyers. The contributions to this book have hopefully contributed to a better understanding of the strengths, but also the methodological weaknesses of the legal origins literature by showing both the problematic nature of attempts to quantify the quality of legal rules, but also the empirical weaknesses and limited robustness of the legal origins literature.

An other reason to pay attention to this topic is that it has strongly influenced the question of what poor countries should do to become rich. The legal origins literature roughly advised not only that legal institutions would generally be important to guarantee economic growth, but that, moreover, institutions originating from the common law may be superior in reaching that goal. These recommendations have been taken seriously at the policy level and have led e.g. via the so called 'Washington consensus' to recommendations to developing countries to focus primarily on the development of stable legal institutions. However, many agree that a few decennia later the results of this policy seem to have been relatively poor. On the one hand not all countries that introduced legal institutions had economic growth and on the other hand some countries (more particularly China) experienced a strong economic growth, even in the absence of legal institutions. Several contributors to this book try to explain this phenomenon, largely arguing that legal institutions may not always be a necessary condition for economic growth (to the extent that other rules or institutions (such as social norms or a strong government) can be adequate substitutes for legal rules); in addition legal rules may not be a sufficient condition for economic growth either since other parameters related to the broad notion of good governance may also be needed to reach a sustained economic growth.

A final reason for this book was that there was apparent mismatch between on the one hand the large debate on the 'law matters' literature in economic and on the other hand comparative law. To a large extent the nuances and differences pointed at in comparative legal scholarship were largely ignored in the legal origins literature. Hence, it remains an open question why legal systems largely differ from each other and whether this can be explained by economics alone. One goal of this book was to somehow bridge this gap and move towards an integration of the economic (statistical) approach and the legal (more qualitative case based) approach.

The contributions to this book have contributed to this important debate on the relationship between legal rules and economic growth, but the issue is of course so demanding and complicated that much more research will be needed. Several contributors to this book have, precisely in an attempt to bridge the legal and the economic approach, provided suggestions on how the statistical approach followed by economists could be supplemented with a more qualitative approach followed by lawyers, e.g. via the use of case studies. Also the chapters looking at the relationship between particular legal rules (in the fields of environmental, corporate and property law) and economic growth show that it is difficult to reach general conclusions and that this relationship may depend upon a number of specific details and circumstances. The key is of course to distinguish these particular circumstances as they may provide more useful insights on how particular legal institutions may, depending upon the circumstances, contribute to economic growth or not.

Given the importance of the role of law in developing countries, but, for example, also in China this topic will undoubtedly remain high on the agenda. METRO and M-EPLI hope to be able to further contribute to this debate in their research.

Bibliography

Armour *et al.* 2009
Armour, J., Deakin, S., Lele, P. & Siems, M., 'How do legal rules evolve? Evidence from a cross-country comparison of shareholder, creditor, and worker protection', *The American Journal of Comparative Law*, 2009, p. 579-629.

Arranuda & Andonova 2005
Arranuda, B. & Andonova, V., 'Market Institutions and Judicial Rulemaking', in: C. Ménard & M.M. Shirley (eds.), *Handbook of New Institutional Economics*, Dordrecht: Springer, 2005, p. 229-250.

Arranuda & Andonova 2008
Arranuda, B. & Andonova, V., 'Judges' Cognition and Market Order', *Review of Law and Economics*, 2008, p. 665-692.

Botero *et al.* 2004
Botero, J., Djankov, S., La Porta, R., Lopez de Silanes, F. & Shleifer, A., 'The Regulation of Labor', *Quarterly Journal of Economics*, 2004, p. 1340-82.

Cooter 2006
Cooter, R.D., 'An Escape from Poverty: Developing Productive Organizations', *South-western Journal of Law & Trade in the Americas*, 2006, p. 181-187.

Cooter & Schäfer
Cooter, R.D. & Schäfer, H.B., *Solomon's Knot: How Law Can End the Poverty of Nations*, Princeton, 2011 (forthcoming).

Davies & Trebilcock 2008
Davies, K.E. & Trebilcock, M.J., 'The Relationship between Law and Development: Optimists versus Skeptics', *The American Journal of Comparative Law*, 2008, p. 895-946.

Djankov *et al.* 2002
Djankov, S., La Porta, R., Lopez-De-Silanes, F. & Shleifer, A., 'The Regulation of Entry', *The Quarterly Journal of Economics*, 2002, p. 1-37.

Djankov *et al.* 2003
Djankov, S., La Porta, R., Lopez-de-Silanes, F. & Shleifer, A., 'Courts', *Quarterly Journal of Economics*, 2003, p. 453-517.

Ellickson 1986
Ellickson, R.C., 'Of Coase and Cattle: Dispute Resolution Among Neighbors in Shasta County', *Stanford Law Review*, 1986, p. 623-687.

Ellickson 1991
Ellickson, R.C., *Order Without Law: How Neighbors Settle Disputes*, Cambridge: Massachusetts: Harvard University Press, 1991.

Fauvarque-Cosson & Kerhuel 2009
Fauvarque-Cosson, B. & Kerhuel, A., 'Is Law an Economic Contest? French Reactions to the Doing Business World Bank Reports and Economic Analysis of the Law', *The American Journal of Comparative Law*, 2009, p. 811-830.

Glaeser & Shleifer 2002
Glaeser, E.L. & Shleifer, A., 'Legal Origins', *The Quarterly Journal of Economics*, 2002, p. 1193-1229.

Klick 2010
Klick, J., 'The Perils of Empirical Work on Institutions', *Journal of Institutional and Theoretical Economics*, 2010, p. 166-170.

Lagarde 2009
Lagarde, X., *Juste Capitalisme*, Paris: Lexis Nexis, 2009.

La Porta, Lopez-De Silanes & Shleifer 2008
La Porta, R., Lopez-De Silanes, F. & Shleifer, A., 'The Economic Consequences of Legal Origins', *Journal of Economic Literature*, 2008, p. 285-332.

La Porta *et al.* 1997
La Porta, R., Lopez-De Silanes, F., Shleifer, A. & Vishny, R.W., 'Legal Determinants of External Finance', *The Journal of Finance*, 1997, p. 1131-1150.

La Porta *et al.* 1998
La Porta, R., Lopez-De Silanes, F., Shleifer, A. & Vishny, R.W., 'Law and Finance', *Journal of Political Economy*, 1998, p. 1113-1155.

Legrand 1996
Legrand, P., 'European Legal Systems Are Not Converging', *International and Comparative Law Quarterly*, 1996, p. 52-81.

Levmore 1986
Levmore, S., 'Rethinking Comparative Law: Variety and Uniformity in Ancient and Modern Tort Law', *Tulane Law Review*, 1986, p. 235-288.

Lipset 1959
Lipset, S.M., 'Some Social Requisites of Democracy: Economic Development and Political Legitimacy', *American Political Science Review*, 1959, p. 69-105.

Michaels 2009
Michaels, R., 'Comparative Law by Numbers? Legal Origins Thesis, Doing Business Reports, and the Silence of Traditional Comparative Law', *The American Journal of Comparative Law*, 2009, p. 765-796.

Ohnesorge 2007
Ohnesorge, J.K.M., 'Developing Development Theory: Law and Development Orthodoxies and the Northeast Asian Experience', *University of Pennsylvania Journal of International Economic Law*, 2007, p. 219-308.

Posner 2011
Posner, R., *Economic Analysis of Law*, 8th edition, New York: Aspen Publishers, 2011.

Roe 2006
Roe, M., 'Legal Origin and Modern Stock Markets', *Harvard Law Review*, 2006, p. 460-527.

Siems 2008a
Siems, M., 'Statistische Rechtsvergleichung', *Rabels Zeitschrift*, 2008, p. 354-390.

Siems 2008b
Siems, M., 'Comparative Law - Who is the Elephant in the Room?', *Edinburgh Law Review*, 2008, p. 334-336.

Smits 2011
Smits, J.M., 'Is Law a Parasite? An Evolutionary Explanation of Differences Among Legal Traditions', *Review of Law & Economics*, 2011 (forthcoming).

Tiebout 1956
Tiebout, C., 'A Pure Theory of Local Expenditures', *Journal of Political Economy*, 1956, p. 416-424.

Ulen 2011
Ulen, T., 'The Uneasy Case for Competition Law and Regulation as Decisive Factors in Development: Some Lessons for China', in: M. Faure & Z. Xang (eds.), *Competition Policy and Regulation. Recent Developments in China, the US and Europe*, Cheltenham: Edward Elgar, 2011, p. 13-44.

Voigt 2008
Voigt, S., 'Are International Merchants Stupid? Their Choice of Law Sheds Doubt on the Legal Origin Theory', *Journal of Empirical Legal Studies*, 2008, p. 1-20.

Wagner 2005
Wagner, G., 'The Virtues of Diversity in European Private Law', in: J. Smits (ed.), *The Need for a European Contract Law: Empirical and Legal Perspectives*, Groningen: Europa Law Publishing, 2005, p. 3-24.

World Bank Group 2010
World Bank Group, *Doing Business 2011: Making a Difference for Entrepreneurs*, Washington: World Bank, 2010.

Zhang & Jing 2007
Zhang, W. & Jing, Y, 'Legal Pluralisme in the Governance of the Transitional China', in: Th. Eger, M. Faure & Z. Naigen (eds.), *Economic Analysis of Law in China*, Cheltenham: Edward Elgar 2007, p. 55-73.

Zweigert & Kötz 1998
Zweigert, K. & Kötz, H., *An Introduction to Comparative Law*, 3rd edition, Oxford: Clarendon , 1998.

PART I

GENERAL

Ralf Michaels

THE FUNCTIONALISM OF LEGAL ORIGINS

1. Introduction

Nothing could better characterize the state of legal studies in general, and comparative law in particular, than the fact that the topic for this jubilee issue of Ius Commune Europaeum is neither European nor actually legal. The legal origins literature has been generated by US-based self-declared 'lawyers wannabe'[1] and discussion among economists continues to pay fairly little attention to the views of legal scholars. The World Bank, which established its 'Doing Business' group to implement and expand on much of this research, employed, for a long time, only economists and no lawyers in the respective research groups.[2] Lawyers have been on the receiving end of this literature. Holmes' prediction, made in 1897, seems finally to have come true: 'For the rational study of the law the blackletter man may be the man of the present, but the man of the future is the man of statistics and the master of economics.'[3] Similarly, Mattei's finding from two decades ago seems true as well: the wind has changed; it is now coming from the United States.[4]

If the use of economics US style still feels relatively new, the outcomes do not. Neither that law matters nor that the common law is superior to the civil law, are new ideas. Nor is the method used satisfactory. From a comparative law perspective, the focus on formal law (law in the books) is too narrow, the use of the civil law/common law distinction is inexcusably simplistic, the understanding of legal transplants is simplistic, and the assumed commensurability between legal systems at least problematic.[5] From a social science perspective, the new literature appears to run into many of the problems that brought the older law and development movement down.

1 Florencio Lopez-de-Silanes, as quoted in Thompson 2005.
2 Disclosure: I am the only lawyer in a newly set up advisory group to the project.
3 Holmes 1897.
4 Mattei 1994.
5 Siems 2007; Siems 2008; Michaels 2009, p. 775-791; Bakardjieva Engelbrekt 2009, p. 225-231.

In this paper, I want to focus on a trope that connects comparative law and social science, namely the use of functional methods,[6] and see what the trope has to say about the legal origins literature. Of course, the legal origins literature is not explicitly functionalist, so both analysis and application of critique require a translation. Yet that translation helps link the legal origins literature to broader debates in the social sciences - and at the same helps explain why it is so successful.

Ultimately, I reach three results. In section 2, I demonstrate that the legal origins literature represents a functionalist method, and that perceived internal inconsistencies and tensions in the legal origins literature match similar inconsistencies between different concepts of functionalism. Although economics does not usually resort to the language of functionalism, ultimately it is a functionalist discipline. In section 3, I show that anti-functionalist critique in the social sciences is similarly powerful against the legal origins literature. In section 4, I suggest that the legal origins literature is more successful than predecessors in the field of law and development not because it has a better theoretical foundation but instead, ironically, because it has less. In short, the objectivity suggested by statistics and rankings blinds for underlying theoretical shortcomings. In a concluding section, finally, I speculate about the limits of such endeavours.

2. Legal Origins as Functionalism

How can we say that the legal origins literature represents a functionalist method? Although it has been remarked before that the legal origins literature has a close affinity with functionalist comparative law or sociological functionalism,[7] this affinity is not explicit. Where La Porta *et al.* cite to Zweigert and Kötz, they cite not to the famous elaboration of the functional method, but mostly to the classification of legal families.[8]

Moreover, the legal origins literature is not uniform, and displays internal contradictions. One such contradiction is this: whereas some articles suggest that 'one size fits all', that best practices and legal rules can be identified and then recommended to all legal systems alike, others suggest, instead, that the best fit is a function of local circumstances and conditions.[9] Another contradiction is this: the legal origins literature claims that, on the one hand, legal origins (i.e. events centuries ago) are still determinative for success today, and, on the other hand, that legal reform can bring about change.[10]

These contradictions are not surprising from the perspective of functionalism. Similar contradictions are known there, arising from unclear and competing con-

6 Michaels 2006; Michaels 2009a, p. 777-779.

7 Michaels 2009, p. 768-769, 777; Cioffi 2009, p. 1520-1526; Whytock 2009, p. 1880; see also Ajani 2009.

8 La Porta, Lopez-de Silanes & Shleifer 2008, p. 286-288. I do not address their treatment of legal families here; for critique, see e.g. Michaels 2009a, p. 780-783; Cioffi 2009; Ramseyer 2009; Bakardjieva Engelbrekt 2009, p. 225-231.

9 As pointed out recently by Bakardjieva Engelbrekt 2009, p. 215-220.

10 E.g. Armour *et al.* 2009, p. 1436-1437.

cepts of functionalism.[11] Between disciplines, the focus differs – more systemic and static in sociology, more teleological and dynamic in political sciences, more instrumentalist in policy studies. Even within one discipline, definitions differ. Thus, when Kingsley Davis famously declared, in 1959, that functional analysis was synonymous with sociology, his point was not to posit a uniform method and theory, but the opposite: There was no one functional method; instead, all sociological methods properly speaking were functionalist, so, important methodological debates were concealed under the label of functionalism.[12] It should be noted that the functional method in comparative law also presents a mix of these concepts.[13]

Here, I want to confine myself to three different concepts.

2.1. *System Functionalism*

A first concept of functionalism is a descriptive one.[14] It is assumed that societies face certain problems, and institutions (in the broadest sense) emerge that respond to these problems. The response to the problem is the function that the institution plays for the society at large. Epistemologically, this means that the institution must be understood with regard to the function it plays. Moreover, the function explains both the existence and the persistence of an institution. At the same time, this implies that society must be understood as a system that is capable of generating problems. And solutions are system-specific – even if problems are universal (a controversial assumption), each society is likely to find the solution best equipped for its own situation. I call this idea system-functionalism.

We can see this concept at work in Glaeser and Shleifer's article on legal origins.[15] The authors ask why different legal systems emerged in England and France in the 12th century and offer a purely functional analysis. They identify a common problem (they say 'goal') all legal systems face, namely 'to protect law enforcers from being bullied with either physical force or bribes by powerful local interests'. The legal regimes are functional responses to this common problem, and they differ according to the respective society:[16] in France, feudal lords feared each other more than a despot, so they delegated lawmaking power to the king. In England, by contrast, feudal landlords were not afraid of each other, so they preferred paying the king so they could adjudicate independently. This is, then, a theory of functional equivalents: both centralized law in France and jury-based law in England fulfil the same function and are in this sense equivalent, not similar.

11 For a longer discussion of different concepts, see Michaels 2006a, p. 343-363.
12 Davis 1959.
13 Michaels 2006a, p. 360-363.
14 The most helpful balanced methodological introduction I know of is Abrahamson 1978; another valuable survey, this one rather a history of ideas, is Münch 2003.
15 Glaeser & Shleifer 2003.
16 For a similar argument, see Djankov *et al*. 2003.

2.2. *Finalism*

A second concept of functionalism follows from the first but is at least partly different and can be called finalism. System-functionalism could be understood as a static theory, where societies are at equilibrium because their problems all find solutions. According to the finalism, however, solutions to problems create new problems that require new solutions. As a consequence, functionalism turns into a dynamic theory that explains and, ideally, predicts, the development of society. The best-known example for such a predictive theory is European integration: once one legal area is harmonized, this creates new pressures toward the harmonization of other areas, with the result that integration becomes ever closer.[17] Often, however, finalism is used in retrospect, to explain developments in the past as somehow necessary.

This strand is clearly present in the legal origins literature, which explains the development of legal systems as determined by their past. Thus, Glaeser *et al.* argue that codification in 19th century French 'naturally follows from the original choice of royal judges over juries': to control these judges further, the sovereign must create clear rules (which they believe to be characteristic of the French Code) that make deviation easily observable. In other words, a problem - independence of courts from local pressure - created a solution - royal judges - which in turn created a new problem - central control of judges - and a new functional response - codification.

2.3. *Instrumentalism*

The third concept of functionalism is different still. Here, the emphasis shifts from an epistemological and descriptive to a normative position. Now, institutions are viewed as tools, introduced by decision makers in order to resolve certain problems or achieve certain goals. 'Law is social engineering', claim Zweigert and Kötz. following Roscoe Pound.[18] The lawyer constructs legal rules in response to societal requirements. I call this third idea instrumentalism.

Instrumentalism is not obvious in most of the economic literature on legal origins, which is, at least on its face, mostly positive not normative. Instrumentalism is, however, clearly present in the World Bank's Doing Business Reports, which are themselves influenced by the legal origins literature. These reports advise underdeveloped countries to adopt legal solutions that have been successful elsewhere. Law reform is viewed in the perspective of social engineering, with a particular comparative and functionalist-instrumentalist bent: what worked elsewhere in a donor country should also work and bring about progress in the receiving country. Remarkably, at least in its early reports, the World Bank suggested 'that when it comes to the manner of regulation, one size often fits all (in many cases there really

17 For recent summary, see Sandholtz & Stone Sweet 2012.
18 Zweigert & Kötz 1996, p. 45; Pound 1954.

is one best practice)'.[19] In other words, not only are problems universal; best solutions are also universal, regardless of their origin or their social and legal context.

2.4. *Interrelations*

It is obviously easy to confuse these ideas. For all of them, institutions relate to, are answers to, problems. In some ways, instrumentalism may look like the normative equivalent of system functionalism. And yet, the difference is relevant. System-functionalism starts from problems faced by the system of society as such; the ultimate function analyzed is, typically, the stabilization of society. Teleological functionalism shares the interest in society as such, but instead of stabilization, focus is on some kind of development. Instrumentalism, by contrast, focuses on smaller, seemingly isolated problems – the reduction of crime, access to the justice system, getting creditors to pay their debts, etc. Such purposes may be related to the general function of society stabilization, but this relation is not a necessary one: we may intend to strengthen the due process rights of men accused for murder even if this is detrimental to societal stability.

System-functionalism and teleological functionalism account not only for manifest functions – those that are known and intended – but also, perhaps particularly, for latent functions – those that institutions perform, although they were not made for those functions and although those functions may not even be recognized within the society.[20] Instrumentalism, by contrast, accounts only for the actual purpose of an institution.[21]

System-functionalism is a theory aimed at understanding what stabilizes societies, without necessarily taking a position on whether such stabilization is desirable, or whether the institutions at stake are actually desirable. Teleological functionalism could likewise be viewed as purely descriptive in this sense, though the open acknowledgment of an intrinsic telos suggests a normative bent. Instrumentalism, by contrast, must necessarily take the desirability of the intended purpose into account.

3. Anti-Functionalist Criticisms

This reconceptualization of legal origins as functionalism is helpful for an assessment of the limits and promises of legal origins because it helps us tap into the rich array of methodological and theoretical debates devoted to functionalism in other disciplines – anthropology, sociology, to some extent also comparative law. Like the concepts of functionalism, critique is somewhat undifferentiated: some criticism is inspired against one kind of functionalism yet voiced against another.

19 World Bank 2004, p. xviii.

20 Merton 1968, reprinted in Demerath & Peterson 1967, p. 9-75.

21 For this reason, Whytock's suggestion that 'functionalist comparative legal scholars should explicitly distinguish between the rule's intended function and its actual consequences' (Whytock 2009, p. 1890) would arguably make sense only for an instrumentalist, not a functionalist comparative law.

3.1. *Society as the Object of Functions*

One challenge against functionalism concerns the idea of society. Legal rules can be responses to societal problems only if societies at large exist and have common problems. Yet different parts of societies may have different, often conflicting, needs, and legal rules may well satisfy some, while running against other needs. At the same time, the instrumentalist idea that problems can be isolated from their broader societal context seems problematic: for example, whether traffic accidents are compensated through tort law or through mandatory insurance has implications on the insurance market, the size of the regulatory apparatus of the state, etc.

To some extent, the legal origins literature takes this into account. Studies of corruption, for example, explain certain rules as performing functions for certain members of society, while being dysfunctional for society at large. However, in the end, the yardstick remains society. This reflects the interest in aggregate welfare over distributive questions that characterizes much of Chicago-style economics more generally. In the legal origins literature, however, the problem is enhanced, because the interest in 'doing business' (obviously a particular interest) is treated as though it were congruent with the interests of society at large. The Doing Business reports have been chided for insufficient attention to labour rights (which may be in tension with investors' interests), but by and large, the focus on entire economies remains.

3.2. *Necessitarianism*

A second frequent criticism of functionalism has been directed against the legal origins literature as well: the assumption that legal institutions necessarily perform certain functions and that certain functions make certain laws necessary.[22] The function of courts is to enforce contracts; the enforcement of contracts requires effective courts. This means, first that other functions of legal rules are ignored: warning functions of formal requirements, social protection in tenancy and employment laws, etc. Cioffi has recently voiced a similar criticism against the legal origins literature.[23] It means, secondly, that functional equivalents are insufficiently accounted for, a point Mathias Siems has made forcefully with regard to the legal origins literature.[24] It means, thirdly, that functionalism does not easily account for dysfunctional rules or for so-called survivals – rules that may at some point have had a function but no longer do.[25] As a consequence, functionalism tends to become apologetic for the status quo. In legal origins, this is strangely half-true: the literature is not at all apologetic of the status quo in underdeveloped countries, but it does accept, at face value it seems, the functionality of most law in the United States.

22 See, most recently, Hyland 2009, p. 69-73.
23 Cioffi 2009, p. 1525.
24 Pistor 2009, p. 1646-1647.
25 Armour *et al.* 2009, p. 1435.

A related problem is the perceived conservative bias of functionalism. System functionalism prioritizes societal cohesion over conflict, so the criticism goes, just as legal origins prioritizes aggregate economic progress over other societal concerns. Teleological functionalism accounts insufficiently for human agency and creativity by suggesting that things could not have developed otherwise than they have, just as legal origins depicts ostensibly necessary trajectories from a system's legal origins.

This criticism of necessitarianism does not apply to instrumentalism, which explicitly favours human agency, but here the criticism is the opposite: the technocratic approach to law as a tool towards the fixing of problems underestimates not only the systemic resistances to such but also the underlying political and social tensions that characterize society.

3.3. *Reductionism*

A third critique goes against the perceived reductionism of functionalism, which reduces legal rules to their functions.[26] Even if reductionism is not necessary for functionalist comparative law,[27] it seems unavoidable for legal origins. Coding as the method of the legal origins literature is necessarily reductionist; its isolation of single elements represents the polar opposite of thick description. Cioffi has rightly pointed out that LLSV 'seeks to reconcile the macro- and micro-level dimensions of law through microeconomic theory and functionalist analysis'.[28] Such combination of micro- and macro-comparison is necessary for proper functionalist comparative law, too.[29] Nonetheless, this means that other considerations, like justice or culture, have no place in the analysis. In one version, culture is absent altogether. In another, culture appears merely as an inadequate representation of what are really functional responses to problems (for example, ritualistic dance is 'really' about social cohesion). In yet another version, culture's irrationality stands in the way of functionalist rationality, as an obstacle to progress. Such criticism has been voiced against the legal origins literature in particular from French critics.[30]

Reductionism may be justifiable, to some extent, to ensure commensurability as a key prerequisite for comparability and therefore a key issue in comparative law. Comparison requires a *tertium comparationis*: we always compare legal systems with regard to a specific factor, be it the performance of a certain function or something else. It follows that findings of similarity and difference are always relative to the specific *tertium* that was chosen. Absolute comparison is impossible. This is even more true for determining the better law: a law can be better than another only with regard to the specific function they both perform. The legal origins literature accepts this restriction, as do the Doing Business reports. However, in the presentation, the

26 Geertz 1983.
27 Michaels 2006a, p. 364-365.
28 Cioffi 2009, p. 1518.
29 Michaels 2006, p. 375.
30 For summaries and evaluations in English, see Fauvarque-Cosson & Kerhuel 2009; Valcke 2010.

relative character of the comparison drops out of sight. This may be the biggest problem with the ranking of countries in the Doing Business reports: they suggest a ranking with regard to the absolute quality of legal systems, and they thereby put pressure on countries to focus their domestic policies on the factors that the Doing Business report measures - and to neglect other functions of the law. It appears as though the common law is better than the civil law tout court, instead of only in promoting economic growth as measured in the project.

3.4. *The Better Law Fallacy*

A fourth critique of functionalism, especially in form of instrumentalism, goes against what is called the 'better law approach'. Zweigert and Kötz argued that a functional comparison can 'suggest[ing] how a specific problem can most appropriately be solved under the given social and economic circumstances'.[31] Functionalism is thus expected to do two ostentatiously incompatible things - to show which legal rules are of equal value ('equivalent') in their responding to a given problem, and at the same time to show which of them is of the highest value, constitutes the best solution. The legal origins literature does the same: it explains legal rules as determined by their origin, while at the same time proclaiming which of them is the best one. On the micro-level, these tend to be the more deregulated solutions. On the macro-level, the general result is that the common law, by and large, performs better than do civil law systems (though among the latter, systems based on German law are said to perform slightly better than those based on French law).[32] This implies the suggestion that the better law can be identified regardless of context (one size fits all)[33] (though they have recently somewhat moderated this claim). This idea runs against a problem known from functionalist comparative law: the quality of a law depends on its context; transplanted laws may perform differently in different legal systems.[34] Strangely, the legal origins literature occasionally concedes this point: legal institutions may function well in developed countries but not in developing countries.

Whytock has recently suggested a way out of this problem: we should not evaluate legal institutions against some assumed objective standard, but rather assess their actual consequences vis-à-vis their purpose (Whytock speaks of 'intended function').[35] This is a valuable suggestion for instrumentalism but not, it seems, for system functionalism that focuses in particular on latent functions. This step also takes away one presumed advantage of functionalist comparative law, namely to identify a factor (function) that is similar in different legal systems. Purposes, by contrast, differ as among legal systems.

31 Zweigert & Kötz 1996, p. 11.

32 La Porta, Lopez-de Silanes & Shleifer 2008, p. 20.

33 But cf. La Porta, Lopez-de Silanes & Shleifer 2008, p. 324: 'the best solutions might differ across legal systems'.

34 Bakardjieva Engelbrekt 2009, p. 222-223.

35 Whytock 2008, p. 1890-1891.

4. The Strange Lure of Economics

None of these critiques is particularly new. For sociology, Merton formulated, and answered, most of them as early as 1949.[36] In comparative law, all of these (and more) have long been voiced as well.[37] Nor is it surprising that they should be applicable to the legal origins literature. What is surprising is that the legal origins literature has, so far, survived these critiques that were damning elsewhere.

4.1. *Legal Origins as Law and Development – a Déjà Vu*

The main focus of the legal origins literature is not on developed economies (though the ferocious defences of French law coming from French comparative lawyers could suggest that).[38] For the descriptive and analytical project the law of developed countries – especially England and France – is used, predominantly, as an exogenous factor to understand the relationship between law and development in former colonies. For the normative project, the main hope is to improve the economies of underdeveloped countries. This is clear especially in the Doing Business project of the World Bank, which focuses predominantly on underdeveloped countries, in accordance with the Bank's mission 'to help *developing* countries and their people reach the goals by working with our partners to alleviate poverty'.[39]

Thus, although the authors do not explicitly acknowledge it both their focus and findings place this literature in the law and development movement.[40] That movement, at least in its US version, pursued many of the same goals as the legal origins literature, albeit mostly with a somewhat different normative bent.[41] Here as well, the hope was to bring about economic success through legal reform. The project was, then, to identify those legal institutions that are conducive to economic success, implement them in developing countries, and then see the economy prosper. Law, understood mostly as formal rules and institutions, was viewed not as a cultural and culture-defined product, but instead as an instrument that could be applied towards development. Because western societies were the most advanced, their legal systems provided the toolbox from which these instruments were chosen.

That first law and development movement, however, withered away, for reasons that were empirical, financial, and theoretical.[42] Empirically, the hopes did not materialize: law reform, widely, did not spur success. The scholars promoting it found themselves in what Trubek and Galanter have called self-estrangement, the realization that they had contributed to something quite different from what they had intended.[43] Financially, support was withdrawn from development projects,

36 Merton 1968.

37 See Michaels 2006a.

38 For summaries in English, see Fauvarque-Cosson & Kerhuel 2009; Valcke 2010.

39 <Web.worldbank.org>.

40 Davis & Trebilcock 2008.

41 See, e.g., Tamanaha 1995.

42 See Davis & Trebilcock 2008, p. 915-938.

43 Trubek & Galanter 1974.

partly for lack of success, party for ideological reasons.[44] Theoretically, the proclaimed direct link between law and societal well-being was found to be too simplistic.

Importantly, much of the theoretical criticism was directed against the simple functionalism underlying law and development. Indeed, we can understand the first law and development movement as a functionalist project. The Ford foundation justified its $ 3 Mio. grant for an International Legal Centre with the clearly functionalist goal 'to help developing countries establish legal institutions essential to the functioning of modern, free societies'.[45] This reflected a widespread understanding at the time of law, in particular Western-type law, as performing necessary functions towards the well-being of society. The hope was that the introduction of Western-style laws and institutions could bring about the same prosperity in underdeveloped countries as existed in the West. The underlying idea that societies must go through various stages of development[46] reflects the teleological worldview that characterizes some social science functionalism. At the same time, law was here understood instrumentally, as a tool to be utilized to bring such success about. Consequently, much of the criticism made against the first law and development movement mirrors, or is borrowed from, critique made against functionalism.

4.2. *The Resilience of Legal Origins*

Why then does the new literature not simply fail to the same type of criticism? One possible explanation would be that the new functionalism is different from the old one. Kerry Rittich has pointed out some differences:[47] the narrow focus on economic success instead of overall societal well-being,[48] the widespread reliance on neoclassical models and statistical research rather than close case studies, the preference for formal rules and institutions (law in the books) over entrenched law (law in action). None of these differences, however, can explain why the new literature can successfully escape the critique that brought the old law and development down. Scholars have pointed out that the new law and development literature suffers from many of the same shortcomings as the old one.

A second explanation is ideological. Where old law and development was predominantly a cause for the political left, the new literature is decidedly market liberal. Perhaps, the first law and development movement failed largely not for theoretical and methodological but for political reasons: it was unable to survive the political shift in the 1970s against the political left. However, such an explanation is insufficient, too. Although the new law and development project relies a lot on markets, it is not confined to the political right: there is broad political support for reform projects.

Both may be good reasons, but I think the most important one is a third one: the decline of sociology and the rise of economics, and with that a change in

44 Merryman 1977, p. 459-460.
45 1966 Ford Foundation Annual Report 23. Cf. Trubek 1982, p. 6-10.
46 Mendelson 1970.
47 Rittich 1995.
48 See also Davis & Trebilcock 2008, p. 898-899.

academic sensitivities. It seems safe to say that economics as a discipline is less occupied with matters of theory than is sociology. Or, put differently, theoretical critique of the assumptions, explicit or not, on which economic modelling rests, has done less against the self-confidence in the mainstream than it did, decades ago, in sociology and anthropology. The ability of economics to show results in objective-looking numbers and rankings has somehow rendered secondary the question whether these numbers and rankings rest on theoretically tenable assumptions. The reductionist quality of rankings is an advantage for their marketability. Rankings are simpler than complex comparisons and look more objective. Only very recently have scholars begun to question the use of indicators, central to both the legal origins literature and the Doing Business Reports, as an undertheorized mode of governance.[49] In particular, anti-functionalist critique has never been damning to economics because functionalism was never explicitly adopted as a method in the first place. Geoffrey Ingham has pointed out that economics as a discipline has so far largely ignored the criticism launched against functionalism within sociology and anthropology, where the theory is practically dead today.[50] This is so although, at its core, the economic method used by the legal origins literature and the Doing Business reports is really a quantitative refinement of the functional method.[51]

This anti-theoretical stance exists not only in economics. If anything, it is even stronger in applied comparative law. Take, for example, the brief section on theory in the otherwise excellent 'Anatomy of Corporate Law' by Kraakman *et al.* They begin by acknowledging that a functionalist project is not unproblemtatic:

> 'We realize that the term "functional", which we have used here and in our title, means different things to different people, and that some of the uses to which that term has been put in the past - particularly in the field of sociology - have made the term justifiably suspect.' [52]

One would, then, expect two things to follow: first, a precision of what is meant by functional here, and second, at least a brief statement as to why the suspicion is unfounded for this book. The authors, however, treat all of this as a mere problem of labelling:

> 'It would perhaps be more accurate to call our approach "economic" rather than "functional", though the sometimes tendentious use of economic argumentation in legal literature has also caused many scholars, particularly outside of the United States, to be as wary of "economic analysis" as they are of "functional analysis".'

Justifiable suspicion for the term 'functional,' regionally confined wariness for the term 'economic' - what is the answer? Surprisingly, it is this: we can engage in functional analysis, as long as we close our eyes to its theoretical problems.

49 See especially Davis, Kingsbury & Engle Merry 2010.
50 See Ingham 1996, p. 251-252. For a very early comparison and critique, see Gregg & Williams 1944.
51 Michaels 2009b.
52 Kraakman *et al.* 2009, p. 4.

> 'For the purposes at hand, however, we need not commit ourselves on fine points of social science methodology. We need simply note that the exigencies of commercial activity and organization present practical problems that have a rough similarity in developed market economies throughout the world, that corporate law everywhere must necessarily address these problems, and that the forces of logic, competition, interest group pressure, imitation, and compatibility tend to lead different jurisdictions to choose roughly similar solutions to these problems.'

How can it be unnecessary to address 'fine' points of social science methodology, if what is 'noted' are all the problematic elements of that methodology - similarity of problems across countries, necessary types of solutions, a teleological confined trajectory of globalization? We are reminded of the anti-theoretical tradition in comparative law, most famously expressed in the statement that disciplines that must deal with their own methods are dead disciplines.[53] Viewed like this, the livelihood of the new law and development literature comes at the expense of theoretical foundations. Ironically, that seems to be to its advantage.

5. Conclusion

What should we follow from this juxtaposition of functionalism and legal origins? My conclusion is ambivalent.

The success may suggest that the critique of functionalism in sociology was overblown. Maybe, a more sophisticated functionalism is actually a promising method and theory at the same time.[54] Such a functionalism would have to take into account at least three insights from the functionalism debate. The first is Merton's suggestion that many of the assumptions of functionalism ought to be treated as no more than testable hypotheses.[55] The second is the emphasis on the possibility of functional equivalents, long a topic in discussions of functionalism, but put at the centre of the theory only, as far as I can see, in Niklas Luhmann's early discussions of functionalism.[56] The third is the need for a systemic perspective, in which individual legal rules interact with the entire legal system.[57]

Progress is made on all three points. The need for more empirics may be the broadest theme: much of the criticism of legal origins questions the assumptions and ask for testing. The second, the focus on functional equivalents, requires special comparative law expertise that non-lawyers often lack, but it seems to me that, for example, the Oxford project around John Armour makes very promising advances in this regards, especially on the level of macro-comparison. Similarly, Gillian Hadfield's macro-comparison, which emphasizes context-specificity and functional

53 Zweigert & Kötz 1996, p. 33.

54 I make this point in Michaels 2006a. For a defence of functionalism in economics, see Jackson 2002.

55 Merton 1968.

56 For discussion, see Michaels 2006a, p. 356-359.

57 I make this point generally in Michaels 2006b, and more specifically with regard to legal origins, in Michaels 2009b.

equivalence more, seems promising.[58] The third point, finally, the sense for a systemic approach, underlies much of Katharina Pistor's recent work.[59]

Pistor's critique of the legal origins literature is also instructive, however, for what might remain a necessary limit of its method: Statistical analysis is necessarily reductionist. Such reductionism may sometimes be helpful;[60] but its use seems limited: by necessity, greater breadth reduces depth. This seems especially problematic in comparative law, where the number of legal systems in the world is too small, the differences between them to great, to yield truly meaningful statistical results, except in a fairly limited number of issues.

Some scholars have suggested, therefore, to move away from quantitative to qualitative analysis, and to focus in particular on case studies. This move resembles the suggested move in comparative law from functionalist to culturalist comparative law, and thereby from explicit comparison to a more hermeneutic approach. In comparative law, such a move comes with a cost, and the same is undoubtedly true in law and development. The challenge for comparative law will be to integrate functionalist and culturalist comparison.[61] In law and development, this might be done through a combination of statistical analysis and case studies, as suggested by Milhaupt and Pistor.[62] Such an approach could save the best of functionalist and culturalist approaches, but it would look very different from the legal origins literature as it exists today.

58 Hadfield 2008.
59 Pistor 2009.
60 Thus e.g. Hadfield 2009; Spamann 2009.
61 My own first suggestion is to use the idea of legal paradigms: Michaels 2006b.
62 Milhaupt & Pistor 2008.

Bibliography

Abrahamson 1978
Abrahamson, M., *Functionalism*, Englewood Cliffs NJ: Prentice-Hall, 1978.

Ajani 2009
Ajani, G., 'Legal Change and Economic Performance: An Assessment', in: A. Bakardjieva Engelbrekt & J. Nergelius (eds.), *New Directions in Comparative Law*, Cheltenham, UK & Northampton, MA: Edward Elgar, 2009, p. 3-18.

Armour *et al.* 2009
Armour, J., Deakin, S., Mollica, V. & Siems, M., 'Law and Financial Development: What We Are Learning from Time-Series Evidence', *Brigham Young University Law Review*, 2009, p. 1435-1500.

Bakardjieva Engelbrekt 2009
Bakardjieva Engelbrekt, A, 'Toward an Instutional Approach to Comparative Economic Law', in: A. Bakardjieva Engelbrekt & J. Nergelius (eds.), *New Directions in Comparative Law*, Cheltenham, UK & Northampton, MA: Edward Elgar, 2009, p. 213-251.

Channell 2006
Channell, W., 'Lessons not Learned about Legal Reform, in: T. Carothers (ed.), *Promoting the Rule of Law Abroad: in Search of Knowledge*, Washington D.C: Carnegie Endowment for International Peace, 2006, p. 137-160.

Cioffi 2009
Cioffi, J.W., 'Legal Regimes and Political Particularism: An Assessment of the "Legal Families" Theory from the Perspectives of Comparative Law and Political Economy', *Brigham Young University Law Review*, 2009, p. 1501-1551.

Davis 1959
Davis, K., The Myth of Functional Analysis as a Special Method in Sociology and Anthropology, *American Sociological Review*, 1959, p. 757-772.

Davis & Trebilcock 2008
Davis, K.E. & Trebilcock, M.J., 'The Relationship between Law and Development: Optimists versus Skeptics, *The American Journal of Comparative Law*, 2008, p. 895-946.

Davis, Kingsbury & Engle Merry 2010
Davis, K.E., Kingsbury, B. & Engle Merry, S., *Indicators as a Technology of Global Governance*, IILJ Working Paper, No. 2, 2010.

Demerath & Peterson 1967
Demerath III, N.J. & Peterson, R.A., *System, Change, and Conflict. A Reader on Contemporary Sociological Theory and the Debate Over Functionalism*, New York: The Free Press, and London: Collier-Macmillan Limited, 1967.

Djankov *et al.* 2003
Djankov, S., Glaeser, La Porta, R., Lopez-de-Silanes, F. & Shleifer, A., 'The New Comparative Economics', *Journal of Comparative Economics*, p. 595-619.

Fauvarque-Cosson & Kerhuel 2009
Fauvarque-Cosson, B. & Kerhuel, A., 'Is Law an Economic Contest? French Reactions to the Doing Business World Bank Reports and Economic Analysis of the Law', *The American Journal of Comparative Law*, 2009, p. 811-830.

Geertz 1983
Geertz, C., *Local Knowledge: Further Essays in Interpretive Anthropology*, New York: Basic Books Inc., 1983.

Glaeser & Shleifer 2003
Glaeser, E.L. & Shleifer, A., 'Legal Origins', *Quarterly Journal of Economics*, 2003, p. 1193-1229.

Gregg & Williams 1948
Gregg, D. & Williams, E., 'The Dismal Science of Functionalism', *American Anthropologist*, 1948, p. 594-611.

Hadfield 2008
Hadfield, G.K., 'The Levers of Legal Design: Institutional Determinants of the Quality of Law', *Journal of Comparative Economics*, 2008, p. 43-73.

Hadfield 2009
Hadfield, G.K., 'The Strategy of Methodology: The Virtues of Reductionism for Comparative Law', *University of Toronto Law Journal*, p. 223-235.

Holmes 1879
Holmes, O.W., 'The Path of the Law', *Harvard Law Review*, 1897, p. 457-478.

Hyland 2009
Hyland, R., *Gifts – A Study in Comparative Law*, Oxford: Oxford University Press, 2009.

Ingham 1996
Ingham, G., 'Some Recent Changes in the Relationship between Economics and Sociology, *Cambridge Journal of Economics*, 1996, p. 243-275.

Jackson 2002
Jackson, W.A., 'Functional Explanation in Economics: a Qualified Defence', *Journal of Economic Methodology*, 2002, p. 169-189.

Kraakman *et al.* 2009
Kraakman, R., Armour, J., Davies, P., Enriques, L., Hansmann, H.B., Hertig, G., Hopt, K.J., Kanda, H. & Rock, E.B., *The Anatomy of Corporate Law. A Comparative and Functional Approach*, second edition, Oxford: Oxford University Press, 2009.

La Porta, Lopez-de-Silanes & Shleifer 2008
La Porta, R., Lopez-de-Silanes, F. & Shleifer, A., 'The Economic Consequences of Legal Origins', *Journal of Economic Literature*, 2008, p. 285–332.

Martindale 1968
Martindale. D. (ed.), *Functionalism in the Social Sciences*, Philadelphia: American Academy of Political & Social Sciences, 1968.

Mattei 1994
Mattei, U., 'Why the Wind Changed: Intellectual Leadership in Western Law', *The American Journal of Comparative Law*, 1994, p. 195-218.

Mendelson 1970
Mendelson, W., 'Law and the Development of Nations', *Journal of Politics*, 1970, p. 223-238.

Merryman 1977,
Merryman, J.H., 'Comparative law and social change: On the origins, style, decline and revival of the law and development movement', *The American Journal of Comparative Law*, 1977, p. 457-491.

Merton 1968
Merton, R.K., *Social Theory and Social Structure*, reviewed editon, New York: The Free Press, 1968.

Michaels 2006a
Michaels, R., 'The Functional Method of Comparative Law', in: M. Reimann & R. Zimmermann (eds.), *The Oxford Handbook of Comparative Law*, Oxford: Oxford University Press, 2006, p. 339-382.

Michaels 2006b
Michaels, R., 'Two Paradigms of Jurisdiction', *Michigan Journal of International Law*, 2006, p. 1003-1069.

Michaels 2009a
Michaels, R., 'Comparative Law by Numbers? Legal Origins Thesis, Doing Business Reports, and the Silence of Traditional Comparative Law', *The American Journal of Comparative Law*, 2009, p. 765-795.

Michaels 2009b
Michaels, R., 'The Second Wave of Law and Economics, *University of Toronto Law Journal*, 2009, p. 197-213.

Michaels 2010
Michaels, R., 'Explanation and Interpretation in Functionalist Comparative Law - a Response to Julie de Coninck', *Rabels Zeitschrift fuer auslaendisches und internationales Privatrecht*, 2010, p. 351-359.

Milhaupt & Pistor 2008
Milhaupt C.J. & Pistor, K., *Law & Capitalism: What Corporate Crises Reveal about Legal Systems and Economic Development around the World*, Chicago IL: University of Chicago Press, 2008.

Münch 2003
Münch, R., 'Funktionalismus - Geschichte und Zukunftsperspektiven einer Theorietradition', in: J. Jetzkowitz & C. Stark (eds.), *Soziologischer Funktionalismus. Zur Methodologie einer Theorietradition*, Opladen: Leske + Budrich, 2003, p. 16-56.

Pistor 2009
Pistor, K., 'Rethinking the "Law and Finance" Paradigm', *Brigham Young University Law Review*, 2009, p. 1647-1670.

Pound 1954
Pound, R., 'The Lawyer as a Social Engineer', *Journal of Public Law*, 1954, p. 292.

Ramseyer 2009
Ramseyer, M., 'Mixing-and-Matching Across (Legal) Family Lines', *Brigham Young University Law Review*, 2009, p. 1701-1712.

Rittich 2005
Rittich, K., 'Functionalism and Formalism: Their Latest Incarnations in Contemporary Development and Governance Debates', *University of Toronto Law Journal*, 2005, p. 853-868.

Sandholtz & Stone Sweet 2012
Sandholtz, W. & Stone Sweet, A., 'Neofunctionalism and Supranational Governance', in: E. Jones & A. Menon & S. Weatherill (eds.), *Oxford Handbook of the European Union*, Oxford: Oxford University Press, 2012.

Siems 2007
Siems, M., 'Legal Origins: Reconciling Law & Finance and Comparative Law', *McGill Law Journal*, 2007, p. 55-81.

Siems 2008
Siems, M., 'Statistische Rechtsvergleichung', *Rabels Zeitschrift für ausländisches und internationales Privatrecht*, 2008, p. 354-390.

Spamann 2009
Spamann, H., 'Large Sample, Quantitative Research Designs for Comparative Law?', *The American Journal of Comparative Law*, 2009, p. 797-810.

Tamanaha 1995
Tamanaha, B.Z., 'The Lessons of Law and Development Studies', *The American Journal of International Law*, 1995, p. 470-486.

Thompson 2005
Thompson, N., 'Common Denominator', *Legal Affairs*, Jan./Feb. 2005, available at: <http://www.legalaffairs.org/issues/January-February-2005/feature_thompson_janfeb05.msp>.

Trubek 1982
Trubek, D.M., 'Towards a Social Theory of Law: An Essay on the Study of Law and Development', *The Yale Law Journal*, 1982, p. 1-50.

Trubek & Galanter 1974
Trubek, D.M. & Galanter, M., 'Scholars in Self-Estrangement: Some Reflections on the Crisis in Law and Development Studies in the United States', *Wisconsin Law Review*, 1974, p. 1062-1103.

Trubek & Santos 2006
Trubek, D.M. & Santos, A., 'An Introduction: the Third Moment in Law and Development Theory and the Emergence of a New Critical Practice', in: D.M. Trubek & A. Santos (eds.), *The New Law and Economic Development – A Critical Appraisal*, New York: Cambridge University Press, 2006, p. 1-18.

Valcke 2010
Valcke, C., 'The French Response to the World Bank's Doing Business Reports', *University of Toronto Law Journal*, 2010, p. 197-217.

Whytock 2009
Whytock, C.A., 'Legal Origins, Functionalism, and the Future of Comparative Law', *Brigham Young University Law Review*, 2009, p. 1879-1905.

Zweigert & Kötz 1996
Zweigert, K. & Kötz, H., *An Introduction to Comparative Law*, 3rd edition, translated by T. Weir, Oxford: Oxford University Press, 1996.

John Armour
Simon Deakin
Viviane Mollica
Mathias Siems

LAW AND FINANCIAL DEVELOPMENT: WHAT WE ARE LEARNING FROM TIME-SERIES EVIDENCE*

1. Introduction

It is widely believed that legal institutions matter for financial development. According to the 'legal origins' hypothesis developed by La Porta *et al.* and their collaborators (LLSV),[1] legal systems vary considerably in the way they regulate economic activity. A principal cause of this diversity is the role played by the different legal traditions or 'origins' of the common and civil law.[2] It is argued that countries whose legal systems have a common law origin emphasize freedom of contract and the protection of private property, whereas those with civil law roots favour an activist role for the state.[3] These legal differences seem to have tangible economic effects. Common law systems have been found to have more dispersed

* This article is a reprint and was first published in the *Brigham Young University Law Review*, 2009, p. 1435-1500.
The work reported here was carried out at the Centre for Business Research, University of Cambridge, as part of the Law, Finance and Development' project (<http://www.cbr.cam.ac.uk/research/programme2/project2-20.htm>). We gratefully acknowledge funding from the ESRC's 'World Economy and Finance' Programme, the Newton Trust, the EU Sixth Research and Development Framework Programme (Integrated Project 'Reflexive Governance in the Public Interest'), and the Oxford-Man Institute of Quantitative Finance. We are also grateful for comments received in the course of presentations of earlier versions of this work at the European Bank of Reconstruction and Development in London, January 2009; at the BYU Law Review Symposium, 'Evaluating Legal Origins Theory', Brigham Young University, February 2009; and at Judge Business School, University of Cambridge, June 2009. We also thank Dominic Chai, Priya Lele, Prabirjit Sarkar and Ajit Singh for helpful comments and discussions, and Rose-Alice Murphy and Phil Fellows for research assistance. Remaining errors are entirely our responsibility.

1 The acronym 'LLSV' refers to the four authors of the first legal origins papers: Rafael La Porta, Francisco Lopez-de-Silanes, Andrei Shleifer and Robert Vishny. See the references to their work, *infra*.

2 La Porta, Lopez-de-Silanes & Shleifer 2008.

3 Glaeser & Shleifer 2002.

share ownership,[4] more liquid and extensive capital markets,[5] and more highly developed systems of private credit,[6] than civilian ones. In part through the Doing Business reports of the World Bank,[7] these findings have come to influence policy reform in 'dozens of countries' over the past decade.[8] Reforms to corporate and bankruptcy law have seen a strengthening of shareholder and creditor rights, particularly the former.[9]

Influential as it is, the legal origins hypothesis has raised more questions than it has answered. The idea that a country's approach to the regulation of the economy is fixed at the point when it first adopts or has imposed upon it, through colonization or conquest, a certain type of legal order, implies that national systems are locked into particular developmental paths. This neglects the possibility of feedback effects between legal change and economic development. It is also points to a potential contradiction in the use of the legal origins hypothesis to generate policy reforms: the common law model, while apparently more conducive to financial development, might not be appropriate for transplantation into civil law regimes. What is at stake here is the degree of fit between substantive rules and the legal structures which are said to underpin them. Adherents of the legal origins hypothesis suggest that legal changes can be undertaken 'without disturbing the fundamentals of the legal tradition' of the countries concerned,[10] a view supportive of the move to align civilian systems with the common law approach.

A further issue is whether the postulated relationship between legal rules and economic outcomes is as tight as has been suggested. A central methodological tenet of the legal origins approach is that legal rules can be coded and the extent of cross-national legal diversity quantified as a preliminary step to testing for the economic effects of certain laws. The legal origins hypothesis was first developed in the context of a legal coding exercise which showed that legal protection of outside investors against the threat of expropriation by corporate insiders was consistently higher in common law countries than in civil law ones. Econometric analysis was then used to show that 'legal investor protection is a strong predictor of financial development',[11] as measured by the level of stock market activity and the degree of dispersion of share ownership.[12] Although the scope of the legal origins claim has since been extended to cover a number of other areas of law and regulation, it is this early work on the relationship between law and finance, as subsequently extended and developed,[13] which has proved most influential on law reform. Yet the

4 La Porta, Lopez-de-Silanes & Shleifer 1999.

5 La Porta *et al.* 1998.

6 Djankov, McLiesh & Shleifer 2007.

7 World Bank, *Doing Business Reports* (various years), available at: <http://www.doingbusiness.org>.

8 La Porta, Lopez-de-Silanes & Shleifer 2008, p. 326.

9 See *infra*, section 4.

10 La Porta, Lopez-de-Silanes & Shleifer 2008, p. 325.

11 La Porta, Lopez-de-Silanes & Shleifer 2008, p. 286.

12 La Porta *et al.* 1998.

13 Djankov, McLeish & Shleifer 2007; Djankov *et al.* 2007; Djankov *et al.* 2008; La Porta, Lopez-de-Silanes & Shleifer 2006.

empirical basis for this finding is limited; it mostly depends on cross-sectional data on the laws of countries in the late 1990s, with no systematic coding of legal change over time.

A decade on from the publication of the first legal origins studies, we are in the position of being able to subject the legal origins hypothesis to tests which measure its validity as an instrument of policy in the law and finance area. In this paper we present time-series evidence of trends in corporate and bankruptcy law in a sample of 25 developed, developing and transition systems over the period 1995-2005. We put this information in the context of a more in-depth study of five countries (France, Germany, India, the UK and USA) over a thirty-six year period, 1970-2005. The evidence from the longitudinal datasets that we report here reveals the far-reaching nature of the legal changes which have occurred over these periods, and in particular the last decade. There has been a consistent rise in levels of shareholder protection that can be seen most clearly in the civil law systems, which have been catching up with their common law counterparts. In the area of creditor rights there has been a less dramatic change, but a significant overall increase in protection has nevertheless occurred, which is particularly marked in transition systems. In short, we see the effects of a process of legal alignment around the idea of legal support for financial development of the kind promoted by the World Bank[14] and given intellectual support by the legal origins hypothesis.[15]

We find, however, that legal convergence has not been translated into financial development of the kind predicted by the legal origins approach, or at least not yet. Econometric analyses that we report here indicate that legal changes of the kind we have tracked have not been reflected in increased levels of stock market activity. We explore why this might be. We look at a number of explanations. One is that laws which might be well suited for the liquid capital markets and dispersed ownership structures of the common law world (in particular Britain and America) are not working as intended in civil law and developing systems where those conditions do not prevail. Another is that the enactment of shareholder rights on the scale that we have seen over the past decade could have been counter-productive, in common law and civil law systems alike.

Our paper aims to make three contributions to the legal origins literature. Our first is theoretical: we show that there are difficulties in viewing the legal system as an entirely 'exogenous' influence on the economy, and it may be more useful to see legal systems as both shaping and being shaped by economic and political factors, an approach we label 'co-evolutionary'. Our second aim is methodological: we demonstrate how the coding and measurement of legal rules can be undertaken on a longitudinal basis and how the resulting data can be used in conjunction with time-series and panel-data econometric techniques to throw light on the direction of causation in the relationship between legal and economic change. Our third aim is normative, in the sense of evaluating how far evidence and analysis of this kind could or should be used to inform the process of legal reform.

14 Through the Doing Business reports, *supra* note 7.
15 La Porta, Lopez-de-Silanes & Shleifer 2008, p. 323-327.

Part 2 below provides an overview of legal origins theory, with the emphasis on the way in which the theory has developed in response to empirical findings and to certain critiques. In section 3 we take a closer look at methodological issues and explain the *leximetric* and econometric techniques which we employ to study legal change and its interaction with economic variables. Section 4 presents our main findings and section 5 offers a theoretical re-evaluation of the legal origins hypothesis in the light of this new empirical evidence. Section 6 concludes.

2. Legal Origins: The Interplay between Evidence and Theory

2.1. *Explaining Legal Origins*

The legal origins literature began with a series of empirical findings requiring explanation; only gradually did a theory emerge which aimed to provide a systematic account of these results. As noted above, the earliest legal origins studies focused on the relationship between legal protection of investor interests and financial outcomes including ownership structure and capital market development. LLSV's 'anti-director rights index'[16] contained six principal indicators of shareholder protection: the extent to which the corporate law of a given system allowed voting by proxy; whether the law prevented the blocking of voting and other rights associated with share ownership prior to a shareholders' meeting; whether it contained a 'cumulative voting' rule which allowed for representation of minority shareholder interests on the board; whether it provided for shareholders' pre-emption rights in respect of new share issues, thereby preventing the dilution of stakes; and the extent of voting rights required to call a shareholders' meeting. Two further indicators, referring respectively to the one-share, one-vote rule and laws on mandatory dividends, were used in some of their analyses. They found, on the basis of legal data collected for 49 countries in the mid-1990s, that low scores on the index were associated with a high concentration of ownership and a low level of stock market development as measured by the ratio of stock market capitalization to GDP.[17] These relationships were especially strong in French civil law systems, justifying the conclusion that 'legal systems matter to corporate governance and... firms have to adapt to the limitations of the systems that they operate in'.[18]

This first 'law and finance' paper proved to be extraordinarily influential in demonstrating the possibilities of quantitative legal analysis. It produced a clear empirical finding with far-reaching implications for policy debates. In subsequent studies, new methods for coding the law were tried out, with the focus on the operation of legal rules in a series of hypothetical cases. Evidence was gathered from surveys of practicing lawyers in a range of countries. This different approach was adopted in order to address some of the criticisms of the early studies. In particular, the new methods, by drawing on survey evidence from legal practi-

16 La Porta *et al.* 1998.

17 La Porta *et al.* 1998, p. 1145.

18 La Porta *et al.* 1998, p. 1117.

tioners, were intended to incorporate evidence concerning the enforcement of legal rules and to avoid undue subjectivity in the coding process. On this basis, a second wave of results essentially confirmed the findings of the early studies: there was a clear divide between the common law and the civil law in respect of rules on self-dealing in corporate transactions,[19] prospectus disclosure,[20] and creditor rights.[21] These legal differences were reflected in financial outcome variables, including, in the context of creditor rights, the size of private debt markets.[22] The common law-civil law divide was also found to operate in related areas of economic life, such as labour regulation[23] and rules on business start-ups,[24] with consequences for unemployment and employment levels, the size of the informal economy, and the level of corruption. In addition, a set of studies looked at aspects of legal institutions including the flexibility of court procedure[25] and the extent of judicial independence;[26] these institutional variables were shown to be linked to contract enforcement and the protection of property rights.[27]

These findings 'raise[d] an enormous challenge of interpretation'.[28] What has emerged from the iteration of theory and evidence over the past decade is a claim that it is not so much legal rules themselves that matter, as the *infrastructure* of the legal system. 'Legal infrastructure' refers to the meta-level rules, norms and practices which determine, in a given national context, the mechanisms for law making and dispute resolution, the competencies of legislatures and courts, and the conception of the role of government in the economy and society, among other things. In this broad sense, 'legal origin' is not confined to formal legal institutions, but may extend to include informal norms and shared assumptions about the prevailing 'style of social control of economic life'.[29] The civil law 'style' is 'associated with a heavier hand of government ownership and regulation than the common law' and, as a result, with 'greater corruption, higher unemployment and a larger informal economy'; the common law, by contrast, 'is associated with lower formalism of judicial procedures and greater judicial independence than civil law', and hence with 'greater contract enforcement and greater security of property rights'.[30]

19 Djankov *et al.* 2008.
20 La Porta, Lopez-de-Silanes & Shleifer 2006.
21 Djankov, McLiesh & Shleifer 2007.
22 Djankov, McLiesh & Shleifer 2007. It should be noted that while there is some evidence that financial development indicators, such as the extent of stock market capitalization and private credit, are correlated with overall levels of economic growth as measured by GDP, it has not proved possible to find a link between legal origins as such and GDP growth: see La Porta, Lopez-de-Silanes & Shleifer 2008, p. 301-302.
23 Botero *et al.* 2004.
24 Djankov *et al.* 2002.
25 Djankov *et al.* 2003.
26 La Porta *et al.* 2004.
27 The evidence is summarized by La Porta, Lopez-de-Silanes & Shleifer 2008, p. 293-298.
28 La Porta, Lopez-de-Silanes & Shleifer 2008, p. 286.
29 La Porta, Lopez-de-Silanes & Shleifer 2008.
30 La Porta, Lopez-de-Silanes & Shleifer 2008.

The persistent influence of legal origin is the result of the tendency of the legal system, in the first instance, to operate as a mechanism for the stabilization of norms and practices. Legal institutions promote particular routines, conventions and distributional compromizes which can understood as providing solutions to various collective action problems and related issues of societal coordination. As such, they display the characteristics of lock-in and path-dependence which are associated with the development of formal institutions:

> 'the reason for persistence is that... beliefs and ideologies become incorporated in legal rules, institutions and education and, as such, are transmitted from one generation to the next. It is this incorporation of beliefs and ideologies into the legal and political infrastructure that enables legal origins to have such persistent consequences for rules, regulations and economic outcomes'.[31]

Legal systems also allow for the transmission of norms and practices across different regulatory spaces. Apart from a few 'parent' systems aside (such as England, France and Germany), most countries have had the basic features of their legal systems imposed upon them by colonization or conquest. When this kind of transplantation occurred at various points in the period from the late eighteenth to the early twentieth centuries, it was not just 'specific laws and codes' that were transmitted but 'more general styles or ideologies of the legal system' along with 'individuals with mother-country training, human capital, and legal outlook'.[32] Over time, the national laws of particular countries might have 'changed, evolved and adapted to local conditions', but 'enough of the basic transplanted elements have remained and persisted to allow the classification [of systems] into legal traditions'.[33] This is the basis for the suggested division of the legal systems of the world into four principal groupings, namely English or common law, and the French, German and Scandinavian variants of civil law.[34]

A key feature of this theorization of the law-economy relationship is the claim that legal origin operates as an 'exogenous' or independent force influencing the path of economic development (see Figure 1). As just stated, legal origins theory acknowledges that legal rules in a given national context may be shaped to some degree by local economic conditions. To that extent, there is mutual feedback between law and economy, and the direction of causation runs both ways. Thus legal origins theory can accept the possibility that many features of modern corporate law regimes can be explained by the particular types of business enterprise that prevailed in certain countries at important points in their development, or that trends in the regulation of financial markets were driven by the emergence of particular types of financial transaction. It can also accommodate the idea that the emergence of interest groups prepared to lobby for laws of a given type, or to litigate particular disputes, in the corporate field as elsewhere, may have been an

31 La Porta, Lopez-de-Silanes & Shleifer 2008, p. 308.
32 La Porta, Lopez-de-Silanes & Shleifer 2008, p. 288.
33 La Porta, Lopez-de-Silanes & Shleifer 2008.
34 La Porta, Lopez-de-Silanes & Shleifer 2008, p. 288-290.

important influence on the content of laws.[35] What is suggested, however, is that these feedback effects do not reach back to the core legal infrastructure of the country concerned, which is unchanging, or at least very slow to change, by comparison both to the legal rules themselves and to the wider economic and social environment: 'the legal system provides the fundamental tolls for addressing social concerns and it is that system, with its codes, distinctive institutions, modes of thought and even ideologies, that is very slow to change'.[36]

Figure 1: Legal *origin as an exogenous influence on legal rules and the economy*

In Figure 1, substantive legal rules provide the 'channel' through which legal origin shapes economic outcomes. Legal rules may not, however, be the only such channel. Legal origins theory raises the possibility that, independently of the content of rules, judicial style and modes of enforcement more generally may impact on the economy. This suggestion is supported by empirical research demonstrating a link between the quality of judicial enforcement of creditor rights and the flow of private credit.[37] Another possible channel is provided by the interpretative rules which courts follow when construing and enforcing contracts. Common law judicial style is, it is argued, more flexible in responding to new types of financial transactions, a flexibility which 'promotes financial development' by legitimising transactional innovation.[38]

2.2. *The Complexity of Legal Origins*

A potential line of criticism of the explanation given by LLSV for their legal origins findings is that the broad-brush descriptions they provide of common law and civilian regulatory 'style' are over-stylised to the point of being inaccurate. The law and finance literature assumes that a clear distinction can be drawn between systems by reference to their membership of one of the four main legal families. The reason for choosing this classification is not explained in detail. Some general references are made to the mainstream comparative law literature,[39] suggesting that this distinction is well established and uncontroversial. However, modern

35 On this, see Coffee 2001, for the United States; Cheffins 2001, for the United Kingdom (discussing the impact of political interest groups on the United Kingdom's form of the dispersed ownership system).

36 La Porta, Lopez-de-Silanes & Shleifer 2008, p. 308.

37 La Porta, Lopez-de-Silanes & Shleifer 2008, p. 299.

38 La Porta, Lopez-de-Silanes & Shleifer 2008, p. 300.

39 Such as: David & C. Brierley 1995; Zweigert & Kötz 1998; Reynolds & Flores 1989.

comparative law scholarship barely recognizes the global classifications and generalizations of the law and finance literature.

On a general level, three degrees of criticism can be distinguished. First, some legal scholars doubt whether even the distinction between 'common law' and 'civil law' can be justified from a historical perspective.[40] Second, others accept the idea of two different legal origins as a historical starting point, but emphasize that, since the end of the twentieth century, legal systems are becoming international, transnational, or even global in nature, so that the idea of a strict common law-civil law divide is an anachronism.[41] Thirdly, even those comparative lawyers who still apply the notion of legal families emphasize the limits of this concept, stating that it is really no more than a didactic device.[42]

More specifically, the law and finance literature overlooks the difficulties involved in classifying many countries as either common law or civil law in origin. The idea that the laws and legal institutions of the parent systems have simply spread to other parts of the world disregards the ongoing influence of pre-transplant laws, the mixtures and modifications which occur at the moment when copying of foreign law occurs, and the post-transplant period, in which the transplanted laws and institutions may be altered (or at least applied differently from in the parent system).[43] Examples of this are legion. For example, the law and finance literature assumes that the transition economies of Eastern Europe are either German or French legal origin countries, whereas in practice they have been influenced by a number of different traditions. Similarly, it is assumed that Japan, South Korea and China are German legal origin countries, whereas a more nuanced analysis would have to take into account the indigenous legal cultures of these legal systems as well as more recent Anglo-Saxon influence. Further, classifying countries such as Iran, Saudi Arabia and Yemen as simply 'common law' in origin underplays the role of religious legal traditions.[44]

A counter-argument to the one just made could be that the law and finance literature is specifically concerned with the rules that are relevant for 'doing business'. Here, it is indeed the case that the law of developed countries has had a discernible influence on most African, Asian and Latin American legal systems. Yet, in these areas of law it is difficult to justify using the suggested distinction between English, French, German, and Scandinavian legal origins. Formally, at least, case law is the primary source of law in common law jurisdictions, whereas in civil law jurisdictions this is constituted by the codes and by related legislation. However, the

40 Vogenauer 2005; Zimmerman 1998.

41 See, e.g., Reimann 2001; Husa 2004.

42 David & Brierley, p. 21 ('it is no more than a didactic device'); Zweigert & Kötz, p. 72 ('... any division of the legal world into families is a rough and ready device. It can be useful for the novice by putting the confusing variety of legal systems into some kind of loose order, but the experienced comparatist will have developed a 'nose' for the distinctive style of national legal systems...').

43 Siems 2007.

44 See Siems 2007, p. 62-70.

sources of corporate law, securities law and bankruptcy law are mainly statutory across the world, even in common law countries.[45]

This is not to say that we should not expect to find some similarities between countries which are regarded as belonging to the same legal family. Countries of the same legal origin often share a common language. So, for example, if Spain amends its corporate law, it is more likely that this reform will diffuse to the Spanish-speaking countries of Latin America than to the Anglophone world.[46] Certain countries have developed a shared legal heritage as a result of coordinated efforts to develop common solutions to legal problems and to systematize the exchange of legal information, as in the case of the Scandinavian systems.[47] It is not necessary to invoke legal origin as an explanation for these trends.

Harmonization of laws and the borrowing of legal concepts and rules from foreign systems may also go on across legal families, particularly in the field of law and finance. There is a long tradition in commercial law of legal transplants, often driven by international trade, to the extent that commentators have questioned the relevance of a strict division between legal families.[48] Some studies suggest that by the end of the nineteenth century the most important features of corporate law were already relatively uniform across countries.[49]

Legal origins theorists have responded to points such as these by conceding that most national legal systems contain hybrid elements, in part as a consequence of the borrowing or voluntary acceptance of regulatory solutions on a cross-country basis. Thus it is accepted that most of securities law, for example, is statutory even in common law systems, and that this is an area of law that was introduced relatively recently 'in response to perceived social needs'.[50] However, the suggestion is then made that laws of this kind 'took different forms in countries with different legal traditions, consistent with broad strategies of how the state intervenes'. In America and Britain, the response to the crisis of the 1930s was 'to rehabilitate and support markets, not to replace them', while in civil law countries it was 'to repress...or to replace [the market] with state mandates'.[51] Thus legal origin, it is claimed, shapes the way in which different systems respond to common crises and new social needs.

The 'exogeneity' of the legal infrastructure with regard to economic development is not simply an incidental feature of legal origins theory. Without it, it would be hard to maintain the view that the legal origins effect apparently identified in the empirical studies is not a proxy for something else. This view, in turn, justifies the use made of legal origins theory to promote institutional reform. Because legal origin locks systems into particular institutional configurations, inefficiencies can result, in particular in the developing world: 'many developing countries today find themselves heavily overregulated in crucial spheres of economic life, in part

45 See e.g. Lele & Siems 2007a, p. 5.
46 For this point see also Spamann 2009; Siems 2008a, p. 138 & 142.
47 On this, see Zweigert & Kötz 1998, p. 281-283.
48 Vagts 2000, p. 598-599.
49 Hansmann & Reinier Kraakman 2001a, p. 439-440. See also Siems 2008b.
50 La Porta, Lopez-de-Silanes & Shleifer 2008, p. 308.
51 La Porta, Lopez-de-Silanes & Shleifer 2008, p. 308.

because of their legal origin heritage'.[52] While common law rules are not 'always'[53] the most efficient, the default position of legal origins theory appears to be that common law solutions are generally to be preferred to civilian ones, not least because the right response to persistent legal inefficiencies 'is simply less government intervention'.[54] Civilian responses are seen as desirable only in a context of extreme crisis and disorder, in which markets break down completely.[55] This is the basis on which the deregulatory reform agenda associated with the Doing Business reports of the World Bank[56] is claimed to be a natural offshoot of legal origins theory.[57]

2.3. *Endogeneity and Co-evolution*

The emergence of 'legal origins theory' as a response to the challenges raised by empirical research on law and development has provided a sounder conceptual foundation for this line of research and has clarified certain aspects of the claims being made. The legal system continues to be at the centre of the analysis, but the idea of legal origin has been broadened to include elements of belief systems, ideologies and social norms, as well as more formal legal institutions. Some limitations of the use of the concept of legal families have been acknowledged, while the underlying value of the division of systems along English, French, German and Scandinavian lines has been reasserted. The exogenous causal influence of legal infrastructure remains, with a reduced role for substantive legal rules in shaping economic outcomes, as alternative channels (enforcement and interpretation) have been proposed.

The critical issue in addressing the legal origins approach at a theoretical level is therefore the question of law's 'exogeneity' with regard to the process of economic development. Notwithstanding the mediation of the effects of legal infrastructure through various channels, the direction of causation can run only one way, from legal origin to the economy. The theory is asymmetrical in its treatment of the legal and economic systems. It requires us to believe that there is some factor which renders the core of the legal system immune from economic influence, but which does not prevent the legal system shaping the economy.

One alternative is to reverse the arrow of causation so that law is shaped by economic or political forces. This is by no means an implausible position; on the contrary, it is one with a long history in certain strands of the sociological and economic analyses of law, and it appears to be widely accepted, if not always explicitly acknowledged, in the social sciences more generally.[58] A good reason for not taking this view, however, is that it would represent something of a step back in

52 La Porta, Lopez-de-Silanes & Shleifer 2008, p. 287.
53 La Porta, Lopez-de-Silanes & Shleifer 2008, p. 309.
54 La Porta, Lopez-de-Silanes & Shleifer 2008, p. 324.
55 La Porta, Lopez-de-Silanes & Shleifer 2008, p. 327.
56 World Bank, *supra* note 7.
57 La Porta, Lopez-de-Silanes & Shleifer 2008, p. 307.
58 For a review of theories which view legal rules as 'epiphenomenal', that is, as a secondary form or expression of 'material' social and economic relations, see Hodgson 2003.

the conceptualization of the law-economy relation. The legal origins literature has, at the very least, done enough to demonstrate that the legal system should be treated as a causal variable in its own right, with the capacity to shape economic outcomes. The claim that, to this extent at least, 'legal systems matter' is one that we share with the founders of the legal origins approach. Where we disagree is in the characterization of the legal system (or, at least, that part of it that can be characterized as 'legal infrastructure') as entirely exogenous with regard to the economy.

In proposing that law is better thought of as, at least in part, 'endogenous' to the economy, we are not arguing that either legal rules or the 'legal infrastructure' are predetermined by economic forces. The claim, rather, is that the dynamic of interaction between law and the economy is one of 'co-evolution', as opposed to linear, uni-directional change.[59] The legal system is, to a certain degree, autonomous from economic relations, and its development is not simply dictated by technological or organizational requirements, or by changes in the composition of supply and demand; legal concepts, processes, and routines form the immediate material from which new solutions are fashioned.[60] Nevertheless, the economy forms part of the context within which legal rules evolve, with pressures for selection being applied by the external environment.[61] These propositions can all be reversed: economic relations evolve, in part, by reference to an institutional context which is set by the legal system, and the same point applies, *mutatis mutandis*, if the political system is included in the model (see Figure 2).[62]

Figure 2. *Co-evolutionary model of the legal, economic and political systems*

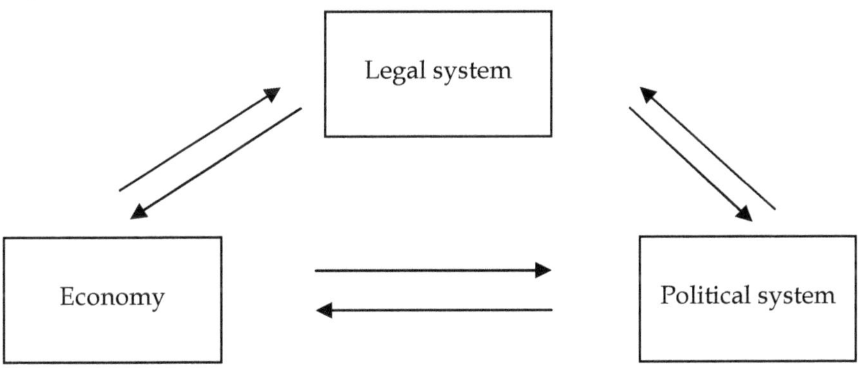

59 The concept of co-evolution has roots in evolutionary biology, game theory and systems theory, and is increasingly applied to explain the evolution of economic and legal institutions. See, e.g. Aoki 2001) (describing evolutionary game theory); Teubner 1993 (describing systems theory). A full account of these theories, and an assessment of the possibilities for synthesis between them, is beyond the scope of this paper.

60 On this 'self-referential' aspect of legal evolution, see Teubner 1993.

61 On the application of the 'Darwinian' evolutionary mechanisms of variation, inheritance and selection to legal change, see Teubner 1993, p. 51; Deakin 2003.

62 The incorporation of political economy considerations into the study of institutions is a core feature of the 'Varieties of Capitalism' approach. See Hall & Soskice 2001. And it is a core feature of Mark Roe's 'political' theory of corporate governance (Roe 2003).

Most scholars of corporate law would accept that there is a link of some kind between the emergence and development of the business enterprise in industrial societies, and the evolution of legal forms, associated with the joint stock company, which have served the needs of entrepreneurs and investors. There is considerable disagreement, however, on the question of whether legal change preceded financial development, or the converse. In the context of the legal origins debate, there is a growing literature looking at the evolution of corporate law in Britain, France, Germany and the United States in the course of the nineteenth and twentieth centuries.[63] One strand of this work argues that financial development in Britain preceded by several decades the passage of laws for shareholder protection, while other studies emphasize that functional equivalents to corporate law,[64] such as stock exchange rules, were already providing a basis for the dispersion of ownership and control in the late nineteenth century.[65] A plausible interpretation of this historical evidence is that 'shareholder rights have improved enormously in Britain over the course of the twentieth century, *parallel to the growth of its markets*.[66] The logic of co-evolution, or mutual influence between law and the economy, better describes this process than one of the linear adjustment of the law to economic imperatives, or vice versa.

It is important to stress that a 'co-evolutionary' conception of legal change is not one which predicts seamless adjustment between the legal and economic systems. It is possible that they will be out of synch with each other for prolonged periods and that, as a result, legal institutions will very often be imperfectly matched for the economic goals they purport to serve. Indeed, in so far as legal concepts are functional, they may well be functional with regard to past environments rather than those in which they currently operate.[67] The efficiency of institutions also needs to be judged in context; particular rules may be more or less efficient depending on the presence of complementary institutions alongside which they have evolved.[68] Thus

> 'it may not be accidental that co-determination in the corporate governance domain and social democratic corporatism in the polity domain co-evolved in Germany, while the main bank system, the lifetime employment system, and the close alliance between industrial associations and relevant administrative bureaux co-evolved in Japan, both in contrast to the so-called Anglo-American model'.[69]

It has been suggested that institutional theories should be evaluated by how well they address two core problems:

63 See, in particular, Lamoreaux & Rosenthal 2005; Hannah 2007.
64 Cheffins 2001.
65 Hannah 2007.
66 La Porta, Lopez-de-Silanes & Shleifer 2008, p. 321 (emphasis added).
67 See Deakin 2002.
68 See Schmidt & Spindler 2002; Ahlering & Deakin 2007.
69 Aoki 2001, p. 17.

> 'the synchronic problem, whereby the goal is to understand the complexity and diversity of overall institutional arrangements across... economies as an instance of multiple *equilibria* of some kind, and the diachronic problem, whereby the goal is to understand the mechanism of institutional evolution/change in a framework consistent with an equilibrium view of institutions, but allowing for the possibility of the emergence of novelty'.[70]

Legal origins theory provides answers to these questions which are in various ways incomplete or unsatisfactory. Its answer to the 'synchronic problem' is that cross-national diversity results from the inherited effect of the transplantation of legal orders. This is potentially a good answer if it is seen as a partial explanation for diversity, but not if it is seen as excluding other possible causes which are derived from cross-national differences in modes of business organization and political organization. Its answer to the 'diachronic problem' is that systems are, for the most part, locked into particular developmental paths, which are the consequence of their legal origin. This lock-in effect is largely detrimental to economic development in the civil law context and largely positive in the common law one. Some movement towards more efficient rules, which legal origins theory tends to identify with convergence on common law practice, may be achieved through the benchmarking of national regulatory regimes by international institutions including the World Bank. From a co-evolutionary perspective, this view is deficient in not allowing for the possibility that legal institutions in civilian systems may be well matched to local economic conditions - or at least as well matched as in common law systems - thanks to mutual feedback with local economic conditions, and to the institutional complementarities to which this gives rise.[71] If that is the case, attempts at convergence which take the common law systems as a model of best practice are likely to be either ineffective or counter-productive.

We now turn to a consideration of how empirical analysis, in particular using quantitative methods, can throw light on these questions.

3. Methodological Issues in the Quantitative Analysis of Law

The initial legal coding exercises carried out by LLSV have been criticized on a number of grounds, including errors in the values attributed to certain specific legal rules and bias in the selection of variables.[72] We do not want to go over this ground again, as it is well known and has to some degree been taken on board by LLSV in their more recent empirical analyses.[73] Instead, our aim is to set out the basis for our own approach to coding, which principally differs from that of LLSV in providing a

70 Aoki 2001, p. 2-3.

71 On this, see Zweigert & Kötz 1998, p. 39-40, suggesting that 'legal systems give the same or very similar solutions, even as to detail, to the same problems of life, despite the great differences in their historical development, conceptual structure, and style of operation', an argument they apply specifically to the manner in which 'developed nations meet the needs of legal business'.

72 Cools 2005; Spamann 2006; Spamann 2008; Braendle 2006.

73 See La Porta, Lopez-de-Silanes & Shleifer 2008.

longitudinal measure of legal variation across systems. We set out below some of the methodological issues encountered in coding the law (*leximetrics*) and in using time-series and panel-data econometric techniques to analyse the resulting legal data.

3.1. *Index Construction: Selection of Variables, Countries, and Time Periods*

All legal indices involve the reduction of a complex institutional reality to a summary form which allows for statistical analysis. The choice of variables, the way in which the indicators are defined, and the algorithms or protocols used for the coding of the legal rules, should each reflect the purpose for which the dataset is constructed. In the case of the datasets we are considering here, the aim of the analysis is to clarify the nature of the relationship between legal and economic change and, more specifically, to examine the impact of law on financial development and vice versa. Accordingly we have constructed datasets which aim to provide an account of how well different legal systems protect certain shareholder and creditor rights. Our guiding assumption in each case is that legal rules are capable of facilitating commercial transactions by reducing agency costs and other frictions in relations between corporate actors. Thus our shareholder protection indices measure how far legal rules protect external shareholders against the risk of expropriation by managers and boards, on the one hand, and dominant blockholders or majority shareholders, on the other, principally in the context of listed companies. The creditor protection indices measure the extent to which aspects of corporate and bankruptcy law rank claims and allocate liabilities between different groups of shareholder and creditors, both while the company is a going concern and in the event of insolvency. The selection of the variables of interest in each case is guided by the comparative law principle of 'functional equivalents', according to which different legal systems may achieve the same end or goal through different means, depending on local contexts and conditions.[74] By including, as far as possible, variables which reflect different legal approaches and traditions, we hope to minimize the risk of 'home-country bias' or the tendency to take the law of one particular country or set of countries as a model or benchmark, thereby distorting the results.[75]

LLSV's anti-director rights index covered 49 countries and some of their later datasets extended to almost 100.[76] Covering as many countries as possible is desirable from the point of view of ensuring a comprehensive or representative sample. However, the more countries that are coded, the greater is the risk that the choice of variables or the definition of the indicators will be inappropriate for some of them.

74 See Zweigert & Kötz 1998, p. 39.

75 For critiques along these lines, in addition to Cools 2005; Spamann 2006; Spamann 2008; Braendle 2006, see Berglöf & Von Thadden 1999; Armour, Cheffins & Skeel 2002; Siems 2005a; Siems 2005b; Lele & Siems 2007b.

76 See, for example, the labour regulation dataset described by Botero *et al.* 2004.

There is also a potential trade-off between the breadth and depth of coverage. For these reasons we proceeded to construct our indices in two stages.

In the first stage we created datasets based on extensive indices for a small number of countries over a lengthy period of time. This allowed us to examine certain countries in depth. We chose countries not because they were representative, but because of their intrinsic interest as 'parent' systems (France, Germany and the United Kingdom), the world's largest and arguably most influential economy (the United States), and its largest democracy by population (India). The period studied was over three decades long (1970-2005), enabling us to chart trends in legal change across a number of economic cycles and major political watersheds, including the fall of the Berlin wall in 1989. Our five-country shareholder protection index contains 60 indicators and the corresponding creditor protection index has 44. As the laws are coded once for each year, we have (60+44)*36*5 = 18,720 observations in these two datasets.[77]

In the second stage, we constructed datasets for a wider range of developing, developed and transition systems, 25 in all, using in each case a reduced-form index and covering a more limited period of time, 1995-2005. This was a period during which most countries were liberalizing their economies and adjusting their regulatory frameworks with a view to promoting private-sector activity and the globalization of markets. It was also a time of sustained economic growth for most systems, although with some interruptions and shocks, including the Asian financial crisis in 1997-1998 and the bursting of the dotcom bubble in 2000-2001. Our reduced-form indices for shareholder and creditor protection contain ten variables each, so that we have (10+10)*11*25 = 5,500 observations. Because they contain fewer variables they do not capture the same range of information as the extended indices for the five-country studies. While covering broadly the same areas of law as the five-country datasets, they also address what we consider to have particularly salient legal issues relating to shareholder and creditor protection in the decade after 1995. For example, the 25-country shareholder protection dataset focuses on change in certain corporate governance standards, such as the presence of independent directors on boards and the mandatory bid rule in takeover bids, which were widely associated with global 'best practice' in this period, and which were incorporated in relevant international standards such as the OECD's corporate governance Principles.[78]

3.2. *Coding the Law*

Our approach to coding has been informed by some of the same methodological considerations that influenced our selection of variables. Thus we have take into account the variety of different legal techniques, ranging from mandatory norms to default rules of different kinds, which are available to legislators. In order to capture the differing degrees of bindingness implied by these techniques, we use graduated

77 In addition, we have constructed a labour regulation dataset for the same five countries and 36-year period. For accounts of this dataset, analysis of which is beyond the scope of the current paper, see Deakin, Lele & Siems 2007; Armour *et al.* 2009a.

78 OECD Principles of Corporate Governance 2004.

variables with scores between 0 and 1, rather than simple binary codings, in appropriate cases. We also code not just for 'positive' legal rules but for standards found in 'soft-law' sources such as corporate governance codes, stock exchange rules and takeover codes.[79] Market participants often regard standards of this type as having the same binding effects as laws, and legislators often defer to industry-level self-regulation on the understanding that resort to statutory solutions may be possible if self-regulatory norms prove to be ineffective.[80]

3.3. *Illustrations: the 25-Country Indices for Shareholder and Creditor Protection*

The definitions of the variables, the coding protocols, the values arrived at through the process of coding, and the detailed legal explanations for these values are available on line for each of our datasets.[81] A previous paper[82] has set out in detail the basis for the coding of the laws in the five-country datasets, so to illustrate our methodology we will focus here on the content of the 25-country indices for shareholder protection[83] and creditor protection, and on the way in which the codings were arrived in two particular cases, those of the United Kingdom (for shareholder protection) and France (for creditor protection).

3.3.1. The 25-country Shareholder Protection Index

The first variable, *powers of the general meeting for de facto changes*, relates to the ability of the shareholders as a collective body to control actions by the board which may substantially alter the company's business profile. The corporate laws of many countries require transactions which exceed a threshold based on a proportion of the company's net assets to be approved by the shareholders. If there is no such threshold, a score of 0 is given. If there is a restriction triggered at a threshold of 50 per cent or lower, then a score of 1 is given. If there is a restriction, but it is triggered at a net asset threshold that is higher than 50 per cent (e.g. 80 per cent), then a score of 0.5 is given. In the UK, the Listing Rules, which apply to publicly-traded firms, specify that any transaction involving more than 25 per cent of the company's net assets must be approved by the shareholders; this rule was present for the entire period 1995-2005.[84] Hence a score of 1 is given for each year.

79 Zweigert & Kötz 1998, p. 39.

80 See Lele & Siems 2007b, for discussion of this point in the context of the coding of the shareholder protection index.

81 See <http://www.cbr.cam.ac.uk/research/programme2/project2-20.html> (homepage of the 'Law, Finance and Development' project on the Cambridge Centre for Business Research website).

82 Armour *et al.* 2009a.

83 The index used to construct the 25-country dataset is also described (more briefly) in Armour *et al.* 2009b.

84 UK Listing Rules 1984 (in force since 1985), s. 6.3.4: major class 1 transactions; Listing Rules, 1993 para. 10.37: super class 1 transactions.

The second variable, *agenda setting power*, relates to the ability of a minority shareholder to have an item put on to the agenda for a shareholders' meeting. The higher the minimum percentage required to have an item put on the agenda, the lower the coded score. For the entire period, the UK's Companies Act 1985 stipulated that a shareholder with 5 per cent or more of the voting rights could have an item put on the agenda for a shareholder meeting.[85] This yields a coding of 0.5 for each year in the period under study.

Our third variable, *anticipation of shareholder decision*, seeks to capture the extent to which the legal regime facilitates participation in shareholder decision-making by those who are unable physically to be present at the meeting. This can be done either by permitting postal voting, or by allowing shareholders to appoint a proxy to represent them in voting at the meeting. Proxy mechanisms can, however, be biased in favour of the board of directors unless the proxies are 'two-way' - that is, they provide for voting both for and against the resolution in question. Moreover, we assume that proxy facilities are more useful to shareholders when accompanied by a 'proxy solicitation' - namely, a circular explaining the background to the particular resolutions in relation to which proxy appointments are sought. In the UK, the Listing Rules required for the entire period under consideration that a two-way proxy form be circulated to shareholders, but there was no requirement that it be accompanied by a proxy solicitation. Hence we code the UK as 0.5 for the entire period.[86]

Fourth, we consider whether, and if so how readily, *multiple voting rights* are permitted - or, put the other way around, whether a one-share-one-vote rule is applied. Multiple voting rights facilitate the aggregation of control in the hands of shareholders with less than equivalent cash-flow rights, and correspondingly disenfranchize shareholders who do not share the enhanced voting capability. In the UK, there has been no legal or other regulatory prohibition of multiple voting rights for the period under consideration, meriting a score of 0.[87]

Our fifth variable relates to the proportion of *independent board members* - that is, who must be free of employment or ownership links to the firm. Independent directors are widely thought to be able to assist shareholders in controlling the actions of managers. We give a score of 1 for jurisdictions in which more than 50 per cent of the board must be independent; a score of 0.5 for jurisdictions in which more than 25 per cent but less than 50 per cent must be independent, and 0 for no requirement relating to independence. For intermediate positions, the score is derived as the percentage of independent board members divided by two. In the UK, the Cadbury Code of Corporate Governance, introduced in 1992, required listed companies to ensure that at least a majority of their non-executive directors be independent. As, at that point, typically half the board would be non-executive directors, we

85 Companies Act 1948, § 140; Companies Act 1985, § 376, 377.

86 UK Listing Rules 1984, § 5.36; UK Listing Rules, § 13.28(a),(b).

87 On the admissibility (in principle) of multiple voting rights, see *Bushell* v. *Faith* [1970] A.C. 1099. Multiple voting rights are rarely observed in UK listed companies, but this appears to be the result of a widely observed social norm which reflects institutional investor opinion on the issue, rather than any legal rule.

code this as 0.25. The Combined Code of Corporate Governance 2003 raised the threshold, requiring that at least half of all the board members be independent. We therefore code the UK as 1 from the following year (2004) onward.[88]

The sixth variable relates to the *feasibility of directors' dismissal* - that is, how readily shareholders may remove board members from their positions. The highest score of 1 is given where directors may be dismissed by shareholders at will, and 0 is given where dismissal may only be effected for cause or an important reason (specified in the law). Intermediate scores are given where although directors may be dismissed at will, this may be accompanied by a financial penalty for the company. Such penalties would be higher where there is no limit to the duration of service contracts, for which a score of 0.5 is given, and lower where there is a fixed duration, for which a score of 0.75 is given. Turning to the UK application, no restrictions were imposed on shareholders' ability to remove directors from office during the study period, but it was possible for directors to enter into service contracts with the firm that contained termination payments, thereby subjecting the company to financial liability. From 1992 to 1995, these were subject to a restriction under the Cadbury Code on Corporate Governance that any service contract for more than a 3-year term must be approved by the general meeting. In 1995, this was reduced to an outright restriction on notice periods of more than one year.[89] The position is thus one in which dismissal is fundamentally straightforward, with the possibility of a financial penalty that is capped by the length of the notice period. We code this variable as 0.75 for 1995, and then, to reflect the reduction in the maximum notice period, 0.875 for the remainder of the study period.

Seventh, we consider the ability of minority shareholders to bring an action to enforce breaches of directors' duties - that is, the extent to which *private enforcement* is facilitated. Here we code as 0 those laws which exclude the possibility of a shareholder suit, 0.5 where there are some restrictions - such as a requirement than the shareholder holds some minimum proportion of the voting rights, and 1 where such an action may be brought readily. In the UK, a minority shareholder action does not depend on having a minimum share qualification, but nevertheless is subject to a significant restriction that the wrong must be sufficiently serious as to constitute a 'fraud on the minority'. As a consequence, only particularly egregious breaches of duty may be enforced by a minority shareholder - misappropriation of assets and the like.[90] We therefore code this as 0.5 for the entire period.

Eighth, we consider the ability of shareholders to file a *personal action* against a resolution of the general meeting—for example, on the basis that it has not been lawfully constituted. Under UK law, every shareholder has the power to bring a

88 Cadbury Committee, Code of Best Practice 1992, § 2.2 (majority of non-executive directors must be independent); Combined Code 2003, A.3.2 (at least half the board members must be independent.

89 This provision originated in the 1995 version of the Code drawn up by the Greenbury Committee and became part of the Combined Code drawn up by the Hampel Committee in 1998 (s. B.1.6).

90 For an overview of this complex area, see Boyle 2002.

personal action,[91] and so a coding of 1 is accorded for the entire period. In other jurisdictions, codings of less than 1 as given where specific percentage thresholds are imposed to bring such actions.

The penultimate variable relates to *mandatory bid* requirements. These compel the purchaser of more than a stipulated proportion of the voting rights of a listed company's share capital to make a tender offer for the remaining shares at a price no lower than what was paid for the initial acquisitions. Such rules are intended to protect minority shareholders by providing them with the option to exit the company - at a price no lower than that which has been paid for the acquisition of a controlling block - rather than be required to continue to participate in the firm under the control of the acquiror. We reason that greater protection is accorded by a lower threshold acquisition level. In the UK, a mandatory bid requirement was triggered under the City Code on Takeovers and Mergers for the entire period following the acquisition of 30 per cent of the voting rights,[92] which we code as 1.

Finally, we consider rules requiring disclosure of *share ownership blocks*. These allow investors to know who has amassed significant stakes in a firm. We reason that greater transparency in this dimension benefits investors. We give the highest score for a 3 per cent threshold, 0.75 for 5 per cent, 0.5 for 10 per cent, 0.25 for 25 per cent and 0 for anything less. In the UK, disclosure of blocks amounting to 3 per cent or more of the voting rights has been mandatory since 1989, meaning that we code this variable as 1 for the entire period.[93]

3.3.2. The 25-Country Creditor Protection Index

The first variable codifies rules on *minimum share capital*. These tend to be regulated by law and fixed at different levels, depending on the type of the company concerned. In continental European countries and civil law systems in general this has been a widely relied on instrument for the protection of creditors' interests. Our approach to coding concentrates on the minimum capital required for establishing a private company, which is interpreted to mean any business vehicle having separate legal personality and providing all its equity investors with limited liability. A score of 1 has been assigned to the law of countries where the minimum capital is fixed at € 25,000 or more, a score of 0 in case of no minimum capital requirements, and a proportional intermediate score in case of a minimum capital set between € 25,000 and 0. In France, the coding for this variable was done with regard to the private limited liability corporate form of the SARL (*Société à responsabilité limitée*). Up to the end of 2003, the law[94] required a minimum capital of 50,000 FF (which is equivalent to approximately € 7,500) in order to form such company, while from January 1 2004 onwards, a SARL could be set up with no mini-

91 See e.g. *Edwards* v. *Halliwell* [1950] 2 All E.R. 1064, 1067.
92 City Code on Takeovers and Mergers, rule 9.1.
93 Companies Act 1985, § 199(2)(a) as amended by the Companies Act 1989.
94 Loi n° 66-537 du 24 juillet 1966 sur les sociétés commerciales, art. 35.

mum capital whatsoever.[95] Therefore, the score for the years 1995-2003 is 0.3, while for the remaining period (2004-2005) it decreases to 0.

The second variable, *dividend restriction*, measures creditor protection by reference to how far the company has an unlimited power to distribute dividends to shareholders, and assigns a score of 0.33 for each of the following provisions: rules on basic dividend payments with limitations on the maximum amount of accumulated net profit which can be distributed as dividends and/or mandatory dividends; restrictions against share repurchase; and rules against disguised dividend distribution. In France, Article L 225-210 of the Commercial Code[96] deals with basic dividend restrictions, defining non-distributable reserves and stating that a company must have reserves, other than the statutory reserve fund, amounting to at least the value of all its shares; Article L 225-209 of the Commercial Code[97] regulates the acquisition by the company of its own shares, by providing that the general meeting of a company whose shares are admitted to trading on a regulated market may authorize the board of directors or the executive board, as applicable, to purchase a number of shares representing up to 10 per cent of the company's capital. In doing so, the general meeting must define the purposes and terms of the transaction, as well as its upper limit, and it cannot give such authorization for a period longer than eighteen months. And, finally, Articles L 232-11 and L 232-12 regulate disguised dividend distributions. Given the presence of these three forms of dividend restriction, and after assigning a score of 0.33 for Art. L 225-210 and Art. L 225-209 and a score of 0.17 for L 232-11, 12, the overall coding is 0.83.

The third variable addresses the issue of *directors' duties towards creditors*. The variable is geared towards the situation of bankruptcy, and gives a score of 1 in the case in which a director has a duty to act in creditors' interests when the company is balance-sheet insolvent. A score of 0.5 is given in a case where the duty is owed in the case of a commercially insolvent company, and, finally, a coding of 0 is given where there is no duty to take creditors' interest into account in these situations. In France, the Commercial Code at Art. L 624-3 rules that, where managerial negligence contributed to a depletion of corporate assets, the court may order that all or some of the debts of the company be borne by its directors. In addition, Article L 624-5 enumerates the circumstances in which the court may institute an administrative order or winding-up proceedings against any (paid or unpaid, *de jure* or *de facto*) directors. These situations include those in which the directors have disposed of the assets of the legal person as their own property, used the assets or credit of the legal person to the detriment of its interests either for personal gain or in order to benefit another legal person or undertaking in which they had a direct or indirect interest, abusively pursued a loss-making operation which was bound to result in the insolvency of the legal person, kept fictitious accounts or removed accounting documents from the legal person, or failed to keep accounts required by law. In the light of these stringent laws, the coding is 1 for the entire period.

95 Art. L 223-2, derived from Loi n° 2003-721 du 1 août 2003, art. 1.
96 Ex art. 217-3, Loi n° 66-537 du 24 juillet 1966.
97 Loi n° 2003-7 du 3 janvier 2003, art. 50 (II).

The fourth variable relates to the possibility offered in various countries of granting *non-possessory security interests* to secure present and/or future debts, thereby providing a security interest in present and future, tangible and intangible collateral. It is well established that most, if not all, jurisdictions allow a non-possessory security to be taken over land. Our coding assigns a score of 0.33 in the case where the law allows the creation of such security interests with regards to personalty (tangible movables), receivables (intangibles) and 'all assets'. In France, with regard to personalty, non-possessory security interests are not generally possible over inventory: the most common form is, instead, the pledge, which requires dispossession of the debtor. Yet, charges are possible over certain assets, including a purchase money security interest over material and equipment.[98] With regard to receivables, the *Loi Dailly* of 1981 establishes a statutory framework specifically for the grant of security over book debts. With regard to 'all assets', it is believed that the notion of a 'floating charge' is foreign to French law',[99] although it is possible to create a comprehensive pledge (which includes the commercial name, goodwill, and intellectual property, and but excludes real estate, book debts, inventory and contractual rights) over the so called *fond de commerce*.[100] In the light of the above, the score attributed to this variable is 0.66.

The fifth variable expands on the fourth and relates to the registration of the type of non-possessory security interests just referred to. In France, registration is required for security over corporeal moveables,[101] but not for incorporeal assets,[102] therefore the coding is 0.33.

The sixth variable is concerned with how far the law allows *out-of-court enforcement of security interests* to be carried out by creditors. Where they have this power, the score is 1; where they can only act through a court order, a score of 0 is given. As for most creditors, out of court enforcement or settlement saves time, cost and human resources, this possibility is viewed as enhancing creditor protection. As in France, out of court enforcement is not possible,[103] the coding is 0.

The seventh variable relates to the degree of the *power to commence bankruptcy proceedings*, and assigns different scores to the cases of a debtor being able to initiate a bankruptcy proceeding unilaterally without any insolvency requirement (when the score will be 0), a debtor being required to initiate bankruptcy proceedings when the company is balance-sheet insolvent (when the score will be 1), and a bankruptcy proceeding being initiated by any creditor able to show that the debtor is insolvent by reference to a relevant criterion (when the score will be 0.5). This variable, therefore, captures the power of the debtor to use bankruptcy as a threat against creditors and, conversely, the power of the creditors to use bankruptcy as a way to compel payment. In France, for the period considered, the Commercial Code envisages that any single creditor may commence an insolvency proceeding, while

98 See Gdanski 2001.
99 Gdanski 2001, p. 59.
100 Gdanski 2001, p. 65-66.
101 Art. 2238 Civil Code.
102 Art. 2361 Civil Code.
103 Gdanski 2001, p. 79.

in the case where the proceeding is started by the debtor, a cash-flow test is deemed to be sufficient, with the criterion being whether the debtor is unable to meet its liabilities out of its disposable assets.[104] Hence, the score is 0.5.

The eighth variable relates to the issue of the stay of *secured creditors* in insolvency proceedings. It distinguishes between situations according to how far there is a compulsory stay where there is a feasible prospect of a corporate rescue or rehabilitation. In France, Commercial Code, Article L 621-40 provides for secured creditors to be stayed: the decision to commence insolvency proceedings prevents any legal action or any application for execution against either the real or personal property of the debtor by any of the creditors whose debts arose before the date of said decision. This provision must, however, be read together with Article L 622-23, which rules that secured creditors may nevertheless exercise individual enforcement in a liquidation, if the liquidator has not sold the assets within three months from the judgment instituting or ordering a court-ordered winding-up. The coding is therefore 0.5.

The ninth variable, *outcome of bankruptcy proceedings*, relates to how and by whom decisions are taken on whether a bankrupt firm continues in operation or has to close down. Where the law grants that role to the court or to the debtor, the score assigned is 0. In situations where the power to decide on the outcome of the bankruptcy proceeding is granted primarily to the creditors, the score will be 1 if the decision rights are allocated to the residual claimants, and 0.5 if the law makes no such specification. In France, the Commercial Code provides for the court to be the primary decision maker regarding the outcome of the proceeding,[105] and so the coding is 0.

The final variable is concerned with the *rank order of secured creditors* during an insolvency proceeding. The division of security interests set out here refers back to the fourth variable, and a coding of 0.25 is assigned for each of the types of secured creditors who are not subordinated by law to preferred claims. In France, the Commercial Code, at Article L 621-32 II, provides that debts secured by specific charges over real or personal property are not subordinated in liquidation.[106] The score for this variable is, therefore, 0.75.

3.4. *Issues Arising in the Econometric Analysis of Longitudinal Data*

As we shall see in more detail in the next section, the presentation of longitudinal data collated in the ways just described can be highly revealing at a purely descriptive level. In addition, once data exist in this form it become possible to undertake

104 Arts. L 620-2, 621-1.

105 Art. L 621-62. See also Arts. L 621-60, 621-61 (explaining that the judicial administrator, in preparing the report, must consult with creditors and employees; the report is influential with respect to the court's decision in the case. This provision was introduced by Loi n° 94-475 du 10 juin 1994 relative à la prévention et au traitement des difficultés des entreprises, *OJ* 134 du 11 juin 1994 p. 8440, in force 21 October 1994).

106 Introduced by Loi n° 94-475, du 10 juin 1994 relative à la prévention et au traitement des difficultés des entreprises, *OJ* 134 du 11 juin 1994 p. 8440, in force 21 October 1994.

econometric analysis aimed at identifying the presence of correlations between legal and economic variables. Time-series and panel-data techniques can be deployed to identify causal relationships in ways which are not possible if cross-sectional data (referring to the state of the law only at a particular point in time) are used. However, these techniques are not straightforward to apply and their use can give rise to difficult issues of interpretation.

In cross-sectional analyses, a statistically significant correlation between an explanatory or 'independent' variable which codes for legal rules, on the one hand, and an outcome or 'dependent' economic variable, on the other, will not necessarily provide good evidence of the direction of causal influence. The explanatory variable may be 'endogenous' to the outcome variable in the technical sense of being correlated to the error term in the regression equation. Where this is the case, a false result may be obtained; for example, it could be the case that a given financial indicator is driving a change in the law rather than the other way round.[107]

There a number of techniques available for getting round this problem of 'reverse' or 'simultaneous' causation. One is to identify a so-called 'instrumental variable' which is correlated with the explanatory variable, but is not correlated with the error term. For example, in the early legal origins literature, the common law or civil law origins of different countries' legal systems were used as instruments for the substance of legal rules on shareholder rights. The assumption being made here was that legal origin was probably linked to the content of legal rules in the countries; but, conversely, that legal origin could not plausibly have been influenced by the economic outcome variables which were the focus of interest (and so could not be correlated with the error term). As we have seen,[108] this was because LLSV took the view that most countries' legal origins were the result of external events such as colonization or conquest which had occurred several decades or even centuries ago, rather than being generated by contemporaneous, country-specific economic forces. By demonstrating a statistical relationship between legal origin and the different outcome variables, they were able to claim that the direction of causation ran from law to the economy rather than vice versa.[109]

However, there are problems with the instrumental variable approach. Not only is a degree of subjective judgement involved in the choice of instrumental variables; a variable will not be a good instrument if it could have influenced outcomes through channels other than that of the proposed explanatory variable. As we have seen, LLSV have more recently come to the view that legal origin might be influencing the economy through a number of routes, including interpretive practices and approaches to enforcement, in addition to that of the content of legal rules. This is the basis on which they have proposed that legal origin should be seen as a causal or exogenous variable in its own right, rather than as an instrument for the content of legal rules.[110] As noted above,[111] this approach creates new difficulties

107 For a general review of problems of endogeneity in growth regressions of the kind which are commonly used in the development literature, see Rodrik 2009.

108 See Rodrik 2009.

109 La Porta *et al.* 1998.

110 La Porta, Lopez-de-Silanes & Shleifer 2008, p. 298.

since it rests on the questionable assumption that legal origin, understood as regulatory style, is not susceptible to feedback effects from the economic environment.

Once longitudinal data become available, a wider range of econometric techniques can be used to address the issue of causal inference. Time series datasets may possess a characteristic known as 'non-stationarity'. These are series which do not follow a regular path, but are prone to irregular deviations, without returning to the previous trend. Where one or both of two time series is non-stationary in this sense, their error terms are liable to auto-correlate, again producing spurious regressions. Techniques for addressing the issue of stationarity through the identification of 'cointegrated' time series - that is to say, times series which are, individually, non-stationary, but are linked by a common, stationary trend - were developed in the 1980s,[112] and these were later combined with methods designed to make it possible to draw causal inferences from correlations in time-series analysis. These mostly involve variants of so-called 'Granger causality' techniques,[113] which, in their basic form, involve regressing current values of the outcome variable against past values of itself and of the explanatory variable. If the addition of the past values of the explanatory variable makes a different to the result, causation is generally assumed, although it may be more accurate to think of the effect in terms of precedence. Cointegration-based techniques are thought to be appropriate where there is a very long time series; conventionally, at least 25 years of annualized data are required. For shorter time periods, panel-data techniques can be used to identify the existence of correlations between legal and economic variables in pooled samples of countries, and Granger causality tests can be deployed to throw light on the direction of causation.

Our five-country datasets, with their very long time series, are non-stationary in the sense just described, and cointegration techniques have been used, as we shall see in more detail below, to deal with the possibility of auto-correlation and to identify causal relationships. For the 25-country dataset, with its shorter time period, we have used panel data techniques in conjunction with Granger causality tests.[114]

4. Empirical Results

4.1. *Leximetric Analysis*

We are now in a position to present our empirical findings. We begin with a *leximetric* account which provides a description of the main trends in legal change that we can identify from our data.

111 Rodrik 2009.
112 Engle & Granger 1987.
113 See Granger 1969.
114 For further details of the panel-data techniques used (in this case involving a random-effects model which is intended to take into account the likelihood that there are unobserved effects which vary both across countries and across time) see Armour, Cheffins & Skeel 2002.

4.1.1. Analysis of Five Countries, 1970-2005

The five-country datasets track the evolution of shareholder and creditor protection between 1970 and 2005 in the UK, the US, France, Germany and India. Aggregating all the variables shows how well these legal systems have protected shareholder and creditor rights over time (see Figures 3 and 4).

Figure 3: *Aggregate Shareholder Protection (60 variables)*

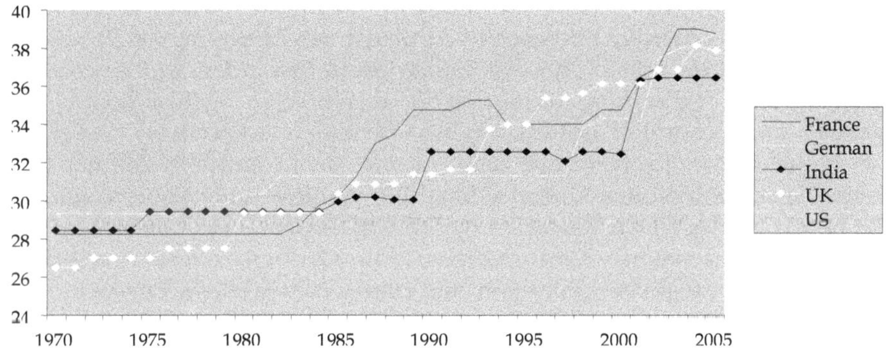

Figure 4: *Aggregate Creditor Protection (44 variables)*

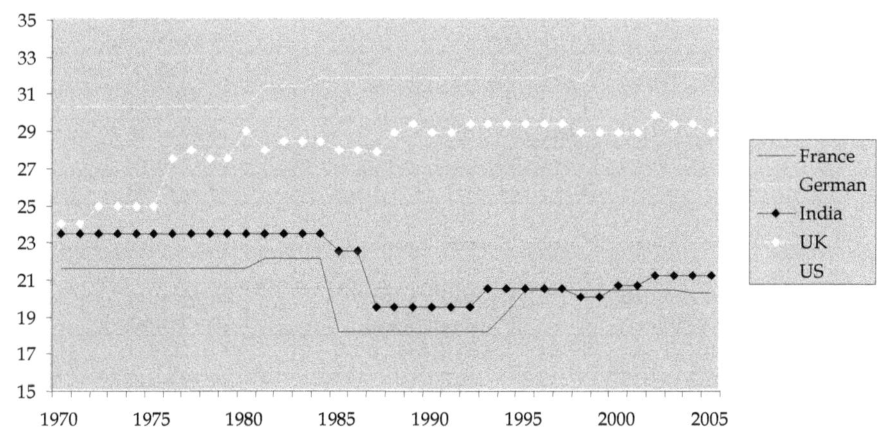

A number of differences between shareholder and creditor protection can be identified. First, shareholder protection has increased in all countries, whereas the development of creditor protection does not show a clear trend. Second, the UK and Germany have strengthened protection for both shareholders and creditors over this period, whereas France, India and the US have a lower level of protection for creditors at the end of the period than at the beginning. Third, shareholder protection has tended to go up incremental steps, whereas the curves on creditor protection have clearer 'plateaux' and 'steps', indicating that change is more episodic and, when it occurs, far-reaching.

These observations are not compatible with a legal origin effect which is time-invariant and constant across closely related areas of law. The rank order of the countries changes over time, and there are very different pictures in respect of shareholder protection and creditor protection. The substance of our findings also differs from those of LLSV. We do not find that shareholders and creditors are better protected in common law countries than in civil law ones. Nor does the pace of change seem to differ with regard to these two broad categories of legal system.

The overall aggregates only provide a highly generalized picture. It is possible to break our results down by reference to particular sub-categories within each of the main indices. In the case of the shareholder protection index, we can consider two sub-categories, concerning protection of shareholders against boards and management and protection against other shareholders respectively.[115] Table 1 presents summary data for these two sub-categories on a country-by-country basis (the deeper shading indicates higher scores). For creditor protection we can distinguish between rules which take effect by limiting the freedom of the debtor firm to engage in activities that may harm creditors, rules which take effect by facilitating creditor contracting for greater protection, and rules which take effect by facilitating creditor power in bankruptcy proceedings.[116] The results of the scores for these sub-categories are summarized in Table 2 on a country-by-country basis.

Table 1: *Shareholder Protection in 5 Countries 1970-2005: Mean (and standard deviation)*

	Protection against boards and management (42 variables)	**Protection against other shareholders (18 variables.)**
France	22.55 (3.12)	9.63 (0.71)
Germany	21.56 (2.03)	10.26 (0.65)
India	23.06 (2.18)	8.27 (0.70)
UK	23.27 (3.44)	8.20 (0.38)
US	21.24 (1.90)	8.69 (0.86)

Table 2: *Creditor Protection in 5 Countries 1970-2005: Mean (and standard deviation)*

	Debtor control (15 variables)	**Credit contracts (10 variables)**	**Insolvency (19 variables)**
France	7.03 (0.17)	4.08 (0.64)	9.26 (1.51)
Germany	11.61 (0.71)	7.06 (0.11)	12.82 (0.66)
India	4.02 (0.14)	7.41 (0.57)	10.33 (1.95)
UK	7.33 (1.90)	7.97 (0.71)	12.78 (0.71)
US	6.06 (1.22)	7.88 (0.65)	8.56 (0.97)

115 Lele & Siems 2007b.

116 Armour *et al.* 2009a.

Related papers have discussed the trends in the sub-indices in some detail,[117] and so we will summarize the main findings here. Once the main indices are broken down into their component parts, we can see that countries can arrive at similar levels of protection overall, through different methods. For example, in the US and the UK creditors have a comparative advantage in mechanisms that facilitate contracting for greater protection, whereas in Germany creditors are better protected than in other countries mainly through controls over debtor activities (see Table 2).

In shareholder protection, we would expect to find that rules protecting minority shareholders against expropriation by majorities would be stronger in jurisdictions in which share ownership was concentrated in the hands of blockholders (Germany, France and India), and that rules protecting shareholders against boards would receive more emphasis in jurisdictions in which dispersed ownership is the norm (the UK and the US). Table 1 suggests that France and Germany higher than average 'minority-majority' protection, but that India does not. This suggests that legal origin may be a force for inertia; India's common law heritage may not have equipped it well to adopt laws, which tend to be found in civilian regimes, for governing minority-majority conflicts. On the other hand, we find that the average level of protection of external shareholders against boards and management is strongest in the UK but weakest in the US. A supposedly core feature of 'Anglo-Saxon' corporate law seems to be only weakly present in the American case, by comparison with the practice in civilian countries. Another way of interpreting this result is that two of the parent civil law regimes, France and Germany, were strengthening the position of minority shareholders with regard to boards and managers over the period of the study, as was the UK, while this aspect of US law changed hardly at all prior to the Sarbanes-Oxley Act of 2002.

4.1.2. Analysis of 25 countries, 1995-2005

In Figures 5-12 we present our 25-country data by reference to the principal legal origin 'families' of English, French and German law, and a fourth category consisting of transition systems, all of which, in this sample, are of German origin.[118] For this purpose, we mostly adopt the classifications of systems used by LLSV. Some of these classifications are problematic, for reasons explored earlier,[119] but this

117 See Armour *et al.* 2009a; Lele & Siems 2007b.

118 While most of the transition systems (and all those in the current sample) can be categorized as having a German-law origin, there is a case for treating them separately from the other categories since their recent evolution has been considerably influenced by American, English and French law, as well as German law, and there is also some residual 'socialist law' influence (on the category of 'socialist law' see La Porta, Lopez-de-Silanes & Shleifer 2008, p. 288).

119 Zweigert & Kötz 1998, p. 279 & 281, treat the Scandinavian systems as a separate category because they are not based on a single civil code model as the French and German systems can be said to be. In practice, the Scandinavian systems have been heavily influenced by German law, and we categorize them as German-origin systems for present purposes, while recognizing that this classification (like all those involving legal 'families') is open to question: see our discussion in section 2, above.

mode of presentation may be useful for the purpose of comparing our results with LLSV's.

The results for shareholder protection indicate a generally rising trend over the period covered. All systems have improved their general level of shareholder protection, with certain variables, particularly those relating to independent board membership and the mandatory bid rule in hostile takeover bids, showing rapid increases. In that sense there has convergence around standards which originated in the common law systems, particularly the UK, and which in the course of the 1990s and 2000s have come to be associated with global 'best practice'.[120] There are however some divergences by reference to legal origin and to the state of transition and development of the different countries.

Figure 5: *Shareholder protection in English legal origin countries (10 variables)*

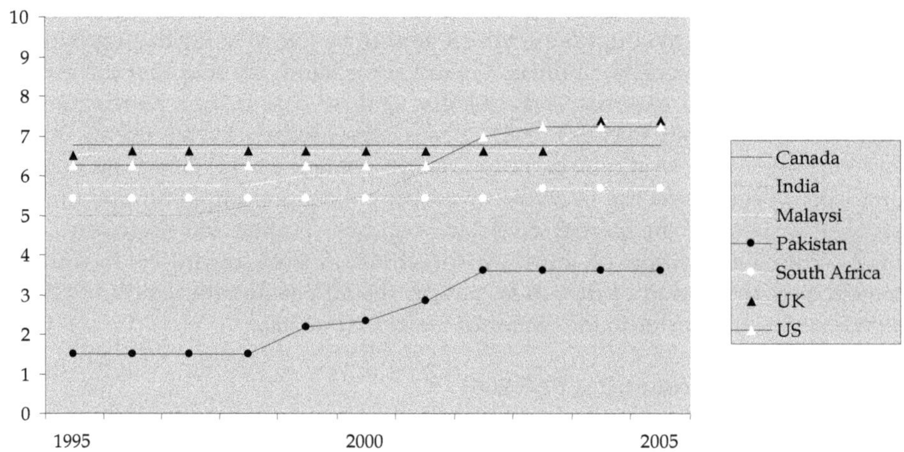

120 While the notion of global 'best practice' in corporate governance is necessarily a rather vague one, it may be relevant to note that the OECD's Principles of Corporate Governance (see *supra* note 77) give prominence to standards on independent boards and the role of the mandatory bid rule in takeover bids (which by requiring the bidder to make an offer for the entire share capital of the company once his holding reaches a certain level, is intended to protect minority shareholders against expropriation). For further discussion, see Armour *et al.* 2009b.

Figure 6: *Shareholder protection in French legal origin countries (10 variables)*

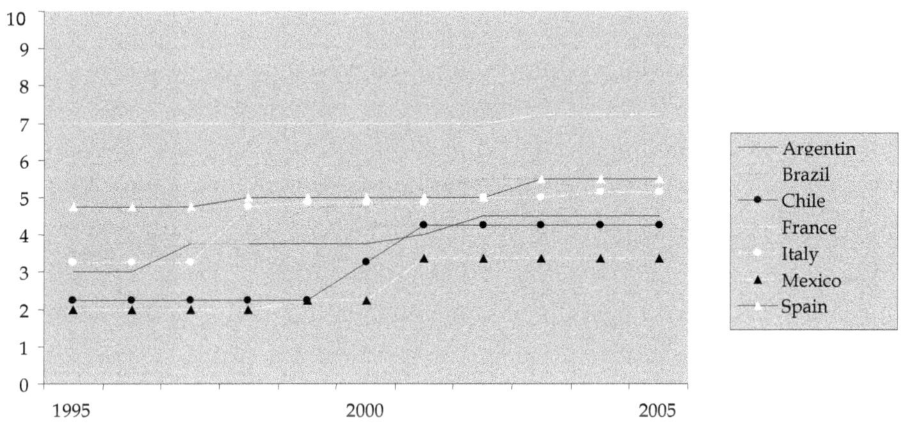

Figure 7: *Shareholder protection in German legal origin countries (10 variables)*

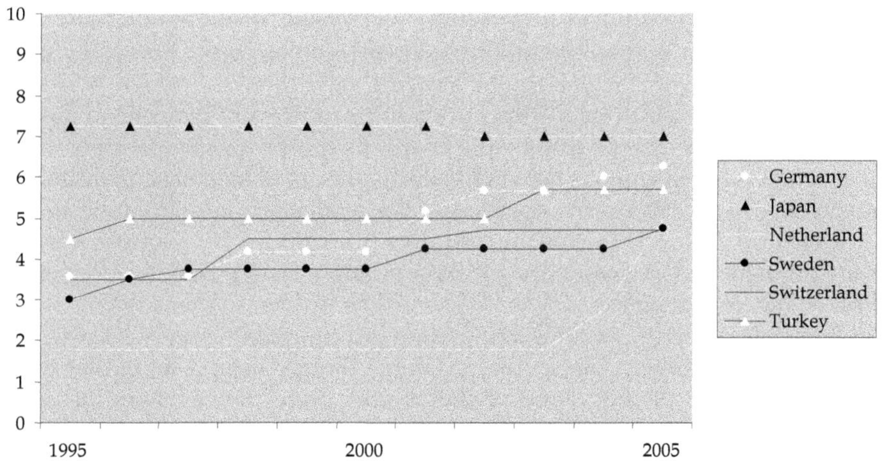

Figure 8: *Shareholder protection in transition countries (10 variables)*

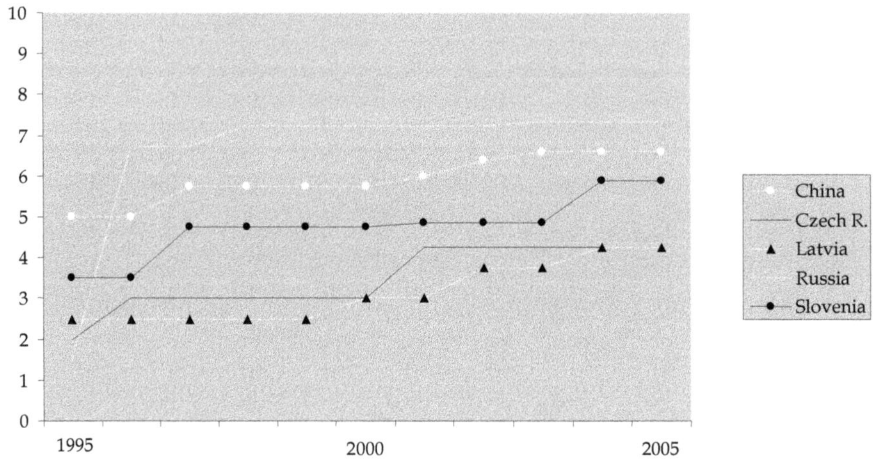

The general rise in protection suggests that legal origin has not been a barrier to convergence and, indeed, it is the case that, on average, civil law countries, both developed and developing, had a faster rate of increase than common law ones. When we break down the sample into individual legal 'families', however, certain differences emerge. The English-origin systems have above average scores for variables 1, 3, 5 and 7 which refer respectively to the powers of the general meeting to control transactions entered into by the board, the power of shareholders to take part in decision-making without being physically present at meetings, requirements for independent directors on the board, and the availability of derivative suits to enforce directors' duties. These are all indicators of corporate law regimes in which the main problem is the possibility of expropriation of shareholder interests by powerful boards or managers.

In French legal-origin systems, the pattern just indicated is reversed: variables 1, 3, 5 and 7 have relatively low scores. Strikingly, France itself is an outlier in this group, indicating that the high level of shareholder protection rights in the parent system has not so far transmitted itself to other members of the group. One possible interpretation of this result is that legal origin is not a strong force here, and that the very concept of a French-origin 'family' makes little sense in this context. An alternative view is that the civil law tradition is proving to be a greater obstacle to convergence outside France than in the system of origin. This seems paradoxical – why should the parent system have been quicker to converge on global corporate governance standards than the rest? One possibility is that a certain regulatory style may be well suited to local conditions in the parent system, alongside which it will have co-evolved,[121] than in systems into which it has been transplanted.[122]

121 On co-evolution, see our discussion in Section 2, above.

German legal-origin systems score strongly on variable 8, which is concerned with the power of minority shareholders to block a resolution of the general meeting. This is not surprising, since such a power would provide an important mechanism for shareholder protection in systems with blockholder forms of ownership. German-origin scores are nevertheless up across the board. In 1995 the scores for German legal-origin systems were below the average for the whole sample; by the end of the period they were above it.

Scores for developing countries are on average below those for developed ones in both the common law and civil law, while transition systems also have low average scores in relation to the sample as a whole. However, some transitions systems are among those undergoing the most rapid movement towards a more shareholder-protective regime, under the influence of external pressures. The jump in the Russian score indicates the influence of western (and, specifically, Anglo-American) models for the Joint Stock Company Law of 1995, while the more incremental rises in the Czech Republic, Latvia and Slovenia are driven in part by the adoption of European Community law standards.[123]

The results for the 25-country creditor protection index are different from those obtained from the five-country study. With this larger sample, certain trends by reference to legal origin become clear. There is no overall common law-civil law divide, but there is evidence of divergence of experience by reference to the legal 'families'. French-origin systems have a significantly lower level of overall creditor protection than either the English-origin of German-origin countries. The French-origin countries are strong on dividend restrictions (variable 2), but relatively weak on minimum capital requirements (variable 1), creditor contract rights variables 4-6), and creditor protection in insolvency (variables 8-10). The English-origin systems tend to stress creditors' contract rights and are weak on minimum capital requirements and rules governing entry into bankruptcy proceedings. German legal-origin countries have high scores on minimum capital requirements, rules on entry into insolvency and the priority of secured creditors, and tend not to have low scores on any of the variables.

122 There is a substantial literature on the difficulties involved in the transplantation of legal institutions. See Berkowitz, Pistor & Richard 2003; Pistor *et al.* 2003. According to Botero *et al.* 2004, p. 1346, 'path dependence in the legal and regulatory styles emerges as an efficient adaptation to the previously transplanted legal infrastructure'.

123 For further analysis of the differences in shareholder protection across countries in this dataset, see Armour *et al.* 2009a; Siems 2008; Schouten & Siems 2009.

Figure 9: *Creditor protection in English legal origin countries (10 variables)*

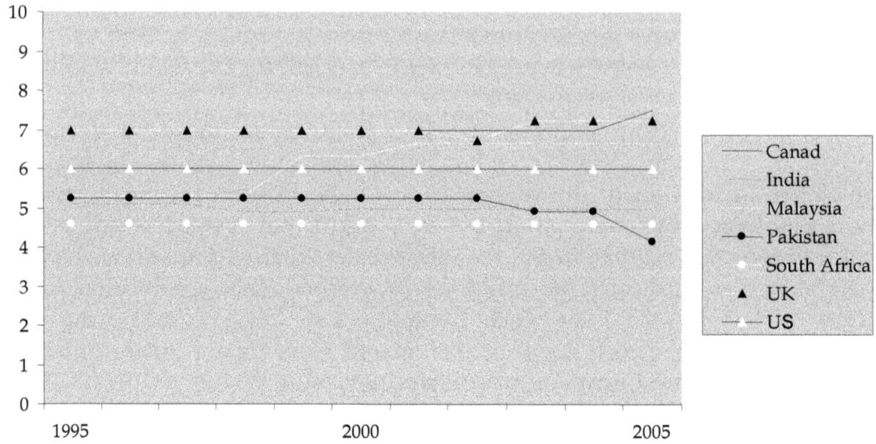

Figure 10: *Creditor protection in French legal origin countries (10 variables)*

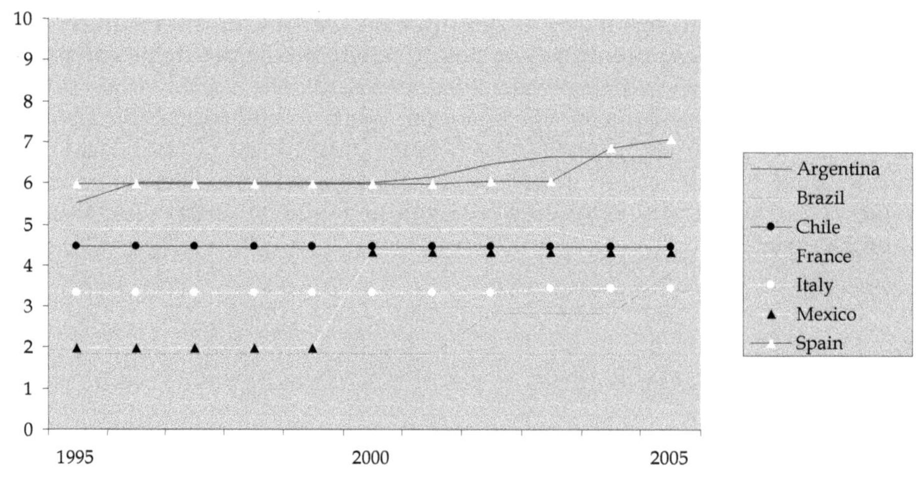

Figure 11: *Creditor protection in German legal origin countries* **(10 variables)**

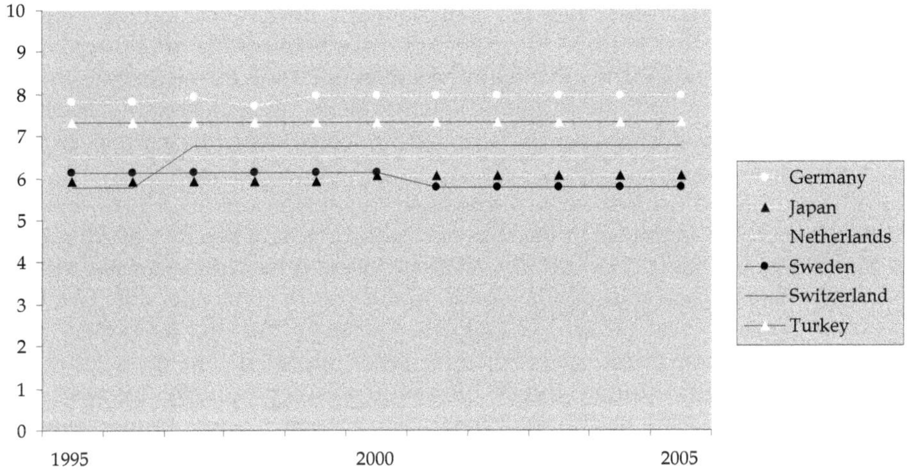

Figure 12: *Creditor protection in transition countries (10 variables)*

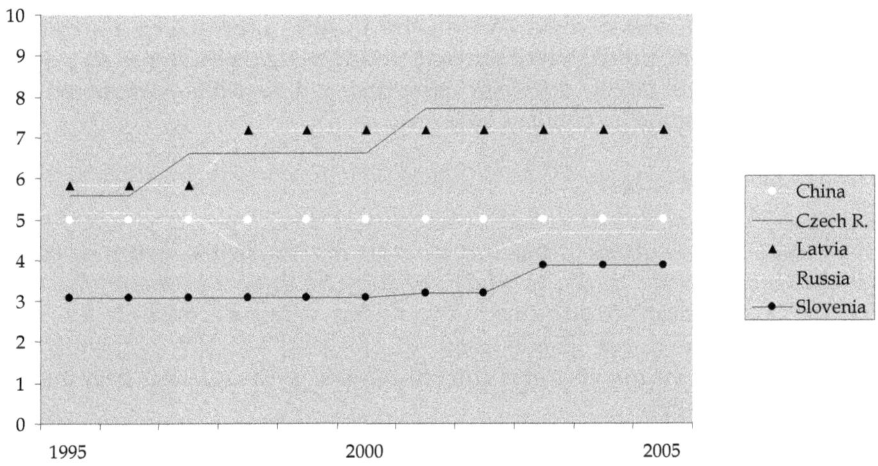

Although the common upwards trend which is found in respect of shareholder protection is absent in the case of creditor rights, most of the countries in the sample have undergone bankruptcy law reforms of some kind over the past ten years, with several of them initiating attempts to speed up or better regulate corporate reorganization procedures. There is a mixed picture on minimum capital requirements; these were abolished in France with effect from 2004, but most other civil law systems have maintained or strengthened this form of protection in the period under review. This kind of protection for creditors is generally absent in the common law systems.

Across the sample as a whole, developing and transition systems have lower scores than developed ones, but the gap between developed and developing/ transition systems is less marked than the difference between the three legal origin 'families'. French legal-origin developing systems have increased their scores the most of any group, in both absolute and relative terms. German-origin developing and transition systems have also increased their scores over this period, whereas those for English-origin developing systems have changed the least.

Why do we find evidence of a strong legal origin effect, at least by reference to the three main legal 'families', in the case of creditor rights when it is missing in the case of shareholder rights? Historically, civil law systems had less extensive systems of security interests than common law ones. In the French civil code, only two types of security interests were recognized, namely mortgage (for non-possessory interests) and pledge (for possessory ones); these were imported directly from Roman law. In French-origin systems, types of non-possessory security interests over property other than land had to be introduced through ad-hoc statutes aimed at facilitating access to credit. While some of these laws included specific provision for registration, others simply relied upon the registration rules already laid down by the various civil codes. The recognition of security interests in the French civil law 'family' has tended to remain limited and unsystematic. In the German-origin countries, by comparison, the courts developed the notion of the 'quasi-floating charge' by way of transfer of title, and a more flexible approach in general was taken with regard to the protection of secured creditors' rights.[124] This is an instance where the division of labour between case law and legislation mattered, but interestingly within the wider civil law category.

4.2. *Econometric Analysis*

With time series data available, it becomes possible to estimate the economic impact of legal change, and, conversely, to study the possible impact of economic conditions on the law. A number of econometric studies using the datasets described above have been carried out. This is work in progress, and it is not possible to report a complete set of results here. Nevertheless, some trends are beginning to emerge from the literature.

The most striking result is the absence of the expected relationship between shareholder protection and stock market development. La Porta *et al.*'s original 'law and finance' study found that a high score on the anti-director rights index was correlated to a number of measures of financial development including stock market capitalization as a proportion of GDP.[125] Fagernäs *et al.*[126] carried out an analysis of the relationship between the five-country shareholder protection index

124 See generally see Pigott 2004.

125 La Porta *et al.* 1998.

126 Fagernäs, Sarkar & Singh 2008.

for the period 1970-2005 and changes in the stock-market turnover ratio for France, Germany, the UK and the US. Stock market turnover ratios measure the relationship between the value of shares traded and stock market capitalization. They have risen in each of the four countries in this study since the 1970s, particularly in France and the US. In Germany there has been a more oscillating pattern, with no clear increase in the turnover ratio since the mid-1980s.

Fägernas *et al.* used the autoregressive distributive lag (ARDL) approach to cointegration to ascertain the existence of a long run relationship between the stock market turnover ratio and the shareholder protection index, together with its different components. In order to take into account the possibility that the overall level of national economic was affecting the stock market behaviour, they included the log-value of GDP in their model. They found that increases in shareholder protection did not appear to have had a positive link with stock market development as reflected in the stock market turnover ratio, irrespective of legal origin. They found a negative relationship between both the index as a whole and its two component elements (protection against boards and protection against majority shareholders) for France and the UK. For Germany and the USA no relationship either way could be identified. In a related paper, Sarkar[127] carried out similar tests to see if there was a relationship between shareholder protection and stock market development in India over the same period. No relationship was found.

Armour *et al.* carried out a panel data analysis to determine whether higher scores in the extended-sample shareholder protection index are correlated with an increased level of stock market development, taking into account a number of other potentially relevant factors including the effectiveness of legal enforcement in the countries concerned (as measured by the World Bank's 'rule of law index').[128] The four measures of stock market development which are available on a longitudinal basis were used: stock market capitalization as a percentage of GDP; shares traded as a percentage of GDP; the ratio of shares traded to real stock market capitalization; and the number of listed companies per million of population. Contrary again to the results from LLSV's cross-sectional study, their analysis finds no statistically significant positive correlation between shareholder protection and the level of stock market development, and a negative correlation in relation to the number of listed companies. Granger causality tests showed that the direction of causation ran from the increase in shareholder protection to the decline in the number of listed companies, not the other way round. These are broadly similar results, in terms of their implications for the relationship between shareholder protection and stock market development, to those obtained by Fagernäs *et al.*[129] and Sarkar[130] in their analyses of the five-country dataset.

127 Sarkar 2008.

128 Armour *et al.* 1992b. This study covers only twenty of the twenty-five countries now contained in the dataset (as only twenty had been coded at that point). The sample of countries analysed by Armour *et al.* is similar, in terms of its composition, to that analysed by La Porta *et al.* in their first 'law and finance' study (La Porta *et al.* 1998); see Armour *et al.* 1992b, p. 360.

129 Fagernäs, Sarkar & Singh 2008.

130 Sarkar 2008.

These findings are open to a number of interpretations. One is that they may reflect difficulty in getting clear-cut results from time-series data, by comparison to cross-sectional analyses. This is refuted by the existence of results from other studies using the five-country datasets. Analysing the five-country labour regulation dataset using the ARDL approach, Deakin and Sarkar[131] found evidence that productivity and employment growth are positively correlated with the strengthening of certain labour standards (mostly those relating to working time and dismissal law) in civil law systems. Similarly, Deakin, Demetriades and James[132] report the findings of a cointegration analysis of creditor protection dataset for India, find evidence that the strengthening of secured creditors' rights was causally related to an increase in banking sector development.

A second possibility is that our longitudinal datasets are in some way defective as an account of legal change. However, by comparison to their only significant rivals, the datasets created by LLSV, they have the advantage of incorporating a wider range of legal information and adopting a more flexible approach to coding. The codings of civil law countries in our 25-country shareholder protection index are significantly higher than those provided by LLSV in their 'law and finance' paper, and the codings of common law systems are, on average, correspondingly lower.[133] We interpret this as evidence for the value of a 'functional' approach to coding which seeks to use indicators which are of potential relevance to a range of different country contexts (or, put slightly differently, avoids 'home-country bias').

Methodological criticisms aside, it is plausible that our results are pointing to findings with real economic significance. The absence of a correlation between corporate law reform and stock market development suggests that the strengthening of shareholder rights which took place in the 1990s and 2000s has not been having its principal intended effect. This could be because national conditions may be setting limits to the effectiveness of legal transplants. Hence, while we report substantial formal convergence of laws, our econometric results suggest that functional discontinuities persist. This result is not incompatible with the legal origins hypothesis, particularly in the modified from presented most recently by La Porta *et al.*[134] It could be that changes in the substantive content of laws, in the form of convergence along the lines of a common law or Anglo-American model, have had little impact in the face of a relatively unchanging 'legal infrastructure' in civil law, developing and transition systems. Legal origin may be working, through channels other than those of the formal content of the law, to frustrate the intentions of law reformers.

However, we also need to take into account the weak evidence (at best) for a positive relationship between stock market development and the strengthening of shareholder rights in common law countries, and not just in civil law and transition ones. In our panel data analysis we found that English legal origin was positively and significantly associated with one of the four measures of stock market develop-

131 Deakin & Sarkar 2008.

132 Deakin, Demetriades & James 2008.

133 Armour *et al.* 1992b, p. 356-357.

134 La Porta, Lopez-de-Silanes & Shleifer 2008.

ment that we were concerned with, namely the number of listed companies.[135] In the case of the other three variables there was no significant relationship. In the case of the time-series analysis, no statistically significant relationship in either direction was found between changes in shareholder rights and the stock market turnover ratio for the United States; in the case of Britain, a statistically significant relationship was found, but the sign was negative. Thus it would seem that greater shareholder protection has not enhanced financial development even in the common law systems. It could be that increases in shareholder protection on the scale witnessed since the mid-1990s have been 'too much of a good thing',[136] imposing undue costs and limiting the attractiveness of the listed company option.

With these possible explanations in mind we are now in a position to re-assess legal origins theory in the light of our empirical results.

5. Theoretical Re-evaluation

As we have seen, the relationship between investor protection rules and the economy has been theorized in a number of ways. The legal origins hypothesis posits a causal role for legal institutions in the creation of legal rules. Early versions of the theory suggested a uni-directional relationship: legal origins, established, in some cases, centuries ago, and transplanted through conquest and colonization, affected the ways in which countries developed their investor protection rules in the course of the nineteenth and twentieth centuries. In this view, legal origins were seen as an exogenous constraint on the extent to which economic forces and interest group politics could shape outcomes.[137] This constraint, it was argued, could lead to differences in investor protection which, in turn, would lead on to differential financial market development.

By contrast, political economy theories view the content of legal rules primarily as a phenomenon engendered by the alignment of interest groups.[138] In this view, the state of the economy is the ultimate cause of legal change, with economic forces operating through the channel of the political system. Thus it is financial market development that stimulates demand for legal protection of investors, not the other way around.[139]

The existence of a link between particular legal institutions and the content or style of legal rules does not, of course, rule out a role for political economy. Rather, legal institutions can be understood as interacting with interest group politics in the production of legal rules.[140] The outcome of previous rounds of political settlements will affect the current allocation of resources, and consequently the relationship between legal rules and the economy can be thought of a bi-, rather than uni-direc-

135 Armour *et al.* 1992b, p. 366-368.
136 Bruno & Claessens 2007.
137 La Porta *et al.* 1998.
138 See, e.g., Rajan & Zingales 2005.
139 Cheffins 2001; Coffee 2001.
140 La Porta, Lopez-de-Silanes & Shleifer 2008.

tional - that is, a 'rolling relation'.[141] Legal origins theorists argue that the nature of a country's legal institutions is nevertheless a more significant determinant of investor protection (and thence financial market) outcomes than its political makeup. The link between origins and rules is thereby viewed as being one about the style of regulation[142] - that is, the processes employed to execute outputs from a policy process.

For economists and development agencies, the most important question concerns the extent to which legal institutions affect financial market development, whether directly or indirectly. In other words, the question is whether differences in regulatory styles are associated with differences in the function of resulting legal rules - that is, differences in the way in which they actually perform in, say, protecting investors and stimulating investment. For comparative lawyers, by contrast, understanding simply the existence and determinants of differences in the form of legal rules may be of interest, even if they are inconsequential for the real economy.[143] Both groups, however, have an interest in clarifying the nature of the law-economy relationship at a conceptual level. Does the empirical evidence that is emerging from time-series datasets assist this process?

5.1. *The Extent of Path Dependencies by Legal Origin*

5.1.1. Legal Origins

Our indexing efforts reveal a number of stylised facts about the evolution of investor protection rules. First, within our time period there are differences between the content of investor protection rules by legal origin. However, the scope of these differences varies considerably depending on the type of rule in question. Differences in shareholder protection by reference to legal origin are relatively modest; moreover, the cross-country differences are much smaller than the intertemporal changes in shareholder protection that have occurred universally in our sample countries during the study period. In creditor protection, however, there are cross-country differences which are persistent over time.[144] Moreover, these differences appear to be related to legal origins, a result emerging from our more extensive 25 country sample. German legal origin countries persistently have the strongest overall protection of creditor rights, closely followed by English legal origin countries; French legal origin countries persistently have the weakest.

Moreover, there is evidence of particular emphases in legal protection styles. Thus within creditor rights, English legal origins have generally stronger protection of creditor contract rights, and generally weaker minimum capital restrictions;

141 See Milhaupt & Pistor 2008. The notion that channels of causation run in both directions between legal institutions and the economy may be traced back to Weber: see Weber 1978.

142 Botero *et al.* 2004.

143 On the significance of the difference between the form and the function of legal rules, see, e.g., Gilson 2001.

144 We observed similar patterns in the evolution of shareholder and creditor protection in our five-country, 36-year dataset: see Armour *et al.* 2009a, p. 609-615.

German legal origins have generally stronger minimum capital requirements and duties on directors to file for insolvency when companies are financially distressed; and French legal origin countries have generally weaker insolvency (or bankruptcy) law protection for creditors.[145]

5.1.2. State of Development

In both our 25 country shareholder and creditor rights indices, developing and transition economies have lower average scores throughout the study period than do developed countries. This is consistent with the claim that greater investor protection is associated with greater financial sector development. However, our econometric tests fail to reject the null hypothesis of no link between these variables.[146] Moreover, variable-by-variable analyses of creditor rights reveal that there is less variance in average scores by variable for developing, as opposed to developed countries, than there is when the analysis is conducted by reference to the legal origin of countries. The fact that differences between the formal structure of legal rules is greater by legal origin than by state of development, and that we find no statistically significant link between development and rule content, is consistent with the ideas that regulatory style (a) exhibits path dependencies (the association with legal origin) but (b) is largely a formal, rather than a functional, matter. In other words, different rule-types (to which we may add, different types of private contracts made in the shadow of the legal rules) are capable of achieving similar outcomes in the real economy, with no corresponding differences in financial development.

5.1.3. Rule types

A novel finding from our data is the way in which indices for different types of rule exhibit different properties both in relation to legal origins and to changes over time. For example, in our 25 country datasets, shareholder rights show relatively little variance by legal origin, and exhibit a relatively high degree of convergence over time. In contrast, creditor rights display a more significant degree of variation by legal origin, and do not converge in any obvious way – differences by origin remain persistent over time. Corresponding differences are also present in our five-country dataset: here, shareholder rights again show more convergence than do creditor rights.[147] No strong relationships with legal origins emerge in either of the two five-country datasets, although this may well simply be an artefact of the small sample size.

Why should different rule-types change at different paces? If legal origins exert a form of path dependency on the content of legal rules, why is this greater in relation to creditor rights than for shareholder rights? Three plausible, and comple-

145 See also Armour *et al.* 2009a, p. 613-614.

146 Fagernäs *et al.* 2008; Sarkar 2008; Armour *et al.* 2009b.

147 Armour *et al.* 2009a, p. 620-625.

mentary, explanations present themselves. The first relates to switching costs. Creditor rights are, in a sense, more fundamental (in the sense of being less susceptible to alteration) than shareholder rights.[148] The latter affect only parties who choose to become shareholders: the relation is essentially voluntary. Thus the role of law in relation to shareholder rights is essentially one of providing standard terms which reduce parties' contracting costs. Parties who do not like these terms may usually contract around them.[149] This means that it is quite straightforward to enhance shareholder rights on a prospective basis. A new form of business organization, a new stock exchange, or a new body of listing rules, may be introduced only for those firms that choose to utilize the new framework – for example, the creation of SEBI in India[150] or the Novo Mercado in Brazil.[151] This involves far lower switching costs.

Secondly, and because of this difference, an improvement in shareholder rights for publicly-traded companies does not entail significant distributional effects for any parties enjoying privileged positions under the existing framework.[152] In contrast, changes to creditor rights affect not only the parties to particular (credit) contracts, but all other actual or potential creditors as well, by altering their potential payoffs in insolvency if the debtor defaults, or the probability that the debtor will in fact default at all.[153] This implies more extensive distributional effects, with consequently greater resistance, for a change in creditor rights.[154] For example, it appears that foreign banks, lacking local knowledge, benefit disproportionately from enhancements of creditor rights in transition economies.[155] Domestic banks may therefore have incentives to oppose improvements in creditor rights for competitive reasons. In contrast, improvements to the rights of shareholders in public firms affect only those firms that choose to go public; in most countries only a minority of large firms are publicly-traded.[156] Hence blockholders who wish to avoid losing out from the new rules need not oppose the rules; they need only avoid an IPO.[157]

5.2. *The Mechanisms of Path Dependencies by Legal Origin*

A recurring weakness in the legal origins literature has been the limitations of theoretical accounts of the mechanisms responsible for the path dependencies associated with legal origins. One way forward, we suggest, is through a more detailed

148 See, e.g., Armour & Whincop 2007; Ayotte & Bolton 2007; Hansmann & Kraakman 2000; Ayotte & Bolton 2007.
149 Armour & Whincop 2007.
150 Armour & Lele 2009.
151 Gilson, Hansmann & Pargendler 2009.
152 Gilson, Hansmann & Pargendler 2009.
153 See Armour & Whincop 2007; Ayotte & Bolton 2007; Hansmann & Kraakman 2000; Ayotte & Bolton 2007.
154 Armour & Lele 2009, p. 504 & 520.
155 Haselmann, Pistor & Vig 2006.
156 See, e.g., Porta, Lopez-de-Silanes, Shleifer & Vishny 1997.
157 Gilson, Hansmann & Pargendler 2009.

account of the institutional mechanisms by which path dependencies may persist. It may be more helpful to proceed by developing categorizations based around measurable indicia of the relevant mechanisms, rather than using the often problematic 'legal families' classification, particularly when the latter lacks a firm theoretical base. Here we sketch the contours of such an account, which is informed by the quantitative and qualitative evidence we have gathered on the processes of legal change. We organize the discussion around three key ideas: mode of lawmaking, mechanisms of enforcement, and sharing of property rights.

5.2.1. Mode of Lawmaking

A leading early account articulates two channels by which legal origin may affect the real economy: the 'adaptability' channel, whereby common law (judicial) lawmaking is associated with greater responsiveness to economic change, and the 'political' or 'judicial independence' channel, whereby common law judges are associated with greater freedom from executive influence and consequently lower propensity to engage in rent-seeking.[158] Both channels focus on the role of judicial, as opposed to statutory, lawmaking. The judicial mode of lawmaking is said to be more responsive to efficiency-enhancing changes (adaptability channel) and less susceptible to capture by interest group politics than statutory law-making (judicial independence channel). What matters from a comparative, systemic perspective, then, is the extent of judicial, versus statutory, lawmaking.

A basic problem with this characterization is that, in relation to investor protection law at least, most - if not all - countries have codified the relevant rules. In other words, the simple extent of judicial, as opposed to statutory, law-making varies little across systems. This is evidenced by the lack of obvious differences in the nature of legal change in our study countries. If there were important differences in the extent of judicial lawmaking, then we would expect to see a pattern of change that differed depending on a country's legal origin: common law countries would be expected to have more rapid accretions of changes in response to development, whereas civilian countries would be expected to have less frequent but more emphatic changes, corresponding to systemic updates of their codes. The results from our five-country and 25-country datasets show, however, no discernible difference in the nature of change by legal origin: shareholder rights have advanced across the board, in a manner that looks roughly similar in all our studied jurisdictions, and to the extent that there is change in creditor rights, its nature and extent does not vary by legal origin.

Acknowledging the near-universal codification of investor protection laws requires a refinement of the function courts are understood as performing in relation to these channels. A revised version of the 'adaptability' channel, for example, would view courts not as providing the bulk of precedents, but rather as providing interstitial decisions on the interpretation or operation of the law.[159] On this view,

158 Beck, Demirgüc-Kunt & Levine 2003.

159 See La Porta, Lopez-de-Silanes & Schleifer 2008.

we should not expect to see differences in the pattern of law production over time, as measured in our indices. This is not, therefore, a mechanism for legal path dependency, but rather an alternate channel (other than via legal rules) through which the structure of legal institutions may affect the real economy. Thus we might expect differences in the functionality of systems of investor protection depending on the degree of efficacy of their courts. To some degree, these differences may be captured by measures of the 'integrity' or independence of courts.[160] However, it seems plausible that there may be other factors at work which make a difference to the operation of courts.

In particular, we consider that there may be important functional consequences flowing from differences in the structure of the courts or tribunals. Variables that may have an impact on court performance include (a) judicial human capital (selection, training, and professional background),[161] which will affect the quality of decisions produced; (b) court procedural rules, including standing, costs, litigation funding, and the availability of class actions, each of which will affect the likelihood that an action will in fact be brought;[162] and (c) the function performed – whether solely for ex post challenge through litigation, or whether the court or tribunal performs an ex ante gatekeeper function.[163]

It is less than clear that these factors match up with the allocation of 'legal origin'. In fact, our case studies cast some doubt on the idea. For example, India, a common law country, suffers from problematic rules of civil procedure that engender delays of 10 years or more in a typical civil trial.[164] Nevertheless, successful development of its stock markets may be explicable in part through the establishment of a dedicated tribunal (the Securities Appellate Tribunal, or SAT, associated with SEBI, the Stock Exchange Board of India), with sector-specific expertise and streamlined procedural rules.[165] There is no reason to suppose that such specialist securities tribunals could only be established in common law countries; nor should we rely, in relation to investor protection, on any measure of the quality of courts that does not code specifically for tribunals that make decisions in relation to this area of law.[166] This may help to explain why, if this is a channel through which legal institutions affect the real economy, we find no empirical association between legal origin and stock market development.[167] A more focused empirical test would code the foregoing differences in the structure of courts directly.[168]

160 See Djankov *et al.* 2002.

161 Hadfield 2008.

162 Hadfield 2008. See also Armour *et al.* 2009c.

163 Armour & Skeel 2007.

164 Armour & Lele 2009.

165 Armour & Lele 2009.

166 For example, in relation to the UK, failure to take into account the Takeover Code, promulgated by the Takeover Panel, which for most of its history has been entirely self-regulatory, would result in a wholly misleading picture of takeover regulation. See Armour & Skeel 2007 p. 1735-38 & 1782-84.

167 See Fagernäs, Sarkar & Singh 2009; Sarkar 2008; Armour, Cheffins & Skeel 2002.

168 See Siems 2006.

For a more nuanced version of the 'judicial independence' channel, an additional set of factors is likely to be significant: namely (d) the status of courts in the constitutional hierarchy. That is, courts with extensive powers of judicial review of primary legislation are able to act as a restraint on the operation of interest group politics, even if the formal (observed) extent of judicial law-making is quite small. This may be expected to have an effect both on the real economy and on the formal content of legal rules. Again, however, this need not vary along the lines of legal origin. For example, in England, despite its status as 'mother country' of the common law legal origin, courts have no constitutional power to strike down primary legislation.[169]

5.2.2. Enforcement

Theory suggests that the efficacy of legal rules at imparting incentives to actors in the corporate sector will be a function not only of their substantive content, but also of their enforcement.[170] In the literature on legal origins, contributions to date have sought to bifurcate enforcement mechanisms into 'public' (initiated by state agencies) and 'private' (initiated by citizens or corporations). Public enforcement agencies typically do not keep the rewards of their efforts, and so have lower incentives to engage in enforcement – and hence a lower deterrent effect – than do private actors.[171]

The measurement of the efficacy of enforcement mechanisms has proved just as difficult as of the quality of law. Early indices based on the extent of enforcement powers[172] asserted the superiority of private enforcement, a preference for which appeared also to be correlated with English legal origin. However, other studies using data based on resources directed toward enforcement[173] or penalties imposed,[174] assert the importance of public enforcement of securities laws. More recent indices distinguish between ex ante and ex post interventions by public and private actors.[175]

However, the full range of mechanisms employed to secure compliance may be larger still.[176] On the one hand, 'public enforcement' may encompass a range of sanctions beyond formal penalties, including reputational sanctions imposed through public censure.[177] On the other hand, 'gatekeeper control'[178] is also a widely-used enforcement mechanism, but is not coded in the existing law and finance

169 See Human Rights Act 1998 (UK), s 4(6).
170 See, e.g., Pound 1910; Becker 1968.
171 La Porta, Lopez-de-Silanes & Schleifer 2006; Hay & Shleifer 1998 (discussing the emergence of private enforcement to address gaps in the system of public enforcement in Russia in the 1990s).
172 La Porta, Lopez-de-Silanes & Schleifer 2006.
173 Jackson & Roe 2008.
174 Coffee 2007.
175 La Porta, Lopez-de-Silanes & Schleifer 2008.
176 See Armour 2009.
177 See, e.g., Liebman & Milhaupt 2008.
178 Kraakman 1986; Coffee 2006.

literature. In particular, a specific type of gatekeeper, the notary, is widely used in civilian, but not in common law, legal systems. The notary charges a fee for verifying the propriety of documentation associated with a range of transactions.[179] In some respects this function is similar to that which might be performed by legal advisers in a common law system. The difference is that referral to a notary is mandatory, and the level of service is centrally prescribed, whereas consultation with a lawyer is voluntary, and can be metered by the client according to the amount at stake. It is plausible that reliance on notaries and other gatekeeper mechanisms associated with formalities might have a significant impact on the efficacy of legal institutions.[180]

An additional factor which should be borne in mind when seeking to quantify enforcement intensity is that there is probably some substitution between aspects of investor protection law and enforcement mechanisms. In particular, shareholder governance rights - that is, decision-making rights and powers to appoint and remove the board, are potentially effective substitutes for enforcement of directors' duties under corporate law, depending on the coordination costs experienced by the shareholders.[181] As a consequence, measuring enforcement intensity in isolation from substantive legal rules may generate results just as potentially misleading as studies based solely on the formal rules.

Not only do enforcement strategies present an additional channel through which legal institutions may affect the real economy, they might also be the source of some path dependencies in the content of legal rules. Consider first the potential substitutability of certain types of substantive rules and enforcement mechanisms. Where such substitution is possible, then this creates a barrier to change in the formal rules. To implement such a change may require not only a change in the formal rules, but also the development of an alternative enforcement mechanism.

Secondly, consider the role accorded to gatekeepers such as notaries in many legal systems. They constitute an interest group, internal to the legal system, who are likely to have a bias against change. Changes to the rules devalue the human capital of all professionals specific to a particular set of transactional rules, and require a further investment in rule-specific human capital. For those whose services are metered (such as business lawyers), these costs can be offset by increased demand for legal services following a change in the law, as clients also need to learn what is involved. For those whose services are not metered, but who operate on the basis of fixed transaction fees (as is the case for notarial services in many countries), the change is simply uncompensated. This may create an additional source of path-dependence for legal systems heavily reliant on notaries as gatekeepers.

179 Arruñada 1996.

180 One might also expect the organization and training of these professions to be relevant variables: see Hadfield 2008.

181 Armour 2009, p. 102-109.

5.2.3. Shared Property Rights

All systems of corporate law involve some partitioning of the rights of ownership to assets between different classes of investor.[182] The property rights in these assets (be they physical or financial) are therefore shared between the participants.[183] Such sharing presupposes some mechanism for dealing with the problem of 'ostensible ownership': that is, where one of the shared owners deals with a third party on the basis that they are sole owner. In this case, either the other shared owners, or the third party, loses out. Legal systems have three basic mechanisms for dealing with this problem, which we may term (i) the *numerus clausus* principle; (ii) selective enforcement or negotiability; and (iii) registration.

The *numerus clausus* approach posits a fixed set of arrangements for sharing property rights. By limiting the set, third parties may be confident that they can limit their due diligence endeavours to enquiries focused on this particular list.[184] Alternatively, selective enforcement involve ex post adjudication by a court as to which of the 'passive' owners or the third party could have avoided the problem at least cost (e.g. by the passive owners doing more to publicize their interest, or the third party making greater enquiries.[185] Thirdly, registration mechanisms provide an authoritative repository of information about the nature of passive ownership interests.[186]

The three mechanisms so described are functional substitutes as regards the resolution of the problem of ostensible ownership: either is capable of reducing the costs thereby incurred to a manageable level. However, they have quite different dynamic properties. The *numerus clausus* approach in particular makes it very costly to introduce new ways in which property rights may be shared, other than those on the existing list. All transacting parties need to add to their list of potential questions if a new entrant is added. In contrast, selective enforcement imposes few additional costs for third parties if a new property-sharing arrangement is introduced: the more unusual the arrangement, the more effort the passive owners must undertake to bring it to others' attention. Registration lies somewhere between these poles, depending on how the mechanism is implemented.[187]

Numerus clausus approaches have traditionally been associated with civil law systems; selective enforcement mechanisms (through the doctrines of 'bona fide purchaser' and 'constructive notice') with the equitable jurisdiction present in 'common law' systems. This therefore constitutes a plausible additional channel through which path dependencies in the content of legal rules might operate. In particular, this could help to explain the relative lack of contractual protections for creditors in French civil law jurisdictions, where reliance is placed on the *numerus clausus* approach.

182 Hansmann & Kraakman 2000.
183 Armour & Whincop 2007.
184 Merrill & Smith 2000.
185 Armour & Whincop 2001.
186 Hansmann & Kraakman 2001b.
187 See Armour 2008.

5.3. *Are Legal Origins 'Endogenous'?*

Summing up this part of our discussion, we have seen that a focus on 'infrastructural' aspects of legal systems can help in explaining some of the mechanisms of legal dependency. A first point to note is that these mechanisms do not always map very well on to the civil law-common law divide. Thus mode of lawmaking (judicial versus statutory), although often referred to in the legal origins literature, is not a convincing explanation for divergences in corporate law, given the predominant role played by statute, and the correspondingly interstitial role of the courts, in all jurisdictions. There is more scope for viewing difference in enforcement strategies and modes of interpretation along legal origin lines. However, more information is needed before we can be sure that the classification of systems by reference to legal 'families' is the right approach to take. A mapping exercise needs to be carried out so that we have an objective basis for differentiating between the 'infrastructural' aspects of different systems. Once that is done, we may have a firmer basis for determining whether the legal families classification is a useful one.

Secondly, a closer identification of the factors that might be driving legal path dependencies will assist us in assessing how far legal systems can be said to 'exogenous' or 'endogenous' with regard to economic development. A possible working hypothesis would be that differences in enforcement strategies (public versus private) and modes of interpretation (open-ended legal categories versus the *numerus clausus* approach) could have an impact on the extent to which the legal system supports transactional flexibility and hence financial innovation. Possible trade-offs between granting transactional flexibility and protecting third party interests have also been noted. If institutional factors such as these have implications for the nature and extent of financial development independently of the operation of formal legal rules, we may have part of the explanation for the limited impact of formal convergence in shareholder protection over the past decade. But if legal infrastructure is linked to economic outcomes in this way, it is also likely that there will have been some matching of legal institutions to economic and political structures over time in the systems concerned. It would, for example, be in the interests of particular interest groups to lobby to defend certain enforcement strategies against changes which would leave them worse off. Thus causal relations may run in both directions.

6. Conclusions

For the past decade or so, legal reforms worldwide have followed a consistent pattern. Shareholder rights and corporate governance standards have been strengthened in the belief that this would lead to more dispersed share ownership and more liquid capital markets, and creditor rights have been enhanced with a view to fostering flows of private credit. A theoretical underpinning for these developments was provided by the legal origins hypothesis, which claims that legal systems affect long-run patterns of economic development. Systems with a common law origin were thought to favour market-facilitating laws, whereas those with roots in the

French or German civil law were seen as tending towards an activist role for the state. These underlying differences of regulatory style were, it was argued, reflected in the contents of the laws governing the business enterprise, and in economic outcomes. As applied by the World Bank through its Doing Business Reports, this approach directly influenced policy initiatives in dozens of countries.

Despite its influence, there are unanswered questions relating to the legal origins hypothesis. At a theoretical level there is a lack of clarity concerning the channels through which legal origins might impact on the substance of legal rules and on economic outcomes. From an empirical viewpoint, a serious shortcoming is that the evidence for the legal origins effect rests on quantitative indicators which offer a cross-sectional view of the law (mostly of the content of laws as they were in the late 1990s). The findings from these studies can only be valid if it is assumed that laws change relatively little and that the rank order of countries, in terms of the impact of regulation on business, do not alter much over time. These are issues which are capable of being tested empirically. We set out to develop longitudinal datasets which could be used to thrown light on the nature and extent of changes to the substantive law and to assess their relationship to legal origins, on the one hand, and to financial development on the other.

We have now produced a number of new datasets tracking legal change over time in the areas of shareholder protection and creditor protection. We have developed indices with up to 60 indicators which code for the law of five significant countries (France, Germany, India, the UK and the US) for 36 years (1970-2005), and reduced-form indices of 10 indicators which code for the laws in a wider sample, 25 countries, for the period 1995-2005. The coding methods we have used incorporate a wider range of legal and regulatory variables than earlier studies and take into account the different ways in which regulatory rules can be expressed (as mandatory rules or as 'defaults' applying in the absence of contrary agreement). We have used time-series and panel data econometric analysis to test for correlations between the changing state of the law over time and economic outcome variables.

Our datasets provide a different picture of the state of the law than that provided by the early legal origins papers. We see considerable change in the area of shareholder protection, with civil law systems catching up with their common law counterparts, in particular over the decade to 2005. This suggests that lock-in through legal origin has not been much of an obstacle to the formal convergence of systems. In the case of creditor protection, we do not see a clear common law/civil law divide, but we do find evidence to support a classification of systems by legal 'families'; German-origin systems have consistently higher scores with English-origin ones in the middle and French-origins systems showing generally low levels support for creditor rights.

What of the impact of legal change? The econometric findings we have reviewed here call into question the widespread assumption that enhancing shareholders' rights has positive economic effects. We find that increases in shareholder protection have not led to greater stock market development, as might have been expected. For some key variables, the relationship between legal change and financial development is negative. One possible interpretation of our results is that a 'one size fits all' approach to corporate governance reforms, stressing elements of British and American practice - the role of independent boards and the market for corporate control - may not be working as intended in civilian and developing systems. Another interpretation is that even in the common law world, shareholder protection can have counter-productive effects, by unnecessarily raising the costs associated with a stock exchange listing.

A theoretical implication of our work is that legal systems are not the independent, 'exogenous' force that legal origins theory takes them to be. Legal systems are, to some degree, 'endogenous' in the sense of being shaped by their economic and political environment. We should expect to see feedback effects not simply between economic and political variables and the content of legal rules, but also between these contextual factors and the 'infrastructural' core of legal systems.

The empirical analysis of legal origins is still, in significant respects, work in progress. The research project initiated just over a decade ago by LLSV shows no sign of running out of steam. On the contrary, with new techniques being deployed and an active theoretical debate going on, it is continuing to progress. Time-series evidence has enhanced our understanding of the legal origins hypothesis, clarifying some the claims with which it is associated while undermining others, but we are still some way from fully understanding the forces at work in the law-economy relation.

Bibliography

Ahlering & Deakin 2007
Ahlering, B. & Deakin, S., 'Labour Regulation, Corporate Governance and Legal Origin: A Case of Institutional Complementarity?, *Law & Society Review*, 2007, p. 865-908.

Aoki 2001
Aoki, M.M., *Toward a Comparative Institutional Analysis*, Cambridghe: MIT Press, 2001.

Armour 2008
Armour, J., 'The Law and Economics Debate About Secured Lending: Lessons for European Lawmaking?', *European Company and Financial Law Review*, 2008, p. 3-29.

Armour 2009
Armour, J., 'Enforcement Strategies in UK Corporate Governance: A Road Map and Empirical Assessement', in: J. Armour & J. Payne (eds.), *Rationality in Company Law: Essays for Dan Prentice*, Oxford: Hart Publishing, 2009, p. 71-120.

Armour & Lele 2009
Armour, J. & Lele, P., 'Law, Finance, and Politics: The Case of India', *Law & Society Review*, 2009, p. 491-526.

Armour & Skeel 2007
Armour, J. & Skeel, Jr., D.A., 'Who Makes the Rules for Hostile Takeovers, and Why? The Peculiar Divergence of US and UK Takeover Regulation', *Georgetown Law Journal*, 2007, p. 1727- 1794.

Armour & Whincop 2001
Armour, J. & Whincop, M.J., 'An Economic Analysis of Shared Property in Partnership and Close Corporations Law', *Journal of Corporation Law*, 2001, p. 101-118.

Armour & Whincop 2007
Armour, J. & Whincop, M.J., 'The Proprietary Foundations of Corporate Law', *Oxford Journal of Legal Studies*, 2007, p. 429-465.

Armour, Cheffins & Skeel 2002
Armour, J., Cheffins, B.R. & Skeel Jr., D.A., 'Corporate Ownership Structure and the Evolution of Bankruptcy Law: Lessons from the UK', *Vanderbilt Law Review*, 2002, p. 1699-1785.

Armour *et al.* 2009a
Armour, J., Deakin, S., Lele, P. & Siems, M., 'How Do Legal Rules Evolve? Evidence from a Cross-Country Comparison of Shareholder, Creditor and Worker Protection', *The American Journal of Comparative Law*, 2009, p. 579-630.

Armour *et al.* 2009b
Armour, J., Deakin, S., Sarkar, P., Siems, M. & Singh, A., 'Shareholder Protection and Stock Market Development: An Empirical Test of the Legal Origins Hypothesis', *Journal of Empirical Legal Studies*, 2009, p. 343-381.

Armour *et al.* 2009c
Armour, J., Black, B.S., Cheffins, B.R. & Nolan, R., 'Private Enforcement of Corporate Law: An Empirical Comparison of the UK and US', *Journal of Empirical legal Studies*, 2009, p. 687-722.

Arruñada 1996
Arruñada, B., 'The Economics of Notaries', *European Journal of Law and Economics*, 1996, p. 5-37.

Ayotte & Bolton 2007
Ayotte, K. & Bolton, P., *Optimal Property Rights in Financial Contracting*, American Law and Economics Association, Working Paper 46, 2007 (available at: <http://repositories.cdlib.org/berkeley_law_econ/Spring2007a/4>.

Beck, Demirgüc-Kunt & Levine 2003
Beck, T., Demirgüc-Kunt, A. & Levine, R., 'Law and Finance: Why Does Legal Origin Matter?', *Journal of Comparative Economics*, 2003, p. 653-675.

Becker 1968
Becker, G., 'Crime and Punishment: An Economic Approach', *Journal of Political Economy*, 1968, p. 169-217.

Berglöf & Von Thadden 1999
Berglöf E. & Von Thadden, E.-L., *The Changing Corporate Governance Paradigm: Implications for Transition and Developing Countries*, Stockholm School of Economics, Working Paper, 1999.

Berkowitz, Pistor & Richard 2003
Berkowitz, D., Pistor, K. & Richard, J.-F., 'The Transplant Effect', *The American Journal of Comparative Law*, 2003, p. 163-203.

Botero *et al.* 2004
Botero, J., Djankov, S., La Porta, R., Lopez-de-Silanes, F. & Shleifer, A., The Regulation of Labor, *Quarterly Journal of Economics*, 2004, p. 1340-1382.

Boyle 2002
Boyle, A.J., *Minority Shareholders' Remedies*, Cambridge: Cambridge University Press, 2002.

Braendle 2006
Braendle, U., *Shareholder Protection in the USA and Germany: on the Fallacy of LLSV*, German Working Papers in Law and Economics 18, 2006, available at: <http://www.bepress.com/gwp/default/vol2006/iss1/art18>.

Bruno & Claessens 2007
Bruno, V. & Claessens, S., *Corporate Governance and Regulation: Can There Be Too Much of a Good Thing?*, ECGI-Finance Working Paper, No. 142/2007. Available on SSRN: <http://ssrn.com/abstract=956329>.

Cheffins 2001
Cheffins, B.R., 'Does Law Matter? The Separation of Ownership and Control in the United Kingdom', *Journal of Legal Studies*, 2001, p. 459-84.

Coffee 2001
Coffee, J., 'The Rise of Dispersed Ownership: The Role of Law in the Separation of Ownership and Control', *The Yale Law Journal*, 2001, p. 1-82.

Coffee 2006
Coffee, J.C., Jr, *Gatekeepers: The Professions and Corporate Governance*, Oxford: Oxford University Press, 2006.

Coffee 2007
Coffee, J.C., Jr, 'Law and the Market: The Impact of Enforcement', *University of Pennsylvania Law Review*, 2007, p. 229-311.

Cools 2005
Cools, S., 'The Real Difference in Corporate Law Between the United States and Continental Europe: Distribution of Powers', *Delaware Journal of Corporate Law*, 2005, p. 697-766.

David & Brierley 1995
David, R. & Brierley, J.E.C., *Major Legal Systems in the World Today*, 3rd edition, London: Stevens & Sons, 1995.

Deakin 2003
Deakin, S., 'Evolution for Our Time: A Theory of Legal Memetics', *Current Legal Problems*, 2003, p. 1-42.

Deakin & Sarkar 2008
Deakin, S.& Sarkar, P., 'Assessing the Long-Run Economic Impact of Labour Law Systems: A Theoretical Reappraisal and Analysis of New Time Series Data, *Industrial Relations Journal*, 2008, p. 453-487.

Deakin, Lele & Siems 2007
Deakin, S., Lele, P. & Siems, M., 'The Evolution of Labour Law: Calibrating and Comparing Regulatory Regimes', *International. Labour Review*, 2007, p. 133-162.

Deakin, Demetriades & James 2008
Deakin, S., Demetriades, P. & James, G., *Creditor Rights and Banking System Development in India*, Working Paper, available on SSRN, <http://ssrn.com/abstract=1208866>.

Djankov, McLiesh & Shleifer 2007
Djankov, S. McLiesh, C. & Shleifer, A., 'Private Credit in 129 Countries', *Journal of Finance*, 2007, p. 299-329.

Djankov *et al.* 2002
Djankov, S., La Porta, R., Lopez-de-Silanes, F. & Shleifer, A., 'The Regulation of Entry', *Quarterly Journal of Economics*, 2002, p. 1-37.

Djankov *et al.* 2003
Djankov, S., La Porta, R., Lopez-de-Silanes, F. & Shleifer, A., 'Courts', *Quarterly Journal of Economics*, 2003, p. 453-517.

Djankov *et al.* 2007
Djankov, S., Hart, O., McLeish, C. & Shleifer, A., *Debt Enforcement Around the World*, ECGI Finance, Working Paper, No. 147, 2007.

Djankov *et al.* 2008
Djankov, S., La Porta, R., Lopez-de-Silanes, F. & Shleifer, A., 'The Law and Economics of Self-Dealing', *Journal of Financial Economics*, 2008, p. 430-465.

Engle & Granger 1987
Engle, R. & Granger, C., 'Cointegration and Error Correction: Representation, Estimation, and Testing', *Econometrica*, 1987, p. 251-276.

Fagernäs, Sarkar & Singh 2008
Fagernäs, S., Sarkar, P. & Singh, A., 'Legal Origin, Shareholder Protection and the Stock Market: New Challenges from Time Series Analysis', in: K. Gugler & B. Yurtoglu (eds), *The Economics of Corporate Governance and Mergers*, Cheltenham: Edward Elgar, 2008.

Gdanski 2001
Gdanski, M., 'Taking Security in France', in: M. Bridge & R. Stevens (eds.), *Cross-Border Security and Insolvency*, Oxford: Oxford University Press, 2001, p. 64-68.

Gilson 2001
Gilson, R.J., 'Globalizing Corporate Governance: Convergence of Form or Function', *The American Journal of Comparative Law*, 2001, p. 329-357.

Gilson, Hansmann & Pargendler 2009
Gilson, R.J., Hansmann, H. & Pargendler, M., *Dual Capital Markets as a Financial Development Strategy: Brazil, the US, and the EU*, Yale Law School Working Paper, 2009.

Glaeser & Shleifer 2002
Glaeser, E. & Shleifer, A., 'Legal Origins', *Quarterly Journal of Economics*, 2002, p. 1193-1229.

Gorga 2009
Gorga, E., 'Changing the Paradigm of Stock Ownership from Concentrated towards Dispersed Ownership? Evidence from Brazil and Consequences for Emerging Countries', *Northwestern Journal of International Law & Business*, 2000, p. 439-554.

Gourevtich & Shinn 2005
Gourevtich, P.A. & Shinn, J.J., *Political Power and Corporate Control. The New Global Politics of Corporate Governance*, Princeton, NJ: Princeton University Press, 2005.

Granger 1969
Granger, C., 'Investigating Causal Relations by Econometric Models and Cross-Spectral Methods', *Econometrica*, 1969, p. 424-438.

Hadfield 2008
Hadfield, G.K., 'The Levers of Legal Design: Institutional Determinants of the Quality of Law', *Journal of Comparative Economics*, 2008, p. 43-73.

Hall & Soskice 2001
Hall, P.A. & Soskice, D., 'An Introduction to the Varieties of Capitalism', in: P.A. Hall & D. Soskice (eds.), *Varieties of Capitalism: The Institutional Foundations of Comparative Advantage*, New York: Oxford University Press, 2001, p. 1-70.

Hannah 2007
Hannah, L., The "Divorce" of Ownership from Control from 1900 Onwards: Recalibrating Imagined Global Trends', *Business History*, 2007, p. 404-438.

Hansmann & Kraakman 2000
Hansmann, H. & Kraakman, R., 'The Essential Role of Organizational Law', *Yale Law Journal*, 2000, p. 387-440.

Hansmann & Kraakman 2001a
Hansmann, H. & Kraakman, R., 'The End of History for Corporate Law', *Georgetown Law Journal*, 2001, p. 439-468.

Hansmann & Kraakman 2001b
Hansmann, H. & Kraakman, R., 'Property, Contract, and Verification: The Numerus Clausus Problem and the Divisibility of Legal Rights', *Journal of Legal Studies*, 2001, p. 373-420.

Haselmann, Pistor & Vig 2006
Haselmann, R., Pistor, K. & Vig, V., *How Law Affects Lending*, Munich Personal RePEc Archive, Working Paper No. 157, 2006, available at: <http://mpra.ub.uni-muenchen.de/157>.

Hay & Shleifer 1998
Hay, J.R. & Shleifer, A., 'Private Enforcement of Public Laws: A Theory of Legal Reform', *American Economic Review*, 1998, p. 398-403.

Hodgson 2003
Hodgson, G.M., 'The Enforcement of Contract and Property Rights: Constitutive versus Epiphenomenal Conceptions of Law', *International Review of Sociology*, 2003, p. 373-389.

Husa 2004
Husa, J., 'Classification of Legal Families Today - Is it Time For a Memorial Hymn?', *Revue internationale de droit comparé*, 2004, p. 11-38.

Jackson & Mark J. Roe 2008
Jackson, H.E. & Roe, M.J., *Public and Private Enforcement of Securities Laws: Resource-Based Evidence*, Harvard Law & Economics Discussion Paper, No. 638, 2008.

Kraakman 1986
Kraakman, R., 'Gatekeepers: The Anatomy of a Third-Party Enforcement Strategy', *Journal of Law Economics and Organization*, 1986, p. 53-104.

Lamoreaux & Rosenthal 2005
Lamoreaux, N.R. & Rosenthal, J.L., 'Legal Regime and Contractual Flexibility: A Comparison of Business Organizational Choices in France and the United States during the Era of Industrialization', *American Law and Economic Review*, 2005, p. 28-61.

La Porta, Lopez-de-Silanes & Shleifer 1999
La Porta, R., Lopez de Silanes, F. & Shleifer, A., Corporate Ownership Around the World, *Journal of Finance*, 1999, p. 471-517.

La Porta, Lopez-de-Silanes & Shleifer 2006
La Porta, R., Lopez-de-Silanes, F. & Shleifer, A., 'What Works in Securities Laws?', *Journal of Finance*, 2006, p. 1-32.

La Porta, Lopez-de-Silanes & Shleifer 2008
La Porta, R., Lopez-de-Silanes, F. & Shleifer, A., 'The Economic Consequences of Legal Origins', *Journal of Economic Literature*, 2008, p. 285-332.

La Porta *et al.* 1997
La Porta, R., Lopez-de-Silanes, F., Shleifer, A. & Visny, R., 'Legal Determinants of External Finance', *Journal of Finance*, 1997, p. 1131-1150.

La Porta *et al.* 1998
La Porta, R., Lopez-de-Silanes, F., Shleifer, A. & Visny, R., 'Law and Finance', *Journal of Political Economy*, 1998, p. 1113-1155.

La Porta *et al.* 2004
La Porta, R., Lopez-de-Silanes, F., Pop-Eleches. C. & Shleifer, A., 'Judicial Checks and Balances', *Journal of Political Economy*, 2004 p. 445-470.

Lele & Siems 2007a
Lele, P. & Siems, M., 'Diversity in Shareholder Protection in Common Law Countries 5/1 DICE-Report', *Journal for Institutional Comparisons*, 2007, p. 3-9.

Lele & Siems 2007b
Lele, P & Siems, M., 'Shareholder Protection - A Leximetric Approach', *Journal of Corporate Law Studies*, 2007, p. 17-50.

Liebman & Milhaupt 2008
Liebman, B.J. & Milhaupt, C.J., 'Reputational Sanctions in China's Securities Market', *Columbia Law Review*, 2008, p. 929-983.

Merrill & Smith 2000
Merrill, T.W. & Smith, H.E., 'Optimal Standardization in the Law of Property: The Numerus Clausus Principle', *Yale Law Journal*, 2000, p. 1-70.

Milhaupt & Pistor 2008
Milhaupt, C. & Pistor, K., *Law and Capitalism: What Corporate Crises Reveal about Legal Systems and Economic Development Around the World*, Chicago, IL: University of Chicago Press, 2008.

OECD 2004
OECD, *OECD Principles of Corporate Governance*, 2nd edition, available at: <www.oecd.org/daf/corporateaffairs/principles/text>.

Pigott 2004
Pigott, H.S., 'The Need for Harmonisation of Collateral Law in Europe', *European Business Law Review*, 2004, p. 871-877.

Pistor *et al.* 2003
Pistor, K., Keinan, Y., Kleinheisterkamp, J. & West, M., 'The Evolution of Corporate Law: a Cross-Country Comparison', *University of Pennsylvania Journal of International Economics and Law*, 2003, p. 791-871.

Pound 1910
Pound, R., 'Law in Books and Law in Action', *American Law Review*, 1910, p. 12-36.

Rajan & Zingales 2005
Rajan, R.G. & Zingales, L., 'The Great Reversals: The Politics of Financial Development in the Twentieth Century', *Journal of Financial Economics*, 2003, p. 5-50.

Reimann 2001
Reimann, M., 'Beyond National Systems: A Comparative Law for the International Age', *Tulane Law Review*, 2001, p. 1103-1119.

Reynolds & Flores 1989
Reynolds, T. & Flores, A., *Foreign Law: Current Sources of Basic Legislation in Jurisdictions of the World*, Buffalo, N.Y.: W.S. Hein, 1989.

Rodrik 2009
Rodrik, D., *Why we Learn Nothing from Regressing Economic Growth on Policies*, Working paper, Harvard University, available at: <http://ksghome.harvard.edu/~drodrik/policy%20regressions.pdf>.

Roe 2003
Roe, M., *Political Determinants of Corporate Governance: Political Context, Corporate Impact*, Oxford, Oxford University Press, 2003.

Sarkar 2008
Sarkar, P., 'Corporate Governance, Stock Market Development and Private Capital Accumulation: A Case Study of India', in: S. Marjit (ed.), *India Macroeconomics Annual 2008*, New Delhi: Sage India, 2008.

Schmidt & Spindler 2002
Schmidt, R.H. & Spindler, G., 'Path Dependence, Corporate Governance and Complementarity', *International Finance*, 2002, p. 311-333.

Schouten & Siems 2009
Schouten, M. & Siems, M., *The Evolution of Ownership Disclosure Rules across Countries*, Working Paper July 14 2009, available at: <http://ssrn.com/abstract=1434144>.

Siems 2005a
Siems, M., 'What Does Not Work in Comparing Securities Laws: A Critique on La Porta *et al.*'s Methodology', *International Company & Commercial Law Review*, 2005, p. 300-305.

Siems 2005b
Siems, M., 'Numerical Comparative Law - Do We Need Statistical Evidence in Order to Reduce Complexity?', *Cardozo Journal of International and Comparative Law*, 2005, p. 521-540.

Siems 2006
Siems, M., 'Legal Adaptability in Elbonia', *International Journal of Law in Context*, 2006, p. 393-408.

Siems 2007
Siems, M., 'Legal Origins: Reconciling Law & Finance and Comparative Law', *McGill Law Journal*, 2007, p. 55-81.

Siems 2008a
Siems, M., 'Shareholder Protection Around the World ('Leximetric II')', *Delaware Journal of Corporate Law*, 2008, p. 111-147.

Siems 2008b
Siems, M., *Convergence in Shareholder Law*, Cambridge: Cambridge University Press, 2008.

Spamann 2006
Spamann, H., *On the Insignificance and/or Endogeneity of La Porta et al.'s 'Anti-director Rights Index' under Consistent Coding*, ECGI Law, Working Paper, No. 67/2006.

Spamann 2008
Spamann, H., *'Law and Finance' Revisited*, Harvard Law School John M. Olin Center Discussion Paper, No. 12, 2008.

Spamann 2009
Spamann, H., *Contemporary Legal Transplants - Legal Families and the Diffusion of (Corporate) Law*, Paper presented to the BYU Law Review Symposium, 'Evaluating Legal Origins Theory', Brigham Young University, February 2009.

Teubner 1993
Teubner, G., *Law as an Autopoietic System*, Cambridge MA: Blackwell Publishing, 1993.

Vagts 2000
Vagts, D., 'Comparative Company Law - The New Wave', in: R. Schweizer (eds.), *Festschrift für Jean Nicolas Druey: Zum 65. Geburtstag*, Zürich: Schulthess Juristische Medien, 2000, p. 595-605.

Vogenauer 2005
Vogenauer, S., 'An Empire of Light? Learning and Lawmaking in the History of German Law', *Cambridge Law Journal*, 2005, p. 481-500.

Weber 1978
Weber, M., *Economy and Society An Outcome of Interpretative Analogy*, edited by G. Roth & C. Wittich, Berkeley: University of California Press, 1978.

Zimmerman 1998
Zimmerman, R., 'Savignys Vermächtnis', *Juristische Blätter*, 1998, p. 273-293.

Zweigert & Kötz 1998
Zweigert, K. & Kötz, H., *Introduction to Comparative Law*, Oxford: Clarendon, 1998.

Eric Helland
Jonathan Klick

LEGAL ORIGINS AND EMPIRICAL CREDIBILITY

1. Introduction

Modern empirical microeconomics is the methodological success story of the profession. Angrist and Pischke suggest the field experienced a 'credibility revolution' starting in the 1990s.[1] Because of this revolution, they argue, decision makers started taking empirical economic analysis seriously in policy discussions in a way they had not previously. Their argument explicitly invokes, endorses, and addresses Leamer's famous criticism of empirical economics which basically dubbed the field a 'con'.[2]

In the midst of this revolution, the legal origins literature starting with La Porta *et al.* indisputably became a juggernaut in both scholarly and policy discussions.[3] La Porta *et al.*[4] is the most cited paper in all of economics since its publication.[5] Organizations like the World Bank used this research to formulate their recommendations concerning institutions to developing countries. From both a scholarship and a practical standpoint, it is not hyperbole to claim that this research has had more impact than anything else done by economists in the past two decades.

Surprisingly, the legal origins literature suffers from the frailties identified by Leamer and Angrist and Pischke.[6] Scholarship on legal origins missed the credibility revolution altogether. Unfortunately, given the nature of legal institutions, the tools of modern micro-econometrics, or statistical tools more generally, are not suited to shed any light on the relationship between legal origins, or even any specific legal institution, and economic or financial development. Thus, even when

1 Angrist & Pischke 2010.
2 Leamer 1983.
3 La Porta *et al.* 1997; La Porta *et al.* 1998.
4 La Porta *et al.* 1998.
5 La Porta *et al.* 1998 has been cited 1,183 times according to <http://ideas.repec.org/top/top.item.nbcites.html> and 1,667 times according to the ISI Web of Science (both as of 20 May 2011).
6 Leamer 1983; Angrist & Pischke 2010.

seemingly sophisticated approaches like the instrumental variables technique used in Acemoglu, Johnson, and Robinson[7] or work using panel data techniques such as that described in Armour *et al.*[8] are used, we learn nothing about the causal impact of legal origins on financial market development.

The fundamental problem is one of statistical identification. That is, while the legal origins literature has identified a number of correlations between various legal institutions and economic outcomes, it is not possible to claim with any confidence that those correlations provide evidence of causality. The estimated relationships may merely be the result of an omitted variable bias. It is problematic then to draw policy conclusions about the kinds of institutions countries should adopt based on the econometric evidence in this literature.

The empirical tools that drove the credibility revolution in applied micro are not suitable for making causal inferences in this context as suggested in Klick.[9] Panel data approaches are unlikely to work since institutions change very slowly over time, whereas the intuition of panel data methods relies on sharp unexpected natural experiments. When there are sharp changes in institutions, for example as the result of conquests or wars, there is significant reason to believe many other factors are changing beyond legal rules. If these factors themselves are related to growth and development, as suggested by Olson,[10] it is not possible to isolate the effects of the institutions separately from the other factors. Similarly, any instrument that is powerful enough to influence legal institutions is surely going to have its own independent effects on development. If the exclusion restriction is not met for the instrument, this instrumental variables approach fares no better than naïve regression analyses. To make matters worse, recent work by Sobel and Coyne demonstrate how many of the commonly used institutional measures are themselves highly related over time, making it unlikely that we could ever parse out very precise policy recommendations about any particular institution even if we had plausible instruments.[11]

Other modern approaches, like regression discontinuity designs and structural modelling, might hold out more hope at least as conceptual matters, but have as of yet not been used in this area. There are also reasons to be pessimistic about these methods in this context. With respect to structural modelling, we do not generally have particularly well defined theoretical models of institutional choice. Such models would be a prerequisite for structural modelling to work. Regression discontinuity designs, on the other hand, are likely to be constrained by data limitations. If a researcher starts with a dataset with a maximum sample size of one hundred or so countries, it is likely that any promising discontinuity would winnow the usable data to a handful of observations at best limiting both the statistical power of the analysis as well as confidence in its generalizability. That is, we would

7 Acemoglu, Johnson & Robinson 2001.
8 Armour *et al.* 2009.
9 Klick 2010.
10 Olson 1984.
11 Sobel & Coyne (forthcoming).

be left with little more than a qualitative case study without any claim to external validity.

This methodological pessimism makes it all the more surprising that La Porta *et al.* claim their work is robust. This chapter questions this claim given criticisms based on omitted variables stories in section 2. We then discuss the fundamental empirical problems in this setting in section 3, including the unsuccessful attempts to solve these problems in this set of articles.

2. The Robustness of Legal Origins

We assume that readers of this volume will be familiar with the claims of the legal origins literature. For the best summary of these claims, see La Porta *et al.*[12] In addition to summarizing their research in this review, La Porta *et al.* address many of the criticisms of their work, especially the claims that legal origins is really proxying for or picking up the effects of some cultural effect. Effectively, these arguments are specific forms of the omitted variables bias problem referred to above. The major criticisms suggest that certain cultural attitudes, including those springing from religious beliefs, are correlated with (or perhaps partially cause or maintain adherence to) legal institutions as well as economic development indicators. While not denying that culture matters for development, La Porta *et al.* argue that these cultural effects are less important than legal origins and controlling for them does not remove the explanatory power of legal origin indicators in regressions of various development metrics.

To make their case, La Porta *et al.*[13] provide Table 4 (p. 312) which presents regressions including various cultural indicators in their original model specifications in explaining the aggregate creditors' rights scores presented in Djankov *et al.*[14] This sensitivity analysis shows that, generally speaking, the cultural variables do not generate statistically significant coefficients, and the negative effect of French and Scandinavian legal origins remains statistically significant and economically important in determining the rights of creditors in various countries as measured in 2002.[15] From this, La Porta *et al.* conclude 'Cultural variables, then, do not make much of a dent in the explanatory power of legal origins'.[16]

This kind of sensitivity analysis is exactly the kind of critical approach suggested in Leamer where scholars were implored to present multiple specifications of their models so readers could judge the underlying robustness of the evidence, adjusting their confidence in any conclusions drawn accordingly.[17] The idea is that in the absence of a credible identification strategy, which Leamer took to mean an experimental design, scholars should test the fragility of the results from their non-

12 La Porta *et al.* 2008.

13 La Porta *et al.* 2008.

14 Djankov *et al.* 2007.

15 The original La Porta *et al.* papers (1997; 1998) examined creditors' rights and this examination was carried out on a broader sample of countries in Djankov *et al.* 2007.

16 La Porta *et al.* 2008, p. 311.

17 Leamer 1983.

ideal designs. Intuitively, in a perfectly designed randomized experiment, specification changes will not change the estimation of treatment effects. Additional (or different) control variables may affect the precision of any estimates, but since randomization ensures there will be no omitted variables bias, the estimates themselves will not change in expectation. If non-experimental results endure through various specifications, we gain confidence by extension from the experimental intuition.

However, La Porta *et al.* do not go as far as Leamer suggested.[18] While they add a cultural variable separately in each specification, Leamer (and other Bayesians) would prefer to see multiple estimates including all the various permutations of the various variables that plausibly affect the outcome variable and might be correlated with the explanatory variable of interest. From these multiple estimates, Leamer suggests that scholars present the bounds of their coefficient estimates.

In Table 1 below, we recreate part of the La Porta *et al.*[19] Table 4.[20] The coefficients presented differ slightly from those presented in their article because of some data revisions that have occurred in the meantime. We use the data conveniently provided by Andrei Shleifer on his website.[21]

The dependent variable is the aggregate creditors' rights score from Djankov which is a 0-4 scale, with a mean of 1.7, where a higher score represents more secure rights.[22] The models also include indicators for French legal origin (mean = 0.59), German legal origins (mean = 0.14), and Scandinavian legal origins (mean = 0.03). The model also controls for 2002 per capita GDP in purchasing power terms (mean = 9048). The cultural variables examined are as follows: 1) % catholic which is an indicator variable taking the value of one if the largest proportion of the country's population practices the Roman Catholic faith (mean = 0.32); 2) power distance index which is a metric indicating the extent to which the individuals in a country submit to authority with a higher score indicating a more authoritarian regime (mean = 56); 3) individualism which captures a country's focus on individual rights and attitudes (higher score) as opposed to a more communal orientation (mean = 45); 4) uncertainty avoidance index which gauges a country's comfort with uncertainty with a higher score indicating a lower comfort level (mean = 66); and 5) masculinity measures the degree to which the country reinforces the traditional role of males with higher scores implying more differentiation in sex roles (mean = 51). Metrics 2 through 5 were developed by Geert Hofstede.[23]

18 La Porta *et al.* 2008.

19 La Porta *et al.* 2008.

20 We omit some of the cultural variables examined but our main point about fragility applies when those variables are examined as well.

21 Available at <http://www.economics.harvard.edu/faculty/shleifer/files/JEL_%20web.xls>. For this analysis, we use the data listed as Table 4, but the income measure included in that worksheet of the spreadsheet is not the one used in the article's Table 4 (the article uses 2002 income but the worksheet includes 1995 income). For the income variable, we use the 2002 income presented in the Table 6 worksheet.

22 Djankov 2007.

23 Data available at <http://www.geert-hofstede.com/hofstede_dimensions.php>.

Table 1: *Replication of La Porta et al. Table 4*[24]

	(1)	(2)	(3)	(4)	(5)
	Dependent Variable: Creditors' Rights in 2002				
% catholic	-0.25 (0.22)				
Power Distance Index		-0.00 (0.01)			
Individualism			-0.01 (0.01)		
Uncertainty Avoidance Index				-0.01 (0.01)	
Masculinity					-0.02* (0.01)
French Legal Origin	-0.76*** (0.24)	-0.84** (0.35)	-0.92** (0.34)	-0.48 (0.40)	-1.02*** (0.37)
German Legal Origin	-0.25 (0.27)	-0.52 (0.45)	-0.56 (0.43)	-0.25 (0.45)	-0.28 (0.43)
Scandinavian Legal Origin	-1.10** (0.48)	-0.87 (0.58)	-0.87 (0.58)	-0.92 (0.55)	-1.69** (0.70)
Log(GDP per capita in 2002)	0.28*** (0.08)	0.19 (0.24)	0.32 (0.21)	0.22 (0.19)	0.20 (0.20)
Constant	0.00 (0.73)	0.65 (2.50)	0.27 (1.80)	0.74 (1.65)	1.70 (1.88)
Observations	136	52	52	52	52
R-squared	20%	14%	15%	16%	19%

Note: Data come from
<http://www.economics.harvard.edu/faculty/shleifer/files/JEL_%20web.xls>.
Heteroskedasticity robust standard errors presented in parentheses.
*** $p < 0.01$ (two sided test of zero null hypothesis)
** $p < 0.05$ (two sided test of zero null hypothesis)
* $p < 0.10$ (two sided test of zero null hypothesis)

In Table 2, however, we show what happens when more than one cultural control is used in any given specification.

24 La Porta *et al.* 2008.

Table 2: *Robustness of La Porta et al. Table 4*[25]

Dependent Variable: Creditors' Rights in 2002	
Catholic	-0.79** (0.36)
Power Distance Index	-0.00 (0.01)
Individualism	-0.00 (0.01)
Uncertainty Avoidance Index	-0.01* (0.01)
Masculinity	-0.02 (0.01)
French Legal Origin	-0.00 (0.39)
German Legal Origin	0.19 (0.39)
Scandinavian Legal Origin	-1.86*** (0.68)
Log(GDP per capita in 2002)	0.33 (0.22)
Constant	1.10 (2.44)
Observations	52
R-squared	29%
Note: Data come from http://www.economics.harvard.edu/faculty/shleifer/files/JEL_%20web.xls. Heteroskedasticity robust standard errors presented in parentheses. *** $p < 0.01$ (two sided test of zero null hypothesis) ** $p < 0.05$ (two sided test of zero null hypothesis) * $p < 0.10$ (two sided test of zero null hypothesis)	

We see that, in this specification, the Catholic indicator, which equals one if the largest proportion of the population practices Catholicism, is statistically significant and quite large in magnitude. In fact, it is of a larger magnitude than the effect of having a French legal origin. The French legal origin indicator is no longer statistically significant and, in fact, is a pretty precisely estimated zero effect. The effect of German legal origin, while still statistically insignificant, now has a point estimate of the opposite sign from the one this variable had in the La Porta *et al.* regressions. The Scandinavian legal origins indicator now carries a negative coefficient with a point estimate that is much larger in magnitude than that estimated by La Porta *et al.*, and it is still statistically significant.

These results belie La Porta *et al.*'s claims of robustness. Note that we are not simply saying that the legal origin variables lose their significance due to multicollinearity or a loss of degrees of freedom. The point estimates themselves change substantially and, in some cases, actually experience sign reversals. Also, as suggested by the Catholic variable above, in some specifications, the cultural variables

25 La Porta *et al.* 2008.

can be statistically significant and suggest practically large effects, though we are quick to point out that the cultural variables do not generate robust effects either.

One response could be that it was appropriate for La Porta *et al.* to leave out the other cultural variables when they test a new one, given that they found those variables to be statistically insignificant. Such an approach would be incorrect.[26] While one might be forced into a trade-off between a better specified model and a more parsimonious one when sample sizes are small, a lack of precision does not seem to be a large problem here. Further, even when one makes such a trade-off, it is important to keep misspecification problems in mind when conclusions are drawn. Also, La Porta *et al.* retained the German legal indicator variable and the income variable in their models despite their general lack of statistical significance, perhaps suggesting a lack of concern regarding degree of freedom or precision problems.

Table 3 provides the results of a more systematic robustness analysis. For the analysis, we ran all permutations of the regression of creditors' rights in 2002 on four core variables that were included in every regression, namely French, German, and Scandinavian legal origins indicators and log GDP per capita in 2002, and all possible combinations of the cultural variables included in La Porta *et al.* Table 4.[27] These cultural variables include the ones investigated above – Catholic, Power Distance Index, Individualism, Uncertainty Avoidance Index, and Masculinity – as well as the six other metrics investigated by La Porta *et al.* in Table 4.[28] These other metrics come from the World Value Survey and represent the fraction of the country's respondents agreeing with the following statements: 1) child obedience is important (mean = 0.37); 2) child independence is important (mean = 0.51); 3) parents must do their best for children (mean = 0.75); 4) parents must be respected regardless of the situation (mean = 0.77); 5) family life is very important (mean = 0.89); and 6) strangers can generally be trusted (mean = 0.28).

The Table provides the following information: 1) the estimated value of the coefficient in a regression that includes none of the cultural control variables (baseline); 2) the mean value of the estimated coefficient (mean); 3) the maximum value of the estimated coefficient (max); 4) the minimum value of the estimated coefficient (min); 5) the average standard error (SE).

26 See, for example, Cameron & Trivedi 2005, p. 286.

27 La Porta *et al.* 2008.

28 La Porta *et al.* 2008.

Table 3: *Bounds of Legal Origins Effects*

	Baseline	Mean	Max	Min	SE
French Legal Origin	-0.85***	-0.05	1.12	-1.04	0.59
German Legal Origin	-0.30	0.07	1.14	-0.82	0.70
Scandinavian Legal Origin	-1.03**	-1.63	-0.56	-2.57	0.82
Log(GDP per capita in 2002)	0.25***	-0.04	0.41	-0.36	0.31
Catholic		-0.86	-0.25	-1.25	0.49
Power Distance Index		-0.02	0.00	-0.03	0.01
Individualism		0.00	0.01	-0.01	0.01
Uncertainty Avoidance Index		-0.01	0.00	-0.02	0.01
Masculinity		-0.02	-0.02	-0.03	0.01
% agree child obedience is important		0.20	1.68	-1.80	1.85
% agree child independence is important		1.93	2.70	1.10	1.16
% agree parents must do their best for children		0.10	2.78	-2.74	2.76
% agree that parents must be respected regardless		-0.93	0.43	-2.17	1.34
% agree family life is very important		1.90	3.47	0.27	2.77
% agree strangers can generally be trusted		0.12	1.97	-1.29	1.47

This sensitivity analysis solidifies the claim that the effect of French legal origin on creditors' rights is not robust. The average effect in a given specification is very close to zero (-0.05) and swings from a maximum of 1.12 to a minimum of -1.04. The German legal origin effect is equally fragile. Only the Scandinavian legal origin effect exhibits any stability with all coefficients bearing a negative sign. By way of comparison, the Catholic cultural indicator, along with a number of the other cultural metrics, always generates a negative sign and exhibits a lower degree of volatility. This is surprising given La Porta *et al.*'s claim that the legal origin effects are robust and maintain their importance when including cultural controls.[29]

29 La Porta *et al.* 2008.

Examining the bounds of effects may be misleading, however, since it could mask a general importance behind some extreme outlier results. Table 4 provides statistics regarding how frequently a coefficient was statistically significant (at the 5 per cent level), and how frequently it took a given sign in the robustness regressions, as well as the average t statistic the coefficient generated.

Table 4: *Distribution of Legal Origins Effects*

	%(Significant)	**%(Positive)**	**%(Negative)**	**Average T**	**Number of Specifications**
French Legal Origin	0.05	0.45	0.55	0.75	2048
German Legal Origin	0	0.50	0.50	0.50	2048
Scandinavian Legal Origin	0.51	0	1	1.96	2048
Log(GDP per capita in 2002)	0.00	0.40	0.60	0.45	2048
Catholic	0.24	0	1	1.771	1024
Power Distance Index	0.21	0.00	1.00	1.67	1024
Individualism	0	0.63	0.37	0.29	1024
Uncertainty Avoidance Index	0	0.00	1.00	0.91	1024
Masculinity	0.05	0	1	1.69	1024
% agree child obedience is important	0	0.61	0.39	0.33	1024
% agree child independence is important	0.23	1	0	1.69	1024
% agree parents must do their best for children	0	0.50	0.50	0.50	1024
% agree that parents must be respected regardless	0.00	0.05	0.95	0.74	1024
% agree family life is very important	0	1	0	0.68	1024
% agree strangers can generally be trusted	0	0.55	0.45	0.36	1024

This table makes it abundantly clear that the effects of the French and German legal origins indicators are not at all robust to the inclusion of La Porta *et al.*'s chosen cultural indicators.[30] The French indicator is statistically significant only 5 per cent of the time, and the German effect is never statistically significant. Furthermore, each is effectively as likely to generate a positive coefficient as the negative coefficient the authors make so much of in their empirical argument. The Scandinavian legal origin effect is robustly negative, always taking a negative sign, and meeting the threshold for statistical significance in half of the specifications. Note that this does not necessarily imply that the true effect of Scandinavian legal origins is negative given the potential for omitted variables bias. It does provide some confidence that there is a systematic effect of Scandinavian, if there is no such bias. A similar claim cannot be made for the French and German indicators.

Contrary to La Porta *et al.*'s claims, some of the cultural variables do appear to have a systematic and potentially important effect (though, of course, the observed effect could suffer from omitted variables bias).[31] For example, the effect of the Catholic indicator is always negative, and it is statistically significant one fourth of the time. The estimated power index effect is almost always negative, and it is statistically significant almost as often. The effect of the variable measuring the fraction of the population agreeing that child independence is important is uniformly positive, and it is a statistically significant predictor in about a quarter of the specifications. The one cultural variable that La Porta *et al.* suggest could be important, masculinity, is statistically significant just 5 per cent of the time, but it does always generate a negative coefficient.[32]

Our purpose in this analysis is not to suggest that the 'right' specification includes these cultural variables or that we can be confident of any particular source of bias. We merely point out that this particular set of estimates, used by La Porta *et al.* to demonstrate robustness falls far short of this aim.[33] Presumably, we could go through the other tables in that article which purport to show that the legal origins results endure when other hypothesized relationships are controlled for, and we could show fragility there too. We refrain from doing so, leaving the results above as an illustration of what we believe is a general phenomenon.

However, even if the results had been shown to be robust, we would still be sceptical of claims of causality. Robustness is a necessary condition for drawing strong causal inferences, but it is not sufficient. Results that are robust to the inclusion of a given set of covariates can still suffer from other sources of bias. Because the La Porta *et al.* results (really all of the results in this literature) lack a reliable research design, there is no confidence in their identification strategy and, therefore, no confidence in the causal inferences drawn.

3. What is the Problem

The fundamental problem in modern empirical economics is one of statistical identification. That is, how can one isolate the causal effect of x on y. If one knew

30 La Porta *et al.* 2008.

31 La Porta *et al.* 2008.

32 La Porta *et al.* 2008.

33 La Porta *et al.* 2008.

everything that affected y, and had data for all of those variables, this would be a trivial problem to solve. In that context, a regression that included all of those variables would yield causal estimates that would be unbiased. Unfortunately, economic theory is not nearly so well developed that any researcher could possibly know all of the important variables affecting the outcome of interest if that outcome is even moderately complex.

Further, even if theory or intuition did provide a well-developed guide, many of the important variables would be difficult to quantify or, at least, to get data that captured them. While proxies sometimes exist, they are never perfect.

If some important variables are left out of the empirical analysis, either due to a failure of theory or a failure of data collection, if any of those omitted variables are correlated with the included variables, the estimates for the included variables will be biased. That is, even in very large datasets, the estimated coefficients will not converge to the true parameter value. The estimates will be systematically too large or too small. While it goes by many names, endogeneity, reverse causality, sample selection, simultaneity, etc., this omitted variable bias problem is ubiquitous.

Intuitively, if an omitted variable is correlated with the outcome variable and a given regressor, the coefficient estimated for the regressor will represent both the true effect of that variable and some portion of the effect of the omitted variable.

While the omitted variable bias problem is wide spread, in some contexts it can be mitigated or eliminated. The credibility revolution referred to above came about due to research designs that were successful in addressing this source of bias. The basic idea behind most of the modern approaches to statistical identification is to mimic an experiment. In an experimental setting, explanatory variables (generally a 'treatment') are randomized across observations or subjects. Because of randomization, any uncontrolled for determinant of the outcome will necessarily be uncorrelated with the analyzed determinants (specifically, administration of the treatment).

Experiments are generally not possible in social science and many policy situations. Random assignment of things like education or health care or political rights is viewed as immoral. Even if this morality constraint is satisfied, it is difficult to ensure random assignment if the subjects have other avenues to receiving the treatment or if the randomization can be undermined. Lastly, cost concerns may limit the ability of researchers to engage in broad social experiments.

To remedy this, modern empirical micro researchers focus on natural experiments or quasi-randomizations wherein some quirk of nature or policy leads some individuals (or jurisdictions) to be affected by a policy while other, presumably comparable, individuals (or jurisdictions) are not. The outcomes for the affected group are examined before and after the quasi-randomization and this difference in outcomes is compared to the simultaneous difference in outcomes in the non-affected group over the same period. The so-called difference-in-difference measure represents the treatment effect of the policy intervention. A similar intuition supports the use of instrumental variables techniques wherein a particular instrument affects the regressor of interest but it does not directly affect the outcome studied. In a two stage process, wherein only the exogenous part of the variation in the regressor is used to explain the outcome (and the exogenous portion is separated from the endogenous portion by modelling the regressor using the instrument) and yield a causal estimate of the effect of x on y.

The use of these natural experiment or instrumental variable techniques is not possible in institutional settings like that found in the legal origins literature. First, because institutions only change slowly over time, and foundational factors like the source of origin of the system do not generally change at all, there is no experiment to examine. In some rare instances where a shock to the institutions might occur, such as happens after a war, it is very likely that the war itself has direct implications for most development indicators. In that case, it will be impossible to parse the effects of the war from the effects of the institutions. Any variable that has the power to change institutions almost certainly will have independent effects on lots of things having to do with the given society. By definition then, the instruments or experiment are not valid and there can be no confidence in any results coming from such designs.

Two other modern approaches offer some hope. Regression discontinuity designs focus on observations just above and below some decision threshold that determines treatment status. The intuition is that if the threshold was arbitrarily chosen (with some general range), subjects just above and just below that threshold are likely to be very comparable with the only difference being that the one group received treatment while the other did not. In the context of legal origins, such a design would require focusing attention on, for example, pairs of colonies where a given country planned to colonize both but for budget reasons chose only one and the choice of which one was decided essentially by a coin flip. Comparing the development of these two places would provide a very nice design for inferring the causal effects of legal origins. The limitation, of course, is that it is unlikely that we have enough information to say with confidence whether any given pair of colonies fits this bill. While historical records may provide clues about which colonies were being considered, it is unlikely that we can confirm that the choice among the set was truly random. If it was not random, the choice was likely influenced by unobservable variables which could have long lasting effects on development. Any estimate of a coefficient would contain part of these effects, depriving us of a causal inference.

Even if we could gain confidence about such pairs, they are likely to be very limited in numbers. This limitation would preclude us from having confidence that our estimated results would be generalizable. Over a large enough sample, idiosyncrasies will wash out, but there is no guarantee of that happening when sample sizes are limited.

One last tool of modern micro-econometrics is structural modelling which attempts to use theory to adjust parameter estimates for any source of bias due to missing data. For example, if we are concerned that self-selection problems bias the estimated treatment effect of a job training program, a structural approach would use microeconomics to model the training enrolment decision and use that information in the estimation process to account for the unobserved heterogeneity that leads to the bias. In the legal origins context, one would need models of legal and institutional development to address the omitted variables problem. While such models exist, they tend to be underspecified, suggesting that much more theory work needs to be done before this becomes a viable approach.

It seems then that the credibility revolution has passed the legal origins literature by primarily because the tools developed in modern empirical micro are not well suited for this application. Unfortunately, there does not appear to be a feasible alternative approach that provides any empirical confidence.

4. Conclusion

Despite its tremendous influence in both academic and policy circles, the empirical estimates from the legal origins literature are simply not credible. The cross sectional research designs used surely suffer from omitted variables biases. As an illustration of this, we showed how La Porta *et al.*'s results, which supposedly showed robustness, are extremely fragile.[34] This is a symptom of a poorly identified relationship. While the legal origins literature raises important, perhaps among the most important, questions, these questions are not amenable to serious empirical examination.

34 La Porta *et al.* 2008.

Bibliography

Acemoglu, Johnson & Robinson 2001
Acemoglu, D., Johnson, S. & Robinson, J., 'The Colonial Origins of Comparative Development: An Empirical Investigation', *American Economic Review*, 2001, p. 1369-1401.

Angrist & Pischke 2010
Angrist, J. &. Pischke, J., 'The Credibility Revolution in Empirical Economics: How Better Research Design is Taking the Con Out of Econometrics', *Journal of Economic Perspectives*, 2010, p. 3-30.

Armour *et al.* 2009
Armour, J., Deakin, S., Mollica, V. & Siems, M., 'Law and Financial Development: What We are Learning from Time-Series Evidence', *Brigham Young University Law Review*, 2009, p. 1435-1500.

Cameron & Trivedi 2005
Cameron, A. & Trivedi, P., *Micro-econometrics Methods and Applications*, Cambridge: University Press, 2005.

Djankov, McLiesh & Shleifer 2007
Djankov, S., McLiesh, C. & Shleifer, A., 'Private Credit in 129 Countries', *Journal of Financial Economics*, 2007, p. 299-329.

Klick 2010
Klick, J., 'The Perils of Empirical Work on Institutions', *Journal of Institutional and Theoretical Economics*, 2010, p. 166-170.

Leamer 1983
Leamer, E., 'Let's take the Con Out of Econometrics', *American Economic Review*, 1983, p. 31-43.

La Porta, Lopez-de-Silanes & Shleifer 2008
La Porta, R., Lopez-de-Silanes, F. & Shleifer, A., 'The Economic Consequences of Legal Origins', *Journal of Economic Literature*, 2008, p. 285-332.

La Porta *et al.* 1997
La Porta, R., Lopez-de-Silanes, F., Shleifer, A. & Vishny, R., 'Legal Determinants of External Finance', *Journal of Finance*, 1997, p. 1131-1150.

La Porta *et al.* 1998
La Porta, R., Lopez-de-Silanes, F., Shleifer, A. & Vishny, R., 'Law and Finance', *Journal of Political Economy*, 1998, p. 1113-1155.

Olson 1984
Olson, M., *The Rise and Decline of Nations: Economic Growth, Stagflation, and Social Rigidities*, London: Yale University Press, 1984.

Sobel & Coyne
Sobel, R. & Coyne, C., 'Cointegrating Institutions: The Time-Series Properties of Country Institutional Measures', *Journal of Law and Economics*, forthcoming.

Mathias M. Siems

MEASURING THE IMMEASURABLE: HOW TO TURN LAW INTO NUMBERS

1. Introduction

According to Lord Kelvin (1883), '(W)hen you can measure what you are speaking about and express it in numbers, you know something about it; but when you cannot measure it, when you cannot express it in numbers, your knowledge is of the meagre and unsatisfactory kind (...).'[1] Lord Kelvin was a natural scientist but today many social scientists would agree that quantitative approaches are central to scientific progress. For instance, in economics John Maynard Keynes was still sceptical about econometrics, asking whether 'this brand of statistical alchemy is ripe to become a branch of science', and adding that he was 'not yet persuaded',[2] whereas today econometrics is accepted in modern economics and forms part of the core undergraduate curriculum. Economists, as well as other social scientists, have also tried to measure legal rules and institutions. Their approach is often a 'just do it' one, implicitly assuming that the complexity of the law does not prevent it from being turned into numbers. Many legal academics, by contrast, have the attitude of 'just don't do it', for instance, bluntly saying that 'law is about things that are not quantifiable'.[3] However, in legal research there have also been some changes, first with socio-legal and then with empirical legal studies.[4] Moreover, as will be shown, not only academics but also policy makers have a strong interest in measuring the quality of legal rules and institutions.

The purpose of this paper is to explain and discuss the different ways how law has been turned into numbers. More briefly it will also be addressed how, in a second step, these numbers can be used to show causal relationships. This second step can be very contentious and complicated; yet, the core interest of this paper is on the preliminary question on how quantitative data on law can be found or constructed. This paper does not attempt a comprehensive review of the literature

1 Quoted in Mager Stellman 1998, p. 197. See also Merton, Sills & Stigler 1984.
2 Keynes 1940, p. 156.
3 Larenz & Canaris 1995, p. 19 (own translation).
4 See, e.g., Lawless, Robbennolt & Ulen 2009.

on quantitative research in law but it will provide representative examples, mainly focussing on comparative legal studies.

Part 2 starts with the presumably easiest path, namely a simple counting of, say, lawyers, cases or laws. Part 3 explains that some studies have measured whether legal rules comply with a particular benchmark. More neutral is a functional approach, showing quantitatively how well legal rules protect certain interest. This is dealt with in Part 4. Moreover, there is not only the positive law: Part 5 discusses studies that try to quantify the practice of private relationships, and Part 6 the ones that try to measure the efficiency of political and legal institutions. Part 7 explains that other studies are based on surveys which show the perceptions of firm managers or the common public about the quality of law or its enforcement. Part 8 concludes.

2. Counting Lawyers, Cases, laws, Words etc.

Socio-legal research has frequently gathered empirical data on the number of lawyers or court decisions in particular jurisdictions. Examples would be legion. In the 1970s John Henry Merryman and colleagues collected time-series data on litigation rates and types of claims in a number of Mediterranean and Latin American jurisdictions.[5] In the 1980s and early 1990s Erhard Blankenburg and colleagues conducted research on the civil litigation rates and the number of judges and lawyers in the Netherlands and Germany (as well as some other countries).[6] A few years later Richard Posner compared the number of lawyers and judges between England and the US.[7] And in the last ten years Rogelio Perez-Perdomo and Lawrence Friedman have provided updated information on Latin America, for instance, the number of law students, lawyers and judges,[8] David Clark has compiled various tables with data on the number of lawyers, judges and legal disputes for a chapter in the *International Encyclopaedia of Comparative Law*,[9] and a project of the University of Oxford has collected data on the costs and funding of civil litigation in various jurisdictions.[10]

There have also been some attempts to count actual legal texts. In a study with the title 'Quantitative Analyses of Law – A Comparative Empirical Study: Sources of Law in Eastern Western Europe' Heinz Schäffer and Attila Racz used questionnaires to estimate the total amount of generally binding normative acts in terms of pages.[11] A related approach was employed by Tom Ginsburg and Robert Cooter who examined whether in Europe the statute length of laws implementing EU Directives varies systematically across countries.[12] Moreover, research can go fur-

5 Merryman, Clark & Friedman 1979. See also Merryman 2000.
6 For a summary see Blankenburg 1997.
7 Posner 1996, p. 28.
8 Perez-Perdomo & Friedman 2003.
9 Clark 2002.
10 Hodges, Vogenauer & Tulibacka 2010.
11 Schäffer & Racz 1990.
12 Cooter & Ginsburg 2003.

ther and count the actual words of legal texts. For instance, it is possible to count the most popular words used in the civil codes of different countries.[13] More frequent are, however, quantitative analyses of court decisions, such as citation statistics[14] or more general forms of content analysis.[15]

All of these 'countings' seem relatively easy and objective in comparison to the measurement and coding approaches outlined in the following parts. However, this is not always the case. For instance, in order to compare the English and US data, Richard Posner contentiously assumed that English barristers are not like attorneys but more like junior judges in the US system.[16] Naturally, such questions become even more challenging if one compares jurisdictions from different legal traditions, such as the number of lawyers in Japan and the United States.[17]

Typically, the numbers of cases, lawyers, citations etc are also only the starting point for further analysis. For instance, Erhard Blankenburg argued that the lower number of lawyers in the Netherlands in comparison to Germany is a result of differences in the supply side, namely the more pronounced infrastructure of filters and alternatives to courts in the Netherlands.[18] However, it is difficult to prove whether there is really a causal relationship. For instance, David Nelken criticized Blankenburg in simply assuming that the demand for litigation is the same in two countries and that structural factors are more important then cultural ones.[19]

Overall, therefore, these simple 'countings' are not as harmless as they seem. Moreover, as such, these numbers do not provide information on the substance of legal rules or the quality of law and law enforcement (however defined), which leads us to the following five approaches.

3. Benchmarking of Legal Rules

Two of William Carney's articles provide good examples of explicit benchmarking of legal rules. In the first one he was interested in the differences between EU and US company law.[20] For this purpose, he undertook a taxonomy of the EU company law directives, divided them into 131 provisions, and searched in the laws of the US states for similar provisions. He found that 95 provisions were in effect in no US state, 14 were in effect in all 50 states, and the remaining 22 provisions were adopted by a random number of states. Since the provisions which were in effect in no US state mainly consisted of protections for creditors and employees, Carney concluded that European law-making was more strongly influenced by interest groups than the US one. In a second article Carney analysed the impact of the

13 See <http://siemslegal.blogspot.com/2009/08/most-common-terms-in-civil-codes.html>.
14 For an example see Gelter & Siems 2010.
15 See Hall & Wright 2008.
16 Posner 1996, p. 22.
17 See Katu 1987.
18 See *supra* note 6.
19 Nelken 1997, p. 78 & 82.
20 Carney 1997.

Model Business Corporation Act on US state law.[21] The general result was that the Model Business Corporation Act is leading to convergence, because 74.4 per cent of its 142 provisions had been taken over by all US states. Since not all provisions are equally important, he also isolated important provisions and found that the Model Business Corporation Act was also leading to convergence with regard to these provisions.[22]

The influential research by a group of financial economists (often cited as La Porta *et al.*, Djankov *et al.*, LLSV, LLS, or DLLS) should be regarded as a form of implicit benchmarking. The first major study of this group was an article by Rafael La Porta, Florencio Lopez-de-Silanes, Andrei Shleifer and Robert Vishny entitled *Law and Finance*.[23] In this article La Porta *et al.* coded the law on shareholder and creditor protection of 49 countries. For instance, with respect to shareholder protection they used eight variables, allocating a country either a '0' or a '1' for each variable. They then drew on these numbers as independent variables for statistical regressions, finding that good shareholder protection leads to more dispersed shareholder ownership, which can be seen as a proxy for developed capital markets. Many subsequent papers by La Porta and colleagues have used a similar methodology for other areas of law. For instance, there are now also datasets on the laws governing civil procedure, securities regulation and labour law.[24]

In these articles the coding of the law has the aim to measure the quality of legal rules. However, this is not based on a comparative analysis of legal tools available in different legal traditions. Rather, La Porta and colleagues usually follow the US model,[25] thus, implicitly benchmarking how similar legal systems are to the US one, and whether this makes a difference in terms of financial development. In this respect this line of research is similar to studies that focus on the effect of a particular legal event. For instance, event studies have investigated whether new laws on company and securities law have had a significant effect on the share price.[26] There are also studies which have examined whether across US states changes in the death penalty and in abortion laws have had a statistically significant effect on the crime rate.[27]

Benchmarking is also used by institutions that want to find out whether they have successfully managed to influence national law makers. In the EU the Commission has a natural interest to monitor how directives have been implemented[28] and whether recommendations have been taken up by national legislators.[29] Benchmarking is also crucial for the work of development agencies. For example, the programme on Commercial Law and Legal Institutions Reform (CLIR) of the United

21 Carney 1998.
22 Carney 1998, p. 731.
23 La Porta *et al.* 1998.
24 Djankov *et al.* 2003; La Porta, Lopez-de-Silanes & Shleifer 2006; Botero *et al.* 2004.
25 See Lele & Siems 2007.
26 See the studies reported in Bhagat & Romano 2007.
27 See, e.g., Donohue & Wolfers 2006; Donohue & Levitt 2001.
28 See, e.g., Commission Staff Working Document 2007.
29 See, e.g., Commission Staff Working Document 2008. Benchmarking is also part of the Open Method of Co-ordination (OMC). See, e.g., Hodson & Maher 2001.

States Agency for International Development (USAID) has examined to what extent developing and transition economies have implemented recommendations, such as the OECD principles of corporate governance.[30] Most importantly, the World Bank has used the La Porta *et al.* studies as a starting point for the World Bank's Doing Business Reports. In these annual reports the World Bank employs various indicators[31] with the aim to measure the quality of legal systems but being clearly based on an Anglo-Saxon model of the legal world.[32]

A technical problem of these studies is whether legal rules really fulfil the requirements of the benchmark. Legal rules are often complex and open to misunderstandings. This was a major problem of the first La Porta *et al.* study since subsequent studies have shown that their coding of foreign laws has been flawed, making their results doubtful.[33]

Further, a discussion of these studies needs to distinguish between explicit and implicit benchmarking. Both forms of benchmarking measure how similar rules are to a particular legal model but only the former studies are transparent about it. In general, this is to be appreciated but it can also have a negative side-effect. Given the benchmark, law makers may feel induced to focus on these criteria only, for instance, in order to get into the list of top-ten performers of the World Bank's Doing Business Report. Such a strategy would, however, be unfortunate since these measures can only capture a small proportion of the legal system.

The studies of implicit benchmarking are open to the challenge that they mislead the reader: they claim to measure the quality of legal rules in an objective way but in reality they only show how much countries deviate from a particular legal model, such as the US one. A possible rejoinder may be that despite the US bias most of the La Porta studies have managed to identify a statistically significant effect of law for financial development. Thus, only the interpretation of their results may change: countries do not benefit from any improvements of their legal system but only such changes which follow the US model. But, again, this is not entirely satisfactory. Legal rules operate differently in different institutional environments. Thus, the fact that legal transplants from US law may have had a positive effect in some countries leaves it open that they may work completely differently in other parts of the world. It is therefore preferable to openly acknowledge the reality of different legal models and to measure legal rules from a functional perspective.

4. Measuring Legal Rules from a Functional Perspective

According to the established methodology of comparative law the initial research question should not just refer to the law of one legal system, but should be posed in

30 See <http://www.bizclir.com/cs/topics/commercial_legal_framework/overview.> See also Taylor 2007.

31 See <http://www.doingbusiness.org/>. The categories are Starting a Business, Dealing with Licenses, Employing Workers, Registering Property, Getting Credit, Protecting Investors, Paying Taxes, Trading Across Borders, Enforcing Contracts, Closing a Business.

32 Fauvarque-Cosson & Kerhuel 2009.

33 Spamann 2010.

functional terms.[34] For instance, following the approach of the Common Core project,[35] a comparative legal researcher may start with a hypothetical problem in order to examine how this problem would be solved in different legal systems. Alternatively, a comparatist can start with a question such as 'how do legal systems protect shareholders?' and then examine the different tools of different legal systems.

Both of these approaches can be used to measure legal rules in a quantitative way. The first one can be found in an article by Simeon Djankov *et al.* on the law and economics of self-dealing.[36] Djankov *et al.* presented a complex hypothetical case of a transaction between two companies to lawyers from 72 countries, and asked them to respond to questions, such as, which body of the companies has to approve the transaction in question or how the transaction's validity could be challenged. Then, Djankov *et al.* coded this information using various indices and sub-indices. Finally, they found that this new dataset predicts stock market development, and generally works better than the initial La Porta *et al.* index.[37]

The second functional approach was used in a project on Law, Finance and Development at the Centre for Business Research (CBR) of the University of Cambridge.[38] The overall aim of the CBR project was to review the mechanisms by which legal institutions influence financial systems and thereby affect economic development. For this purpose the CBR researchers constructed time-series indices on shareholder, creditor and worker protection in 25 countries. Importantly, the selection of the variables considered that the same functional role may be performed in different jurisdictions by rules with different formal classifications. The main aim was therefore that the indices should get as close as possible to representing a coherent and meaningful characterization of the law in any given jurisdiction. Subsequently, the CBR researchers examined the claim that the quality of the law is reflected in a country's financial development. This could, however, only be confirmed in some cases.[39] As a possible explanation it was offered that legal rules are, to a significant degree, endogenous to the economic and political economy context of the systems in which they operate, and therefore the causal models on which statistical regressions are based may be unsuitable.[40]

Is one of these two techniques preferable? The first approach seems more straight-forward but there are at least two problems. First, evidence on the state of law as seen by practising lawyers is not available on an historical basis. Thus, the case-based approach cannot collect time-series data, making claims about causal relationships between law and finance doubtful. Second, this approach has to assume that the same type of problem exists in all of the legal systems examined. This is far from obvious since social and economic structures differ widely between

34 See Zweigert & Kötz 1998, p. 38 & 43.
35 See <http://www.common-core.org/>.
36 Djankov *et al.* 2008.
37 *Supra* note 23.
38 See <http://www.cbr.cam.ac.uk/research/programme2/project2-20.htm>.
39 Summary in Siems & Deakin 2010.
40 Deakin 2009.

countries. Thus, instead of relying on just one case, a comprehensive index is better able to capture how different legal tools may reflect different types of problems.

However, the second approach too has its shortcomings which it shares with many other quantitative studies. The index construction and the coding of variables may have the aim to be as objective as possible, but since the legal world is very complex it inevitably involves some subjective element. Once the data are collected, the most common procedure is to aggregate the numbers of all variables. This, however, raises the question of whether all variables are really equally important. Going further, the same variable may play a completely different functional role in different countries, or different variables may play the same role, with their relative importance varying from one context to another.[41] Finally, treating functionality seriously, it is not sufficient just to look at the positive legal rules but one also has to consider private contracting and differences in law enforcement, as will be discussed in the following parts.

5. Quantifying the Practice of Private Legal Relationships

Interviews or questionnaires are a common tool in socio-legal research. They can also be used to identify, and if appropriate to quantify, how contractual parties respond to the positive law. The path-breaking study on the relevance of contract law was Stewart Macaulay's interview-based research of 68 businessmen and lawyers.[42] His general finding was that many exchanges reflect only a minimal amount of planning, especially concerning legal sanctions and the effect of defective performances. In his article Macaulay provides some quantitative data on these interviews but his main approach is qualitative. Many subsequent projects have more strongly relied on quantitative evidence. An interesting comparative article is the one by Alessandro Arrighetti *et al.* on contractual drafting in the UK, Germany and Italy.[43] Based on 60 interviews they found considerable diversity in the form, duration and substance of contracts. For instance, Arrighetti *et al.* report how often parties use written contracts and how often certain clauses, such as retention of title, are included. Finally, they relate these practical differences to the positive contract law of the three countries.

Research in corporate governance often uses documents, for instance, the articles of associations or annual reports of companies, in order to quantify topics such as investor protection across firms. There are also some professional providers, such as Standard & Poor's, Governance Metrics International and Riskmetrics, that make such information available.[44] In academic research, most important is the study by Paul Gompers *et al.* which uses 24 governance rules to construct a governance index for the level of shareholder rights at about 1500 large US firms. They

41 Ahlering & Deakin 2007, p. 884.

42 Macaulay 1963.

43 Arrighetti, Bachmann & Deakin 1997. See also Burchell & Wilkinson 1997; Deakin & Michie 1997; Deakin 2006.

44 See <http://www.governance.standardandpoors.com/>; <http://www.gmiratings.com>; <http://www.riskmetrics.com/>.

found that firms with stronger shareholder rights had higher firm value, higher profits, higher sales growth, lower capital expenditures, and made fewer corporate acquisitions.[45] Subsequently, a study by Lucian Bebchuk *et al.* examined which of these 24 rules are likely to drive the results.[46] There has also been some empirical research on firm-level corporate governance in Europe. For instance, Iain MacNeil and Li Xiao have studied how UK firms have implemented the non-binding Combined Code on Governance,[47] and Axel von Werder *et al.* have done the same for the German counterpart.[48]

These studies are very interesting but it is clear that such research can only present a partial picture of the way how contractual parties or companies work. The research on corporate governance is closely related to other questions of how firms are structured, managed and financed. Thus, it is difficult to establish of whether there is really an identifiable causal relationship between the corporate governance indices and other firm characteristics.[49] The studies on contractual practices can show that contract law in practice may be quite different from the law in the books. However, as such, they can only provide some clues on why this may be the case. From a comparative perspective it likely matters that the quality of political and legal institutions differs widely across the world. Attempts to measure such variations are discussed in the next two parts.

6. Measuring the Quality of Political and Legal Institutions

As with the benchmarking of legal rules (see 3, above), many policy markers, groups and academics try to measure the quality of political and legal institutions. Often this has the explicit or implicit purpose to improve these institutions, which is why Davis *et al.* develop the concept of indicators as a technology of global governance.[50] It is also revealing to quote the World Bank:

> 'Measuring the performance of the various elements of the justice sector is crucial for any justice reform. Empirical research and court statistics are key in this context. Benchmarks and comparative data are invaluable tools for justice reform practitioners working on evaluations.'[51]

The Freedom House and the Political Risk Services are two private entities that provide general quantitative information on political and legal institutions. The former produces the Freedom in the World, which rates from 1 to 7 the political rights and civil liberties of countries.[52] The latter produces a Political Risk Index, including a

45 Gompers, Ishii & Metrick 2003.
46 Bebchuk, Cohen & Ferell 2009.
47 MacNeil & Xiao 2006.
48 Von Werder, Talaulicar & Kolat 2005.
49 See Bhagat, Bolton & Romano 2008.
50 Davis, Kingsbury & Merry 2010.
51 See <http://go.worldbank.org/LRFA0Q06E1> and the World-Bank funded research by Dakolias 1999.
52 See <http://www.freedomhouse.org/template.cfm?page=351&ana_page=364&year=2010>.

variable which rates countries from 0 to 6 on law and order. One of the law and order sub-variables examines the independence of the judiciary, for instance, based on questions such 'are judges appointed and dismissed in a fair and unbiased manner?' and 'is the judiciary subject to interference from the executive branch of government or from other political, economic, or religious influences?'[53]

The efficiency of courts is also a natural point of interest for governments and other public entities. The Netherlands Council for the Judiciary assigned a study to 'design and implement a method to periodically compare the judiciary system of the Netherlands with that in other countries'[54] and the European Commission for the Efficiency of Justice (CEPEJ) undertakes 'a regular process for evaluating judicial systems of the Council of Europe's member states'.[55] These two studies contain comparative information on the number lawyers, judges, cases etc. similar to other mere countings (2, above). But, additionally, these studies also have a clear policy dimension. For instance, the Dutch study includes a performance index calculated by the number of concluded cases per judge and per Euro spent on the judiciary. And the European study reports data such public budget allocated to all courts per inhabitant, level of computerization of courts, number of cases violating the right to a speedy trial, and clearance rate of litigious and non litigious civil cases.

There is also academic research on the quality of legal institutions. Two articles by Djankov *et al.*, which have also found their way into the World Bank's Doing Business Report (see 3, above), deal with the efficiency of courts and the regulation of entry of start-up firms across countries.[56] The main focus is on the speed of proceedings. In the article on courts this relates to the duration of trial and enforcement for hypothetical cases to evict a tenant for non-payment of rent and to collect a bounced check, and in the article on regulation of entry they examine the number of procedures, official time, and official cost that a start-up must bear before it can operate legally. Another study is the one by Howell Jackson and Mark Roe who are interested in the public enforcement of securities law.[57] The information used in this article are resource-based securities law enforcement data, namely the staffing of securities regulators per population and its budget per GDP.

However, again, a number of critical comments can be made. The first type of measurements, by Freedom House and the Political Risk Services, uses a Western model of law, rights and democracy as benchmark. Thus, they can only tell readers how different other countries are to the West. Moreover, the aggregate nature of these indices makes them even more subjective.[58] One may therefore prefer the latter studies which aim to measure more precisely how courts and other institutions work. Here too, however, the main problem is that the indicators are far from

53 See <http://www.prsgroup.com/ICRG_Methodology.aspx>.

54 Blank *et al.* 2004, p. 7.

55 See <http://www.coe.int/t/dghl/cooperation/cepej/evaluation/default_en.asp>. The most recent version is European Commission for the Efficiency of Justice 2008.

56 Djankov *et al.* 2003; Djankov *et al.* 2002.

57 Jackson & Roe 2009.

58 This is a frequent point of criticism. See, e.g., Skaaning 2010; Voigt 2009. More specifically, Davis 2004 criticises the combination of legal data with non-legal one (such as the crime rate).

straight-forward. For instance, most of the studies seem to assume that it is good to have cheap courts which decide many cases in a short time. But is this really desirable? The apparent danger of this kind of 'justice light' is that the quality of decisions suffers. Thus, one could equally make the opposite case, namely, that it is preferable to have a relatively expensive court system where judges can take their time to decide few cases as good as possible. A way forward may be not to rely on these performance data but to survey how people actually think about their legal systems.[59] This leads to the final type of measurement.

7. Surveying Perceptions about Law and its Enforcement

A first group of surveys is based on the perceptions of firm managers. For instance, the World Bank's World Business Environment Survey (WBES) 2000 surveyed over 10,000 firms in 80 countries. Topics related to law included taxes and regulations, functioning of judiciary, corruption, collateral requirements, property rights, public services, legal predictability and government intervention.[60] A successor of this survey is now administered by the Enterprise Analysis Unit of the World Bank, again covering a broad range of topics, such as corruption, legal infrastructure and crime. For instance, one of the questions asks participants whether they agree or disagree that the court system of their country is 'fair, impartial and uncorrupted'.[61] Another survey has been jointly undertaken by the European Bank for Reconstruction and Development (EBRD) and the World Bank. This Business Environment and Enterprise Performance Survey (BEEPS) has specifically examined the quality of the business environment in transition economies, for example, asking whether participants perceive courts as honest, quick and affordable (with the options: always, usually, or frequently).[62] Finally, the World Economic Forum's Global Competitiveness Reports are based on an executive opinion survey. Participants are asked to rank their legal system from 1 to 7 on questions such as 'is the judiciary independent from political influences of members of government, citizens, or firms?', 'is the legal framework for private businesses to settle disputes and challenge the legality of government actions and/or regulations efficient and follows a clear, neutral process' and 'are property rights clearly defined and well protected by law'.[63]

A second group of surveys examines the views of general members of the public. A well-known private opinion survey is Transparency International's Global Corruption Barometer. This survey is supplemented by expert assessments and the resulting data are consolidated into a Corruption Perception Index.[64] More general in scope is the World Value Survey, being based on 256,000 interviews across the world. Some of its questions relate to legal issues, for instance, participants are

59 Of course, it is also possible to combine these two approaches, as done by the World Justice Project for its Rule of Law Index, <http://www.worldjusticeproject.org/rule-of-law-index/>.
60 See <http://go.worldbank.org/RV060VBJU0>.
61 See <http://www.enterprisesurveys.org>.
62 See <http://www.ebrd.com/pages/research/economics/data/beeps.shtml>.
63 See <http://www.weforum.org/reports>.
64 See <http://www.transparency.org/policy_research/surveys_indices/cpi/2005>.

asked to rate from 1 to 4 whether they have confidence in their justice system and whether they think that human rights are respected in their country.[65] Similar, but restricted to European countries, is the European Social Survey. Here too there is for instance a question which asks to scale from 0 to 10 whether they have trust in their legal system.[66] More specific data are also collected by individual governments: as the aforementioned study of the European Commission for the Efficiency of Justice (CEPEJ) indicates, 28 out of 46 Member States of the Council of Europe survey court users or legal professionals in order to assess the functioning of the judicial system.[67]

Finally, some datasets 'just' aggregate perception and performance data collected by other organizations. This is the case for the Fraser Institute's report on Economic Freedom of the World.[68] Most famous are the World Bank Governance Indicators, developed by Kaufmann *et al.*[69] The WBGI contain aggregate indicators on voice and accountability, political stability and absence of violence, government effectiveness, regulatory quality, rule of law, and control of corruption, for instance, being based on the aforementioned research by the Freedom House, Political Risk Services and Transparency International.

These surveys have collected an impressive amount of information but they are not without problems. Here again, it matters which topics are included in the survey. For instance, the World Bank's rule of law variable has been criticized as mainly being interested in the protection of property rights and not the equal application of the law.[70] There can also be problems with the collection and aggregation of the data. Naturally, participants may be reluctant to disclose participation in illegal behaviour, such as corruption.[71] It has also been shown that indices such as the Corruption Perception Index are very sensitive to the way how the different expert ratings and surveys are aggregated.[72] More generally, it is difficult to assess whether perceptions can really be used to assess the quality of legal systems. Sceptics also point out that participants are typically coloured by cultural differences and recent economic performance.[73] Thus, surveys cannot replace objective forms of measurement, outlined in the previous parts.

65 See <http://www.wvsevsdb.com/wvs/WVSData.jsp>. Ivanyna & Shah 2010 construct a new governance index based on these data.

66 See <http://ess.nsd.uib.no/>. See also Gibson & Caldeira 1996 (using data from the Eurobarometer surveys).

67 European Commission for the Efficiency of Justice 2008, p. 69.

68 See <http://www.fraserinstitute.org/research-news/display.aspx?id=16613>.

69 See <http://www.worldbank.org/wbi/governance/govdata/>, <http://www.govindicators.org/> and Kaufmann, Kraay & Mastruzzi 2009. For a critical assessment see Thomas 2010.

70 Perry-Kessaris 2011. But note that economists often use the term 'property rights' to denote the strength of law enforcement in general. For a legal approach to measuring property rights see however Fedderke, De Kadt & Luiz 2001; Fedderke & Garlick 2011.

71 Perry-Kessaris 2003, p. 688.

72 Hawken & Munck 2011 (which also identifies considerable differences between the expert assessment and the surveys).

73 Kurtz & Schrank 2007 citing Seligson 2006.

8. Conclusions

Following the studies cited in this paper, one has to conclude that it is not impossible to measure legal rules and its enforcement. That may come as a surprise to traditional legal academics, but even recent publications in mainstream legal journals indicate that approaches such as 'numerical comparative law' cannot be ignored anymore.[74] However, the 'just do it' attitude of some economists and other social scientists is also to be criticized. The measurement of law is not straightforward. Thus, collaboration across disciplines should not be a one-way traffic, since economists and other social sciences may also benefit from lawyers' more sceptical attitude towards quantification.[75]

More specifically, researchers should reflect on different forms of measurement. None of the six approaches outlined in this paper is without problems, and often a combination may be useful. For instance, a researcher interested in the effect of legal rules across countries may start with a functional measurement of these rules (4, above), but then she may also examine quantitatively whether and how private parties deviate from these rules (5, above), and she may count the court decisions on these issues (2, above). In addition, she may reflect on the quality of enforcement of these rules, using both performance and perception data (6 & 7, above). With appropriate econometric tools (which are not the topic of this paper) it may then be found that a certain set of rules does indeed have a favourable effect, and that, possibly, it can therefore serve as a benchmark (3, above).

74 See Michaels 2009a; Spamann 2009a; Fauvarque-Cosson & Kerhuel 2009; Milhaupt 2009; Reitz 2009a; the contributions by Reitz 2009b; Michaels 2009b; Legrand 2009; Hadfield 2009; the contributions by Aguilera & Williams 2009; Armour *et al.* 2009; Cioffi 2009; Engert & Smith 2009; Fairfax 2009; Ohnesorge 2009; Okamoto 2009; Pistor 2009; Puri 2009; Ramseyer 2009; Sokol 2009; Spamann 2009b; Whytock 2009. The term 'numerical comparative law' was introduced in Siems 2005.

75 See already Goodhart 1997.

Bibliography

Aguilera & Williams 2009
Aguilera, R.V. & Williams, C.A., '"Law and Finance": Inaccurate, Incomplete, and Important', *Brigham Young University Law Review*, 2009, p. 1413-1434.

Ahlering & Deakin 2007
Ahlering, B. & Deakin, S., 'Labour Regulation, Corporate Governance and Legal Origin: A Case of Institutional Complementarity?, *Law & Society Review*, 2007, p. 865-898.

Armour *et al.* 2009
Armour, J., Deakin, S., Mollica, V. & Siems, M., ' Law and Financial Development: What We Are Learning from Time-Series Evidence', *Brigham Young University Law Review*, 2009, p. 1435-1500.

Arrighetti, Bachmann & Deakin 1997
Arrighetti, A., Bachmann, R. & Deakin, S., 'Contract Law, Social Norms, and Inter-Firm Cooperation', *Cambridge Journal of Economics*, 1997, p. 171-195.

Bebchuk, Cohen & Ferrell 2009
Bebchuk, L.A., Cohen, A. & Ferrell, A., 'What Matters in Corporate Governance?', *Review of Financial Studies*, 2009, p. 783-827.

Bhagat & Romano 2007
Bhagat, S. & Romano, R., 'Empirical Studies of Corporate Law', in: A.M. Polinsky & S. Shavell (eds.), *Handbook of Law and Economics*, Amsterdam: Elsevier, Volume 2, 2007, p. 945-1012.

Bhagat, Bolton & Romano 2008
Bhagat, S., Bolton, B. & Romano, R., 'The Promise and Peril of Corporate Governance Indices', *Columbia Law Review*, 2008, p. 1803-1882.

Blank *et al.* 2004
Blank, J., Van der Ende, M., Van Hulst, B. & Jagtenberg, R., *Bench Marking in an International Perspective: An International Comparison of the Mechanisms and Performance of the Judiciary System*, 2004, available at <http://www.rechtspraak.nl/NR/rdonlyres/7DAF9378-1142-4D39-BFF3-F78277821565/0/BenchMarkingInternationalPerspective.pdf>.

Blankenburg 1997
Blankenburg, E., 'Civil Litigation Rates as Indicators for Legal Culture', in: D. Nelken (ed.), *Comparing Legal Cultures*, Aldershot: Dartmouth, 1997, p. 41-68.

Botero *et al.* 2004
Botero, J., Djankov, S., La Porta, R., Lopez-de-Silanes, F. & Shleifer, A., 'The Regulation of Labor', *Quarterly Journal of Economics*, 2004, p. 1340-82.

Burchell & Wilkinson 1997
Burchell, B. & Wilkinson, F., 'Trust, Business Arrangements and Contractual Environment', *Cambridge Journal of Economics*, 1997, p. 217-237.

Carney 1997
Carney, W.J., 'The Political Economy of Competition for Corporate Charters', *Journal of Legal Studies*, 1997, p. 303-329.

Carney 1998
Carney, W.J., 'The Production of Corporate Law', *Southern California Law Review*, 1998, p. 715-780.

Cioffi 2009
Cioffi, J.W., 'Legal Regimes and Political Particularism: An Assessment of the "Legal Families" Theory from the Perspectives of Comparative Law and Political Economy', *Brigham Young University Law Review*, 2009, p. 1501-1553.

Clark 2002
Clark, D.S., 'The Organization of Lawyers and Judges', in: *International Encyclopedia of Comparative Law*, Tübingen: Mohr, 2002, Volume 16, Chapter 3.

Commission Staff Working Document 2007
Commission Staff Working Document, *Report on the implementation of the Directive on Takeover Bids of 21 February 2007*, SEC(2007) 268, available at <http://ec.europa.eu/internal_market/company/docs/takeoverbids/2007-02-report_en.pdf>.

Commission Staff Working Document 2008
Commission Staff Working Document, *Report on the application by the Member States of the EU of the Commission Recommendation on the role of non-executive or supervisory directors of listed companies and on the committees of the (supervisory) board of 13 July 2008*, SEC(2007) 1021, available at <http://ec.europa.eu/internal_market/company/docs/independence/sec20071022_en.pdf.>.

Cooter & Ginsburg 2003
Cooter, R.D. & Ginsburg, T., *Leximetrics: Why the Same Laws are Longer in Some Countries than Others*, Research Paper 2003, available at <http://ssrn.com/abstract=456520>.

Dakolias 1999
Dakolias, M., 'Court Performance Around the World: A Comparative Perspective', *Yale Human Rights and Development Law Journal*, 1999, p. 87-142.

Davis 2004
Davis, K.E., 'What Can the Rule of Law Variable Tell Us About Rule of Law Reforms?', *Michigan Journal of International Law*, 2004, p. 141-161.

Davis, Kingsbury & Merry 2010
Davis, K.E., Kingsbury, B. & Merry, S.E., *Indicators as a Technology of Global Governance*, NYU Law and Economics Research Paper No. 10-13, available at <http://ssrn.com/abstract=1583431>.

De Coninck 2010
De Coninck, J., 'The Functional Method of Comparative Law: Quo Vadis?', *Rabels Zeitschrift*, 2010, p. 318-350.

Deakin 2006
Deakin, S., 'Learning about Contracts: Trust, Cooperation and Contract Law', in: R. Bachmann & A. Zaheer (eds.), *Handbook of Trust Research*, Cheltenham: Edward Elgar, 2006, p. 218-232.

Deakin 2009
Deakin, S., 'Legal Origin, Juridical Form and Industrialisation in Historical Perspective: The Case of the Employment Contract and the Joint-Stock Company', *Socio-Economic Review*, 2009, p. 35-65.

Deakin & Michie 1997
Deakin, S. & Michie, J. (eds.), *Contracts, Cooperation and Competition: Studies in Economics, Management and Law*, Oxford: Oxford University Press, 1997.

Djankov *et al.* 2002
Djankov, S., La Porta, R., Lopez-de-Silanes, F. & Shleifer, A., 'The Regulation of Entry', *Quarterly Journal of Economics*, 2002, p. 1-37.

Djankov *et al.* 2003
Djankov, S., La Porta, R., Lopez-de-Silanes, F. & Shleifer, A., 'Courts', *Quarterly Journal of Economics*, 2003, p. 453-517.

Djankov *et al.* 2008
Djankov, S., La Porta, R., Lopez-de-Silanes, F. & Shleifer, A., 'The Law and Economics of Self-Dealing', *Journal of Financial Economics*, 2008, p. 430-465.

Donohue III & Levitt 2001
Donohue III, J.J. & Levitt, 'The Impact of Legalized Abortion on Crime', *Quarterly Journal of Economics*, 2001, p. 379-420.

Donohue III & Wolfers 2006
Donohue III, J.J. & Wolfers, J., 'Uses and Abuses of Empirical Evidence in the Death Penalty Debate', *Stanford Law Review*, 2006, p, 791-846.

Engert & Smith 2009
Engert, A. & Smith, D.G., 'Unpacking Adaptability', *Brigham Young University Law Review*, 2009, p. 1554-1570.

European Commission for the Efficiency of Justice 2008
European Commission for the Efficiency of Justice (CEPEJ), *European judicial systems, Edition 2008 (data 2006): Efficiency and quality of justice*, Strasbourg: Council of Europe Publishing, 2008.

Fairfax 2009
Fairfax, L.M., 'The Legal Origins Theory in Crisis', *Brigham Young University Law Review*, 2009, p. 1571-1618.

Fauvarque-Cosson & Kerhuel 2009
Fauvarque-Cosson, B. & Kerhuel, A.J., 'Is Law an Economic Contest? French Reactions to the Doing Business World Bank Reports and Economic Analysis of the Law', *The American Journal of Comparative Law*, 2009, p. 811-829.

Fedderke & Garlick 2011
Fedderke, J. & Garlick, J., *Measuring Institutions: Indicators of Political and Property Rights in Malawi*, Working Paper 2011, available at <http://ssrn.com/abstract=1809887>.

Fedderke, De Kadt & Luiz 2001
Fedderke, J.W., De Kadt, R. &. Luiz, J., 'Indicators of Political Liberty, Property Rights and Political Instability in South Africa', *International Review of Law and Economics*, 2001, p. 103-134.

Gelter & Siems 2010
Gelter, M. & Siems, M., *Language, Legal Origins, and Culture before the Courts: Cross-Citations between Supreme Courts in Europe*, Fordham University Law School Working Paper 2010, available at <http://ssrn.com/abstract=1719183>.

Gibson & Caldeira 1996
Gibson, J.L. & Caldeira, G.A., 'The Legal Cultures of Europe', *Law & Society Review*, 1996, p. 55-86.

Goodhart 1997
Goodhart, C.A.E., 'Economics and the Law: Too Much One - Way Traffic?', *Modern Law Review*, 1997, p. 1-22.

Gompers, Ishii & Metrick 2003
Gompers, P., Ishii, J.L. & Metrick, M., 'Corporate Governance and Equity Prices', *Quarterly Journal of Economics*, 2003, p. 107-155.

Hadfield 2009
Hadfield, G., 'The Strategy of Methodology: The Virtues of Being Reductionist for Comparative Law', *University of Toronto Law Journal*, 2009, p. 223-235.

Hall & Wright 2008
Hall, M.A. & Wright, R.F., 'Systematic Content Analysis of Judicial Opinions', *California Law Review*, 2008, p. 63-122.

Hawken & Munck 2011
Hawken, A & Munck, G.L., *Does the Evaluator Make a Difference? Measurement Validity in Corruption Research*, Committee on Concepts and Methods Working Paper Series, No. 48, March 2011.

Hodges, Vogenauer & Tulibacka 2010
Hodges, C., Vogenauer, S. Tulibacka, M., *The Costs and Funding of Civil Litigation: A Comparative Perspective*, Oxford: Hart, 2010.

Hodson & Maher 2001
Hodson, D & Maher, I., 'The Open Method as a New Mode of Governance', *Journal of Common Market Studies*, 2001, p. 719-745.

Ivanyna & Shah 2010
Ivanyna, M. & Shah, A., *Citizen-centric Governance Indicators: Measuring and Monitoring Governance By Listening to the People and Not the Interest Groups*, The World Bank, Policy Research Working Paper 2010, 5181.

Jackson & Roe 2009
Jackson, H.E. & Roe, M.J., 'Public and Private Enforcement of Securities Laws: Resource-Based Evidence', *Journal of Financial Economics*, 2009, p. 207-238.

Katu 1987
Katu, M, 'Role of Law and Lawyers in Japan and the United States', *Brigham Young University Law Review*, 1987, p. 627.

Kaufmann, Kraay & Mastruzzi 2009
Kaufmann, D., Kraay, A. & Mastruzzi, M., *Governance Matters VIII: Aggregate and Individual Governance Indicators, 1996-2008*, World Bank Policy Research Working Paper No. 4978 (June 29, 2009), available at <http://ssrn.com/abstract=1424591>.

Kelivn 1883
Kelivn, Lord, Lecture on 'Electrical Units of Measurement' (3 May 1883), published in *Popular Lectures*, Vol. I, 1883, p. 73.

Keynes 1940
Keynes, J.M., 'On Method of Statistical Research: Comment', *Economic Journal*, 1940, p. 154-156.

Kurtz & Schrank 2007
Kurtz, M.J. & Schrank, A., 'Growth and Governance: Models, Measures, and Mechanisms', *The Journal of Politics*, 2007, p. 538-554.

La Porta, Lopez-de-Silanes & Shleifer 2006
La Porta, R., Lopez-de-Silanes, F. & Shleifer, A., 'What Works in Securities Laws?', *Journal of Finance*, 2006, p. 1-32.

La Porta *et al.* 1998
La Porta, R., Lopez-de-Silanes, F., Shleifer, A. & Vishny, R., 'Law and Finance', *Journal of Political Economy*, 1998, p. 1113-1155.

Larenz & Canaris 1995
Larenz, K. & Canaris, K.W., *Methodenlehre der Rechtswissenschaft*, 3rd edition, Berlin: Springer, 1995.

Lawless, Robbennolt & Ulen 2009
Lawless, R.M., Robbennolt, J.K. & Ulen, T.S., *Empirical Methods in Law*, New York: Aspen, 2009.

Legrand 2009
Legrand, P., 'Econocentrism', *University of Toronto Law Journal*, 2009, p. 215-222.

Lele & Siems 2007
Lele, P & Siems, M., 'Shareholder Protection – A Leximetric Approach', *Journal of Corporate Law Studies*, 2007, p. 17-50.

Macaulay 1963
Macaulay, S., 'Non-Contractual Relations in Business: A Preliminary Study', *American Sociological Review*, 1963, p. 1-19.

MacNeil & Xiao 2006
MacNeil, I. & Xiao, L., 'Comply or Explain: Market Discipline and Non-Compliance with the Combined Code', *Corporate Governance: An International Review*, 2006, p. 486-496.

Mager Stellman 1998
Mager Stellman, J., *Encyclopaedia of Occupational Health and Safety*, Geneva: International Labour Office, 1998.

Merryman 2000
Merryman, J.H., 'Law and Development Memoirs II: SLADE', *The American Journal of Comparative Law*, 2000, p. 713.

Merryman, Clark & Friedman 1979
Merryman, J.H., Clark, D. & Friedman, L., *Law and Social Change in Mediterranean Europe and Latin America: A Handbook of Legal and Social Indicators for Comparative Study*, Stanford, CA: Stanford Studies in Law and Development, 1979.

Merton, Sills & Stigler 1984
Merton, R.K., Sills, D.L. & Stigler, S.M., 'The Kelvin Dictum and Social Science: An Excursion into the History of an Idea', *Journal of the History of the Behavioral Sciences*, 1984, p. 319-331.

Michaels 2006
Michaels, R., 'The Functional Method of Comparative Law', in: M. Reimann & R. Zimmermann (eds.), *The Oxford Handbook of Comparative Law*, Oxford: Oxford University Press, 2006, p. 339-382.

Michaels 2009a
Michaels, R., 'Comparative Law by Numbers? Legal Origins Thesis. Doing Business Reports, and the Silence of Traditional Comparative Law', *The American Journal of Comparative Law*, 2009, p. 765-796.

Michaels 2009b
Michaels, R., 'The Second Wave of Comparative Law and Economics?', *University of Toronto Law Journal*, 2009, p. 197-213.

Milhaupt 2009
Milhaupt, C.J., 'Beyond Legal Origin: Rethinking Law's Relationship to the Economy – I mplications for Policy, *The American Journal of Comparative Law*, 2009, p. 831-846.

Nelken 1997
Nelken, D., 'Puzzling Out Legal Culture: A Comment on Blankenburg', in: D. Nelken (ed.), *Comparing Legal Cultures*, Aldershot: Dartmouth, 1997, p. 69-92.

Ohnesorge 2009
Ohnesorge, J., 'Legal Origins and the Tasks of Corporate Law in Economic Development: A Preliminary Exploration', *Brigham Young University Law Review*, 2009, p. 1619-1634.

Okamoto 2009
Okamoto, K.S., 'A "Law & Personal Finance" View of Legal Origins Theory', *Brigham Young University Law Review*, 2009, p. 1635-1646.

Perez-Perdomo & Friedman 2003
Perez-Perdomo, R. & Friedman, L., 'Latin Legal Cultures in the Age of Globalization', in: L.M. Friedman & R. Perez-Perdomo (eds.), *Legal Culture in the Age of Globalization: Latin America and Latin Europe*, Stanford: Stanford University Press, 2003, p. 1-19.

Perry-Kessaris 2003
Perry-Kessaris, A., 'Finding and Facing Facts about Legal Systems and Foreign Direct Investment in South Asia', *Legal Studies*, 2003, p. 649-689.

Perry-Kessaris 2011
Perry-Kessaris, A., 'Prepare Your Indicators: Economics Imperialism on the Shores of Law and Development', *International Journal of Law in Context*, forthcoming 2011.

Pistor 2009
Pistor, K., 'Rethinking the "Law and Finance" Paradigm', *Brigham Young University Law Review*, 2009, p. 1647-1670.

Posner 1996
Posner, R., *Law and Legal Theory in England and America*, Oxford: Clarendon, 1996.

Puri 2009
Puri, P., 'Legal Origins, Investor Protection, and Canada', *Brigham Young University Law Review*, 2009, p. 1671-1700.

Ramseyer 2009
Ramseyer, J.M., 'Mixing-and-Matching Across (Legal) Family Lines', *Brigham Young University Law Review*, 2009, p. 1701-1712.

Reitz 2009a
Reitz, J., 'Legal Origins, Comparative Law, and Political Economy', *The American Journal of Comparative Law*, 2009, p. 847-862.

Reitz 2009b
Reitz, J., 'Toward a Study of the Ecology of Judicial Activism?', *University of Toronto Law Journal*, 2009, p. 185-196.

Schäffer & Racz 1990
Schäffer, H. & Racz, A. (ed.), *Quantitative Analyses of Law – A Comparative Empirical Study: Sources of Law in Eastern Western Europe*, Budapest: Akademiai Kiado, 1990.

Seligson 2006
Seligson, M., 'The Measurement and Impact of Corruption Victimization: Survey Evidence from Latin America', *World Development*, 2006, p. 381-404.

Skaaning 2010
Skaaning, S.-E., 'Measuring the Rule of Law', *Political Research Quarterly*, 2010, p. 449-460.

Siems 2005
Siems, M., 'Numerical Comparative Law - Do We Need Statistical Evidence in Order to Reduce Complexity?', *Cardozo Journal of International and Comparative Law*, 2005, p. 521-540.

Siems & Deakin 2010
Siems, M. & Deakin, S., 'Comparative Law and Finance: Past, Present and Future Research', *Journal of Institutional and Theoretical Economics*, 2010, p. 120-140.

Sokol 2009
Sokol, D.D., 'Competition Policy and Comparative Corporate Governance of State-Owned Enterprises', *Brigham Young University Law Review*, 2009, p. 1713-1812.

Spamann 2009a
Spamann, H., 'Large Sample, Quantitative Research Designs for Comparative Law?', *The American Journal of Comparative Law*, 2009, p. 797-810.

Spamann 2009b
Spamann, H., 'Contemporary Legal Transplants: Legal Families and the Diffusion of (Corporate) Law', *Brigham Young University Law Review*, 2009, p. 1813-1878.

Spamann 2010
Spamann, H., 'The 'Antidirector Rights Index' Revisited', *Review of Financial Studies*, 2010, p. 468-483.

Taylor 2007
Taylor, V., 'The law reform Olympics: Measuring the effects of law reform in transition economies', in: T. Lindsey (ed.), *Law Reform in Developing and Transition States*, London: Routledge, 2007, pp. 83-105.

Thomas 2010
Thomas, M.A., 'What do the Worldwide Governance Indicators Measure?', *European Journal of Development Research*, 2010, p. 31-54.

Voigt 2009
Voigt, S., *How to Measure the Rule of Law*, Working Paper 2009, available at <http://ssrn.com/abstract=1420287>.

Von Werder, Talaulicar & Kolat 2005
Von Werder, A., Talaulicar.T. & Kolat, G.L., 'Compliance with the German Corporate Governance Code: An Empirical Analysis of the Compliance Statements by German Listed Companies', *Corporate Governance: An International Review*, 2005, p. 178-187.

Whytock 2009
Whytock, C.A., 'Legal Origins, Functionalism, and the Future of Comparative Law', *Brigham Young University Law Review*, 2009, p. 1879-1906.

Zweigert & Kötz 1998
Zweigert, K. & Kötz, H., *Introduction to Comparative Law*, Oxford: Clarendon, 1998.

Giuseppe
Dari-Mattiacci
Carmine
Guerriero

LAW, ECONOMICS AND HISTORY: ENDOGENOUS INSTITUTIONAL CHANGE AND LEGAL INNOVATION

1. Introduction: The Endogenous Institution Approach

Understanding the origins of formal and informal institutions of cooperation and regulation and their long-lasting impact on market exchange and technological investment is the most pressing questions in law, economics and history. Accordingly, despite the different angles considered by different disciplines, the notion that institutions emerge endogenously in the face of both welfare-enhancing and rent-seeking motives has recently come to be an accepted paradigm. Yet, despite this convergence, an even more vigorous effort in inquiring the determinants and the effects of institutional change is needed in order to guide legal and political reforms: the aim of this chapter is to substantiate this desideratum and, at the same time, to provide a new interdisciplinary research agenda.

The need to understand institutional genesis is innate to human thinking. Already Aristotle, referring to the constitution of Athens, discussed a common belief held by many who thought that Solon had 'deliberately made the laws indefinite, in order that the final decision might be in the hands of the people'[1] and contrasted it with an alternative explanation based on the inherent incompleteness and, at times, internal inconsistency of the law. In modern words, Aristotle's problem concerned the factors determining the emergence and the functioning of the key institution of his time. Similarly, Justinian' codification of Roman law was motivated by the need to affect the path of unregulated development of Roman law, as the emperor found 'the whole extent of our laws which has come down from the foundation of the city of Rome and the days of Romulus to be so confused that it extends to an inordinate length and is beyond the comprehension of any human nature'.[2] An urgent need for consolidation (of the achievements of the revolution, in this case) also inspired the Napoleonic codification.[3] Codifications provide but an

1 Aristotle 350 BC, Sec. 1, Part 9.
2 *Const. Deo auct.* § 1 (translation from Watson 2009).
3 Holtman 1967.

example of a more general class of legal, cultural and political institutional changes, including the enlargement of the suffrage, the protection of minorities, the abolition of slavery, the development of social capital, the emergence of the modern business formats, and the rise of the regulatory state among other equally important issues. Institutional genesis occurs not only at the juncture of demand for institutional change from one or several sectors of society and of supply of such changes by another sector, but also depends on the complex interaction of other factors such as path dependence, exogenous shocks, technological constraints and international or domestic political competition. This complex web of simultaneous forces unveils the crucial challenges analysts face: when the same primitive forces shape at the same time institutions and economic development or when the latter feeds back to institutions, a source of 'exogenous variation' in institutional change is needed to correctly assess the relation between the economy and the shared rules of conduct. In the following we show how an increasing legacy of research has started to tackle this issue combining in novel ways insights from legal scholarship, economic theory and history. Our illustration is not meant to be an exhaustive account of the relevant contributions but rather to highlight, through some interesting examples, the challenges faced by the endogenous institutional analysis literature in delivering both a serious historic and institutional reconstruction and a rigorous economic analysis. In section 2 we will first look at the origins and evolution of legal institutions and then shift our attention to the more long-lasting political ones. In section 3, we will build on this discussion to propose an interdisciplinary approach to the analysis of institutional change and legal innovation based on a deeper study of history. Finally, we will conclude in section 4 highlighting how this approach could be applied to several open research questions that naturally lend themselves to an interdisciplinary inquiry.

2. The Origin and Impact of Shared Rules of Conduct

2.1. *Legal Institutions*

Two are the sets of historical factors affecting the functioning of the legal system: those that shape the way in which the law is created and those that determine the social approach to the regulation of a particular harmful act. We will look at very recent literature dealing with each of them in turn.

2.1.1. Endogenous Legal Systems: Beyond the Civil vs. Common Law Divide

From an abstract standpoint, the legal system is a mechanism aggregating social preferences into a level of deterrence for harmful conduct; the gears of such mechanism are the lawmaking rules fixing the identity of the lawmaker – for instance, the Legislator or appellate judges – and the procedures of dispute adjudication. Such rules are so long-lasting that comparative legal scholars have referred to them as a unitary bundle of institutions called 'legal origins'. Two are the most widespread legal origins worldwide: the civil law and the common law.[4] While the latter originated in thirteen-century England and has been transplanted through colonization into England's ex-colonies, the former has its original roots in Roman law and has been imported through the Napoleonic codes to Italy, Belgium, the Netherlands, Spain and Portugal. These last four powers, along with France, spread it to the Near East, Latin America, Northern Africa and Indochina. While common law recognizes a key role to precedents and allows more procedural discretion to lower adjudicating courts, civil law relies on legal codes and bright-line adjudication rules.[5] Building on these deep differences, a massive literature, started almost 15 years ago, proposed the idea that the exogenous transplantation process brought into the colonies not only specific laws, but also a more 'general style of the legal system' as well as the mother-country human capital.[6] Hence, even if the original transplanted laws adapted to local circumstances and technological progress, the bundle of lawmaking and adjudication rules, with their ideological content and their impact on the judiciary, remained unaltered, continuing to shape the quality of the new laws. Accordingly, the 'legal origins' movement has provided evidence suggesting that, compared to the countries to which the French civil law was originally transplanted, those that initially received common law show:

> '(a) better investor protection, which in turn is associated with improved financial development [...], (b) lighter government ownership and regulation, which are in turn associated with less corruption, better functioning labour markets, and smaller unofficial economies, and (c) less formalized and more independent judicial systems, which are in turn associated with more secure property rights and better contract enforcement'.[7]

In the last few years, however, an increasing legacy of legal studies have criticized the 'legal origins' maintained assumption that the transplanted legal infrastructures remained unchanged over time, noticing, in the first place, the growing importance of legislation in common law countries.[8]

Inspired by this crucial observation, the 'legal origins' project has been challenged on both theoretical and empirical grounds by studies aimed at proving the basic point that different bundles of legal institutions are optimal in different social contexts. First, more careful historical analyses have refuted the medieval-grounded primacy of common law in protecting private ordering.[9] Second, consistent with recent evidence, a growing number of models have clarified that the evolutionary

4 'The following factors [crucially shape] the style of a legal system [...]: (1) its historical background and development, (2) its predominant and characteristic mode of thought in legal matters, (3) especially distinctive institutions, (4) the kind of legal sources it acknowledges and the way it handles them, and (5) its ideology' (Zweigert & Kötz 1998, p. 68).

5 See Zweigert & Kötz 1998. See also Guerriero 2010b, for a more articulated analysis.

6 See for a review of the literature La Porta, Lopez-de-Silanes & Shleifer 2008 and Guerriero 2010b.

7 La Porta, Lopez-de-Silanes & Shleifer 2008, p. 298.

8 See, for instance, the anecdotal evidence on corporate governance discussed in Roe 2004.

9 See the historical comparison of the evolution of courts in England and in France in Klerman & Mahoney 2007.

efficiency of case law is far from obvious at the theoretical level.[10] Third, the initial partition in countries that inherited the civil law tradition and countries that inherited the common law tradition has been proved inconsistent with the fact that a large number of countries effectively chose whether to retain the originally transplanted institution or shift. This critique to the 'legal origins' project has been based on both a more detailed process of data gathering and a deeper theoretical inquiry into the comparative properties of the two legal traditions.[11]

This work has recorded: 1) the lawmaking institution in place at independence and in 2000 in 156 countries that received their initial legal order externally; 2) the four most relevant adjudication institutions in place in 98 of these 156 countries at the same points in time. Contrary to the 'legal origins' maintained hypothesis, 26 countries have reformed their lawmaking institution and 91 their lawmaking and/ or at least one of the adjudication procedures in such a way that: 1) reforms toward case law in countries to which statute law was imposed by continental European colonizers are more likely the weaker democracy and the broader cultural heterogeneity; 2) symmetrically, moves toward statute law in England's ex-colonies are found where the cultural differences among subgroups are the smallest.

Culture is the main driver of this pattern. Recent psychological studies suggest that humans have well defined preferences over the harshness of punishment for dangerous actions, and that these tastes are modulated by the cultural biases of the group to which individuals pertain.[12] Under case law appellate judges bring the bias of their own group into the law. Yet, the institutional relevance recognized to precedents moderates them. Thus, opposing biases balance one another over time leading to the socially optimal rule, which is the mean of those preferred by each group. This comes at the cost of everlasting uncertainty over the law. Under statute law, instead, legal rules are selected by a Legislator, who weights the welfare of society against the perquisites obtained favouring a cultural group and has as outside option the optimal law. When the disagreement among social groups is limited, the costs that a collective action requires discourage bribing; hence, statutes are contemporaneously certain and optimal, and statute law outperforms case law. When, however, cultural heterogeneity is sufficiently high, statutes become more biased the lower the quality of the political process – i.e., democracy. In this case, it can be shown that case law prevails over statute law when political institutions are sufficiently weak. This model also shows that the use of limited discretion by adjudicating courts increases appellate judges' overruling costs and makes statute

10 Gennaioli & Shleifer 2007a, Anderlini, Felli & Riboni 2010 and Baker & Mezzetti 2010 provide different justifications to the lack of convergence toward efficiency of precedents shown by Niblett, Posner & Shleifer 2010.

11 See Guerriero 2010a. Dari-Mattiacci & Guerriero 2011 confirm these patterns looking at roman law and exploiting the fact that between the fifth century B.C. and the fifth century A.D. Rome went through two momentous law making reforms. Finally, Guerriero 2011b exploits the exogenous instruments identified in Guerriero 2010a to measure the truly exogenous impact of the transplanted legal tradition on economic outcomes.

12 See Herrmann, Thöni & Gächter 2008.

law volatile. Thus, a pure common (civil) law tradition where case (statute) law is used along with flexible (bright line) adjudication rules will endogenously arise.

These results cast two fundamental doubts on the 'legal origins' approach. First, how can we give a causal interpretation to the impact of institutions which were not even in place?[13] Second, how can we defend the exogeneity assumption if the evolution of legal systems is driven by primitive forces affecting also the performances we want to explain? These are two of the key questions that the approach proposed in this chapter can help to tackle.

2.1.2. Endogenous Laws and Regulations: Understanding Comparative Variation

Even if the presence of different law-making and adjudication institutions can explain the distance between the prevailing laws and the socially optimal ones,[14] there is still unexplained variation in the regulations adopted by legal systems pertaining to the same legal origins. Again the endogenous institutions framework has been fruitfully employed to identify primitive forces, such as the relative power of different social groups and their preferences for wrong-doing, in order to shed more light on these regularities. This can be seen as a relevant progress upon the traditional comparative law and economics approach, which has been functional in spirit and, thus, prone to look for regularities more than differences. Such an approach has maintained that, if laws in different countries are meant to provide solutions to very similar problems, they have to be similar.[15] As a result, only two are the possible justifications to comparative variation: a disagreement about the optimal solution and the functional equivalence of different solutions. While the former reduces to admit that the existing variation is a temporary state deriving from human limitations in quickly grappling with important issues,[16] the latter justification touches the heart of the problem. Essentially, saying that different rules

13 A similar criticism is proposed by those contributions showing that the initial 'legal origins' codification was picking a correlation between specific features of colonization - like human capital and the enforcement of property rights - and economic development (Perotti & Von Thadden 2006; Garoupa & Gomez Liguerre 2010; Musacchio 2010).

14 Another dimension determining the overall quality of the law is the degree of government centralization. While a centralized government fares better in terms of reducing inter-jurisdictional externalities and preventing races to the bottom (see *Louis K. Liggett Co.* v. *Lee* - 288 U.S. 517 [1933], 558-559 - and *New State Ice Company* v. *Liebmann* - 285 U.S. 262 [1932], 311), local governments exploit local knowledge (Tiebout 1956; Oates 1972), respect heterogeneous preferences, diversify the risk of taking bad decisions (Arcuri & Dari-Mattiacci 2010), and can engage in a healthy competition to the top (Romano 1985; Breton 1996) in providing the best rules.

15 Levmore 1987 applies this principle in explaining the variation in the good-faith purchaser rules around the world.

16 Hence, a temporary mismatch between problems and optimal rules generates an equally temporary variety of laws. This theory fits well with the federalist idea that, once the solution is found in one jurisdiction, it will easily spread to other countries, pushed by competitive forces.

in different countries are functionally equivalent is to say that, from a functional perspective, there is no variation at all.[17]

The difficulties in accepting this conclusion and the inability of the legal origins scholarship in explaining different regulations across societies within the same legal tradition have led several social scientists to propose path dependence as an explanation:[18] laws today are different because they were different in the past. Yet, path dependence only moves the question back in time without solving the fundamental issue of the origins of legal rules. In the following, we document how the endogenous institutions framework has provided some preliminary, interesting insights in the understanding of comparative variation by way of a recent example, looking at the observed differences in the rules concerning good-faith purchase of stolen goods by an innocent buyer. Different countries balance the interests of the buyer and of the original owner of the good in different ways, ranging from full protection of the owner to full protection of the buyer. The most recent contribution in the law and economics literature has evidenced that the theoretically optimal rule – balancing the owner's incentives to protect his property and the buyer's incentives to inquire about title – differs from any of the solutions adopted in reality.[19] As a consequence, societies around the world should try to convergence towards the optimal rule, as the theory of temporary disagreement would suggest. Yet, this conclusion would imply that comparative variation in such a crucial piece of market regulation has originated randomly around the world and that the push towards efficiency has nowhere been met by reform.

A recent study addresses this issue by systematically coding the extent of protection of the owner vs. the buyer for over one hundred countries and by explaining the large comparative variation with reference to the quality of the public enforcement of the law and the level of morality in society.[20] Crucially, this theory is based on: 1) the observation that, given uncertainty in the roles that each individual will take in a transaction (either buyer or seller), individuals are essentially behind a veil of ignorance and their best option is to favour the optimal rule; 2) the quality of the public enforcement of the law and the level of morality in society are likely to be independent from the rules of private law.[21] The testable predictions are confirmed by the empirical investigation.

17 Acemoglu & Johnson 2005 also show that, once the effects of private law and the public provisions protecting private property are separated, only the latter seem to have a sizable effect on performance. The argument here is not functional identity, but rather the ability of parties to contracting around the inefficiencies of private law.

18 Roe 1996 proposes path dependence, chaos and evolutionary theory as tools in the economics of legal evolution.

19 Schwartz & Scott 2011 derives the theoretically optimal rule for good-faith purchase and argues that reforms should make the observed variety of legal solutions converge towards this rule.

20 Dari-Mattiacci, Guerriero & Huang 2011.

21 The key model's results are that: 1) there are equilibria in which moral intermediaries – who suffers a moral cost from stealing – signal their good title by charging higher prices, provided that the moral cost is sufficiently high; 2) a society should accept more coercion, if buyers value the good more than owners, and less coercion, otherwise; 3) in the last case, the market →

As this example reveals, the endogenous institutions approach is able to generate testable predictions concerning comparative variation starting from allegedly exogenous factors and offering a third way to justify comparative variation, next to functional equivalence and institutional disagreement.[22] In the case of the good-faith purchase problem, this third explanation coincides with an efficient response to two exogenous constraints. In the conclusions we will propose other possible applications of the endogenous legal institutions approach.

2.2. *Political Institutions*

A plethora of contributions have documented that informal - i.e., a culture of cooperation - and formal political institutions - i.e., a democratic government - are the two key factors favouring economic development: while the former facilitates cooperation, the latter helps enforcing property rights.[23] Yet, only recently social scientists have begun to uncover the origins of these institutions in order to figure out the chain of causality - i.e., whether political institutions drive development or the other way round, to isolate the individual contributions of each type of institution - i.e., informal and formal - and to characterize their interaction.

A first strand of literature has proposed the idea that an historical experience of an efficient political organization, such as the free city-state in medieval Italy, can permeate the long-run institutional development and economic success of a society.[24] However, documenting that the two types of settings reinforce one another and are persistent explains neither the primitive forces producing each of them nor the way in which they interact with each other and affect economic outcomes. A first step along these lines has been taken by two recent papers. According to one of them,[25] democracy expands where it helps the existing elite to credibly convince the citizens that their property rights will not be expropriated. A case in point is the political evolution of Athens and Sparta at the end of the Dark Ages. While the terrain in Sparta was plain, in Athens it was hillside; this geographic characteristic made investments in new harvesting technologies by the farmers more difficult to monitor by the landowners. Hence, the elite in Athens, differently from its counterpart in Sparta, extended the franchize in order to credibly enforce property rights

shrinks because moral types refrain from stealing. So, mature economies - those for which, due to preference heterogeneity, owners value goods more than the buyer - will move toward buyer protection, the higher is the share of moral types (lower extent of coercion) and the less efficient is public enforcement (lower impact of owner protection).

22 This result belongs to a series of other findings showing that regulatory institutions arise as the rational attempt of a society to solve a technological failure - e.g., preventing the majority of market participants from being coerced by a subgroup of more powerful special interests (Glaeser & Shleifer 2003; Djankov *et al.* 2003; Benmelech & Moskowitz 2010; Guerriero 2011a) or of similarly powerful untrustworthy agents (Aghion *et al.* 2010).

23 Guiso, Sapienza & Zingales 2006 review the contributions looking to the relation between culture and the economy, Persson & Tabellini 2009 document the role of democracy in pushing development via property rights protection.

24 See the evidence discussed in Guiso, Sapienza & Zingales 2008 and Tabellini 2010.

25 Fleck & Hanssen 2006.

and, thus, stimulate difficult-to-monitor investments. Building on a similar intuition, a second study shows that regions with more volatile climate in the growing seasons of the period 1500-1750 present today stronger norms of cooperation. In other words, the latter developed in preindustrial times as a result of episodes of mutual insurance against climatic risk.[26] Yet, even if innovative, these papers neither clarify whether forces shaping one type of institution affect also the other type nor characterize the full set of interactions among culture, democracy and the economy.

An even more recent contribution has shed more light on these points, bridging together the intuitions of the two papers just discussed and looking at the experience of 100 European regions between the 11th and 17th centuries.[27] From a theoretical point of view, this study argues that: 1) exogenous geographical factors have a first order effect only on the institution more related to the economic activity it determines - risk sharing for culture and investment for democracy; 2) cultural formation and democratization reinforce each other working as commitment devices in the intermediate situations - when showing commitment to cooperate in the future, by either assuring property rights as elite or cooperating in investment as citizens, is crucial in favouring investments; 3) technological shocks could destroy valuable institutions by affecting the related economic activity. Estimates based on the geographical features and institutions of the regions studied are consistent with this prediction. Crucially, the mix of clear-cut predictions and the identification of the roots of institutional formation will allow future contributions to characterize the role of each type of institution in shaping economic development and to identify the best public policies to implement.

3. Learning from History

The endogenous institutions approach naturally extends to history and, vice versa, insights from history cross-fertilize modern theories on how institutions emerge and develop. Ancient economies, in particular in the Greco-Roman world, were technologically and organizationally very different from modern ones. Not only did they heavily rely on chattel slavery as a mean of production, but they also lacked many of the tools - including both technology and accounting techniques, such as double entry book-keeping - that appeared only later during the middle ages and the industrial revolution. This observation has induced many scholars (the 'primitivists') to claim that the Roman economy was essentially a household economy and denied any role for market exchange.[28] In contrast, 'modernists' have argued that also ancient economies were based on regular markets and that market exchange played an important role.[29] The debate has become ideologically and terminologically loaded and scholars are trying to go beyond it, in order to inquire to what extent - between the two extreme views taken by the primitivist and modernist

26 Durante 2010.
27 Boranbay & Guerriero 2011.
28 Finley 1973; Pearson 1957.
29 Rostovtseff 1957.

positions – market exchange played a role in ancient economies.[30] Once reformulated, the inquiry on the structure of ancient economies reveals very interesting issues for the legal economist as to exactly how market exchange was organized and especially how the institutions supporting such an exchange emerged and evolved in a technologically-constrained environment. Also, the needs and the characteristics of the economy may have fed back into the institutions generating further change. One example of such fruitful interdisciplinary is provided by inquiries into the genesis of the corporate form.

An Example: The Origins and Evolution of the Modern Corporate Form

The emergence of the legal infrastructure supporting the modern corporate form is one of the most influential legal innovations, one that broke with the past and spurred a host of further changes in the law and in society. The corporate form has proven to be essential for business for it allows broad participation of diffuse investors in risky business endeavours, facilitate financing and allows for long-term investments that transcend the live-spans of the individual investors or managers. Despite its downsides, this business format has dominated economic life in the western world for at least three centuries. A famous and somewhat abused quote from Justice Holmes states that 'The life of the law has not been logic; it has been experience'.[31] Yet, the challenge is precisely to find a logic in how experience guides the development of the law through time. It is important to understand why a certain legal change occurred in a specific jurisdiction or at a specific point in time, why it was not imitated elsewhere and, most interestingly, why it had not occurred earlier.

The origin of the corporate form is usually identified in the Dutch East India Company (VOC, 1602), which also gave birth to the first stock market. An analysis of the historical pattern that brought about the VOC reveals two interesting facts. First of all, other countries were in the same business of East Asian trade at the same time as the Dutch Republic, but organized their business in a different way. Second, trade with Asia had been going on for a while and companies were usually dissolved at the end of each voyage and then reformed again. The creation of the VOC breaks both with the Dutch Republic own past and with the strategies employed by competing countries. In the natural world such changes occur because of random variation, but this does not seem to be the case here. A recent study explains this legal innovation with reference to, on the supply side, the political situation of the Dutch Republic and, on the demand side, the specific commercial and military conditions of the time.[32] The prospects of enormous gains in the Asian trade were essentially aligned with the military interests of the Dutch Republic at war with Spain. Uniting commercial and military interests required a commitment on the part of the government not to expropriate merchants once the investments had been

30 See Andreau 1999; Maucourant 2004; Temin 2006; Scheidel, Morris & Saller 2007.

31 Holmes 1881, p. 1.

32 Dari-Mattiacci *et al.* 2011.

made. Such commitment required in turn a relatively weak and accountable government. Strong monarchies in Spain, Portugal and England were unable to commit not to expropriate the gains from trade, while the essentially federal structure of the Dutch Republic limited the possibility for the government to act against the interests of the majority of the merchant community. In turn, the ability to commit allowed the state to step in and provide a path-breaking legal structure for the VOC, one that (next to monopoly rights for the exploitation of the Asian trade) conferred on the company limited liability and a medium-term life-span (initially 10 years, later made indefinite), preventing individual investors from requiring the drawing of accounts (and hence liquidation) during this period. Such a degree of long-term commitment and limited liability would not have been possible by private contracting due to prohibitive coordination costs.[33] This approach leverages on the institutional context in which legal change occurs and allows institutions to evolve endogenously in response to changing external conditions. Nevertheless, it does not disregard the importance of cultural transmission, legal traditions and technology. In fact, demand for a business format guaranteeing asset partitioning and continuity had been felt for quite some time before the creation of the VOC.

A proof of it can be indirectly obtained from business practices in ancient Rome (between the second century BC and the second century AD). A business format allowing for asset partitioning and continuity (in addition to a form of direct representation) was constructed around the attribution of dedicated assets to a slave. These assets, autonomously managed by the slave, were essentially a functional equivalent of a modern limited-liability company. In contrast, partnership contracts were a purely private affair and did not confer limited liability, did not imply representation and were dissolved if any of the partners died or exited. One explanation for this asymmetry is the fact that separating liability from management ran against strong cultural beliefs, holding that losses should fall where profits accrue (*ubi commoda ibi incommoda*). Businesses run by slaves were subject to a legal regime that circumvented these restrictions. As a default, the master was not liable for obligations contracted by his slave. Thus, legal evolution went in the direction of extending the liability of the master for debts generated by the slave. Being an extension of liability (rather than a restriction), the evolution of this business format went along the cultural constraints, for it attributed more liability to the master (rather than less).[34]

After the end of classical slavery, the evolution of a (functionally) similar format based on the participation of free individuals as managers (rather than slaves) required several centuries. The VOC was only the first step. An additional innovation was made with the general incorporation statutes in the 19th century, which lifted state discretion in the concession of the corporate status and made this format available for a wide variety of businesses.[35] Even if much work is needed, these studies suggest that a crucial import of the focus on endogenous institutional

33 Hansmann & Kraakman 2000.

34 Abatino, Dari-Mattiacci & Perotti 2011.

35 See, for instance, Harris 2000, p. 277-285.

development is the unveiling of the mechanisms that bring the system in disequilibrium and spur change. These forces do not operate in a vacuum. Rather, context and culture are important constraints.

4. Conclusions

Interdisciplinary research at the juncture of law, economics and history has shown great potential in providing a new perspective on important research issues. This potential is even greater if measured in terms of new challenging questions arising at the interface of these three disciplines. Next, we offer some considerations on three clusters of questions. The list is by no means exhaustive but should provide three interesting directions for the drafting of innovative research agendas.

4.1. *Emergence and Impact of Lawmaking Institutions*

The literature on the economic effects of different lawmaking institutions - namely, common vs. civil law - and the literature on their origins can be taken further by both integrating these two perspectives and broadening the scope of the inquiry. The focus has been almost exclusively on common vs. civil law, but modern societies witness a wide variety of sources of law besides courts and legislatures; moreover, different modes of production of legal rules exhibit much more nuances than this traditional divide can possibly embed. This observation suggests that the inquiry could be profitably both broadened and deepened in order to take into account the internal functioning of lawmaking institutions, their accountability to a constituency and their ability to process information,[36] and to include in the analysis the complex interaction among sources of law.[37]

4.2. *Relative Weight of Demand-Side and Supply-Side Drivers of Legal Change*

Inquiries into the explanation of comparative legal variation face two main challenges. On the one hand, understanding the effects of change in fact means assessing the (potential) demand for change in society (or a portion of society). On the other hand, only by assuming a strong drive towards efficiency can one use the (social) demand for institutional change as an accurate description of the forces determining change. In reality, important factors affect the emergence of such demand, how it is channelled through the existing institutions and whether and how it will be received and, possibly, met. Integrating demand- and supply-side aspects of institutional development provides a richer picture than simply looking

36 See, for instance, the analysis of the interaction between judicial incentives and legal human capital in Hadfield 2011.

37 For instance, Pistor & Xu 2003 examine the interaction of legislation and regulation.

at either of them in isolation; for it is at the juncture of demand and supply that institutional and legal change occur.[38]

4.3. *Formal and Informal Institutions*

Next to the technological determinants of institutional change, a very important and often neglected engine of evolution is culture. Lawyers typically look at the law as a cultural phenomenon and it is reasonable to think that slow cultural development accompanies, facilitates or at times hinders reforms. This implies that, on the one hand, culture should feature as an important explanatory variable in model of legal and political institutional change; on the other, however, economic development, the opening of markets, or changes in the institutional structure of society are likely to feedback on cultural norms, spur change or, possibly, break firmly-held beliefs. In this perspective, the challenge of future studies on formal and informal institutions is to build and test models in which, given a parsimonious set of truly exogenous forces, culture, laws and the economy interact.

[38] For instance, Parisi & Fon 2003 stress the importance of supply in the evolution of precedents.

Bibliography

Abatino, Dari-Mattiacci & Perotti 2011
Abatino, B., Dari-Mattiacci, G. & Perotti, E., 'Depersonalization of Business in Ancient Rome,' *Oxford Journal of Legal Studies*, 2011, forthcoming.

Acemoglu & Johnson 2005
Acemoglu, D. & Johnson, S., 'Unbundling Institutions,' *Journal of Political Economy*, 2005, p. 949-995.

Aghion *et al.* 2010
Aghion, P., Algan, Y, Cahuc, P. & Shleifer, A., 'Regulation and Distrust,' *Quarterly Journal of Economics*, 2010, p. 1015-1049.

Andreau 1999
Andreau, J., *Banking and Business in the Roman World*, Cambridge: Cambridge University Press, 1999.

Arcuri & Dari-Mattiacci 2010
Arcuri, A. & Dari-Mattiacci, G., 'Centralization versus Decentralization as a Risk-Return Trade-off', *Journal of Law and Economics*, 2010, p. 359-378.

Aristotle 1994
Aristotle, *The Athenian Constitution* (F.G. Kenyon trans.). MIT, The Internet Classics Archive, classics.mit.edu, 1994.

Baker & Mezzetti 2010
Baker, S. & Mezzetti, C., *A Theory of Rational Jurisprudence*, Working Paper, 2010.

Benmelech & Moskowitz 2010
Benmelech, E. & Moskowitz, T.J., 'The Political Economy of Financial Regulation: Evidence from U.S. State Usury Laws in the 19th Century', *Journal of Finance*, 2010, p. 1029-1073.

Boranbay & Guerriero 2011
Boranbay, S. & Guerriero, C., *Endogenous (In)Formal Institutions*, Working Paper, 2011.

Breton 1996
Breton, A., *Competitive Governments*, Cambridge: Cambridge University Press, 1996.

Dari-Mattiacci & Guerriero 2011
Dari-Mattiacci, G. & Guerriero, C., *Fiat Lex: Lawmaking, Politics, and Cultural Heterogeneity in Ancient Rome*, Working Paper, 2011.

Dari-Mattiacci, Guerriero Huang 2011
Dari-Mattiacci, G., Guerriero, C. & Huang, Z., *The Good-Faith Purchaser: Markets, Culture, and the Legal System*, Working Paper, 2011.

Dari-Mattiacci *et al.* 2011
Dari-Mattiacci, G., Gelderblom, O., Jonker, J. & Perotti, E., *Institutional Discontinuity: The Twisted Emergence of Legal Personality in the Dutch East India Company*, Working Paper, 2011.

Deakin 2011
Deakin, S., 'Legal Evolution: Integrating Economic and Systemic Approaches', *Review of Law and Economics*, 2011, forthcoming.

Djankov *et al.* 2003
Djankov, S., Glaeser, E., La Porta, R., Lopez-de-Silanes, F. & Shleifer, A., 'The New Comparative Economics,' *Journal of Comparative Economics*, 2003, p. 595-619.

Durante 2010
Durante, R., *Risk, Cooperation and the Economic Origins of Social Trust: an Empirical Investigation*, Working Paper, 2010.

Fernandez & Ponzetto 2008
Fernandez, P.A. & Ponzetto, G.A.M., 'Case Law vs. Statute Law: an Evolutionary Comparison', *Journal of Legal Studies*, 2008, p. 379-430.

Fleck & Hanssen 2006
Fleck, R.K. & Hanssen, F.A., 'The Origins of Democracy: A Model with Application to Ancient Greece', *Journal of Law and Economics*, 2006, p. 115-146.

Fleck & Hanssen 2010
Fleck, R.K. & Hanssen, F.A., *How Tyranny Paved the Way to Wealth and Democracy: A Model with Application to Ancient Greece*, Working Paper, 2010.

Fon & Parisi 2003
Fon, V. & Parisi, F., 'Litigation and the Evolution of Legal Remedies: A Dynamic Model', *Public Choice*, 2003, p. 419-433.

Garoupa & Gomez Liguerre 2011
Garoupa, N. & Gomez Liguerre, C., 'The Syndrome of the Efficiency of the Common Law', *Boston University Journal of International Law*, 2011, p. 287-335.

Guerriero 2010a
Guerriero, C., *Democracy, Judicial Attitudes and Heterogeneity: the Civil Versus Common Law Tradition*, Working Paper, 2010.

Guerriero 2010b
Guerriero, C., 'Legal Traditions and Economic Performances: Theory and Evidence,' in B. Bouckaert & G. De Geest (eds.), *Encyclopedia of Law and Economics*, Cheltenham: Edward Elgar, 2nd edition, 2010, forthcoming.

Guerriero 2011a
Guerriero, C., *The Political Economy of (De)Regulation: Theory and Evidence from the U.S. Electricity Market*, Working Paper, 2011.

Guerriero 2011b
Guerriero, C., *Endogenous Legal Traditions and Economic Outcomes*, Working Paper, 2011.

Guiso, Sapienza & Zingales 2006
Guiso, L., Sapienza, P. & Zingales, L., 'Does Culture Affect Economic Outcomes?', *Journal of Economic Perspectives*, 2006, p. 23-48.

Hadfield 2011
Hadfield, G.K., 'The Dynamic Quality of Law: The Role of Judicial Incentives and Legal Human Capital in the Adaptation of Law', *Journal of Economic Behavior and Organization*, 2011, forthcoming.

Hansmann & Kraakman 2000
Hansmann, H. & Kraakman, R.H., 'The Essential Role of Organizational Law', *Yale Law Journal*, 2000, p. 387-440.

Harris 2000
Harris, R., *Industrializing English Law: Entrepreneurship and Business Organization, 1720-1844*, Cambridge: Cambridge University Press, 2000.

Henry & Miller 2009
Henry, P.B. & Miller, C., 'Institutions versus Policies: A Tale of Two Islands', *American Economic Review*, 2009, p. 261-267.

Herrmann, Thöni & Gächter 2008
Herrmann, B., Thöni, C. & Gächter, S., 'Antisocial Punishment Across Societies', *Science*, 2008, p. 1362-1367.

Holmes 1881
Holmes, O.W., *The Common Law*, Boston: Little Brown, and Co., 1881.

Holtman 1967
Holtman, R.B., *The Napoleonic Revolution*, New York: J.B. Lippincott, 1967.

Klerman & Mahoney 2007
Klerman, D. & Mahoney, P.G., 'Legal Origin?', *Journal of Comparative Economics*, 2007, p. 278-293.

La Porta, Lopez-de-Silanes & Shleifer 2008
La Porta, R., Lopez-de-Silanes, F. &. Shleifer, A., 'The Economic Consequences of Legal Origins', *Journal of Economic Literature*, 2008, p. 285-332.

La Porta *et al.* 1998
La Porta, R., Lopez-de-Silanes, F., Shleifer, A. & Vishny, R.W., 'Law and Finance', *Journal of Political Economy*, 1998, p. 1113-1155.

Levmore 1987
Levmore, S., 'Variety and Uniformity in the Treatment of the Good-Faith Purchaser', *Journal of Legal Studies*, 1987, p. 43-65.

Maucourant 2004
Maucourant, J., 'Rationalité économique ou comportements socio-économiques', in: J. Andreau, J. France & S. Pittia (eds.), *Mentalités et choix économiques des Romains*, Bordeaux: Ausonius, 2004, p. 227-240.

Moses 1973
Moses, I.F., *The Ancient Economy*, London: Chatto & Windus, 1973.

Musacchio 2010
Musacchio, A., *Law and Finance C. 1900*, Working Paper, 2010.

Oates 1972
Oates, W.E., *Fiscal Federalism*, New York: Harcourt Brace, 1972.

Pearson 1957
Pearson, H.W., 'The Secular Debate on Economic Primitivism' in: K. Polany, C.M. Arensberg & H.W. Pearson (eds), *Trade and Market in the Early Empires. Economies in History and Theory*, Glencoe: The Free Press, 1957, p. 3-11.

Perotti & Von Thadden 2006
Perotti, E. & Von Thadden, E.-L., 'The Political Economy of Corporate Control and Labor Rents', *Journal of Political Economy*, 2006, p. 145-174.

Persson & Tabellini 2009
Persson, T. & Tabellini, G., 'Democratic Capital: The Nexus of Political and Economic Change', *American Economic Journal: Macroeconomics*, 2009, p. 88-126.

Pistor & Xu 2003
Pistor, K. & Xu, C., 'Incomplete Law', *New York University Journal of International Law and Politics*, 2003, p. 931-1013.

Roe 1996
Roe, M.J., 'Chaos and Evolution in Law and Economics', *Harvard Law Review*, 1996, p. 641-668.

Romano 1985
Romano, R., 'Law as a Product: Some Pieces of the Incorporation Puzzle', *Journal of Law, Economics and Organization*, 1985, p. 225-283.

Rostovtseff 1957
Rostovtseff, M.I., *The Social and Economic History of the Roman Empire*, Oxford: Oxford University Press, 1957.

Scheidel, Morris & Saller 2007
Scheidel, W., Morris, I. & Saller, R.P., *The Cambridge Economic History of the Greco-Roman World*, Cambridge: Cambridge University Press, 2007.

Schwartz & Scott 2011
Schwartz, A. & Scott, R.E., 'Rethinking the Laws of Good Faith Purchase', *Columbia Law Review*, 2011 (forthcoming).

Smits 2011
Smits, J.M., 'Is Law a Parasite? An Evolutionary Explanation of Differences among Legal Traditions', *Review of Law and Economics*, 2011 (forthcoming).

Tabellini 2010
Tabellini, G., 'Culture and Institutions: Economic Development in the Regions of Europe', *Journal of European Economic Association*, 2010, p. 677-716.

Temin 2006
Temin, P., 'The Economy of the Early Roman Empire', *Journal of Economic Perspectives*, 2006, p. 133-151.

Tiebout 1956
Tiebout, C.M., 'A Pure Theory of Local Expenditures', *Journal of Political Economy*, 1956, p. 416-433.

Watson 2009
Watson, A. (ed.), *The Digest of Justinian*, Philadelphia (PA): University of Pennsylvania Press, 2009.

Zweigert & Kötz 1998
Zweigert, K. & Kötz, H., *Introduction to Comparative Law*, Oxford-New York: Oxford University Press, 1998.

Robert D. Cooter
Hans-Bernd
Schäfer

MAKE OR TAKE, WHY LAW CAN CAUSE GROWTH

1. Introduction

In a coral reef, an animal (polyp) creates a hard shell around itself that protects many single-celled plants (zooxanthellae) living within its flesh. The plants produce most of the animal's food and energy. Similarly, the state is needed to protect the makers of society's wealth from the takers. Most rich nations today became wealthy because the state and social norms channelled the efforts of their citizens into making wealth. Conversely, many poor nations stay that way because the state and social norms channel too much effort into taking wealth from others.

All countries have makers and takers of wealth, but the balance between them differs by place and time. In striking the balance, much depends on law. The types of law needed to protect the makers of wealth include property, contracts, crimes, finance, corporations, regulation, antitrust, labour law, taxation, and torts. When law enables creative people who make wealth to keep much of it, the state channels their energies into enriching the nation by enriching themselves. Conversely, when laws allow the strong to take wealth from its makers, the state channels the energies of people into enriching themselves by impoverishing the nation. In these countries, taking less from entrepreneurs would cause wealth to grow, like catching fewer anchovies would cause the stock of fish to grow in the ocean off Peru.[1]

We cannot explain how nations grow rich without distinguishing between making and taking wealth. This distinction engages the deepest political disagreements between left and right about the worth of different groups and classes in society. We trespass reluctantly on this contested ground. This chapter begins with a satellite's view of the productivity of wage earners, capitalists, and innovators. We explain two classical theories – the labour theory of value and marginal productivity theory. We also explain a novel theory about the productivity of entrepreneurs who supply many economic innovations.

1 All the world's fisheries are beyond the maximum sustainable yield. For theory and data, see Tietenberg 1992.

2. Who takes Wealth?

Distinguishing wealth-making from wealth-taking is easy when the contrast is stark. In the years before 1220, artisans and merchants in Bukhara on the 'Silk Road' enriched their city, but that year Bukhara opened its gates to an over-powering army sent by Genghis Khan. Instead of leniency, the invaders took Bukhara's wealth, enslaved the useful population, and reduced the city to a gravel pit. Similarly people who take wealth from others in the modern economy include gangsters, frauds, autocrats, commissars, cartels, stock manipulators, corrupt unions, bribe-seeking politicians, and monopolists of many kinds. We will distinguish three ways to take wealth from others: theft and bribes (criminal), subsidies and regulations (political), and cartels and monopolies (market power).

2.1. *Theft and Bribes*

Mineral resources are the most saleable assets in many poor countries. After communism collapsed in Russia in 1989, gangster-capitalists looted the state's mineral resources and sold them abroad. The richest 300 people in the world in 2003, according to Forbes Magazine, included 16 Russians, 11 of whom made their wealth in oil. Mikhail Khodorkovsky, the richest of the gangster capitalists, was arrested in 2005, sentenced to nine years in prison, and the Russian state expropriated his company. Commentators disagree about whether Khodorkovsky behaved worse or better than the state officials who prosecuted him.[2]

Khodorkovsky was a private businessman, whereas some mineral thieves are government officials. Forbes magazine makes an annual guess of the world's 10 richest 'kings, queens, and dictators'. Most people on the list rule oil-rich countries (but not all - the 2006 list includes the Queen of England and Fidel Castro). To illustrate how power makes politicians rich, after oil was discovered in 1995 in Equatorial Guinea, its ruler, Teodoro Obiang, and his government deposited $ 700 million in private accounts in the Riggs Bank of Washington, D.C. These facts surfaced when regulators fined the bank for not reporting possible money laundering. Similarly, Sese Seku Mobutu, Congo's president from 1960-1997, held billions of dollars in Swiss Bank accounts that he had ransacked from his country.[3]

While oil-rich government officials mostly take their wealth from the state, other government officials take wealth from private citizens. Most constitutions require the state to compensate private owners for taking their property. Some politicians, however, are above the constitution. When power outweighs law, politicians can expropriate private citizens, especially their enemies. In 2000 President Mugabe of Zimbabwe encouraged his political allies to expropriate the

2 Khodorkovsky's opponents believe that he was correctly convicted for his criminal actions related to the privatization of state assets during the 1990s. Khodorkovsky's supporters, however, believe that Vladimir Putin, the Russian President, was retaliating for Khodorkovsky's support of political groups that oppose the government's policies.

3 For the whereabouts of Mobutu's billions, see Wrong 2007.

farms of white citizens. The Zimbabwe constitution prohibited the state from taking land without compensation, so Mugabe amended the constitution.[4]

Instead of stealing oil or land, however, many corrupt officials extort small sums of money from people who need something from them. The officials may demand a bribe for a license, performance of a duty, over-looking a regulatory violation or tax liability, obtaining a state document, granting a variance, or holding a hearing. A 'corruption tax' i.e. the cost of pervasive petty bribes, can be imposed on businesses. The corruption tax slows growth like an under-inflated tire slows an automobile.

2.2. *Subsidies and Regulations*

We discussed illegal ways to take wealth from others, notably stealing and extracting bribes. Alternatively, instead of breaking the law, people can use law to take wealth from others. Thus privileged industries and firms extract state subsidies at the expense of taxpayers. Farmers subsidized city workers in Peron's Argentina and Stalin's Russia, whereas city workers subsidize farmers in the U.S. and the European Union. In Tanzania protective tariffs kept a company in the business of assembling bicycles from imported components that cost more than importing assembled bicycles.[5] One country or another subsidizes telephones, banking, railroads, electricity, steel manufacturing, airplane flights, windmills, coalmines, southern industries, northern industries, core industries, export industries, green industries, minority businesses, majority businesses, and so forth.

Subsidies are part of the government's budget. Alternatively, special interests often disguise subsidies as when lobbyists riddle tax codes with special provisions. To disguise tax subsidies, loopholes are called 'incentives' that allegedly serve national goals like oil exploration, energy conservation, self-sufficiency in food, small business development, small-scale farming, and home ownership. A clever accountant smiles slyly when he says to his client, 'There are no tax loopholes, only tax incentives'.

Besides tax loopholes, the state directs money from citizens to its favourites by restricting competition. To get rich by restricting competition, obtain an exclusive license to operate cabs at an international airport, sell road signs to a city through closed bidding, own all of a country's electro-magnetic spectrum for mobile phones, or build cars behind tariff walls in a country with two automobile plants. One country or another requires farmers to sell coffee beans exclusively to a state exporter at prices below world market prices, forbids selling aspirin without a pharmaceutical license, prohibits optometrists and lawyers from advertising their prices, requires

4 The amendment shifted the responsibility for compensating white farmers from Zimbabwe to its former colonial power, Britain. In the end, no one compensated them, most of them were robbed and exiled, and some of them were murdered. For a popular memoir of these events, see Godwin 2006. For facts about compensation, see Pan 2005.

5 Other studies have found goods assembled in developing countries whose imported components cost more than importing the assembled good. The validity of these results has also been challenged. For a survey see Bruton 1998.

banks to lend to political favourites at below-market rates, and forbids dry cleaners from locating within a mile of each other.

Restrictions on competition are usually disguised through licenses, charters, permits, restrictions, regulations, orders, variances, privileges, and government contracts.[6] By such devices, administrators and politicians determine where a factory can locate, what goods it can produce, to whom it must sell, and whom it employs. These devices shield the friends of politicians from competition, and the friends repay the politicians with donations, bribes, and electoral support. Political power can restrict competition and create market power for politically favoured factions of all kinds - entrepreneurs, unions, the upper class, the working class, the ethnic majority, the ethnic minority, men, women, optometrists, pharmacists, defence contractors, religious schools, state schools, to name a few. The authors and beneficiaries of these restrictions justify them in the name of fairness, employment, economic growth, national security, equal opportunity, public health, consumer protection, pollution abatement, and so on.

2.3. *Cartels and Monopolies*

Whenever executives in competing firms talk to each other, consumers are in peril. Talk leads to constraints on trade - businessmen set prices and divide territory like European colonialists divided Africa in the 19th century. To combat this problem, most countries enacted statutes in the 20th century that prohibit firms from collaborating to set prices or divide territory. If enforced impartially, these statutes can benefit the public, but administering them is often politicized. The simplest and most reliable antitrust policy for most sectors of an economy is free trade and removal of administrative barriers to firms entering and exiting from markets.

While antitrust law forbids private businesses from organizing cartels, governments routinely do so. The firms in an industry sometimes capture its regulator, who operates a cartel on their behalf. To illustrate, a plane flight from Boston to Washington, which passes over several states, cost about twice as much in 1980 as a flight of similar distance from San Francisco to San Diego, which remains within the state of California. The fact that the federal government regulated air travel between states, and not within California, explains the price difference. On Boston-to-Washington flights that cross state lines, federal law allowed competing airlines to ask their regulator to increase the legal fares charged to passengers. On San-Francisco-to-San-Diego flights, however, the presidents of competing airlines who had such a discussion risked fines or imprisonment for violating antitrust laws.

We have discussed three harmful ways that people take wealth from each other: illegally through theft and bribes, legally through state subsidies and regulations, and by monopolies and cartels that can be legal or illegal. Whereas innovators get paid less than the wealth that they make for society, businesses that take wealth get paid more than they make. Furthermore, people who make wealth must use some of it to fend off those who take wealth. Thus laws which encourage people to

6 See Dixit 1987; Olson 1971; Stigler 1971.

make wealth enrich the nation, whereas laws which encourage people to take wealth, impoverish it. Many business fortunes come from a combination of making and taking wealth, and law determines the balance between them.

3. Who makes Wealth?

We have discussed easy examples of people who take wealth from others. In contrast, entrepreneurs, industrialists, farmers, labourers, shopkeepers, scientists, programmers, and teachers mostly make wealth. However, the division of labour obscures exactly how much most people make in a complex economy. Sorting out their contributions is a fundamental task of economic theory. We will frame the problem and discuss some theories.

3.1. Are Workers exploited?

A factory in Mumbai (formerly Bombay) makes cloth from Egyptian cotton and German dyes. It sells the cloth to a factory in Kolkata (formerly Calcutta). A seamstress in the Kolkata factory uses the cloth, a pattern, a sewing machine, a building, and electricity to sew jackets. She sews 10 jackets per week and her weekly wages equals 600 rupees. The Kolkata factory sells the jackets to an Italian wholesaler for 2,500 rupees each. Does the factory owner keep most of the wealth that seamstress makes, or does the factory owner pay most of it to her in wages?

Before answering, we remark on the meaning of these numbers. In India a person can survive on 600 rupees per week by buying in local markets. 600 rupees exchanges roughly for 10 U.S. dollars, which will not buy enough in U.S. markets to survive. For comparing living standards in different countries, wages should be compared according to their local purchasing power, not international exchange rates. However, we convert rupees to U.S. dollars to make our calculations more transparent for most readers. Thus the seamstress sews 10 jackets per week, which the factory sells for $ 50 each or $ 500 for all 10. Out of the $ 500 in revenues, the factory pays the Kolkata seamstress $ 10 per week.

Does the wage of $ 10 per week approximately equal the wealth that the seamstress makes, or does the factory owner pay her a fraction of what she makes? Two classical theories give opposite answers. The first is due to Karl Marx, who remains an icon in many universities in developing countries (although seldom in their economics departments). Besides being influential, Marxist theory is useful intellectually because of its logical purity. According to Marx's labour theory of value, workers make everything and capitalists receive too much of it.[7] To simplify a complicated theory, say that the factory owner supplies the seamstress with inputs such as cloth and electricity, and these inputs cost $ 400 per week. Her weekly output of 10 jackets sells for $ 500. The factory owner pays her $ 10 per week

7 This is the 'emiseration hypothesis'. Note that Marx also predicted rising production and declining profits. Noting the inconsistency of these prediction, Robert Solow remarked that Marx made one prediction too many.

in wages and keeps $ 90 for himself. According to Marxist theory, the value of her work is closer to $ 100 per week than to her wage of $ 10. The difference of $ 90 measures the extent of her exploitation by the factory owner.

Turning from Marx to microeconomics, its basic theory of wages is marginalism, which parses these numbers differently. Besides buying inputs from others, the factory owns some of the inputs that it supplies to the seamstress, such as the sewing machine and the building where she works. Capital was needed to buy them. The owner could liquidate these assets and invest the money elsewhere. Thus the capital used by the seamstress has an opportunity cost – the cost of the opportunity foregone by not investing the capital elsewhere. If all the relevant markets are competitive, then the $ 90 that the factory owner keeps from sales revenues equals the opportunity cost of his capital. Thus Marxism and marginalism disagree over whether the factory exploits workers or gets paid the value of his capital. In general, marginalism holds that competition causes the price of each factor of production (capital, labour, land, and so on) to equal the value of its marginal product. If the workers wage equals her marginal product, then she is not exploited. And if the capitalist's marginal product equals his profits, then he is not an exploiter.

Which theory of wage determination is more nearly correct? Most modern economists think that the answer depends on the structure of labour markets. When employers must compete with each other to hire able workers, they lose the power to pay someone less than the market value of what she makes.[8] Competition roughly equates wages and marginal product. Later we review some data showing that in large cities or in countries where people can move and freely choose their working place, marginal productivity theory is approximately correct and the pay of most workers roughly equals the market value of what they produce.

In contrast, keeping wages below marginal productivity requires thwarting competition by cartels, serfdom, bonded labour, and the like.[9] Without competition, employers can exploit workers. Thus millions of people in India, Pakistan and Nepal are trapped in debt bondage and forced to work for an individual employer to repay loans, even though international conventions ban bonded labour.[10] Bonded labour concentrates in villages where competition is weak, but it also exists in big cities where people work as 'slum dogs'. Such victims include some textile workers. The problem would disappear if effective laws allowed debtors to escape their creditors through bankruptcy.

8 Here is how it works. The employer pays the seamstress her wage and sells her product. If her product exceeds her wage, the employer earns a profit from her labour. Competition will prevent him from doing so. If her employer pays her a wage that is below the value of her product, another employer can profit by inducing her to change jobs at a slightly higher wage. Competition among employers should bid up her wage until it approaches her marginal value product, which is $ 10 per week.

9 For a Marxist theory that focuses on monopoly power, see Baran & Sweezy 1966.

10 UN Sub-Commission on the Promotion and Protection of Human Rights, February 2001 The Enslavement of Dalit and Indigenous Communities in India, Nepal and Pakistan through Bondage.

Modern labour economics is much more complicated than the contrast between Marx and marginalism. It encompasses many departures from marginal productivity theory such as cartels, regulations, tariffs, unions, minimum wage legislation, and executive compensation in public companies. It also encompasses a hot political issue in many countries - discrimination that favours men over women, high caste over low caste, and the dominant ethnicity or tribe or religion over the subordinate ones.[11] Theories of modern labour economics explain earnings below marginal product as with discrimination, or earnings above marginal product as sometimes happens with executives, unionized workers, and the beneficiaries of quota systems.

3.2. *Are Entrepreneurs too Rich? Are Workers exploited?*

We asked, 'How much does a worker make and how much does she keep?' Now we ask the same question about an innovator. To answer it, we divide the life-cycle of an innovation into phrases as depicted in Figure 1. Before the innovation, the industry is in competitive equilibrium and its firms receive the normal rate of profit. In the first phase of innovation, one firm has a new idea and invests money to develop it. Many innovators try and few succeed. Thus recent U.S. data suggests that 40 per cent of new businesses survive and 60 per cent disappear within four years.[12] If development succeeds, the innovator goes to the second phase and launches the innovation in the market. On launch, the innovator earns extra-ordinary profits because the product has no competitors. In the third phase, the new idea disseminates to imitators, whose competition causes a fall in the innovator's profits. In the fourth and final phase, the industry settles into equilibrium like the crowd that eventually stops yelling after a goal is scored at a football match. The innovator's profits fall to the normal rate of return, as they were in the beginning.

Figure 1: Life-Cycle of an Innovation

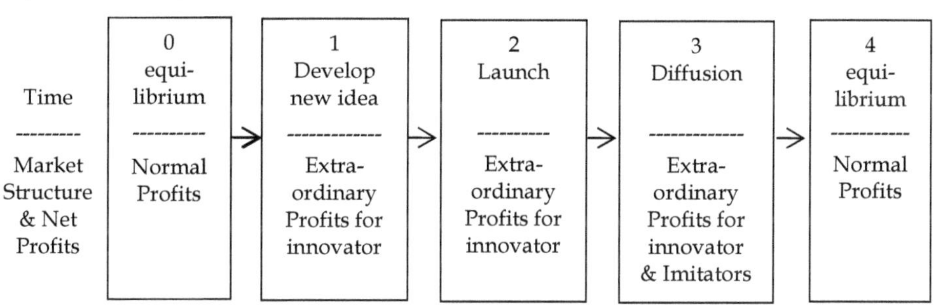

[11] For a summary of economic theories of discrimination as market imperfections, see Cooter 2000, Chapter 14.

[12] 44 per cent of U.S. businesses started in the 1990s still existed 4 years afterwards. See Knap 2005. The number given by Dun and Bradstreet is 37 per cent as cited in 'Some of the Reasons Why Business Fail and How to Avoid Them', *Entrepreneur Weekly*, Issue 36, 3-10-96.

Averaged over the life-cycle, the successful innovator receives extraordinary profits, which exceed the normal profits earned by non-innovators. However, even the most successful innovator earns much less than the innovation's economic value to society. When the innovator sells the innovative product to buyers, they presumably value it more than they pay for it. Otherwise they would not buy it. The 'consumer's surplus' is the difference between an innovation's value to a buyer and the price he pays for it. In addition, as the innovation disseminates, some of its value goes to the imitators as extraordinary profits. Thus the innovation's social value is divided among innovators, imitators, and consumers.

Whenever law and policy creates incentives that cause another innovation, the innovator benefits and so do the imitators and consumers. Law and policy affect the shares of these three groups in the social value of innovations. Is the share of innovator too high or too low? Few people will object to small producers keeping much of the value of their innovations, like Indian farmers adapting 'miracle wheat' to local conditions, or Beijing shopkeepers discovering that their customers will buy coffee, or a Malaysian converting a craft shop into a textile factory.

What about rich people? A few stars in the Milky Way are brightest, and a few entrepreneurs are richest. The five richest people in the world in 2008 were, in order, Warren Buffett, Carlos Slim, Bill Gates, Lakshmi Mittal, and Mukesh Ambani. They averaged approximately $ 50 billion in wealth each.[13] If you invested that much money in no-risk bonds, you would have to spend approximately $ 4,500 per minute to keep your wealth from growing larger.[14]

Besides great wealth, these five people have something else in common: They did not inherit vast agricultural estates like Indian maharajas in colonial times, or own desert sands that float on oil like Saudi princes, or divert taxes into Swiss bank accounts like African dictators, or collect massive bailouts from taxpayers like American investment bankers. Rather, they created extraordinarily profitable businesses.[15] To become super rich, you should identify companies that will grow fastest and invest in them (Warren Buffett), supply mobile phone service to Mexicans (Carlos Slim), develop a computer operating system that becomes a world standard (Bill Gates), reorganize steel manufacturing in the world's rust belts (Lakshmi Mittal), or develop the Indian petrochemical industry (Mukesh Ambani).

For all five, a significant portion of their wealth apparently came from developing new ideas. As explained in this chapter's prelude, innovation benefits the nation as a whole and causes wealth to accumulate unimaginably quickly. Presumably they also gained from unproductive advantages like natural monopoly, political patronage, or regulatory favouritism. We can only guess at the combination of creative and non-productive sources of their wealth. In any case, their creativity

13 Forbes magazine annually estimates the wealth of the world's richest people and ranks them.

14 $ 50 billion invested at 5 per cent per year yields enough interest to spend roughly $ 4.500 per minute for a year.

15 Three of the five started life relatively poor and made all of their wealth. Two of the five started life with modest wealth and then added vastly to it. Forbes magazine's list of people with at least $ 1 billion in personal wealth in 2006 consisted of 746 people, most of whom made their money through business.

benefitted consumers, producers, and themselves by billions of dollars. Such is the power of innovation and compound growth.

4. Conclusion

Clear thinking about the economy requires skepticism about people. For predictive accuracy, economic theorists since Adam Smith in the 18th century assume that most people want more wealth, and they will devote talent and energy to getting it. Oliver Wendell Holmes, the American legal theorist and Supreme Court Justice, thought that law should aim at bad people who will disobey unless coerced, not good people who obey willingly. Combining Smith and Holmes, law and economics scholars usually assume that most people devote talent and energy to getting more wealth, and law's coercive force must channel and constrain their pursuit of it.

People can acquire wealth by making or taking it. If businessmen and entrepreneurs mostly get their wealth by taking it from others, then abolishing capital markets should cause faster economic growth, like killing parasites in a puppy's intestines. Conversely, if businessmen and entrepreneurs mostly get their wealth by making it, then securing their property through law will cause faster growth, like feeding a puppy. This requires institutions in the sense of norms, which protect investors and whose violation is sanctioned. It does not imply a particular institutional form.

Bibliography

Baran & Sweezy 1966
Baran, P.A. & Sweezy, P.M., *Monopoly Capital; An Essay on the American Economic and Social Order*, New York: Monthly Review Press, 1966.

Bruton 1998
Bruton, H.J., 'A Reconsideration of Import Substitution', *Journal of Economic Literature*, 1998, p. 903-936.

Cooter 2000
Cooter's, R. *The Strategic Constitution*, Princeton: Princeton University Press, 2000.

Dixit 1987
Dixit, A., 'On Pareto-Improving Distributions of Aggregate Economic Gains', *Journal of Economic Theory*, 1987, p. 133-153.

Godwin 2006
Godwin, P., *When a Crocodile Eats the Sun: A memoir of Africa*, New York: Little Brown and company, 2006.

Knap 2005
Knap, A.E., 'Survival and Longevity in the Business Employment Dynamics Data', *Bureau of Labour Statistics of the U.S. Department of Labour*, 2005.

Olson 1971
Olson, M., *The Logic of Collective Action: Public Goods and the Theory of Groups*, (revised edition edition.), Cambridge: Harvard University Press, 1971.

Pan 2005
Pan, E., *Africa: Mugabe's Zimbabwe*, available at: <http://www.cfr.org/publication/7723/africa.html>, Council on Foreign Relations, 2005.

Stigler 1971
Stigler, G., 'The Theory of Economic Regulation', *Bell Journal of Economics and Management Science*, 1971, p. 3-18.

Tietenberg 1992
Tietenberg, T., *Environmental and Natural Resource Economics*, 3rd edition, New York, NY: Harper Collins Publishers, 1992.

Wrong 2007
Wrong, M., 'Mystery of Mobutu's Millions', *New Statesman*, 26 July 2007, available at: <http://www.newstatesman.com/africa/2007/07/wrong-mobutu-congolese>.

Anthony Ogus

LEGAL SYSTEMS AS NETWORKS

1. The Background

Within the past thirty years or so, the information technology revolution and the increasing integration of markets across national boundaries have changed what economic actors are seeking from law and legal systems.[1] In Hadfield's words, the new economy is 'knowledge-based, transaction-driven, high velocity, highly fluid, highly differentiated, emergent - and increasingly hard to predict'.[2] In a world in which transactions often take place across jurisdictional boundaries, legal solutions and legal procedures designed by a particular legal system for phenomena within its own territory may prove to be inadequate or inappropriate. So also, as the nature of many transactions changes to accommodate technological developments, traditional legal formats become quickly outdated. How well can and do legal systems perform in meeting these challenges? How adept are they at reducing legal transactions costs and legal dispute-resolving costs?

Two areas of debate are related to these questions. Concern with them led legal policymakers, during the last decade of the twentieth century, to press for harmonization of, or at least greater compatibility between, national legal systems on instruments and principles that vitally affect transboundary transactions.[3] Others, however, viewed such policies, imposed from the top, as unnecessary, since the force of market pressure from below and the presence of competition between national legal orders should determine what degree of harmonization or compatibility is desirable.[4] And for a third group, harmonization was, in any event, inherently impossible given the fundamental differences between legal cultures, notably those of the common law and the civil law.[5]

A second area of debate was provoked by a series of studies, emerging principally from the World Bank, purporting to show that common law systems have

1 Hadfield 2010.
2 Hadfield 2010, p. 4.
3 Hartkamp & Von Bar 1998.
4 Van den Bergh 1996.
5 Legrand 1996.

been more successful in fostering economic development than civil law systems.[6] While the methodology involved in these studies has been sharply criticized,[7] and the findings challenged on other grounds,[8] the ensuing debate has stimulated much interest in the question posed in the first paragraph of how legal systems in general perform in meeting the challenges posed by technical change and economic development; so also what are the variables within particular legal systems which determine success or otherwise.

In a previous publication,[9] I attempted to make a modest contribution to this last debate. I argued that it was helpful to recognize the network qualities of particular legal cultures. The characterization of legal culture as a network provided not only a means of understanding how legal systems develop to meet the demands made of them. It also facilitated identification of the key players in these developments and their motivation for furthering, or conversely hindering, reform. In this paper, I seek to build on this idea, to show how network characteristics may apply to features within a legal system as well as to systems as a whole. I address the normative question of the extent to which legal networks are desirable and how they may be contained by competition both internal and external to a particular legal system. In the latter half of the paper, I move to some generalizations on how legal networks might predictably affect legal evolution. I conclude with some implications which this analysis might have both for harmonization policies and the current debate on the importance of legal origins.

2. The Basics of Networks

A network is a system providing links, often of a technical character, for users of a product or service[10] - the fax (or facsimile) means of communication is a good example. Since the value to a single user depends on the number of other users, so therefore the social value of the network increases as more users adopt it. In other words, significant positive externalities are generated by individual adherents to the system.[11] It follows that demand for a network reflects not only the preferences of individual users but also their prediction of how many other users will opt for the system. This leads to another important feature which has been referred to as the 'tippy' quality of networks.[12] Once a particular system begins to acquire a degree of popularity, it can benefit from a spiralling of demand, as that popularity will render it attractive to an increasing number of users. Conversely, once demand begins to drop, a vicious circle can ensue as, for that reason, it loses its value for other users.

The dominance of a particular network in a market may enable its suppliers to enjoy monopolistic profits, but these are unlikely to be sustainable for a substantial

6 La Porta, Lopez-de-Silanes & Shleifer 2008.
7 Armour *et al.* 2009.
8 Berkowitz, Pistor & Richard 2003.
9 Ogus 2002.
10 Economides 1996.
11 Page & Lopatka 2000.
12 Shapiro & Varian 1998.

period as the prospect of such profits will lure other suppliers to develop rival systems which might eventually supplant the incumbent's product or service. Also it may be possible for an alternative system to be rendered compatible with the latter. On the assumption that consumers value a variety, this will be socially beneficial.[13] Prospective suppliers have, in consequence, a delicate choice: either to go for an incompatible alternative to the incumbent system, hoping to oust it and secure the monopolistic profits; or, which may be particularly attractive to those who are risk-averse, to render the new system compatible and share the profits with the incumbent. And the incumbent supplier has an equivalent dilemma, whether or not to resist compatibility. An important consideration for these purposes is the extent to which usage is constrained by technological paradigms. Where these are prevalent, the costs of switching from one network to another will be high and developments within the industry will be path dependent.[14]

Industries in which networks arise are indeed generally technologically sophisticated and one tends to associate them with modern communication systems, but they occur also in relation to some infrastructure services which have been around for a long time. Take the railways, the development of which well illustrates the features of networks. At first, largely dependent on private initiative, there was competition between services operating different technical specifications, notably the 'broad' and 'standard' gauges. However, as the demand for intercommunication between the services increased, so there was pressure for one set of specifications to be come dominant, and the 'standard' gauge prevailed, first within national boundaries and subsequently for transfrontier traffic.[15]

Although most networks comprise 'physical' entities, they need not be so confined. Languages are effectively networks. So, for example, while the positive externalities associated with English internationally have led to a spiralling upwards in its use, Esperanto has moved in the opposite direction.[16] Within national borders, where there is significant competition between two or more languages, network analysis can have important implications for language policy.[17] So, what about law?

3. Network Characteristics of Legal Phenomena: Standard Terms and Precedent

Let us begin with a relatively simple example of legal phenomena operating as a network. A well-known feature of legal practice is the creation and use of standard-form contracts and standard-form terms in contracts and other legal transactions, such as wills and articles of incorporation. Standardization of these instruments obviously creates benefits for those engaged in the transactions: it lowers the cost of drafting, and it reduces uncertainty regarding interpretation, since reference can be made to prior decisions on the same terms. But it also generates network benefits

13 Katz & Shapiro 1994.
14 Arthur 1989.
15 Wedgewood 1946.
16 Shapiro & Varian 1998.
17 For Canada, see Church & King 1993.

since it reduces the cost of professional legal services in the future for others involved in similar transactions.[18] If the parties to those transactions and their legal advisers can free ride on the investment and experience of the earlier formulations, and if the value to them is not taken into consideration by the originators of the standard, these network benefits become network externalities.[19]

Precedents created by judicial decisions can be analysed in a similar way. At least in those legal systems relying on stare decisis, these decisions have a social value for third parties active in the relevant area of law.[20] An accumulation of case law thus serves to provide information to market actors about the nature of legal obligations, and the more sensitive the decisions are to the preferences of those actors, the greater the adherence to the body of law.[21] In theory, then, a case-law system, as with other networks, can generate a beneficial spiral, with increasing use of the precedent by some attracting even greater use by others.

The normative question of the extent to which legal phenomena of this kind giving rise to network benefits should be encouraged is not however straightforward. In some contexts, standardization is not optimal.[22] First, early adopters of a term, or creators of a precedent, may not appreciate the social benefits dimension and in consequence may opt for a formulation which maximizes the value for them but not for third parties. Secondly, the principal-agent problem which afflicts legal professional work may mean that lawyers working for subsequent actors may too readily opt for the existing precedent rather than customize the terms for their clients.[23] It will be less costly for them to do so not only for the obvious reason that they will not have to spend time and effort drafting the bespoke terms; but also because, in comparison to the standard term, there will be greater uncertainty regarding judicial interpretation of unfamiliar formulations. In addition, there is the phenomenon of herd instinct, better known in the behaviouralist literature as conformity or status quo bias, clients' preferences being to stick to what they know or has been done before, rather than risk novelty.[24] Path dependency, then, can play a key role in networks of this kind, inhibiting evolution of efficient choices.

When inefficiency results from the presence of a network externality, there has been some discussion of how this might be corrected.[25] One suggestion is that, with or without legislative aid, judges should be given greater discretion to adjust standard terms to meet the assumed intentions of the parties to a particular transaction. Another is that publicly funded bodies should undertake the task of creating default standard terms because these organizations might be in the best position to determine what will maximize social value.

18 Kahan & Klausner 1997.
19 Ribstein & Kobayashi 2001.
20 Harnay & Marciano 2003.
21 Chen 2010.
22 Kahan & Klausner 1997.
23 Kahan & Klausner 1996.
24 Kahan & Klausner 1996.
25 Ribstein & Kobayashi 2001.

4. Legal Systems as Networks

It is a more ambitious exercise to consider legal systems as a whole, or significant parts of them, as distinctive networks, but in the light of the previous section, it is not difficult to imagine how such networks might evolve.[26] In all societies there is a need for disputes over resources to be resolved and specialists emerge who are particularly adept at carrying out this task. To economize on their costs of decision-making, these individuals will over time develop not only standard terms and rules to deal with frequently recurring situations but also linguistic concepts (to reduce communication costs) and procedures and formalities (to reduce fact-finding error costs).[27] Although a single set of concepts, procedures and formalities may not be adopted exclusively within a particular territory, nevertheless, because of the network externalities which its use generates, social value increasing as more adhere to it, one such set is likely to become dominant. The larger the number of transactions designed for this set and the larger the number of disputes resolved by it, the higher the expectation that future transactions and disputes will be governed by the same system.

In some territories the dominance of a particular legal network may be reinforced by political forces. Rulers need law to control activities within their domain and although public law might be the subject of an independent network, because of overlap of functions, there may be scale economies in having some communality of concepts and procedures, or at least compatibility between the two sets. We thus arrive at the notion of some constitutional authorization of the dominant legal network.

Political involvement may extend to the authorized network being granted monopoly status, in the sense that other systems are prohibited from being invoked to determine the legal validity of transactions or legally to resolve disputes. But this is not inevitable. Within a nation state, some degree of competition between different legal networks may be tolerated or even favoured by political rulers. Whether monopoly or competition prevails may depend on cultural or historical factors. For example, different sets of concepts and procedures may have developed in different ethnic communities or as a consequence of successive occupation by different colonial powers - such circumstances often give rise to what have been referred to as hybrid legal systems.[28] But much will also depend on the relationship between governments and the suppliers of legal services.

The suppliers of legal services, legal practitioners, are indeed important for an understanding of the development of legal networks. Most obviously, since their income is derived from operating a particular network, they will seek to acquire for it monopoly status, thus ousting competitors from rival networks. Further, as I have demonstrated in an earlier publication,[29] if they are able to control key features of the network, and their clients cannot transfer business to an alternative network,

26 Ogus 2002.
27 Posner 1973.
28 Örücü, Attwooll & Coyle 1996.
29 Ogus 2002.

they may be able to enhance their profits. For example, if they are able to insist that certain transactions require a substantial amount of legal formalities or if they can ensure that the law in a given area is very complicated, they can increase demand for their services.

Nor is it difficult to understand how legal practitioners may gain control over the rules governing the network. Rulers who seek the cooperation of lawyers in order to exercise their authority, as a price for that support, may be willing to confer on them, explicitly or tacitly, power to regulate the content of the network. Even if this is not the case, and the matter is in principle to be determined by democratic processes, legal practitioners are normally able to exert considerable influence during the legislative process to move the law to outcomes which they regard as desirable simply because of the principal-agent problem. They can claim that they alone have sufficient mastery of the technicalities of the law to be able to make judgements on what legal reforms are and are not feasible. All of this suggests that, unless constrained by external forces, legal networks serve the private interests of legal practitioners as much as, or more than, the interests of their clients. To investigate this further, we need to address more generally the normative dimension of legal networks and the role of competition between them.

5. Legal Networks: the Normative Dimension and Competition

From an economic perspective, the normative basis of legal networks is self-evident: they should meet the preferences of consumers of them at lowest cost. Within a dynamic framework, they should respond innovatively to meet changes in those preferences over time, particularly – as indicated in the first section of this paper – as increasing globalization of markets has placed new demands on legal services.

We saw, when considering networks generally, that though suppliers may be lured by the prospect of monopoly profits, the monopoly status should only be temporary, as rival suppliers have the similar incentive to introduce alternative, or at least compatible networks. Therefore innovation to meet consumer preferences should not be thwarted. Obviously the relevant market being open to competition is crucial for the purpose of this prediction.

If, as we have seen, legal practitioners can exercise control over the content of legal networks and are motivated to further their own interests rather than meeting the preferences of their clients at lowest cost, to what extent is the potential inefficiency of the network constrained by competition? To answer this question, we have to take account of challenges to an existing network both internal and external to the relevant legal system.

Hitherto I have tended to equate legal networks with legal systems, implying that there is likely to be a single legal network within each nation state. In fact, as we have also seen, this is rarely the case because most legal systems embrace a number of legal sub-systems. Historically, in England there were two such parallel systems administered, respectively by the courts of chancery (or equity) and the courts of common law. Now, while the former tended towards greater flexibility, discretion and therefore also uncertainty, the latter applied more rigid, but also more certain, rules.[30] To some extent, litigants could choose which forum would resolve their dispute and it might not be too fanciful to suggest that competition between the two jurisdictions led each of them to converge towards some optimal mix of flexibility and certainty. So also, and not only in England, the law merchant and canon law penetrated the legal system and provided some alternative mode of resolution for certain areas of dispute.[31]

In civil law countries, private law and public law have their own sets of principles, adjudicatory processes, and culture. Now, though these systems might not compete directly for custom, there is some overlap of jurisdiction and thus some competitive pressure at the boundaries of their respective territories. So, for example, there may be some competition between regulatory agencies and the courts for adjudicating on cases involving commercial and industrial activity.[32]

Even where this is not the case, there may be so-called 'yardstick competition', a concept which has played an important role in the regulation of social services.[33] Where each of two or more suppliers has a local monopoly, a regulator can compare what they offer in terms of price and quality in order to ensure that this meets consumer preferences. By way of analogy, if independent legal networks offer significantly different prices and quality, consumer pressure may force them to make adjustments.

In the modern, globalized economy, competition from networks external to the jurisdiction have nevertheless been more important than internal competition. Just as the crossing of national boundaries by a railway service requires technical specifications which are compatible with the systems prevailing both sides of that boundary, so also transfrontier trade necessitates the adoption of legal instruments which can accommodate preferences from either side of the border.

Technically, the matter is governed by private international law which in some areas allows freedom of choice of law for the parties involved in the international transaction. So, in American law, corporations can choose the state whose laws are to govern their organization, and because the governments of the chosen state normally gain tax and other revenue from the decision to incorporate there, they are motivated to attract corporations by making their laws meet the preferences of the corporate decision-makers.[34] Competition between legal networks leading to more efficient law may also be driven by legal practitioners. Most legal systems allow freedom for choice of law clauses in contracts and since those deriving income from legal services arising from the transaction will benefit from their jurisdiction being chosen, they will seek to render the contract law and its procedures attractive to the contracting parties.[35]

30 Plucknett 2010.
31 Plucknett 2010.
32 Chen 2010.
33 Revelli 2006.
34 Romano 1985.
35 Ogus 1999.

Even where there is no direct '*lex*-shopping' of this kind, practitioners who appreciate that, for particular commercial purposes, a foreign jurisdiction offers a more attractive set of legal rules or principles, will want to see some equivalent transplanted in their own system. The endeavours in European jurisdictions to emulate the Anglo-Saxon trust provides an obvious example.[36] Whether such a transplant will succeed is another matter, to which I will return in the following section.

6. Legal Networks and Legal Evolution

Viewing legal systems as legal networks, in the way suggested above, can generate important predictions for legal evolution. It suggests, for example, that if, in relation to particular areas of law, the volume of transfrontier transactions increases relative to purely domestic transactions, so there will be greater competition between networks. Consequently, in those areas, we would expect such competition to push legal systems to greater efficiency in meeting the preferences of market actors, since the benefits of adaptation increase while the costs of adaptation diminish. Thus, to take two examples from the extremes of the transfrontier domestic spectrum, competition between networks should ensure that contract law evolves towards efficiency, whereas within a particular jurisdiction the lack of competition in relation to the law governing immovables will enable practitioners to exploit the network characteristics of that law, enabling them to earn monopolistic rents. It should also be the case that legal networks within smaller jurisdictions, subject to larger volumes of transfrontier commerce, will be more sensitive to competitive pressures than those within larger jurisdictions, and thus more responsive to the preferences of market actors.

Such predictions are nevertheless subject to an important caveat, relating to path dependency.[37] The costs of switching between networks is in general high, and in legal networks these may be particularly high. We have already identified some of the reasons for this: there are the costs of uncertainty in moving away from familiar, often standardized principles and procedures; and there are behavioural phenomena, such as status quo bias. But there are also other explanations.

A long-standing literature,[38] asserts that there are often cultural obstacles to transplants, especially between common law and civil law jurisdictions. For example, the trust may be so inimical to the basic structure of any receiving Continental European legal system that it does not take there. Strategic considerations may also be relevant. Rendering one legal network compatible with another by means of transplant normally requires unilateral reform by one of the two jurisdictions: the other jurisdiction will benefit from compatibility but will not incur the costs. That may lead to an impasse, neither jurisdiction being willing to take the

36 Graziadei, Mattei & Smith 2009.

37 Eckardt 2008.

38 E.g. Legrand 1996.

initiative.[39] If that is the case, then there may be perverse incentives for politicians and legal practitioners to engage in a hand-tying exercise of resisting legal change.[40]

Account must also be taken of organizational factors. The development of legal networks and their potential evolution to efficiency by meeting market actors' preferences depend crucially on the availability of information and how it is disseminated and that depends on how the system's institutions are organized.[41] To take one important dimension, in terms of law-making and law enforcement, a legal system may be more or less centralized. A centralized legal system uses primarily governmental or public agencies to evaluate existing legal principles and institutions, to acquire information as to how responsive these are to the needs of market actors and on what alternatives are used in other systems, to formulate reform proposals, to draft legislative or administrative instruments to implement the proposals, and to enforce those instruments. A decentralized system relies much on independent agencies, even private actors and institutions, to carry out these functions; and, in contrast to centralized institutions which are typically monopolistic, there is often some degree of competition between decentralized institutions. For this, and for other reasons, a decentralized system is likely to be more sensitive to the demands of market actors for legal change.[42]

7. Conclusions: Harmonization and Legal Origins

Network analysis and the predictions articulated in the last section also have implications for the two areas of debate to which I referred in the introduction to this paper. Take first the question of harmonization. Provided that the principles of conflicts of law are sufficient to foster genuine competition between different legal networks, then the content of national legal systems governing areas where there is a significant amount of transboundary transactions should evolve towards meeting market actors' preferences at lowest cost, and interventionist measures of harmonization will be unnecessary. But this is subject to a major caveat, that of path dependency. Some features of an existing legal network may be so deeply entrenched, or so idiosyncratic, that the cost of rendering them compatible with another network may be very high - the Anglo-Saxon trust with its interplay between legal and equitable interests may be an example of this. In such a case, transplants, whether by evolutionary processes or by interventionist harmonization measures, are likely to fail. The consequence is that some degree of incompatibility between legal networks will remain, though this will not necessarily be detrimental to transboundary trade, provided that market actors can opt for the legal network which best meets their preferences.

What then of legal origins? There is relatively little in network analysis to support the somewhat simplistic hypothesis that common law systems invariably facilitate economic growth better than civil law systems. True, the common law has

39 Garoupa & Ogus 2006.

40 Carbonara & Parisi 2009.

41 Chen 2010.

42 Milhaupt & Pistor 2008.

traditionally placed greater reliance on judicial activism and stare decisis which, as we have seen, can generate important network effects. But as we have also seen, since practitioners may be motivated unduly to rely on judicial precedents - which may be the case in some common law jurisdictions - efficiency cannot be guaranteed.

A more nuanced approach to network analysis might nevertheless produce some insights for the debate. A - perhaps the - key variable in assessing the impact of legal systems on economic growth in developing countries is how well a legal network originally externally imposed by colonialist regimes is adaptable to local conditions and pre-existing local legal networks.[43] There are, indeed, two dimensions to this issue. The first relates to compatibility. While the imposed colonialist regime becomes the dominant network and, as such, governs most major transactions within the territory, it must be sufficiently flexible to accommodate, perhaps by some form of authorized recognition, transactions couched in the local network. For their part, practitioners both of the imposed legal network and of the local legal network must recognize that adaptation to the other network and cooperation with its practitioners will be mutually beneficial.

The second dimension relates to competition. An important theme of this paper has been that, for a dominant legal network to evolve efficiently to meet market actors' preferences, it must be subject to competition, internal or external. Now in circumstances when a colonialist power asserts control over a territory, and imposes its legal network upon it, it will generally be the case that it will not tolerate competition from other external networks. However, some degree of competition may be tolerated and even encouraged with local pre-existing networks, perhaps indigenous to the territory, or resulting from previous colonial occupation. If this occurs, as we have seen in section 5, it should thwart the ability of practitioners to capture rents by manipulating the law and its procedures to serve their own interests rather than those of their clients and the local economy more generally.

43 Berkowitz, Pistor & Richard 2003.

Bibliography

Armour *et al.* 2009
Armour, J., Deakin, S., Lele, P. & Siems, M., 'How Do Legal Rules Evolve? Evidence from a Cross-Country Comparison of Shareholder, Creditor, and Worker Protection', *The American Journal of Comparative Law*, 2009, p. 579-629.

Arthur 1989
Arthur, W.B., 'Competing Technologies, Increasing Returns, and Lock-in by Historical Events', *The Economic Journal*, 1989, p. 116-131.

Van den Berg 1996
Van den Berg, R., 'Economic criteria for applying the subsidiarity principle in the European community: The case of competition policy', *International Review of Law and Economics*, 1996, p. 363-383.

Berkowitz, Pistor & Richard 2003
Berkowitz, D., Pistor, K. & Richard, J.-F., 'Economic Development, Legality and the Transplant Effect', *European Economic Review*, 2003, p. 165-195.

Carbonara & Parisi 2009
Carbonara, E. & Parisi, F., 'Choice of Law and Legal Evolution: rethinking the market for legal rules', *Public Choice*, 2009, p. 461-492.

Chen 2010
Chen, R., *The Information Challenge and a Market Solution to Legal Development – A Case Study of Overseas IPOs of China's State Owned Enterprises*, Available at SSRN: <http://ssrn.com/abstract=1665435>, 2010.

Church & King 1993
Church, J. & King, I., 'Bilingualism and Network Externalities', *Canadian Journal of Economics*, 1993, p. 337-345.

Eckardt 2008
Eckardt, M., 'Explaining Legal Change from an Evolutionary Economics Perspective', *German Law Journal*, 2008, p. 437-464.

Economides 1996
Economides, N., 'The Economics of Networks', *International Journal of Industrial Organization*, 1996, p. 673-699.

Garoupa & Ogus 2006
Garoupa N. & Ogus, A., 'A Strategic Interpretation of Legal Transplants', *Journal of Legal Studies*, 2006, 339-363.

Graziadei, Mattei & Smith 2009
Graziadei, M., Mattei, U. & Smith L. (eds.), *Commercial Trusts in European Private Law*, Cambridge: Cambridge University Press, 2009.

Hadfield 2011
Hadfield, G., *Law for a Flat World: Legal Infrastructure and the New Economy*, USC Law Legal Studies Paper No. 10-8. Available at SSRN: <http://ssrn.com/abstract=1567712>.

Harnay & Marciano 1994
Harnay, S. & Marciano, A., 'Judicial Conformity Versus Dissidence: an Economic Analysis of Judicial Precedent', *International Review of Law and Economics*, 1994, p. 405-420.

Hartkamp & Von Bar 1998
Hartkamp, A.S. & Von Bar, C. (eds), *Towards a European Civil Code*, 2nd edition, The Hague: Kluwer, 1998.

Kahan & Klausner 1996
Kahan, M. & Klausner, M., 'Path Dependence in Corporate Contracting: Increasing Returns, Herd Behavior and Cognitive Biases', *Washington University Law Quarterly*, 1996, p. 347-366.

Kahan & Klausner 1997
Kahan, M. & Klausner, M., 'Standardization and Innovation in Corporate Contracting (Or The Economics of Boilerplates)', *Virginia Law Review*, 1997, p. 713-770.

Katz & Shapiro 2008
Katz, M.L. & Shapiro, C., 'Systems Competition and Network Effects', *Journal of Economic Perspectives*, 1993, p. 93-115.

La Porta, Lopez-de-Silanes & Shleifer 2008
La Porta, R., Lopez-de-Silanes, F. & Shleifer, A., 'The Economic Consequences of Legal Origins', *Journal of Economic Literature*, 2008, p. 285-332.

Legrand 1996
Legrand, P., 'European Legal Systems are Not Converging', *International and Comparative Law Quarterly*, 1996, p. 52-81.

Milhaupt & Pistor 2008
Milhaupt, C.J. & Pistor, K., *Law and Capitalism: What Corporate Crises Reveal about Legal Systems and Economic Development around the World*, Chicago: Chicago University Press, 2008.

Ogus 1999
Ogus, A., 'Competition between National Legal Systems: A Contribution of Economic Analysis to Comparative Law, *International and Comparative Law Quarterly*, 1999, p. 405-418.

Ogus 2002
Ogus, A., 'The Economic Basis of Legal Culture: Networks and Monopolization', *Oxford Journal of Legal Studies*, 2002, p. 419-434.

Örücü, Attwooll & Coyle 1996
Örücü, E., Attwooll, E. & Coyle, S. (eds.), *Studies in Legal Systems: Mixed and Mixing*, The Hague: Kluwer, 1996.

Page & Lopatka 1999
Page, W. & Lopatka, J., 'Network Externalitiies', in: B. Bouckaert & G. De Geest (eds.), *Encyclopedia of Law and Economics*, Cheltenham: Edward Elgar, vol. 1, p. 952-980.

Plucknett 2010
Plucknett, T.F.T., *A Concise History of the Common Law*, 3rd edition, Indianapolis: Liberty Fund, 2010.

Posner 1973
Posner, R., 'An Economic Approach to Legal Procedure and Judicial Administration', *Journal of Legal Studies*, 1973, p. 399-458.

Revelli 2006
Revelli, F., 'Performance Rating and Yardstick Competition in Social Service Provision', *Journal of Public Economics*, 2006, p. 459-475.

Ribstein & Kobayashi 2001
Ribstein, L.E. & Kobayashi, B.H., 'Choice of Form and Network Externalities', *William and Mary Law Review*, 2001, p. 79-140.

Romano 1985
Romano, R., 'Law as a Product: Some Pieces of the Incorporation Puzzle', *The Journal of Law, Economics & Organization*, 1985, p. 225-283.

Shapiro & Varian 1999
Shapiro, C. & Varian, H., *Information Rules: A Strategic Guide to the Network Economy*, Cambridge Mass: Harvard Business Press, 1999.

Wedgewood 1946
Wedgewood, R.L., *International Rail Transport*, Oxford: Oxford University Press, 1946.

Thomas S. Ulen

THE ROLE OF LAW IN ECONOMIC GROWTH AND DEVELOPMENT[1]

1. Introduction

Why some nations have grown and prospered and others have not is one of the most remarkable puzzles of modern scholarship and one of the most pressing issues in public policy. And considering how long the topic has fascinated scholars, it is surprising how little we truly know about the subject. What we do know is that modern growth is very different from episodes of growth in the past: those historical episodes (the Roman Empire, the Holy Roman Empire, the triumphs of Ozymandias, Spain in the 16th and 17th centuries; the ancient Mayan, Aztec, and Incan empires; and those who developed Angkor Wat in Cambodia) were all transitory, based on conquest of other peoples, and premised on a finite store of valuable natural resources; modern growth is sustained, cumulative, driven by technology, discovery, (largely) private enterprise, and facilitating public legal and governance institutions. We know that the sustained growth that characterizes the last two centuries began: in the early 19th century in northern Europe - most notably in the United Kingdom and the Netherlands.

But there is no consensus on much else about modern economic growth and development. For instance, while there are, as we shall see, many theories of the causes of growth, none of those theories commands universal favour. Nor is there much agreement about what should be done to help the most distressed, the poorest people and countries in the world to begin the process of growth.[2] And there is

1 Portions of this paper draw on a paper presented at a symposium at the University of Hyderabad and subsequently published in an edited volume by Oxford University Press. I am grateful to the Law and Economics Workshop at the University of Bonn, the Universidad Torcuato di Tella Faculty of Law, the Comparative Law and Economics Forum, the Atlantic Corridors Program, the University of Illinois College of Law Faculty Retreat, the University of Toronto Faculty of Law, the University of Maryland Carey School of Law Faculty Workshop, and the Williams College Department of Economics for comments on an earlier draft. I also want to thank Brian Doxey of the University of Illinois College of Law Class of 2009 for his research assistance.

2 See Collier 2007, for thoughtful proposals for helping the poorest one-sixth of humanity.

great controversy about why some areas of the world - central Asia, sub-Saharan Africa, and much of the Arab world - seem to be nearly immune to modern growth.[3] Nor do we fully understand why some countries that were once relatively prosperous, such as Argentina and Spain, lost much of their wealth and then seem to have begun to regain prosperity.[4]

The search for explanations of what causes growth and how growth can become the standard human condition has ranged far and wide and has recently looked to law as a central causal factor.[5] In this essay I want to assess the role of law in fostering or sustaining economic growth. My view is that law is important but not central. Bad law (including no law) can certainly stifle growth or even reverse it, but the positive case for law as a central force in development is not, I argue, strong.

The essay proceeds in the following steps. In the next section I briefly review the most recent patterns of economic growth and some theories of economic growth, and identify some recent issues in development. Section III considers the role that law in its many forms might play in fostering development and prosperity. A concluding section summarizes the argument.

2. Patterns of Recent Economic Growth

Economic growth has long fascinated scholars. Arguably, the modern science of economics began - in Adam Smith's An Inquiry into the Nature and Causes of the Wealth of Nations (1776) - with a treatise on economic growth. Since then, the profession's concern with explaining and fostering growth and development has been episodic. We appear to be in a phase now in which economists (and others) are devoting a great deal of time to the subject. Before we turn to a summary of those efforts, let me first sketch the very long-run patterns of economic growth and then turn to consideration of the very recent record.

3 I shall also contend later that even the poorest regions of the world have recently experienced upsurges of growth that inspire hope for their continued betterment.

4 The instances of Argentinian and Spanish decline are distinguishable. Spanish decline in the 16th and 17th centuries follows the pattern of pre-modern growth - betterment got through conquest and exploitation followed by decline as the resources run out and the conquest is challenged. Argentina's case is different: it was a relatively early participant in modern growth (which I further define in the a following section); indeed, Argentina was one of the wealthiest countries in the world in the 1930s; unlike almost any other participant in modern economic growth, Argentina then began a 70-year period of decline that has only begun to reverse itself within the last decade. For a persuasive theory of why Argentina stagnated and declined, see Alston & Gallo 2010.

5 There was a 'first' law and development movement in the early and mid-1970s. That literature, to which David Trubek and Marc Galanter of the University of Wisconsin School of Law were prominent contributors, sought to explore the transferability of the great successes that U.S. law had worked in civil rights in the 1960s and 1970s to similar rights issues in developing countries. For a critical review of that earlier literature, see Tamanaha 2009.

2.1. *The Long View*

Modern economic growth, by which I mean 'sustained economic growth', began in the early 19th century (or possibly the late-18th century) in northern Europe, principally in the United Kingdom and the Netherlands.6 There had been no discernible increase in human well-being during the first millennium of the modern era, and the best estimate is that average per capita income increased by 50 per cent during the 800 years between 1000 A.D. and 1800 A.D. There were differences in average per capita income across the world in 1800, but those differences were not that substantial.[7] The world's richest economy in roughly 1800, the United Kingdom, had an average per capita income that was approximately four times that of the then (and still) poorest region in the world, Africa.[8]

Between 1820 and 2000 average per capita income and total world output of goods and services increased substantially.[9] For the world as a whole, average per

6 Angus Maddison, who died in late April, 2010, dates the beginning of modern growth from 1820. See Maddison 2007a, and Maddison 2007b.

7 See Maddison 2007a, and Sachs 2006.

8 Sachs 2006.

9 Here is a brief primer on growth accounting. There are two standard measures of economic growth – the annual growth rate of Gross Domestic Product (GDP), which is the value of all goods and services produced in the economy, and the annual growth rate of GDP per capita, which is equal to the difference between the growth rate of GDP and the growth rate of population. For cross-country comparisons of GDP, adjustments are made to take account of price level differences in different countries, so that, after the adjustments are made, GDP is said to be measured at 'purchasing power parity' or PPP. For the purposes of benchmarking, the annual growth rate of the United States has been in the range of 3.1 – 3.5 per cent since, we believe, the early 17th century. (The U.S. growth rate in the first quarter of 2010 was recently reported to have been 3.2 per cent, on an annual basis.) At that rate, real (that is, adjusted for price changes) GDP doubles approximately every 20 years – approximately once each generation or, if that rate is sustained and if average lifespan is 80 years, real GDP quadruples in the course of an average U.S. lifetime. (According to the rule of thumb known as the 'Rule of 72', anything growing at the annual rate of r per cent will double in $72/r$ years.)

Simply looking at GDP growth may be misleading because it does not tell us, among other things, the share of GDP potentially available to the average resident of the nation. To get that figure, we need to divide GDP by the population. And recall that the growth rate of GDP per capita (or income per capita) is the growth rate of GDP minus the growth rate of population. Population growth rates of approximately 2 per cent per year are common in developed countries (and lead to what is called 'steady state population'). So, in a country with that population growth rate and a GDP growth rate of 3.5 per cent per year, GDP per capita is growing at a rate of 1.5 per cent per year – doubling in approximately 48 years.

There is dissatisfaction in some quarters with reliance on GDP and GDP per capita as summary measures of the well-being in a society. Three recent attempts at supplemental or substitute measures of how well a society is doing are the UN Development Program's Human Development Index (first introduced in 1990 and recomputed annually), the World Values Surveys of subjective measures of well-being, and the recent report commissioned by President Nicolas Sarkozy of France (Joseph Stiglitz, Amartya Sen & Jean-Paul Fitoussi, *Report of the Commission on the Measurement of Economic Performance and Social Progress* (2009)).

To give an example of an alternative measure, the UN Development Program developed the HDI in response to Amartya Sen's arguments that the principal goal of economic develop- →

capita income during this period increased by nine-fold. But some countries prospered far more than that. In the United States, average per capita income increased 25-fold; in Western Europe, 15-fold. For the world as a whole (world GDP, if you will), the total value of all goods and services increased by a factor of almost 50. We do not yet fully understand why some countries grew faster than others.

An important implication of this broad, long-term view of economic growth is that the phenomenon of increasing societal well-being is modern. For the vast stretch of human history, human beings did not have a reasonable expectation that their standard of living or per capita income would increase over the course of their lifetimes, nor that their children or grandchildren could anticipate easier, healthier, wealthier, or longer lives than they lived.

Increasingly since the early 19th century, the notion of growth in well-being and per capita income has come to be a reasonable expectation. And that expectation is not just reasonable in the developed economies; it has also become a reasonable expectation of those in the poorer, developing countries. And in some instances the expectation is not just of gradual increases in well-being or increases that will accrue to one's children and grandchildren but of rapid and palpable increases for each generation. Some economies, such as India and China, which contain 40 per cent of the 6.5 billion people on Earth, are growing at annual rates on the order of 8-10 per cent. Growth in Gross Domestic Product at that pace implies that GDP will double each 7 to 9 years.[10] Supposing that population growth is not too great, this rate of increase in GDP suggests that average per capita income could double every decade or 15 years. As health improves and life-span increases, this means that

ment should be the expansion of human capabilities. Each country's HDI is a weighted sum of the citizenry's life expectancy at birth (meant to be a proxy for health), education (a composite of the adult literacy rates, weighted two-thirds, and the combined elementary, secondary, and tertiary gross enrolment rate - the percentage of children enrolled as a percentage of those eligible to be enrolled - weighted one-third), and the standard of living (measured as the natural log of GDP per capita). In the most recent HDI rankings (published in October, 2009, based on data of 2007), Norway ranked first at 0.971, Australia ranked second at 0.970, and the United States ranked thirteenth at 0.956.

All this having been said, it nonetheless appears to be the case (see Justin Wolfers, Freakonomics blog, January, 2010) that there is a very high correlation among all these different measures. As a result, perhaps we may rely after all on GDP and GDP per capita as indicators of societal well-being.

See also Gertner 2010.

10 The People's Republic of China, which is, as we will see, anomalous in the standard account of growth has been growing at a real annual rate of 9 per cent for almost 30 years. The most recent quarterly figure suggests that China will grow at a rate of greater than 10 per cent in 2010. Growth rates of this magnitude have never been sustained for such long periods of time. The United States, for the sake of comparison, has only had one year of 9 per cent real growth (in the late 1930s) in its history.

India has been growing at a more modest, but still relatively rapid, rate of 8 per cent per year since the early 1990s, after the introduction of reforms by Manmohan Singh. In the development community there is a great deal of interest in speculating about which of these giants - the messy Indian democracy or the centrally controlled Chinese economy - will prove to be the better model for other developing countries.

individuals could see their annual incomes double or even quadruple during a single lifetime. That is demonstrable improvement in matters that creates strong expectations. And those expectations can and do give rise to societal disruptions and political pressures.[11]

To put the matter succinctly, the 190-year-long period of modern economic growth began with all countries roughly in equal conditions of well-being. The richest country in the world had an average per capita income in 1820 that was about 90 per cent of that in a modern African country. The ratio between the average per capita income in the wealthiest country in the 1820 world and the poorest was on the order of four to one. And average life expectancy in Japan and Western Europe was approximately 40 years.

But by 2000, the picture was very different. Approximately one-sixth of humanity had risen to high-income status, levels of well-being hardly imaginable at the beginning of the 19th century. Approximately two-thirds of humanity had risen to middle-class status, with comfortable but not extravagant levels of well-being. And approximately one-sixth of humanity is stuck in extreme poverty - stuck, that is, at the same levels of well-being that characterized the entire world at the beginning of the modern period.[12]

11 To my knowledge, no one has written about how the experience of modern economic growth has changed the average person's expectations for his or her life's accomplishments and how those changes then give rise to political action. But the topic is a potentially important one and ought to command scholarly attention.

12 Since the early 1990s, the development community has measured extreme poverty in two tranches - those who live on $ 1 per day (approximately $ 500 per year) and those who live on $ 2 per day (approximately $ 1,000 per year). There is now a consensus that the total number of people living in dire poverty has fallen dramatically since the 1980s. This wonderful accomplishment is largely due to the remarkable record of economic growth in the two largest (by population) countries in the world - India and China. Their sustained growth since the early 1980s or early 1990s has lifted a very large number of very poor people out of poverty and put them well on the way to middle income.
For a more detailed account of the lives of the poorest billion, see Banerjee & Duflo 2007.
Although the total number of destitute human beings has fallen significantly over the past 30 years, there are still approximately one billion people who are living on $ 1 or $ 2 per day. Here are a few facts about the experience of those who remain desperately poor. About 70 per cent of them live in sub-Saharan Africa. (See Collier 2007). During the 1970s the per capita income of the bottom billion rose at the rate of 0.5 per cent per year; during the 1980s, it *declined* at the rate of 0.4 per cent per year so that by 1990 the poorest people on the planet were literally back at the point at which they had begun the 1970s. During the 1990s, which most scholars reckon to have been a golden decade of growth between the bookends of World War II and 9/11, the per capita income of the poorest declined at an even faster rate than it had in the 1980s - at 0.5 per cent per year. Thus, in 2000 the bottom billion were literally worse off than they had been in 1970. There have been glimmers of hope for the worst off in the first decade of this century: since 2004 many sub-Saharan African countries have been growing at a rate of 6 per cent per year, and the income per capita of the poorest has grown at 1.7 per cent per year. There is some skepticism among development scholars about the sustainability of these figures in that they may simply be due to the discovery of valuable natural resources and the increase in world prices for those resources. It is not at all →

2.2. *The Scholarly Literature on the Causes of Growth*

When modern economists, beginning with Sir Roy Harrod, Evsey Domar, and Robert Solow, first turned their attention to economic growth, they characterized the growth process as one that was technical and, at root, driven by improvements in the technology of production. But these improvements were modelled to be exogenous - that is, while there was a certainly a logic to the pattern of technological improvement,[13] Harrod, Domar, and Solow assumed that it simply appeared, as if thrown from the sky by the gods. Growth was a technical matter of organizing production so as to use society's resources more efficiently. An excess of income over expense (or profit over cost) could be used to invest in expansion for greater output and greater income and profit in the future.

In Solow's famous and innovative attempt to test the applicability of the model's predictions to the record of 20th century U.S. growth, the vast bulk of growth - well more than 50 per cent - was attributable to the 'residual' - that is, to the growth of 'total factor productivity', the accumulated improvement in the efficiency with which resources were organized for production (as opposed to growth occurring through increases in the quantities or productivity of individual factors of production, such as land, labour, and capital).[14] But, as noted, this clearly vital engine of growth was not explained within the model. Technological change was exogenous to the model.

The policy implications of the Harrod-Domar and Solow models of economic growth were seized upon in the 1960s and 1970s to guide aid and advice to the developing countries. The central policy recommendation that advisors gave to the developing world was to increase the amount of productive capital equipment, such as dams, roads, factories, power generation, and the like so as to put in place a capital infrastructure that would encourage entrepreneurial activity and raise the capital-labour ratio to levels that would sustain higher growth rates. Because the developing world did not have sufficient domestic savings to invest in capital accumulation, the developed world filled this 'financing gap' through aid that was to be invested in massive capital-accumulation projects.

The result of this (perhaps misguided) application of the Harrod-Domar and Solow models to development was grim failure. There was no discernible growth in the countries that received aid; nor was growth demonstrably faster in those countries that received more aid; nor was there any other empirical indication that the aid based on the 'financing gap' model was helpful.[15]

certain that the revenues from the international sale of these resources is widely distributed so as to make a significant difference in the lives of the poor.

13 For example, a labour-scare and resource-abundant society, like the 19th-century United States, looked for technological improvements that substituted for labour. In contrast, a labour-abundant and resource-poor society, like England in the 19th century, looked for technological change that saved resources and capital.

14 Solow 1956, and Solow 1957.

15 The story is marvellously told in Easterly 2002. In more recent work, Easterly 2006 and others (see Moyo 2009) have argued that the most productive way forward in development is for the West to stop giving foreign aid; not to make it conditional on the adoption of better policies →

The lack of progress of development in the poorest countries through the 1980s gave rise to searches for better theories of growth and better methods of helping the poor nations. Among scholars there was great interest in two strands of thought. The first was the elaboration of 'endogenous growth' (or 'new growth theory') models. The innovation of those models was to bring technical change within the model so that real factors in an economy determined the rate of technical change and, through that rate and other real factors, the nation's growth rate.[16] Although these new growth models were a tremendous scholarly advance, they have not had a deep impact on the policy of advising or aiding developing economies.

The second strand of academic thought on economic growth that gave rise to excitement was the interest in 'institutions' as a fundamental determinant of national growth and development. Douglass North, a co-winner of the 1993 Nobel Memorial Prize in the Economic Sciences, had long been associated with the 'new institutional economics', which holds, among other things, that the legally and otherwise-determined rules that govern economic activity have a profound influence on the ability of an economy to prosper.[17] For example, the mechanisms by which a society encourages and rewards risk-taking will have a deep effect on investments that might be necessary for growth. If a society discourages economic risk-taking or does not have appropriate safety nets to catch those who take risks and fail, then that society may not have sufficient investment in entrepreneurial activity. In theory, economists could identify the institutions that are necessary for a nation to grow and prosper, see if a given nation has those institutions, and if it does not, suggest means by which it might acquire those vital institutions.[18]

One of the most interesting strands of scholarship to emerge from the institutional literature is the work of Daron Acemoglu, James A. Robinson, and Simon Johnson. In a series of insightful articles,[19] they have argued that there is persuasive theoretical and empirical evidence that those nations that have strong legal and social institutions have prospered and that those nations that do not have strong and stable institutions have not prospered. Consider the phenomenon they characterize as the 'reversal of fortune'.[20] The starting point for the article is the observation that in the 16th, 17th, and 18th centuries there were some colonies of European

but simply to stop giving it. In contrast, Jeffrey Sachs (see Sachs 2006) has urged the West to make a stronger commitment to give aid, carefully targeted to the most promising ends, such as health and education.

16 Romer 1986, and Romer 1990. For a nontechnical discussion, see Romer 2007.

17 North 2005, and North & Thomas 1976. See also Parente & Prescott 2000. In his wonderful survey of economic thinking about growth, Elhanan Helpman concludes that the technical models had not provided the explanatory power and guidance for practical policymaking that developing countries desire. But, he wrote, the interest in institutions as a bedrock of growth holds great promise for both explaining and directing growth. See Helpman 2004.

18 The 'Washington consensus', which I shall discuss shortly, was the policy implementation of this view. Dani Rodrik of the Kennedy School of Government, Harvard University, has been a consistent champion of the view that institutions are central to economic prosperity. See Rodrik 2004 and Rodrik, Subramanian & Trebbi 2004. See also Spence 2008.

19 See, for example, Acemoglu, Johnson & Robinson 2005 and Acemoglu, Johnson & Robinson 2001. See Acemoglu & Robinson 2005 and Acemoglu 2009.

20 Acemoglu, Johnson & Robinson 2002.

countries that were extremely wealthy (such as some Caribbean islands) and others that were relatively poor (such as North America). But by the late 20th century, these roles had been reversed: the former colonies that had been relatively wealthy were now relatively (and in some cases absolutely) poor and those that had been poor were now wealthy. What explains this reversal of fortune?

According to Acemoglu, Johnson, and Robinson, the key difference between the two groups of colonies is the presence of institutions that would facilitate long-run growth. The colonies that used to be wealthy were 'extractive': they had substantial deposits of valuable natural resources that the European colonizers wanted to get out of the colony, onto ships, and into markets in Europe as quickly as possible. Because these colonies were valued only to the extent that they had valuable natural resources and those resources were finite, the colonizers did not have a long-term interest in the colony. As a result, there was no reason for the colonizers to invest in establishing and nurturing stable and valuable institutions. For example, there was nothing to be said for establishing representative and responsive governance structures in the extractive colonies. The inhabitants of the colonies were to be exploited, not encouraged to be self-governing. Nor was there much to be said for encouraging widespread and secure property interests or the other institutions of a well-functioning civil society. Nor was there an incentive to facilitate consensual agreements through third-party enforcement of contracts.

As a result, when the natural resources ran out, the Europeans left, and these extractive colonies began a long slide into poverty with no stable institutions to arrest that slide or to provide alternative sources of economic growth.

Contrast this account of the history of extractive colonies with that of what Acemoglu, Jonson, and Robinson call 'settler colonies'. In the 16th, 17th, and 18th centuries these colonies - such as Canada, the United States, and New Zealand - had no immediately valuable natural resources that could be extracted for transportation to markets in Europe.[21] In order to become valuable to their European

[21] It is instructive to consider, in broad outline, the history of one of the most prominent early American colonies. Virginia was founded as a profit-maximizing enterprise by London and Bristol investors who had reason to believe, on the basis of reconnaissance reports, that there were mulberry trees in Virginia suitable for producing silk. The gentlemen who first populated that colony intended to be silk producers, with labour for gathering and weaving to be supplied by enslaved Indians. Things did not work out that way. First, there was no silk - there were mulberry trees but no silk worms. Second, the Indians refused to be enslaved and, indeed, fought back against such attempts. Third, the gentlemen had no experience with farming and so nearly died when their initial supplies and the willingness of the Indians to help them were exhausted. The venture was saved from complete failure by Captain John Smith, who organized everyone in the colony with military efficiency (and tolerated little dissent), married an Indian woman, and put the gentlemen to work planting tobacco as a cash crop, against the express wishes of the King (who thought tobacco to be a society-rotting habit and wrote a pamphlet against tobacco use). The King's objections vanished when the tax revenues and import duties on tobacco proved to be a welcome source of revenue in his battle with Parliament. Tobacco and indigo were the chief cash or export crops of the southern colonies until after the American Revolution of 1776-1783. And cotton did not become a viable cash crop for large numbers of farmers until after the invention and dissemination of the cotton gin in the early 1970s. Think, in light of Acemoglu, Johnson, and →

masters, these colonies would require longer-run development. In particular, they would need to become populated with people who could develop the colony so that it would become valuable to the mother country. So, these colonies sought to encourage emigration from the mother country (and other European countries). And the settlers would be more eager to come to the extent that there were attractive prospects of success in the colony.[22] This fact, argue Acemoglu, Johnson, and Robinson, explains why these colonies developed stable, attractive, citizen-empowering institutions. And those institutions served the long-run interests of the colonists so well that over the long haul those colonies became wealthy.[23]

The recognition that institutions may be an important - and, possibly, the most vital - aspect of economic growth is the reason that there is now such elevated interest in the role of law in fostering development. Law is, after all, the institution that may be the one most under human control and the most amenable to change (by comparison to, say, cultural and religious institutions).

The interest in the role of institutions in furthering economic growth also had a great impact on the methods by which international organizations extended aid to developing countries. For example, the 'Washington consensus' of the early 1990s held that aid should be conditional on the recipient's adopting institutions that were thought to be conducive to modern economic growth - such institutions (and policies) as fiscal discipline, privatization of state-owned enterprises, trade liberalization, and deregulation. There is now general agreement that the reform experiences of the 1990s, conducted under the Washington consensus, were not successful.[24]

Robinson's distinction between extractive and settler colonies, how very different matters might have been for the U.S. if Virginia had become an extractive colony, rather than, as it became, a settler colony.

22 An important statistic distinguishing the extractive from the settler colonies was the rate of European mortality: it was much higher in the extractive colonies.

23 For a sceptical view of the role of institutions, see Glaeser *et al.* 2004.

24 See World Bank 2005. See also Rodrik 2006. At the conference in Hyderabad at which I presented a very early version of this paper, Hans-Bernd Schaefer commented that the Washington consensus was not merely neutral (in the sense of doing no harm even if it did not do much good): it actually did harm in some areas of the world, notably Latin America and Russia (both of which implemented 'big bang' policies to move to more 'Washington-consensus friendly' policies). Bernd noted that two dire consequences of the implementation in Russia were that life expectancy went from 63 to 55 and per capita income fell dramatically.
It is not clear that these well-known statistics are a fair characterization of the Russian record of growth after the fall of communism and the Soviet Union in 1991. Shleifer & Treisman 2005 argue that although some aspects of the transition from communism were painful, Russia has made significant economic and social progress, reaching, for example, the middle level of developing countries (with a GDP per capita of $ 8,000) and that Russia's crime and corruption and other problems are 'normal' for a country at that level of development. They attribute the despair over Russia's post-communist development to the widespread misconception that pre-1991 Russia, with its brilliant physicists, world chess champions, space program, and global military presence was a relatively wealthy country. In fact, Shleifer and Treisman show, 1991 Russia was not wealthy; it was more like Argentina or Mexico, in the middle ranks of developing countries.

→

The scholarly literature on the causes of economic growth and the practical policy advice that might follow from it are still evolving. Even so, there are two fundamental points about the causes of growth about which there is a general consensus. The first point is that there is no persuasive evidence that the more successful countries achieved their growth by exploiting other countries. The rich came by their wealth relatively honestly (although we are not precisely sure how they managed it). There is great hope in this observation: economic growth is not a zero-sum game in which some are destined to prosper and others not; it is not the case that the only viable path to sustained growth and prosperity is to take from others, thereby impoverishing them until they have the strength to take from you. Rather, the hopeful pattern is, to paraphrase Deng Xiaoping, that 'All will be wealthy; some will be first'.[25]

A second point worth making is that among the many possible causes of growth, one that almost no serious student of the process takes seriously is that some portions of humanity - races, religions, ethnic groups - are more adept at growth than are others.[26] Economic growth, prosperity, and happiness are achievable by all humans. This hopeful point should not be taken to undermine the earlier point about the possible importance of institutions: all human societies may grow so long as they have growth-favouring institutions. The reconciliation of the points may lie in the observation that all human societies are capable of finding and implementing those institutions.

2.3. *More Recent Experience*

As I indicated above, roughly all countries began the modern period of growth at the same level of well-being. But they did not end at the same level. Indeed, one of the most significant results of this 190-year period of modern economic growth is

On the bad effects of the adoption of 'Washington-consensus friendly' policies in Latin America, see Fukuyama 2008.

25 I am grateful to Hans-Bernd Schaefer for this paraphrase. I don't mean to be Pollyanna-ish about the prospects for growth. Some countries and regions have greater resource endowments than others; some have greater access to trade than others; and so on. Nonetheless, if it is institutions that are more important than geography, the prospects for meaningful growth are good everywhere.

26 There is an important strain in the economic development literature that has held that 'culture' is an under-appreciated force in economic growth and development. Weber 1904 argued that northern Europe developed before southern Europe because the prevalent Protestant religions of the north urged its adherents to work hard in this life so as to reveal through their degree of worldly success the extent to which they were God's chosen. In contrast, Weber argued that the fatalistic theism of the Catholic religion prevalent in southern Europe created no incentive for hard work in this life. A more modern proponent of the view that 'culture matters' is the great economic historian David Landes. In Landis 1999, Landes argues that culture is the most important factor in explaining and predicting national prosperity. He notes, as have many others, that it is not mere coincidence that the countries that are the wealthiest have a connection to English culture. See also Landes 2001. Finally, see Fukuyama 1995. I will address an interesting recent attempt to show how historical events can determine current culture (and thereby affect growth) in the next section.

the fact that the gap between the richest and the poorest has widened throughout that period. Today the richest country in the world, the United States, has a per capita income that is between 50 and 100 times greater than that of the poorest countries.[27]

The clearest-eyed view of the current state of comparative development holds that all nations follow the same general path from underdevelopment to sustained growth but that (as Deng Xiaoping saw) some began a long time ago and others have begun the process at later dates.[28] For example, the leaders (the United States, Canada, and the countries of northern Europe) began the process in the late 18th or early 19th century.[29] Mexico began the process in the mid-19th century. Japan began with the Meiji Restoration of the 1860s. Brazil began in the 1920s. The 'late starters', such as India and China, began their sustained, modern growth only in the last two decades of the 20th century. And there is now some hope that the heretofore chronically poor sub-Saharan African nations have initiated the modern growth process in the first decade of the 21st century.[30]

There are good reasons for believing that the experience of the leaders will be replicated among the late starters, subject, of course, to the fact that there are different resource and other constraints, different technologies, and different policy concerns (such as global warming) facing the late starters than faced the leaders when they began the process.[31] Indeed, it might be the case that getting a late start may have some advantages. For example, rather than work their way through the various technologies of communication in the same order that the leaders have done, late starters can go straight to the mobile phone and the dizzying array of communications possibilities that the near future holds out.[32]

27 The per capita income in the United States is (or was before the current Great Recession) almost $ 50,000, and the annual income of the very poorest is between $ 500 and $ 1,000.

28 Parente & Prescott 2005. See also Parente 2008.

29 Sachs 2006, p. 33-40. Sachs asks, 'Why was Britain first?' And he gives six reasons for Britain's being a leader in modern economic growth. (1) 'British society was relatively open, with more scope for individual initiative and social mobility than most other societies of the world'. At 33. (2) 'Britain had strengthening institutions of political liberty. Britain's parliament and its tradition of free speech and open debate were powerful contributors to the uptake of new ideas. They were also increasingly powerful protectors of private property rights'. Id. (3) 'Britain became one of the leading centers of Europe's scientific revolution'. Sachs counts this factor as being critically important. Id. (4) 'Britain had several crucial geographical advantages. It had low-cost sea trade routes with most of Europe and proximity to North America, where the 'new settlements ... provided vast new territories for food production and raw materials such as cotton for British industry'. Those settlements also provided a 'safety valve that facilitated the exodus of impoverished people from the British countryside'. Id. (5) 'Britain remained sovereign and faced lesser risk of invasion than its neighbours'. At 34. And (6) 'Britain had coal'. At 35. Sachs concludes his enumeration of these advantages with this marvellous observation: 'When a society is economically dominant, it is easy for its members to assume that such dominance reflects a deeper superiority - whether religious, racial, genetic, cultural, or institutional - rather than an accident of timing or geography'. At 39.

30 See Young 2009; Arbache, Go & Page 2008; and Pinkovskiy & Sala-i-Martin 2010.

31 Parente & Prescott 2000.

32 Jensen & Oster 2009 show that the introduction of cable television into rural areas of India has led, by showing viewers new sources of information, to 'significant decreases in the →

Do we know what the state of development is in the countries that are and have been seeking to grow? Yes, and the record is somewhere between mixed and encouraging. The 'mixed' part is that there are some identifiably poor regions of the world – that is, serious difficulties with growth appear to be confined now to only certain areas rather than to be a pervasive and nearly worldwide phenomenon. To the extent that we now know where the worst poverty is – in the central Asian republics, some of the 22 Arab-speaking countries, and sub-Saharan Africa – we can target aid and other policies designed to address the particular problems of those areas.

The 'encouraging' part of the current record is that there is evidence to suggest that the world distribution of income is improving – that is, that the relative and absolute numbers of the poorest people in the world has been declining and declining rapidly. Xavier Sala-i-Martin of Columbia University has argued that 'the proportion of the world's people living in acute poverty (on less than a dollar a day) fell from 17 per cent in 1970 to 7 per cent in 1998; the proportion living on less than $ 2 a day fell from 41 per cent to 19 per cent'.[33] Sala-i-Martin further contends that the absolute number of people in the world who were living at the lowest level of well-being (one dollar per day or an annual income of $ 500) fell by 200 million over the same period and that the absolute number of people living at the intermediate level of poverty (two dollars per day or an annual income of $ 1,000) also fell by 350 million over the same period.[34]

This finding is controversial. There are obvious measurement problems having to do with the validity and comparability of statistics from different countries. But the biggest controversy has to do with the underlying issue of whether to compute poverty using national income statistics (as Sala-i-Martin does) or using household surveys of consumption (as others have done).[35] Calculation of poverty levels by Chen and Ravallion at the World Bank using household survey data show little improvement in world poverty in the 1990s (and beyond).[36] They find that the percentage of world population living on less than a dollar a day in 1987 was 28 and that that figure had fallen by 1998 to only 24 per cent of world population. In

reported acceptability of domestic violence towards women and son preference, as well as increases in women's autonomy and declines in fertility'. Jensen 2007 has shown that the introduction of mobile phones in south India has allowed fishers, while at sea, to call the various coastal market towns to find out where the best prices and thinnest markets are and then to go to those markets, has greatly increased the efficiency of fresh fish markets (in the sense that there is much greater availability, less wastage, and lower prices and higher incomes for fishers).

33 See Sala-i-Martin 2006. The quotation is from a summary of an earlier version of Sala-i-Martin 2004.

34 Some commentators, such as Bhalla 2002, argue that these data indicate that the U.N. Millennium Development Goal of reducing the number of people living on one dollar a day or less to half its 1990 level by the year 2015 had already been achieved by the time that goal was announced.

35 There is no consensus among those learned in these matters about which source of data is preferable.

36 See Chen & Ravallion 2001, and Chen & Ravallion 2004. The authors have updated their work to the present and have found similar discouraging results in Chen & Ravallion 2008.

contrast, Sala-i-Martin, using national income data, had found a decline to 7 per cent of world population and a decline in the absolute number of people in poverty.

Finally, some commentators note that while income inequality may be lessening across all poor nations, it may be widening among all nations - that is, while there may be improvement among the poorest world population, the rich are getting richer at a faster rate. And this trend might be replicated within the nations that are making progress in improving the well-being of the worst off. That is, even within the poorest countries, the income of the well-to-do could be increasing at a faster rate than that of the very poorest so that the degree of inequality within the poorest nations may be worsening. These critics ask then what sense it makes to be cheerful about the reduction in the proportion or absolute number of the poorest people in the world if both the gap in income between the richest and the poorest nations and the gap in income between the richest and the poorest within nations have widened.

These are vexing issues to which there appear to be no simple answers. Perhaps the most appropriate stance is to be cautiously optimistic about improvement in the condition of the very poorest but not to relax further efforts to continue those improvements. One encouraging way to look at recent developments is this one from Jeff Sachs:

> 'Approximately 4.9 billion people live in countries where average income - measured by GDP per person - increased between 1980 and 2000 An even larger number, roughly 5.7 billion people, live in countries where life expectancy increased'.[37]

There is one sure method to improvement on which all thoughtful commentators agree: reduce population growth in the very poorest countries. There is no doubt at all that those countries that have managed to reduce their fertility rates are the ones that are either wealthy or are experiencing sustained economic growth. Half of the roughly 200 nations in the world, including the entire developed world, is at the zero population growth level of two children per couple, one of which children is female. By contrast, the poorest countries in the world have fertility rates of five or more, with the result that national populations are doubling every 20 or so years.[38] Of particular note in this regard are the poor countries that have made the demographic transition from high fertility rates to the lower rates that characterize the wealthy countries. And note how rapidly these changes have occurred. Bangladesh, for example, reduced its fertility rate from 6.6 in 1975 to 3.1 in 2000. Iran reduced its fertility rate from 6.7 in 1980 (just after the Islamic Revolution of 1979) to 2.6 in 2000.[39]

There is a chicken-and-egg problem with fertility declines: will higher growth cause a fertility decline or will an earlier fertility decline lead to higher economic growth? Whichever the direction of causation or whether the changes are complementary, a demographic transition is an almost essential part of national growth

37 Sachs 2006, p. 51.
38 Sachs 2006, p. 64.
39 Sachs 2006.

and development.[40] There is evidence to suggest that a global demographic transition has begun. China, the most populous country, has already begun that transition. And there are worries in some developed countries that there will not be a sufficient labour force in the future. Japanese newspapers have reported that, at current trends, there will be no Japanese people in the year 2569.

2.4. *Some Recent Developments in the Scholarship of Modern Growth*

In this section I want to give a brief account of three recent developments in the scholarship of economic growth and development. The first is the introduction of randomized field experiments to gauge which policies work and which do not. The second is a discussion of some new work that seeks to offer a novel explanation for some of the particular development problems of sub-Saharan Africa. And the third is a description of the economic conditions of the 22 Arab-speaking countries between Morocco and Iraq.

2.4.1. Randomized Experiments

In a previous section I referred to the fact that scholarly attempts to provide grand theories of economic growth and development have generally come to a halt. However, there is still much fascinating scholarship being done on development issues, but it has shifted its central focus from the consideration of grand, macroeconomic issues (as in the Solow and Romer models) to consideration of small-scale experiments.[41]

The key tool in this new literature is the randomized field experiment.[42] To illustrate, suppose that one is eager to discover how to induce people in climates where malaria and other insect-borne diseases are endemic to use insecticide-

40 This is another example of a very common issue in talking about development – what is cause and what is effect? Does a decline in fertility cause growth, or does growth cause a decline in fertility? As I mentioned in my discussion of the relationship between democracy and growth above, many of these simultaneity problems are explained by the fact that the particular issue and growth are co-evolutionary. To take an important policy to which this matter applies, consider corruption. Corruption is clearly an impediment to growth, but we are not certain how best to reduce corruption so that growth may proceed. See, for example, Svensson 2005. Nonetheless, we do know that higher levels of national income per capita are associated with lower levels of corruption. So, as with many bad things, their cure is economic growth.

41 See, for example, Easterly & Cohen 2009, the website of the Abdul Latif Jameel Poverty Action Laboratory (J-PAL) at the MIT Department of Economics, and the work of Abhijit Banerjee and Esther Duflo of MIT (such as Banerjee & Duflo 2008). See also Parker 2010.

42 The randomized experiment is the gold standard of experimental methods. An experimenter who wants to discover the effects of some event or food or other 'treatment' randomly divides his experimental subjects into two groups. If the division has been truly random, then each group should have roughly the same general characteristics as the entire group, such as the same distribution of gender, age, height, education, income, and so on. One group, called the 'control group', does not receive the treatment; the other, the 'treatment group', does.

→

treated nets (ITNs) at night. Netting is cheap by Western standards (approximately $ 1) but expensive by the standards of the sub-Saharan African countries where their use would do the most good. Should Western aid organizations give away the insecticide-treated nets for free or engage in cost-sharing (having the people bear some fraction of the cost, in the hope that this will establish an ownership claim that will increase use)?

This matter - whether to make the netting free or cost shared - cannot be resolved by appeal to theoretical argument. One can think of reasons why use would be greater under either scenario. But there may be some enlightenment to be had by performing a careful randomized field experiment. That is precisely what Jessica Cohen and Emil Dupas did:

> 'Working with twenty prenatal clinics [in western Kenya] to offer ITNs at varying prices, they divided the clinics randomly into five groups of four, with four of the groups offering the ITNs at a (single) price ranging from $ 0 to $ 0.60 per ITN and the fifth serving as the control. They then measured the uptake of ITNs from the clinics and also spot-checked for usage (whether the nets were hanging on beds or not). In addition, they checked the hemoglobin levels (anemia rates) of women getting ITNs to see if cost sharing does a better job of selecting women at greater risk for malaria'.[43]

The results were clear: cost sharing was on every measure less successful than free distribution of the ITNs. Specifically, the large social benefits that came from greater use under free distribution swamped the increased budgetary costs of free distribution.

This is only one example of many that could illustrate the great value of randomized field experiments in refining development policy.[44]

There are, of course, cautions that have been raised. Experiments tend to focus on small-scale development policies, not the grand strategies and policies that have been the focus of development studies over the past 60 years or more. But that is only a lament for things past; perhaps the appropriate focus for these studies right now is precisely the small scale experiment. It is hard to argue with the clear results that have come from the experiments that have been done just in the past decade.

Another concern - one that must always be raised with respect to experimental results - is whether the randomized field experiments have internal and external validity. Consider whether, in the Cohen and Dupas study, the fact that they focused on prenatal clinics as their distribution point might temper their results. Perhaps pregnant women who are willing to go to prenatal clinics are a select group that is not representative of the greater population for whom ITNs are desirable. And consider whether the results have external validity: do they, for example, apply just to western Kenya? Or would we expect the same results in a

Because the only difference between the two groups is whether they received the treatment, the experimenter can attribute any observed differences - typically, the 'mean effect' of the treatment - between the groups to the treatment and not to other factors. See Lawless, Robbennolt & Ulen 2010.

43 See Rodrik 2009.

44 For others, see Banerjee & Duflo 2008, and Rodrik 2009.

comparison between free and cost-shared ITNs in, say, central India? And what about the applicability of the results to some other desirable policy that one might either give away for free or cost-share, such as elementary education?

Finally, Dani Rodrik points out that there may be issues of scale that the experiments do not adequately treat but that might matter a great deal to a policymaker. That is, would we really expect the same results if, instead of dealing with 20 relatively small prenatal clinics in western Kenya, we were to scale up the program to cover the entire country of Kenya? Or would there be, for example, such large administrative costs or so much corruption if the program were to go large scale that the benefits of free distribution would no longer exceed budgetary costs?

Some of these perfectly reasonable concerns can be addressed simply by doing more experiments. If, for example, one worries that the Kenyan results might not apply in Uttar Pradesh in India, one can do another experiment in India to find out. And if one wonders about the applicability of Cohen and Dupas' result to elementary education, one can do another experiment. But for other concerns, such as Rodrik's worries about scale effects, it may not be possible to resolve those issues prior to implementing the program on a large scale.

2.4.2. The Long-Lasting Effects of History as Impediments to Growth

In 1976, shortly before his death, the Chinese leader Chou En-Lai was asked by an interviewer what effect he thought that the French Revolution had had on the modern world. Chou answered, 'It's too soon to tell'. This remark might strike an American as both wise and weary - yes, there are long-lasting effects of historical events, but typically, historical events play out relatively quickly; at least they seem to most Americans to have done so.

So, many would think that distant historical events would be unlikely to have a controlling hold on current events. Specifically, one might be sceptical of a claim that events - even traumatic events - of more than 100 years ago might help to explain current difficulties in economic development.

But that is precisely the claim of Nathan Nunn and Leonard Wantchekon regarding Africa's historical experience with the slave trades and its current difficulties with economic growth.[45] Specifically, they claim that cultural attitudes today that impede economic growth in sub-Saharan Africa may have their origin in cultural attitudes developed during the 400 years of the various waves of slave trades that washed over Africa between the 15th and late 19th centuries.

The authors note that in the first three great waves of the slave trades in Africa, slaves tended to be captured and sold into slavery by state-organized raiding parties and through warfare. This itself engendered a great deal of social insecurity. In all the waves of the slave trade, there was such a ubiquitous sense of insecurity that individuals began to turn on one another - on their neighbours and

45 See Nunn & Wantchekon 2009 (currently under review at the *American Economic Review*), and Nunn 2008. Nunn is an Assistant Professor in the Department of Economics, Harvard University, and Wantchekon is a Professor in the Departments of Political Science and Economics at New York University.

even on their family members – to supply slaves through kidnapping, trickery, and deceit:

> 'We hypothesize that in this environment, where everyone had to constantly be on guard against being sold or tricked into slavery by those around them, a culture of mistrust may have evolved, and that this mistrust may continue to persist today'.

To test this hypothesis, Nunn and Wantchekon use data from the 2005 Afrobarometer survey as their dependent variable. That survey asked respondents to rate, on a scale of 1 to 5, their trust in their relatives, their neighbours, and their local government councils. They knew the ethnic affiliation of the respondents and where they lived. The authors regressed these trust responses on a set of independent variables that included the percentage of ethnicities and of geographic populations that were taken in the various waves of the slave trade. Their hypothesis is that ethnicities and regions that were the subject of greater takings for slaves will exhibit a higher level of distrust in their relatives, neighbours, and local government councils than will ethnicities and regions that did not give up large numbers to the slave trade. And that is precisely what they found.[46]

The authors then try to distinguish between two different channels by which the slave trade could have been changed cultural norms of trust. The first of those channels posits a direct effect – namely, that it was the trickery of the slave trade that directly and adversely affected the cultural norms of trust in the groups most exposed to the trade. The second channel posits an indirect effect – the loss of one's relatives and neighbours to the slave traders highlighted the ineffectualness of the political and legal institutions to protect people. They conclude that the first channel accounts for about 75 per cent of the distrust currently observed in sub-Saharan Africa and that the second channel accounts for the remaining 25 per cent.

As a result, Nunn and Wantchekon conclude that today sub-Saharan Africans distrust one another and legal and political institutions because of the events of the 400 years of the slave trades and that this pervasive distrust helps to explain the difficulties of sustaining modern economic growth and development in that region.

2.4.3. The Arab Economies

I have already mentioned several times that the 22 Arab-speaking states between Morocco and Iraq are typically included among the portions of the world in which modern sustained economic growth has not begun. These statements may seem to be at odds with widespread perceptions of, at least, the oil-rich Gulf states. But those perceptions are inaccurate.

[46] The authors are aware that their implicit causal relationship might have run the other way – that is, that ethnicities that, prior to the slave trade and for reasons predating the slave trade, exhibited high levels of social distrust were more actively involved in the slave trade. They try to instrument for this alternative causation by using distance from the coast as their instrument for trust because they find a strong positive relationship between distance from the coast and trust.

The view that these 22 countries are very poor was brought into public discourse by the 2002 *Arab Human Development Report*, a report authored by scholars from the Arab countries. Among the startling testaments to the poverty in the region were these assertions:

(1) if one were to add the GDPs of the 22 Arab-speaking countries, the sum would be less than the GDP of Spain, which is, of course, not one of the wealthier countries in Western Europe, and
(2) there are more books translated into Greek from all other languages each year than have been translated into Arabic from all other languages over the past several hundred years.

These and other facts (for example, about extreme gender inequality) have given rise to a picture of the Arab-speaking world as one that is extraordinarily different from the rest of the world, even from the rest of the developing world. But as with many summary statements, this picture is not entirely fair or accurate. There are signs that the Arab-speaking world has begun the process of modern economic growth.

To begin, one should avoid the view that there is a uniformity of culture among the 22 Arab-speaking countries. Indeed, there is probably as much variety among those countries as there is among such English-speaking countries as India and Scotland and the United States, or as there is among the countries of Latin America.[47]

In a recent article James Rauch and Scott Kostyak divide their survey of the Arab countries into three 'worlds': Arab sub-Saharan Africa, Arab fuel-endowed economies, and the Arab Mediterranean. They then assess the recent record of economic growth in each of those 'worlds' with the records of the non-Arab countries in those areas. So, for instance, they compare the record of the Arab countries in sub-Saharan Africa with that of the non-Arab countries in that same region, and they compare the record of the Arab Mediterranean countries with that of the European countries that border the Mediterranean. These comparisons seem fairer than the comparison that lumps together the very different Arab-speaking countries and compares them to other developing countries that may not share much in the way of resource, population, education, or other important characteristics.

Rauch and Kostyak compare some elements of the UN's Human Development Index in 1970 and again in 2006 for the three Arab worlds. In almost every one of the comparisons, each section of the Arab world was doing significantly worse than its non-Arab reference group in 1970 but had caught up with the reference group or surpassed it by 2006. For instance, life expectancy in the three Arab worlds was lower than in their reference groups in 1970, but by 2006 life expectancy in two of

47 'The range of Arab values is more than double the range of Latin American values for life expectancy, more than 25 per cent higher for literacy, more than triple for school enrolment, and more than six times greater for income (adjusted for purchasing power)'. Rauch & Kostyak 2009, p. 170.

the Arab worlds - sub-Saharan Africa and the fuel-endowed economies - exceeded that in their reference groups.

Similarly with education:

> 'By 2000, the Arab fuel-endowed economies and Arab Mediterranean [economies]... had caught up with the comparison country groups substantially, with the Arab Mediterranean [economies] almost equaling the educational attainment of Latin America. Arab sub-Saharan Africa, on the other hand, fell further behind non-Arab sub-Saharan Africa, though in this case due to limited data Arab sub-Saharan Africa is represented by only one country, Sudan. The lower levels of educational attainment for the Arab and non-Arab fuel economies relative to the remainders of the Arab and non-Arab worlds, respectively, are consistent with one of the common explanations for the oil/natural resources curse: abundant natural resources lower the return to obtaining an education by increasing wages for unskilled workers'.[48]

Finally, with respect to GDP per capita, the picture is mixed. As with other elements of the HDI, GDP per capita in two of the three parts of the Arab worlds was less in 1970 than in their comparison groups. Only in the fuel-endowed Arab countries was GDP per capita higher in 1970 than in non-Arab fuel-endowed countries. Growth in those natural-resource-rich countries has been approximately equal between 1970 and 2006 so that by the close of the period, GDP per capita in the Arab fuel-endowed countries was still higher than in the non-Arab fuel-endowed economies. Arab sub-Saharan Africa has grown more rapidly than has non-Arab sub-Saharan Africa so that by 2007, income per capita in the Arab and non-Arab countries of sub-Saharan Africa was roughly equal. Finally, growth in the Arab Mediterranean countries between 1970 and 2007 has not been as rapid as in the reference countries so that the GDP per capita in that part of the Arab world was even further behind its comparison group than it had been in 1970.

With respect to two indicators, the state of the Arab worlds by comparison to their reference groups is not good. The first of those is population growth. Only in the sub-Saharan Arab world has population growth been lower than in its reference group. But in the other two Arab worlds the rate of population growth (at 3 per cent per year) has been much higher than the rates in their reference countries. Indeed, population growth is so high in some countries in the Arab world that half of the population in those countries is younger than 15 years-old.

The second indicator on which the Arab countries do not do well is with regard to females, although here the picture has some nuanced aspects. First consider females in education. Female participation at all levels of education was much lower in all three Arab worlds in 1970 than in each of the comparison groups. However, in the Arab Mediterranean countries the rate of female participation in primary, secondary, and tertiary education had, by 2006, caught up to or surpassed its reference group. is much lower than in the non-Arab Mediterranean countries and the gap has widened over the period 1970-2006. Female educational participation in Arab sub-Saharan Africa is much higher at both dates than in non-Arab sub-Saharan African countries. Female participation in education in the Arab fuel-

48 Rauch & Kostyak 2009, p. 170.

endowed economics was substantially behind that in the non-Arab fuel-endowed economies in 1970 and was no further behind in 2006.

Next, consider female labour force participation rates. In this category, the record of all three of the Arab worlds is poor:

> 'The Arab gender gaps exceed those in the comparison country groups across the board, and by extraordinarily large margins. Latin America, southern Europe, and the non-Arab fuel economies all reduced their labor force participation gender gaps since 1980 far more than any of the Arab worlds. Arab convergence in the near future seems unlikely'.[49]

So, the picture of economic growth and development in the Arab-speaking countries that Rauch and Kostyak paint is less distressing than the picture that appears from the various Arab Human Development Reports.[50]

2.4.4. The Limits of Modern Growth

I cannot leave this mixed and encouraging news about modern economic growth without mentioning the fact that there may be limits to growth and that those limits may be real, binding, and very, very troublesome.

One of those limits may be imposed by global climate change. The problem is that development, under our current technologies, involves a nation's using increasing per capita amounts of fossil fuels. Burning coal to generate electricity and using refined petroleum to provide transportation are putting ever-increasing amounts of carbon dioxide (CO_2) (and other greenhouse gases) into the atmosphere. And that CO_2 traps heat from the Sun close to the Earth's surface, leading to a rise in the average temperatures on the planet. There is a clear positive correlation between the concentrations of CO_2 in the atmosphere and Earth's average temperature. Since the dawn of modern growth in the late 18th century till today, concentrations of CO_2 have risen from approximately 275 parts per million (ppm) to approximately 380 ppm. If current rates of growth in usage of fossil fuels continue and, indeed, increase through 2050, the concentrations of CO_2 are expected to reach 500 ppm.

49 Rauch and Kostyak regress the gender differences in labour force participation rates on the percentage of the national population that is Muslim. They find that 'a country that is 100 per cent Muslim will have a gender gap that is 18.3 percentage points higher than a country that is zero per cent Muslim'. But when they add a second independent variable that is a dummy for whether the country is Arab-speaking, the Muslim effect becomes insignificant. (Rauch & Kostyak 2009, p. 182.)

50 And less distressing than the pictures presented by Kuran 2001 (arguing that institutional bottlenecks prevented Islamic countries from fostering large-scale private economic enterprises and governments from providing an optimal number of public goods; Kuran finds nothing in Islam that is inherently antithetical to modern economic growth[; indeed, the largest Muslim nation by population, Indonesia, has had a sustained annual GDP growth rate of 6 per cent for several decades, and Turkey is one of the wealthiest countries in the Middle East]), and Ayres & Macey 2005 (stressing the general lack of pro-growth policies in the Middle Eastern countries and the particular failure to adopt policies favourable to the creation of innovative new business entities).

The results of those increases are somewhat in controversy, but all serious students agree that the rise in concentrations is anthropogenic and that it could have serious, unforeseen, and costly consequences for the entire planet.[51]

Adding to the problem of fossil-fuel use is that the Earth's ability to absorb CO_2 through forests and the oceans is either compromized or decreasing. Deforestation to provide additional living space is removing one of the most effective methods of 'carbon sequestration'.

Let me relate this issue more clearly to modern economic growth. The current population of the Earth is approximately 7 billion. Of those, about one billion live in developed countries where the annual per capita income is $ 20,000 and above. About one billion live in poor countries where the annual per capita income is $ 1,000 or less. The remaining 4.5 billion live in countries whose annual per capita income lies between $ 1,000 and $ 20,00 and that are experiencing sustained economic growth.

These broad generalizations hide the fact that the average consumer of fossil-fuel-related products and services in the wealthy countries annually consumes 32 times the quantity of those resources than does the average person in the developing world.[52] Put dramatically, each one of the over 300 million U.S. citizens annually consumes as much fossil-fuel-related goods and services as 32 Kenyans. Presumably, those Kenyans and others in the 5.5 billion below U.S. consumption standards aspire to emulate the consumption patterns or wealth positions of the average U.S. citizen.

Imagine what would happen to the amount of fossil-fuel consumption if only one country, China, reached the U.S. level of consumption. China has a population of approximately 1.5 billion, and per capita consumption rates of fossil-fuel-related goods and services there are only one-eleventh of what they are in the U.S. (even though China has recently become, by volume, the greatest emitter of greenhouse gases in the world) Suppose, for the sake of argument, that China continues its remarkable growth of almost 10 per cent per year into the near future so that their annual per capita consumption levels rise to ours. That fact alone (and assuming no other changes in the world) would double world consumption rates of oil, electric power, metals, plastics, and other greenhouse-gas emitting products and services. If India, with a current population of one billion people, were also to grow so that their annual per capita consumption rates rose to current U.S. levels, then world consumption rates would triple. Finally, suppose that the entire developing world of 5.5 billion people were to grow to U.S. annual per capita consumption levels. World consumption rates would increase to 11 times their current levels. This would be the equivalent of the world's population increasing, at current consumption levels, to 72 billion people from its current level of 6.5 billion.[53]

51 See, for example, Kolbert 2005. See also Stern 2007. Eleven of the 12 warmest years in recorded history have occurred in the last 12 years.

52 Much of what follows is based on Diamond 2008.

53 This frightening thought experiment assumes that there are no dramatic technological changes that replace 'carbon dioxide and other greenhouse-gas emitting' technologies. Of →

The clear problem that global warming poses is whether increasing wealth is consistent with widespread concerns for the stability of the environment. We know that development improves lives considerably, but we now also know (or strongly suspect) that it may do so at a significant cost. A planet that in the year 2100 or beyond is, on average, 5° C warmer than it is today will cause climatic change that has large costs for large numbers of human beings. For example, sea levels may rise, causing extraordinary expenses of shoring up large coastal cities or large costs of relocating population and fixed capital away from the coasts; growing seasons are likely to change, making some areas of agricultural productivity inhospitable but opening up other areas (such as Siberia) to cultivation; droughts are likely to become more common in areas, such as the Sahel, that are already hard pressed; and the melting of snows and glaciers could threaten the water supplies of South and East Asia where 40 per cent of the human population lives.

The distressing aspect of these thoughts is that the problem is a worldwide one, and yet we have international institutions agreements that address the issues only marginally. Nor is there any realistic prospect of creating such institutions or agreements. In the words of one careful student of global warming, 'This is the most serious problem to face humanity'.[54]

3. Law and Economic Growth

As we have seen, the most promising recent literature in economics on the causes of sustained modern growth focuses on institutions. In this section I draw a connection between 'institutions' and law. I shall ultimately conclude that however important institutions may be to growth, the aspects of law to which people frequently point as being vital to national development are unlikely to be as flexible or as crucial as some other factors that I seek to identify.

I begin with an overview of the supposed or hypothesized relationship between law and economic growth. I then turn to a consideration of the most striking case of growth without the foundations of strong property, contract, and other legal protections – the People's Republic of China. And I conclude this section with a brief consideration of four factors that argue against the centrality of law in economic development.[55]

course, there may be such changes. Indeed, there almost have to be in order for widespread growth leading to current resource-consumption levels to succeed.

54 Farber 2008.

55 Nuno Garoupa has convinced me that I need to include a section on the 'legal origins' literature. That literature finds, speaking broadly, that the countries with a common law system have grown faster than have countries with a civil law system. This is the finding, for example, of Mahoney 2001. Other entries in this literature worth noting are La Porta *et al.* 1998, Glaeser & Shleifer 2002, and La Porta, Lopez-di-Silanes & Shleifer 2008. The finding might be dismissed as indicative of correlation but not causation; some of the literature has argued that specific substantive areas of the common law system, such as its law of corporate governance, can be demonstrated to be more efficient than other corporate governance regimes.

3.1. *Overview*

One of the shortcomings of the literature on institutions is its failure to be specific about just what counts as an 'institution'. A core understanding is that 'institution' refers to the practices and organizations of public life - the societal, regional, and local governance organizations; and the executive, legislative, and judicial organs of government. But the literature seems to spread out from that core to encompass the institutions of civil society,[56] private religious institutions, and commercial institutions. And even beyond those private institutions the literature sometimes cites the structure of the family and extended clan and social norms. We might further include 'culture', that elusive but suggestive term that encompasses shared notions of right conduct or behaviour, of ethical and moral values, and of senses of beauty, euphonious music, and art.

So broadly conceived, the idea of 'institutions' seems to swallow up all categories of explanation and, in so doing, to become an ultimately useless catch-all. We have to have a clearer and more exclusive notion of an 'institution' in order for that notion to be useful in explaining and predicting modern growth. As an important adjunct of this more precise notion, we ought to be able to explain how those institutions that favour growth come into being, why they finally appeared in northern Europe in the late 18th and early 19th centuries, why they have appeared only later in the 'late starters', how inappropriate institutions give way to those that favour growth, and how, if at all, human intervention can consciously create growth-enhancing institutions.

This is a formidable list of questions and a demanding research agenda - both far beyond the scope of this essay. I want to look at a more limited subset of the possible meanings of 'institutions' in order to see the extent to which that meaning of the word is vital to the onset and continuation of modern growth.

The subset of 'institutions' upon which I want to concentrate are those gathered under the rubric 'law'. So as to be inclusive, I mean that term to include both the organizations that make and enforce the law (the legislature, administrative agencies, executive, and judiciary; the private legal profession; and the police) and the substantive content of the law. I want to include the realms of private law that seek to govern relationships between private parties, such as contract, tort, and property law. I also want to include public law - criminal law, corporation law, bankruptcy law, and so on. In addition, I want to include the general governance

56 See, for example, the path breaking work on the vital role of civil society: Putnam 1992. Putnam compared similarly sized towns in northern Italy, some of which were well-governed and others of which were not. His attempt to explain the differences in why democracy worked in some towns and not in others focused on the role of the institutions of civil society - the clubs, choir groups, soccer team fan clubs, commercial organizations, neighbourhood associations, and other informal groups that operated in the space between the families of the towns and their government and served to unify families and individuals. Where those intermediate civic organizations were present, democracy worked well; where they were absent or weak, democracy did not work very well. Putnam's hypothesis is that intermediate civic groups provide connections and cross relationships that are essential to a well-functioning democracy.

structure of the society - whether there is meaningful democracy; whether political considerations are suitably under control or inappropriately intrude into decisions that would better be decided on principled, neutral grounds. Despite my attempt to focus on a limited set of institutions, this is a wide-ranging set.

Let me begin with a statement of the case that there is a connection between these legal institutions and modern growth. The broadest view holds that law is vital to national growth to the extent that it creates incentives for people to behave in a growth-enhancing manner. This means, among other things, harnessing individual self-interest to serve the public good, inducing people to 'do good by doing well'. Thus, a business organization must have the appropriate incentives to produce and market so as to make a profit but, in doing so, must respect the interests of their customers and employees in not being harmed unreasonably by the products they are purchasing or producing. And the production process must not result in unwanted and uncompensated pollution of the air or water. Those seeking to make agreements that will bind them for a period of time so as to secure a benefit from another similarly and reciprocally bound for a period of time must have confidence that those agreements will be kept or, if broken, result in adequate compensation. Those artists and inventors who seek to create new expressive works or new, useful, and non-obvious inventions (and in so doing, forego other profitable employment opportunities) should have reasonable expectations of being able to enjoy the economic benefits of their expressive and creative activities. Property owners should have reasonable security in their assets and know themselves to be free from unreasonable interference in the enjoyment and employment of those assets from other individuals, organizations, and the government.

There are, of course, many details to be added to this account, such as provisions for education of the populace, subsidies for basic scientific research, well-functioning financial intermediaries, an equitable taxation system, a reasonable health-care system, security for foreign investors, bankruptcy, and so on. But the core of the argument linking economic prosperity to legal institutions is the one in the previous paragraph.

One elaboration on this argument that is often left unstated but is implicit is that the governance structure of the system - including the judiciary who will decide private litigation - must be reasonably stable, inclusive, and productively and prudently responsive to the real events of the nation. Put in the negative, the government ought not to be cravenly corrupt.[57]

The key to implementing this view of the vital role of these legal institutions in fostering economic growth is the discovery of a mechanism for getting a low- or no-growth society to adopt these legal institutions. And so far, no obvious mechanism has presented itself. An important part of the Washington consensus was the attempt to condition aid from the international organizations on the adoption of some of the policies and institutions noted above. And as we have seen, that

57 There may be such a thing as 'optimal corruption'. The intuition is that some corruption is both inevitable and good and that attempts to zero-out corruption will be excessively costly and, among other social costs, may lead to discouraging otherwise talented people from devoting their energies to politics.

conditionality was not successful and, indeed, detrimental to sustained growth in several instances. As I also indicated above, we do not yet have a clear account of why these legal institutions - assuming for the moment that they are, in fact, essential to sustained modern growth - were adopted in northern Europe in the late 18th and early 19th centuries, nor why some former colonies (mostly former English colonies) saw fit to adopt those legal institutions while others did not. We do not know, in the parlance of comparative law, why some legal institutions are attractive as transplants and others are not. And because of our lack of knowledge about the reasons for the evolution or adoption of growth-enhancing legal institutions, we are at a loss as to how to persuade developing countries to follow the developed world's lead in this regard.

3.2. *The Anomalous Example of the People's Republic of China*

I have already remarked on the fact that the annual GDP growth rate of the People's Republic of China has been a staggering 9 per cent for most of the past 30 years. This is not only the highest current economic growth rate; it is also one of the highest and most sustained growth rates ever recorded. So, if we are eager to pursue the hypothesis that law can have a particularly benign effect on fostering and sustaining growth, we ought to examine China closely. Our initial hypothesis might be that China's rapid and continuous growth is in substantial part attributable to its having efficiently defined and enforced property interests, provided for the neutral enforcement of consensual agreements, established an independent judiciary committee to the rule of law, made provisions for training an effective and competitive legal profession, and has done most of the other legal reforms that, by hypothesis, are important for growth.

There is an immediate question with which we must deal. Among the many legal reforms that one might imagine is growth-enhancing is the creation of an effective participatory regime of societal governance - in a word, democracy. And whatever else China may have done to spur growth, it has not adopted democratic values. But, as it happens, this is not fatal to the hypothesis. That is because, to summarize a vast literature boldly, participatory political regimes are not a precondition of growth.[58]

Let us turn to a consideration of the more central private law areas (property and contracts) to see if they can be shown to have played a significant role in Chinese economic growth. Before turning to the specific case of China, I begin with

58 This is the famous Lipset hypothesis: see Lipset 1959. (That article was recently announced to be the seventh most cited article in the first 100 years of the *American Political Science Review*). Lipset argued that democracy (and some other social effects) were co-evolutionary with growth - that is, that democracy was both created and consolidated by growth. That, I venture to say, is the consensus opinion among students of economic growth. In Acemoglu, Johnson & Robinson 2008 the authors use fixed-effects and instrument-variables approaches to show that the obvious correlation between income and democracy is not causal, either way.

a recent research paper by Michael Trebilcock and Paul-Erik Veel that considers the general case for defining and enforcing property interests as a growth strategy.[59]

The case for replacing informal or tradition-based property interests with formal property rights is straightforward. On the assumption that formal property interests are clearer than traditional interests, the owners can make more efficient use of the resource if the physical, temporal, and other extents of their interest in the resource are more certain. Moreover, potential lenders are likely to be more generous in lending to a property-owner whose interests are more certain and therefore easier to evaluate to plan for the contingency of default.[60] Finally, clear, formal property interests make it less expensive for alternative uses - potentially more valuable uses - of the resource to be easier to evaluate and therefore lower the costs of negotiating between the current possessor and a higher-valuing user about a change in ownership. All of that is part of the central canon of property law through the lens of law and economics.[61]

Trebilcock and Veel acknowledge these benefits of formalization, but they also note that the process of formalization may be costly. Specifically, they note two potential costs: (1) that complementary social, economic, political, and legal arrangements in a developing society may not be sufficiently elaborated in order for a formal property regime to work efficiently (as might be true if there is no method of registering property claims, only a rudimentary legal profession, and no independent judiciary before whom to assert and defend property claims); and (2) that the transition costs from a traditional property rights regime (in which, for example, many different individuals and families may have fractional interests in the same piece of land) to a formal property regime in which interests are concentrated in an efficient manner may be so substantial that the benefits of formality are less than the costs.

The import of these eminently sensible observations is that there are costs and benefits to the formalization of property interests and that it may be the case that the benefits of formalization exceed the costs but that it may be that the costs exceed the benefits. In brief, the case for formalization depends on the specifics of a given instance.

These considerations also suggest that where formalization generates no net social benefits, it may be the case that a system of informal or incomplete or ill-defined property interests may be efficient.

Trebilcock and Veel use these general observations to consider the recent record of property interests in China. They begin with the observation that China ef-

59 Trebilcock & Veel 2007.

60 See Besley 1995 for an empirical study of the relationship between clearer property interests and incentives to invest.

61 And also part of the standard institutional argument about the importance of efficiently defining and enforcing property interests as a condition for modern economic growth. See, for example, Barro 1991 (showing a statistically significant correlation between strongly enforced property interests and a nation's economic growth rate). See also Rodrik, Subramanian & Trebbi 2004, and Acemoglu & Johnson 2005 (both articles also finding a strong positive relationship between strong property interests and national economic growth rates, investment rates, and the strength of credit markets).

fectively abolished private property rights in land in 1956. Instead, rural production of agricultural goods was organized around communes and collectives. Not surprisingly, from an economic point of view, grain production grew very modestly from the mid-1950s till the early 1970s.[62]

Along with other reforms that appeared in the late 1970s when Deng Xiaoping consolidated power, there was an important alteration in the status of rural property. The Household Responsibility System, introduced in the early 1980s, allowed the village collective to retain legal ownership of land but encouraged the collective to make contracts to provide individuals and families with use rights, initially for a term of five years. In 1984 the allowable term was extended to 15 years, and in 1993, to 30 years. Tenure security was an issue; the revisions to the Land Management Act of 1998 strengthened tenants' security interests by being more explicit about those interests and by greatly narrowing the circumstances in which adjustments to a lease could be made. The Rural Land Contracting Law of 2002 further narrowed the circumstances in which long-term leases could be adjusted to a few exceptional instances. And finally, a further revision of 2007 gave farmers the right to renew a 30-year lease for another 30 years upon the first lease's expiration.

All of this notwithstanding, Trebilcock and Veel find four reasons why this increasing formalization has failed to provide the benefits posited to come from formal property interests. First, village leaders commonly redistributed land, giving rise to insecurity of tenure. A 2005 survey found that 74.3 per cent of villages had had at least one round of redistribution since the institution of the Household Responsibility System in the mid-1980s and that 55 per cent of villages had had two or more such rounds of redistribution.

Second, throughout China, both in urban areas and in rural areas, the expropriation of property without compensation is relatively common.[63]

Third, land transfers are becoming more common, but there are still significant impediments to the development of an active market in land and in land-use rights.

Fourth, the ability of private citizens to access the courts to seek enforcement of their property claims is severely limited. Not only is it difficult for peasants, in particular, to assert a legal claim, the evidentiary basis for their doing so is thin. Many land-tenure agreements were never written down or recorded. A 2006 survey found that only about 10 per cent of farmers had a written contract or certificate that fully specified their rights and contained all the provisions that the various land-management acts required.[64]

62 Indeed, there was a devastating famine in China from 1958 to 1961 in which between 20 and 43 million people are thought to have perished.

63 See Wines & Ansfield 2010, p. 5 (describing incidents in an area of west Beijing where the Chinese national government has sold land to developers who must then buy out residents, sometimes resorting to 'squads of toughs' to encourage sale).

64 There is additional sceptical scholarly work on the relationship between formal legal protections and the process of economic development in China. For example, Michael Trebilcock & Leng 2006 argue that it is difficult to find evidence of the importance of formal contract law in development outside the financial sector of developing countries. And Clarke, Murrell & Whiting 2006 examine three areas of substantive law – property rights, agreements →

3.3. *Why Good Law is not Sufficient to Growth*

A previous section laid out the argument linking law to the view that the correct institutions are vital for growth and also noted that we do not know how to implement this view in the slow-developing countries or 'late starters'. But the previous section made the case that formal legal rules have not contributed significantly to the remarkable record of growth in China over the past 30 years.

In this section I want to express a more general skepticism about the relationship between growth-enhancing legal institutions and modern growth. My sense is that the arguments above about the vital role of private and public law and the legal profession are overblown and possibly inaccurate and misleading. This intuition takes some force from the evidence that the Washington consensus was not a successful growth plan and from the remarkable record of Chinese growth in the absence of formal legal protections. Nonetheless, my skepticism is not solidly grounded in either theory or thorough empirical evidence. As a result, these suggestions are preliminary and tentative, subject to revision in light of clearer theoretical and empirical arguments.

My arguments are three-fold. First, the view that law is central to growth ignores the fact that there are alternatives to law that can and do serve the same general functions as law. Second, the view ignores the great contribution that stability, in and of itself, can make to national growth and development. And third, the view underestimates the things that can go wrong in a society, even one that seems to have a well-functioning legal system, and also underestimates the value that a courageous political leader can have in fostering growth.

3.3.1. Alternatives to Law

The great psychologist Abraham Maslow memorably said, 'If the only tool you have is a hammer, every problem is a nail'. Lawyers have law as their principal tool, and, as a result, lawyers see every problem as amenable to legal solution. This 'legal centrism', as Robert Ellickson called it,[65] suggests that other forms of ordering society are either ineffectual, unjust, or uncontrollable or all three. But we now know that those alternatives to law are not only possible but that in many instances are the driving force in social organization.

Bob Ellickson's study of social norms in Shasta County, California, made this point eloquently.[66] Ellickson discovered that the law on the books regarding damage done by cattle to private property was different in two halves of a large county in northern California. In one half, the cattle-owner could be held liable for damage done by his unsupervised cattle to another person's property – say, a homeowner's garden; in the other half, the cattle owner could not be held liable for

to trade, and corporate governance; they find that while law has been playing an increasingly important role in Chinese economic development, 'formal legal institutions have not made a critical contribution to China's remarkable economic success'.

65 Ellickson 1991.

66 Ellickson 1986.

similar damage. Ellickson's hope was that if the costs of bargaining between cattle-owners and other property owners were low in both halves of the county, then the same practices for dealing with cattle damage might prevail, regardless of the law. If so, this would be a real-world indication that the Coase Theorem is correct.[67]

What Ellickson found was that the practices were identical in the two halves but that the reason was not that the Coase Theorem was correct. Rather, cattle-owners and private property owners in the two halves were seeking to conform to a clear and dominant social norm of being a 'good neighbour'. That norm required that if a cow strayed onto your property, you should take steps to protect that cow – by, for example, moving your car out of your garage and moving the cow in – call the cow's owner to tell him that you have the cow, and feed and protect the cow until the owner could come to pick it up. You should not remonstrate with the owner about the costs you were incurring; nor should you seek to get compensation from the cow-owner for any minor damage that you might have suffered.

Of course, the 'good neighbour' norm placed duties on the cow-owner, too. He should apologize for the inconvenience, offer to compensate the protector for the damage and the costs of housing and feeding his stray cow, and seek to come to retrieve the cow as quickly as possible. But so long as the norm was being observed by both sides, there was no talk of or need for lawyers. Indeed, Ellickson found that people in Shasta County only resorted to the law when people (typically recent immigrants from another region of the country) failed to obey the 'good neighbour' norm.

The central point of this famous example and of much subsequent work on similar topics is that for most people social norms, not law, are the principal governing rules of their lives. Law is invoked only in unusual situations where social norms have broken down or are not being followed.

How is this literature relevant to the role of law in economic development? The obvious connection is that social norms appear to be a close substitute for the law. Put a little more forcefully, formal law may not be necessary for a well-ordered society; social norms may serve perfectly well. In fact, it may be the case that where the institutions of law are either absent or ill-managed, social norms become elaborate enough to perform many of the functions that a well-functioning legal system would have provided.

It may be, then, that the absence of a well-functioning legal system should not be taken as a signal that a society cannot sustain modern economic growth. It is possible that in developing societies, social norms are the principal guide to good behaviour, as they appeared to be in Shasta County, California, and that they perform well in guiding behaviour into efficient, growth-enhancing channels.

I am well aware that there can be detrimental social norms that impede growth as well as the beneficial social norms that substitute for law. Critics, such as Richard McAdams,[68] have noted, for example, that racism was a social norm in

67 The Coase Theorem holds that 'when transaction costs are zero, an efficient allocation will result, regardless of the law'. See, for an extended discussion, Cooter & Ulen 2007.

68 McAdams 1995.

much of the United States that had a very toxic effect on society and required correction through concerted legal action. It is easily conceivable that developing countries or regions have deleterious social norms that prevent efficient investment or other growth-enhancing activities and that law might correct those adverse effects.

Nonetheless, a modern legal system may be a product of development, not a prerequisite to it. Until we know much more about the role of social norms in developing countries, we should not be so certain that social norms are not fulfilling the same societal functions that a well-functioning modern legal system might fill.

3.3.2. Stability and Growth

Decades ago Joseph Schumpeter characterized the capitalist system as one in which there was 'creative destruction'.[69] That wonderful phrase evokes the swirl of success and failure of new enterprises, the rise and fall of industries, the unsettling effects of new technologies that seems to many critics of capitalism to be chaotic and, therefore, undesirable. Modern growth brings along with it an unavoidable ferment and barely controlled chaos. There is no all-seeing institution in any society that can predict which enterprises should succeed and which should fail, which new technologies are going to have far-reaching effects, and which are going to stir minor ripples in the social and commercial fabric.

Nonetheless, stability is a valuable background condition for long-term growth. Investors, both foreign and domestic, must have reasonable assurances that next year will be much like this year. Too much uncertainty about fundamental conditions in which economic calculations are made will discourage anything other than very short-term decision-making. And that short-term decision-making is not conducive to the longer-range planning that seems such an essential part of modern growth.

How should a developing country seek to strike a sensible balance between allowing the ferment of modern growth and creating the stability within which that ferment may proceed? That is, of course, the key. And my central point here is to draw attention to this obvious and central point that may be lost in the literature on the salutary effects of good institutions and of good law – stability of background conditions is extremely important to long-run growth. Indeed, there may be a tension between having the correct legal institutions and having stable institutions such that stable-but-not-ideal institutions are more conducive to growth than less-stable-but-ideal institutions.[70]

We do not know the relative merits of stability versus correctness. But we have a hint that there is this trade-off in the literature on the role of democracy in

69 Schumpeter 1942. See also McCraw 2007.

70 I am grateful to Katharina Pistor for suggesting that I look at Bates 2009 on this matter – a suggestion I have not yet followed. I am also mindful of the hypothesis in Gilson & Milhaupt 2010, that '[s]ome autocratic regimes have fundamentally transformed their economies [for the better], despite serious deficiencies along a range of other dimensions' and will incorporate that material into subsequent drafts of this article.

fostering economic growth. Democracy is, like sound legal institutions, thought in some quarters to be a necessary precondition of modern growth. However, the great sociologist Seymour Martin Lipset noted in 1959 that democracy is typically a product of modern growth, not a precursor.[71] Because democracy can be an untidy system of government, societies just embarking on modern growth may prefer societal governance that is more stable than democracy and only tolerate the vagaries of democracy when the process of growth has taken such firm hold that stability of the background conditions (if not of the actual people in government) has been secured.

3.3.3. Political Courage

Modern growth unsettles society. The swirl of 'creative destruction' raises some and dashes others; it elevates some sectors of the economy at the expense of others; it may expose previously secure domestic producers to withering competition from foreign enterprises; and so on. Accepting these and other changes is not at all easy. The prospect for betterment resulting from a change must be substantial for individuals to prefer the maelstrom of creative destruction to the less rewarding but comfortable life of low- or no-growth stasis. And most people prefer the known present to the unknown future, even with assurances of betterment. Change will command widespread approval or toleration only if it will positively affect the vast majority of people and that betterment is far more likely than not.

Regardless of what form of government a developing nation has, navigating the politics of modernization is extremely taxing on political skills. Indeed, the social strains of modernization can result in rioting and rebellion.[72] But even if they do not, modernization can place responsive politicians into very difficult situations. Growth involves change, and where there is change, there are gainers and losers. The gainers will surely encourage and accept the change, but the losers may fight to prevent their losses from becoming permanent or crippling. And because the losers are likely to have been people with considerable power in the pre-growth regime, they may begin their campaign to stall change from a very powerful position.[73]

There are two important implications of these observations. First, if change is disruptive and people are likely to resist it forcefully, is this not an argument for having a dictatorship or other form of nonresponsive government when modern growth begins?[74] This would certainly seem to follow, but I am sure that the suggestion in favour of dictatorship goes too far. It is true that a dictatorship could ignore the protests of those who are hurt by modernization or compensate them in some way. That is, the political costs of managing the transition to modernization might be lower under a dictatorship than under a responsive government. But the

71 As noted above, the 'Lipset hypothesis', sometimes called the 'hypothesis', appeared in Lipset 1959 and was elaborated in Lipset 1960. For modern, empirical confirmation of the Lipset hypothesis, see Przeworski *et al.* 2000.

72 See, for example, Chua 2002. See also Ginsburg 2004.

73 Acemoglu & Robinson 2000.

74 I am grateful to Ajit Mishra for posing this important question.

catch is that the dictatorship would have to be convinced that it would be better off under modern growth than under the alternative. And it is not at all clear that a dictator would always or even usually conclude that calculation in favour of modernization. Some, perhaps most, dictatorships will focus on what is best for them, not on what is best for the entire society. So, to be more precise, the argument in favour of overcoming political opposition to modernization's changes makes a case for an enlightened dictator, one who sees the benefits to all of the changes and subordinates his or her own desires in favour of that social good. Such dictatorships exist, but they are rare.

To be fair, it is not clear that a responsive government will opt for modernization either. It may mistakenly conclude that the costs of modern growth exceed the benefits. But it seems more likely that a responsive government will respond in favour of sustained growth when the benefits far exceed the costs. As I said above, there are good reasons for believing that a dictatorship will only take into account is own costs and benefits, not societal benefits.

Second, a further implication of the points above about the political costs of modernization is that nearly every society will opt for growth when the costs are small and the benefits large or when the gap between costs and benefits are very large and where the benefits will be widespread and when the likelihood of the benefits' being realized are high.[75] But this is a formidable list of preconditions, and in real-world situations, these preconditions may either not exist or may be attended by a large degree of uncertainty. For instance, it may be the case that the benefits are distant and hazy, while the costs are vivid and immediate.

What is to be done in those circumstances? I believe that in those instances a society needs leaders with extraordinary courage, vision, and determination. They need vision to see the benefits of modern growth, courage to take on the costs of battling the political losers from modernization, and determination to continue the battle to victory. These are, needless to say, rare qualities in anyone and perhaps rarer still in professional politicians. Nonetheless, a developing society that can identify and encourage courageous politicians is likely to make the transition to modern growth quickly and with a minimum of pain.[76]

Every society would like to have courageous and far-seeing leaders. But how often does an Abraham Lincoln or a Deng Xiaoping come along? And that fact that great leaders are rare leads to the question of how a society is supposed to identify great leaders. How does a society select for political courage? Is its appearance random or due to luck? Or do dire circumstances create them, as the trauma of the

75 I demonstrated above that the very rapid growth that has characterized the modern experience of India and China has created an easily seen indication of the benefits of growth to the citizens of those societies. Presumably, people in a participatory regime can be enlisted to favour a policy that, although it does not make them wealthier, will make their grandchildren wealthier. But even that deferred benefit is often not enough to command current political support.

76 In Hyderabad, Hans-Bernd Schaefer noted that politician who are frequently credited with being great leaders – such as Nehru and Gandhi in modern Indian history – have in fact been disastrously wrong-headed, from an economic point of view, while spectacularly successful leaders, such as Manmohan Singh, are frequently undervalued.

U.S. Civil War may have made Abraham Lincoln?[77] Can a society establish processes or institutions that train political leadership and courage?

4. Conclusion

This essay began with a review of the record of modern growth, noting that the experience of the past 190 years or so is fundamentally different from any preceding episodes of national wealth in human history in that this modern growth is sustained, not exploitative, and open to all nations and all humanity. I also briefly rehearsed the various academic theories of the causes of modern growth and how those theories have been instantiated in policies. I noted that there is an emerging consensus among students of growth and development that 'institutions' are a vital ingredient, and I argued that among the various possible organizations and practices that the word 'institution' might encompass, 'law' and 'legal institutions' seem to occupy a core position in fostering national growth.

Nonetheless, I expressed some skepticism about the ability of legal institutions to be the 'golden key' to growth that has so long been sought. My skepticism centers on three factors – that there are suitable alternatives to growth-facilitating legal institutions and that many societies have found those alternatives, that just as important as the right institutions is social and national stability, and that focusing on the role of institutions and law as engines of growth draws attention away from the crucial role that political factors and particularly political courage can play in fostering a nation's growth and development.

77 'Some are born great; some achieve greatness; and some have greatness thrust upon them'. William Shakespeare, *Twelfth Night*, Act II, Scene V (1602).

Bibliography

Acemoglu 2009
Acemoglu, D., *Introduction to Modern Economic Growth*, New Jersey: Princeton University Press, 2009.

Acemoglu & Johnson 2005
Acemoglu, D. & Johnson, S., 'Unbundling Institutions', *Journal of Political Economy*, 2005, p. 949-995.

Acemoglu & Robinson 2000
Acemoglu, D. & Robinson, J.A., 'Political Losers as a Barrier to Economic Development', *American Economic Review*, 2000, p. 126-130.

Acemoglu & Robinson 2009
Acemoglu, D. & Robinson, J.A., *Economic Origins of Dictatorship and Democracy*, New York: Cambridge University Press, 2005.

Acemoglu, Johnson & Robinson 2001
Acemoglu, D., Johnson, S. & Robinson, J.A., 'The Colonial Origins of Comparative Development: An Empirical Investigation', *American Economic Review*, 2001, p. 1369-1401.

Acemoglu, Johnson & Robinson 2002
Acemoglu, D., Johnson, S. & Robinson, J.A., 'Reversal of Fortune: Geography and Institutions in the Making of the Modern World Income Distribution', *Quarterly Journal of Economics*, 2002, p. 1231-1294.

Acemoglu, Johnson & Robinson 2005
Acemoglu, D., Johnson, S. & Robinson, J.A., 'The Rise of Europe: Atlantic Trade, Institutional Change and Growth', *American Economic Review*, 2005, p. 546-579.

Acemoglu, Johnson & Robinson 2008
Acemoglu, D., Johnson, S. & Robinson, J.A., 'Income and Democracy', *American Economic Review*, 2008, p. 808–842.

Alston & Gallo 2010
Alston, L.J. & Gallo, A.A., 'Electoral Fraud, the Rise of Peron, and the Demise of Checks and Balances in Argentina', *Explorations in Economic History*, 2010, p. 179–197.

Arbache, Go & Page 2008
Arbache, J. Go, D.S. & Page, J., *Is Africa's Economy at a Turning Point?*, The World Bank, Africa Region, Office of the Chief Economist, Policy Research Working Paper, No. 4519, February 2008.

Ayres & Macey 2005
Ayres, I. & Macey, J.R., 'Symposium: National Building in the Middle East: Institutional and Evolutionary Failure and Economic Development in the Middle East', *Yale Journal of International Law*, 2005, p. 347-472.

Banerjee & Duflo 2007
Banerjee, A. & Duflo, E., 'The Economic Lives of the Poor', *Journal of Economic Perspectives*, 2007, p. 141-167.

Banerjee & Duflo 2008
Banerjee, A. & Duflo, E., *The Experimental Approach to Development Economics*, Centre for Economic Policy Research Discussion Paper, October 2008.

Barro 1991
Barro, R., 'Economic Growth in a Cross-Section of Countries', *Quarterly Journal of Economics*, 1991, p. 407-443.

Bates 2009
Bates, R.H., *Prosperity and Violence: The Political Economy of Development*, 2nd edition, New York, London: W.W. Norton & Company, 2009.

Besley 1995
Besley, T, 'Property Rights and Investment Incentives: Theory and Evidence from Ghana', *The Journal of Political Economy*, p. 903-937.

Bhalla 2002
Bhalla, S.S., *Imagine There's No Country: Poverty, Inequality, and Growth in the Era of Globalization*, Washington DC: Peterson Institute, 2002.

Chen & Ravallion 2001
Chen, S. & Ravallion, M., 'How Did the World's Poor Fare in the 1990s?', *Review of Income and Wealth*, 2001, p. 283-300.

Chen & Ravallion 2004
Chen, S. & Ravallion, M., 'How Have the World's Poorest Fared Since the Early 1980s?', *World Bank Research Observer*, 2004, p. 141-169.

Chen & Ravallion 2008
Chen, S. & Ravallion, M., *The Developing World Is Poorer Than We Thought, But No Less Successful in the Fight Against Poverty*, World Bank, Development Research Group, Policy Research Working Paper, No. 4703, August 2008, available at: <http://www-wds.worldbank.org/external/default/WDSContentServer/IW3P/IB/2008/08/26/000158349_20080826113239/Rendered/PDF/WPS4703.pdf> (last accessed, 21 October 2009).

Chua 2002
Chua, A., *World on Fire: How Exporting Free-Market Democracy Breeds Ethnic Hatred and Global Instability*, New York: Doubleday Publishing, 2002.

Clarke, Murrell & Whiting 2006
Clarke, D., Murrell, P. & Whiting, S., *The Role of Law in China's Economic Development*, SSRN Working Paper, 27 January 2006, available at: <www.ssrn.com>.

Cohen & Easterly 2009
Cohen, J. & Easterly, W. (eds.), *What Works in Development?: Thinking Big and Thinking Small*, Washington DC: Brookings Institution Press, 2009.

Collier 2007
Collier Paul, *The Bottom Billion. Why the Poorest Countries are Failing and What Can Be Done About It*, New York: Oxford University Press, 2007.

Cooter & Ulen 2007
Cooter, R.D. & Ulen, T.S., *Law and Economics*, 5th edition, Boston: Addison Wesley, 2007.

Diamond 2008
Diamond, J., 'What Is Your Consumption Factor?', *The New York Times*, 2 January 2008.

Easterly 2002
Easterly, W., *The Elusive Quest for Growth: Economists' Adventures and Misadventures in the Tropics*, Cambridge, Massachusetts: The MIT Press, 2002.

Easterly 2006
Easterly, W., *The White Man's Burden: Why the West's Efforts to Aid the Rest Have Done So Much Ill and So Little Good*, New York: The Penguin Press, 2006.

Ellickson 1986
Ellickson, R.C., 'Of Coase and Cattle: Dispute Resolution Among Neighbors in Shasta County', *Stanford Law Review*, 1986, p. 623-687.

Ellickson 1991
Ellickson, R.C., *Order Without Law: How Neighbors Settle Disputes*, Cambridge: Massachusetts, 1991.

Farber 2008
Farber, D., 'Modeling Climate Change and Its Impacts: Law, Policy, and Science', *Texas Law Review*, 2008, p. 1655-1699.

Fukuyama 1995
Fukuyama, F., *Trust: The Social Virtues and the Creation of Prosperity*, New York: Free Press, 1995.

Fukuyama 2008
Fukuyama, F. (ed.), *Falling Behind: Explaining the Development Gap Between Latin America and the United States*, New York: Oxford University Press, 2008.

Gertner 2010
Gertner, J., 'The Rise and Fall of the GDP', *New York Times Sunday Magazine*, 16 May 2010, available at <www.nytimes.com/2010/05/16/magazine> and <www.stateof theusa.org/>.

Gilson & Milhaupt 2010
Gilson, R. & Milhaupt, C., *Economically Benevolent Dictators: Lessons for Developing Democracies*, Columbia and Stanford Law and Economics Working Paper, August 2010.

Ginsburg 2004
Ginsburg, T., 'Democracy, Markets and Doomsaying: Amy Chua's World on Fire', *Berkeley Journal of International Law*, 2004, p. 310-335.

Glaeser & Shleifer 2002
Glaeser, E. & Shleifer, A., 'Legal Origins', *Quarterly Journal of Economics*, 2002, p. 1193-1229.

Glaeser *et al.* 2004
Glaeser, E., La Porta, R., Lopez-de-Silanes, F. & Shleifer, A., 'Do Institutions Cause Growth?, *Journal of Economic Growth*, 2004, p. 271-303.

Helpman 2004
Helpman, E., *The Mystery of Economic Growth*, Harvard: Belknap Press of Harvard University Press, 2004.

Jensen 2007
Jensen, R., 'The Digital Provide: Information (Technology), Market Performance, and Welfare in the South Indian Fisheries Sector', *Quarterly Journal of Economics*, 2007, p. 879-924.

Jensen & Oster 2009
Jensen, R. & Oster, E., 'The Power of TV: Cable Vision and Women's Status in India', *Quarterly Journal of Economics*, 2009, p. 1057-1094.

Kolbert 2005
Kolbert, E., *Field Notes from a Catastrophe: Man, Nature, and Climate Change*, New York: Bloomsbury USA, 2005.

Kuran 2001
Kuran, T., 'Why the Middle East is Economically Underdeveloped: Historical Mechanisms of Institutional Stagnation', *Journal of Economic Perspectives*, 2001, p. 71-90.

Landes 1995
Landes, D., 'Culture Makes Almost All the Difference', in: L.E. Harrison & S.P. Huntington (eds.), *Culture Matters. Culture Matters: How Values Shape Human Progress*, New York: Basic Books, 2001, p. 2-13.

Landes 1999
Landes, D., *Wealth and Poverty of Nations: Why Some Are So Rich and Some So Poor*, New York, London: W.W. Norton & Company, 1999.

La Porta, Lopez-de-Silanes & Schleifer 2008
La Porta, R., Lopez-de-Silanes, F. & Schleifer, A., 'The Economic Consequences of Legal Origins', *Journal of Economic Literature*, 2008, p. 285-332.

La Porta *et al.* 1998
La Porta, R., Lopez-de-Silanes, F., Schleifer, A. & Visny, R., 'Law and Finance', *Journal of Political Economy*, 1998, p. 1113-1155.

Lipset 1959
Lipset, S.M., 'Some Social Requisites of Democracy: Economic Development and Political Legitimacy', *American Political Science Review*, 1959, p. 69-105.

Lipset 1960
Lipset, S.M., *Political Man: The Social Bases of Politics*, Garden City, New York: Doubleday, 1960.

Lawless, Robbennolt & Ulen 2010
Lawless, R.M., Robbennolt, J.K. & Ulen, T.S., *Empirical Methods in Law*, New York: Aspen Publishers, 2010.

Maddison 2007a
Maddison A., *The World Economy: A Millennial Perspective / Historical Statistics*, Paris: OECD Publishing, 2007.

Maddison 2007b
Maddison A., *Contours of the Word Economy 1-2030 AD: Essays in Macro-Economic History*, New York: Oxford University Press, 2007.

Mahoney 2001
Mahoney, P.G., 'The Common Law and Economic Growth: Hayek Might be Right', *Journal of Legal Studies*, 2001, p. 503–525.

McAdams 1995
McAdams, R.H., 'Cooperation and Conflict: The Economics of Group-Status Production and Race Discrimination', *Harvard Law Review*, 1995, p. 1003-1084.

McCraw 2007
McCraw, T.K., *Prophet of Innovation: Joseph Schumpeter and Creative Destruction*, Cambridge, Massachusetts and London: The Belknap Press of Harvard University Press, 2007.

Moyo 2009
Moyo, D., *Dead Aid: Why Aid is not Working and How there is a Better Way for Africa*, New York: Farrar, Straus and Giroux, 2009.

North 2005
North, D.C., *Understanding the Process of Economic Change*, New Jersey: Princeton University Press, 2005.

North & Thomas 1976
North, D.C. & Thomas, R.P., *The Rise of the Western World: A New Economic History*, Cambridge: Cambridge University Press, 1976.

Nunn 2008
Nunn, N., 'The Long-Term Effects of Africa's Slave Trades', *Quarterly Journal of Economics*, 2008, p. 139-176.

Nunn & Wantchekon 2009
Nunn, N. & Wantchekon, L., *The Slave Trade and the Origins of Mistrust in Africa*, Working Paper, February 2009 (currently under review at the American Economic Review).

Parente 2008
Parente, S.L., 'Narrowing the Economic Gap in the 21st Century', in: K.R. Holmes, E.J. Feulner & M.A. O'Grady (eds.), *Index of Economic Freedom*, 2008, available at: <http://www.heritage.org/Index/> (last accessed, 21 October 21 2009).

Parente & Prescott 2000
Parente, S.L. & Prescott, E.C., *Barriers to Riches*, Cambridge, Massachusetts: The MIT Press, 2000.

Parente & Prescott 2005
Parente, S.L. & Prescott, E.C., 'A Unified Theory of the Evolution of International Income Levels', in: Ph. Aghion & S. Durlauf (eds.), *The Handbook of Economic Growth*, Amsterdam: Elsevier B.V., 2005, p. 1371-1416.

Parker 2010
Parker, I., 'The Poverty Lab', *The New Yorker*, 17 May 2010.

Pinkovskiy & Sala-i-Martin 2010
Pinkovskiy, M. & Sala-i-Martin, X., *African Poverty Is Falling ... Much Faster than You Think!*, Columbia University Working Paper, 17 January 17 2010.

Przeworski *et al.* 2000
Przeworski, A., Alvarez, M.E., Cheibub, J.A. & Limongi, F., *Democracy and Development: Political Institutions and Well-Being in the World*, 1950-1990, New York: Cambridge University Press, 2000.

Putnam 1992
Putnam, R., *Making Democracy Work: Civic Traditions in Modern Italy*, Princeton, New Jersey: Princeton University Press, 1992.

Rauch & Kostyak 2009
Rauch, J. & Kostyak, S., 'The Three Arab Worlds', *Journal of Economic Perspectives*, 2009, p. 165-188.

Rodrik 2004
Rodrik, D., *Getting Institutions Right*, April 2004, available at: <http://ksghome.harvard.edu/~drodrik/ifo-institutions%20article%20_April%202004_pdf> (last accessed, 21 October 21 2009).

Rodrik 2006
Rodrik, D., 'Goodbye Washington Consensus; Hello Washington Confusion?: A Review of the World Bank's Economic Growth in the 1990s: Learning from a Decade of Reform', *Journal of Economic Literature*, 2006, p. 973-987.

Rodrik 2009
Dani, 'The New Development Economics: We Shall Experiment, But How Shall We Learn?', in: Cohen, J. & Easterly, W. (eds.), *What Works in Development?: Thinking Big and Thinking Small*, Washington DC: Brookings Institution Press, 2009, p. 24-47.

Rodrik, Subramanian & Trebbi 2004
Rodrik, D., Subramanian, A. & Trebbi, F., 'Institutions Rule: The Primacy of Institutions over Geography and Integration in Economic Development', *Journal of Economic Growth*, 2004, p. 131-165.

Romer 1986
Romer, P., 'Increasing Returns and Long-Run Growth', *Journal of Political Economy*, 1986, p. 1002-1037.

Romer 1990
Romer, P., 'Endogenous Technological Change', *Journal of Political Economy*, 1990, p. 71-102.

Romer 2007
Romer, P., 'Economic Growth', in: D.R. Henderson (ed.), *The Concise Encyclopedia of Economics*, Indianapolis: Liberty Fund, 2007.

Sachs 2006
Sachs, J., *The End of Poverty: Economic Possibilities for Our Time*, New York: Penguin Press, 2006.

Sala-i-Martin 2004
Sala-i-Martin, X., 'More or less equal', *The Economist*, 11 March 2004.

Sala-i-Martin 2006
Sala-i-Martin, X., 'The World Distribution of Income: Falling Poverty and ... Convergence, Period', *Quarterly Journal of Economics*, 2006, p. 351-397.

Schumpeter 1942
Schumpeter, J.A., *Capitalism, Socialism, and Democracy*, New York: Harper & Row 1942.

Shleifer & Treisman 2005
Shleifer, A. & Treisman, D., 'A Normal Country: Russian after Communism', *Journal of Economic Perspectives*, 2005, p. 151-174.

Solow 1956
Solow, R.M., 'A Contribution to the Theory of Economic Growth', *Quarterly Journal of Economics*, 1956, p. 65-94.

Solow 1957
Solow, R.M., 'Technical Change and the Aggregate Production Function', *Review of Economics and Statistics*, 1957, p. 312-320.

Spence 2008
Spence, M., *The Growth Report: Strategies for Sustained Growth and Inclusive Development*, 2008, (available at <http://www.growthcommission.org/index.php?option=com_content&task=view&id=96&Itemid=169> (last accessed, 21 October 21 2009).

Stern 2007
Stern, N., *The Economics of Climate Change: The Stern Review*, New York, Cambridge University Press, 2007.

Svensson 2005
Svensson, J., 'Eight Questions About Corruption', *Journal of Economic Perspectives*, 2005, p. 19-42.

Tamanaha 2009
Tamanaha, B., *The Primacy of Society and the Failures of Law and Development*, SSRN Working Paper, October 2009.

Trebilcock & Leng 2006
Trebilcock, M. & Leng, J., 'The Role of Formal Contract Law and Enforcement in Economic Development', *Virginia Law Review*, 2006, p. 1517-1580.

Trebilcock & Veel 2007
Trebilcock, M. & Veel, P., *Property Rights and Economic Development: The Contingent Case for Formalization*, SSRN Working Paper, December 2007.

Weber 1904
Weber, M., *The Protestant Ethic and the Spirit of Capitalism*, 1904.

Wines & Ansfield 2010
Wines, M. & Ansfield, J., 'Resisting Bulldozers in a Push for Property Rights', *International Herald Tribune*, 29 April 2010.

World Bank 2005
World Bank, *Economic Growth in the 1990s: Learning from a Decade of Reform*, Washington: World Bank, 2005.

Young 2009
Young, A., *The African Growth Miracle*, Working Paper, September 2009.

PART II

COMMON LAW, CIVIL LAW AND CHINA

Nuno Garoupa
Carlos Gómez
Ligüerre

EFFICIENCY OF THE COMMON LAW*

1. Introduction

The efficiency of the common law generated discussion among legal economists quite early in the law and economics literature. The controversial thesis was introduced by Judge Posner in the first edition of his seminal book.[1] His main argument was that there is an implicit economic logic to the common law. In his view, the doctrines in common law provide a coherent and consistent system of incentives which induce efficient behaviour, not merely in explicit markets but in all social contexts (the so-called implicit markets). For example, common law reduces transaction costs to favour market transactions when that is appropriate. Quite naturally, Judge Posner recognized that not all doctrines in common law are economically justifiable or even easy to understand from an economic perspective. Economics does not offer a complete and exhaustive theory of the common law, but his view is that it offers a balanced and significant explanation.

The hypothesis suggested by Judge Posner can be traced back to the evolutionary theory of the common law suggested by Justice Holmes in the 1880s.[2] His main argument was that the development of the common law was driven by judicial responses to public policy rather than some internal logic. According to him, the ability of the common law to adjust appropriately to external needs relied on the recruitment of the judiciary as representatives of the community. Notably the theory developed by Holmes vehemently opposed the codification movement in the United States in those days.[3] Justice Holmes never used an efficiency argument for the common law (and against codification). Notwithstanding, it is clear that Judge Posner's understanding of the common law is very close to the theory developed by Justice Holmes.

* This article is based on our previous work: Garoupa & Gómez Ligüerre 2011a; Garoupa & Gómez Ligüerre 2011b; Garoupa & Gómez Ligüerre 2012. Roya H. Samarghandi has provided superb research assistance. The usual disclaimers apply.

1 Posner 2010 (the first edition was published in 1972).

2 Holmes 1881.

3 Novick 1991.

It is important to stress that the common law Justice Holmes and Judge Posner are considering goes back to the Blackstonian definition. According to Sir William Blackstone, the common law consists of general customs by which the judges and the courts are guided and directed.[4] Alternatively, the common law includes all legal doctrines that do not require a written form to be valid, but rather rely on the usage by courts.[5] Therefore, statutes have a secondary and subordinate role. They are essentially declaratory (to restate the common law) or remedial (to correct the flaws of the common law).

However, in American legal history, the Blackstonian understanding of the common law has not been without controversy. For example, Justice Cardozo saw clear advantages in the codification process and recognized some advantages to the French legal method in shaping judgments.[6] The American codification debate in the nineteenth century shows clearly that there are multiple understandings of the role of the common law. By proposing the efficiency hypothesis of the common law, Judge Posner noticeably opts for one side of the discussion. Unfortunately most legal economists have not realized that the Posnerian hypothesis has to be understood in the context of a richer debate.[7] Looking at the debates in the past, the traditional arguments for the Blackstonian common law included flexibility, stability, and ability to develop better rules without the need for statutes.[8] The conventional arguments against the Blackstonian common law mentioned uncertainty (because of conflicting precedents), difficulty of non-lawyers to understand the law (higher transaction costs in modern economic language), and incorrectly allowing judges to legislate.[9]

In this context, consider the analytical models developed by legal economists. They discuss under which conditions respect for precedent generates evolution to efficiency (hence supporting the Posnerian hypothesis). They never consider the limitations imposed by multiple and conflicting precedents. Inadvertently, or not, legal economists have disregarded the different arguments for and against the Blackstonian common law. They have entered the discussion on the common law without paying enough attention to the numerous existing viewpoints.

This article goes as follows. We start by discussing the efficiency of the common law hypothesis in the following section. Next, we discuss the evolution of the common law and efficiency in more detail. In section 4, we debunk the relationship between the efficiency of the common law hypothesis and the legal origins literature. In section 5, we assess mixed jurisdictions. Section 6 concludes the article.

4 Blackstone 2005.
5 Blackstone 2005.
6 Cardozo 2009.
7 See, among others, Morriss 1999. For a more detailed discussion about the influence of civil law in the U.S., see Clark 2006.
8 *Ibidem.*
9 *Ibidem.*

2. The Efficiency of the Common Law Hypothesis

If the common law is to be efficient, certainly there must be strong reasons to support such an assertion. One immediate explanation for the Posnerian hypothesis is that judges have a preference for efficiency.[10] If judges pursue efficiency as the goal of law, it is no surprise that the common law is efficient. However, this does not seem to be a persuasive argument. Why would judges care about efficiency rather than equality or other possible goals? Moreover, from an empirical perspective, we now have an extensive literature showing that ideology and other significant non-efficiency oriented variables play a major role in explaining judicial behaviour.[11]

A second possible explanation is that efficiency is promoted by the prevalence of precedent (more efficient rules are more likely to survive through a mechanism of precedent).[12] Another explanation relies on the incentives to bring cases and the role of court litigation (since inefficient rules are not welfare maximizing).[13] Nevertheless, these two explanations require a particular mix of case litigation in order to derive an efficient outcome. In fact, the search for a more convincing setup for the efficiency of the common law hypothesis has sparked important academic work. This literature essentially looks at how litigation improves the law, or some specific legal doctrine, taking into consideration that only a self-selected number of cases is actually litigated.[14]

The efficiency of the common law must be unequivocally related to the observation that litigation follows private interests.[15] Presumably it is true that bad rules are challenged more often than good rules, so naturally court intervention could improve the overall quality of the law. However, this line of reasoning is not without problematic shortcomings. It could be that the subset of cases that are actually litigated are not representative enough to trigger the necessary improvements, hence biasing evolution of legal rules against efficiency.[16] Furthermore, the emergence of efficiency in common law necessarily depends on a number of factors in the evolutionary mechanism, namely initial conditions, path dependence and random shocks.[17]

More recent work has provided a more comprehensive analytical framework to show under which precise (mathematical) conditions the evolution of the common law tends toward efficiency. For example, even if judges are ultimately efficiency-seeking, precedent and overruling must be balanced in an appropriate way.

10 Posner 1979.
11 See, among others, B. Friedman 2005.
12 Rubin 1977.
13 Priest 1977.
14 See, among others, Goodman 1978; Cooter & Kornhauser 1980; Terrebonne 1981; Rubin 1983; Von Wangenheim 1993; Fon & Parisi 2003; Depoorter, Fon & Parisi 2005; Fon & Parisi 2006; Niblett, Posner & Shleifer 2010 (showing empirically that rules fail to converge with significant inconsistencies across states).
15 Landes & Posner 1979 (also making the point that judicial opinions are a public good that arbitration fails to provide).
16 Hadfield 1992.
17 Roe 1996; Hathaway 2001.

A judicial bias might distort the law in the short run but at the same time provide the mechanism to improve the law in the long run, depending on critical elements of the evolution of the common law.[18] The possibility of selective litigation driven by private interests (likely to be misaligned with social interests) just makes the whole process more complex; convergence to efficiency is still possible as long as the biases are not overwhelming to the point of hurting the likelihood that inefficient laws will be more often litigated. Naturally strong precedent could be socially valuable if judges are significantly biased.[19]

3. The Evolution of the Common Law and Efficiency

If the common law is evolutionarily efficient, we are left with no explanation for the important doctrinal differences across common law jurisdictions. Furthermore, the *de jure* initial condition was the same for all common law jurisdictions, namely English law. Alternatively, we could consider adaptation to distinct local circumstances across the Anglo-American world, but such explanation is exogenous to the original model.

In this respect, we take a particular understanding of the original common law. In fact, one of the many problems with the economic literature on this topic is the confusing use of 'common law' to describe different legal features. Our definition is the standard one: A body of general rules prescribing social conduct, originally enforced by the ordinary royal courts in England (as opposed to equity, local or ecclesiastical courts), and characterized by the development of its own principles in actual legal controversies (through the use of judicial precedents), by the procedure of trial by jury, and by the doctrine of the supremacy of law (all agencies of government are subject to court review and compelled to follow legal procedure such as due process).[20]

It is known historically that the development of the common law in the thirteen colonies followed different paths that were not only distinct from the original English common law, but also between the colonies themselves.[21] To start with, unlike the English tradition, all colonial law tended to be codified with the exception of Maryland. Some of these colonial law codes departed significantly from the English common law, in particular in New England (Massachusetts most importantly) and Pennsylvania.[22] In other cases, such as Virginia and the Carolinas, English law was influential in adjudication, for example, but subsidiary to colonial law.

18 See Gennaioli & Shleifer 2007a; Gennaioli & Shleifer 2007b; Niblett 2011 (polarization concerning precedent depends on judicial preferences, cases that get litigated, and cost of adhering to precedent).

19 See Miceli 2009 & Anderlini, Felli & Riboni 2011.

20 We follow closely Hogue 1966. The author considers the survival and shaping of the common law in the early stages. He argues that the common law showed early maturity by the end of the thirteenth century. According to Hogue, significant economic interests with political influence dominated the early evolution of the common law.

21 See Reinsch 2010.

22 Although there were standard provisions to ensure that colonial law would not be radically in conflict with English common law. See *Ibidem*.

Finally, appeals from colonial courts to the English Privy Council were generally not allowed and drastically discouraged given the generalized respect for self-rule.[23] As a consequence, the development of the general reasoning and principles of the American common law were shaped by local determinants that were potentially quite different from the English common law.[24]

Colonial laws could not be contrary to the laws of England but could be diverse for local reasons. We could say that colonial laws were as close as possible to English law subject to the local needs. The English Privy Council deferred to local circumstances and did not impose English law in a strict binding way even when scrutinizing colonial statutes. Apparently the English Privy Council was less deferential in private litigation but that could be the result of an implicit dispute over judicial supremacy between the Council itself and the colonial courts.[25]

It is unquestionable that the English common law influenced and formed the American common law.[26] No doubt there were political and economic factors helping the convergence with English law.[27] But the very different realities faced by the colonies and the metropolis led to significant departures from the English common law in many fields of law, notably property (including inheritance, alienability and trespass), contracts (including remedies and restitution), torts (from negligence rules to proximate causation), slavery laws, and family (marriage and divorce rules).[28]

In fact, we could describe the early stages of American common law more accurately by recognizing the existence of thirteen different legal systems with different degrees of codification (quite significant in Massachusetts due to the Puritan distrust of lawyers).[29] English law was important more in the sense of providing a background and legal method as opposed to the elements of substantive law. Apparently the situation changed in the eighteenth century, when colonial courts become more English in nature.[30] The British developed more interventionist methods of governing the colonies, which resulted in a strengthening of the executive power. Although the British did not opt for a model of giving the courts in London jurisdiction over colonial courts, the role of the Privy Council was enhanced.[31] Colonial statute law was subject to review by the Privy Council. A process of convergence in substance and style was imposed by the Privy Council. Yet frequent delays and the permissive attitude of the Council (more political than

23 But not impossible, see Langbein *et al.* 2009.

24 See Reinsch 2010; L. Friedman 2005.

25 See Bilder 2004.

26 See Langbein *et al.* 2009.

27 *Ibidem.*

28 *Ibidem.*

29 See L. Friedman 2005. Many colonial statutes have not been studied by modern legal historians because they have disappeared. See, for example, the recent discovery of the Laws and Liberties of Massachusetts (1648).

30 *Ibidem.*

31 *Ibidem.*

truly judicial) undermined the possibility of full conformity of the colonial courts by the time of independence.[32]

Similar trends are found in other common law jurisdictions such as Australia, Canada, New Zealand and Ireland. Their common law systems have been formed and shaped by the English common law. Yet local determinants and different historical events have determined important departures from the original law in significant areas.[33]

It seems clear that the common law adjusts to local determinants that vary across the world, therefore producing different doctrines and legal outcomes. One immediate explanation for observed differences across common law countries could be the asymmetric role of statute law. Even if statute law prevails over judge made law in all common law jurisdictions nowadays, such preponderance varies. In that case, the potential inefficiencies could be possibly unrelated to the common law itself, in particular, if we take the view suggested by legal economists that statute law is intrinsically less efficient than judge made law.[34] However, we recognize that using statute law as the main source to explain differences across common law jurisdictions would be self-defeating in the eyes of those who believe in the efficiency hypothesis of the common law.

Our approach in this article does not mean we reject the view held by other legal scholars that the interaction of judge made law and statute law might actually improve rather than hurt convergence for efficiency. Most likely an appropriate mix of judicial precedent and statute rule should be the efficient outcome.[35] Otherwise, given the growth of statute law in all common law jurisdictions, the obvious conclusion should be that the overall efficiency has been reduced considerably in recent times.[36] This drastic conclusion seems to be reinforced by the argument that the efficiency of the common law is not really demand-side induced (i.e., through the incentives provided by litigation) but supply-side induced. According to this version, the historical competition between common law and equity courts was the driving force; once these courts were merged and a monopoly had been achieved, the efficiency forces had lost stimulus.[37]

32 *Ibidem.*

33 The specific case of Ireland is already mentioned by Hale 1971.

34 See, among others, Landes & Posner 1975; Tollison & Crain 1979; Crain and Tollison 1979; McChesney 1987 (discussing several theories of capture in rulemaking); Merrill 1997a; Merrill 1997b.

35 See a technical model by Ponzetto & Fernandez 2008 (predicting the progressive convergence of common and civil law toward a mixed system) and Guerriero 2009 (arguing that case law outperforms statute law when political institutions are weak).

36 See Rubin 1977, noting that the common law might have been more efficient in the past when the organization of interests was more costly, but not now. Also, these arguments face a serious challenge in areas such as antitrust law that might be statute law precisely because the traditional principle of fair trade in common law did not protect market competition and courts were excessively deferential to monopolies.

37 Zywicki 2003. He argues for supply-side explanations based on the competition between several court systems, in particular common law and equity. A more comprehensive discussion is provided by Klerman 2007, who argues that institutional structures that were able to produce more innovative legal rules tended to prevail in English law. However, he chal-
→

The central question is why common law jurisdictions have different doctrines in property, in contracts and in torts. When common law jurisdictions have a different doctrine in a particular relevant area of the law there could be two possible interpretations. The first interpretation is that the evolution of the common law to efficiency generates multiple equilibria. Therefore, each common law jurisdiction is potentially efficient and there are multiple efficient doctrines depending on local determinants. The second interpretation is that there is one and only one efficient equilibrium, and many common law jurisdictions simply fail to achieve it. We use the analytical models developed in the law and economics literature to identify the two possibilities and to understand the implications.[38] Note that these possibilities are not mutually exclusive; quite the contrary. Hence, we conclude this section by addressing the more realistic model which allows for the coexistence of both interpretations.

When the fundamentals of the model vary across jurisdictions, we could have multiple efficient equilibria. Each jurisdiction converges to an efficient doctrine and rule in the long run, but they are not the same because there are local conditions and aspects that vary significantly. The process of convergence to an efficient and stable equilibrium is based on selective litigation. The selective litigation could be different across the common law world in response to local conditions and asymmetric shocks caused by local historical events. The circumstances under which an original rule or doctrine in common law is applied in different jurisdictions varies dramatically since different sets of cases are litigated. As a consequence the conditional probability that a given inefficient rule is challenged is not the same.[39] Therefore, the evolution of the common law follows different paths. Necessarily the pattern of path dependence will be consistently diverse leading to distinctive (but equally efficient) equilibria.[40]

Legal historians seem to perceive this effect in explaining the development of the English common law and the early American common law. Colonial law responded mainly to local problems and conditions faced by the European settlers which were radically distinct from the realities of the English (and possibly the Irish) society. However, relying on these differences that resulted in dissimilar selective litigation to explain significant variations across the American colonies, Canada, Australia and New Zealand seems less persuasive.

If there are multiple efficient equilibria due to distinctive selective litigation, the implications for the efficiency hypothesis of the common law are twofold. First, there is no single or unique common law as assumed by the economic literature, but a multiplicity of common law systems. The focus on a particular doctrine or rule is

lenges the efficiency of the supply-side competition between these courts. He notes that there was a pro-plaintiff bias that generated certain (hardly efficient) rules given the way judges were paid. Important changes to judicial compensation and salaries corrected the pro-plaintiff bias in the 19th century.

38 In particular, we focus on Gennaioli & Shleifer 2007a & Gennaioli & Shleifer 2007b; Miceli 2009; Ponzetto & Fernandez 2008; Von Wangenheim 1993.

39 See Miceli 2009; von Wangenheim 1993.

40 See, among others, Roe 1996; Hathaway 2001.

not very informative concerning the efficiency of legal arrangements since the appropriate response varies across the common law jurisdictions. Second, under the efficiency hypothesis of the common law, when a particular jurisdiction adopts the common law approach as suggested by the legal origins literature, the (efficient) outcome is difficult to predict since particular local determinants might generate yet another (completely new) path.

Multiple efficient equilibria signal that the world is more complex than the approach taken by the legal origins literature. A mistaken focus on legal outcomes hides the interaction of different local determinants with dissimilar path dependencies. Under the current analytical models, the assessment of legal outcomes concerning efficiency cannot be disentangled from the varying selective litigation in each jurisdiction. Certainly that has not been the approach taken by the legal origins literature.

Another possibility is that there is a single efficient equilibrium. Immediately we recognize that some common law jurisdictions seem to develop the efficient doctrine or rule, whereas others do not. There are several possible explanations for why some common law jurisdictions fail to achieve efficiency. One possible reason is that the distribution of relevant attributes of judicial preferences is not the same. For example, the proportion of pro-plaintiff and pro-defendant judges varies, with the consequence that the number of pro-efficient rule judges is different, and in some cases insufficient to force convergence to efficiency.[41] Alternatively, the biases favouring certain types of rules vary across the population of judges. In particular, more polarized judiciaries are less likely to achieve efficient doctrines and rules. Efficiency requires a more unbiased judiciary and therefore more judicial polarization leads to significant social welfare losses.[42] At the same time, a varying degree of influence of special-interest groups in judicial politics could contribute toward shaping behaviour in different ways that preclude some particular institutional arrangements from converging to efficiency.[43] Moreover, the concern about the future evolution of the law measured by a specific discount factor (for example, how forward looking judges are) plays an important role in explaining efficiency. A judiciary too focused on the short run and less so on the long run is less likely to generate an efficient legal outcome.[44]

There are good reasons to think that indeed the distribution of relevant judicial attributes varies across common law jurisdictions, with the U.S. judiciary probably being distinct from other common law judiciaries.[45] From the perspective of the current available models, these differences could be a by-product of specific appointment mechanisms (that can polarize the judiciary or empower the influence of special-interest groups), judicial tenure (including mandatory retirement), promotion and retention policies, or recruitment strategies (a wider or narrower pool of potential candidates to the judiciary that breeds different degrees of heterogeneity

41 See Miceli 2009.

42 See Gennaioli & Shleifer 2007a & Gennaioli & Shleifer 2007b.

43 See Ponzetto & Fernandez 2008.

44 See Ponzetto & Fernandez 2008.

45 See Posner 1996.

in the bench). The most interesting implication of these considerations is that most probably the U.S. is the jurisdiction with the least likely judiciary (within the common law jurisdictions) to promote efficient legal outcomes according to the mathematical models.

Another reason for why some common law jurisdictions fail to converge to efficiency is the role of precedent. If the cost of changing precedent is too low, judicial biases prevail and the legal outcome in the long run is unlikely to be efficient.[46] To put it differently, the judicial gains from getting closer to an efficient outcome are insufficient when it is easy to change precedent.[47] Consequently the value of precedent plays an important role. Frequent defections from an established precedent undermine the process of converging to efficiency. In the context of the common law jurisdictions, there are important differences on how precedent is respected. U.S. judges seem to be more willing to change precedent than the English judiciary as a general observation (with particular reference to horizontal precedent).[48] Again, if that is so, it seems likely that the American common law is less likely to achieve efficiency than the English common law.

There are important implications stemming from a model with a single efficient equilibrium. The most immediate is that if doctrines and rules vary across the common law jurisdictions, only one is efficient and the remaining has failed to achieve it. Given that the initial condition was presumably the same (English law) we can conclude that some judicial intervention helps efficiency but, under different conditions, judicial intervention is detrimental.

Another inference from this model is that the common law is efficient only under certain conditions. Not all common law jurisdictions satisfy those conditions, both in terms of judicial attributes and cost of changing precedent. A comparison across common law jurisdictions demands a focus on the local judiciary and the stickiness of precedent.

Combining the two possible models we have considered so far, we derive a more complex and realistic overview of the efficiency hypothesis of the common law. First, there is not a single efficient rule or doctrine, but a multiplicity of possible equilibria depending on selective litigation. Second, for each specific set of selective litigation, there is no guarantee that there will be convergence to efficiency, depending on judicial attributes and the preponderance of precedent.

The most important consequence is that the identification of the efficiency of the common law is much more intricate and multifaceted than anticipated by the literature. A mere comparison of how a specific predicament is addressed in each jurisdiction, as inspired by the legal origins literature, is not only insufficient but also likely to produce gross mistakes. The observation that each jurisdiction provides a different legal outcome says very little about efficiency. First, due to the existence of multiple efficient solutions. Second, because the variables that determine efficient outcomes vary. A proper analysis requires a clear understanding of local

46 See Miceli 2009; Gennaioli & Shleifer 2007a; Gennaioli & Shleifer 2007b.

47 See von Wangenheim 1993.

48 See Posner 1996. See also, Wise 1975; Lee 1999.

determinants, including judicial preferences, before we can jump to the conclusion that the common law is undoubtedly efficient.

Elsewhere we have discussed relevant examples to illustrate the difficulties of the exercise.[49] They show that once we depart from a general and undefined efficiency hypothesis of the common law into specific doctrines and rules, the analysis is complex, dense and less clear than the legal origins literature portrays. They also illustrate situations where multiple equilibria are more likely and where a single efficient equilibrium is probable.

4. The Efficiency Hypothesis of the Common Law and Legal Origins

The literature on the efficiency of the common law that followed Posner's hypothesis is not comparative in nature, but effectively looks at judge-made law. Therefore, the alleged efficiency should hold in any jurisdiction with respect to either judge-made law or general principles of law developed by courts (as it is better known in civil law jurisdictions). In fact, from the perspective of civil law countries, the argument could be rephrased as court interventions improve the overall efficiency of the legal system because of the common biases of litigation (i.e., more inefficient laws will be subject to more court intervention than less efficient laws). It is well known that tort law is an area of French law that has been systematically developed by case law given the absence of specific codification in the 1804 Civil Code (all French tort law is based on article 1382 and following of the Civil Code). As a consequence, we should treat torts from the perspective of the efficiency of the common law much in the same way in the United States as in France. The only relevant question then is the extent to which the litigation biases in the area of torts increase or decrease efficiency of the law.

Let us suppose that there are more occasions for court intervention and judgment in a common law legal system than under code law. It could be argued that the appropriate mutation towards efficiency will be faster in common law than in civil law. In other words, even if both systems move closer to efficiency induced by judge-made law, due to the more significant influence of judge-made law in the common law, such evolution will be faster and quicker. However such a conclusion relies on the inability or the incapacity of statute creation and modification to supplement any 'delays' in the evolutionary process.

At the end of the day, the Posnerian hypothesis does not set common law in a better position than civil law in the evolution towards efficient rules. It does not provide a convincing framework to argue that judicial precedent is a superior way to promote an efficient solution than a statutory rule precisely because the focus is on judge-made law.[50] Under the common law reasoning, bad decisions are over-

49 Garoupa & Gómez Ligüerre 2012.

50 See a technical model by Ponzetto & Fernandez 2008 (predicting the progressive convergence of common and civil law toward a mixed system); Dari-Mattiacci, Deffains & Lovat 2011 (explaining the relationship between high litigation rates and the balance between case law and legislation) and Guerriero 2009 (arguing that case law outperforms statute law when political institutions are weak).

ruled, in the same way that under civil law, bad statutes can be effectively corrected by the judiciary.[51] There is no (theoretical or empirical) basis to assert that courts and juries are in a better position in common law than in civil law jurisdictions to calculate the consequences of their decisions more appropriately than the government.[52] Moreover, that judge-made law can be better understood as a set of rules designed to maximize economic efficiency, as Judge Posner proposed, is not an exclusive feature of common law jurisdictions. Furthermore, Judge Posner finds important functional systematic differences between the United States and Britain, and recognizes important similarities between the current institutional arrangements in Britain and in continental Europe.[53]

If the Posnerian hypothesis is true, at least in the long run, rules that do not promote efficient results should be repealed in any legal system. Therefore, the central question is not whether one legal family or the other promotes an economic efficiency solution, but which of these two main legal families reaches the adequate result (always from the economic perspective) at a lower cost in terms of delays and opportunity costs.[54] From a cost perspective solely, it is not clear that the type of cost attached to general axiomatic legal solutions, characteristic of civil law approaches, is necessarily higher than litigation costs incurred in the approach developed by common law.[55]

Our emphasis is that the next step, that is, arguing that judge-made law is more efficient than statute law, requires further reasoning. The mere Posnerian efficiency hypothesis of the common law cannot alone support the conclusion that lawmaking by legislation is necessarily less efficient than court intervention. One of the main arguments for the superiority of judge-made law is that private interests are more likely to capture the legislature than the courts, although such argument is debatable at the theory as well as at the empirical level.[56] In fact, there is no systematic evidence that rent-seeking is more persistent with the legislature than with the courts, since demand and supply conditions are fundamentally different.[57] Moreover, courts and legislators have their own goals in terms of enhancing their influence which complicates the potential effect of private interests in lawmaking.[58]

Notice that the relative efficiency of judge-made versus statute law by itself does not provide a good framework to justify the superiority of the common law system as compared to the civil law system. First, statute law is important in common law jurisdictions and many important areas of private law such as torts or even

51 See, for example, Fon & Parisi 2006 (discussing *jurisprudence constant*).

52 On the more general question, see Van Caenegem 1987.

53 See Posner 1996. Also see more generally Levitsky 1994.

54 See the critique to Posner's argument in Friedman 2001.

55 A different perspective is defended by Dawson 1968.

56 See Crew & Twight 1990, (arguing that common law is less subject to rent-seeking than statute law); Rubin 1982 (arguing that both are influenced by private interests to advance their goals). The most devastating criticism is Tullock 1997; Tullock 2005. See also Luppi & Parisi 2011.

57 See citations *supra* note 34.

58 See discussion by Pritchard & Zywicki 1999. For a very interesting comparison between lawmakers and its influence under English and French systems, see Allison 1996.

commercial law are essentially case law in civil law jurisdictions. Second, the biases of legislation and litigation are not qualitatively and quantitatively similar in both legal systems due to procedural and substantive differences. Once again the efficiency hypothesis of the common law coupled with the alleged bias of legislation for private capture are insufficient to support the argument that French civil law is necessarily inferior to the common law.

In fact, the traditional Posnerian analysis could be transposed to French civil law in many ways and multiple forms. It could be argued that general law (Code) is more efficient than specific statutory interventions (potentially prone to more capture). It could be also said that bottom-up law (for example, case law pilling up under general code provisions such as tort law under article 1382 of the French Civil Code) is more appropriate than top-down law (including very detailed code provisions as well as specific statutes). Nothing in the discussion so far makes the argument unique to common law or provides a complete framework to derive implications for comparative law.

Elsewhere we have provided detailed examples where French law is more efficient than Anglo-American law.[59] The purpose is not to argue that French law is superior to Anglo-American law, but rather to illustrate that the Posnerian account can be easily applied within the French legal system. There is simply no relationship between the efficiency hypothesis of the common law and the alleged superiority of the common law legal family in terms of economic growth.

5. The Efficiency Hypothesis of the Common Law and Mixed Jurisdictions

In this section, we focus on mixed, pluralist or hybrid jurisdictions. These are jurisdictions that mix elements of civil law and common law (and eventually elements from a third legal system). Given the alleged superiority of the common law system, one should expect the civil law to fade away. Moreover, the common law being the legal system of the later, stronger colonizer or occupier, we should suppose the civil law to be in a difficult position to survive. Such predictions are broadly speaking inconsistent with reality. We discuss the reasons for that with an economic model.

The comparative law literature does not provide for any precise definition of a mixed jurisdiction. The reason is that all jurisdictions are likely mixed in the sense that they are informed by indigenous legal tradition and transplants in relevant areas of the law. Jurisdictions interact for multiple reasons and, as a consequence, conscious or not, by statute, by case law or by legal practice, are influenced by other jurisdictions.[60] If every jurisdiction is mixed, then the classification of legal families must be based on a matter of degree.[61]

The first distinction is between those jurisdictions that mix legal systems in a systematic way and those that do not. Within those jurisdictions that do not mix

59 Garoupa & Gómez Ligüerre 2011b.

60 For a general discussion, see Garoupa & Ogus 2006.

61 See Mattei 1997.

legal systems in a systematic way, we include the vast majority of the world that is usually affiliated to a particular legal family. They occasionally and opportunistically transplant laws and legal institutions from a different legal family, but overall they follow a particular dominant tradition. Obviously such classification does not occur without problems, but very much fits with the traditional division between civil and common law legal families.[62] The focus of our article is on those jurisdictions that combine legal systems in a systematic way, and therefore cannot be regarded as either civil or common law.

A second important distinction is between those jurisdictions that have a structured mix and those that have an unstructured mix. By unstructured mixed legal system, comparativists understand an overlap of two traditions, with no clear or evident application of one or the other to all legal subjects. There is no formal articulation or coordination between the two legal traditions. The obvious example is European law and indigenous law in many African countries. In contrast, in a structured mixed legal system, there is some coordination. Such coordination can take different complementary forms. It could be established by conceptual boundaries (such as private and public law). It could be categorized even if within areas where the overlap is unclear (such as commercial law or procedure). Alternatively, a legal tradition could dominate in certain areas of the law with legislative enclaves of the other legal family. Finally, both legal traditions may coexist under a process of mutual recognition of structured boundaries and sources.[63]

Structured mixed legal systems can be pluralist (usually dualist) or hybrid. By pluralist, we envisage the case where the different legal families operate side by side, in well-defined contained areas of the law. For example, private law follows the civil law tradition whereas public law follows the common law tradition. By hybrid, we consider the possibility of blending together those legal traditions. A possibility is that contract law, or more generally private law, combines both common and civil law doctrines.[64]

The terminology in comparative law is not without problems. In fact, some comparitivists have criticized the standard vocabulary. For example, legal scholars refer to 'mixed jurisdictions' when they use common and civil law traditions, rather than 'mixed legal systems' as it would be more appropriate. 'Mixed jurisdictions' seems to presuppose a degree of hybridism which is usually absent. 'Mixed legal systems' anticipates legal pluralism which is more frequent than hybridism.[65]

Jurisdictions of a mixed legal family were not originally founded as such.[66] Their mixed nature is the product of a later change. Following the insights of a famous legal scholar, we could define these jurisdictions to be 'basically a civilian system that had been under pressure from the Anglo-American common law and

62 Mattei 1997.

63 We follow here Glenn 1996. See also general discussion by Smits 2001; Örücü 2008.

64 Here we rely on Örücü 2010.

65 See Palmer 2010.

66 See Palmer 2001.

has in part been overlaid by that rival system of jurisprudence'.[67] The civil law is not necessarily the original legal tradition (since many of these countries had some aboriginal or indigenous law before European colonization), but it was implemented before the arrival of British common law.

Legal scholars have traced back the combination of civil and common law to two distinct possible historical reasons:

(i) *Intercolonial transfer* (losses from France, Spain, the Netherlands or the Ottoman Empire; gains to Britain or the U.S.). There is usually little influence of Anglo-American law before the transfer of sovereignty. The new sovereign is established in a strong political position but avoids or fails to effectively impose the common law because of a large non-Anglophonic community that is socially and economically dominant. The English speaking community initially is a minority who communicates in a different language that does not dominate the life of the jurisdiction. However, the common law expands due to a well developed colonial administration and the local (business) interests of the small English speaking community.[68]

(ii) *Merger of sovereignties* (mainly Scotland): the Act of Union of 1707 keeps strict separation between Scottish and English law. Scottish private law is respected but the Union effectively merges public law and public institutions. The new political and judicial institutions promoted the reception of English law, although it is debatable if the combination of legal traditions was already there before the Union due to trade and political and economic influence.[69]

The importance of precedent with binding effect even in areas of traditional civil law has been recognized as the main source to combine substantive civil law with a common law approach in Scotland. However, some areas have been largely immune to legislative incursion from English law unless and when absolutely necessary (such as criminal or family law). Legal scholars mention the Scottish examples as a unique voluntary combination of civil and common law that struggles for legal consistency.[70]

67 A general definition provided by Sir Thomas Smith in 1965, cited by Palmer 2010, having the case of Scotland in mind.

68 *Ibidem*. Such constraint could explain why Spanish civil law faded away in Florida, Texas or California, Dutch civil law in New York and German (Japanese) civil law in the Mariana Islands, but not in South Africa, Louisiana, Quebec, Puerto Rico, Malta and the Philippines. For the case of South Africa, see Miller 1996.

69 See Palmer 2010. For a more detailed discussion, see White & Willock 2006; Clark 2009.

70 See Attwooll 1996.

In most cases of mixed legal systems around the world, there are significant common elements that have been identified by comparativists to explain the patterns of development of a mixed legal family. The most immediate is language as we already mentioned. Usually there is a linguistic factor which requires, at least in early stages, for the law to be in a language different from English.[71]

A second aspect is the influence of Anglo-American law on legal institutions and procedure which is usually determined by the political power of the English-speaking community: powerful courts, influential judges, some form of *stare decisis* where judicial decisions are accepted as a source of law (*de facto* or *de jure*) and bind inferior courts (in a much less flexible way than the Spanish *doctrina jurisprudencial* or the French *jurisprudence constante*), assimilation of common law rules of civil procedure, although usually no formal separation between common law and equity.[72]

A third element is the slow penetration of common law in the context of private law. According to legal scholars, the patterns of common law influence in private law are usually the following: some in torts, less so in contracts, even less in quasi-contracts and unjust enrichment, very little to nothing in property.[73] Commercial law tends to adhere to common law more easily, generally not by imposition, but due to self-interested economic reasons and the inadequacy of the old civil law.[74]

As we have noted, comparative law has identified general patterns of development of a mixed legal family. Civil law arrives first due to the initial colonization or political influence (in the case of Scotland). Common law follows after some transfer of sovereignty. Common law is not developed because the local community is unsatisfied with civil law but due to political and military reasons. Not surprisingly, common law dominates legal institutions, procedure and public law. However, common law does not easily penetrate private law.

An immediate explanation for the observed pattern could be mere path dependence. Alternatively, in other words, mixed legal families are still in a process of transformation. Common law will eliminate civil law in some distant future much the same way it has happened in some southern American states. The reason for this delay would be the codification of civil law principles in many of those jurisdictions. Codification encroaches civil law and therefore reinforces path dependence. The problem with this explanation is that legal scholars do not detect such a trend in those jurisdictions. Civil law seems to be there to stay.

Absent mere path dependence, if we take literally the legal origins movement, common law should replace civil law in the areas of private law. Common law is more efficient. Common law is better for business interests and conducive to economic growth. The persistence and survival of civil law is therefore puzzling from

71 See Palmer 2010.

72 *Ibidem*. The distinction between common law and equity was eliminated in the Confederate States of America in 1861 because it was considered unjustified given the civil law tradition of many Southern states. See Robinson 1941.

73 *Ibidem*.

74 *Ibidem*.

that perspective. Why would a second-best legal tradition persist in private law when a first-best legal alternative is already available in public law?

A possible explanation is that mixed legal families are locked in to an inefficient institutional arrangement and cannot move out. There is some market failure that inhibits the common law to take over civil law in the areas of tort, contracts and property. The costs of switching are so immensely large that mixed legal families cannot easily abandon the old civil law and adhere to common law.

It is difficult to see what these significant costs can be. Legal economists have recognized that changing legal regimes has important disadvantages, but they do not seem to be as significant in this context as they are in the economic literature of transplants.[75] However, in all these jurisdictions, there is a central government that was able to impose common law on areas of legal institutions, public law and procedure. Presumably the same central government could easily internalize these externalities, solve the public good under provision of legal change, and consequently impose common law in the area of private law.

In sharp contrast to the legal origins movement, forcing mixed legal families to abandon the civil law aspect in search of the efficiency of the common law would probably be detrimental for economic growth since it would violate current institutional arrangements based on local determinants. Elsewhere we detail the significant economic costs of imposing the elimination of civil law in mixed jurisdictions.[76] It suffices to say that there are good economic arguments to explain why the civil law is useful in complementing the common law under some local conditions.

6. Concluding Remarks

This paper has discussed the efficiency hypothesis of the common law from the perspective of comparative law. We argue that the general treatment of this hypothesis by legal economists leaves unanswered many questions regarding the significant variations across the common law jurisdictions, the persistence of mixed jurisdictions and the implications for the legal origins literature.

Other authors have attacked the legal origins literature as a bad exercise in comparative law and shortage of details.[77] The problem with this line of inquiry is that it inevitable concludes that legal systems are not comparable and efficiency or economic growth are not useful to understand legal systems.[78] We disagree with such criticism. In fact, our work avoids the excruciating details of a more traditional comparative law precisely because, in our view, such an approach does not help in understanding the limitations of the legal origins literature and self-defeats any meaningful and tractable efficiency analysis.

75 See Garoupa & Ogus 2006.
76 Garoupa & Gomez Ligüerre 2011a.
77 See, among others, Engelbrekt 2010. She points out the following problems: fallacies in classifying or measuring legal families, legal dynamics and transplants (difficulty of attributing law to legal families), ideal types.
78 For a different perspective, see Glenn 2001; Siems 2005; Spamann 2009. See also Siems 2008.

The identification of the efficiency of the common law is much more intricate and multifaceted than anticipated by the literature. A mere comparison of how a specific predicament is addressed in each jurisdiction, as inspired by the legal origins literature, is not only insufficient but likely to produce gross mistakes. The observation that each jurisdiction provides a different legal outcome says very little about efficiency. First, there are multiple efficient legal solutions. Second, the variables that determine efficient outcomes vary significantly across the common law jurisdictions (England and Wales, U.S., Canada, Australia, New Zealand and Ireland). A proper analysis requires a clear understanding of local determinants, including judicial preferences, before we can jump to the conclusion that the common law is undoubtedly efficient (or more precisely, which common law is undoubtedly efficient).

Bibliography

Allison 1996
Allison, J.W.F., *A Continental Distinction in the Common Law: A Historical and Comparative Perspective on English Public Law*, Oxford: Clarendon Press, 1996.

Anderlini, Felli & Riboni 2011
Anderlini, L., Felli, L. & Riboni, A., *Why Stare Decisis?*, CEPR Discussion Papers, No. 8266, 2011.

Attwooll 1996
Attwooll, E., 'Scotland: A Multi-Dimensional Jigsaw', in: E. Orücü, E. Attwooll & S. Coyle (eds.), *Studies in Legal Systems: Mixed and Mixing*, Boston: Kluwer Law International, 1996.

Bilder 2008
Bilder, M.S., *The Transatlantic Constitution: Colonial Legal Culture and the Empire*, Cambridge, MA: Harvard University Press, 2008.

Blackstone 2005
Blackstone, W., *Commentaries on the Laws of England*, Oxford: Clarendon Press, 2005.

Cardozo 2009
Cardozo, B.N., *The Nature of the Judicial Process*, New York: Cosimo, Inc., 2009.

Clark 2009
Clark, B., *Scottish Legal System*, Dundee: Dundee University Press, 2009.

Clark 2006
Clark, D.S., 'Development of Comparative Law in the United States', in: M. Reimann & R. Zimmermann (eds.), *The Oxford Handbook of Comparative Law*, Oxford: Oxford University Press, 2006, p. 175-214.

Cooter & Kornhauser 1980
Cooter, R.D. & Kornhauser, L.A., 'Can Litigation Improve the Law without the Help of Judges?', *Journal of Legal Studies*, 1980, p. 139-163.

Crain & Tollison 1979
Crain, W.M. & Tollison, R.D., 'The Executive Branch in the Interest-Group Theory of Government', *Journal of Legal Studies*, 1979, p. 555-567.

Crew & Twight 1990
Crew, M.A. & Twight, C., 'On the Efficiency of Law: A Public Choice Perspective', *Public Choice*, 1990, p. 15-36.

Dari-Mattiacci, Deffains & Lovat 2011
Dari-Mattiacci, G., Deffains, B. & Lovat, B., 'The Dynamics of the Legal System', *Journal of Economic Behaviour and Organization*, 2011, p. 95-107.

Dawson 1968
Dawson, J.P., *The Oracles of Law*, Ann Arbor: University of Michigan, 1968.

Depoorter, Fon & Parisi 2005
Depoorter, B., Fon, V. & Parisi, F., 'Litigation, Judicial Path-dependence, and Legal Change', *European Journal of Law and Economics*, 2005, p. 43-56.

Engelbrekt 2010
Engelbrekt, A.B., 'Toward an Institutional Approach to Comparative Economic Law?' in: A.B. Engelbrekt & J. Nergelius (eds.), *New Directions in Comparative Law*, Cheltenham, UK: Edward Elgar, 2010, p. 213-227.

Fon & Parisi 2003
Fon, V. & Parisi, F., V. Fon and F. Parisi, 'Litigation and the Evolution of Legal Remedies: A Dynamic Model', *Public Choice*, 2003, p. 419-433.

Fon & Parisi 2006
Fon, V. & Parisi, F., 'Judicial Precedents in Civil Law Systems: A Dynamic Analysis', *International Review of Law and Economics*, 2006, p. 519-535.

Friedman 2005
Friedman, B., 'The Politics of Judicial Review', *Texas Law Review*, 2005, p. 257-337.

Friedman 2001
Friedman, D.D., *Law's Order: What Economics Has to Do with Law and Why it Matters*, Princeton: NJ, Princeton University Press, 2001.

Friedman 2005
Friedman, L.M., *A History of American Law*, New York: Simon & Schuster, 2005.

Garoupa & Gómez-Ligüerre 2011a
Garoupa, N. & Gómez-Ligüerre, C., *The Efficiency of the Common Law: The Puzzle of Mixed Legal Families*, unpublished manuscript, 2011.

Garoupa & Gómez Ligüerre 2011b
Garoupa, N. & Gómez Ligüerre, C., 'The Syndrome of the Efficiency of the Common Law', *Boston University. International Law Journal*, 2011, p. 287-335.

Garoupa & Gómez Ligüerre 2012
Garoupa, N. & Gómez Ligüerre, C., 'The Evolution of the Common Law and Efficiency', *Georgia Journal of International and Comparative Law*, 2012 (forthcoming).

Garoupa & Ogus 2006
Garoupa, N. & Ogus, A., 'A Strategic Interpretation of Legal Transplants', *Journal of Legal Studies*, 2006, p. 339-363.

Gennaioli & Shleifer 2007a
Gennaioli N. & Shleifer, A., 'The Evolution of Common Law', *Journal of Political Economy*, 2007, p. 43-68.

Gennaioli & Shleifer 2007b
Gennaioli N. & Shleifer, A., 'Overruling and the Instability of Law', *Journal of Comparative Economics*, 2007, p. 309-328.

Glenn 1996
Glenn H.P., 'Quebec: Mixité and Monism', in: E. Orücü, E. Attwooll & S. Coyle (eds.), *Studies in Legal Systems: Mixed and Mixing*, The Hague: Kluwer Law International, 1996, p. 1-15.

Glenn 2001
Glenn, H.P., 'Are Legal Traditions Incommensurable?' *The American Journal of Comparative Law*, 2001, p. 133-145.

Goodman 1978
Goodman, J.C., 'An Economic Theory of the Evolution of the Common Law', *Journal of Legal Studies*, 1978, p. 393-406.

Guerriero 2009
Guerriero, C., *Democracy, Judicial Attitudes, and Heterogeneity: The Civil versus Common Law Tradition*, Cambridge Working Paper, No. 917, 2009.

Hadfield 1992
Hadfield, G. K., 'Biases in the Evolution of Legal Rules', *Georgetown Law Journal*, 1992, p. 583-616.

Hale 1971
Hale M., *The History of the Common Law of England*, Chicago: University of Chicago Press, 1971.

Hathaway 2001
Hathaway, O.A., 'Path Dependence in the Law: The Course and Pattern of Legal Change in a Common Law System, *Iowa Law Review*, 2001, p. 601-665.

Hogue 1996
Hogue, A.R., *Origins of Common Law*, Bloomington, IN: Indiana University Press, 1966.

Holmes 1881
Holmes, O.W., *The Common Law*, Boston: Dover Publications, 1881 (reprinted 1991).

Klerman 2007
Klerman, D., 'Jurisdictional Competition and the Evolution of the Common Law', *University of Chicago Law Review*, 2007, p. 1179–1226.

Landes & Posner 1975
Landes, W.M. & Posner, R.A., 'The Independent Judiciary in an Interest Group Perspective', *Journal of Law & Economics*, 1975, p. 885-887.

Landes & Posner 1979
Landes, W.M. & Posner, R.A., 'Adjudication as a Private Good', *Journal of Legal Studies*, 1979, p. 235-284.

Langbein, Lerner & Smith 2009
Langbein, J.H., Lerner, R.L. & Smith, B.P., *History of the Common Law: The Development of Anglo-American Legal Institutions*, New York: Aspen Publishers, 2009.

Lee 1999
Lee, T.R., 'Stare Decisis in Historical Perspective', *Vanderbilt Law Review*, 1999, p. 647-735.

Levitsky 1994
Levitsky, J E., 'The Europeanization of the British Legal Style', *The American Journal of Comparative Law*, 1994, p. 347-380.

Luppi & Parisi 2011
Luppi, B. & Parisi, F., 'The Case against Gordon Tullock Forty Years Later', *Public Choice*, 2011 (forthcoming).

Mattei 1997
Mattei, U., 'Three Patters of Law: Taxonomy and Change in the World's Legal Systems', *The American Journal of Comparative Law*, 1997, p. 5-44.

McChesney 1987
McChesney, F.S., 'Rent Extraction and Rent Creation in the Economic Theory of Regulation, *Journal of Legal Studies*, 1987, p. 101-118.

Merrill 1997a
Merrill, T.W., 'Does Public Choice Theory Justify Judicial Activism After All?' *Harvard Journal of Law and Public Policy*, 1997, p. 226-227.

Merrill 1997b
Merrill, T.W., 'Institutional Choice and Political Faith', *Law & Social Inquiry*, 1997, p. 959-998.

Miceli 2009
Miceli, T.J., 'Legal Change: Selective Litigation, Judicial Bias, and Precedent', *Journal of Legal Studies*, 2009, p. 157–168.

Miller 1996
Miller, D.C., 'South Africa: A Mixed System Subject to Transcending Forces', in: E. Orücü, E. Attwooll & S. Coyle (eds.), *Studies in Legal Systems: Mixed and Mixing*, The Hague: Kluwer Law International, 1996, p. 165-191.

Morriss 1999
Morriss, A.P., 'Codification and Right Answers', *Chicago-Kent Law Review*, 1999, p. 355-391.

Niblett 2011
Niblett A., *Case-by-Case Adjudication and the Path of the Law*, unpublished mimeograph, 2011.

Niblett, Posner & Shleifer 2010
Niblett, A., Posner, R.A. & Shleifer, A., 'The Evolution of a Legal Rule', *Journal of Legal Studies*, 2010, p. 325-358.

Novick 1991
Novick, S.M., 'Introduction to the Dover Edition', *The Common Law by Oliver Wendell Holmes*, Dover Publications, 1991.

Orücü 2008
Orücü, E., 'What is a Mixed Legal System: Exclusion or Expansion?' *Electronic Journal of Comparative Law*, 2008 <http://www.ejcl.org/121/art121-15.pdf>.

Orücü 2010
Orücü, E., 'General Introduction: Mixed Legal Systems at New Frontiers', in: E. Orücü (ed.), *Mixed Legal Systems at New Frontiers*, London: Wildy, Simmonds and Hill Publishing, 2010, p. 1-18.

Palmer 2001
Palmer, V.V., *Mixed Jurisdictions Worldwide: The Third Legal Family*, Cambridge, UK: Cambridge University Press, 2001.

Palmer 2010
Palmer, V.V., 'Two Rival Theories of Mixed Legal Systems', in: E. Orücü (ed.), *Mixed Legal Systems at New Frontiers*, London: Wildy, Simmonds and Hill Publishing, 2010, p. 19-52.

Ponzetto & Fernandez 2008
Ponzetto, G.M. & Fernandez, P.A., 'Case Law versus Statute Law: An Evolutionary Comparison', *Journal of Legal Studies*, 2008, p. 379-430.

Posner 1996
Posner, R.A., *Law and Legal Theory in England and America*, Oxford: Clarendon Press, 1996.

Posner 1979
Posner, R.A., 'Utilitarianism, Economics and Legal Theory', *Journal of Legal Studies*, 1979, p. 103-140.

Posner 2010
Posner, R.A., *Economic Analysis of Law*, New York: Aspen Publishers, 2010.

Priest 1977
Priest, G.L., 'The Common Law Process and the Selection of Efficient Rules', *Journal of Legal Studies*, 1977, p. 65-82.

Pritchard & Zywicki 1999
Pritchard, A.C. & Zywicki, T.J., 'Finding the Constitution: An Economic Analysis of Tradition's Role in Constitutional Interpretation', *North Carolina Law Review*, 1999, p. 409-522.

Reinsch 2010
Reinsch, P.S., *English Common Law in the Early American Colonies*, Whitefish, MT: Kessinger Publishing, 2010.

Robinson 1941
Robinson, W.A., *Justice in Grey: A History of the Judicial System of the Confederate States of America*, Cambridge: Harvard University Press, 1941.

Roe 1996
Roe, M.J., 'Chaos and Evolution in Law and Economics', *Harvard Law Review*, 1996, p. 641-668.

Rubin 1977
Rubin, P.H., 'Why is the Common Law Efficient', *Journal of Legal Studies*, 1977, p. 51-63.

Rubin 1982
Rubin, P.H., 'Common Law and Statute Law', *Journal of Legal Studies*, 1982, p. 205-223.

Rubin 1983
Rubin, P.H., *Business Firms and the Common Law: The Evolution of Efficient Rules*, New York: Praeger Publishers, 1983.

Siems 2005
Siems, M.L., 'Numerical Comparative Law – Do We Need Statistical Evidence in Order to Reduce Complexity?', *Cardozo Journal of International & Comparative Law*, 2005, p. 521-540.

Siems 2008
Siems, M.L., 'Legal Originality', *Oxford Journal of Legal Studies*, 2008, p. 147-164.

Smits 2001
Smits, J., 'Mixed Legal Systems and European Private Law', in: J. Smits (ed.), *The Contribution of Mixed Legal Systems to European Private Law* (Ius Commune Europaeum 36), Antwerp: Intersentia, 2001, p. 1-13.

Spamann 2009
Spamann, H., 'Large Sample, Quantitative Research Designs for Comparative Law?', *The American Journal of Comparative Law*, 2009, p. 797-810.

Terrebonne 1981
Terrebonne, P.R., 'A Strictly Evolutionary Model of Common Law', *Journal of Legal Studies*, 1981, p. 397-407.

Tollison & Crain 1979
Tollison, R.D. & Crain, W.M., 'Constitutional Change in an Interest-Group Perspective', *Journal of Legal Studies*, 1979, p. 165-175.

Tullock 1997
Tullock, G., *The Case against the Common Law*, Durham, NC: Carolina Academic Press, 1997.

Tullock 2005
Tullock, G., 'Rent-Seeking and the Law', in: C.K. Rowley (ed.), *The Selected Works of Gordon Tullock*, Indianapolis, IN: Liberty Fund, Inc., 2005, p. 184-195.

Van Caenegem 1987
Van Caenegem, R.C., *Judges, Legislators and Professors: Chapters in European Legal History*, Cambridge, UK: Cambridge University Press, 1987.

Von Wangenheim 1993
Von Wangenheim, G., 'The Evolution of Judge Made Law', *International Review of Law & Economics*, 1993, p. 381-411.

White & Willock 2006
White, R.M. & Willock, I.D., *The Scottish Legal System*, London: Tottel Publishing, 2006.

Wise 1973
Wise, E.M., 'The Doctrine of Stare Decisis', *Wayne Law Review*, 1973, p. 1043-1060.

Zywicki 2003
Zywicki, T.J., 'The Rise and Fall of Efficiency in the Common Law', *Northwestern University Law Review*, 2003, p. 1551-1634.

Bertrand Crettez
Bruno Deffains
Guillaume Leyte
Laurent Pfister

ON THE LAW AND ECONOMICS OF THE ORIGINS OF THE FRENCH CIVIL CODE

1. Introduction

The economic analysis of legal systems is an important field for research. The first arguments developed by Posner,[1] Rubin[2] or Priest[3] have tried to demonstrate the efficiency of the common law. They explain how market forces (supply and/or demand sides) contribute to the selection of efficient legal rules. However, these authors were not interested in the comparison between common law and civil law traditions.

Such a comparison is the object of the *New comparative economics* whose main objective is to explain differences in countries economic and financial performances considering their legal origins. As noted by La Porta *et al.*: 'if we find that legal rules differ substantially across legal families and that financing and ownership patterns do as well, we have a strong case that legal families, as expressed in the legal rules, actually cause outcomes'.[4] In other words, legal origins imply differences in terms of private property rights protection. These authors show that the common law system generates historically greater judicial independence and more developed financial markets. The effect of legal systems would be bolstered in institutional settings where the judiciary is more independent.[5] According to them, common law has evolved to protect property rights whereas civil law was constructed mainly to solidify State power. Thus, the difference of legal systems originates in the difference in the objective of the rule-makers. For a literature survey of these findings, see for example, La Porta *et al.*[6]

1 Posner 2003.
2 Rubin 1977.
3 Priest 1977.
4 La Porta *et al.* 1998.
5 La Porta *et al.* 2008.
6 La Porta *et al.* 2008.

Another analysis of the *effects* of different legal systems has been proposed by Beck, Demircug-Kunt and Levine.[7] They consider that legal systems differ in their abilities to adapt to changing economic and financial conditions. More precisely, legal systems that embrace adjudication and do not rely excessively on changes in statutory law will tend to evolve more efficiently to changing conditions than legal systems that reject adjudication or require strict adherence to statutes. In a way, it is another version of the Posnerian hypothesis of the efficiency of the common law (if one considers that adaptability implies a reduction of transaction costs). The problem with these explanations is that they cannot completely capture the complex interaction between legal and socio-economic conditions. Moreover, it left unexplained the difference in the design of legal systems.

This is certainly the reason why new perspectives are developed that focus on the importance of the political process to establish causal relations between Law and Economics. Many authors reject the law and finance's view that legal origin is a central determinant of investor protection laws and financial development.[8] Indeed, political decisions could determine the degree of investor or labour protections and legal rules from a political agreement between entrepreneurs and workers. Trade unions and social democratic parties are expected to oppose shareholder-orientated corporate governance reforms.[9]

However, the reasons for the differences between legal systems remain 'not entirely clear yet nor, in general, are the causal mechanisms that link either legal system to economic performance'.[10] There is a need for a theoretical approach of the legal systems that insists on the respective roles of judges and legislators. This is also the opinion expressed by Hadfield:

> 'the more fundamental difficulty in the existing framework, ..., has to do with the stylized theoretical relationship that is assumed to exist between how legal regimes, particularly judges, behave and the institutions that identify the regime as a "civil code" or a "common law" system'.[11]

Glaeser and Shleifer offer an explanation of why legal origins were different.[12] They assert that a key point in the design of a legal system is to know if law enforcers can be protected from coercion by litigants from either violence or bribes. They argue that when this is not possible, it is best to have law enforcers beholden to the state (as in thirteen century France). If this is possible, using decentralized juries is the

7 Beck, Demircug-Kunt & Levine 2003.

8 Roe 2003; Roe 2007; Rajan & Zingales 2003; Pagano & Volpin 2006.

9 See, notably, Roe 2003. Roe explains the differences between insider-orientated corporate governance regimes, where ownership is concentrated and minority shareholders have few legal protections, on the one hand, and shareholder-orientated regimes on the other, by the varying strength of social democratic parties. Pagano & Volpin 2006.

10 Ponzetto & Fernandez 2008.

11 Hadfield 2008.

12 Glaeser & Shleifer 2002.

best solution (as in thirteen century England). For a critical assessment of this idea, see Roe,[13] Klerman and Mahoney.[14]

To the best of our knowledge, attempts at explaining the differences in legal systems based on economic reasoning are scant.[15] So are the discussions of these attempts by specialists of Legal History. In this connection, two attempts at explaining the drawing of the *Code Civil* are worth considering. A common feature of these explanations is that they take care of the societal background in the economic analysis of law.

The first explanation proposed by Arrunada and Andonova concentrates on judges' behaviour.[16] In a nutshell, before the French Revolution, French judges were not very friendly with the market system. To enhance growth, it was necessary to control their choices by forcing them to make pro-market decisions. The drawing of the *Code Civil* was necessary to control these decisions.

The second explanation, proposed par a French in Law Professor, Xavier Lagarde, addresses the separation between the *bonus pater familias* (the *Code Civil*) and the merchant (the *Code de Commerce*). This explanation explores the role of the *Code Civil* as a model of low risk-taking relationships.

This paper unfolds as follows. In the next section (section 2), we will present the Arrunada and Andonova analysis and we will assess it from an historical perspective. In section 3 we present Lagarde's explanation and, again, an historical assessment of its relevance. Section 4 contains some concluding remarks.

2. The Code Civil: An Engine of Growth?

In two recent contributions, Benito Arrunada and Veneta Andonova have reconsidered the links between legal systems and growth.[17] In a somewhat revisionist way, they have reconsidered the idea that the common law is everywhere, every time the best system to spur growth. In contrast, these authors argue that legal systems are not independent of society's values and therefore that there is no reason why there should be a unique legal system to promote economic growth.

The original stance of Arrunada and Veneta is that there is a connection between the *Code Civil*, the centralized way in which it was drew and its very impact on growth, at least in continental Europe (and particularly in France). Their thesis is that a system in which law is produced in a more decentralized way, giving more freedom to judges, would have been essentially ill adapted to France.

The thesis of Arrunada and Veneta can be developed in three steps.

13 Roe 2007.

14 Klerman & Mahoney 2007.

15 Maybe we could make an exception with Dam 2008 who finds that the legal tradition view inaccurately portrays how legal systems work, how laws developed historically, and how government power is allocated in the various legal traditions. Yet, after probing the legal origins' literature for inaccuracies, Dam does not deeply develop an alternative hypothesis to explain the world's differences in financial development.

16 Arrunada & Andonova 2005; Arrunada & Andonova 2008.

17 Arrunada & Andonova 2005; Arrunada & Andonova 2008.

1. Judges of the Ancien Regime were fundamentally hostile to a free market economy.
2. The Post-Revolution elites were in contrast strong supporters of free markets.
3. To enhance growth it was necessary to promote a free market economy and thus to limit the power of judges, which has been possible by the drawing of the Civil Code.

Let us now consider each of these steps in more details.

2.1. *'Rulemaking Power' and Economic Development*

To begin with, following Arrunada and Andonova, it is useful to recall that the creation of wealth depends on the very possibility to exchange.[18] But exchanges are stimulated when there exists a legal environment which enables agents to define and conceive their best opportunities and to enforce legal agreements.

The legal environment comprises rules as well as courts. While rules are instrumental to define standard contracts, courts intervene when contracts are incomplete (because of unforeseen contingencies or simply because legal arrangements are unclear and ambiguous). Agents rely on courts as a last resort mean to interpret and to enforce contracts. Without rules and courts, agents would have to bear huge transaction costs to simply write and to enforce contracts.

In that connection, it is important to notice that rules may either be elaborated by parliament, or by courts (through jurisprudence). In the first case, the production of rules is centralized, it is decentralized in the second one.

The interesting issue raised by Arrunada and Andonova consists in identifying the characteristics of legal rulemaking that best spur growth. To answer this question it is crucial to know who are the judges.

2.2. *Hostility of Ancien Regime's Judges to Free Markets*

The main argument of Arrunada and Andonova is that, in contrast to British judges, judges of the Ancien Regime were not well informed about the economic organization and were hostile to markets. There are two reasons to explain why French judges were not well acquainted with the economy.

1. The first explanation is that Judges were noble[19] (or at least were members of the administrative nobility). As a consequence their incomes came from land and urban rents, and from venal offices.[20] They despised the risks taken by traders, industrialists and bankers (whose incomes were incompatible with a noble statute.[21] In a way, they preferred statute to income. Moreover, judges

18 See Arrunada & Andonova 2005, p. 231.

19 See Arrunada & Andonova 2008, p. 14.

20 A venal office was a position in the pre-revolutionary French royal administration which was both hereditary, and able to be bought and sold.

21 Bluche 1960.

were unlikely to be fully respectful of private property. This is because, as owner of venal offices, they were often themselves victims of King's actions infringing their assets (for instance, through the creation of new offices).

2. Second, judges' attitudes and beliefs derived from their education.[22] Judges were educated in Law schools, in French Universities, where they studied the *ius commune*, a doctrine emanating from Roman and Canon Laws.

In addition to their hostility to a market economy, grounded on an ignorance of economic life, Arrunada and Andonova suggest that judges could have suffered from cognitive bias.[23]

More precisely, judges were inclined to favour redistributive justice, by intervening in contract disputes, often by changing the terms of contracts. They were supposed to be mentally used to an economy where exchanges were infrequent, simple, concrete, often concerned with physical items, made by people knowing each other. Judges would have been unaware of the rapid development of a market economy around the middle of the seventeen-century, which relied on numerous anonymous and frequently complex exchanges. The higher the degree of complexity of contracts,[24] the lower the probability that a judge were able to understand them.

According to Arrunada and Andonova, judges tend to favour the weakest part of a contract. They overlook the fact that by doing so, they could weaken this part (by deteriorating the terms of contract in future transaction, terms which would take into account the risk of conflict and trial).[25]

2.3. *Centralization of Rule-Making in Civil Law and Growth*

What were the consequences of judges' hostility to markets on the optimal level of rules-making?

It is clear that, based on what we have seen above about the desirability of a stable legal environment to enhance growth, this hostility had to be reigned. To achieve this, there were two solutions. First, one has to make the law and contracts as rigid as possible, so as to prevent judges' discretion. Second, one could simply remove the judges.

For the authors, the post-revolution elites held pro-market views. This was particularly true in the case of representatives, who, through the working of an income-based voting system, were wealthier than the general population, and therefore pro-markets. It is those elites who decided to re-organize the legal system.

22 See Arrunada & Andonova 2005, p. 235.
23 See Arrunada & Andonova 2008, p. 7.
24 By which, we mean long-term contract, involving considerations of risks, and then of risk premium and interest rates.
25 Cf. Arrunada & Andonova 2008, p. 5.

On the one hand, the hiring of judges was changed. The venal offices system was removed. Judges became ordinary civil servants, whose careers could be controlled (needless to say, judges were by no means independent).

On the other hand, judge's freedom of action was tightly controlled. What was at stake was to control the arbitrariness of judges' decisions (from the business view point). To achieve this aims, the elites resorted to two means.

First, judges' decisions had to be made only with regard to statutes laws, or adjudication. This is where the draft of the *Code Civil* (and the codification policy) plays a role. References to such notions as the just price (and the 'doctrine de la lesion')[26] were banished. Appeal courts were specially supervised and warranted a uniform application of legal rules (insuring the stability and security of exchanges).

The draft of the *Code de Commerce* in 1808 served the same purpose. In particular it made harder for judges to make moratoriums in favour of indebted agents. It was also made harder to make winding-up agreements (concordat).[27]

2.4. *Legal History Assessment of the Arrunada-Andonova Thesis*

While original and insightful, the Arrunada-Andonova thesis is far from being completely supported by facts. A few comments are in order.

First, it is difficult to infer what were the beliefs of judges of the Ancien Regime. We do not know for sure what was their knowledge in economic matters, nor do we know what they thought of wealth, money, risk and so on. It is then difficult either to confirm or to refute the idea that they were not market friendly.

Judges were not that different from the other agents. They were living in a society in which it was considered as normal to intervene in the economy (e.g., Colbert). In this respect, they surely did not have the feeling to live in an economy without markets. Notice also that at least before the revolution, even the noble were doing business. So, it is unclear that judges were necessarily anti-capitalists. In fact, viewing judges as anti-capitalists is a bit of an anachronism.

Second, what were judges supposed to do? Should have they simply apply the law or do something else such as play an active role of legal interpret and/or legal producer? It fact, judges took the context into account. They took into account the consequences of their decisions on plaintiffs and defendants. However, since their decision were not motivated, it is difficult to settle the issue.[28]

Even if what Arrunada and Andonova assert about judges beliefs is correct, their whole thesis relies on shaky ground. The *Code Civil* only concerned ordinary citizens. Before and after the Revolution, commercial laws were special laws that only concern merchants. As far as business life was concerned, judges were chosen from businessmen.

26 Lesion means the injury suffered in consequence of an inequality of situation.

27 See Arrunada & Andonova 2008, p. 16.

28 Moreover, a distinction must be made between Parliaments' judges who could choose the interpretation of legal norms, from ordinary judges whose hands were tied by the letter of the law.

So, while the *Code de Commerce* limited judges' choices, the latter, being active businessmen where unlikely to be anti-markets. Perhaps judges of civil issues were less market-friendly, but their decisions were unlikely to concern directly businessmen (at least as long as their business, as opposed to their civil life, was concerned). Therefore, their hostility was not a cause of concern. Finally, as far as the *Code Civil* is concerned, one has to notice that some parts of it cannot be considered as business-friendly. For instance this is the case of the principle of equal inheritance.

In the same vein, it is difficult to assert that judges in the post-revolution time were different than those of the Ancien Regime. This is because they were largely the same individuals. Of course, in the long-run, because of the removal of the venal offices system, some changes certainly occurred.

Next, it is disputable to argue that the centralization of rule making was consciously done to spur growth. The drawing of the *Code du Commerce* has probably been stimulated by a surge of bankruptcies (especially in 1805). But if anything can be said, it is that judges' concerns were more of moral than economic nature. They sought to morally and socially condemn people who fooled their customers or their shareholders. They did not try to find beneficial arrangements for stakeholders. As far as commercial is concern, it is difficult to go beyond this remark. In civil matters, in fact, judges had recovered their freedom of interpretation ever since the Consulat.

Finally, one may observe that it is a general fact that law follows the customs. More precisely, the rule is that the economic movement precedes the legal one (and not the reverse). So perhaps we do overestimate the influence of legal institution on growth. After all, growth was a European phenomenon (even though the growth rates differed in Europe) that took place in European nations having different legal systems.

3. The Code Civil, Risk and Growth

As was seen above, we are far from sure that the introduction of the Civil Code was made on economic ground, at least in view of enhancing growth. Yet, another hypothesis deserves some attention.

This hypothesis is connected with an old issue, which is the rationale for having a civil law distinct from the commercial law. To put it another way, why has there been first a *Code Civil* (1804) and then a *Code de Commerce* (1807)? Concerning the common law, especially in British Law, there is no distinction between these two laws (such distinction however exists in the USA).

A possible explanation of the distinction between civil law and commercial law has been introduced recently by a French Professor in Law, Xavier Lagarde.[29]

The major point in Lagarde's reasoning is that 'what is risky does not concern civil law. Therefore, it is hardly surprising that the later relies on commercial law to take care of the regulation of actions which, by definition, involve taking risk'.[30]

29 See Lagarde 2010.

30 '... Ce qui est risqué n'intéresse pas le droit civil. Il n'est dès lors pas surprenant que ce dernier laisse au droit commercial le soin de régler les activités qui reposent par principe sur une prise de risque'. See Lagarde 2005.

More precisely, the *Code Civil* contains, illustrates and advocates some models of contracts involving low risk taking. The will to encourage people not to take excessive risks was a political objective whose aim was to insure social stability.

Thus, of necessity, risky contracts had to be relegated to other codes.

Incidentally, we see that Lagarde's thesis is somewhat connected with the issues raised by Arrunada and Andonova. Indeed, discouraging people to engage in risky business may have an impact on growth, on its rhythm and nature.

3.1. *Portalis and the Distinction between Civil and Commercial Laws*

Lagarde strongly relies on Portalis, one of the writers of the French *Civil Code*, to develop his reasoning. Portalis makes a difference between *everyday trade*, linked to the civil life and *trade*, which means in fact international trade. For Portalis, trade must be ruled by different laws than the civil laws. In his terms, 'the spirit of these rules differs essentially from the spirit of the civil laws'.[31]

A main difficulty with this statement has to do with the definition of the spirit of a law. An easy answer, perhaps not an entirely satisfactory one, is to assimilate the spirit of a law with the goals of the legislators. At the very least, there must exist a link between the spirit and the goals of a law.

3.2. *The Goals of the Code Civil*

As was mentioned above, the goal pursued by the writers of the *Code Civil*, as well as of Napoleon, was mainly to restate a durable civil peace.

In these post-revolution times, the orders of the Ancien Regime, did not exist anymore. Therefore, it was necessary to provide people with institutions to insure a minimal level of stability (indeed, if everything is possible, making expectations is impossible).

According to Lagarde, the *Code Civil* was set to create tight links between individuals so as to create and promote social cohesion. More specifically, the links between individuals would rely on contracts. Lagarde also notices that a contract should not be seen primarily as a way of making profits. Its main aim is to make people feeling closer, by making possible enduring relationships.

Quite surprisingly, for Portalis himself, the marriage contract 'provides us with the fundamental idea of a contract properly said, and of a perpetual contract from the onset'.[32]

Relationships among citizen must build on the development of exchange of goods, and by the use of contracts. Indeed, contracts are considered as being a substitute for a social pact. A contract is thought as a kind of constitution on which

31 'L'esprit de ces lois diffère essentiellement de l'esprit des lois civiles', see Portalis 1827, p. 513.

32 '[Le mariage] nous offre l'idée fondamentale d'un contrat proprement dit et d'un contrat perpétuel par sa destination', see Portalis 1827, p. 485.

two (or more) individuals agree (see, e.g., Art. 1134 of the *Code Civil*: 'Agreements lawfully entered into take the place of the law for those who have made them…').[33]

To sum up, the relationships between individuals through the use of contracts should be stable and strong. They contribute to social order.

At this stage, we still have to explain why social stability is incompatible with risk. Why, to put it differently, should individual engage in low-risk taking contracts ?

3.3. *Risk and the Code Civil*

There are at least two reasons why the *Code Civil* is not concerned with risky contracts.

A first one, which is not presented by Lagarde, can again be attributed to Portalis.[34] This reason is in our view connected to the analysis of bets and games of chance made by Portalis in his evaluation of the social value of risky contracts.

In a famous text, 'On random contracts',[35] Portalis concedes that random contracts, namely those contracts whose effect on the stakeholders depends on an uncertain event, may be welfare enhancing. But in fact, in his discussion Portalis only considers bets, games of change, and life annuity (relegating insurance and bottomry loan[36] to another code, the *Code Maritime* (Maritime Law)).

On the bets and game of change, Portalis writes: 'What do two bettors? They respectively engage themselves to deliver a given amount of money whose provision is left to the blindness arbitrary of chance. Where is the cause of the engagement? We hardly see one'.[37]

As the contract has no object, without mediation, the reverse of the transaction can lead to conflict: 'At the difference of ordinary contract, which make people closer, gambling debts divide and isolate them, …, all social links are broken'.[38]

Without doubt, this position explains the consideration on gambling debt that is found in the *Code Civil* (see Art. 1965: 'Legislation does not grant any action for a gaming debt or for the payment of a bet').[39]

33 'Les conventions légalement formées tiennent lieu de loi à ceux qui les ont faites ...'.

34 In passing, Lagarde observes that there is no mention of the term entrepreneur in the *Code Civil*. In contrast, use is made of the term prudent administrator (the so called *bon père de famille*, or *pater familias* (Art. 1728 of the *Code Civil*), who only seeks to preserve his assets. Lagarde wonders why is the term entrepreneur not mentioned in the 'the social game defined by the Code civil' (see Lagarde 2009, p. 41).

35 'Des contrats aléatoires', Fenet 1827, Vol. XIV, p. 675.

36 Prêt à la grosse aventure.

37 'Que font deux joueurs qui traitent ensemble? Ils se promettent respectivement une somme déterminée dont ils laissent la disposition à l'aveugle arbitraire du hasard. Où est donc la cause de l'engagement ? On n'en voit aucune' (see Fenet 1827, Vol. XIV, p. 539).

38 'A la difference d'un contrat ordinaire qui rapproche les gens, les promesses contractées aux jeux les divisent et les isolent, …, tout lien social est rompu' (see Fenet, Vol. XIV, p. 539).

39 'La loi n'accorde aucune action pour une dette de jeu ou le paiement d'un pari'.

Portalis arguments on risk help us understand the reluctance to include risky contracts in the *Code Civil*. Promoting risky contracts leads to conflictual relations which is precisely what the *Code Civil* is trying to avoid.

The second reason put forward by Lagarde relies strongly on a Fernand Braudel vision of trade and capitalism.[40]

Let us go back to the distinction between *every day trade* and properly *trade* made by Portalis. According to Braudel a major difference between these two activities is that trade, and especially long-run trade, requires a larger amount of capital than every day trade.

As a consequence, trade must be profitable (not the least because it is risky). This is why encounters between entrepreneurs and ordinary citizens are potentially conflictual. Trade is thus not made to strengthen social links. Its main purpose is to make profits, possibly at the expense of ordinary citizens, because exchanges and contracts are unequal. As a consequence, once again, social order is put at risk by risky trade.

In Lagarde's terms:

> 'Whereas ordinary traders, being aware of their interdependence, multiply links between them, the agents of the big firm only look for a mean to increase the invested capital. The time of exchange is for them the time for the return on investment. Since the Code Civil aims at founding a peaceful society by providing the model of relationships between individuals, it is understandable that is has nothing to do with trade properly said.'[41]

3.4. *Legal History Assessment of Lagarde's Thesis*

Even though Lagarde's thesis is brilliant and stimulating, it remains disputable.

Even if the *Code Civil* were written to define and illustrate socially beneficial relationships, what are the exact mechanisms by which these relationships were encouraged? Why should the fact of not mentioning risky contracts deter individuals to undertake them?

Were two codes necessary to make people aware of difference of risks between civil and commercial activities?[42]

40 Braudel 1979.

41 'Alors que les acteurs du petit commerce vont au contact les uns des autres et que, conscients de leurs interdépendance, ils multiplient les liens entre eux, les agents de la grande entreprise ne cherchent chez les autres que le moyen d'accroître le capital investi. Le moment de l'échange est pour eux le temps du retour sur soi. L'on comprend donc que le code civil, dont le projet est de définir les fondements d'une société pacifiée et qui, de ce fait, a pour principal objet d'établir un modèle de relation entre les individus n'ai que faire de ce qu'il appelle le commerce proprement dit' (see Lagarde 2009, p. 46).

42 Were the very existence of the two codes a nudge in the sense of Thaler & Sunstein 2008? ('A nudge is a small change in the social context that makes behaviour very different without forcing any one to do any thing. The concept behind libertarian paternalism is that it's possible to maintain freedom of choice – that's libertarianism- while also moving people in directions that make their own lives a bit better- that's paternalism').

Yet, one can observe that at the time of the inception of the *Code Civil*, most of the population was living and working in rural areas. Rural and agricultural activities are hardly qualified as riskless. Illness, bad harvests, wars and so on were quite common. As a consequence people were used to bear risks and to embark on high risk-taking activities. It is therefore difficult to conceive why they were unable to assess the risks involved by embarking on risky contracts, even with entrepreneurs/traders.

From a pure historical ground, what can be said from the *Code Civil* writers' political aims? Was social stability their main goal? Were the writers of the Code civil really willing to eliminate excessive risk-taking? If so, was this will linked to the political goal of social stability?

Lagarde is right when he supports that one of the main goals of the *Code Civil* was to contribute to social order. In fact, after 10 years of French Revolution, the Napoleon's regime wanted to restore social peace and stability. The *Code Civil* is one of the means to *recomposer une société* (rebuild a society). It is driven by a clear will to stop the weakening of individual ties. It has a vocation to stabilize and to strengthen the links between individuals for the common good. That is why it grants strength and guarantee to the *pater familias*, to the owners, to the respect of contracts.[43]

However, regarding the link between risk and contractual relations, Lagarde is only partly right. It is true that risky contracts like life or maritime insurance did not find place in the *Code Civil*. The first one was considered as being immoral (one shall not speculate on another's death). But, even if bets and games of chance were considered as a threat to social cohesion, they were not forbidden, only indirectly discouraged (since gambling-debt had no legal value).[44]

Nevertheless, there was another risky contract, life annuity, which remained perfectly legal for citizens and introduced in the *Code Civil*. Yet, a life annuity is a contract where the interests of one part are opposed to those of the other part. That is a risky contract. In this way, some contracts which were risky and probably antagonistic were not legally forbidden. In this mater, the rule-maker hoped that stakeholders would find a mutual beneficial arrangement. He trusted their goodwill.

Moreover, and more fundamentally, we may observe that every contract produces some risks. Risk is inherent to contracts.

Contracts between merchants are not the only risky ones. On one hand, a corporation act is a civil contract, regulated by the *Code Civil*, and so open to citizens and not only to merchants. Yet it is not considered as a random contract though the result of such a contract is certainly random. In addition, this kind of contract is made in the hope to be profitable. Being a partner in a company is not exactly the same thing as being a *pater familias*. Partners take risks after all! And the benefits should be shared in proportion to the risk taken by each civil partner.[45] On the other

43 About this lecture of the *Code Civil* of 1804, see Martin 2003.

44 Recall Art. 1965: 'Legislation does not grant any action for a gaming debt or for the payment of a bet'.

45 'Il faut une proportion équitable entre la mise et le profit de chaque associé; il faut que la différence dans la répartition des bénéfices, s'il en existe une, soit fondée ou sur une mise →

hand, in order to stimulate private borrowing, the *Code Civil* contains some legal instruments like deposit, caution, which helps to make less risky loans.

Finally, the thesis which defends the fact that commercial law is considered by the law-maker as autonomous from the civil law is disputable. It's very important to underline that the distinction between civil and commercial law is not a new distinction. Moreover the formal distinction, i.e., the existence of two codes, does not necessary implies substantial differences.

Firstly, the distinction already existed before the Revolution (e.g., merchants law). Merchants were submitted to special jurisdictions and to special rules. Revolutionary assemblies decided to write two codes, one for the civil law, another for the commercial law. However they never wrote these two codes. Then the existence of two codes is not an innovation of the Napoleon's regime. And in substance, the *Code de Commerce* in 1807 appears less as a new codification than as a 'revision' of the old laws. It is particularly true when we look at the *Ordonnance sur le Commerce* written in 1673.[46]

Secondly, according to most of the *Code de Commerce* makers and commentators and in opposition with Portalis, maker of the *Code Civil*, commercial law is not autonomous but only an exception to the civil law. That means that the *Code Civil* is the common law for the commerce and has to be applied when there are no special rules planned by the *Code de Commerce*.[47] For example, the *Code de Commerce* refers explicitly to the civil law for regulation of corporation contract.[48] And many contracts used in business stem from civil law (e.g., loan contracts, sales contract: these contract are not in the *Code de Commerce*).

Moreover, moral considerations were present during the writing of both codes. Both are promulgated to fight against consequences of the social, politic and

plus forte, ou sur des risques plus grands, ou sur de plus éminents services, ou enfin sur toute autre cause légitime en faveur de celui qui est le plus avantagé'. See Treilhard, 1er mars 1804, *Corps législatif*, Fenet 1827, Vol. XIV, p. 398.

46 'Dans leur ensemble, la plupart des dispositions qu'il [le Code de commerce] renferme, ont été extraites de l'édit de 1673, de l'ordonnance de 1681 et de divers réglements qui sont intervenus postérieurement'. See Chaptal 1802 and Gorneau, Legras & Roux 1802, both in the Projet de Code du Commerce, p. XV and XXVII-XXVIII. About this point, see Hilaire 1986. See also, J.-L. Thireau 2008.

47 'Le premier objet dont les commissaires rédacteurs ont eu à s'occuper, a été de fixer ceux des principes de la législation civile qui doivent conserver leur force dans la législation commerciale (...) Ils ont laissé à la législation civile tout ce qui lui appartient; ils ont circonscrit les lois commerciales aux objets pour lesquels la loi leur a paru insuffisante, et à ceux qui, par leur nature et par les besoins du commerce, exigent des dispositions particulières'. See Chaptal 1802, p. XII. Also Delpierre 1807, who speaks about a 'régime d'exception'. Also Locré 1811, Vol. I, Introduction: 'Le Code Napoléon, contenant l'universalité des règles du droit civil qu'il constitue, se suffit à lui-même, et devient ainsi la loi unique et principale. Le Code de commerce, au contraire, n'étant qu'une loi d'exception destinée à régler des affaires d'une nature particulière, ne peut se suffire à lui-même, vient s'enter sur le droit commun, laisse sous l'empire de ce droit tout ce qu'il n'excepte pas, et s'y réfère, même pour ce qu'il excepte'.

48 See Livre 1, Titre III, Art. 18, *Code de Commerce*: 'Le contrat de société se règle par le droit civil, par les lois particulières au commerce, et par les conventions des parties'.

economic troubles and to reintroduce morality. The *Code du Commerce* of 1807 contains a lot of very strong rules. Adopted after recrudescence of bankruptcy as was already seen, the code, which followed the will of Napoleon himself, punished the bankrupt very rigorously. The claim of good faith is stronger than in civil relations and every society founded in an anonymous form must be approved by the administration.[49]

4. Concluding Remarks

In this paper, we have presented and discussed the historical relevance of two recent opinions in the literature about the creation of the *Napoleonic Code*.

The first explanation focused on judges' behaviour and on the *Code Civil* as a mean to control their decisions.

The second explanation pays attention to the role played by the *Code Civil* as a mean to insure social order in a post-revolutionary era.

In a way, both explanations are insightful. Yet, they are not totally in line with what we know of the historical evidence. For sure, legal systems are so complex that no single explanation can be totally relevant. However, the hypotheses presented in this paper, while not totally convincing, shed some light on the reasons and the effects of the drawing of the *Code Civil*.

49 See Padoa-Schioppa 1982; Sgard 2006.

Bibliography

Arrunada & Andonova 2005
Arrunada, B. & Andonova, V., 'Market Institutions and Judicial Rulemaking', in: C. Ménard & M.M. Shirley (eds.), *Handbook of New Institutional Economics*, Berlin, Dordrecht, Heidelberg, New York: Springer, 2005, p. 229-250.

Arrunada & Andonova 2008
Arrunada, B. & Andonova, V., 'Judges' Cognition and Market Order, *Review of Law and Economics*, 2008, p. 665-692.

Beck, Demirguc-Kunt & Levine 2003
Beck, T., Demirguc-Kunt, A. & Levine R., *Bank Supervision and Corporate Finance*, NBER Working Papers 9620, National Bureau of Economic Research, Inc., 2003.

Bluche 1960
Bluche, F., *Les magistrats du parlement de Paris au XVIII siècle (1715-1771)*, Paris, 1960.

Braudel 1979
Braudel, F., *Civilisation matérielle, économie et capitalisme (XVe-XVIIIe siècles)*, Tomme 3, Paris: Armand Colin, 1979.

Chaptal 1802
Chaptal, J.A., *Rapport présenté aux Consuls de la république sur le projet du Code de Commerce*, Paris, 1802.

Dam 2006
Dam, K., *The Law-Growth Nexus: The Rule of Law And Economic Development*, Washington: Brookings Institution Press, 2006.

Delpierre 1807
Delpierre A.F., *Rapport sur la seconde partie du livre IV du Code de commerce présenté le 14 septembre 1807 devant le Corps législatif*, 1807.

Fenet 1827
Fenet, P.A, *Recueil Complet des Travaux Préparatoire du Code Civil*, Paris, Au dépot, Rue Saint-André-des-Arcs, n° 51 (15 volumes), 1827.

Gorneau, Legras & Roux 1802
Gorneau, P.J., Legras, P. & Roux, V., *Discours préliminaire*, Paris, 1802.

Glaeser & Shleifer 2002
Glaeser, E. & Shleifer, A., 'Legal Origins', *Quarterly Journal of Economics*, 2002, p. 1193-1229.

Hadfield 2008
Hadfield, G.K., 'The Levers of Legal Design: Institutional Determinants of the Quality of Law', *Journal of Comparative Economics*, 2008, p. 50-56.

Hilaire 1986
Hilaire, J., *Introduction historique au droit commercial*, Paris: PUF, 1986.

Klerman & Mahoney 2007
Klerman, D. & Mahoney, P., 'Legal Origins?', *Journal of Comparative Economics*, 2007, p. 278-293.

La Porta *et al.* 1998
La Porta, R., Lopez de Silanes, F., Shleifer, A. & Vishny, R.W., 'Law and Finance', *Journal of Political Economy*, 1998, p. 1113-1151.

La Porta, Lopez-de Silanes & Shleifer 2008
La Porta, R., Lopez-de Silanes, F. & Shleifer, A., 'The Economic Consequences of Legal Origins', *Journal of Economic Literature*, 2008, p. 285-332.

Lagarde 2005
Lagarde, X., 'Brèves réflexions sur l'attractivité économique du droit français des contrats', *Recueil Dalloz*, 2005, p. 2745-2747.

Lagarde 2009
Lagarde, X., *Juste Capitalisme*, Litec, 2009.

Locré 1811
Locré, J.G., *Esprit du code du commerce*, Paris, 1811.

Martin 2003
Martin, X., *Mythologie du Code Napoléon. Aux soubassements de la France moderne*, Paris: Bouère, Dominique Martin Morin, 2003.

Padoa-Schioppa 1982
Padoa-Schioppa, A., 'Napoleone e il Code de commerce', in: *Diritto e potere nelle storia europea. Atti in onore di Bruno Paradisi*, Volume II, Florence: Leo Olschki, 1982, p. 1041-1067.

Pagano & Wolpin 2006
Pagano, M. & Wolpin, P., 'The Political Economy of Corporate Governance', *American Economic Review*, 2006, p. 1005-1030.

Ponzetto & Fernandez 2008
Ponzetto, A.M. & Fernandez, P.A., 'Case Law vs. Statute Law: An Evolutionary Comparison', *Journal of Legal Studies*, 2008, p. 379-430.

Portalis 1827
Portalis, J., 'Discours préliminaire', in: Fenet, P.A. (ed.), *Recueil complet des travaux préparatoires du Code civil*, I, Paris, p. 464-490.

Posner 2003
Posner, R.A., *Economic Analysis of Law*, 6th edition, New York: Aspen, 2003.

Priest 1977
Priest, G.L., 'The Common Law Process and the Selection of Efficient Rules', *Journal of Legal Studies*, 1977, p. 65-82.

Rajan & Zingales 2003
Rajan, R.G. & Zingales, L, 'The Great Reversals: the Politics of Financial Development in the Twentieth Century', *Journal of Financial Economics*, 2003, p. 5-50.

Roe 2003
Roe, M., 'Delaware's Competition', *Harvard Law Review*, 2003, p. 610-634.

Roe 2007
Roe, M., 'Juries and the Political Economy of Legal Origins', *Journal of Comparative Economics*, 2007, p. 294-308.

Rubin 1977
Rubin, P.H., 'Why Is the Common Law Efficient', *Journal of Legal Studies*, 1977, p. 51-63.

Sgard 2006
Sgard, J., 'On Legal Origins and Bankruptcy Laws: the European Experience (1808-1914)', *European Review of Economic History*, 2006, p. 389-419.

Thaler & Sunstein 2008
Thaler, R. & Sunstein, C., *Nudge: Improving Decisions about Health, Wealth, and Happiness*, New Haven & Londres: Yale University Press, 2008.

Thireau 2008
Thireau, J.L., *Un Code traditionaliste pour un droit nouveau, D'un code à l'autre: le droit commercial en mouvement*, Paris: LGDJ, 2008.

Julan Du

DOES CHINA NEED LAW FOR ECONOMIC DEVELOPMENT?

1. Introduction

The importance of law for economic development is a longstanding issue in economics, sociology and legal studies. Weber argues for the necessity of rational law as well as the well-known Protestant ethics for the emergence of modern capitalism.[1] In his view, legal rationalization could shape culture and institutions, particularly the hierarchically organized state administration. Rational institutions are technically superior, efficient and therefore supportive of economic growth and facilitative of capitalism. This line of thoughts has been revived in recent decades. By comparing economic performance in different countries, North argues forcefully that countries having provided property rights protection and having established predictable rules for resolving contract disputes delivered a better environment for economic growth than those having not.[2] This view points to the central importance of economic institutions supported by formal legal institutions for economic development. In the past decade or so, a growing literature has demonstrated that formal institutions or the rule of law are crucial to long-term economic growth, and a large portion of the variation in economic growth performances across countries can be accounted for by the differences in legal institutions strength.[3] This finding derived from the experience of a large number of countries has been regarded as one general principle and a widely applicable policy recipe for policymakers around the world. It also becomes an integral part of the Washington Consensus that summarizes the established wisdom regarding growth-promoting public policies.[4]

1 Weber 1958.
2 North 1990; North 1991.
3 E.g. Hall & Jones 1999; Acemoglu, Johnson & Robinson 2001; Rodrik, Subramanian & Trebbi 2004.
4 Washington Consensus refers to a set of neoliberal, market-friendly and laissez-faire-oriented policies that was influential among mainstream economists, politicians, journalists and global institutions such as the International Monetary Fund and World Bank. It constitutes the cornerstone of policy advices for developing countries and transition economies in the period →

Nonetheless, China, the fastest growing economy in the past few decades, produces a picture that seems inconsistent with this general pattern. Since the outset of economic reforms in 1978, China has witnessed a spectacular, large-scale and prolonged economic growth. It has registered an annual average GDP growth rate of 9.5 per cent since 1978, which is in sharp contrast to an average of 4.4 per cent before 1978. The tremendous growth has transformed China from one of the poorest countries in the world into the second largest economy in the world in 2010. At the same time, the Chinese per capita GDP increased by almost eight-fold in the reform period, which helped lift millions of people out of poverty at a scale unparalleled in world history. Even more impressively, the quality of economic growth has improved considerably. It is estimated that the contribution of total factor productivity (TFP) to output growth has increased from 11 per cent prior to 1978 to more than 40 per cent afterwards.[5]

However, China has achieved its impressive economic growth record in the absence of adequate legal institutions. Based on commonly-applied standards, China is rated below average on various measurements of rule of law, property rights protection, contracting institutions, etc.[6] By examining the relationship between legal system development and economic development, Clarke, Murrell, and Whiting reach the conclusion that it is impossible to claim that formal legal institutions development has contributed much to economic development in China.[7] In this sense, China seems to be an outlier that deviates from the general patterns on law and development observed across countries over the past centuries of capitalist development. The coupling of economic success and weak legal institutions in the Chinese economic growth experience poses a great challenge to the conventional wisdom on the relationship between law and development as contained in the aforesaid academic studies as well as in the Washington Consensus.

What accounts for the China puzzle? A growing literature on China's economic and institutional development[8] has pointed out that some alternative mechanisms must have substituted for the formal legal institutions to provide a reasonable level of property rights protection and contract enforcement and to generate expectations of reasonable and predictable returns from investments and transactions. The literature has pointed to the political structure and governments at both the national and sub-national levels that play a substituting role in providing reasonable security for private property rights and resolving business disputes to ensure the smooth execution of contracts.

In this chapter, we provide a further interpretation of the role of government as a substitute for formal legal institutions in maintaining a stable business environ-

1980-2008. It advocates 'stabilize, privatize, and liberalize', that is, maintaining macroeconomic balances by means such as reducing fiscal deficits, taking the state out of business through privatization and deregulation, and freeing up domestic prices and international trade and investment (Williamson 1989; Rodrik 2006).

5 Perkins & Rawski 2008.

6 Allen, Qian & Qian 2005.

7 Clarke, Murrell & Whiting 2008.

8 For a survey see, e.g., Clarke, Murrell & Whiting 2008; Xu 2010.

ment. We argue that the success of Chinese economic reforms in the presence of notoriously weak legal institutions lies in that China has adopted a helping hand regulatory state model as a target model of market economy for economic transition and reforms, which turns out to suit well China's situations. In this model, major institutional changes to support market economy development have been first reflected in the shift in ideologies and government policies initiated by the national government. To implement policy changes, the administration system introduces a series of regulatory changes to cater to the policy shift. In practice, the national government often carries out some experiments with policy changes in some pilot experimental areas. After getting ensured that these changes are feasible and well received, the national government extends the policy reform to the whole nation. China's authoritarian administration regime provides an institutional support to ensure that the regulatory state model turns out to be primarily a helping-hand regulatory state model by controlling bureaucratic corruption at a tolerable level.

Then the regulatory changes guide the economic activities of economic agents, particularly the non-state sector. After these changes have been widely accepted and proved feasible and suitable, the legislature would enact or revise laws to reflect these changes. This procedure of going from state policy shifts to regulatory changes and eventually to legislation is a natural outcome of China's political structure where the Communist Party and its administration are the leading force in shaping socioeconomic transitions. Laws have so far been treated as instruments to implement state policy changes rather than as the way to impose constraints upon governments and bureaucrats and protect the rights of citizenry.

This helping-hand regulatory state model has contributed considerably to China's economic development. Nonetheless, it is currently facing the threat of degrading into a grabbing-hand regulatory state model if we cannot effectively control rampant corruption and various practices of bureaucratic capitalism. Hence, a readjustment of the power of the state vis-à-vis the market in the regulatory state model is direly needed at present.

The rest of this chapter is organized as follows. Section 2 discusses the general features of a helping-hand regulatory state model. Sections 3-5 present three cases to illustrate how the regulatory state works in China. Section 6 discusses the institutional foundation for the formation of a helping-hand regulatory state. Section 7 discusses the relationship between statist legalism and regulatory state. Section 8 concludes the chapter by discussing the current challenges facing the regulatory state model.

2. A Helping-hand Regulatory State Model

The choice of a suitable target model of market economy is by no means an easy task. The experience of economic reforms and liberalization in many countries in the past few decades demonstrates the overarching importance of the choice of an appropriate target model. Dissatisfied with failed experiments in state ownership during the 20th century, developing economies embraced ideals of private ownership and market competition as part of their efforts to promote market economies.

The means and goals of transition from state ownership to a market economy, however, have varied widely. At one end of the spectrum was the Washington Consensus, which sought to minimize state intervention in the economy. Its purpose was to 'stabilize, privatize, and liberalize', i.e. maintain macroeconomic stability, push for domestic liberalization, privatization and openness in international trade, and drastically reduce the role of the state in the economic sphere. This has been the guiding principle for economic reforms in most of the former socialist economies in Europe, Latin America, Africa, and South and East Asia.[9] At the other end of the spectrum were countries like China, where the role of government in the economy has remained constant and significant throughout three decades of economic reform.[10]

These diverse approaches to establishing a market economy appear to reflect fundamental differences over the understanding of what a market economy should look like, particularly for transition and developing economies. Theoretically speaking, we can have several variant models of market economy depending on the relative power of the state vis-à-vis the market. Glaeser and Shleifer,[11] and Djankov *et al.*[12] lay out a general framework of market economy models that can help us think about this issue systematically. In their view, market economy can range from models with low state intervention, which are called private orderings and private litigation through courts, to the model with high state intervention that is referred to as regulatory state. They classify distinct market economy models from the perspective of how closely the state is involved in helping private contracting parties to resolve business disputes. However, this aspect of state intervention could reflect in general the degree of state involvement in guiding economic activities.

These authors point out a central trade-off in weighing the merits and demerits of different models of market economy, that is, the trade-off between market disorder costs and state dictatorship costs. They complement Hobbes' assertion that the proper function of a market economy requires governments to protect investors against expropriation by thieves, competitors, or tortfeasors that leads to 'disorder costs'.[13] At the same time, to facilitate the development of a market economy, governments themselves need to refrain from expropriation where it leads to 'dictatorship costs'. These authors characterize the challenge to establishing a market economy as a balancing act, wherein the government must follow a path between disorder costs arising from inadequate control over the market and dictatorship costs that arise from government excess.

The differences in the conduct and impacts of state intervention for market economy development result in two possible variants of the regulatory state model, i.e. the helping-hand model and the grabbing-hand model. In both models, bureaucrats intervene extensively in economic activities. Nonetheless, in the helping-hand model, bureaucrats suffer from relatively limited corruption and can largely

9 Williamson 1989; Blanchard *et al.* 1992; Blanchard *et al.* 1993; Rodrik 2006.
10 Walder 1995; Rodrik 2006.
11 Shleifer 2002; Shleifer 2003.
12 Djankov *et al.* 2003.
13 Hobbes 1651.

promote private economic activity. In the grabbing-hand model, corrupt bureaucrats establish various predatory regulations to seek rents.[14] Obviously, the helping hand model brings into play the function of state intervention in precluding market disorder costs and at the same time keeps dictatorship costs under control. In contrast, the grabbing hand model enables state expropriation to disrupt the proper functioning of a market economy.

Most of the developing and transition economies started to carry out their economic reforms from a status quo of excessive state regulations and state ownership. Naturally, they often regard economic reforms as equivalent to withdrawing the state from the economic sphere. The Washington Consensus clearly reflects this ideology in advocating for privatization and liberalization. In this sense, it leans toward the less invasive private orderings and private litigation through courts models of a market economy. Both target models, however, require that a host of preconditions are met before they can be implemented. Specifically, private orderings can be an efficient choice of market economy model only after systems to protect private property rights of market participants are in place. Correspondingly, the private litigation model assumes the existence of a judiciary composed of competent, independent judges, immune to influence from the rich and politically connected. In the former socialist economies, of course, these preconditions were not met at the outset of transition. Property rights protections for private enterprises had yet to be formally established, and the independence of members of the newly created judiciaries was dubious at best.[15] Nor was this an isolated phenomenon. Most developing economies suffered the same failure to meet preconditions of the market economy models embraced by the Washington Consensus (i.e. private orderings and private litigation through courts). Under this circumstance, any radical transition towards a laissez-faire capitalism would disrupt the existing state institutions without an adequate replacement market-supporting institution being available. In light of this observation, it is hardly surprising that developing economies following the Washington Consensus have posted less-than-stellar performances.[16]

Similarly, the successes of economic reforms in China, India and Vietnam are usually credited to incremental implementation of policies and a cautious reform approach. Could it also be, however, that this success stems in part from targeting an appropriate market economy model for the transition?

The path of ideological changes of the Chinese leadership demonstrates that China has never regarded laissez-faire style models as an ideal target model for its transition toward a market economy. At the end of the 1970s and in the early 1980s, China introduced some elements of private sector, market transactions and free prices to complement its dominant centrally planned economy. In 1984, the ruling Communist Party issued 'Decisions on the Reforms of the Economic System', in which the leadership asserts that China's socialist economy is a socialist commodity

14 Frye & Shleifer 1997; Shleifer & Vishny 1998.

15 Clarke, Murrell & Whiting 2008.

16 Rodrik 2006.

economy built on the basis of state ownership and a central planning system. In early 1992, the Chinese senior leader Mr. Deng Xiaoping claimed that the target model of the Chinese economic restructurings was the socialist market economy with Chinese characteristics. In October 1992, the Chinese leaders formally confirmed that China's economic reforms and open-up were aimed at building up a socialist market economy. This model tries to incorporate the market into the then planned economy in China. In the process of its implementation, the state sector has gradually dwindled, whereas the private sector has grown rapidly and accounted for the majority of China's GDP. In nature, China's socialist market economy model is a regulatory state model where the state retains considerable control over economic activities. It bears some resemblance to the Western socialist market economy in terms of the mixed economic model. Nonetheless, the two differ considerably in terms of the political structure where China remains an authoritarian regime with the Communist Party keeping the political monopoly, fundamentally different from the Western notions of democracy, individual rights and the rule of law.

Interestingly, in the absence of the rule of law, multiple party elections, and individual rights, China's regulatory state still turns out to be a primarily helping-hand regulatory state. In hindsight, the state regulation of the economy proves mainly efficiency-enhancing rather than being driven by predatory rent-seeking. In Section 6, we will discuss the institutional foundations for China to build up a helping-hand regulatory state.

In the following, we first present several cases to illustrate whether and how state regulation of the economy in China works and contributes to the development of the market economy. These cases are related to the role of the state in helping resolve business disputes and creating a good business environment, in strengthening corporate governance system through regulatory innovation, and in regulating the listing and stock issuances of listed firms. From these cases, we can see how the helping-hand regulatory state tries to establish a sound microeconomic foundation and supportive business environment for economic growth in China.

3. Case 1: Business Dispute Resolution

An essential element of a good environment for the development of market economy is the effective resolution of disputes that may arise from business transactions. In principle, corresponding to the three models of market economy laid out in Section 2, there are three distinct methods of resolving business disputes, i.e., private orderings, private litigation through courts, and regulatory state. These methods differ from each other in the degree of government involvement in dispute resolution.

In private orderings, contracting parties resolve business disputes through private negotiations. The primary force enabling private settlement of disputes is market discipline. For instance, reputational concern may lead contracting parties to reach a compromise when their stakes in an individual transaction is smaller than the benefits of keeping a long-term business relationship. In this sense, no formal legal institutions and governments are needed.

In private litigation through courts, the judicial system helps resolve business disputes according to laws, and the government plays a minimal role through invisible hand by providing basic public goods such as law and order.

In a regulatory state, the government is heavily involved in commercial dispute resolutions where the adjudication reflects the will of the government, while the legal framework plays a limited part. There are various ways for the government to help resolve commercial disputes. It could directly intervene in the disputes to suggest some solutions to the disputing parties and prompt them to accept the solutions. It could indirectly contribute to dispute resolution. For instance, the government could encourage local banks to extend loans or loan guarantees to the enterprises involved in disputes. The provision of financial support could help resolve business disputes.

Clearly, going from private orderings to regulatory state involves an increasing power of the state vis-à-vis the market in the economy. Nonetheless, it is not obvious which model is superior. A strong role of the state helps to resolve business disputes expediently thereby minimizing the disorder costs associated with the dispute resolution by the market.[17] On the other hand, there are concerns about whether the strong state can refrain itself from becoming an expropriator, which could lead to dictatorship costs. Hence it is not clear a priori whether a strong role of the state in resolving business disputes is conducive to the development of market economy.

In controlling both the market disorder costs and state dictatorship costs, we face a crucial question, i.e. whether the regulatory state model turns out to be a helping-hand model or a grabbing-hand model. In both models, bureaucrats rather than courts and judges are decisive in adjudicating many commercial disputes. Nonetheless, in the helping-hand model, bureaucrats suffer from relatively limited corruption and can largely promote private economic activity. In the grabbing-hand model, corrupt bureaucrats exercise discretion to impose their own will in commercial disputes and establish various predatory regulations to seek rents.[18]

To address this intriguing and important question, in Du, Lu and Tao,[19] we conduct a systematic empirical investigation by quantifying the power of the state vis-à-vis the market in resolving business disputes. Using a firm-level survey dataset from China, we investigate how the role of state in resolving business disputes affects enterprise performance.

The data used in this study comes from a survey conducted in 1999 containing a sample of 3,073 privately-owned enterprises in China. We choose private enterprises for our study because in general they do not have government backing and protection, and hence they are most vulnerable to both disorder costs and dictatorship costs. Examining the impacts of different dispute resolution modes on private enterprise performance can most accurately demonstrate whether the government

17 Hobbes 1651.

18 Frye & Shleifer 1997; Shleifer & Vishny 1998.

19 Du, Lu & Tao 2010.

involvement in dispute resolution promotes or hinders firm performance, which in turn facilitates or deters the national economic growth.

The dataset provides information on the ways that these private entrepreneurs resolved business disputes. In the survey, there is a question regarding how an entrepreneur would resolve business disputes with others. The available answers are: (i) doing nothing; (ii) negotiating between themselves; (iii) seeking help from private networks; (iv) court ruling; and (v) seeking help from the provincial/local government. It turns out that these answers correspond well to the three modes of dispute resolution in a market economy listed above. We therefore group these answers into three categories. We treat answers (i), (ii), and (iii) as private orderings, answer (iv) as private litigation through courts, and answer (v) as regulatory state.

We first assign an ordinal value to each enterprise corresponding to the specific category of the response made by the entrepreneur. Because these three resolution methods correspond to an ascending order of state involvement, we assign value 1 for private orderings, value 2 for private litigation through courts, and value 3 for regulatory state. Then we take the average of such values of enterprises located in a province (weighted by the number of employees) to quantify the power of the state vis-à-vis the market in resolving business disputes in that region, with a higher value indicating a greater power of the state vis-à-vis the market.

Next we examine the relationship between the indicator of the power of the state vis-à-vis the market in dispute resolution and firm performance measured as output per worker. By carrying out a series of regression analyses, we find that private enterprises located in provinces with greater powers of the state vis-à-vis the market turned out to have better enterprise performance. These findings remain robust when the regression models are modified to address typical technical concerns in empirical studies, such as omitted variables and reverse causality issues, alternative measures of the power of the state vis-à-vis the market, and different sub-samples.

The positive net effects of state involvement in business dispute resolution on firm performance suggest a beneficial role played by the state in promoting the development of the market economy. We interpret our results as that a higher power of the state vis-à-vis the market in adjudicating commercial disputes enhances property rights protection and improves contracting environment, which in turn promotes enterprise performance.

To substantiate our conclusion, however, we need to consider a potential competing explanation. One possible alternative interpretation of our findings is that those enterprises located in regions with greater powers of the state vis-à-vis the market conducted more rent seeking activities and thus achieved better performance by receiving government favours. In other words, the strong performances of those firms seeking government help in resolving business disputes could reflect the rewards extended by corrupt bureaucrats for entrepreneurs' bribes instead of superior performances from a fair and contestable market. Clearly, distinguishing between these two opposing interpretations is instrumental to our understanding of whether the regulatory state in China serves as a helping hand or a grabbing hand for private enterprises.

Because of the secret nature of bribery, we can only infer the existence and severity of bribery in an indirect manner. To see whether rent seeking is the driving force behind our results, we examine the various channels in which enterprises may obtain favours through rent seeking activities. These channels include input procurement, availability of production locations, supply of electricity and water, recruitment of skilled labour, sales of products, sales of services, and access to bank loans. These channels are related to the supply of production factors (costs) and the sales of products (revenues). If private entrepreneurs received favours from local bureaucrats, we should be able to detect traces from these channels. Hence, we are interested in learning whether enterprises located in provinces with greater powers of the state vis-à-vis the market showed any sign of having received government favours along these lines. Nonetheless, our results fail to show that firms in regions with more state involvement in business disputes obtained any favours along any of these channels, thereby largely ruling out the possibility of the rent seeking interpretation of our results being the primary underlying rationale.

Our results suggest that the role of the state in resolving business disputes in China is conducive to enterprise performance. Given that private enterprises have been accounting for an ever increasing share of the national output growth, we can conclude that the state's initiative in business dispute resolution has been beneficial to economic growth, which implies that China has been implementing a helping-hand regulatory state model.

To help readers to get a sense of how state intervention in business dispute resolution works, we discuss a short case of a commercial dispute that happened in South China's Guangdong province in 2009.[20] Yangpu Zhonghe Petrochemical Co. Ltd. signed two crude oil transactions contracts with Zhenhua Petrochemical Co. Ltd. located in Zhongshan City, Guangdong Province in November and December, 2008, respectively. Another company, Zhenhua Lubricating Oil Company, is based in Dongfeng Town, Zhongshan City in Guangdong Province. It is a private company owned by Mr. Liang Hengrong. This company provided guarantee for Zhenhua Petrochemical Co. Ltd for the fulfilment of contract obligations, and hence took on legal obligations.

Because of the breakout of the global financial tsunami in 2008-2009, Zhenhua Petrochemical Co. could not honour its contract obligations. Consequently, in January, 2009, Yangpu Zhonghe Petrochemical Co. sued the three defendants, i.e., Zhenhua Petrochemical Co. Ltd, Zhenhua Lubricating Oil Company, and Mr. Liang Hengrong, and asked the local court to freeze the assets of these three parties.

The local court made investigations into the contract default and concluded that it was not caused by malicious fraud on the part of the three defendants. On the contrary, it was true that global financial tsunami caused the breakdown of the value chain of the defendants, and resulted in their inability to fulfil the contractual obligations.

[20] This case is based on an essay entitled *A Documentary of a Commercial Transaction Dispute Triggered by the Global Financial Tsunami* written by Shen Meiping on May 17, 2010, which is available online in Chinese at <http://www.hicourt.gov.cn/theory/artilce_list.asp?id=5476 &l_class=1>.

In view of the facts that the contract default was triggered by global economic recession and the survival of these enterprises was important for local economic development and social stability, the government of Dongfeng Town, where Zhenhua Lubricating Oil Company is located, decided to intervene in the disputes. The township government worked closely with the local court to negotiate with the plaintiff and the defendants. After long negotiations, the township government used funds from other channels to help the defendant to pay around 25 million Yuan (around 3.6 million US dollars) to the plaintiff. With the funds secured, the plaintiff agreed to withdraw the petition and let the court free up the defendants' assets. Consequently, the two defendant firms were able to resume production, and all parties eventually gained from this resolution. By forcefully intervening into the disputes, the Dongfeng township government successfully prevented the local economy and local employment from being adversely affected by the incident.

This case illustrates several points. First, government intervention helps resolve business disputes and promote economic efficiency. Clearly, the two defendant firms met financial distress under unexpectedly harsh macroeconomic environment following the global financial tsunami. Without the rescue efforts of the government, the plaintiff firm would keep freezing the defendants' assets. The situation would remain at a dead end: the defendant firms were not able to resume production and compensate the plaintiff fully; the stability of local economy and local employment would be undermined. Hence, the township government's intervention in this suit broke the deadlock, improving the situations of all parties as well as the local economy.

Second, government intervention in commercial disputes is targeted at some significant, unconventional, controversial and politically sensitive cases. Consistent with the legal literature on China, our study finds that the legal courts have dealt with the majority of regular and routine commercial disputes. Government intervention in commercial disputes primarily takes place when the case is politically sensitive or hits the boundary of the established concepts of legality. In this illustrated case, following the call of the central leadership, the local government treated the provision of assistance to firms adversely affected by the global financial tsunami as a political task to maintain the stability of the local economy and local employment. Hence, the government stepped in under these circumstances.

It is worth pointing out that the three distinct modes of dispute resolution in our study share some common features with the concept of *guanxi* (social network) but the two have significant differences. The literature on *guanxi* emphasizes that *guanxi* is mainly interpersonal or social connections implicitly based on mutual interest and benefit, i.e., one party can ask a favour of the other with the expectation that the debt incurred will be repaid sometime in the future. Various studies[21] show that entrepreneurs and managers in China cultivated personal connections with other business people and government officials to smooth business operation, facilitate dispute resolution, and secure property rights protection in a business environment with weak formal institutions. Actually, *guanxi* is regarded as a possible

21 E.g., Xin & Pearce 1996.

substitute for a reliable government and rule of law in developing countries and transition economies where adequate formal institutions are yet to be established.

Clearly, private ordering in our framework has quite many commonalities with *guanxi* between business people. In private ordering, entrepreneurs can utilize social network to resolve commercial disputes. *Guanxi* could also matter to some extent when private businesses resort to courts or governments for dispute resolution. It is always the case that the existence of good personal connections with judges and bureaucrats could smooth the judicial or administrative process.

Nonetheless, *guanxi* is primarily a non-institutionalized scheme. When we talk about *guanxi* between business people and courts or governments, it is at most a type of lubricating oil that smoothes the adjudication process. In contrast, the distinct modes of dispute resolution in our study emphasize more the role of courts and governments in helping resolve business disputes in an institutionalized manner. It is quite clear that government intervention in dispute resolution involving so many administrative and financial resources as illustrated in the above case could not be primarily motivated by the personal connections between the entrepreneur and local bureaucrats. Instead, the political and economic legitimacy becomes the driving force for government intervention in private business disputes. Hence, in this study, we focus more on the involvement of governments or courts in dispute resolution in a systematic and institutionalized way.

4. Case 2: Independent Director System in Corporate Governance Reform

The second aspect of the regulatory state model we look at is the regulatory innovation in the independent director system. The Chinese economy and corporate China are experiencing an unparalleled fast growth. The mandate to improve the corporate governance of Chinese companies as part of the government's efforts to develop the financial market has become a top priority on the Chinese national agenda. Because most of the listed firms in China were converted from one or several large state-owned enterprises, which have become the controlling shareholders after listing, corporate management is basically controlled by and comprises the representatives from the dominant shareholders. The resultant potential problem of controlling shareholders' expropriation of minority shareholders has been a dominant issue in corporate governance. This is similar to the situation in many other emerging market economies where dominant shareholders can make a wide range of self-dealing transactions to extract private benefits from the firms they control.[22]

To strengthen the corporate sector, most emerging markets have transplanted a host of corporate governance measures from developed economies. Nonetheless, under weak legal institutions, the transplanted corporate governance measures cannot deliver the desirable outcomes. How to improve the monitoring efficiency and protect the interests of minority shareholders remains a daunting task in emerging market countries.

22 See, e.g., Johnson *et al.* 2000; Djankov *et al.* 2008.

Since the re-opening of stock markets in 1990, China has installed a supervisory board system in addition to the board of directors to fulfil the function of corporate monitoring. Following the German model of corporate governance, the Chinese regulators tried to use the supervisory board to complement the board of directors to monitor corporate management. But the results are by no means encouraging. Supervisory boards proved far from effective to curb self-dealing transactions conducted by controlling shareholders. Supervisory boards were usually served by the leaders and active members of labour unions or worker representatives in the controlling shareholder's parent company. These supervisors typically got used to the subordinate role they played in the parent company, and did not have sufficient incentives, courage and expertise to protect minority investors.

In view of this serious situation, the Chinese regulators were seeking new ways to strengthen the corporate governance system. At the turn of the century, there was a wave of corporate governance reforms across countries led by the Sarbanes-Oxley Act in the U.S. and the Cadbury Committee Report in the U.K. To tackle the primary issue of the threat of controlling shareholders' expropriation of minority shareholders, China introduced the independent director system on top of the existing supervisory board system in hope of utilizing external monitoring forces to create checks and balances in the power structure of the board of directors so as to improve minority shareholder protection.

On August 16, 2001, the China Securities Regulation Commission (CSRC) released a regulation called the 'Guidance Opinion on the Establishment of an Independent Director System in Listed Companies' (the Guidance Opinion). The Guidance Opinion requires that listed firms appoint at least two independent directors by June 30, 2002 and have no less than one third of the board made up of independent directors by June 30, 2003. There are also qualifications requirements. At least one independent director should be an accountant. Independent directors must have basic knowledge relevant to the operations of the listed company. They must have relevant work experience, possess professional qualifications, and so on.

On January 7, 2002 the CSRC released its Corporate Governance Principles (the Principles) for listed companies. The Principles require listed companies to 'establish an independent director system in accordance with relevant rules'. The Principles define independent directors as those who do not assume any position with the company other than that of director. Independent directors should be sufficiently independent to enable them to function without being subject to the influence of the company's major shareholders.

In spite of these regulatory measures, independent directors are far from effective in monitoring the management of Chinese firms. In compliance with regulatory requirements, the number and proportion of independent directors in the board are almost invariably high in China's listed firms. Nonetheless, these features are often window dressing tactics of corporate management and controlling shareholders. Compared with their U.S. counterparts, Chinese 'independent' directors are often appointed not because of their professional qualifications but due to their close relationships with executives or government officials. Some independ ent directors are former executive directors who become outside directors to satisfy regulatory requirements. There are frequent media reports of collusion between independent directors and top management to expropriate minority shareholders. Furthermore, the last thing wanted by those who currently control a company and are systematically corroding the firm's assets is for a 'competent' independent director to join the board. Independent directors are sometimes bribed to gain their complicity in management exploitation.[23]

Given the dominance of major shareholders over corporate management, the primary issue of corporate governance is to constrain the self-dealing activities of major shareholders, for which independent directors are expected to play a key role. Nonetheless, whether independent directors can fulfil their mission is dubious. To strengthen the independent director system, the Chinese regulatory authorities established the mandatory reporting scheme of independent directors' opinions towards major corporate events. This is an innovative regulatory device. It requires that independent directors should express and publicly release their independent opinions regarding major corporate events, particularly those corporate activities such as related party transactions that are highly likely to be associated with the self-dealing transactions of the controlling shareholders.

This new corporate governance mechanism is expected to achieve two primary objectives. First, this mandatory reporting scheme provides a platform for independent directors to voice their opinions regarding corporate events, especially those negative ones, to the investing public and the regulatory authorities, which helps fulfil their role of preventing the dominant shareholders from expropriating minority shareholders. In poorly governed companies, the controlling shareholders often attempt to conduct self-dealings through related party transactions etc. Naturally, they are not supportive of independent directors when the latter carry out their monitoring work. They tend to hide corporate information from independent directors, and turn a deaf ear to the warnings and suspicions expressed by independent directors. Taking advantage of the opinion issuance scheme, independent directors can send a warning signal to the market and the regulatory authorities for those problematic companies. The ensuing market reactions and regulatory interventions would discipline controlling shareholders and corporate management.

Second, the regulatory authorities also employ this mandatory reporting scheme to discipline the behaviour of independent directors. In both developed and developing countries, independent directors are widely believed to not have played an effective role in corporate monitoring. One important reason is that independent directors have failed to actively exercise their duty. They could be appointed because of personal relationships in the first place; they could be too busy to spend enough time monitoring corporate activities; they could intend to avoid infuriating corporate management and dominant shareholders in order to maintain good relations and keep their posts; they could lack relevant expertise to assess the impacts of corporate events on minority shareholder interests. To push independent directors to carry out corporate monitoring more actively, the regulatory authorities

23 Clarke 2003.

in China established this mandatory reporting scheme to enhance the accountability of independent directors. If independent directors fail to voice negative opinions for companies that subsequently turn out problematic, they may suffer reputation losses and incur legal liability. Hence, independent directors need to weigh the costs and benefits of remaining silent for problematic companies in determining whether they would issue negative opinions.

To a large extent, this corporate governance reform experiment attempts to create a role of whistleblower for independent directors, and to utilize the stock market disciplinary power and the regulatory enforcement actions to curb the expropriation of minority shareholders by controlling shareholders.

Taking advantage of the publicly released records of the independent opinions issued by the independent directors in China, in Du, He and Rui[24] we carry out systematic studies to assess whether this corporate governance reform has worked, and if so, to what extent.

Our empirical analysis proceeds along two lines. First, we examine the link between negative opinion issuances and the personal characteristics of independent directors, the corporate governance structure and regional institutions strength. Second, we investigate the economic consequences and implications of the issuance of negative opinions. By analyzing these two aspects, we address the questions of whether the issuance of negative opinions truly represented effective monitoring and how effective is negative opinion issuance in strengthening corporate governance and improving firm performance.

Our results show that independent directors in a typical listed corporation seldom issued negative opinions in the period 2001-2009. The negative opinions accounted for only a tiny proportion (3%) of the total number of opinions issued. This is not so surprising. Issuing negative opinions requires substantial efforts to seek and study corporate information and runs the risk of infuriating dominant shareholders and losing their positions. On the other hand, ignoring corporate problems and expressing positive opinions for problematic corporations do not involve high risks of legal costs given that the whole system of formal legal institutions remains weak.

We then analyze where negative opinions came from. Those independent directors who have more political background and political connections, such as former government officials, and those who have similar industry working experience, were more likely to issue a negative opinion. Moreover, board structure and ownership structure also cast impacts on the issuance of negative opinions. Independent directors in poorly governed corporations and provinces were more likely to issue negative opinions.

The issuance of negative opinions sent a strong alert to the market about the problems in business operations. It led to a significant negative stock price reaction to the announcement of negative opinions. This shows that the negative opinions expressed by independent directors truly contained some new and useful information for the investing public to assess firms' business prospects. Furthermore, we

24 Du, He & Rui 2011.

examine the role of independent directors issuing negative opinions in strengthening corporate governance and improving firm performance by investigating the changes of operating performance around the public release of negative opinion issuance. We find that firms' accounting performance deteriorated on average in the two years following the issuance of negative opinions. We further show that the negative opinions issued by independent directors carried some useful information to predict the adverse outcomes for firms such as financial distress and regulatory enforcement. That is, firms having received negative opinions from independent directors were more likely to fall into financial distress and be detected for having committed corporate frauds by the CSRC.

Combining the findings from these two lines of analysis, we can assess whether and to what extent the two objectives of the mandatory reporting scheme have been achieved. On the one hand, we find that the negative opinions of independent directors' truly targeted poorly governed firms and their serious corporate problems. Those firms underwent a long-term deterioration in corporate performance. The negative opinions alerted the investing public by arousing significant negative market reactions. Firms having received negative opinions were often subsequently detected with corporate fraud and incurred regulatory enforcement actions. This suggests that the mandatory reporting scheme has at least partially realized its objectives. It has made independent voices be heard by the market and the regulatory authorities, and has prompted independent directors to carry out monitoring task more diligently.

On the other hand, the negative opinion issuance was mainly confined to those independent directors who have political capital and similar industry working experience. Independent directors' negative opinions primarily took place in those companies that subsequently experienced long-term deterioration in performance, fell into financial distress, met regulatory enforcement, etc. In this sense, independent directors' negative opinions could not effectively correct corporate problems and reverse earnings decline. They only targeted those companies with very serious problems. This suggests that negative opinion issuance only played a rather limited role in strengthening corporate governance and improving firm performance. Many constraints such as limited time, limited access to corporate information and the wish to maintain good relations with corporate management made independent directors treat negative opinion issuance as an extreme way and a last resort in exercising corporate monitoring that is only used when corporate problems are rather serious. In some sense, negative opinion issuance could be a means for independent directors to escape their potential legal liability held for the failing firms.

5. Case 3: Administration-based Decentralized Regulation System

To achieve the goals of regulations in the helping-hand regulatory state model, China introduced an administration-based decentralized regulation system. In this scheme, the central regulatory authorities break down the regulatory tasks and delegate them to sub-national governments. With the support of regional competi tion, the central regulatory authorities solicit the assistance and cooperation of sub-national governments for the implementation of national regulations. Hence, the regulation system runs in parallel to the administration system. In this system, one of the major instruments deployed is the quota system, i.e. the central government controls the total size of some resources, and allocates them to different sub-national governments according to regional economic development plans and the performance of different regions.

One example is the bank credit quota system. It was utilized by China's central bank, the People's Bank of China, to control the aggregate supply of money until 1998. In this scheme, the People's Bank of China formulated the national credit plan under the guidance of the central government first, and then allocated credit quotas to the headquarters of all major state banks, which in turn reallocated these to their regional branches and subsidiaries that operated under the guidance of the respective sub-national governments. The allocation of bank credit quotas across regions depends largely upon regional banking business performance which is measured by various indicators such as the amount of deposits taken by regional banks in the previous year, regional economic performance, and a wide variety of other metrics.

The bank credit quota system was a major instrument for the implementation of monetary policy. On the one hand, it helped fulfil the goal of controlling the aggregate money supply, and on the other hand, it channelled bank credit to different regions on 'merit' basis so as to maintain a reasonable level of efficiency of credit allocation.

The evolution of China's financial market regulation is another example. China's securities markets were formerly re-opened in 1990 and 1991 with the establishment of the Shanghai and Shenzhen Stock Exchanges respectively. Initially, the national government delegated the regulatory power over these exchanges to the municipal governments of Shanghai and Shenzhen. In 1993, China introduced the quota system of equity share issuance to its stock markets. The quota system was designed to control the size of financial markets to maintain balance among regions and to preserve the dominant position of state ownership in listed firms. The central government would determine the national aggregate number of shares to be issued and then would allocate stock issuance quotas to regions. Sub-national governments in turn would allocate stock issuance quotas to selected state-owned enterprises for public listing or to listed companies seeking seasoned equity offerings. The sub-national governments would collect information on these firms and submit it to the CSRC. After reviewing the company information, the CSRC would give its approval to companies to issue shares in the public equity markets. The quota system served as a major regulatory instrument for equity markets from 1993 to 2000, and it actually governed financial markets up until around 2003.

The quota system was not designed as a means to deal with the incentive and information problems in equity market regulation. However, in practice it played a significant part in creating incentives for regional competition and decentralized information collection in stock issuance.

In a systematic study of listed firms in China that controls for political factors and macroeconomic variables,[25] we find that firms located in regions with better performance of listed firms in the preceding periods obtained more quotas in subsequent periods. This is a reward incentive scheme. Interestingly, we also find that firms administered by regions where a larger proportion of listed firms met regulatory enforcement actions for corporate frauds in the previous periods were allocated with less stock quotas in subsequent periods. This is a punishment-based incentive scheme.

We then explore various other aspects of provincial/regional performances. Firms in provinces with better economic performances in previous years reflected in higher GDP growth, industrial output growth, foreign direct investment inflow, etc. obtained more stock issuance quotas in the ensuing years. In addition, the data demonstrate that everything else being equal, listed firms coming from provinces where listed firms had on average better information disclosure were rewarded with more stock issuance quotas in the later periods.

These findings point to one conclusion that provinces which performed better (worse) in various aspects previously would be given a higher (lower) stock issuance quota later on from the central government. This indicates that the stock issuance quota allocation process had functioned as a de facto incentive device that motivated sub-national governments to select better-performing firms for initial public offerings or seasoned equity offerings. This incentive scheme encourages sub-national governments to assist the central regulatory authorities in collecting firm-level information, selecting well-performing firms for stock issuance, and monitoring firm performance.

6. Institutional Foundations for China's Helping-Hand Regulatory State Model

We have discussed three cases of China's regulatory state model. They show that government officials replace court judges in adjudicating business disputes to create a friendly and supportive business environment, the central regulatory authorities carry out corporate governance reforms by introducing some innovative regulatory device, and the central regulatory authorities make use of the central-local administration hierarchy to implement a decentralized regulation system to facilitate various regulations. These findings suggest that a regulatory state model helped fill the void left by the absence of formal legal institutions and law enforcement, and the role of the state in guiding economic activities is conducive to economic performance in China. In short, China's regulatory state model lends a helping hand to private entrepreneurs.

A natural question is why China chose the regulatory state model as the target model for its economic transition. At the end of 1978, China initiated its economic reforms and started the transformation from a state-ownership-dominated central planning system towards a market economy system. For the Chinese reformers, the

25 Du & Xu 2008.

model of private litigation through courts might not be a feasible target model for economic transition.

Firstly, the institutional preparation is far from adequate for adopting this model. For private litigation through courts to function properly, we need the institutional support of adequate legislatures and courts. However, the formal legal institutions (i.e., courts) are far from being independent and impartial in China.[26]

Secondly, the gradualist approach to economic reforms is inconsistent with this model. It is well-known that China's economic transition has been a gradual one with strong characteristics of path dependence in institutional evolution. It did not radically dismantle the pre-existing political and economic structure inherited from the central planning system. Instead China introduced a market sector into the country by keeping it outside the state-controlled sector and incrementally utilizing the market sector to push for reforms in the state sector.

Hence, both the weak legal court system and the gradualist reform philosophy illegitimatized the model of private litigation through courts that leans towards the laissez-faire capitalism.

Compared with legal courts, government regulations could play a more proactive role in guiding economic restructurings in a transition economy like China. China's legal system basically follows the civil law tradition. Laws and national ordinances are typically too passive, reactive and slow to respond to the new innovations in socioeconomic activities and take on the role of a harbinger for economic reforms.

As we know, laws and national ordinances enacted by the national legislature and the central government tend to be sketchy and incomplete. On the one hand, China is a large country with substantial variations in endowments, socioeconomic development and culture across regions. Thus it is difficult for the central government to enact unified laws and national ordinances applicable to all regions. On the other hand, it is challenging to develop comprehensive laws and national ordinances that could cope with fast-changing socioeconomic environment as experienced during China's economic transition. For example, it took 12 years for the National People's Congress to pass the Law on Township and Village Enterprises.[27] In addition, there are many unfilled gaps in the laws and national ordinances in the sense that some of the relevant issues are not stipulated in the laws and national ordinances.[28]

As laws and national ordinances are sketchy and incomplete, they are not applicable to specific cases without further clarification of the meaning of laws and national ordinances. Under this situation, the power to interpret the existing laws and national ordinances, to adapt them to the changing circumstances, and to extend their application to new cases constitutes the de facto lawmaking power, which in turn is the cornerstone of maintaining a reasonable level of property rights protection and contract enforcement.[29]

26 Clarke, Murrell & Whiting 2008; Cohen 2008.
27 Clarke, Murrell & Whiting 2008.
28 Eggleston, Posner & Zeckhauser 2000.
29 Pistor & Xu 2002.

In the face of a complicated and fast-changing environment, courts appear too slow to adapt to changes because they are designed to be reactive contract enforcers in the sense that they would not initiate legal proceedings but only respond to the initiative of another party. In contrast, government officials can exercise de facto lawmaking power by adapting rules to changing situations on a continuous basis and initiating enforcement procedures. They can proactively resolve business disputes and enforce contracts by interpreting laws and national ordinances, monitoring behaviour, launching investigation and enjoining or sanctioning actions on their own initiative.[30] Given that China's reforms typically start with policy shift following ideological changes, adjustments in government regulations and the exercise of de facto lawmaking power by bureaucrats are the best ways to implement policy innovation. Hence, the regulatory state model becomes an ideal choice in response to the substantial regional variations and fast-changing environment.

A further question is how China could successfully implement a regulatory state model in a vast country undergoing tremendous socioeconomic reforms. To ensure that the regulatory state model turns out to be a helping-hand one, the Chinese central government has successfully implemented a decentralized regulation system based on regional competition.

In view of the size of the Chinese territory and population and the formidable task of economic administration, China's central government has developed a decentralized regulation system where regional government officials are motivated to assist the central government in drafting and enforcing regulations. Regional bureaucrats often issue local regulations on the basis of national ordinances in order to adapt the national regulations to local circumstances. The central government also relies on regional governments to enforce and implement regulations on a daily basis. The central government has successfully utilized regional competition and the merit-based bureaucratic promotion system to motivate regional government officials to help carry out central government regulations.[31]

Moreover, regional government officials are granted discretionary power to adopt local decrees and rules on their own initiatives to promote local market economy development.[32] The People's Congress at the provincial level may enact 'local regulations' to govern local issues, and they are enforceable by courts in the province. Local governments can enact rules, which are not generally enforceable by courts but can substantially alter the rights of individuals and could well be appealed to by one party in private litigation against another.[33]

In addition, regional government officials used administrative power to considerably promote local economic development and transition. They advocated entrepreneurship via policies and enhanced social awareness of a market economy through media and education; they promoted non-state ownership and provided reasonable protection for private property rights well before private property was legally acknowledged; they controlled the pace of marketization and economic

30 Du and Xu 2009.

31 Clarke, Murrell & Whiting 2008; Du & Xu 2008; Xu 2010.

32 Wu 2007.

33 Clarke, Murrell & Whiting 2008.

liberalization with the purpose of conducting economic reform in an orderly manner; and they carried out industry entry regulations, and issued industrial policies to make structural adjustment of industries.[34]

The involvement of regional government officials in guiding private economic activities, resolving commercial disputes, providing protection for private property rights proves quite effective on average and is the most widely accepted system received by the public in China. This is particularly the case when the business dispute involves politically sensitive issues or hits the boundary of the established concepts of legality.[35] This fully reflects the typical sequence of institutional changes in China, that is, the ruling Communist Party and its administrative system initiates policy shifts based on ideological changes, and local bureaucrats implement these policy changes through adjustment in regulations, and finally the laws incorporate these changes after they become stable and widely accepted.

The leading role of local bureaucrats is also especially effective in regions lagging behind in marketization because local courts in those regions have less experience in handling private business disputes etc. due to slower market economy development. Hence, in deciding cases, regional courts may have to refer certain issues to regional government officials and to defer to their interpretations.

The regional government regulations, directives and guidelines have become China's 'living constitution'.[36] Over the years, the Chinese public has become used to rely on regional governments rather than on regional courts for dispute resolution and contract enforcement.

Then what motivates local bureaucrats to extend a helping hand to business activities? To answer this question, we need to resort to a large literature on Chinese economic reforms, which points to two noteworthy features of the political-economic structure in China.[37] The first is the political power of the central government to select and appoint provincial and local leaders through the cadre evaluation system. Through this evaluation and promotion system, the central leadership, e.g. the politburo of the Communist Party, sets criteria for and monitors the performance of leading officials in the Party and governments. The Organization Department of the Communist Party is in charge of implementing this evaluation and selection process. Officials in the state administrative hierarchy seek to maintain their positions of power and advance within the system. Since the beginning of economic reforms, the overarching objective of the Chinese leadership has shifted unwaveringly from class struggle to economic development. Consequently, regional economic performance, primarily reflected in GDP growth rate, has become the leading criterion in assessing the administrative performance and determining the chances of promotion of provincial and local leaders. The fact that the central government keeps a firm grip on the power to make political appointments of provincial governors and local bureaucrats is widely regarded as an effective means of

34 Wu 2007; Fu & Peerenboom 2008.

35 Wu 2007.

36 Fu & Peerenboom 2008.

37 See, e.g., Qian 2002; Clarke, Murrell & Whiting 2008; Xu 2010.

ensuring that the development policies of the central government can be largely implemented at local level in China.

The second institutional feature is the fiscal system. China is said to be characterized by fiscal federalism where the fiscal contracting system in place until 1994 featured high marginal revenue retention rates for local governments that encouraged local officials to promote economic activity within their jurisdictions. Although the 1994 tax sharing reform that divides the tax revenues between the central and local governments enhanced the tax capacity of the central government, the incentive for local governments to increase local tax revenue is still retained.

The ways for local governments to promote economic growth and employment to meet performance criteria and generate revenue were constrained by the nature of available resources and the broader political environment. Generally, there was a trend of shifting from relying on the state sector to promoting the non-state sector. In areas with a significant legacy of state investment and state enterprises, local officials often sought to develop and protect state firms under their administration by channelling loan capital to them via the state-run banking system. In areas with little legacy of the state sector, by contrast, local officials typically showed enthusiasm in actively courting private investment, from which they could extract tax and fee revenues.[38] So, it is exactly the GDP growth criterion and the local tax incentive that prompted local bureaucrats to create a business-friendly environment by providing property rights protection and contract enforcement. In this sense, the administrative system has established an incentive scheme that develops an interest for local bureaucrats to substitute for formal legal institutions in maintaining a reasonable local business environment.

7. Statist Legalism and the Regulatory State Model

As observed by Clarke, Murrell, and Whiting,[39] formal legal institution development has not made much contribution to economic reform and growth in contemporary China. Nonetheless, as documented by these authors, China has made big strides on the front of strengthening and improving the formal legal system. Then how can we compromise these seemingly contradictory findings?

Actually we say that law did not make considerable contributions to economic development in China because almost all the prominent institutional changes in the transition towards a market economy were not initiated by changes of laws. In other words, China's socioeconomic reforms did not follow the sequence of reforming laws before implementing system changes. In this sense, law is seen as having followed the market rather than led the market.[40] As discussed above, this passive and reactive role is consistent with the regulatory state model that has guided China's economic reforms and fits well the political structure of China as an authoritarian regime. China's socioeconomic reforms have been driven by the ideological

38 Clarke, Murrell & Whiting 2008.
39 Clarke, Murrell & Whiting 2008.
40 Clarke, Murrell & Whiting 2008.

changes and policy shifts of the ruling Communist Party. Because of the reactive nature of courts, state regulations serve as the primary instruments of implementing the shifts in state policies. Only when these policy changes prove effective, well accepted and stable are they enacted into formal laws and rules. Hence, regulations play the part of proactive enforcers and experimenters for state policy shifts, whereas courts deal with numerous routine cases when new policies have been stabilized and accepted.

In this process of state-led socioeconomic reforms, the judiciary is subordinate to the executive. Law serves as an instrument of state power rather than a means of constraining the state. First, the Chinese judicial system is characterized by the dependence of courts on local governments. The power of appointment and dismissal rests with the local Communist Party organizational department. Courts remain weak and have low status in the political system. They are simply one bureaucracy among a multitude of other entities without overarching authority. The state and its officials treated courts as a tool of governance and control.

On the rule-making side, the legislative and regulatory drafting process remains opaque. The bureaucracy in charge of drafting any particular piece of legislation has no obligation to consult the public for comment. On the rule-implementation side, the state remains wary of excessive citizen litigation. Thus, many ostensibly mandatory norms in legislation can be enforced only through action by the appropriate government agency, and do not confer a private right of action. Under this circumstance, the increasing number of legislations and de jure rights remain largely laws and rights on paper that do not necessarily correspond to an increased volume of *de facto* legal rights.[41]

Thus, from the Western perspective, the judiciary in China is extremely weak. Nonetheless, this does not mean that the judicial system in China is a total failure. China's judiciary has played a positive role in implementing new state policies when policy changes have established legality for many new phenomena, although courts are not expected to establish new concepts of legality for the changing society of China. This is the statist legalism where legal rationality is imposed by and for the purposes of the state.

We generally observe a typical sequence of legalizing new initiatives in socioeconomic reforms in China's regulatory state model. Under this model, formal legal rules could not make an initiative in endorsing institutional changes and promoting rapid economic growth. Economic growth was largely generated by the changes of leadership ideology and government policies. To implement these changes, governments first resort to making corresponding changes in state regulations. It is these changes in regulations that reflect the shift in statist policies. Only when certain changes become mature and widely accepted does the government defer the power to administer these routine cases to the legal courts. It is therefore not surprising that the court system in China is found to have competently handled a fairly large number of routine cases such as routine business dispute cases in which judicial

41 Ginsberg 2000; Clarke, Murrell & Whiting 2008.

independence is not an issue.[42] With the progress of economic reforms and market economy development, a constantly growing set of legal issues has become routine ones and required the legal courts to deal with them on a daily basis. This means that the market economy development itself created demands on the legal system. In this sense, law mattered for economic development in the period after the policy shift.

The policy debate over, regulatory experimentation with, and legislation of the bankruptcy law illustrate this typical sequence in China's statist legalism model. The legislation process for the bankruptcy law started as early as 1986, but it was not finalized until 2006. Following the shift of focus of economic reforms from the rural agricultural sector to the state industrial sector in urban areas in the early 1980s, the Chinese leadership started to give high priority to the restructuring of state-owned enterprises. Implementing bankruptcy for those loss-making state firms was one of the issues on agenda. Nonetheless, facing tremendous political risks, Chinese leadership was cautious in carrying out bankruptcy reform. In 1986, the first bankruptcy law, the 'Experimental Bankruptcy Law' was passed, but it only served as a guideline for policy experiments in a small number of selected localities. From 1986 to the early 2000s, the State Council issued various new regulations to modify the law, implementing many new procedures. During this period, formal bankruptcy proceedings in courts only played a minor part. It is the central government and local bureaucrats in the experimental areas that constantly implemented the bankruptcy procedures and adjusted regulation practices. After long years of reform experiments and regulation adjustments, the final version of the Bankruptcy Law was enacted in 2006.[43]

This example illustrates the typical sequence of socioeconomic system reforms in China. Ideological breakthrough and policy shift initiated the whole process. Regulations implement policy shifts, and adjustments to regulations are made to reflect the modification of practices based on feedback from policy experiments in some locations. When policy changes become mature, legislature endorses them by enacting or modifying laws accordingly.

This statist legalism is not unique to China. Actually many countries in East and Southeast Asia have implemented variants of this statist legalism in the process of socioeconomic development.[44] This can be regarded as one prominent feature of the Asian model of capitalism. This model has achieved some success because the leadership role of the developmental state in socioeconomic transition and development has promoted economic growth in Asia. Nonetheless, the side effects of this statist legalism are also evident. The massive state intervention in the economy could give rise to rampant bureaucratic corruption and collusion between businesses and bureaucrats. This is exactly the threat that China is facing now. In Section 8, we will discuss how the regulatory state model in China can be readjusted to cater to the new developments in the economy and society.

42 Pei 2001; Fu 2003.
43 Heilmann 2008; Xu 2010.
44 Ginsburg 2000.

8. Concluding Remarks

In this chapter, we examine the question whether China needs law for economic development. We demonstrate that formal legal institutions have made small contributions to China's spectacular economic growth, but a helping-hand regulatory state model has largely filled the void left by the absence of a functioning formal legal system. We discuss the institutional foundations for China's regulatory system to be a helping-hand one. We also discuss the interrelationships between state policy shift, regulation changes and judicial system in the context of China's statist legalism.

So far, our case studies demonstrate that the net effect of China's regulatory state model is positive, which leads to a helping-hand regulatory state. Nonetheless, it does not guarantee that this model will continue to be beneficial. In fact, the possible arrival of a grabbing hand regulatory state has always posed a threat to the regulatory state model in China. Over years, bureaucratic corruption has kept being prevalent. The collusion between local bureaucrats and private entrepreneurs in expropriating the interests of ordinary citizens has aroused public discontent. For example, local bureaucrats used state power to take over the land from peasants in rural areas and the housing units from urban residents with extremely low land requisition compensation, which gave rise to numerous cases of social unrest. Then, local governments sold the rights to use the land to real estate developers at a much higher price, and the developers in turn sold apartments and office buildings at an even higher price. This created a vicious cycle in which the local government budget relied heavily on the revenue from selling land use rights, and it is the ordinary people bore most of the costs eventually by paying extremely high prices to buy or rent apartments. This kind of disturbing development has led many economists to worry about the rise of the bureaucratic capitalism in China, which is essentially a grabbing-hand regulatory state model.

To prevent the helping-hand regulatory state model from degrading into a grabbing-hand one, great efforts are needed to modify the regulatory state model in China. In essence, a readjustment of the relative power of the state vis-à-vis the market is direly needed. That is, we need to accelerate the development of the legal system and improve state regulation in China. Generally speaking, we had better pay attention to the following two aspects. First, the state and the government regulations should withdraw from those areas where bureaucratic initiatives are no longer needed. With the deepening of market economy reforms, an increasingly wide spectrum of economic activities has become standard and routine ones, for which government policy support is no longer essential. Under this circumstance, if local bureaucrats continue to intervene in these activities, the risks of rent seeking will rise sharply. In other words, the development of the market economy would reduce the scope of beneficial state regulation but increase that of predatory state intervention. At this critical moment, the governments at various levels should leave most of the routine economic activities to the oversight of the judicial system. The regulatory state model should be focused on those most innovative market institution reforms where government policy support is most needed to help pro mote and preserve market development, whereas the majority of standard market economy activities can be handled by the judicial system. Reducing the scope and extent of state regulations could preclude the negative effects of a grabbing-hand regulatory state model, and preserve the positive role of the regulatory state model in initiating and supporting market economy reforms.

Second, the central leadership should gradually change the statist legalism model to the standard model of the rule of law. Rather than being regarded as instruments to implement the will of the state administration system, laws should be treated as ways to create effective constraints on executive power. The judicial system should be given not only an expanding scope of oversight but also independence and overarching political status.

In this Chapter, we demonstrate that the China miracle of economic development in the absence of adequate formal legal institutions is achieved through a regulatory state model. The Chinese political and administration systems ensure that this regulatory state model is a helping-hand one. Whether China can continue to implement a helping-hand regulatory state model is of central importance to the future of China. If China can successfully establish a new helping-hand regulatory state model based on rule of law, the Chinese experience in this regard will certainly have profound implications for other countries, especially the developing and transition economies.

Bibliography

Acemoglu, Johnson & Robinson 2001
Acemoglu, D., Johnson, S. & Robinson, J.A., 'The Colonial Origins of Comparative Development: An Empirical Investigation', *American Economic Review*, 2001, p. 1369-1401.

Allen, Qian & Qian 2005
Allen, F., Qian, J. & Qian, M., 'Law, Finance, and Economic Growth in China', *Journal of Financial Economics*, 2005, p. 57-116.

Blanchard *et al.* 1992
Blanchard, O.J. *et al., Reform in Eastern Europe*, Cambridge Mass., London: MIT Press, 1992.

Blanchard *et al.* 1993
Blanchard, O.J. *et al., Post-Communist Reform: Pain and Progress*, Cambridge Mass., London: MIT Press, 1993.

Clarke 2003
Clarke, D.C., 'Corporate Governance in China: An Overview', *China Economic Review*, 2003, p. 494-507.

Clarke, Murrell & Whiting 2008
Clarke, D., Murrell, P. &. Whiting, S., 'The Role of Law in China's Economic Development', in: L. Brandt & T.G. Rawski (eds.), *China's Great Economic Transformation*, Cambridge: Cambridge University Press, 2008, p. 375-428.

Cohen 2008
Cohen, J.A., 'China's Reform Era Legal Odyssey', *Far East Economic Review*, 2008, p. 34-38.

Djankov *et al.* 2003
Djankov, S. *et al.*, 'New Comparative Economics', *Journal of Comparative Economics*, 2003, p. 595-619.

Djankov *et al.* 2008
Djankov, S. *et al.*, 'The Law and Economics of Self-Dealing', *Journal of Financial Economics*, 2008, p. 430-465.

Du & Xu 2009
Du, J. & Xu, C., 'Which Firms Went Public in China? A Study of Financial Market Regulation', *World Development*, 2009, p. 812-824.

Du & Xu 2010
Du, J. & Xu, C., *Regional Competition and Regulatory Decentralization: The Case of China*, Working Paper, Chinese University of Hong Kong and University of Hong Kong, 2010.

Du, He & Rui 2011
Du, J., He, Q. & Rui, O.M., *Whose Voice Prevails in the Board Room? China's Corporate Governance Reform Experiment with the Independent Director System*, Working Paper, Chinese University of Hong Kong, 2011.

Du, Lu & Tao 2010
Du, J., Lu, Y. & Tao, Z., *Property Rights Protection and Enterprise Performance: the Role of the State in Resolving Business Disputes*, Working Paper, Chinese University of Hong Kong and University of Hong Kong, 2010.

Eggleston, Posner & Zeckhauser 2000
Eggleston, K., Posner, E.A. &. Zeckhauser, R.J., *Simplicity and Complexity in Contracts*, Working Paper, John M. Olin Law and Economics, 2000.

Frye & Shleifer 1997
Frye, T. & Shleifer, A., 'The Invisible Hand and the Grabbing Hand', *American Economic Review*, 1997, p. 354-358.

Fu & Peerenboom 2008
Fu, Y. & Peerenboom, R., *A New Analytic Framework for Understanding and Promoting Judicial Independence in China*, Working Paper, La Trobe University School of Law, 2008.

Ginsburg 2000
Ginsburg, T., 'Does Law Matter for Economic Development? Evidence from East Asia', *Law and Society Review*, 2000, p. 829-856.

Glaeser & Shleifer 2002
Glaeser, E. & Shleifer, A., 'Legal Origins', *Quarterly Journal of Economics*, 2002, p. 1193-1229.

Glaeser & Shleifer 2003
Glaeser, E. & Shleifer, A., 'The Rise of the Regulatory State', *Journal of Economic Literature*, 2003, p. 401-425.

Hall & Jones 1999
Hall, R. & Jones, C., 'Why Do Some Countries Produce So Much More Output Per Worker Than Others?', *Quarterly Journal of Economics*, 1999, p. 83-116.

Heilmann 2008
Heilmann, S., *Experimentation under Hierarchy: Policy Experiments in the Reorganization of China's State Sector, 1978-2008*, CID Working Paper, No. 172, 2008.

Hobbes 1651
Hobbes, T., *Leviathan*, reprinted in: R. Tuck (ed.), *Leviathan*, New York: Cambridge University Press, 1651.

Johnson *et al.* 2000
Johnson, S., LaPorta, R., Shleifer, A. & Lopez-de-Silanes, F., 'Tunneling', *American Economic Review*, 2000, p. 22-27.

North 1990
North, D., *Institutions, Institutional Change, and Economic Performance*, Cambridge: Cambridge University Press, 1990.

North 1991
North, D., 'Institutions, Institutional Change, and Economic Performance', *Cato Journal*, 1991, p. 477-487.

Perkins & Rawski 2008
Perkins, D. & Rawski, T., 'Forecasting China's Economic Growth to 2025', in: L. Brandt & T. Rawski (eds.), *China's Great Economic Transformation*, Cambridge: Cambridge University Press, 2008, p. 829-886.

Pistor & Xu 2002
Pistor, K. & Xu, C., *Incomplete Law – A Conceptual and Analytical Framework – And its Application to the Evolution of Financial Market Regulation*, Working Paper No. 204, The Center for Law and Economic Studies, Columbia Law School, 2002.

Qian 2002
Qian, Y., *How Reform Worked in China*, Working Paper No. 473, William Davidson Institute, 2002.

Rodrik 2006
Rodrik, D., *Goodbye Washington Consensus, Hello Washington Confusion?*, Working Paper, Harvard University, 2006.

Rodrik, Subramanian & Trebbi 2004
Rodrik, D., Subramanian, A. & Trebbi, F., 'Institutions Rule: The Primacy of Institutions over Geography and Integration in Economic Development', *Journal of Economic Growth*, 2004, p. 131-165.

Shleifer & Vishny 1998
Shleifer, A. & Vishny, R., *The Grabbing Hand: Government Pathologies and Their Cures*, Cambridge, Mass: Harvard University Press, 1998.

Walder 1995
Walder, A.G., 'China's Transitional Economy: Interpreting its Significance', *China Quarterly*, 1995, p. 963-979.

Weber 1958
Weber, M., *The Protestant Ethic and the Spirit of Capitalism* (translation Talcott Parsons), New York: Scribner's, 1958.

Williamson 1989
Williamson, J., 'What Washington Means by Policy Reform', in: J. Williamson (ed.), *Latin American Readjustment: How Much has Happened,* Washington, Institute for International Economics, 1989, p. 5-38.

Wu 2007
Wu, Q., 'The Making of a Market Economy in China: Transformation of Government Regulation of Market Economy', *European Law Journal*, 2007, p. 750-771.

Xin & Pearce 1996
Xin, K.R. & Pearce, J.L., 'Guanxi: Connections as Substitutes for Formal Institutional Support', *Academy of Management Journal*, 1996, p. 1641-1658.

Xu 2010
Xu, C., 'The Institutional Foundations of China's Reforms and Development', *Journal of Economic Literature,* forthcoming, 2010.

PART III

SPECIFIC FIELDS OF LAW

Alessio M. Pacces

HOW DOES CORPORATE LAW MATTER? 'LAW AND FINANCE' AND BEYOND

1. Introduction

What is efficient corporate law? The safest answer is, the law supporting efficient corporate governance. Matters start being complicated from here. Not only opinions differ as to what corporate governance exactly is, but legal and economic commentators also disagree upon what corporate governance should aim to.[1] This chapter does not aim to discuss, let alone resolve, these differences. Rather, it purports to review critically the strand of literature that for the first time attempted to identify efficient corporate law on objective, statistical grounds. Named after the first of a series of influential articles, this literature is known as 'law and finance'.[2]

The success of this scholarship partly depends on a clear-cut response to the above questions about the meaning and the goals of corporate governance. Corporate governance is understood as a synthesis of investor protection devices vis à vis the company's management.[3] The goal of corporate governance is to protect a specific class of investors, the shareholders, for they are the residual claimants on the corporate assets and thus they have the right incentives to maximize firm value.[4] Consequently, corporate law is efficient when it protects shareholders well.

The simplicity of this framework is both the advantage and the limitation of this approach. On the one hand, it reduces corporate governance to a straightforward principal-agent problem; with the obvious consequence that law should minimize agency costs. This allows laws to be measured across different jurisdictions according to the ability to reduce agency costs. On the other hand, this approach neglects two important complications of the real world. First, agency problems in corporate governance differ, particularly depending on the presence of controlling

1 Compare, on the economists' side Zingales 1998 with Shleifer & Vishny 1997; on the legal side, Blair & Stout 1999 with Easterbrook & Fischel 1991. For a recent survey, see Becht, Bolton & Röell 2007.

2 La Porta *et al.* 1998.

3 Shleifer & Vishny 1997.

4 Fama & Jensen 1983.

shareholders.[5] Second, agency problems may be not the only issue in corporate governance. Particularly when the management is exposed to shareholder opportunism, excessive investor protection may undermine efficiency.[6]

Perhaps the main achievement of the law and finance scholarship is the empirical proof that 'law matters' for efficient finance, in terms – as the authors argue – of dispersion of ownership, stock market development, and thus growth of companies and of the countries where they are established.[7] The importance of this claim explains the enormous controversy on the items of corporate law that matter. I will review this debate in section 2, paying particular attention to the issue of how the quality of corporate law is measured and to the attempts that have been made to improve the consistency of this measurement. It is worth noting that the evolution of the law and finance scholarship now points to the legal origin characterizing a certain style of regulating business, rather than to a specific set of rules, as the main determinant of certain economic consequences, including financial development.[8] However, because the legal origins theory is discussed in other chapters of this volume, it will be not dealt with here.

How does law corporate matter is the next question, which is also the main focus of this chapter. The question is relevant for both positive and normative analysis of corporate governance. In section 3, I will review the positive issues, focusing on the relationship between legal investor protection and concentration of the company's ownership, which initially motivated the law and finance scholarship. Over time, the impact of corporate law on ownership concentration has become the weakest part of the law matters proposition. First, the effectiveness of laws protecting investors strictly depends on the ownership structure. It is immediately clear that protecting investors from managers or from controlling shareholders requires different legal tools.[9] Second, separation of ownership and control may depend on factors other than investor protection, partly extralegal like the impact of social democracy on corporate governance,[10] partly legal like the power of management to secure control and its benefits from interference by shareholders.[11]

One major problem with the law matters thesis is that the ownership structure is endogenous,[12] that is, it is affected by a number of economic factors acting together with corporate law. This leads me to the normative question, how should corporate law intervene with the ownership structure, which I will address in section 4. Differently from the implicit background of law and finance, shared by

5 Kraakman *et al.* 2009.
6 Pacces 2011; Bratton & Wachter 2010.
7 See particularly La Porta *et al.* 1998 on ownership concentration and La Porta *et al.* 1997 on stock market development. Other applications to different measures of financial performance are surveyed in La Porta, Lopez-de-Silanes & Shleifer 2008. For the extension of the law and finance argument to economic growth, see Levine 1999.
8 La Porta, Lopez-de-Silanes & Shleifer 2008.
9 See Bebchuk & Hamdani 2009.
10 Roe 2003.
11 Cools 2005.
12 Demsetz 1983.

part of the corporate law and economics scholarship,[13] I see no convincing theoretical and empirical argument for the superiority of dispersed ownership. Not only have decades of literature failed to identify a robust relationship between ownership and performance,[14] but also casual observation suggests that both management and controlling shareholder models can be successful in corporate governance.

The endogeneity of ownership structure does not imply that corporate law does not matter for efficient corporate governance. On the contrary, corporate law may fail to support the efficient choice of ownership structure at the firm level, not only because insufficient investor protection undermines separation of ownership and control - as the law and finance scholarship contends - but also because excessive investor protection may rule out certain ownership structures when securing control from outside shareholders' interference is important. Boards that are legally 'weak' relative to shareholders (for instance because directors can be fired at will and/or cannot fend off a hostile takeover) may make controlling shareholders necessary to maintain control. Conversely, shareholders who are prevented from growing too large (for instance because of mandatory bid obligations) may bias corporate control towards dispersed ownership structures. Based on my previous work,[15] I will contend that corporate law should be neutral to the ownership structure and enable both controlling shareholders and managers to be in control while committed not to expropriating investors.

In section 5, I will conclude with some reflections on the future of law and finance, particularly regarding its implications for convergence of corporate laws worldwide, after the global financial crisis.

2. The Measurement of Corporate Law

2.1. Theoretical Background

The idea that law plays a role in corporate governance comes from the application of the agency theory to an incomplete contracts setting.[16] Under asymmetric information, shareholders (the principals) cannot perfectly monitor the manager's (the agent's) behaviour; therefore they are willing to buy stock only at a discount. The source of the discount is the agency cost.[17] In theory, agency costs could be minimized by an incentive-compatible contract between shareholders and the manager. If the corporate contracts were complete, minimization of agency costs would take place without the aid of mandatory legal rules, because it is in the common interest of both parties.[18] However, given contractual incompleteness, optimal shareholder protection cannot be specified ex-ante in detailed corporate contracts.[19] What is

13 Hansmann & Kraakman 2001.
14 Becht, Bolton & Röell 2007.
15 Pacces 2007.
16 Shleifer & Vishny 1997.
17 Jensen & Meckling 1977.
18 Easterbrook & Fischel 1991.
19 Becht, Bolton & Röell 2007.

optimal today might not be optimal tomorrow. For this reason managers are vested with discretionary authority in corporate governance. Consequently, minimization of agency costs requires that some external constraints on the managers' behaviour be established by institutions, in particular by corporate law.

The theoretical underpinning of the 'law matters' proposition[20] is that when these legal constraints are insufficient to discipline the managers' conflicts of interest with the shareholders, separation of ownership and control will be impaired. On the one hand, shareholders fearing managerial misbehaviour would be willing to pay less for the company's stock. When the discount becomes high enough, selling shares to the investing public would become unattractive for the entrepreneur, and therefore ownership could not further separate from control. On the other hand, in the absence of reliable legal protection of the shareholder interest, maintaining a large stake is the only way for the shareholders, including the controlling shareholder, to discipline management.

Consistent with the agency framework, the logic underlying law and finance is that unconstrained opportunities for the managers to abscond with shareholders' money, or to place them to suboptimal use, make investors unwilling to sink equity capital in the firm. More technically, too a high risk of moral hazard and adverse selection going unchecked contractually limits the corporate controller's ability to raise equity through separation of ownership and control, making equity capital much costlier. 'Law matters' is an appealing way to say that failure of national corporate laws to protect non-controlling shareholders from expropriation is responsible of ownership concentration and stock market underdevelopment. To the extent that external equity funds are needed to finance uncertain growth opportunities available to the firm, this would ultimately lead to inefficient allocation of financial resources within an entire economy.[21]

In this perspective, the law matters proposition has an implicit normative flavour: it suggests that enhancing shareholder protection is efficient and should be the goal of corporate law. I will discuss this point in the following sections. Yet the main achievement of the law and finance scholarship is having ranked corporate laws on this basis and having shown that the effect of law on finance can be captured – statistically, at least – by such rankings expressed in the form of legal indices. The first and still the best known of these indices – the 'Anti-director Rights Index'[22] – included only a few specific corporate law rules. But it was shown to significantly and substantially affect ownership concentration, the relative availability

20 La Porta *et al.* 1998.

21 The law and finance scholarship occupies a prominent position in the theory of legal origins (La Porta, Lopez-de-Silanes & Shleifer 2008) not only because it started the empirical inquiry on the effects of law on economic performance, but also – and perhaps more importantly – because financial development is the most plausible channel through which efficient law affects economic growth. This empirical validity of this channel has been demonstrated by Rajan & Zingales 1998 and subsequently tested, among others, by Levine, Loayza & Beck 2000.

22 La Porta *et al.* 1998.

of external equity funds to firms situated in different countries of the world, and a number of other indicators of financial performance.[23]

A group of financial economists led by Andrei Shleifer managed to empirically prove that different patterns and performances of corporate governance systems depend on a few representative items of corporate law and on the quality of their enforcement, which were both determined, in turn, by the historical tradition of the legal system. According to these findings, good law and good enforcement of shareholder rights characterize legal systems whose roots lie in the English common law, while the reverse holds true for systems based on the French civil law tradition. That should explain why Anglo-American firms have typically diffuse ownership and managers in control, whereas the lower quality of corporate law only allows for controlling shareholders and concentrated ownership in continental Europe.

The impact of these findings has been enormous, not only in the academic debate, but more importantly in policymaking. Many developed and developing countries have engaged in legal reforms with the goal to improve their score on the Anti-director Rights Index. After over a decade since the publication of Law and Finance, the indices have evolved, they have been improved or replaced. Anyway they have become part of the investors' and the policymakers' thinking about regulation of corporate governance. Prominent examples of this influence are the Doing Business project of the World Bank, the EU Directive on Shareholders' Rights and, to a lesser extent, the OECD Principles of Corporate Governance.[24] A brief review of these indices and of their limitations is thus necessary to appreciate their actual relationship with the question, what is efficient corporate law?

2.2. *Indices of Corporate Law's Quality*

La Porta *et al.* reported many statistics on alternative sources of legal protection of shareholders.[25] However, it was a particular combination of substantive rules in corporate law that had the strongest explanatory power in the econometric analysis. Such a combination apparently explained why ownership is dispersed in some countries and concentrated in some others; and, similarly, why some countries have more developed stock markets than others.[26] The combination at issue was based on a selection of six legal rules allowing shareholders to constrain managerial power as exercised via the board of directors (by assumption, captured by the management). The quality of law was measured by an index ranging from zero to six, where a score of one or zero was assigned depending on whether a certain 'anti-director' rule was present or not in national corporate law. Legal systems whose origins lies in the common law tradition scored much better on the Anti-director Rights Index than those based on a civil law tradition, and in fact, the former have on average

23 See *supra* note 2.

24 See e.g. World Bank 2011. All of the Doing Business reports since 2004, the data, and the methodological notes are downloadable from the World Bank website: <http://www.doingbusiness.org>. See also European Commission 2006 and OECD 2004.

25 La Porta *et al.* 1998.

26 La Porta *et al.* 1997.

much lower ownership concentration and better developed stock markets than the latter. Thus, superiority of the Anglo-American legal origin in the regulation of corporate finance sprang out as a powerful corollary of the 'law matters' thesis.

In the original econometric setup, legal origins were an instrumental variable used to overcome concerns of reverse causality between law and financial performance. Because legal origins pre-existed to the development of stock markets, they had to be exogenous in the statistical model. Short of the doubts on whether legal origins capture any meaningful legal pattern,[27] it is worth noting that the authors themselves have ultimately come to the conclusion that legal origins are not a good instrument for assessing the relation between law and finance, but remain a causal determinant of this and other relations between law and economic outcomes.[28] Given our interest in the substantive elements of good corporate law, it is worth focusing on the construction of the indices rather than on the causal determinants of its scores.

There are a number of issues with this construction, which have been variously emphasized during over a decade of debate on the Anti-director Rights index.[29] First, there are problems of coding. The same variable may be given inconsistent scores across jurisdictions, for instance because the distinction between default rules and/or the impact of case law is neglected. The second problem is the selection of the index components, as it has been argued that the Anti-director Rights index suffers from a strong 'US bias' and fails anyhow to identify the most important legal tools for investor protection. The third problem is weighting. Intuitively, the impact of different rules for investor protection varies, so it is arbitrary to put all of them on equal footing - as it would be arbitrary to assign specific weights. The final issue can be understood as a combination of the above problems. Legal comparison should be performed functionally, this implying that the coding, selection and weighing of legal rules affecting investor protection in different jurisdictions can diverge substantially, although the effects may be similar.[30] This critique casts serious doubts on the possibility to measure the quality of legal rules, and particularly on the validity of the Anti-Director Rights Index as a prototype of this measurement.

The problems with coding have been documented with respect to several countries.[31] Some countries received a score of 1 on shareholder rights which are only optional under corporate law, whereas some others scored zero on shareholder rights that are not codified but are nonetheless plainly granted by courts. The most serious issue in coding is inconsistency as, for instance, default rules received different scores depending on the jurisdiction. Technically speaking, both case law and

27 On which see e.g. the contributions of John Armour *et al.* and Eric Helland & Jonathan Klick to this volume.

28 La Porta, Lopez-de-Silanes & Shleifer 2008, p. 298.

29 For a recent survey, see Siems & Deakin 2010.

30 See the comprehensive qualitative study performed by Kraakman *et al.* 2009, focusing more on the similarities than on the differences across corporate laws in addressing agency problems.

31 Spamann 2006; Cools 2005; Braendle 2006.

the distinction between mandatory, default, and optional rules are not accounted for in the definition of components of the Anti-director Rights Index, even though this distinction clearly matters for shareholder protection particularly when those who are in control can engage in opportunistic charter amendments.[32]

Coding problems with the Anti-director Rights Index were ultimately addressed by the law and finance scholarship,[33] although according to the critics they were never completely overcome.[34] The other points of criticism are more radical. First, who tells that in every country shareholder protection depends on exactly the same rules to the same extent? And why should they be just those six rules? Could not an equivalent degree of protection be granted by a different, but neglected set of rules? And how should the importance of each rule in a given country be weighted within each set? These problems are much harder to cope with than coding, since they cast doubt on the very relevance of each component of the index as to investor protection. The six equally weighted components of the Anti-director Rights Index are the following: (i) the right of shareholders to mail their proxy vote to the firm; (ii) the individual right to participate in the general meeting without having shares blocked in advance; (iii) proportional shareholder representation in the board of directors (or so-called 'cumulative voting'); (iv) judicial venues against unfair conduct by directors actionable by shareholders accounting for no more than 10 per cent of share capital; (v) pre-emptive rights in new issues of stock; (vi) the right to call an extraordinary general meeting granted to shareholders representing no more than 10 per cent of share capital.

The relevance of the above rights as to shareholder protection was questioned even for the US, on whose typical corporate governance model the selection of rules was based.[35] A few American scholars stressed that corporate lawyers would not consider any of the components of the Anti-director Rights Index among the principal tools of investor protection provided for by US law.[36] The criticism went even further in Europe. Not only rules other than those considered by La Porta *et al.* seemed to be actually responsible of the quality of outside shareholder protection, but some of the rules included in the Anti-director Rights Index were even going in the opposite direction.[37]

One important example is proxy voting. This is allowed in many countries but does not have always to do with investor protection. In France and in Germany, for instance, proxy voting is regulated in such a way that it can only support incumbent controllers.[38] To be sure, proxy voting most often works to the advantage of insiders rather than of outside investors, and this is also the case in the US and in the UK.[39] Another example of a shareholder right that may turn out against outside investor

32 Bebchuk & Hamdani 2002.
33 Djankov *et al.* 2008.
34 Spamann 2009.
35 Paredes 2004.
36 See Coffee 2001; Roe 2002.
37 See Baums & Scott 2005; Cools 2005.
38 Kraakman *et al.* 2009.
39 Pacces 2007.

protection is proportional representation in the board, or cumulative voting. This might be helpful for minority shareholders in concentrated ownership structures, but is counterproductive where ownership is dispersed and shareholder empowerment depends on the ability to coalesce and take full control of the board.[40] Similarly, pre-emptive rights are supposed to protect minority shareholders from dilution, but are irrelevant to this purpose in a dispersed ownership structure. Only in the UK pre-emptive rights perform another function, namely supporting the bargaining power of institutional blockholders vis à vis the management when the company is short of funding.[41] Elsewhere the problem of investor dilution by controlling shareholders is addressed by functionally equivalent rules.[42]

Problems of this kind are probably impossible to overcome within any 'indexing' methodology unless indices are allowed extraordinary wideness and complexity. Taking stock of the decennial experience of the law and finance scholarship, a group of more legally oriented scholars have tried to construct broader and more sophisticated indices.[43] However, it is at least doubtful that more fine-grained indices, allowing for 60 instead of six components, can overcome the critique of lack of functional approach by comparative lawyers.[44] Even if the selection of corporate law items effectively accounted for all the relevant tools of investor protection across different countries, the problem with weighting the items would remain. Still, the advantage of these more recent studies is not just that they are more sophisticated, but that they are less ambitious. They seek to describe patterns of legal evolution and their economic effects across countries and over time, instead of claiming that one model of investor protection is better than another. This approach remains instead the major weakness of the law and finance scholarship, despite the improvements in methodology.

Professor Shleifer and his co-authors ultimately acknowledged the limitations of the Anti-director Rights Index, particularly its ad hoc character and the mistakes in coding. The more recent articles of the law and finance scholarship[45] sought to improve on these two issues by surveying, with the help of local lawyers, the legal response to key problems in a number of jurisdictions. However, short of a more precise problem definition, the methodology and the ambition of the law and finance approach remained unchanged. New measures of investor protection were crafted in order to address the two main venues of shareholder expropriation, namely security fraud and self-dealing. According to the authors, investors are concerned about expropriation even more than of their powers relative to the management, and thus legal tools aimed at countering expropriation illustrate better how law 'matters' for finance.

As a result, the Anti-director Rights Index was still revised for reason of continuity, but it was effectively replaced by two new indices of investor protection

40 Easterbrook & Fischel 1991.
41 Franks, Mayer & Renneboog 2001.
42 Kraakman *et al.* 2009.
43 See Siems & Deakin 2010.
44 Hertig 2010.
45 La Porta, Lopez-de-Silanes & Shleifer 2006; Djankov *et al.* 2008.

under securities law[46] and a compounded index of protection from self-dealing under corporate law.[47] These indices had stronger and sometimes even more statistically significant effects on stock market development and dispersion of corporate ownership. They continued to support the view that the common law tradition outperforms civil law countries as to the quality of investor protection and the availability of equity finance to the corporate enterprise. The impact of the new indices went beyond academia, as this time they were endorsed by the World Bank in the Doing Business project. This project has the great ambition of leading improvement in the legal infrastructure worldwide. To this purpose, the World Bank calculates and publishes yearly a series of indices of quality of business law. Investor protection is one of these indices, and it is based - as most of the other Doing Business indices - on the work of the law and finance scholarship.[48]

It must be acknowledged that the last indices developed by the law and finance scholarship follow a somewhat more functional approach to legal comparison. The two indexes of quality of securities law refer to categories of tools available to investors for preventing or challenging a standard securities fraud. The Anti Self-Dealing Index is based on a number of ex-ante and ex-post remedies in the face of a stylized case of self-dealing. Unfortunately, not all possible reactions of each legal system to either securities fraud or related-party transactions are accounted for, which still undermines the legal comparison. A second problem is that the weighting of each kind of reaction is standardized, although it is likely that the relative importance of each category of remedies varies from country to country.[49]

As far as the first problem is concerned, the statistical approach to legal comparison may overlook important issues. For instance, both American and comparative lawyers acknowledge that a major strength of investor protection under US securities law comes from a rather unique combination of class action suits with the lawyers' contingent fees.[50] However, this issue is deliberately dismissed from the quantitative assessment of the quality of securities law on grounds that, statistically, it bears no significant relation with stock market development across countries.[51] A similar point can be made about the Netherlands, whose collective enforcement tools are becoming increasingly popular among disgruntled investors worldwide. However, La Porta *et al.*[52] present the Netherlands as one typical case of under-enforcement of securities law.[53]

46 'Disclosure in Prospectus' and 'Prospectus Liability' - La Porta, Lopez-de-Silanes & Shleifer 2006.

47 'Anti Self-Dealing Index' - Djankov *et al.* 2008.

48 See particularly the construction of the Investor Protection index within Doing Business (<http://www.doingbusiness.org/methodology/protecting-investors>).

49 I discuss both problems in greater detail in Pacces 2007.

50 Coffee 2001; Kraakman et *al.* 2009.

51 La Porta, Lopez-de-Silanes & Shleifer 2006.

52 La Porta, Lopez-de-Silanes & Shleifer 2006.

53 It must be acknowledged that the legal information underlying the indices in La Porta, Lopez-de-Silanes & Shleifer 2006 refer to 2000. The international relevance of the Netherlands for securities law enforcement is much more recent (see Kortmann & Bredenoord-Spoek 2011). Still, the gist of the law and finance approach is that legal investor protection is quite →

As far as weighting is concerned, how effectively self-dealing is policed by the legal system is not just a matter of how many safeguards are available but rather, of how they are combined. For instance, in Djankov *et al.*,[54] the Swedish score on the Anti Self-Dealing Index was even lower than the Italian one (33% and 42% respectively, as opposed to 65% for the US and 95% for the UK) whereas the Netherlands scored as bad as developing countries (20% – that is, less than a half of the world average). Based on some qualitative research I have undertaken in the past,[55] both the Netherlands (by means of a special procedure and a specialized Court) and Sweden (by means of severe public enforcement supporting powerful social norms) functionally provided investors with good protection from expropriation. These findings match the perception of international investors. However, the Anti Self-Dealing Index overlooks these circumstances. On the contrary, the index correctly assigns a low score to Italy – which Djankov *et al.*[56] describe in detail as a 'bad law' situation opposed to the UK example of 'good law' – because anti self-dealing provisions used to be (and to some extent still are) under-enforced.[57]

The problem with weighting is well illustrated by the performance of the above countries on the Doing Business index of investor protection.[58] This index is officially based on Djankov *et al.*,[59] but the scores differ significantly. Specifically, as of 2006,[60] the UK scores 80 per cent instead of 95 per cent; the US, 83 per cent instead of 65 per cent; Italy and Sweden, 57 per cent instead of 42 per cent and 33 per cent respectively; the Netherlands, 47 per cent instead of 20 per cent. Given that both the source of legal information and the methodology of calculation is the same for both indices, there is no reason why the output should differ, particularly regarding the ranking of countries. The reason of difference is indeed a trivial one: the scores of sub-indices are aggregated with two different formulas in Djankov *et al.*[61] and in Doing Business. This is sufficient evidence that arbitrary weighting may have a very significant impact on the final scores.[62]

From the first attempts to measure the quality of corporate and securities law it can be concluded that the results of this exercise are considerably less objective than they look. Thus, they should be taken with a lot more caution. The second generation of comparative law and finance, which remains indeed a valuable exercise, seems to be going exactly in this direction.[63] Particularly noticeable is a shift of

stable over time as it is strongly influenced by the legal origin. The Dutch case contradicts this argument on a number of counts, including the enforcement of securities law.

54 Djankov *et al.* 2008.

55 Pacces 2007.

56 Djankov *et al.* 2008.

57 Enriques & Volpin 2007.

58 See *supra* note 48.

59 *Djankov et al.* 2008.

60 The reference year of Djankov *et al.* 2008.

61 Djankov *et al.* 2008.

62 In this regard, it is also remarkable that the country scores were ultimately removed from the published version of Djankov *et al.* 2008. As a matter of academic policy, however, Professor Shleifer has always made these data available on his homepage.

63 Siems & Deakin 2010.

focus from the aprioristic selection of legal institutions that are supposed to 'matter' for financial development to the study of how corporate and securities laws have actually evolved across countries, possibly to reflect converging legal patterns in investor protection.

The more recent approach acknowledges that indices, however sophisticated, can never replicate a fully-fledged functional comparison. Because selection of legal variables must allow from some arbitrariness, these indices cannot reveal more than trends. For this reason, the time-series dimension is currently receiving more attention than the cross-country dimension. In this regard, it is worth noting that legal investor protection ceases to have statistically significant effects on financial development once the legal indices are allowed more complexity; some specifications even reveal that investor protection may be excessive and then undermine efficiency.[64] It remains to be established whether our ability to measure the quality of corporate law is simply too limited or whether there are factors other than legal investor protection which determine financial development and the prevalence of one ownership structure over another. We now turn to this question.

3. The Effects of Corporate Law

3.1. *Law and Ownership Concentration*

The fundamental claim by the law and finance scholarship, that law 'matters', was based on the observation that separation of ownership and control is very rare outside the Anglo-Saxon world.[65] Controlling shareholders effectively dominate corporate governance worldwide. This is not necessarily an inefficient outcome under the agency approach to corporate governance. Because controlling shareholder have stronger incentives to monitor, it may be efficient to trade this advantage against lower liquidity and diversification of the controller's investment.[66] The problem, correctly identified by Shleifer and Vishny,[67] is when concentrated ownership is chosen because the law is too weak to support monitoring of management by dispersed shareholders. This intuition, which is theoretically valid, had to be significantly stylized in order to fit the empirical setup of law and finance and its progeny discussed earlier. This had important consequences for the definition of both the dependent and the independent variables of the law and finance regressions.

To begin with, the dependent variable - ownership concentration - was oversimplified in the whole series of articles based on the findings of La Porta *et al.*,[68] which were the first to document the dominance of blockholders in the largest companies listed outside the US and the UK. However, the measure of ownership concentration in that study (mean ownership of the three largest shareholders in the ten largest listed companies) was much too coarse to allow for an effective descrip-

64 Armour *et al.* 2009.

65 La Porta, Lopez-de-Silanes & Shleifer 1999.

66 See Bratton & McCahery 2002.

67 Shleifer & Vishny 1997.

68 La Porta, Lopez-de-Silanes & Shleifer 1999.

tion of the degree of separation of ownership and control in the countries of the sample. The problem is that controlling shareholders exist in virtually any corporate law jurisdiction, including the US and the UK, but their actual frequency across countries is difficult to estimate with a standardized methodology. In addition, not all blockholders are controlling shareholders. Although there are more accurate studies of comparative ownership and control,[69] a precise understanding of concentration of ownership and voting powers has not yet been synthesized in one single measure applicable worldwide. Perhaps for this reason, despite wide availability of data, previous comparative statistics on ownership and control have not been updated and they have never been relied upon by the law and finance scholarship.

As a result, all the articles of the law and finance series show effects of corporate law on ownership concentration that would be questionable even in the absence of controversy on the accuracy of the legal indices. For instance, in the US corporate ownership is considered as dispersed as in the UK, but recent studies document a much higher frequency of controlling shareholders in American companies.[70] Likewise, the Netherlands is considered a country with highly concentrated ownership whereas Sweden is presented as a moderately concentred ownership jurisdiction; in reality, the opposite is true.[71] Most importantly - as the law and finance scholarship explicitly recognized - there is nothing bad with ownership concentration per se; the problem is when ownership concentration depends on the law. Two wrongs do not make one right. Because both ownership concentration and legal investor protection were not measured precisely, the message came through that ownership concentration mainly depended on the bad quality of corporate law. La Porta *et al.* never denied the virtues of ownership concentration outside that perverse relationship; more simply, they ignored ownership concentration not determined by bad law.

The implications of this omission for the independent variable - the legal indices - have been recently emphasized by.[72] They have argued that legal investor protection (as well as the investor friendliness of corporate charters) cannot be assessed in the same fashion when the management is in control and when there is a controlling shareholder. The essential difference is that, while the management can always be replaced - in principle - by a takeover, this is normally not the case for a controlling shareholder. On the other hand, while managers may care too little about maximizing shareholder value due to their limited ownership, the interest of controlling shareholders is better aligned with that of the other shareholders, unless controlling shareholders can engage in unconstrained self-dealing and/or control-enhancing mechanisms. These aspects are all dealt with by different legal rules and enforcement mechanisms.

The essential point of this argument is that the law and finance scholarship managed, at best, to capture one half of the story. Particularly, the Anti-Director rights index was well suited to a dispersed ownership structure, but its features are

69 E.g. Barca & Becht 2001; Faccio & Lang 2002.
70 Holderness 2009.
71 Barca & Becht 2001; Pacces 2007.
72 Bebchuk & Hamdani 2009.

largely irrelevant in a concentrated ownership structure. The opposite conclusion holds for the more recent Anti Self-Dealing Index, whose design is based on a stylized case of self-dealing by a controlling shareholder. But if the law and finance scholarship only included investor protection in one setting (say, concentrated ownership), how could they possibly claim that the same variable simultaneously affected the frequency of the other setting (dispersed ownership)? Despite all the reservations on the accuracy with which both independent and dependent variables are measured, indeed this ambiguity has an impact in the last findings of the law and finance scholarship. In Djankov *et al.*,[73] for the first time a legal variable (the Anti Self-Dealing Index) has no statistically significant effect on ownership concentration.[74]

The argument that the quality of corporate law needs to be verified for at least two different models of corporate governance - one with concentrated, one with dispersed ownership - can be carried further. Not only does investor protection mean different things depending on who is effectively in control, which implies that legal discipline of both management and controlling shareholder matters for stock market development. Also, investor protection could be excessively demanding, in either the concentrated or the dispersed ownership setting, and induce companies to select an inefficient ownership structure or to forego separation of ownership and control altogether in order to avoid overly burdensome regulations. Although this proposition has never been tested empirically, it is in line with the recent findings that excessive investor protection may even impair stock market development.[75]

3.2. *What is missing from the Law Matters Framework?*

It would be premature to conclude that, if only the features of legal protection of outside shareholders were measured with more precision, this account of corporate law would explain the variation in corporate governance patterns around the world and particularly between continental Europe and the US/UK. Indeed, the problem with the law matters argument may be not technical, but conceptual: legal protection of outside shareholders may be just not the only institutional factor affecting the choice of corporate governance arrangements. Even aside from the weakness of comparative law analysis, the argument seems to be incomplete because it fails to explain a few facts of corporate governance in the real world, let alone their efficiency or inefficiency.

To begin with, there are some countries where, regardless of the scores on the various indices of the law and finance scholarship, investor protection appears to be functionally equivalent.[76] Nonetheless, the ownership and control structures of publicly held companies differ significantly. For instance, in both Sweden and the

73 Djankov *et al.* 2008.

74 Curiously, however, a different result is reported by La Porta, Lopez-de-Silanes & Shleifer 2008, where the Anti Self-Dealing Index has a slightly significant effect on ownership concentration.

75 Armour *et al.* 2009.

76 Gilson 2006.

US expropriation of minority shareholders does not appear to be a major problem. However, while the typical Swedish company has a controlling shareholder, the vast majority of US listed companies do not have one.[77] Based on the theoretical framework underlying the law and finance literature, one could hardly explain that result. Neither, of course, could one say which system is the best.

Conversely, in some other countries, investor protection is achieved in completely different ways, for instance because corporate laws put different emphasis on litigation versus effective governance by non-controlling shareholders. Contrary to a long-lived misconception, the two countries where dispersed corporate ownership is most pervasive in the world - the US and the UK - actually provide outside shareholders with different modes and intensity of legal protection.[78] Once again, how do these results possibly obtain? Even more importantly, is the British system any better than the American one, or it is just the other way around?

These and other observations have led many commentators, on both the economic and the legal side, to conclude that the impact of legal rules on corporate governance has been exaggerated. Alternative hypotheses thus emerged on the institutional determinants of corporate governance. They are too many to be reviewed here. Two of these hypotheses are particularly interesting for the potential implications on efficiency. The first hypothesis deals with the broader institutional determinants of private benefits of control; the second hypothesis concerns the politics of corporate governance, i.e. the constituencies in whose interest companies are supposed to be managed.

3.3. *Private Benefits of Control*

A broader and, in a sense, less rudimentary account of the 'law matters' story is based on the bearing of a number of institutions (including the law) on private benefits of control. Private benefits of control are utilities enjoyed exclusively by the corporate controller, which can mean one or more controlling shareholders or the managers depending on the ownership structure. Because private benefits of control include different things, their extraction can be efficient or inefficient.[79] In the mainstream agency framework, however, private benefits of control can only be extracted at the expenses of non-controlling shareholders and this is inefficient because it leads to either underproduction of the firm's surplus or to its outright diversion from investors (who then become less willing to invest). The agency view completely neglects the possibility that extraction of private benefits of control may be efficient, for instance because it supports unverifiable investments in entrepreneurship whose value could not be captured by investors otherwise. I will discuss this limitation in section 4.

Regardless of whether private benefits are efficient or inefficient, their presence in corporate governance naturally leads to concentrated ownership. However,

77 For recent evidence on the ownership and control structure prevailing in Sweden, see Henrekson & Jakobsson 2011.

78 Armour & Skeel 2007.

79 Coates 2004.

this is not just because shareholders refrain from investing in listed companies for fear of being expropriated. More importantly, the entrepreneur who expects to enjoy high private benefits of control will not be willing to deconcentrate ownership beyond a certain extent, for this would involve leaving corporate control and its private value up for grabs.[80] Therefore, the ultimate reason of ownership concentration is that protection of control rents requires that contestability of corporate control be ruled out at the outset. Now, assume that these private benefits of control depend on the controlling shareholder's inability to commit to a policy of no-investor-expropriation when it would be efficient to do so. Then gains from trading equity between the entrepreneur and outside investors are foregone because institutions, including corporate law, fail to police inefficient extraction of private benefits, which leads in turn to suboptimal separation of ownership and control.[81] This is the point of tangency with the law and finance scholarship. However, the notion of private benefits of control can tell us more about the institutional determinants of corporate governance.

A few attempts have been made to quantify private benefits of control empirically, on a cross-country basis.[82] These studies capture pecuniary values realized or traded on the stock market which should account for the present value of expected diversion of cash flow from non-controlling shareholders. These studies have some methodological problems, making comparisons between developed countries particularly difficult.[83] Nevertheless, even this rather crude proxy for the real size of private benefits of control appears to be more significantly related to ownership concentration than 'poor' legal protection of outside shareholders as measured by the Anti-director Rights Index. Since these indicators essentially point at expropriation of non-controlling shareholders from two different angles, this implies that corporate law - at least as measured by the law and finance scholarship - is not the only institutional factor that affects shareholder expropriation.[84]

The empirical analysis of private benefits of control reveals that the latter depends not only on the quality of legal investor protection and of its enforcement, but also on a number of other factors like social norms, product market competition, an independent financial press, and a high rate of tax compliance.[85] By enhancing the protection of shareholders' investment, these factors contribute to the minimization of agency costs. A remarkable result is that, once the effect of extralegal institutions is included in the regressions, the size of private benefits of control is no longer correlated with the origin of each country's legal system. That is to say, systems based on English common law fare no better in policing private benefits of

80 Bebchuk 1999.

81 Gilson 2006.

82 Nenova 2003; Dyck & Zingales 2004.

83 See Nicodano 1998; Nicodano & Sembenelli 2004.

84 However, it is worth noting that the last paper of the law and finance scholarship Djankov *et al.* 2008) find that the measure of private benefits of control estimated by Dyck & Zingales 2004 is significantly determined by the Anti-Self-Dealing Index and it is strongly correlated with the legal origin.

85 Dyck & Zingales 2004.

control and in fostering dispersion of ownership. The only group of countries that have some statistically significant advantage in this regard is Scandinavia, where some peculiar extralegal institutions are likely to drive the result.

These findings have important implications for the law matters argument. First, there is no one-size-fits-all model of legal investor protection promoting financial development. The statistical effects of corporate law on financial performance are best captured by a measure of private benefits of control, but the size of those is determined by combinations of legal and extralegal factors varying considerably across countries. A second implication is that, because abnormally high levels of private benefits of control do not allow ownership to separate from control, legal curbs on shareholder expropriation indeed 'matter' for financial development, although not necessarily according to the indices of the law and finance scholarship. The third implication is a puzzle. Moderately low levels of private benefits of control are observed both in countries with typically dispersed ownership (like the US) and in countries where ownership is typically concentrated (like Sweden). This suggests that, as soon as shareholder expropriation ceases to be the determinant of large private benefits of control, the relationship between investor protection and the ownership structure becomes ambiguous.

3.4. *Political Theory*

The political hypothesis does not only claim that institutions other than corporate law matter for investor protection, but more importantly that politics shapes corporate law and its evolution.[86] While corporate law may and should indeed protect investors from expropriation, shareholders do not simply care of not being expropriated; they want the value of their investment to be maximized. Corporate law, especially if regarded as a mere anti-expropriation tool, seems to be far less important than politics in the second respect. On the one hand, social democracy brings stakeholders, like the employees, into corporate governance. If shareholders want to keep their primacy and, more importantly, to have the firm managed in their interest, they need to be large enough to resist stakeholders' impact. On the other hand, this process creates vested interests resistant to legal changes that would involve redistribution of economic rents.[87] Specifically, established controlling shareholders and labour unions oppose dispersed ownership as much as managers of free-standing companies resist concentration of ownership.

This approach contends that ownership did not separate from control in continental Europe because stakeholders were entitled to various degrees of interference in corporate governance and they would have prevailed in the companies' management in the absence of controlling shareholders. The same account suggests that the emphasis of courts and legislatures on shareholder value maximization, instead of protection of employees, enabled dispersion of ownership and managerial control in both the US and in the UK. In this perspective, politics matters more

86 Roe 2003.

87 Pagano & Volpin 2005.

than law for corporate governance. At the end of the day, how friendly to shareholders the institutional environment is seems to depend on politics, first, and on the law only consequently.

Yet the idea that the regulation and the patterns of corporate governance are determined by politics, in particular by social democracy, seems to fly in the face of reality.[88] Stakeholder involvement in corporate governance is compatible both with systems characterized almost exclusively by the presence of controlling shareholders (like Sweden and Germany) and with those supporting also managerial control (like the Netherlands). On the contrary, the absence of stakeholder involvement in corporate governance comes with ownership structures that are either very dispersed (like in the UK) or very concentrated (like in Italy). One may of course disagree on the precise meaning of stakeholder involvement and on how this should be measured in empirical analyses. But it seems fair to conclude that, while politics has undeniable influence on corporate governance, the choice of ownership structure is not entirely determined by politics.

3.5. *May Law Still Matter?*

The foregoing analysis suggest that, contrary to the claim by the law and finance scholarship, certain features of corporate and securities law do not unambiguously determine the shape of corporate governance, particularly the ownership structure. However, neither do other institutional factors like, for instance, politics and social norms. If anything, the empirical evidence shows important effects of all these factors, which, however, are not easy to disentangle.

Especially on historical grounds, some commentators have pushed the argument so far as to claim that law may not matter at all for separation of ownership and control.[89] Particularly in the UK, separation of ownership and control had emerged in the absence of meaningful legal protections of outside shareholders.[90] These protections were subsequently bargained for by institutional investors. Also in the US, separation of ownership and control seems to have preceded the establishment of strong shareholder rights.[91] Finally, in the beginning of the 20th Century, there was more separation of ownership and control in Continental Europe than in the US and in the UK, despite the allegedly low quality of investor protection outside the common law tradition.[92] The law and finance scholarship ultimately replied that none of these argument shows that law does not matter.[93] Legal investor protection did arise in the US and the UK to support models of corporate governance based on dispersed ownership, and subsequently both the degree of investor protection and separation of ownership and control became significantly higher in the Anglo-Saxon world than in Continental Europe. Whatever the historical factors

88 Gilson 2006.
89 See Cheffins 2008.
90 Franks, Mayer & Rossi 2005.
91 Coffee 2001.
92 Rajan and Zingales 2003.
93 La Porta, Lopez-de-Silanes & Shleifer 2008.

behind separation of ownership and control, this separation would have evolved differently and perhaps even failed to persist, in the absence of legal support. Therefore, law does play a role.

What this role exactly is and under which conditions corporate law improves the efficiency of corporate governance outcomes, remains an open question. The answer by the law and finance scholarship[94] is that legal origins determine whether the regulatory style is oriented to sustain markets (like in the common law tradition) or rather to replace them (like in the civil law tradition). Powerful legal tools for investor self-help naturally emerge only in the first situation, because in the other situation governments play a direct role in the production of goods and in its financing. At least when financial markets work without major crises, countries in the first situation outperform those in the second one. Without entering the controversy on the legal origin theory, there is one important truth in this kind of reasoning: legal systems are path-dependent.[95] If that is the case, the impact of law on corporate governance always depends on a particular combination of legal and extralegal factors that make almost impossible, at least statistically and on a cross-country basis, to show what determines what.

While this insight casts some doubts on the prospect of international convergence of corporate laws to a single model, it does not undermine the quest for efficient rules in corporate governance. The only problem is that these rules may 'matter' differently in different institutional contexts, for instance because one country guarantees good investor protection only in concentrated ownership structures and another one only in dispersed structures. This is after all the essence of the functional critique to the measurement of the quality of law. From a normative perspective, however, corporate law may still aim to the same goals and be functionally efficient to the extent that these goals are achieved. Protection of outside investors is certainly one of these goals. But it might be not the only one.

4. What is Efficient Corporate Law?

4.1. Why Legal Protection of Outside Shareholders is Important, but it is not Enough

One limitation of the law matters thesis is that it does not distinguish 'stealing' from 'shirking' in corporate governance.[96] Both are sources of agency costs that should be minimized through protection of outside shareholders. While appropriate legal rules can possibly contain the diversion of the firm's surplus once it is produced (stealing), no legal mechanism can substitute for the suboptimal exercise of business judgment over the production of the same surplus (shirking). Conversely, ownership concentration provides high-powered incentives to put effort in the firm's management, but does not limit the controlling shareholder's ability to divert cash

94 La Porta, Lopez-de-Silanes & Shleifer 2008.
95 Bebchuk & Roe 1999.
96 Roe 2002.

flow from minority shareholders. As a result, an effective legal protection of non-controlling shareholders does not necessarily lead to dispersion of ownership, whereas ownership concentration alone provides no guarantee against minority shareholders expropriation. As Mark Roe[97] has efficaciously pointed out, protection of investors from outright expropriation does not automatically explain separation of ownership and control.

Another issue is whether separation of ownership and control is always desirable. This is the case according to the standard principal-agent approach to corporate governance, which supports efficient separation of management from risk-taking. In this perspective, all private benefits of control deriving from agency problems are unambiguously inefficient. It makes no difference whether they are obtained by outright expropriation of the company's cash flow (stealing) or, rather, by on-the-job consumption of the assets under management (shirking). Limiting the extraction of private benefits of control by the corporate controller and minimizing agency costs are in fact two sides of the same coin.[98] This means that promotion of equity finance by the legal system requires not only behavioural constraints on shareholder expropriation by the management but, even more so, allocation of control rights to shareholders: shareholders should be entitled to replace the management when they are stealing or shirking too much.[99]

The only legal implication from this framework is that law should support hostile takeover.[100] That would be sufficient to support separation of ownership and control. Contestability of corporate control would ultimately make sure that no private benefits of control can be secured by the management, for this would immediately attract a takeover bid.[101] The mere threat of hostile takeovers encourages separation of ownership and control. Alternatively, inasmuch as corporate control can be shield from hostile takeover, selling shares to the investing public may not be profitable enough for the entrepreneur to give up his private benefits of control, and ownership will remain concentrated.[102]

Why then the law and finance scholarship focused on expropriation of outside shareholder to identify efficient corporate law? The reason is that the hostile takeover mechanism does not really work in practice.[103] The threat of hostile takeover can be avoided essentially in two ways. The first is permissible takeover defences that can be credibly operated by the management through their control of the board. The second is simply one or more controlling shareholders acting as a coalition to stop changes in control not previously agreed upon. Most companies around the world can and do avail themselves of these control entrenchment devices, often supplemented by legal rules that make hostile acquisitions even costlier (like for instance, the mandatory bid). This explains why hostile takeovers have become too

97 Roe 2002; Roe 2003.
98 Shleifer & Vishny 1997.
99 Becht, Bolton & Röell 2007.
100 Easterbrook & Fischel 1991.
101 Macey 2008.
102 Bebchuk 1999.
103 Becht, Bolton & Röell 2007.

rare to constitute a credible threat, which makes investors dependent on other tools to secure a return from their investment.[104]

Entrenchment of corporate control is allowed on different conditions by legal systems, but it is ultimately a matter of choice. From the entrepreneur's standpoint, insulating from hostile takeovers when going public must be preferable to committing to a policy of contestable control. Even in those jurisdictions, like the UK, making it difficult for listed companies to avoid exposure to hostile takeovers, entrepreneurs always have the choice to keep or take their company private. But the real question is what is so important about control to induce entrepreneurs to forego the profit of selling valuable equity to the investing public. The answer is the presence of private benefits of control.[105] As I mentioned, private benefits of control come in different forms, but those arising from investor expropriation are the greatest source of inefficiency because market mechanisms cannot correct a stealing problem without institutional support.

Unconstrained opportunities for expropriating outside shareholders imply that hostile takeovers be ruled out by the corporate controller. Any different commitment would not be credible.[106] Private benefits from stealing are perfectly transferable control rents, so why should an incumbent controller leave them up for grabs while she can always trade them for a control premium? This of course implies that investors will heavily discount non-controlling stock. As a result, separation of ownership and control will always occur to a limited extent, if not at all, in the presence of expropriation of non-controlling shareholders. The key finding of the law and finance scholarship is that a commitment that investors will not be expropriated must be supported by corporate law in order to be credible. For this reason a good quality of legal investor protection is a precondition for separation of ownership and control and a defining feature of efficient corporate law.

If that was the whole story of private benefits of control, however, we should observe dispersed ownership and contestable control in every jurisdiction that protects investors well. This is not the case.[107] In the US, for instance, a sizeable number of listed companies have a controlling shareholder. More importantly, the vast majority of listed companies are under management control, but they are mainly incorporated in Delaware whose courts allow boards to fend off hostile takeovers. This circumstance is very hard to reconcile with a principal-agent paradigm, because an undisciplined management can consume perquisites and engage in value-destroying projects. In this situation, concentrated ownership and closer monitoring by a controlling shareholder should be preferable for efficiency. Another puzzling example is Sweden, where despite the perceived high quality of (legal and extralegal) investor protection, there is hardly any company with a fully dispersed ownership structure. It seems that even in those countries where shareholder investment is well protected from expropriation, corporate control remains an issue

104 Shleifer & Vishny 1997.

105 Hart 2001.

106 Bebchuk 1999.

107 This paragraph draws on Pacces 2007 where I elaborate on the evidence underlying the examples in the text.

and both managers and controlling shareholders are unwilling to leave it up for grabs. This implies that there must be some other kind of private benefits of control, unrelated to expropriation, which managers and controlling shareholders care for.

As we know, private benefits of control can also be extracted in the form of on-the-job consumption, or shirking in the broad sense. Differently from the benefits from stealing, however, it is always profitable for an entrepreneur to commit not to benefit from shirking in the future by opting for a contestable ownership and control structure.[108] Once stealing is ruled out, committing to a no-shirking policy via exposure to hostile takeover should allow entrepreneurs to sell more equity for a higher price. The other outcomes we observe more frequently in the real word, namely managerial control with at least moderate antitakeover protection or straightforward controlling shareholdings, are simply unexplainable under the standard principal-agent approach in the absence of expropriation of non-controlling shareholders.

4.2. *Private Benefits of Control and the Legal Support for Entrepreneurship in Corporate Governance*

Law may not matter much for efficiency apart from preventing shareholder expropriation. Then the actual patterns of corporate governance that we observe around the world would be determined by how the remainder of agency costs (shirking) are dealt with by different, and typically non-legal, institutional factors. For instance, efficient corporate governance could be dependent on the political support for shareholder value maximization as opposed to the protection of different constituencies of firm's stakeholders. Another important factor affecting efficient separation of ownership and control could be the social norms embedded in each country's financial community which may, or may not, provide the same support.

While I do not doubt the importance of these and other non-legal institutions in shaping corporate governance, I believe that consideration for one important element of the theory of the firm is missing from the analysis, which is entrepreneurship.[109] This element operates at the firm level, which explains the variety of corporate governance patterns in individual countries - an issue systematically neglected by the law and finance scholarship. However, corporate law also affects the way in which entrepreneurship can be implemented in corporate governance. If that is the case, corporate law may fail to support entrepreneurship in certain ownership structure, which provides an explanation of why certain models of corporate governance do not emerge in some countries even in the absence of shareholder expropriation.

The reasons why entrepreneurship matters in corporate governance has nothing to do with agency costs.[110] Actually, when they perform some entrepreneurial function, managers or controlling shareholders are not acting as share-

108 Grossman & Hart 1988.
109 For a comprehensive illustration, see Pacces 2009.
110 Mayer 2001.

holders' agents. Rather, they foresee some potential from running the company that are not yet visible to anyone else, including the owners.[111] The value of this potential must be appropriable in order to generate incentives to uncover it. The problem is that entrepreneurship is a factor of production that cannot be fully rewarded contractually. Contracts are incomplete for exactly the same reason why entrepreneurship exists and it is valuable: the future is uncertain and therefore, it is not possible to specify a perfectly state-contingent system of remuneration.[112] The implication of this circumstance for corporate governance is that private benefits of control do not only arise from misalignment of managerial incentives, but also from the need to combine entrepreneurship with separation of ownership and control. In this perspective, extraction of private benefits of control is efficient and may justify legal support for control powers.[113]

To see why this is the case one should consider the entrepreneurial talent of managers and/or controlling shareholders as a firm-specific investment under structural uncertainty about whether this investment will pay off. It is a bet on the firm's success along some management strategy that nobody else than the entrepreneur in question is prepared to place. In the spirit of Williamson,[114] this investment for the firm's success by the management or the controlling shareholder would be both idiosyncratic (i.e., non redeployable outside the relationship with the company) and unverifiable (i.e., non contractible with the company's owners). Therefore also the reward of this investment should come in the form of idiosyncratic control rents, which can be regarded as the psychic benefits of control that only the entrepreneur can enjoy.[115] Because these benefits have no opportunity costs for investors, they are not a source of agency costs. How large are idiosyncratic control rents relative to the verifiable stream of profits that can be expected from a business venture, and therefore be contracted upon with investors, is a key determinant of the firm's optimal ownership structure.

As argued by Demsetz[116] and Demsetz and Lehn,[117] this approach implies that the ownership structure is endogenous. The more uncertain are the business prospects of the company, the higher will be the subjective value of entrepreneurship and the lower the future verifiable income that may be pledged to outside investors. Therefore, the amount of outside equity that can be traded is limited and ownership will remain relatively concentrated. Conversely, when the valuation of the company's outlook does not differ considerably between the entrepreneur and outside shareholders (i.e. the idiosyncratic private benefits of control are low), ownership can be more dispersed.

This mechanism has two prominent implications. First, because we are assuming no prospective expropriation of outside investors, the choice of ownership and

111 See Kirzner 1979.
112 Aghion & Bolton 1992.
113 See e.g. Schnitzer 1995.
114 Williamson 1979.
115 See Gilson 2006.
116 Demsetz 1983.
117 Demsetz & Lehn 1985.

control structure is certainly efficient *ex ante*, but it might become inefficient *ex post*, typically because the company value is no longer maximized under the entrepreneur's control.[118] This problem can be solved by an appropriate design of the market for corporate control, which I discuss elsewhere.[119] The second implication is that protection of idiosyncratic investments in entrepreneurship requires control rights in order to prevent ex-post expropriation by outside investors, regardless of the ownership structure. When corporate law prevents shareholders from freely negotiating the allocation of control rights with the management, this may result in the selection of a suboptimal ownership structure. This issue deserves a little elaboration.

An entrepreneur concerned with her firm-specific investment cannot choose an ownership structure where control is contestable because that will not allow securing a control premium as a reward for (successful) entrepreneurship. This control premium will instead be auctioned to the best bidder by shareholders as a group, who will then appropriate the value of the entrepreneur's private benefits of control that motivated the initial investment. Obviously, no rational entrepreneur is willing to invest in this situation. The consequence of this is not lack of entrepreneurship in corporate governance, but rather the choice of potentially suboptimal ownership structures. As I mentioned, it is always possible to shield corporate control from takeover. But corporate law sometimes makes this option prohibitively costly, or impossible, with certain ownership structures.

For instance, under Swedish law securing control and its private benefits is only possible with concentration of voting power in the hands of a controlling shareholder.[120] In the Netherlands and in the US, managerial control is also an option because takeover defences are allowed along with a number of control-enhancing mechanisms available to the management as well as to controlling shareholders. In the UK, however, the control powers of managers essentially depend on a regulatory disfavour towards controlling shareholders, whose prominent illustration is the mandatory bid. Shareholder protection in Britain may go as far as to restrict even efficient extraction of private benefits of control,[121] particularly when this extraction requires concentrated ownership.[122]

It may seem counterintuitive to conclude that efficient corporate law needs not just to protect investors from expropriation, but also to enable the exercise of control powers and the protection of a control premium with different ownership structures. This conclusion, however, arises from the empirical observation that good quality of investor protection is no sufficient condition for separation of ownership and control. This casts doubts on the validity of the mainstream agency approach to corporate governance. If we depart from that framework, there can be indeed too much of investor protection, particularly when this is achieved by restricting the control powers of those – managers or controlling shareholders – who are supposed

118 Gilson 2006.
119 Pacces 2009.
120 See Pacces 2007.
121 Mayer 2001.
122 Pacces 2011.

to be running the company. When this protection is too costly to opt out under the applicable corporate law, a suboptimal ownership structures may be chosen just in order to protect control and its benefits from outside interference. Therefore, efficient corporate law should support freedom of contract on the allocation of control rights between investors and the controlling managers or shareholders. However, because this freedom should not result in expropriation of outside shareholders via self-dealing and similar conflicts of interest, mandatory rules are still necessary to prevent the abuse of control powers.

The details of this delicate balance between enabling and mandatory rules in corporate law are better left for another day.[123]

5. Beyond Law and Finance

To sum up, the question 'how does corporate law matter?' does not have a single answer. If anything, the observation that law matters functionally already suggests that there is no one-size-fits-all solution to certain problems in economics and finance. This does not detract form the utility of the comparative law and finance exercise. The major achievement of the law and finance scholarship is to have established the importance of legal investor protection for efficient corporate governance. This importance, however, lies more in the ability of corporate law to support commitments that outside shareholders will not be expropriated than on specific legal rules or enforcement patterns. The ambition of the law and finance scholarship to identify the 'best' instruments for the legal protection of investors remains the most controversial part of their work.

The quest for efficient corporate laws by academics had a lot of impact in policymaking. In a sense, the law and finance scholarship has set the standards for legal reform across the globe. La Porta *et al.*[124] correctly consider this an important achievement of their work, which goes beyond the scientific controversy upon whether they really captured the key aspects of legal investor protection: the latter has improved anyhow. The impact of the law and finance scholarship on convergence of corporate laws is confirmed by the second generation of law and finance studies, which focuses more on time series and on the positive aspects of legal comparison.[125] But legal change has not implied significant changes in patterns of corporate governance around the world.[126]

There are two, somehow complementary, explanations for this outcome. One is that legal reform is driven by considerations of political economy, so that the international emphasis on investor protection produces local reforms that are not harmful for the beneficiaries of the status quo, be them the managers or the controlling shareholders.[127] The second explanation is that investor protection is not

123 For an illustration of the main issues in the areas of distribution of powers, self-dealing, and control transactions, see Pacces 2007. See also Kraakman *et al.* 2009.

124 La Porta, Lopez-de-Silanes & Shleifer 2008.

125 Siems & Deakin 2010.

126 Bebchuk & Weisbach 2010.

127 Bebchuk & Neeman 2009.

always efficient and there may be too much of it. When this is the case, the path-dependency of corporate laws turns out to preserve the virtues of corporate governance models under attack. The improvements in legal investor protection during the last decade have not undermined the persistence of concentrated ownership in continental Europe.[128]

In the aftermath of the global financial crisis, one could even argue that the failure of corporate governance to converge towards a single model, despite the globalization of corporate governance rules and standards, ultimately saved the world. One remarkable finding about banks is that those having more investor-friendly corporate governance experienced significantly worse performance during the crisis.[129] Writing before the crisis, La Porta *et al.*[130] presciently acknowledged that the market-harnessing regulatory style associated with the common law origin may not work in situations of financial or social turmoil. One explanation becoming increasingly popular in the literature[131] is that strong investor protection, especially when it is interpreted as managerial accountability for stock returns, tends to undermine the ability of management to focus on long-term goals. As I have suggested elsewhere,[132] the legal possibility for managers and controlling shareholders to extract private benefits of control without expropriating investors may allow them to resist the pressure of short-termist capital markets. Although it is unlikely that private benefits of control could have avoided the financial crisis, the implications of their appropriability for efficiency and stability are an open territory for future research in law and finance.

128 Kraakman *et al.* 2009.
129 Beltratti & Stulz 2010.
130 La Porta, Lopez-de-Silanes & Shleifer 2008.
131 See Bratton & Wachter 2010.
132 Pacces 2010.

Bibliography

Aghion & Bolton 1992
Aghion, P. & Bolton, P., 'An Incomplete Contracts Approach to Financial Contracting', *Review of Economic Studies*, 1992, p. 473-494.

Armour & Skeel 2007
Armour and, J. & Skeel, D.A., 'Who Writes the Rules for Hostile Takeovers, and Why? The Peculiar Divergence of US and UK Takeover Regulation', *Georgetown Law Journal*, 2007, p. 1727-1795.

Armour *et al.* 2009
Armour, J., Deakin, S., Sarkar, P., Siems, M. & Singh, A., 'Shareholder Protection and Stock Market Development: An Empirical Test of the Legal Origins Hypothesis', *Journal of Empirical Legal Studies*, 2009, p. 343-381.

Barca & Becht 2001
Barca, F. & Becht, M. (eds.), *The Control of Corporate Europe*, Oxford: Oxford University Press, 2001.

Baums & Scott 2005
Baums, T. & Scott, K.E., 'Taking Shareholder Protection Seriously? Corporate Governance in the U.S. and Germany', *The American Journal of Comparative Law*, 2005, p. 31-76.

Bebchuk 1999
Bebchuk, L.A., *A Rent-Protection Theory of Corporate Ownership and Control*, NBER Working Paper, No. 7203, 1999, available at: <http://ssrn.com/abstract=168990>.

Bebchuk & Roe 1999
Bebchuk, L.A. & Roe, M.J., 'A Theory of Path Dependence in Corporate Ownership and Governance', *Stanford Law Review*, 1999, p. 127-170.

Bebchuk & Hamdani 2002
Bebchuk, L.A. & Hamdani, A., 'Optimal Defaults for Corporate Law Evolution', *Northwestern Law Review*, 2002, p. 489-520.

Bebchuk & Hamdani 2009
Bebchuk, L.A. & Hamdani, A., 'The Elusive Quest for Global Governance Standards', *University of Pennsylvania Law Review*, 2009, p. 1263-1317.

Bebchuk & Neeman 2010
Bebchuk, L.A. & Neeman, Z., 'Investor Protection and Interest Group Politics', *Review of Financial Studies*, 2010, p. 1089-1119.

Bebchuk & Weisbach 2010
Bebchuk, L.A. & Weisbach, M.S., 'The State of Corporate Governance Research', *Review of Financial Studies*, 2010, p. 939-961.

Becht, Bolton & Röell 2007
Becht, M., Bolton, P. & Röell, A., 'Corporate Law and Governance', in: A.M. Polinsky & S. Shavell (eds.), *Handbook of Law and Economics*, Amsterdam: Elsevier, 2007, p. 829-943.

Beltratti & Stulz 2010
Beltratti, A. & Stulz, R.M., *The Credit Crisis Around the Globe: Why Did Some Banks Perform Better?*, Working Paper Dice Center WP, No. 5, 2010, available at: <http://ssrn.com/abstract=1572407.

Blair & Stout 1999
Blair, M.M. & Stout, L.A., 'A Team Production Theory of Corporate Law', *Virginia Law Review*, 1999, p. 247-328.

Braendle 2006
Braendle, U.C., 'Shareholder Protection in the USA and Germany – "Law and Finance" Revisited', *German Law Journal*, 2006, p. 257-278.

Bratton & McCahery 2002
Bratton, W.W. & McCahery, J.A., 'Incomplete Contracts Theories of the Firm and Comparative Corporate Governance', *Theoretical Inquiries into Law*, 2002, p. 745-782.

Bratton & Wachter 2010
Bratton, W.W. & Wachter, M.L., 'The Case Against Shareholder Empowerment', *University of Pennsylvania Law Review*, 2010, p. 653-728.

Cheffins 2008
Cheffins, B.R., *Corporate ownership and control*, Oxford: Oxford University Press, 2008.

Coates 2004
Coates, J.C., 'Ownership, Takeovers and EU Law: How Contestable Should EU Corporations Be?', in: G. Ferrarini *et al.* (eds.), *Reforming Company and Takeover Law in Europe*, 2004, Oxford: Oxford University Press, p. 677-709.

Coffee 2001
Coffee Jr., J.C., 'The Rise of Dispersed Ownership: The Roles of Law and the State in the Separation of Ownership and Control', *Yale Law Journal*, 2001, p. 1-82.

Cools 2005
Cools, S., 'The Real Difference in Corporate Law between the United States and Continental Europe: Distribution of Powers', *Delaware Journal of Corporate Law*, 2005, p. 697-766.

Demsetz 1983
Demsetz, H., 'The Structure of Ownership and the Theory of the Firm', *Journal of Law and Economics*, 1983, p. 375-390.

Demsetz & Lehn 1985
Demsetz, H. & Lehn, K., 'The Structure of Corporate Ownership: Causes and Consequences', *Journal of Political Economy*, 1985, p. 1155-1177.

Djankov *et al.* 2008
Djankov, S., La Porta, R., Lopez-de-Silanes, F. & Shleifer, A., 'The Law and Economics of Self-Dealing', *Journal of Financial Economics*, 2008, p. 430-465.

Dyck & Zingales 2004
Dyck, A. & Zingales, L., 'Private Benefits of Control: An International Comparison', *Journal of Finance*, 2004, p. 537-600.

Easterbrook & Fischel 1991
Easterbrook, F.H. & Fischel, D.R., *The Economic Structure of Corporate Law*, Cambridge, Mass.: Harvard University Press, 1991.

Enriques & Volpin 2007
Enriques, L. & Volpin, P., 'Corporate governance reforms in continental Europe', *Journal of Economic Perspectives*, 2007, p. 117-140.

European Commission 2006
European Commission, *Impact Assessment on the Proposal for a Directive on the Exercise of Shareholders' Voting Rights*, Commission Staff Working Document, available at: <http://ec.europa.eu/internal_market/company/shareholders/indexa_en.htm>.

Faccio & Lang 2002
Faccio, M. & Lang, L.H.P., 'The Ultimate Ownership of Western European Corporations', *Journal of Financial Intermediation*, 2002, p. 365-395.

Fama & Jensen 1983
Fama, E.F. & Jensen, M.C., 'Separation of Ownership and Control', *Journal of Law and Economics*, 1983, p. 301-325.

Franks, Mayer & Renneboog 2001
Franks, J., Mayer, C. & Renneboog, L., 'Who Disciplines Management in Poorly Performing Companies?', *Journal of Financial Intermediation*, 2001, p. 209-245.

Franks, Mayer & Rossi 2005
Franks, J., Mayer, C. & Rossi, S., 'Spending Less Time with the Family: The Decline of Family Ownership in the UK', in: R. Morck (ed.), *A History of Corporate Governance Around the World: Family Business Groups to Professional Managers*, Chicago, IL: University of Chicago Press, p. 581-607.

Franks, Mayer & Rossi 2009
Franks, J., Mayer, C. & Rossi, S., 'Ownership: Evolution and Regulation', *Review of Financial Studies*, 2009, p. 4009-4056.

Gilson 2006
Gilson, R.J., 'Controlling Shareholders and Corporate Governance: Complicating the Taxonomy', *Harvard Law Review*, 2006, p. 1641-1679.

Grossman & Hart 1988
Grossman, S.J. & Hart, O., 'One Share-One Vote and the Market for Corporate Control', *Journal of Financial Economics*, 1988, p. 175-202.

Hansmann & Kraakman 2001
Hansmann, H. & Kraakman, R.H., 'The End of History for Corporate Law', *Georgetown Law Journal*, 2001, p. 439-468.

Hart 2001
Hart, O., 'Financial Contracting', *Journal of Economic Literature*, 2001, p. 1079-1100.

Henrekson & Jakobsson 2011
Henrekson, M. & Jakobsson, U., *The Swedish Corporate Control Model: Convergence, Persistence or Decline?*, IFN Working Paper, No. 857, 2011, available at: <http://ssrn.com/abstract=1734149>.

Hertig 2010
Hertig, G.A., 'Comparative Law and Finance: Past, Present, and Future Research: Comment', *Journal of Institutional and Theoretical Economics*, 2010, p. 145-148.

Holderness 2009
Holderness, C.G., 'The Myth of Diffuse Ownership in the United States', *Review of Financial Studies*, 2009, p. 1377-1408.

Jensen & Meckling 1976
Jensen, M.C. & Meckling, W.H., 'Theory of the Firm: Managerial Behavior, Agency Costs and Ownership Structure', *Journal of Financial Economics*, 1976, p. 305-360.

Kirzner 1979
Kirzner, I.M., *Perception, opportunity, and profit: studies in the theory of entrepreneurship*, Chicago, IL:University of Chicago Press, 1979.

Kortmann & Bredenoord-Spoek 2011
Kortmann, J.S. & Bredenoord-Spoek, M.G., 'The Netherlands: hotspot for class actions?', *Global Competition Litigation Review*, 2011, p. 13-17.

Kraakman *et al.* 2009
Kraakman, R., Armour, J., Davies, P., Enriques, L., Hansmann, H.B., Hertig, G., Hopt, K.J., Kanda, H. & Rock, E.B., *The Anatomy of Corporate Law. A Comparative and Functional Approach*, 2nd edition, Oxford: Oxford University Press, 2009.

La Porta, Lopez-de-Silanes & Shleifer 1999
La Porta, R., Lopez-de-Silanes, F. & Shleifer, A., Corporate Ownership Around the World, *Journal of Finance*, 1999, p. 471-517.

La Porta, Lopez-de-Silanes & Shleifer 2006
La Porta, R., Lopez-de-Silanes, F. & Shleifer, A., 'What Works in Securities Laws?', *Journal of Finance*, 2006, p. 1-32.

La Porta, Lopez-de-Silanes & Shleifer 2008
La Porta, R., Lopez-de-Silanes, F. & Shleifer, A., 'The Economic Consequences of Legal Origins', *Journal of Economic Literature*, 2008, p. 285-332.

La Porta *et al.* 1997
La Porta, R., Lopez-de-Silanes, F., Shleifer, A. & Visny, R., 'Legal Determinants of External Finance', *Journal of Finance*, 1997, p. 1131-1150.

La Porta *et al.* 1998
La Porta, R., Lopez-de-Silanes, F., Shleifer, A. & Visny, R., 'Law and Finance', *Journal of Political Economy*, 1998, p. 1113-1155.

Levine 1999
Levine, R., 'Law, Finance, and Economic Growth', *Journal of Financial Intermediation*, 1999, p. 8-35.

Levine, Loayza & Beck 2000
Levine, R., Loayza, N. & Beck, T., 'Financial intermediation and growth: Causality and causes', *Journal of Monetary Economics*, 2000, p. 31-77.

Macey 2009
Macey, J.R., *Corporate Governance: Promises Kept, Promises Broken*, Princeton, N.J.: Princeton University Press, 2009.

Mayer 2001
Mayer, C.P., 'Firm Control', in: J. Schwalbach (ed.), *Corporate Governance: Essays in Honor of Horst Albach*, Berlin: Springer-Verlag, 2001, p. 69-90.

Nenova 2003
Nenova, T., 'The Value of Corporate Votes and Control Benefits: A Cross-Country Analysis', *Journal of Financial Economics*, 2003, p. 325–351.

Nicodano 1998
Nicodano, G., 'Corporate Groups, Dual-class Shares and the Value of Voting Rights', *Journal of Banking and Finance*, 1998, p. 117-137.

Nicodano & Sembenelli 2004
Nicodano, G. & Sembenelli, A., 'Private Benefits, Block Transaction Premiums and Ownership Structure', *International Review of Financial Analysis*, 2004, p. 227-244.

OECD 2004
OECD, *OECD Principles of Corporate Governance*, 2nd edition, available at: <www.oecd.org/daf/corporateaffairs/principles/text>.

Pacces 2007
Pacces, A.M., *Featuring Control Power – Corporate Law and Economics Revised*, PhD dissertation, Rotterdam Institute of Law and Economics, 2007, available at <http://hdl.handle.net/1765/10907>.

Pacces 2009
Pacces, A.M., *Control Matters: Law and Economics of Private Benefits of Control*, ECGI Law Working Paper, No. 131, 2009, available at: <http://ssrn.com/abstract=1448164>.

Pacces 2010
Pacces, A.M., 'Consequences of Uncertainty for Regulation: Law and Economics of the Financial Crisis', *European Company and Financial Law Review*, 2010, p. 479–511.

Pacces 2011
Pacces, A.M., 'Controlling the Corporate Controller's Misbehaviour', *Journal of Corporate Law Studies*, 2011, p. 177-214.

Pagano & Volpin 2005
Pagano, M. & Volpin, P.F., 'The Political Economy of Corporate Governance', *American Economic Review*, 2005, p. 1005-1030.

Paredes 2004
Paredes, T.A., 'A Systems Approach to Corporate Governance Reform: Why Importing U.S. Corporate Law Isn't The Answer', *William and Mary Law Review*, 2004, p. 1055-1157.

Rajan & Zingales 1998
Rajan, R.G. & Zingales, L., 'Financial Dependence and Growth', *American Economic Review*, 1998, p. 559-586.

Rajan & Zingales 2003
Rajan, R.G. & Zingales, L., 'The Great Reversals: The Politics of Financial Development in the Twentieth Century', *Journal of Financial Economics*, 2003, p. 5-50.

Roe 2002
Roe, M.J., 'Corporate Law's Limits', *Journal of Legal Studies*, 2002, p. 233-271.

Roe 2003
Roe, M.J., *Political Determinants of Corporate Governance: Political Context, Corporate Impact*, Oxford: Oxford University Press.

Roe 2006
Roe, M.J., *Political Determinants of Corporate Governance: Political Context, Corporate Impact*, Oxford: Oxford University Press, 2006.

Schnitzer 1995
Schnitzer, M., '"Breach of Trust" in Takeovers and the Optimal Corporate Charter', *Journal of Industrial Economics*, 1995, p. 229-259.

Shleifer & Vishny 1997
Shleifer, A. & Vishny, R.W., 'A Survey of Corporate Governance', *Journal of Finance*, 1997, p. 737-783.

Siems & Deakin 2010
Siems, M. & Deakin, S., 'Comparative Law and Finance: Past, Present, and Future Research', *Journal of Institutional and Theoretical Economics*, 2010, p. 120-140.

Spamann 2006
Spamann, H., *On the Insignificance and/or Endogeneity of La Porta et al.'s 'Antidirector Rights Index' under Consistent Coding*, ECGI Working Paper, No. 67, 2006, available at: <http://ssrn.com/abstract=894301>.

Spamann 2009
Spamann, H., 'The "Antidirector Rights Index" Revisited', *The Review of Financial Studies*, 2009, p. 467-486.

Williamson 1979
Williamson, O.E., 'Transaction-Cost Economics: The Governance of Contractual Relations', *Journal of Law and Economics*, 1979, p. 233-261.

World Bank 2011
World Bank, *Doing Business 2011: Making a Difference for Entrepreneurs*, 2011, available at <http://www.doingbusiness.org>.

Zingales 1998
Zingales, L., 'Corporate Governance', in: P. Newman (ed.), *The New Palgrave Dictionary of Economics and the Law*, New York: Palgrave Macmillan, 1998, p. 497-503.

Guangdong Xu

THE ROLE OF PROPERTY LAW IN ECONOMIC GROWTH

The institution of property rights is as old and ubiquitous as humankind. Even in aboriginal societies where formal legal authorities were not in place, some sort of claim to land and other objects emerged as a consequence of an adaptive response to the natural environment and can be explained in efficiency terms.[1] Those old precepts, like the Eighth Commandment prohibiting theft, clearly illustrate the value of property rights to our ancestors as a means to establish and maintain basic social order. The importance of property rights has increased with the growing complexity of human societies driven by the dynamic relationship between population growth, economic development, and resource exploitation. Rising population pressure means more severe scarcity of resources and calls for more intensive utilization of those resources, which in turn necessitates a well designed property rights system to guide people's behaviour in a more productive, cooperative, and innovative direction.

Property rights also reveal their power in one of the greatest events of the twenty century, the fall of centrally planned economies. In addition to the informational limitations of planning (and the superiority of market prices in conveying decentralized information) emphasized by Hayek,[2] the preponderance of state ownership over private property in planned economies contributed significantly to the economic failure of communist regimes all over the world. As Demsetz[3] puts it clearly, the larger a society, the more likely it is that underlying conditions favour private ownership. Societies as large as those of China and Russia simply cannot function well on a centralized, state-controlled basis, because the bureaucracy lacks incentives to manage assets efficiently without bearing the consequences of their actions, and finally the accumulative bureaucratic costs result in the downfall of planned economies.

While never underestimating the significance of property rights, economists paid little attention to the origins, operations, and consequences of property rights

1 Bailey 1992; Bailey 1998.

2 Hayek 1945.

3 Demsetz 1988.

for a long time; rather, they simply assumed that the property rights system was exogenously determined and focused on understanding the price mechanism from different angles.[4] A fatal flaw then followed: owing to its treatment of property rights, neo classical theory was unable to discriminate between certain economic situations that are in reality quite different. For example, a private property based economy could not be distinguished from a communist economy, and the price theory would seem applicable to a socialist as well as to a capitalist society.[5] Consequently, traditional economic theory neglected to understand the various institutional settings in the real world, failed to predict the collapse of planned economies, and opened the door for ineffective policy suggestions for transitional and developing countries.[6]

Though this topic was not completely ignored by economists, the path-breaking economic analysis of property rights did not occur until 1960, when Ronald Coase published *The Problem of Social Cost*. Coase's seminal work was gradually extended and refined by Alchian,[7] Demsetz,[8] Furubotn & Pejovich,[9] De Alessi,[10] and Barzel,[11] among others, and eventually gave birth to a general approach which focuses on the relationship between property rights and the allocation and use of resources. According to the Coasean analysis of property rights, property rights are crucial to economic performance: 'in all societies, primitive and modern, property rights are an important part of social technology that helps to determine economic efficiency'.[12]

Thanks to the growing literature on the economic analysis of property rights over the past several decades, our understanding of the nature, evolution, and effects of property rights has been greatly enriched. In addition, property rights based policy options have been proposed to solve the problem of market failure in a broad array of areas, like fisheries management, pollution control, etc. Nevertheless, when we look at the specific area of property law rather than the broad domain of property rights, the situation is distinctively different. As Lueck and Miceli[13] admit, the economic analysis of property law is substantially less well developed than the economic analysis of property rights, and there is a longstanding disconnection between these two fields.

Current economic analysis of property law manifests its insufficiency most obviously when we try to explore the role of property law in economic growth. First, there is no general theoretical framework available for understanding property law as a whole, not to mention the complicated interrelationship among law, political systems, and economic forces. Second, great attention is paid to property laws in

4 Demsetz 1998.
5 Lerner 1944; Lange 1936 and Lange 1937.
6 Roland 2000; Easterly 2002 and Easterly 2006.
7 Alchian 1965.
8 Demsetz 1967.
9 Furubotn & Pejovich 1972.
10 De Alessi 1980.
11 Barzel 1997.
12 Bailey 1998.
13 Lueck & Miceli 2007.

developed countries, especially in common law countries like the U.S., while transitional and developing countries where the property law is supposed to be more important, are virtually ignored. Finally, property law is treated as static rather than dynamic, hence the time dimension is missing from these analyses and history is ignored in descriptions of the transformation of property law. In view of the aforementioned problems, it is necessary to look beyond the literature of the economics of property law and bring contributions from the economics of property rights, development economics, economic history, comparative law and economics, etc., into our study of the role of property law in economic growth, so that a more comprehensive and profound understanding of the value of property law may be reached.

The rest of the chapter is organized as follows. Section 1 discusses the definition and taxonomy of property rights. Section 2 reviews theoretical arguments and empirical studies on the relationship between property rights and economic performance. Section 3 offers some explanations on the failure of formal property rights in most developing countries. Finally, we conclude in section 4.

1. Some Basics of Property Rights and Property Law

1.1. Definition

It is important, yet seemingly difficult, to offer an incontrovertible definition of property rights, given the fact that property rights are specified variously and inconsistently in the law and economics literature and no consensus appears to exist. As Eggertsson[14] and Cole and Grossman[15] point out, the principal disagreement about the concept of property rights is rooted in the incompatibility of economic and conventional legal conceptions of the nature and scope of property rights. For economists, property rights are nothing but a mechanism which can be used to allocate authority for the access to and use of resources. This mechanism may or may not be related to and supported by formal law: for example, Allen[16] regards property rights as 'the ability to freely exercise a choice over a good or service', with no reference to any social institutions;[17] on the other hand, Demsetz[18] describes property rights as 'socially acceptable uses to which the holder of such rights can put the scarce resources to which these rights refer', and therefore suggests the importance of social underpinnings,[19] formal or informal.

14 Eggertsson 1990, p. 34.

15 Cole & Grossman 2002.

16 Allen 1999.

17 Umbeck 1981 expresses a similar view by arguing that 'a person may acquire rights in coconuts simply because he is the only one who can climb a tree. Similarly, an individual may have rights to fish because he alone knows where to catch them. Or, a pretty woman may have the rights to a seat on a crowded bus because she is pretty'.

18 Demsetz 1998.

19 This understanding of property rights echoes the arguments in Alchian 1965 that property rights are related to selecting specific uses from an unprohibited class of uses; Alchian 1977, p. 129-130, which emphasized that property rights are to be construed as supported by the →

For legal scholars, however, property rights have a different meaning: they are relations between people respecting things. As Cole and Grossman[20] put it clearly, if A holds a 'right' to something, at least one other person must have a corresponding duty not to interfere with A's possession and use. If A claims a 'right', but cannot point to a corresponding duty that is enforceable against at least one other person, then what A possesses may not be a 'right' at all but some lesser entitlement such as a privilege, liberty, or mere use. Consequently, to assert a property right is to assert a claim enforceable against others by formal law, or by some other social alternatives which inevitably involve public authority of some kind. Anyway, doing something, or having the ability to do something, has nothing to do with the (legal) *right* to do something.

Barzel[21] tries to clear up the confusion by introducing a taxonomy of economic (property) rights and legal (property) rights, and defines the economic (property) rights an individual has over a commodity or an asset 'to be the individual's ability, in expected terms, to consume the good (or the services of the asset) directly or to consume it indirectly through exchange'. Moreover, legal rights, recognized and enforced by the government, as a rule, enhance economic rights, but the former are neither necessary nor sufficient for the existence of the latter. An example which can be used to clarify the distinction between economic and legal rights is theft: thieves lack legal rights over the goods they steal, but they are able to consume the goods, to exclude others from using them, to derive income from them, and to alienate them; each of these capabilities is an attribute of ownership and hence thieves have economic rights over stolen property. Posner[22] makes a similar distinction between formal legal rights and de facto rights, and argues that formal legal rights are just a subset of property rights in a broader economic sense.

It is true that 'when transaction costs are positive, rights to assets will not be perfectly delineated',[23] and therefore a legitimate claimant will never fully own a commodity or an asset from an economic perspective. It is also true that some entitlements created by legislation, regulation, or even community-based norms, demonstrate the same features as legal property rights, such as transferability, exclusivity, and perpetuity, though without being recognized as legal rights. Hence we need to extend the definition of property rights to incorporate the complexity of the real world which had been disregarded by traditional legal understanding for a long time. Nevertheless, to say that thieves have economic rights over stolen property, or that a person may acquire rights in coconuts simply because only he can climb a tree, is so aberrant from common sense and contrary to legal practice that any resulting research will risk being rejected by the public and being considered irrelevant to social policies. In addition, the equation of property rights

force of informal mechanisms, such as social custom and ostracism, and formal legally enacted laws; and Furubotn & Pejovich 1972, who underlined the social context of property rights.

20 Cole & Grossman 2002.

21 Barzel 1997.

22 Posner 2002, p. 46-47.

23 Barzel 1997, p. 4.

with ability or use also leads to inefficient economic outcomes, since ability - or use - based property rights are not entitled to compensation and other remedies in the face of encroachment, expropriation, etc., and such weak, and insecure property rights will in turn discourage investment, production, and exchange.

In one word, we cannot talk about property rights without referring to enforcement mechanisms, remedial methods, and legitimacy or social reorganization. We therefore prefer definitions relating property rights to social underpinnings or public authority, such as the aforementioned definition provided by Demsetz; Libecap's[24] definition which describes property rights as 'the social institutions that define or delimit the range of privileges granted to individuals to specific assets'; or Pipes'[25] definition which emphasizes the importance of formal acknowledgement by public authority, etc. Property law is thus a set of rules which are enforced by courts and govern the acquisition, use, and transfer of property rights to specific assets.

1.2. *Taxonomy*

Basically, four types of property rights are identified in law and economics, namely open access, private property rights, common property rights, and state property rights.[26] Open access can be defined as a state under which 'there is no delimitation or delineation of its use rights to any private party, and hence no one has the right to exclude others from using it and all are free to compete for its use'.[27] The adverse consequences of open access can be summarized under two headings: supply effects and demand effects.[28] On the supply side, aggregate wealth is not maximized because of an insufficient supply of resource units caused by inadequate provision, maintenance, and investment in improvement, while on the demand side excessive withdrawal of resource units means a loss of wealth. Open-access resource values also fall because exchange is limited due to the absence of property rights; in addition, under open access, competing claimants will divert labour and capital inputs from socially-valued production to predatory and defensive activities.[29] In sum, the problem of open access can be formalized as a prisoner's dilemma, whereby the lack of cooperation among users of a open-access resource leads to the

24 Libecap 1989, p. 1.

25 Pipes 1999, Introduction and Definitions.

26 Lueck & Miceli 2007.

27 Cheung 1987. In his analysis, Cheung imprudently uses the term 'common property rights' to define a state of open access, a move which inevitably leads to some confusion that clouds his argument. For extensive discussions on the difference between open access and common property rights, see Ostrom 1999 and Eggertsson 2003. The confusion may be traced back to Hardin's (Hardin 1968) famous *The Tragedy of the Commons*, which uses the term 'commons' to describe a situation of actual open access, in which rational individuals, acting independently without any restrictions or regulations, will ultimately deplete a shared limited resource on which their collective long-term interests depends heavily.

28 Eggertsson 2003.

29 Libecap 1998.

least-optimal result for all, or, in Harding's classic term, the tragedy of the commons.[30]

The most salient open access resources are those that exist in a vacuum of effective rules defining property rights, such as marine resources in international waters, the air, the atmosphere, etc. Some other open access resources are the consequence of conscious public policies to ensure the access of all stakeholders (real or potential) to the domain of a resource. In addition, even those resources with *de jure* clear property rights may be transformed into *de facto* open access resources when the claims are ill defined and/or ineffectively enforced. For example, in many poorly protected national parks and forest reserves, villagers from the surrounding areas may perceive it as legitimate and of little risk to encroach on resources.[31]

It is also necessary to make a clear distinction between open access (a property regime) and common pool resources (a resource system). Common pool resources defined by Ostrom,[32] are natural or human-constructed resources in which (1) exclusion of beneficiaries through physical and institutional means is especially costly, and (2) exploitation by one user reduces resource availability for others. Typical common-pool resources include irrigation systems, fishing grounds, pastures, forests, water, and the atmosphere. Sharing with public goods the difficulty of developing physical or legal barriers to exclude beneficiaries and sharing with private goods the attribute that one person's consumption subtracts from the quantity available to others, common pool resources are subject to congestion, overuse, and potential destruction.[33] However, there is no automatic match between common pool resource and open access, or any other specific type of property rights aforementioned.[34] Whatever the property regime actually in place, without effective rules regarding access to and use of the resource, a common pool resource will finally degenerate into open access resource and rent-dissipation follows.

In the state of open access, nobody owns the resource and hence the external cost in terms of reduced resource availability is not internalized by individual users. An obvious and straightforward solution to open access is to create and distribute private ownership through which an externality can be internalized to a great extent: under perfect private ownership, owners capture the full benefits of their decisions and bear corresponding costs by excluding anyone else from using the resource, and hence face a strong incentive for optimal asset use, maintenance, and investment.[35] In addition, private property rights are extolled because resources governed by this regime are transferable from owners to others by sale or gift at mutually agreed upon terms. Transferability, then, acts as an effective mechanism

30 Harding 1968.
31 Heltberg 2001 & Heltberg 2002.
32 Ostrom 1999.
33 Ostrom 1999; Ostrom 2008; Faysse 2005.
34 Thus common pool resources may be owned by governments, by communal groups, by private individuals or corporations, or used as open access. For successful and unsuccessful examples of governing and managing common pool resources under different property regimes, see Bromley 1992; Ostrom 1990 and Singh 1994.
35 Demsetz 1967; Pejovich 1990, p. 28; Lueck & Miceli 2007.

through which resources can move from less productive to more productive owners.[36] Compared with other forms of property rights such as common property regimes, private ownership saves on the costs of delineating rights and monitoring for compliance, since 'monitoring boundary crossings is easier than monitoring the behaviour of persons situated inside boundaries'.[37]

Generally speaking, private property rights pave the way for the operation of market mechanisms, which make full use of available knowledge,[38] especially dispersed and tacit information that by its nature cannot be measured, processed, and integrated by any central authority;[39] realizes the fruits of specialization and division of labour by coordinating decisions and activities among different parties in a cost-effective way,[40] or in North's term,[41] by reducing the costs arising from specialization; and encourages organizational and technical innovations by rewarding productive entrepreneurship rather than unproductive rent-seeking activities.[42]

Unfortunately, private property rights are not a panacea for all economic problems resulting from open access or other market failures. First, it is not free to create, distribute, and enforce private property rights. In other words, cost benefit calculations will leave some resources, or some attributes of a resource, unregulated and relinquish them to what Barzel named the 'public domain' where unproductive wealth capture prevails.[43] Second, some well-organized interest groups can maximize their wealth by seeking favourable changes in legal rules and policies with a negative influence on the structure of property rights in a given society. Finally, when government acts as a definer and enforcer of rights, information costs, rent-seeking costs, and agency costs as results of bureaucratic incompetence and opportunism will frequently render the definition and enforcement of rights ineffective or invalid, and in some extreme cases lead to the partial or complete destruction of private property.[44]

When private property rights are not available or do not allocate resources efficiently owing to the aforementioned problems, other forms of property rights, such as common property rights and state property rights can be relied upon to address the open access problem. Common property rights may be viewed as an intermediate step between open access and private ownership, emerging as an institutional solution when a resource is sufficiently valuable to justify the cost of organizing a user group but not the cost of defining and enforcing private property rights. More specifically, five attributes are most conductive to the development of common property rights: (1) low value of production per unit of area; (2) high variance in the availability of resource units on any one parcel; (3) low returns from

36 Posner 2002, p. 33; Pejovich 1990, p. 29.
37 Ellickson 1993.
38 Cheung 1970.
39 Hayek 1945.
40 Demsetz 2002.
41 North 1981, p. 209.
42 Baumol 1990; Murphy, Shleifer & Vishny 1991; Murphy, Shleifer & Vishny 1993.
43 Barzel 1997.
44 McChesney 2003.

intensification of investment; (4) substantial economies of scale by utilizing a large area; and (5) substantial economies of scale in building infrastructure to utilize the large area.[45]

A typical common property regime does not give members full rights of alienation even though they can bequeath their rights to members of their family. In other words, they can not transfer their rights to outsiders of the group. This attribute of a common property regime is related to a fundamental problem faced by the community members, by which we mean the task of designing an effective internal governance structure to prevent excessive use and to ensure continued maintenance and improvement. The most common method of allocating the use of common property is to grant equal access to all members of the group. This avoids the explicit cost of measuring and enforcing individual use (when the access to the resource is shared) or effort (when final output is shared) but, in a group with heterogeneous members creates an incentive for overuse in the former case and shirking in the latter.[46] Fortunately, inefficiencies arising from the equal sharing rule can be moderated by homogenous membership requirements. This provides an economic rationale for preserving homogeneity by screening potential members, by indoctrination, or by restricting the transfer of memberships.[47]

Despite obvious weaknesses such as the absence of the right to transfer ownership shares and the internal governance costs incurred to reach a collective agreement and organize a community of users, a common property regime is recognized to be an efficient institutional solution to the tragedy of the commons in many cases.[48] Taking irrigation as example, a series of studies of the performance of communal proprietorship systems as contrasted to government-owned and - managed systems clearly demonstrate the higher productivity of the communal systems, controlling for relevant variables.[49]

In traditional law and economics, state ownership is justified in view of its function in correcting market failures arising from the provision of public goods. The value of state ownership may be better understood in the theoretical framework of the so-called new comparative economics.[50] To Djankov *et al.*[51] there are two central dangers that any society faces, i.e., disorder and dictatorship.[52] Four social

45 Ostrom 1999.
46 Lueck 1994.
47 Lueck & Miceli 2007.
48 Fitzpatrick 2006.
49 Ostrom 1999.
50 Djankov *et al.* 2003.
51 Djankov *et al.* 2003.
52 Disorder refers to the risk to individuals and their property of private expropriation in such forms as banditry, murder, theft, violation of agreements, torts, or monopoly pricing. Disorder is also reflected in the private subversion of public institutions, such as courts, through bribes and threats, which allows private violators to escape penalties. Dictatorship refers to the risk to individuals and their property of expropriation by the state and its agents in such forms as murder, taxation, or violation of property. Dictatorship is also reflected in expropriation through, rather than just by, the state, such as occurs when state regulators help firms to restrict competitive entry.

strategies, namely private orderings, private litigation, regulation, and state ownership, can be used to control the twin dangers of dictatorship and disorder. These four strategies are ranked in terms of the growing powers of the state vis-à-vis private individuals: while no public involvement is required with private orderings, the government takes complete control over an activity with state ownership. Given a fundamental trade-off between dictatorship and disorder inherent in such control strategies, the efficient strategy for a given society is that which could minimize the total social costs of dictatorship and disorder. In some situations, if disorder is too high for private orderings or courts or regulations to counter successfully, government ownership stands as a last resort. For example, Hart *et al.* argue that prisons should be publicly-owned because the risk of private jailers mistreating inmates is too high.[53] Compared with a government employee, the private prison owner has a stronger incentive to engage in cost reduction, which can at least in principle substantially reduce quality in some important dimensions, such as prison violence and the quality of personnel.

Even in most of the situations where state ownership is apparently desirable because cost reduction has adverse consequences, private ownership is still superior for several reasons.[54] First, in industries where innovation is crucial, the greater incentives of private entrepreneurs to innovate may shift the efficiency balance in their favour. Second, the adverse effects of cost reductions present less a problem when there is enough competition between private suppliers who would face lower demand as a result of worse quality. Third, some private firms may work hard to establish a reputation for quality so that they can have customers in the future. These considerations point to a rather narrow set of circumstances in which state ownership is likely to be efficient: (1) opportunities for cost reductions that lead to non-contractible deterioration of quality are significant; (2) innovation is relatively unimportant; (3) competition is weak and consumer choice is ineffective; and (4) reputational mechanisms are also weak. In addition, once politics is taken into account, the case for government ownership is further weakened. In an economy with weak institutions, government may use its control of state firms and other assets as a means of channelling benefits to its political supporters.

2. Property Rights and Economic Performance: Theory and Evidence

2.1. *Theory*

It has become conventional wisdom among economists and lawyers that effective property rights, especially private property rights, play a fundamental role in economic development by shaping the incentives of individuals to carry out productive activities such as investment, trade, and wealth creation. In Eggertsson's words, 'subtle changes in the content of property rights can change the macro-performance

53 Hart *et al.* 1997.
54 Shleifer 1998.

of an economic system and lead to economic growth or stagnation'.[55] This proposition has been confirmed by numerous theoretical and historical works. However, when we look at the empirical studies concerning the effects of private property rights, particularly those conducted on the micro level in developing countries, the picture is mixed: while many of the studies report positive and significant effects of private property rights on investment and other measures of economic performance, others fail to find a strong link between property rights and economic outcomes. Consequently, as Besley admits, in spite of its theoretical importance, empirical support for the significance of private property to economic outcomes is still limited.[56]

Theoretically, there are five channels through which private property rights can affect economic activities.[57] The first claim is that private property encourages individuals to use their resources in the most socially efficient way since under a private property regime, all costs and benefits of individual action are internalized by decision makers.[58] As the instance of open access indicates, without private property rights, resources are highly prone to over-exploitation and degradation, especially when population densities increase or if resources are commercially valuable.

The second mechanism through which private property influences economic efficiency is that where property is relatively secure, resources will be maintained in productive uses rather than being diverted to unproductive uses such as invasion and self-defence.[59] It's not uncommon to find that even in developed countries with well-functioning governments, private protection of property rights, such as private security guards hired by firms and neighbourhood-watch groups organized by homeowners, abounds in the economy. In some extreme cases where governmental enforcement of property rights is unavailable, individuals will seek out an alternative enforcer of property rights who frequently employs the threat and sometimes the actuality of violence, just like organized crime in Japan and the mafia in Sicily.[60]

The third channel concerns the effects of property rights on investment, a channel that has attracted the most attention in both theoretical and empirical studies. Investment decisions can be influenced by property rights, or more precisely, security of property, in two ways.[61] First, the values of all investments attached to an asset will decline when the asset faces the risk of expropriation and hence the volume of such investments will be reduced. Second, the risk of expropriation changes the relative returns on different investments and therefore diverts investments toward assets that are less uncertain but less productive: for example, from fixed assets such as trees and irrigation to more portable assets such as livestock, and from long-term projects to short-term projects.

55 Eggertsson 1990, p. 40.
56 Besley 1998.
57 Johnson 1972; Besley 1998; Besley & Ghatak 2010; Trebilcock & Veel 2008.
58 Demsetz 1967; Alchian & Demsetz 1973.
59 Skaperdas 1992; Grossman & Kim 1995.
60 Milhaupt & West 2000; Gambetta 1993.
61 Johnson 1972; Besley 1995; Besley 1998.

Assets with formal titles, for example, registered or titled lands, are widely believed to improve access to credit for asset owners.[62] When a lender is assured that an asset pledged as a collateral is secure and free of competing claims, he will become more willing to make loans based on the collateral which can be relied on to reduce the lender's cost of information regarding the borrower's creditworthiness and the risk of default. Consequently, the interest rate faced by the borrower is lowered and the volume of credit is expanded, which in turn encourages investment in assets. According to de Soto, the most influential advocate of formal property rights in spurring economic development, it is the lack of formal titles to land and other assets that has prevented the poor in the developing world from using the asset as collateral and thereby capturing the full value of their assets. These assets therefore become 'dead capital', rather than capital-generating assets prevailing in the developed countries which, in de Soto's words, 'is the life blood of the capitalist system'.[63]

Finally, when property rights are clear and secure, transaction costs in identifying the real owner of the property and making and enforcing a lease or sale contract will be reduced to the extent that property markets can function effectively in transferring the property from less efficient uses to more efficient uses.[64] In addition, improving the transferability of property can improve investment incentives when the gains from trade raise the owner's marginal return to the property;[65] a well developed property market is also conductive to the development of financial markets by making collateral-based credit more extensive.

2.2. *Historical and Cross-Country Evidence*

The significance of property rights for economic development has been an appealing subject in economic history studies, among which the works of North stand out as the most path-breaking and influential contributions. In *The Rise of the Western World*, North and Thomas[66] attribute the rise of the western world, and more precisely, the success of the Netherlands and England versus the failure of France and Spain, to the creation and evolution of an efficient property rights regime, which provided the incentives necessary for sustained economic growth. In *Structure and Change in Economic History*, North provided a neoclassical theory of the state and argued that the existence of a state is essential for economic growth since 'it is the state that is responsible for the efficiency of the property rights structure, which causes growth or stagnation or economic decline'.[67] The theory of the state is then used to explore human history from the Neolithic Age to the beginning of the twentieth century, in which two major

62 Atwood 1990; Besley 1998; Deininger 2003.
63 Soto 2000, p. 4.
64 Johnson 1972; Barrows & Roth 1990; Deininger 2003.
65 Besley 1998.
66 North & Thomas 1973.
67 North 1981, p. 17.

discontinuities in the population/resource rates, namely the First (Neolithic or Agricultural) and Second (Industrial) Economic Revolutions are paid the most attention and explained by the complicated interaction between property rights and organizations. In *Constitutions and Commitment*, North and Weingast argue that the Glorious Revolution of 1688 gave rise to some fundamental constitutional changes that allowed the government to commit credibly to upholding property rights.[68] The resultant decrease in risk premiums enabled the government to borrow at an unprecedented level, advanced the development of a market for private debt, and finally led to a financial revolution which in turn triggered the industrial revolution.

A long line of economic research has continued to support North's conclusions, from the general understanding of the importance of property rights to the more specific issue of the economic effects of the Glorious Revolution. For example, Rosenberg and Birdzell argue that the immediate sources of economic growth in Western countries are innovations in trade, technology, and organization, which in turn rely on effective property rights to grant decision-making power to entrepreneurs rather than some political or religious authorities and protect the fruits of innovation from expropriation.[69] Pipes reviews the development of property in mankind's history with special attention to the institutional difference between England and Russia, and concludes that the different status of private property against the threat of appropriation from the state lay a corner stone in different historical paths of social, political, and economic development in the two countries.[70] The significance of property rights in explaining economic history is also endorsed by Jones,[71] Mokyr,[72] and Landes.[73]

Moreover, North's propositions are backed by some empirical studies indirectly. For example, Klerman and Mahoney find that abnormal equity returns around the time of the 1701 Act of Settlement which mandated that judges enjoy tenure during good behaviour rather than at the pleasure of the Crown are large and statistically significant, a result that is consistent with the view that judicial independence as a shield for private property should have a beneficial economic impact which in turn can be reflected in equity returns.[74] Another empirical study conducted by Delong and Shleifer shows that over the period 1050 to 1800, absolutist governments are associated with low economic growth, as measured by city growth.[75] They therefore conclude that the rise of absolutism in regions like Italy and Spain, and absolutism's failure to enrich itself in Holland and early modern England, diverted the economic centre of Europe from the Mediterranean to the English Channel and the Atlantic.

68 North & Weingast 1989.
69 Rosenberg & Birdzell 1986.
70 Pipes 1999.
71 Jones 1981.
72 Mokyr 1990.
73 Landes 1998.
74 Klerman & Mahoney 2005.
75 Delong & Shleifer 1993.

However, North's theory, especially his interpretation of the Glorious Revolution has been criticized from different perspectives. For example, Quinn provides evidence to show that while the risk premium on sovereign debt declined after the Glorious Revolution, interest rates on private debts increased.[76] Sussman and Yafeh find that the level of interest rates in Britain continued to be fairly high for several decades following the Glorious Revolution, and increased substantially in response to the outbreak of military conflicts.[77] Stasavage argues that the British state's credibility as borrower was only consolidated after 1715, once the Whig party which was intimately associated with government creditors established lasting political supremacy.[78] About the effect of institutional reform on property rights, Clark finds that the Glorious Revolution had no significant impact on either rates of return on capital or land values, and concludes that

> 'stable property right may have been a necessary condition for the Industrial Revolution, but, since they had existed in England and Wales for more than 200 years prior to the Industrial Revolution, they were certainly not a sufficient condition'.[79]

The importance of the patent system in encouraging innovation in the British Industrial Revolution is also doubted.[80] All the evidence leads Mokyr to caution that 'the traditional emphasis on formal institutions has been over emphasized, and the enforcement of property rights by the state was less crucial than the Northian interpretation has suggested'.[81]

The relationship between property rights and economic development has been examined in some empirical studies[82] using cross country data. The most influential may be Knack and Keefer (1995), who use institutional indicators compiled by two private international investment risk services (ICRG and BERI) to measure the security of property rights in individual countries, and find significant correlation between institutions and economic growth. The same indicators are used by Clague *et al.*,[83] Hall and Jones,[84] Acemoglu *et al.*,[85] among others, who confirm the property rights have a positive and important effect on growth. The cross-country studies on the institutional foundations of growth, however, have been challenged by recent literature.[86] As Glaeser *et al.* argue, most indicators of institutional quality used to establish the proposition that institutions (property rights) cause growth are constructed to be conceptually unsuitable for that purpose.[87] These measures of institu-

76 Quinn 2001.
77 Sussman & Yafeh 2006.
78 Stasavage 2003 & Stasavage 2007.
79 Clark 1996.
80 Mokyr 2009.
81 Mokyr 2008.
82 For a comprehensive review on the macroeconomic literature on institutions and growth relying on cross-country regression study, see Pande & Udry 2006.
83 Clague *et al.* 1999.
84 Hall & Jones 1999.
85 Acemoglu *et al.* 2001.
86 Glaeser *et al.* 2004; Pande & Udry 2006.
87 Glaeser *et al.* 2004.

tions reflect what actually happened in a country, or *ex post* outcomes of institutions, rather than institutions per se. As such, these measures change with per capita income and are highly volatile; in addition, they cannot be used to differentiate a dictator's choice of respecting property rights from a democratic government's obligation to protect private property. The indicators are also criticized by Pande and Udry for their coarseness, their inability to capture institutional quality, and their neglect of within-country heterogeneity in the characteristics and operation of particular institutions.[88]

2.3. *Micro Evidence*

Numerous academic efforts have examined the effects of property rights on economic performance empirically along the five dimensions we have discussed. As for the relationship between property rights and resource management, some studies confirm the superiority of private property rights over open access (and communal ownership) in guiding efficient resources use. In one of the pioneer works, Bottomley finds that in the Libyan province of TripoliTania, Arab tribesman used communal land for low-valued uses such as growing occasional crops of barley and grazing privately owned sheep and goats rather than more profitable activities such as almond-tree planting.[89] Using both cross-section and time series data from the U.S. East and Gulf coast oyster industry, Agnello and Donnelley show that labour productivity (measured by average physical product of labour, i.e. total weight of oyster meat harvested divided by total labour force in the oyster industry in each state) was higher in privately leased oyster grounds versus government-regulated open access grounds.[90] Anderson and Lueck[91] exploit a sample of thirty nine Indian reservations to estimate the impact of land tenure on the agricultural productivity, and find that the per-acre value of agricultural output is 85-90 per cent lower on tribal-trust land[92] than on fee-simple land[93] and 30-40 per cent lower on individual-trust land[94] than on fee-simple land. Grafton, Squires, and Fox[95] test for changes in efficiency in the same common pool resource (the British Columbia halibut fishery), following privatization of the property rights, and find that privatization leads to not only efficient input usage, but also substantial producer surplus.[96] In addition to negative effects on productivity, common ownership is demonstrated to be ineffec-

88 Pande & Udry 2006.
89 Bottomley 1963.
90 Agnello & Donnelley 1975.
91 Anderson & Lueck 1992.
92 Tribunal-trust land is managed by the tribe subject to trust constraints administered by the Bureau of Indian Affairs (BIA).
93 Under fee simple, the land is privately owned by individuals who are free to use, lease, and sell it.
94 Under individual trust, the land is held by individual Indians but their rights are subject to trust constrains administered by BIA.
95 Grafton, Squires & Fox 2000.
96 For more evidence on the productive gains from private property, see De Alessi 2003.

tive in controlling resource over-exploitation problems and hence conducive to land degradation and resource depletion.[97]

There are plenty of cases, however, that challenge the reported inefficiency of common property in resource allocation and exploitation.[98] For example, in Töbel, Switzerland, a village of only 600 people, communal space for cattle grazing is regulated by an Alp association which is governed by the villagers themselves. Although yields are relatively low, the land in Töbel has maintained its productivity for many centuries and overgrazing has been prevented by tight controls. Successful management of common property resources can also be found in Nepal,[99] in Japan,[100] in Turkey,[101] in India,[102] and in medieval North Europe,[103] among others. Furthermore, some studies find that privatization of resources has not served as a panacea for their conservation; in fact, in many cases it has contributed to a more rapid destruction of resources. For example, in India, privatization of land accelerated more rapid destruction of native vegetation.[104] In view of negative evidence for the role of private property, Cole doubts the suggestion that private ownership is the best solution to resource allocation problems in most cases since 'private resource owners are, indeed, often short-sighted, and they discount future costs and benefits quite heavily'.[105]

The apparently conflicting conclusions about the efficiency of private property relative to common property can be reconciled when the context-contingent or environment-dependent nature of property rights is taken into account.[106] First, when a natural resource (land, for example) is relatively abundant, private property rights are not useful nor economically justifiable and common ownership prevails. Second, when population pressure on the resource intensifies and commercialization of its products increases, the advantages of private property in inducing resource users to internalize externalities and avoiding governance costs under common ownership become more appealing; such advantages, however, may be outweighed by the values inherent in common property regimes, such as the presence of scale economies and function of risk-reduction. Finally, even if a direct economic cost-benefit calculation favours private property, some social and political considerations, such as social status (or identity) attached to land, unacceptable distributive consequences of privatization, and malpractice of the government, will paralyze the functioning of private property.

There is clear evidence that when property rights are insecure, individuals will divert resources to unproductive uses, such as inefficient investment, expensive

97 López 1995; López 1997; Ahuja 1998.

98 Ostrom 1990, Ostrom 1999; Baland & Platteau 1996.

99 Arnold & Campbell 1986.

100 Mckean 1982.

101 Berkes 1992.

102 Wade 1994.

103 Smith 2000.

104 Jodha 1992.

105 Cole 2002, p. 96.

106 Platteau 2000, Chapter 3.

self-protection, and even violent conflict. For example, De Vany and Sanchez[107] find that *ejidatarios*[108] in Mexico exhibit higher fertility than other comparable groups, since children help the parents to secure their rights to land.[109] The relationship between land security and fertility can also be found in Thailand, the Philippines, Iran, Egypt, and India.[110] By a similar token, Field shows that a titling program issued by the Peruvian government with the aim of converting informal property in urban squatter settlements into formal property, has greatly reduced the human resources devoted by untitled households to maintaining tenure security through informal means, and hence resulted in a combination of an increase in total labour force hours and a reallocation of work hours from inside the home to the outside labour market.[111] In Buenos Aires, Argentina, when squatters obtained formal land rights as a result of an expropriation law enacted by the Congress in 1984, they are found to increase housing investment, reduce household size, and improve the education of their children.[112] In Brazil, unfortunately, the inconsistency between civil law that supports the title held by land owners and constitutional law that supports the right of squatters leads to pervasive violence between landowners and squatters.[113] Violence resulting from squatting was also universal in California and other western states of the U.S. in 1860; in addition, squatters are found to have lower production than non squatters, since squatters have to allocate part of their labour to protection of property rights.[114]

The empirical linkage between property rights and investment has been of the greatest concern to economists and hence is the subject of numerous studies covering the majority of developing countries; unfortunately, the evidence does not systematically confirm the linkage as the theory suggests. The evidence from Asian and Latin American countries is stronger.[115] For example, in Thailand, Feder and Onchan find that in two provinces, farm land security (possession of land title)

107 De Vany & Sanchez 1979.

108 An *ejidatario* is a member of an *ejido*, an agrarian community that has received and continues to hold land in accordance with the agrarian law growing of the Mexican Revolution. In 1991, President Carlos Salinas de Gortari eliminated the constitutional right to *ejidos*. Since then some of the *ejido* land has been sold to corporations, although most of it is still in the hands of farmers. In a typical *ejido*, all rights to crop lands are granted to individual families on a usufruct basis. The land cannot be sold, leased, mortgaged or disposed of in any similar fashion. Rights to these lands may be passed on to heirs, but they may also be lost if the land is not under cultivation for two consecutive years.

109 Since the land and other resources of the *ejido* are rationed by non-price means through a political body, a large family will find it less difficult to form a coalition that could block moves to reduce its land holding or use of *ejido* resources.

110 Stokes *et al.* 1986.

111 Field 2007.

112 Becker & Lewis 1973: there is a trade-off between the quantity and quality of children faced by parents. Therefore, if land titling causes a reduction in fertility, it could so induce households to increase educational investments in their children. Galiani & Schargrodsky 2006.

113 Alston, Libecap & Mueller 1999; Alston, Libecap & Mueller 2000.

114 Clay 2006.

115 For a more extensive review on Asian and Latin American countries, see Feder & Nishio 1999; for reviews on African countries, see Besley 1998; Platteau 2000, Chapter 4; Place 2009.

implies greater capital formation and higher capital/land ratios, as well as higher levels of land improvement.[116] In China, Li *et al.* and Jacoby *et al.*[117] use household data from northeast China to show that land tenure security[118] significantly affects land-specific investment, specifically investment in soil quality (organic fertilizer). In India, Pender and Kerr find that soil and water conservation investment is significantly lower on leased land in two of the study villages and lower on plots that are subject to sales restrictions in one village.[119] In Vietnam, the land law of 1993 which gave households the power to exchange, transfer, lease, inherit and mortgage their land-use rights, is found to lead to a significant increase in the share of total area devoted to multi-year crops, as well as some increase in irrigation investment.[120] In Brazil, the results of the household survey confirm that ownership security (whether the farmer holds title to his land or not) plays an important role in promoting investment in land improvements.[121] Land titling and registration are also found to be associated with increased investments in Guatemala and Nicaragua.[122] In addition to rural areas, tenure security is demonstrated to influence residential investment in urban squatter neighbourhoods in Peru and Argentine.[123]

When we turn to Africa, however, the picture is more mixed. An early study reviews empirical evidence from Kenya, Uganda, and Zimbabwe, and concludes that 'there is little empirical evidence to support the hypothesis that registration, through increased tenure security, has increased investment in agriculture'.[124] Migot-Adholla *et al.* uses cross-sectional evidence from Ghana, Kenya, and Rwanda in 1987-1988 to show that the relationship between land rights (the level of individualization of land rights, especially the extent of transfer or alienation rights) and land improvements is far from clear.[125] In a book based on eight case studies in seven African countries (Burkina Faso, Rwanda, Ghana, Kenya, Uganda, Somalia, and Senegal), several cases confirmed the positive impact of land rights on investment[126] while others failed to do so. The relative insignificance of the effects of land ownership on investments is further supported by findings from Uganda[127] and

116 Feder & Onchan 1987.

117 Li *et al.* 1998; Jacoby *et al.* 2002.

118 Most cultivated land in rural China remains collectively owned and the state has purposely provided localities flexibility in land management and has explicitly allowed leaders the right to make periodic adjustments to household land holdings if conditions so require. Tenure insecurity induced by frequent reallocation by local leaders of collective land is thus believed to weaken farmer investment incentive in the land, especially in longer-term, land-saving investments (Wen 1995). By contrast, some scholars suggest that the inefficiencies are not so great and that even farmers are not in favour of tenure reform (Kung 1995).

119 Pender & Kerr 1998.

120 Do & Iyer 2003.

121 Alston *et al.* 1996.

122 Schweigert 2006; Deininger & Chamorro 2004.

123 Field 2005; Galiani & Schargrodsky 2006.

124 Barrows & Roth 1990.

125 Migot-Adholla *et al.* 1991.

126 Matlon 1994 on Burkina Faso; Blarel 1994 on Rwanda, and Roth *et al.* 1994 on Uganda.

127 Place & Otsuka 2002; Pender *et al.* 2004.

Madagascar.[128] By contrast, in a very influential paper, Besley uses data from two different regions of Ghana (Wassa and Angola), and finds that land improvements in Wassa (in the form of tree planting) are significantly related to land rights, whereas land improvements in Angola (including drainage, continuous fertilizing, etc.) have no such relationship.[129] Similarly, Gavian and Fafchamps find evidence that tenure insecurity incites farmers to divert scarce manure resources to more secure fields (owned fields rather than borrowed fields) whenever they can;[130] Place and Otsuka confirm the impacts of tenure security on incentives for making long-term investments to boost agricultural production in their study of Malawi;[131] and Deininger and Jin show that compared with tenure security, transfer rights have a higher and unambiguous impact on productivity-enhancing investments.[132]

Even if investment is empirically confirmed to be positively correlated with tenure security in general, and land titling in particular, it is too early to conclude a causal relationship from that. As Sjaastad and Bromley argue, the causal direction may be from investment to tenure security rather than vice versa.[133] In other words, investment, especially the 'conspicuous' investment, such as planting leguminous trees (relative to 'inconspicuous' investment like fallows), can be viewed as a commitment to the long-term productive use of the land, and hence undertaken to increase tenure security. Some empirical evidence, for example, Gray and Kevane and Brasselle *et al.* on Burkina Faso,[134] Quisumbing *et al.* on Ghana,[135] and Place and Otsuka on Uganda,[136] seems to be consistent with this hypothesis.

There are several reasons that can be presented to explain the ambiguous relationship between property rights and investment found in Africa. First, as Feder and Feeny state, most of the impact of land ownership 'stemmed from the fact titles increased farmer's access to credit, rather than from the elimination of actual risk to the land rights of the farmers'.[137] Therefore, the malfunctioning or even non-existence of factor markets, especially financial markets, a phenomenon prevailing in African countries, tends to invalidate the effects of land rights. Second, in most cases, customary land ownership continues to be more important in governing land issues than formal property law.[138] In addition, the customary law tenure is found to be flexible enough to adapt to a new environment, and secure enough to warrant

128 Jacoby & Minten 2007.
129 Besley 1995.
130 Gavian & Fafchamps 1996.
131 Place & Otsuka 2001.
132 Deininger & Jin 2006.
133 Sjaastad & Bromley 1997.
134 Gray & Kevane 2001; Brasselle *et al.* 2002.
135 Quisumbing *et al.* 2001.
136 Place & Otsuka 2002.
137 Feder & Feeny 1991.
138 Generally, in most African countries, the outreaches of formal land system covers at most between 2 and 10 per cent of the total land area (Deininger 2003, p. 62). Barrows & Roth 1990; Pinckney & Kimuyu 1994.

land-related investments.[139] By contrast, the introduction of a modern titling and registration system to replace a customary land regime may lead to undesirable economic and social outcomes, such as unfair allocation of land resources,[140] deprivation of some (informal) derived or secondary rights,[141] and pervasive and continuous land conflicts.

The evidence on the credit effects of formal property rights is also ambiguous. An early study conducted by Feder and Onchan shows that in Thailand, farm land security (possession of land title) increased access to institutional credit and therefore resulted in greater capital formation.[142] In Peru, land titling is found to be associated with a 9-10 percentage point increase in loan approval rates from the public sector bank for housing construction materials.[143] In Argentina, the evidence indicates a positive (but modest) effect of land titling on access to mortgage credit, and no impact on access to other forms of credit, such as credit card and banking accounts.[144] Again, empirical studies in rural Africa fail to find a significant relationship between the possession of title and use of formal credit.[145] A more subtle conclusion is reached by Carter and Olinto, who find that land titling has differential effects across wealth classes and disproportionately benefit larger scale farmers (farms in excess of 15 hectares).[146]

The ambiguous linkage between land titling and credit access can be understood from both demand and supply sides.[147] On the demand side, small holders, especially those subsistence-constrained farmers, may fail to apply for loans because they perceive a high risk of losing their land through foreclosure; additionally, farmers may be unlikely to respond to credit availability because of the lack of attractive investment opportunities or the absence of conditions critical for their successful exploitation. On the supply side, failures may arise from different sources. First, titled land will not be considered as reliable collateral by credit-givers if it is difficult to foreclose. Second, in many countries, especially African countries, financial market distortions prevent increased agricultural lending.[148] Third, financial institutions are likely to accept land as collateral only in situations where the land market is sufficiently active for foreclosed land to be disposed of fairly

139 Atwood 1990; Pinckney & Kimuyu 1994; Sjaastad & Bromley 1997; Deininger & Binswanger 1999; Platteau 2000; Place 2009.

140 This phenomenon is labelled 'land grabbing' by Feder & Nishio 1999, who define the grabbers as 'those who are better informed, are more familiar with formal processes, and have better access to officials and financial means to undertake procedures for registration'.

141 Women, pastoralists, hunter-gathers, casted people, former slaves and serfs, people belonging to minority tribes, etc., who have traditionally enjoyed subsidiary or derived (usufruct) rights to land, face a serious risk of being denied legal recognition of their customary rights to land during the registration process (Platteau 2000, p. 164).

142 Feder & Onchan 1987.

143 Field & Torero 2004.

144 Galiani & Schargrodsky 2006.

145 Migot-Adholla *et al.* 1991; Place & Hazell 1993; Bruce & Migot-Adholla 1994; Pinckney & Kimuyu 1994.

146 Carter and Olinto 2003.

147 Platteau 2000, p. 143-150.

148 Atwood 1990.

easily, while such a land market will not be created by land titling itself. Finally, where informal credit markets function well and can substitute for the formal ones to a great extent, land titling will also be of limited value.

In some studies, land titling is claimed to stimulate land transactions, and increase the value of titled property relative to untitled property. For example, Jimenez compares unit housing prices between the non-squatter (formal) sector and squatter (informal) sector in the city of Davao, the Philippines, and finds that formal sector unit dwelling prices are 58 per cent higher than in the informal sector.[149] Based on interviews with real estate brokers in Jakarta, Dowall and Leaf show that land prices were affected strongly by the level of tenure security.[150] Feder and Nishio report that in Thailand, 3-4 years after the issuance of title deeds under the Land Titling Project, the land market was more active in the project area compared with the non-project area.[151] In Brazil, Alston *et al.* find that the effect of title on land value is positive and significant, but distance-varying.[152] In Nicaragua, registration is found to increase land values by 30 per cent.[153] In Ecuador, Lanjouw and Levy find that having title is associated with a sizable increase in the market value of properties (on average 23.5 per cent of untitled property values).[154]

On the other hand, there is also evidence showing that formal property rights are not a prerequisite for the development of an active land market, especially in, but not limited to African countries. In Ho Chi Minh City(HCMC) of Vietnam, Kim shows that a real estate market continued to flourish in spite of the fact that about half of houses did not have legal title.[155] In Kenya, a well-functioning land market has not been created as a result of land registration.[156] From a survey of sixteen different areas belonging to six African countries with titling programs (Kenya, Rwanda, Burundi, Uganda, Malawi, and Zambia), it came out that on average, only 16 per cent of the land parcels have been acquired though market purchases, while 63 per cent have been obtained through inheritance and various kinds of gift transfers, and the rest through other means among which state allocation stands foremost.[157] A comprehensive review conducted by Chimhowu and Woodhouse indicates that in the nineteenth century African farmers were actively engaged in market transfers of land under customary tenure; the commercialization of land, much of which is carried out in vernacular markets (informal markets), has been accelerated in response to social and economic change in the twentieth century.[158]

It is not surprising to find an ambiguous relationship between land markets and land titling, given the fact that market-style land transfers have developed in customary regimes, especially where land is relatively scarce and hence the efficien-

149 Jimenez 1984.
150 Dowall & Leaf 1991.
151 Feder & Nishio 1999.
152 Alston *et al.* 1996.
153 Deininger & Chamorro 2004.
154 Lanjouw & Levy 2002.
155 Kim 2004.
156 Barrows & Roth 1990.
157 Platteau 2000, p. 151-152.
158 Chimhowu & Woodhouse 2006.

cy gains from market transfers are high.[159] In addition, the positive effect of land titling on land markets should not be taken for granted, in view of the number of factors that can influence the functioning of land markets and the complicated interaction between them. For example, land rental markets will not work well if there are imperfections in labour markets, capital markets, and insurance markets.[160] Land sales markets will also be influenced by market imperfections or distortions in other markets, and can hence give rise to some inefficient outcomes.[161] Even where land markets function well, the land may in many cases fail to fall into efficient hands because the motives behind land purchases are not driven by efficiency.[162]

3. Why Formal Property Rights fail in Most Developing Countries

In this section, we will try to solve the apparent puzzle revealed by the aforementioned empirical evidence, namely the failure or insignificance of formal property rights in general, and land titling in particular in most developing countries, in spite of the advantages of formal ownership claimed by economists and lawyers for a long time in the literature. We have discussed some factors contributing to the puzzle, such as the persistence of customary land tenure, the malfunctioning of other factor markets, etc., and will therefore pay more attention to the benefits, costs, and preconditions of formal property rights per se, especially the problematic role played by the state in defining and enforcing property rights here. A more nuanced and balanced understanding of the relationship between economic development and formal property regime, or property law in a broad sense, will then be reached.

3.1. *Benefits of Formal Property Rights*

Generally speaking, formal property rights are considered synonymous with private ownership, and hence share the same merits as private ownership in terms of exclusivity, transferability, and transaction costs reduction (see section 1). Moreover, formal property rights, defined and enforced by the state - an organization 'which has a comparative advantage in violence'[163] - are believed to be clearer and more secure than informal property rights enforced by private power or community-based norms, and hence more helpful for economic growth. For one thing, as a (credible) third party, the state can lower the transaction costs related to property rights through the development of an impersonal judicial system, which will help to capture important economies of scale[164] by providing more people with more stan-

159 André & Platteau 1998; Platteau 2000, p. 158-159.

160 Deininger 2003, Chapter 3; Deininger & Feder 2001.

161 Deininger 2003, Chapter 3; Deininger & Feder 2001.

162 Platteau 2000, p. 161-162.

163 North 1981, p. 21.

164 For a more extensive discussion on the economies of scale in public enforcement of property rights, see Bell & Parchomovsky 2005. They argue that, first, given that a single transgressor typically threatens multiple property owners, centralized monitoring, which is more easily →

dardized enforcement of property rights in a broader territory, as well as to make the punishment of wrongdoing more credible by isolating the enforcers from the enforced parties. For another, informal substitutes for legal enforcement of property rights can function only to a limited extent, and result in inefficient outcomes in some cases: reliance on extralegal norms for enforcement may limit one's business partners to a small number of individuals with whom one is familiar and forego potentially mutually beneficial exchanges when strangers are involved, and therefore mean a shortage of new firms, a dearth of new ideas and entrepreneurship, and an inability to adopt and develop complex technologies; there is also a risk that the extralegal norms created by the close-knit groups may not be in the more general interest;[165] in some extreme cases, private enforcers resort to the threat and sometimes the actuality of violence, an unproductive and inefficient approach to economy.[166]

Formal property rights can also be justified from other perspectives. For example, as Merrill and Smith argue, if property owners are allowed to create idiosyncratic rights to property at will, they will not take into account the full magnitude of the measurement costs they impose on strangers to the title.[167] In that case, property law can be relied on to address this measurement-cost externality problem though compulsory standardization of property rights. Moreover, property law can be expected to limit the right to subdivide private property into wasteful fragmentations and keep resources well-scaled for productive use.[168] Finally, the security and stability of property rights provided by legal provisions makes possible the temporary separation of ownership and possession which in turn increases the joint wealth of the parties, allows for increased net value resulting from learning how best to use assets, especially those complex assets whose full economic potential can not be realized right away, and helps to extract more utility from other interoperable assets.[169]

The alleged benefits of formal property rights cannot be taken for granted when such factors as the cost of creating and maintaining a formal property regime, the complicated interaction between law and social norms, and the effectiveness of the state are taken into consideration. In other words, property rights will not emerge just because they are *demanded;* they have to be *supplied* by the state in a cost-effective manner. States in the developing world, however, frequently fail to complete this task because they lack either sufficient resources (physical and

achieved by the state, could detect these crimes more cheaply. Second, centralized apprehension will reduce the cost of prosecuting repeat violators and enable the specialization of agents to pursue violators more effectively than individual property owners. Finally, judicial decisions give new content and meaning to property rights and thus affect parties beyond those involved in the immediate dispute. In addition, certain network externalities and free-riding problems also suggest that public enforcement of property rights should be provided.

165 Ellickson 1993: 'norm of "honoured among thieves" may well be welfare maximizing for thieves, but welfare diminishing for society at large'.

166 Cross 2002.

167 Merrill & Smith 2000.

168 Heller 1998; Heller 1999.

169 Bell & Parchomovsky 2005.

human) or suitable 'social technologies'[170] which can be used to transform resources into institutional outcomes efficiently, or both. The failure in the supply side of property rights therefore implies that, in many developing and transitional countries, formal property rights might be the cause rather than the solution to economic problems.

3.2. *Costs of Formal Property Rights*

There are a variety of costs in terms of creating and maintaining a formal property regime, including the costs of establishing a property registration system. Taking land registration as an example, there are two different systems of land registration, namely a land records system prevailing in the United States and France (and some other countries, most of them having a French legal background), and a land title registration system, which was created within the German legal tradition, and is now used in most of the world.[171] According to Miceli, the land records system, which originated with the recording acts, requires the maintenance of a public record of land transfer that can be inspected by prospective buyers to establish evidence of good title, thereby easing land transfer.[172] However, examination of the record does not guarantee title; depending on the thoroughness of the search and differences in lawyer's opinions about the title history, the risk of a claim to title remains.[173] As a result, the history is searched anew with each land transfer, and owners typically purchase private title insurance to provide monetary compensation in the event of future claim. In contrast, under the land title registration system, a landowner registers his land with the government, at which time a legal proceeding is undertaken to determine the status of title. In the absence of a legitimate claim, the government issues a certificate that gives the owner good title against any

170 See Eggertsson 2005, who divides technologies into production technologies and social technologies and describes social technologies as methods or mechanisms whereby social institutions create patterns of behaviour. In addition, production technologies need the support of appropriate social institutions to function effectively, which means that production technologies and social technologies complement each other. However, compared with production technologies, social technologies do not travel well from one country to another, because pre-existing institutional arrangements often undermine the transplanting effort.

171 Land titling systems also include the Australian 'Torrens' variety, which has been introduced in some other common law jurisdictions. The term 'Torrens' derived from the name of Sir Robert Torrens, who created a system of registration of title to land in Australia while he was serving as Register General of the Province of South Australia in 1858. Arruñada 2003; Arruñada & Garoupa 2005; Hanstad 1998; Miceli 1998.

172 Miceli 1998.

173 Under records system, title disputes are solved by using a property rule. If the seller's right is shown to be defective, the buyer loses the property right to the benefit of the true owner. The buyer is left with contractual rights against the seller, the title examiner, and/or title insurer (Arruñada 2003). By contrast, the use of a liability rule for solving title disputes dominates in the title registration system. That is to say, a good faith buyer requires a property right if the purchase is based on the information provided by the register. If the seller's right is later shown to be defective, the buyer keeps the property right and the true owner gets a contractual right against the seller and the register.

future claims. Subsequent purchasers need only inspect the certificate to verify ownership and if a claimant should appear, he is only entitled to monetary compensation from a public fund financed by registration fees.

There have been long debates over the comparative merits of these two systems. On the one hand, a land records system is believed to be less costly and more flexible.[174] Under a records system, some minor defects not worth clarifying can be insured either by the parties or a third-party insurer, which helps to avoid holdout problems (and associated substantial bargaining costs) in title purging. Moreover, costs will tend to be minimized and flexibility (in terms of rapid innovation and adaptation to changes in technology and demand) achieved, given title examination and clarification are conducted by business firms or professionals who are paid with a residual profit, at least when the competition is sufficiently strong. On the other hand, a land title registration system is advocated because it can provide more security for property rights, as well as realize economies of scale in information production which has to be forgone under a land records system. A land title registration system is also given credit for the fact that it awards the land to the party who values it most (the current owner rather than the claimant),[175] induces optimal investment in land improvement,[176] and reduces dynamic inefficiency in land development.[177] To sum up, a land title registration system is favoured by the majority of scholars, since it 'not only makes land titles more reliable, but is also simpler, more logical, and less costly',[178] and therefore is recommended by most land registration projects funded by multilateral agencies in developing countries as a more efficient policy option.[179]

However, an effective land title registration system is expensive. Establishment of the system will likely take several years to complete and will consume valuable physical and human resources which can be used for other socially desirable projects. Moreover, operation and maintenance of the system, once established, will require significant additional costs. In the World Bank's 2008 *Doing Business* report, the mean cost associated with property registration in 173 countries amounted to 6.6 per cent of the property's value, and the mean waiting time was 81 days. The cost of registering property is highly bimodal; while it is 2 per cent or less of property values in 32 cases it amounts to 5 or 10 per cent and more of property values in 92 and 41 of the cases respectively.[180] In some extreme cases, such as Syria, the costs of registering property is about 28.05 per cent of property value, while in Kiribati it takes 523 days to register property. Consequently, as Barnes and Griffith-Charles

174 Arruñada 2003.

175 Miceli & Sirmans 1995.

176 Miceli, Sirmans & Turnbull 1998.

177 Miceli, Sirmans & Turnbull 2000.

178 Hanstad 1998. One empirical study conducted by Janczyk 1977 shows that, in Cook County, Illinois, where the two title systems coexist, the cost of transferring a title in the records system was about twice that of a transfer in the Torrens system. In addition, Cook County could have saved $ 76 million once all of the property in the records system was registered into the Torrens system.

179 Deininger & Feder 2009.

180 Deininger & Feder 2009.

show, when the costs exceed the benefits (in terms of increased security) which users obtain from registering, they will return to the informal system to convey and divide their land and the sustainability of land registry system will be seriously compromised by this process of 'deformalization'.[181]

In addition to the direct costs related to a land registration system, the discrepancies between title documents and reality resulting from ineffective operation of this system constitute another major disappointment of the land titling program in developing countries.[182] Without sufficient administrative capabilities, succession and other transfers of title have gone largely unregistered, as a result of which the land registration system hardly reflects the present day reality, thus destroying the utility of the system and engendering new uncertainties. In some other cases, such as in Nicaragua and Bolivia, title of the same piece of land is delivered to separate parties when more than one government agency has the authority to title land, but there is no clear distinction between their geographic jurisdiction nor is there any cooperation between the two agencies.[183] Finally, in some Latin American countries such as Guatemala, over-centralization of registry institutions renders the registration service highly inaccessible for persons living in remote areas.

3.3. *Property Law and Customary Land System*

When the state in the developing world tries to replace customary land tenure with formal property law, but fails to fill the gap in important social service provision left by the withdrawal of a communal regime, such as the social safety net function performed by communal land, a significant efficiency loss will be incurred. As Bromley and Chavas states, 'the absence of a right to exclude someone desperately in need of the means of life means that risks are more effectively pooled', and a common property regime can therefore 'be seen as an integral part of risk sharing strategies'.[184] Commonly held land can provide insurance against external shocks in two different manners.[185] First, communal land usually act as the 'asset of last resort': those who work on communal land receive not only a return on their labour, but also an imputed form of resource rent, and the amount of rent they obtain is directly proportional to their labour contribution; those in most need, i.e., those with relatively poor outside earnings chances who allocate relatively more effort to gathering resources from the common property, obtain a relatively higher share of the resource rent. Second, communal land can fulfil a role as 'employer of last resort': across individuals, the productivity of labour allocated to the common land is relatively homogeneous in comparison with productivity outside; this feature allows the commons to provide a fall-back form of employment in cases where labour cannot find profitable employment elsewhere. Therefore, where there exist incomplete insurance markets because of either information asymmetries or limits

181 Barnes & Griffith-Charles 2007.

182 Platteau 2000, p. 146-147; Trebilcock & Veel 2008.

183 Barnes, Stanfield & Barthel 2000.

184 Bromley & Chavas 1989.

185 Platteau & Francois 2005.

on contract, if individuals are sufficiently risk averse and the efficiency gains from privatization are sufficiently limited, privatization of communal land can be welfare-decreasing.[186]

Plenty of empirical studies have confirmed the insurance-providing role of common property resources (CPRs). For example, Ellickson shows that in each of the three pioneer settlements in U.S history (the Jamestown settlement of 1607, the Plymouth settlement of 1620, and the Mormon settlement at Salt Lake in 1847), settlers started with group ownership of land as a response to an environment characterized as highly dangerous.[187] In the context of the modern developing world, this insurance function performed by CPRs is shown to be in favour of the poor: Jodha reveals significant contribution of CPRs towards the employment and income generation for the rural poor in India;[188] in the Tapajos region of Brazil, where there are 18 traditional communities along the border of the Tapajos National Forest, Pattanayak and Sills find that non-timber forest products have played a large role in providing local people with a form of 'natural insurance' against agricultural risk;[189] in Zimbabwe, Cavendish shows that communally owned environmental resources, such as forests, fisheries, soils and water, make a significant contribution to average rural incomes, especially to the well-being of the poorer households.[190] Therefore, when common property resources are privatized and the vulnerable segments of the community (the poor) can not be adequately compensated, they will try to resist the alleged efficiency-increasing institutional change.

As Meinzen-Dick and Mwangi show, in many rural communities which continue to be dependent to a large extent on agriculture and nature resources for their livelihoods, property rights to land are better understood as a 'web of interests', with many different parties having a right to use, regulate, or manage the resource.[191] Therefore, most land is subject to multiple and overlapping claims by several different kinds of groups. In addition, customary land tenure is claimed to be adaptive, flexible, and dynamic, given the fact that 'land rights are subject to intermittent or on-going negotiation, and tenure security depends on a person's standing with his/her relatives and neighbours than on the way in which a claim was originally acquired'.[192] It is very hard or even impossible to codify and register such complex bundles of rights associated with given parcels, especially in view of the high information and transaction costs faced by most less developed countries. When customary group rights are extinguished by a procedure of formalization, the state's failure to record all existing land rights will therefore lead to a cutting of this web, and legitimate claimants, such as women, youth, and seasonal users, among others, may be denied legal recognition of their traditional rights to land. The formalization of property right thus becomes an important source of social conflict.

186 Platteau & Francois 2005.
187 Ellickson 1993.
188 Jodha 1992.
189 Pattanayak & Sills 2001.
190 Cavendish 2000.
191 Meinzen-Dick & Mwangi 2008.
192 Berry 1997.

In some other cases, land tenure formalization may even be regard as illegitimate when the titling programs are manipulated by the elites to the extent that the poor or otherwise vulnerable land users are dispossessed of their rights to land. In Barrows and Roth's words, 'registration effectively provided a mechanism for transfer of wealth to those with better social or economic positions, thereby creating tenure insecurity for less influential right-holders'.[193] This phenomenon is pervasive in the developing world. For example, in Thailand, land records have been manipulated by government officials so as to allow elites with a high level of political connections to obtain ownership of land that, under the traditional system, would have been controlled by homesteading cultivators, while original occupants (especially when they belong to non-Thai minorities) found it difficult to protect their customary rights owing to land dispute claimants' differential access to the Thai bureaucracy; in Kenya, those few well-connected Kenyans who succeeded in having pasture lands registered in their own names on the grounds that they would bring them into cultivation, were finally found to use the land as collateral in order to obtain loans from banks in Nairobi and to use proceeds of these loans to finance their children's university studies abroad, with the intention of shunning repayment and letting the land be foreclosed; in Mauritania, good irritated lands traditionally claimed by local Negro-African communities have been adjudicated to private owners with a view to encouraging their efficient exploitation, but in the end these lands were allocated to people of Moorish origin by an essentially Moorish administration and in many instances were not actually brought into cultivation.[194]

Therefore, the transition from customary land tenure to formalized individual ownership becomes a 'race for the prize', and 'it is mostly the wealthy, the powerful, and the informed who succeed in a race contested under such murky conditions'.[195] Insofar as it encourages unequal capture of land by powerful elites, formalization of land rights will inevitably be rejected by those whose traditional claims are weakened or even denied in the process of formalization (by accident or design), and debates and conflicts will then continue to plague the society. As a consequence, valuable resources are wasted on unproductive uses, such as pervasive recourse to courts, exclusion of other users through various types of enclosure, and even illicit and semi-criminal acts of theft.[196] Output on land is also detrimentally affected by conflicts.[197] In some extreme cases, even apparently trivial land conflicts can be kept alive for generations and may suddenly erupt into large-scale civil strife and violence.[198]

Generally speaking, when most developing countries try to replace the customary land system with formal (individualized) land rights, their supply-side constraints, such as insufficient budget, incompetent agencies, and inadequate

193 Barrows & Roth 1990.
194 Platteau 2000, p. 165-167.
195 Benjaminsen & Sjaastad 2002.
196 Peters 2004.
197 Deininger & Castagnini 2006.
198 André & Platteau 1998; Fred-Mensah 1999.

legitimacy, will frequently cause so called 'legal pluralism'.[199] For example, in Kenya, Barrows and Roth show that

> 'the land law failed to gain popular understanding or acceptance, individuals continued to convey rights to land according to customary law, and a gap developed between the control of rights as reflected in the land register and as recognized by most local communities'.[200]

Under legal pluralism, which institution can be relied on to define and enforce property rights becomes ambiguous since 'traditional authorities have lost much of their power of control over land, but the state has not developed the capacity to take full control'.[201] Instead of complementing each other, formal and informal land institutions compete with each other, and this parallel system will give rise to 'institutional shopping', a term used to describe the situation that different parties pursue disputes through different channels (formal vs. informal, legal vs. administrative, etc.).[202]

Legal pluralism, institutional ambiguity, and institutional shopping, will further undermine social conditions that enable customary land tenure to function effectively, such as norms of reciprocity and cooperation, low-cost internal governance mechanisms, and informal sanction systems, etc.[203] Norm-based common property arrangements may therefore become dysfunctional,[204] or even break down, especially under pressure from rising resource values. On the other hand, legal pluralism may also damage the legitimacy and credibility of formal property systems, and hence leads to efficiency costs, in view of determined resistance of local people to drastic reshuffling of land rights. In the worst scenario, there will be a disintegration of the norm-based resource governance system without the provision of effective substitutes by the state, and open access (as well as resource depletion) then follows.

3.4. *Property Law and the State*

The aforementioned discussions finally lead us to an evergreen issue attracting much attention from scholars of law and economics as well as new institutional economics, namely the relationship between property rights and the state. As

199 Fitzpatrick 2006.
200 Barrows & Roth 1990.
201 Fred-Mensah 1999.
202 Deininger 2003, p. 35; Deininger & Feder 2009.
203 Fitzpatrick 2006.
204 For example, Besteman notes that customary land tenure in Somalia was quite secure and that titling programs actually decreased security by calling into question the applicability of customary law and creating the possibility of dispossession of unregistered farmers who continued to abide by customary law (Trebilcock & Veel 2008). See also Lanjouw & Levy 2004, who argue that 'if one takes an area with a long-standing and well-understood customary property rights system and overlays a formal state titling program. it can make residents less secure because they are unsure which system will apply in any given situation'.

Eggertsson puts it clearly, 'the property rights approach is not complete without a theory of the state', since 'without the state, its institutions, and supportive framework of property rights, high transaction costs will paralyze complex production systems, and specific investments involving long-term exchange relationships will not be forthcoming'.[205] In North's words, 'A theory of the state is essential because it is the state that specifies the property rights structure. Ultimately it is the state that is responsible for the efficiency of the property rights structure, which causes growth or stagnation or economic decline.'[206] Finally, the state is a two-edged sword: 'The existence of a state is essential for economic growth; the state, however, is the source of man-made economic decline'.[207]

The importance and desirability of the state has long been endorsed by social scientists since Thomas Hobbes, given its allegedly irreplaceable role in maintaining social order, providing public goods and services, and redressing market failure. While far from perfect, states in the developed world indeed conform to such stereotypes and function effectively in fulfilling their responsibilities. Unfortunately, if the whole world is taken into consideration, well-functioning governments that protect property rights and supply public goods are the exception, not the rule.[208] For example, according to 2010 Failed States Index[209] compiled by the Foreign Policy magazine and the Fund of Peace, nearly 21 per cent of the world's countries (37 countries) have 'failing states'. In them, governments are often ultra-predatory, dysfunctional, and threatening to collapse. Another 51 per cent of the world's countries (91 countries) have states in imminent danger of failing. If these measures are correct, in over half of the world, states are either critically or dangerously dysfunctional.

Weak and failed states can not be expected to perform the functions that they are supposed to carry out, such as defining and protecting property rights, given the fact that their governments lack either the capacity or the incentives required by an effective governance mechanism.[210] Weak countries therefore fail to create and maintain a variety of institutions which are directly or indirectly responsible for the functioning of a formal property rights regime, such as a reliable and inexpensive land titling system, a competent and uncorrupt judiciary, and a functional police

205 Eggertsson 1990, p. 40 & 317.

206 North 1981, p. 17.

207 North 1981, p. 20.

208 Leeson 2007; Leeson & Williamson 2009.

209 The index's ranks are based on twelve indicators of state vulnerability: four social, two economic and six political. Social indicators include demographic pressures, massive movement of refugees and internally displaced persons, legacy of vengeance-seeking group grievance, and chronic and sustained human flight. Economic indicators consist of uneven economic development along group lines and sharp and/or severe economic decline. Political indicators is comprised of criminalization and/or delegitimization of the state, progressive deterioration of public services, widespread violation of human rights, security apparatus as 'state within a state', rise of factionalized elites, and intervention of other states or external factors.

210 As Acemoglu 2005 shows, when the state is excessively weak, the ruler anticipates that he will not be able to extract rents in the future and under-invest in public goods, which are important for the efficient functioning of the economy.

force, etc.[211] In some extreme cases, the consequences of weak states are so detrimental that they are claimed to 'kill growth',[212] and are better replaced by a state of anarchy.[213]

More generally, weak states are susceptible to capture by powerful elites and therefore easily become a vehicle for rent-seeking and free loading.[214] As the models of Glaeser *et al.*, Polishchuk and Savvateev, and Sonin have shown, in an institutional environment where the state is likely to be captured, influential elites and/or rich agents can subvert the political, regulatory, and legal institutions of society for their own benefit.[215] In that case, they have no interest in, and even object to strong protection of property rights provided by the state in a non-discriminatory manner. On the one hand, they can protect their own property by appealing to their *de facto* political power, or other available strategies that can be used to shelter them from expropriation.[216] On the other hand, they will benefit from weak protection of property rights which allows them to engage in profitable but unproductive activities such as rent-seeking or other redistributive action. In Gradstein's words, 'When the political machinery is controlled by small wealthy elite, it will not be interested in state protection against appropriate rent seeking despite its growth enhancing potential because rent seeking benefits the rich relatively more'.[217]

Evidence from transition economies shows that in high-capture economies, including Azerbaijan, Bulgaria, Croatia, Georgia, Kyrgyzstan, Moldova, Romania, Russia, Slovakia, and Ukraine, public officials appear to have created a private market for the provision of typically public goods, such as the security of property rights, and for rent-seeking opportunities that a relatively small number of firms can obtain through capture. State capture generates individualized gains to captor firms, while at the same time it is associated with large social costs for the rest of the economy in deteriorating sales and investment growth.[218] In Russia, the public property rights enforcement mechanism has been replaced by private (mafia-type)

211 Trebilcock & Veel 2008.

212 Easterly 2002, Chapter 11.

213 Leeson 2007 compares the state of 18 key development indicators in Somalia before and after its government collapse and finds that on nearly all indicators Somalia is doing significantly better under anarchy than it was under government. See also Powell *et al.* 2008, who rank Somali welfare on 13 development indicators before and after anarchy relative to 41 other Sub-Saharan Africa (SSA) countries, and find that on five of the indicators, Somalia is in the top half of SSA countries. In addition, Moselle & Polak 2001 provide a theoretical model demonstrating that if a state is highly predatory and its behaviour goes unchecked, government may not only fail to add to social welfare, but may actually reduce welfare below its level under anarchy.

214 Braguinsky 1999; Hellman *et al.* 2003.

215 Glaeser *et al.* 2003; Polishchuk & Savvateev 2004; Sonin 2003.

216 For example, during the political instability resulting from the Mexican Revolution, the Mexican oil industry effectively defended its property rights by making use of two powerful weapons (Haber *et al.* 2003). First, the oil companies could make effective appeals to the U.S. government to intervene on their behalf. Second, they were able to coordinate their moves, which meant that they could threaten the Mexican government with production boycotts.

217 Gradstein 2007.

218 Hellman *et al.* 2003.

enforcement to the extent that the state and the government are claimed to have effectively been 'privatized'.[219] Consequently, markets are subject to extremely high transaction costs, since the number of participants in each segment of the divided market (caused by private enforcement) is strictly limited and the flows of goods, capital, labour and information are severely disrupted; the intrinsic uncertainty inherent in the private enforcement systems makes the economy oriented toward extremely short-term profit maximization; and many small businesses and much of the population are driven to the shadow economy when they feel that they are being unfairly taxed and exploited by small but well-organized pressure groups.[220]

In the developing world, especially the post colonial states of Africa, rulers rely on alliances with local strongmen whom they allow to exploit local economic opportunities, and hence create a so-called 'neo-patrimonial' system of governance. In some extreme cases, as with Mobutu Sese Seko of Zaire, a neo-patrimonial regime results in the theft of a large part of society's resources by a single individual, while in others, it merely amounts to rent-seeking-that is, use of the public sector to reallocate property rights to the benefit of a particular interest.[221] For example, in Northwest Cameroon, land conflicts have increased since local elites seek to acquire large tracts of land under individual title, a process facilitated by the 1974 land ordinance and by the links between local elites and national politics; in Kenya, a critical contributing factor to the growing social inequality in access to land is the capacity of the patron-client chains that link the national elite to the local level to gain control over resources that offer opportunities for accumulation; in Nigeria, political and civil elites benefit disproportionately from the 1978 Land Use Decree by manipulating the allocation authorities; in Somalia, the tragic civil strife is rooted in earlier process of land occupation and expropriation by the Somalia state and its governing elites, in particular, the Land Law of 1975 which enables those with privileged access to the mechanisms of registration to obtain titles to land that had been used for generations by local farmers.[222]

In summary, good governance, such as a consistent legal and institutional framework, broad access to information, and competent and impartial agencies, is the precondition for the functioning of formal property rights. However, many developing countries can be characterized by serious deficiencies in governance, and the state's monopoly on the exercise of power may therefore be abused to appropriate property or to assist in the unfair acquisition of land by elites.[223] The property law enacted and enforced by the state will then become a so-called 'empty institution',[224] rather than a credible institution which can be appealed to by proper-

219 Braguinsky 1999.

220 See also Frye & Zhuravskaya 2000, who find that in three cities of Russia, shopkeepers who faced particularly extensive (predatory) regulations were more likely to have had contact with private protection rackets than shopkeepers who faced a lighter regulatory burden. The Sicilian mafia is also understood as a substitute for public enforcement of property rights at a time when state provided security was scarce and banditry widespread (Bandiera 2003).

221 Fukuyama 2004, p. 16.

222 Peters 2004.

223 Deininger & Feder 2009.

224 Ho 2005, p. 13.

ty owners in case of being invaded, regardless of who the invader is, a government official or ordinary citizen. In that case, property law 'remains nothing more than a paper agreement or a hollow shell with little or even a negative effect on the actions of social actors'.[225]

4. Conclusion

For a long time in economics and jurisprudence, property rights in general and property law in particular are regarded as the fundamental precondition for sustainable economic growth, and are used to explain the differences in economic performance across countries. Property rights, or more precisely, those formal, individualized property rights are expected to encourage efficient resource management, to stimulate investments in production and innovation, and hence to push the economy to a faster growth trajectory. The alleged desirability of formal private ownership has been embraced by a large number of economists and lawyers, who present numerous supportive evidence from historical and comparative perspectives (basically on the macro level), and finally become theoretical foundation for policy recommendations submitted to developing countries.[226]

When we look at those studies conducted on the micro level, especially those from African countries, however, the picture is more mixed. While some of the studies report positive and significant effects of formal private ownership on investment and other measures of economic performance, others fail to find a strong link between individualized property and economic outcomes. In general, three factors can be identified to account for the failure or insignificance of formal property rights in most developing countries. First, the malfunctioning or even nonexistence of other factor markets, particularly financial markets, tends to invalidate the effects of formal property ownership. Second, the merits of formal property rights may frequently be overweighed by their costs, which include both the direct costs of defining, measuring, and enforcing property rights through the use of state power, and opportunity costs in terms of the forgone benefits supplied by customary (common) property regime, such as scale economies, risk reduction, etc. Finally, when the state is captured by the elites and degenerates into a machine of rent seeking, or when the state itself acts as a tyrannical leviathan whose interests are mainly in exploitation, plunder, and confiscation, property law will only be regarded as a scrap of paper by property owners who will then be driven to the underworld economy and rely completely on private enforcers.

The main point here is not a simple conclusion, such as that property rights do or do not matter, but rather an exhortation to pay more attention to the complexity inherent in the functioning of property rights, such as their dependence on the extent and depth of the market, their dynamic rather than static characteristic, and their complicated interactions with the economy, polity, and society. It is therefore too optimistic, or even naïve, to embrace property privatization and formalization

225 Ho & Spoor 2006.

226 World Bank 2002.

as a panacea for economic backwardness, given the context-contingent and environment-dependent nature of property rights which is hard to generalize into an optimal model of a property regime.

As Rodrik indicates, as a first-order economic principle, property rights should be protected so that individuals will be induced to act productively and cooperatively;[227] however, such a principle does not map onto any unique institutional framework; on the contrary, there may be multiple ways of overlaying such principle onto institutional arrangements. Therefore, 'There is no unique correspondence between the *functions* that good institutions perform and the *form* that such institutions take'.[228] In other words, one size can not fit all. At least for some countries, economic growth can be achieved despite apparently weak *de jure* property rights, provided that some substitute strategies can be found to assure investors and entrepreneurs that their fruits will not be appropriated in the future, such as the Mexican oil industry's reliance on the U.S government's intervention,[229] or some unorthodox institutional practices adopted in China's transition.[230] On the other hand, as our study has shown, well-designed property law may be proved to be *de facto* dysfunctional or impractical, if it is not supported by effective enforcement mechanisms, or not compatible with local norms and traditions.

It is hence not a surprise to find that property law seems inessential in some scenarios, at least in the short term. In the long run, however, it is more plausible to argue that an impartial and effective property law is irreplaceable and indispensable, in view of the fact that 'igniting economic growth and sustaining it are somewhat different enterprises'.[231] More specifically, the former generally requires a limited range of (often unconventional) reforms that need not overly tax the institutional capacity of the economy. The latter challenge is in many ways harder, as it requires constructing a sound institutional underpinning to maintain productive dynamism and endow the economy with resilience to shocks over the longer term. Therefore, less developed countries do not need an extensive set of institutional reforms in order to start growing, since 'when a country is so far below its potential steady-state level of income, even moderate movements in the right direction can

227 Rodrik 2007.

228 Rodrik 2007, p. 15 (italics in original).

229 Haber *et al.* 2003.

230 For example, the township and village enterprises (TVEs) were the growth engine of China until the mid-1990s, with their share in industrial value added rising to more than 50 per cent by the early 1990s. However, TVEs had a very special ownership structure: property rights were vested not in private hands or in the central government, but in local communities (townships or villages). According to Qian 2003, in the environment characteristic of China, property rights were effectively more secure under direct local government ownership than they would have been under a private property regime. The efficiency loss caused by the absence of private control rights was probably outweighed by the implicit security guaranteed by local government control (Rodrik 2007, p. 24). In addition, fiscal decentralization combined with mobile capital has created intense regional competition for private capital (for example, foreign direct investment-FDI) in China, leading local governments to provide strong de facto protection for business investment, which can be used as a substitute for the weak formal property rights and legal systems that prevail in China (Zhang 2007).

231 Rodrik 2005.

produce a big growth payoff'.[232] By contrast, sustaining growth is more difficult, and an economy may finally find itself having outgrown its institutional underpinnings without extensive institutional reform. As a part of these growth-sustaining institutions, property law will justify itself if the observation period is long enough, as we have seen from the historical evidence.

232 Rodrik 2007, p. 39.

Bibliography

Acemoglu 2005
Acemoglu, D., 'Politics and Economics in Weak and Strong States', *Journal of Monetary Economics*, 2005, p. 1199-1226.

Acemoglu, Johnson & Robinson 2001
Acemoglu, D., Johnson, S. & Robinson, J.A., 'The Colonial Origins of Comparative Development: An Empirical Investigation', *American Economic Review*, 2001, p. 1369-1401.

Agnello & Donnelley 1975
Agnello R.J. & Donnelley, L.P., 'Property Rights and Efficiency in the Oyster Industry', *Journal of Law and Economics*, 1975, p. 521-533.

Ahuja 1998
Ahuja, V., 'Land Degradation, Agricultural Productivity and Common Property: Evidence from Côte d'Ivoire', *Environment and Development Economics*, 1998, p. 7-34.

Alchian 1965
Alchian, A.A., 'Some Economics of Property Rights', *Il Politico*, 1965, p. 816-829.

Alchian 1977
Alchian, A.A., *Economic Forces at Work*, Indianapolis: Liberty Press, 1977.

Alchian & H. Demsetz 1973
Alchian, A.A. & Demsetz, H., 'The Property Rights Paradigm', *Journal of Economic History*, 1973, p. 16-27.

Allen 1999
Allen, D.W., 'Transaction Costs', in: B. Bouckaert & G. De Geest (eds.), *The Encyclopedia of Law and Economics*, Chelthenham: Edward Elgar, 1999, p. 893-926.

Alston, Libecap & Schneider 1996
Alston, L.J., Libecap, G.D. & Schneider, R., 'The Determinants and Impact of Property Rights: Land Titles on the Brazilian Frontier', *Journal of Law. Economics, and Organization*, 1996, p. 25-61.

Alston, Libecap & Mueller 1999
Alston, L.J., Libecap, G.D. & Mueller, B., 'A Model of Rural Conflict: Violence and Land Reform Policy in Brazil', *Environment and Development Economics*, 1999, p. 135-160.

Alston, Libecap & Mueller 2000
Alston, L.J., Libecap, G.D. & Mueller, B., 'Land Reform Policies, the Sources of Violent Conflict, and Implications for Deforestation in the Brazilian Amazon', *Journal of Environmental Economics and Management*, 2000, p. 162-188.

Anderson & Lueck 1992
Anderson, T.L. & Lueck, D., 'Land Tenure and Agriculture Productivity on Indian Reservations', *Journal of Law and Economics*, 1992, p. 427-454.

André & Platteau 1998
André, C. & Platteau, J., 'Land Relations under Unbearable Stress: Rwanda Caught in the Malthusian Trap', *Journal of Economic Behaviour and Organization*, 1998, p. 1-47.

Arnold & Campbell 1986
Arnold, J.E.M. & Campbell, J.G., 'Collective Management of Hill Forests in Nepal: The Community Forestry Development Project', in: *Proceedings of the Conference on Common Property Resource Management* (April 21-26, 1985), Washington D.C.: National Academy Press, 1986.

Arruñada 2003
Arruñada, B., 'Property Enforcement as Organized Consent', *Journal of Law, Economics, and Organization*, 2003, p. 401-444.

Arruñada & Garoupa 2005
Arruñada, B. & Garoupa, N., 'The Choice of Titling System in Land', *Journal of Law and Economics*, 2005, p. 709-727.

Atwood 1990
Atwood, D.A., 'Land Registration in Africa: The Impact on Agricultural Production', *World Development*, 1990, p. 659-671.

Bailey 1992
Bailey, M., 'The Approximate Optimality of Aboriginal Property Rights', *Journal of Law and Economics*, 1992, p. 183-198.

Bailey 1998
Bailey, M., 'Property Rights in Aboriginal Societies', in: P. Newman (ed.), *The New Palgrave Dictionary of Economics and Law*, London: Macmillan Reference LTD, Volume 3, 1998. p. 155-157.

Baland & Platteau 1996
Baland, J. & Platteau, J., *Halting Degradation of Natural Resources: Is There a Role for Rural Communities*, Oxford, FAO and Clarendon Press, 1996.

Bandiera 2003
Bandiera, O., 'Land Reform, the Market for Protection, and the Origins of the Sicilian Mafia: Theory and Evidence', *Journal of Law, Economics and Organization*, 2003, p. 218-244.

Barnes & Griffith-Charles 2007
Barnes, G. & Griffith-Charles, C., 'Assessing the Formal Land Market and Deformalization of Property in St. Lucia', *Land Use Policy*, 2007, p. 494-501.

Barnes, Stanfield & Barthel 2000
Barnes, G., Stanfield, D. & Barthel, K., 'Land Registration Modernization in Developing Economies: A Discussion of the Main Problems in Central/Eastern Europe, Latin America, and the Caribbean', *URISA Journal*, 2000, p. 33-42.

Barrows & Roth 1990
Barrows R. & Roth, M., 'Land Tenure and Investment in African Agriculture: Theory and Evidence', *Journal of Modern African Studies*, 1990, p. 265-297.

Barzel 1997
Barzel Y., *Economic Analysis of Property Rights*, Cambridge: Cambridge University Press, 1997.

Baumol 1990
Baumol, W.J., 'Entrepreneurship: Productive, Unproductive, and Destructive', *Journal of Political Economy*, 1990, p. 893–921.

Becker & G. Lewis 1973
Becker, G. & Lewis, G., 'On the Interaction between the Quantity and Quality of Children', *Journal of Political Economy*, 1973, p. 279-288.

Bell & Parchomovsky 2005
Bell, A. & Parchomovsky, G., 'A Theory of Property', *Cornell Law Review*, 2005, p. 531-615.

Benjaminsen & Sjaastad 2002
Benjaminsen, T.A. & Sjaastad, E., 'Race for the Prize: Land Transactions and Rent Appropriation in the Malian Cotton Zone', *European Journal of Development Research*, 2002, p. 129-152.

Berkes 1992
Berkes, F., 'Success and Failure in Marine Coastal Fisheries of Turkey', in: D.W. Bromley (ed.), *Making the Commons Work: Theory, Practice, and Policy*, San Francisco: ICS Press, 1992, p. 161-182.

Berry 1997
Berry, S., 'Tomatoes, Land and Hearsay: Property and History in Asante in the Time of Structural Adjustment', *World Development*, 1997, p. 1225-1241.

Besley 1995
Besley, T., 'Property Rights and Investment Incentives: Theory and Evidence from Ghana', *Journal of Political Economy*, 1995, p. 903-937.

Besley 1998
Besley, T., 'Investment Incentives and Property Rights', in: P. Newman (ed.), *The New Palgrave Dictionary of Economics and the Law*, Volume 2, London: Macmillan Reference LTD, 1998, p. 359-365.

Besley & Ghatak 2010
Besley, T. & Ghatak, M., 'Property Rights and Economic Development', in: D. Rodrik & M.R. Rosenzweig (eds.), *Handbook of Development Economics*, Volume 5, Amsterdam: Elsevier B.V., 2010, p. 4525-4595.

Blarel 1994
Blarel, B., 'Tenure Security and Agricultural Production under Land Scarcity: The Case of Rwanda', in: J. Bruce & S. Migot-Adholla (eds.), *Searching for Land Tenure Security in Africa*, Dubuque: Kendall/Hunt, 1994, p. 71-96.

Bottomley 1963
Bottomley, A., 'The Effect of the Common Ownership of Land Upon Resource Allocation in TripoliTania', *Land Economics*, 1963, p. 91-95.

Braguinsky 1999
Braguinsky, S., 'Enforcement of Property Rights during the Russian Transition: Problems and Some Approaches to a New Liberal Solution', *Journal of Legal Studies*, 1999, p. 515-544.

Brasselle, Gaspart & Platteau 2002
Brasselle, A., Gaspart, F. &. Platteau, J., 'Land Tenure Security and Investment Incentives: Puzzling Evidence from Burkina Faso', *Journal of Development Economics*, 2002, p. 373-418.

Bromley 1992
Bromley, D.W. (ed.), *Making the Commons Work: Theory, Practice, and Policy*, San Francisco: ICS Press, 1992.

Bromley & Chavas 1989
Bromley, D.W. &. Chavas, J., 'On Risk, Transactions and Economic Development in the Semiarid Tropics', *Economic Development and Cultural Change*, 1989, p. 719-736.

Bruce & Migot-Adholla 1994
Bruce J.W. & Migot-Adholla, S. (eds.), *Searching for Land Tenure Security in Africa*, Dubuque: Kendall/Hunt, 1994.

Carter & Olinto 2003
Carter, M.R. & Olinto, P., 'Getting Institutions 'Right' for Whom? Credit Constraints and the Impact of Property Rights on the Quality and Composition of Investment', *American Journal of Agricultural Economics*, 2003, p. 173-186.

Cavendish 2000
Cavendish, W., 'Empirical Regularities in the Poverty-Environment Relationship of Rural Households: Evidence from Zimbabwe', *World Development*, 2000, p. 1979-2003.

Cheung 1970
Cheung, S.N.S., 'The Structure of a Contract and the Theory of a Non-Exclusive Resource', *Journal of Law and Economics*, 1970, p. 49-70.

Cheung 1987
Cheung, S.N.S., 'Common Property Rights', in: J. Eatwell, M. Milgate & P. Newman (eds.), *The New Palgrave: A Dictionary of Economics*, Volume 1, London, Macmillan, 1987, p. 504-506.

Chimhowu & Woodhouse 2006
Chimhowu, A. & Woodhouse, P., 'Customary vs. Private Property Rights? Dynamics and Trajectories of Vernacular Land Markets in Sub-Saharan Africa', *Journal of Agrarian Change*, 2006, p. 346-371.

Clague *et al.* 1999
Clague, C. *et al.*, 'Contract-Intensive Money: Contract Enforcement, Property Rights, and Economic Performance', *Journal of Economic Growth*, 1999, p. 185-211.

Clark 1996
Clark, G., 'The Political Foundations of Modern Economic Growth: England, 1540-1800', *Journal of Interdisciplinary History*, 1996, p. 563-588.

Clay 2006
Clay, K., *Squatters, Production, and Violence*, Working Paper Carnegie Mellon University, 2006.

Cole 2002
Cole, D.H., *Pollution and Property, Comparing Ownership Institutions for Environmental Protection*, Cambridge: Cambridge University Press, 2002.

Cole & Grossman 2002
Cole, D.H. & Grossman, P.Z., 'The Meaning of Property Rights: Law versus Economics', *Land Economics*, 2002, p. 317-330.

Cross 2002
Cross F.B, 'Law and Economic Growth', *Texas Law Review*, 2002, p. 1737-1775.

De Alessi 1980
De Alessi, L., 'The Economics of Property Rights: A Review of the Evidence', *Research in Law and Economics*, 1980, p. 1-47.

De Alessi 2003
De Alessi, L., 'Gains from Private Property', in: T.L. Anderson & F.S. McChesney (eds.), *Property Rights: Cooperation, Conflict, and Law*, Princeton: Princeton University Press, 2003, p. 90-111.

Deininger 2003
Deininger, K., *Land Policies for Growth and Poverty Reduction*, Washington, D.C.: The World Bank, 2003.

Deininger & Binswanger 1999
Deininger, K. & Binswanger, H., 'The Evolution of the World Bank's Land Policy: Principles, Experience, and Future Challenges', *World Bank Research Observer*, 1999, p. 247-276.

Deininger & Castagnini 2006
Deininger, K. & Castagnini, R., 'Incidence and Impact of Land Conflict in Uganda', *Journal of Economic Behaviour and Organization*, 2006, p. 321-345.

Deininger & Chamorro 2004
Deininger, K. & Chamorro, J.S., 'Investment and Equity Effects of Land Regularisation: The Case of Nicaragua', *Agricultural Economics*, 2004, p. 101-116.

Deininger & Feder 2001
Deininger, K. & Feder, G., 'Land Institutions and Land Markets', in: B.L. Gardner & G.C. Rausser (eds.), *Handbook of Agricultural Economics*, Volume 1, Amsterdam, Elsevier Science, 2001, p. 288-331.

Deininger & Feder 2009
Deininger, K. & Feder, G., 'Land Registration, Governance, and Development: Evidence and Implications for Policy', *World Bank Research Observer*, 2009, p. 233-266.

Deininger & Jin 2006
Deininger, K. & Jin, S., 'Tenure Security and Land-Related Investment: Evidence from Ethiopia', *European Economic Review*, 2006, p. 1245-1277.

Delong & Shleifer 1993
Delong, J.B. & Shleifer, A., 'Princes and Merchants: European City Growth before the Industrial Revolution', *Journal of Law and Economics*, 1993, p. 671-702.

Demsetz 1967
Demsetz, H., 'Toward a Theory of Property Rights', *American Economic Review*, 1967, p. 347-359.

Demsetz 1988
Demsetz, H., 'A Framework for the Study of Ownership', in: H. Demsetz (ed.), *Ownership, Control, and the Firm*, Oxford: Basil Blackwell, 1988, p. 12-27.

Demsetz 1998
Demsetz, H., 'Property Rights', in: P. Newman (ed.), *The New Palgrave Dictionary of Economics and Law*, London: Macmillan Reference LTD, Volume 1, 1998, p. 144-154.

Demsetz 2002
Demsetz, H., 'Toward a Theory of Property Rights II:The Competition between Private and Collective Ownership', *Journal of Legal Studies*, 2002, p. S653-S672.

De Soto 2000
De Soto, H., *The Mystery of Capital: Why Capitalism Triumphs in the West and Fails Everywhere Else*, New York: Basic Books, 2000.

De Vany & Sanchez 1979
De Vany, A. & Sanchez, N., 'Land Tenure Structures and Fertility in Mexico', *Review of Economics and Statistics*, 1979, p. 67-72.

Djankov *et al.* 2003
Djankov, S. *et al.*, 'The New Comparative Economics', *Journal of Comparative Economics*, 2003, p. 595-619.

Do & Iyer 2003
Do, Q. & Iyer, L., *Land Rights and Economic Development: Evidence from Vietnam*, World Bank Policy Research Working Paper No. 3120, 2003.

Dowall & Leaf 1991
Dowall, D.E. & M., 'The Price of Land for Housing in Jakarta', *Urban Studies*, 1991, p. 707-722.

Easterly 2002
Easterly, W., *The Elusive Quest for Growth: Economist's Adventures and Misadventures in the Tropics*, Cambridge: MIT Press, 2002.

Easterly 2006
Easterly, W., *The White Man's Burden: Why the West's Efforts to Aid the Rest Have Done So Much Ill and So Little Good*, New York: The Penguin Press, 2006.

Eggertsson 1990
Eggertsson, T., *Economic Behaviour and Institutions*, Cambridge: Cambridge University Press, 1990.

Eggertsson 2003
Eggertsson, T., 'Open Access versus Common Property', in: T.L. Anderson & F.S. McChesney (eds.), *Property Rights: Cooperation, Conflict, and Law*, Princeton: Princeton University Press, 2003, p. 73-89.

Eggertsson 2005
Eggertsson, T., *Imperfect Institutions: Possibilities and Limits of Reform*, Ann Arbor: University of Michigan Press, 2005.

Ellickson 1993
Ellickson, R.C., 'Property in Land', *Yale Law Journal*, 1993, p. 1315-1400.

Faysse 2005
Faysse, N., 'Coping with the Tragedy of the Commons: Game Structure and Design of Rules', *Journal of Economic Surveys*, 2005, p. 239-261.

Feder & Feeny 1991
Feder, G. & Feeny, D., 'Land Tenure and Property Rights: Theory and Implications for Development Policy', *World Bank Economic Review*, 1991, p. 135-153.

Feder & Nishio 1999
Feder. G. & Nishio A., 'The Benefits of Land Registration and Titling: Economic and Social Perspectives', *Land Use Policy*, 1999, p. 25-43.

Feder & Onchan 1987
Feder, G. & Onchan, T., 'Land Ownership Security and Farm Investment in Thailand', *American Journal of Agricultural Economics*, 1987, p. 311-320.

Field 2005
Field, E., 'Property Rights and Investment in Urban Slums', *Journal of the European Economic Association*, 2005, p. 279-290.

Field 2007
Field, E., 'Entitled to Work: Urban Property Rights and Labor Supply in Peru', *Quarterly Journal of Economics*, 2007, p. 1561-1602.

Field & Torero 2004
Field, E. & Torero, M., *Do Property Titles Increase Credit Access Among the Urban Poor? Evidence from a Nationwide Titling Program*, Working paper, Harvard University, 2004.

Fitzpatrick 2006
Fitzpatrick, D., 'Evolution and Chaos in Property Rights Systems: The Third World Tragedy of Contested Access', *Yale Law Journal*, 2006, p. 996-1048.

Fred-Mensah 1999
Fred-Mensah, B.K., 'Capturing Ambiguities: Communal Conflict Management Alternative in Ghana', *World Development*, 1999, p. 951-965.

Frye and E. Zhuravskaya 2000
Frye, T. & Zhuravskaya, E., 'Rackets, Regulation, and the Rule of Law', *Journal of Law, Economics and Organization*, 2000, p. 478-502.

Fukuyama 2004
Fukuyama, F., *State-Building: Governance and World Order in the 21st Century*, Ithaca: Cornell University Press, 2004.

Furubotn & Pejovich 1972
Furubotn, E.G. & Pejovich, S., 'Property Rights and Economic Theory: A Survey of Recent Literature', *Journal of Economic Literature*, 1972, p. 1137-1162.

Galiani & Schargrodsky 2006
Galiani S. & Schargrodsky, E., *Property Rights for the Poor: Effects of Land Titling*, Working Paper, Universidad Torcuato Di Tella, 2006.

Gambetta 1993
Gambetta, D., *The Sicilian Mafia: the Business of Private Protection*, Cambridge: Harvard University Press, 1993.

Gavian & Fafchamps 1996
Gavian, S. & Fafchamps, M., 'Land Tenure and Allocative Efficiency in Niger', *American Journal of Agricultural Economics*, 1996, p. 460-471.

Glaeser *et al.* 2004
Glaeser, E.L. *et al.*, 'Do Institutions Cause Growth', *Journal of Economic Growth*, 2004, p. 271-303.

Glaeser, Scheinkman & Shleifer 2003
Glaeser, E.L., Scheinkman, J. & Shleifer, A., 'The Injustice of Inequality', *Journal of Monetary Economics*, 2003, p. 199-222.

Gradstein 2007
Gradstein, M., 'Inequality, Democracy and the Protection of Property Rights', *Economic Journal*, 2007, p. 252-269.

Grafton, Squires & Fox 2000
Grafton, R.Q., Squires, D. & Fox, K.J., 'Private Property and Economic Efficiency: A Study of a Common-Pool Resource', *Journal of Law and Economics*, 2000, p. 679-713.

Gray and M. Kevane 2001
Gray, L.C. & Kevane, M., 'Evolving Tenure Rights and Agricultural Intensification in Southwestern Burkina Faso', *World Development*, 2001, p. 573-587.

Grossman & Kim 1995
Grossman, H.I. & Kim, M., 'Swords or Plowshares? A Theory of the Security of Claims to Property', *Journal of Political Economy*, 1995, p. 1275-1288.

Haber, Maurer & Razo 2003
Haber, S., Maurer, N. & Razo, A., 'When the Law Does Not Matter: The Rise and Decline of the Mexican Oil Industry', *Journal of Economic History*, 2003, p. 1-32.

Hall & Jones 1999
Hall, R.E. & Jones, C.I., 'Why Do Some Countries Produce So Much More Output Per Works than Others', *Quarterly Journal of Economics*, 1999, p. 83-116.

Hanstad 1998
Hanstad, T., 'Designing Land Registration Systems for Developing Countries', *American University International Law Review*, 1998, p. 647-703.

Hardin 1968
Hardin, G., 'The Tragedy of the Commons', *Science*, 1968, p. 1243-1248.

Hart, Shleifer & Vishny 1997
Hart, O. Shleifer, A. & Vishny, R., 'The Proper Scope of Government: Theory and an Application to Prisons', *Quarterly Journal of Economics*, 1997, p. 1127-1161.

Hayek 1945
Hayek, F.A., 'The Use of Knowledge in Society', *American Economic Review*, 1945, p. 519-530.

Heller 1998
Heller, M.A., 'The Tragedy of the Anticommons: Property in the Transition from Marx to Markets', *Harvard Law Review*, 1998, p. 621-688.

Heller 1999
Heller, M.A., 'The Boundaries of Private Property', *Yale Law Journal*, 1999, p. 1163-1223.

Hellman, Jones & Kaufmann 2003
Hellman, J.S., Jones, G. & Kaufmann, D., 'Seize the State, Seize the Day: State Capture and Influence in Transition Economies', *Journal of Comparative Economics*, 2003, p. 751-773.

Heltberg 2001
Heltberg, R., 'Determinants and Impact of Local Institutions for Common Resource Management', *Environmental and Development Economics*, 2001, p. 183-208.

Heltberg 2002
Heltberg, R., 'Property Rights and Natural Resource Management in Developing Countries', *Journal of Economic Surveys*, 2002, p. 189-214.

Higgs 1982
Higgs, R., 'Legally Induced Technical Regress in the Washington Salmon Fishery', *Research in Economic History*, 1982, p. 55-86.

Ho 2005
Ho, P., *Institutions in Transition: Land Ownership, Property Rights, and Social Conflict in China*, New York: Oxford University Press, 2005.

Ho & Spoor 2006
Ho, P. & Spoor, M., 'Whose Land? The Political Economy of Land Titling in Transitional Economies', *Land Use Policy*, 2006, p. 580-587.

Jacoby, Li & Rozelle 2002
Jacoby, H.G., Li, G. & Rozelle, S., 'Hazards of Expropriation: Tenure Insecurity and Investment in Rural China', *American Economic Review*, 2002, p. 1420-1447.

Jacoby & Minten 2007
Jacoby, H.G. & Minten, B., 'Is Land Titling in Sub-Saharan Africa Cost-Effective? Evidence from Madagascar', *World Bank Economic Review*, 2007, p. 461-485.

Janczyk 1977
Janczyk, J.T., 'An Economic Analysis of the Land Title Systems for Transferring Real Property', *Journal of Legal Studies*, 1977, p. 213-233.

Jimenez 1984
Jimenez, E., 'Tenure Security and Urban Squatting', *Review of Economics and Statistics*, 1984, p. 556-567.

Jodha 1992
Jodha, N.S., *Common Property Resources: A Missing Dimension of Development Strategies*, World Bank Discussion Paper, No. 169, 1992.

Johnson 1972
Johnson, O.E.G., 'Economic Analysis, the Legal Framework and Land Tenure Systems', *Journal of Law and Economics*, 1972, p. 259-276.

Jones 1981
Jones, E.L., *The European Miracle: Environments, Economies, and Geopolitics in the History of Europe and Asia*, Cambridge: Cambridge University Press, 1981.

Kim 2004
Kim, A.M., 'A Market without the 'Right' Property Rights: Ho Chi Minh City, Vietnam's Newly-Emerged Private Real Estate Market', *Economics of Transition*, 2004, p. 275-305.

Klerman & Mahoney 2005
Klerman, D.M. & Mahoney, P.G., 'The Value of Judicial Independence: Evidence from Eighteenth Century England', *American Law and Economics Review*, 2005, p. 1-27.

Knack & Keefer 1995
Knack S. Keefer, P., 'Institutions and Economic Performance: Cross-Country Tests Using Alternative Institutional Measures', *Economics and Politics*, 1995, p. 207-227.

Kung 1995
Kung, J.K.S., 'Equal Entitlement versus Tenure Security under a Regime of Collective Property Rights: Peasants' Preference for Institutions in Post-Reform Chinese Agriculture', *Journal of Comparative Economics*, 1995, p. 82-111.

Landes 1998
Landes, D.S., *The Wealth and Poverty of Nations: Why Some Are So Rich and Some Are So Poor*, New York: W.W. Norton & Company, 1998.

Lange 1936
Lange, O., 'On the Economic Theory of Socialism: Part One', *Review of Economic Studies*, 1936, p. 53-71.

Lange 1937
Lange, O., 'On the Economic Theory of Socialism: Part Two', *Review of Economic Studies*, 1937, p. 123-142.

Lanjouw & Levy 2002
Lanjouw, J.O. & Levy, P.I., 'Untitled: A Study of Formal and Informal Property Rights in Urban Ecuador', *Economic Journal*, 2002, p. 986-1019.

Lanjouw & Levy 2004
Lanjouw, J.O. & Levy, P.I., 'A Difficult Question in Deed: A Cost-Benefit Framework for Titling Programs', *William and Marry Law Review*, 2004, p. 889-952.

Leeson 2007
Leeson, P.T., 'Better Off Stateless: Somalia Before and After Government Collapse', *Journal of Comparative Economics*, 2007, p. 689-710.

Leeson & Williamson 2009
Leeson, P.T. & Williamson, C.R., 'Anarchy and Development: An Application of the Theory of Second Best', *Law and Development Review*, 2009, p. 76-96.

Lerner 1944
Lerner, A., *The Economics of Control*, New York: The Macmillan Company, 1944.

Li, Rozelle & Brandt 1998
Li, G., Rozelle, S. & Brandt, L., 'Tenure, Land Rights, and Farmer Investment Incentives in China', *Agricultural Economics*, 1998, p. 63-71.

Libecap 1989
Libecap, G.D., *Contracting for Property Rights*, New York: Cambridge University Press, 1989.

Libecap 1998
Libecap, G.D., 'Common Property', in: P. Newman (ed.), *The New Palgrave Dictionary of Economics and Law*, London: Macmillan Reference LTD, Volume 1, 1998, p. 317-324.

López 1995
López, R., *Resource Degradation, Community Controls and Agricultural Production in Tropical Areas*, Working Paper, Department of Agriculture and Resource Economics, University of Maryland, 1995.

López 1997
López, R., 'Environmental Externalities in Traditional Agriculture and the Impact of Trade Liberalization: The Case of Ghana', *Journal of Development Economics*, 1997, p. 17-39.

Lueck 1994
Lueck, D., 'Common Property as an Egalitarian Share Contract', *Journal of Economic Behaviour and Organization*, 1994, p. 93-108.

Lueck & Miceli 2007
Lueck. D. & Miceli, T., 'Property Law', in: A.M. Polinsky & S. Shavell (eds.), *Handbook of Law and Economics*, Amsterdam: Elsevier B.V., 2007, p. 183-257.

Matlon 1994
Matlon, P., 'Indigenous Land Use Systems and Investment in Soil Fertility in Burkina Faso', in: J. Bruce & S. Migot-Adholla (eds.), *Searching for Land Tenure Security in Africa*, Dubuque: Kendall/Hunt, 1994, p. 41-69.

McChesney 2003
McChesney, F.S., 'Government as Definer of Property Rights: Tragedy Exiting the Commons', in: T.L. Anderson & F.S. McChesney (eds.), *Property Rights: Cooperation, Conflict, and Law*, Princeton: Princeton University Press, 2003, p. 227-253.

Mckean 1982
Mckean, M.A., 'The Japanese Experience with Scarcity: Management of Traditional Common Lands', *Environmental Review*, 1982, p. 63-88.

Meinzen-Dick & Mwangi 2008
Meinzen-Dick, R. & Mwangi, E., 'Cutting the Web of Interests: Pitfalls of Formalizing Property Rights', *Land Use Policy*, 2008, p. 36-43.

Merrill & Smith 2000
Merrill, T.W. & Smith, H., 'Optimal Standardization in the Law of Property: The *Numerus Clausus* Principle', *Yale Law Journal*, 2000, p. 1-70.

Miceli 1998
Miceli, T.J., 'Land Title Systems', in: P. Newman (ed.), *The New Palgrave Dictionary of Economics and Law*, Volume 2, London: Macmillan Reference LTD, 1998, p. 433-437.

Miceli & Sirmans 1995
Miceli, T.J. & Sirmans, C.F., 'The Economics of Land Transfer and Title Insurance', *Journal of Real Estate Finance and Economics*, 1995, p. 81-88.

Miceli & Sirmans 1998
Miceli, T.J. & Sirmans, C.F., 'Title Assurance and Incentives for Efficient Land Use', *European Journal of Law and Economics*, 1998, p. 305-323.

Miceli, Sirmans & Turnbull 2000
Miceli, T.J., Sirmans, C.F. & Turnbull, G.K., 'The Dynamic Effects of Land Title Systems', *Journal of Urban Economics*, 2000, p. 370-389.

Migot-Adholla *et al.* 1991
Migot-Adholla, S. *et al.*, 'Indigenous Land Rights Systems in Sub-Saharan Africa: A Constraint on Productivity', *World Bank Economic Review*, 1991, p. 155-175.

Milhaupt & West 2000
Milhaupt, C.J. & West, M.D., 'The Dark Side of Private Ordering: An Institutional and Empirical Analysis of Organized Crime', *University of Chicago Law Review*, 2000, p. 41-98.

Mokyr 1990
Mokyr, J., *The Lever of Richs: Technological Creativity and Economic Progress*, New York: Oxford University Press, 1990.

Mokyr 2008
Mokyr, J., 'The Institutional Origins of the Industrial Revolution', in: E. Helpman (ed.), *Institutions and Economic Performance*, Cambridge: Harvard University Press, 2008, p. 64-119.

Mokyr 2009
Mokyr, J., 'Intellectual Property Rights, the Industrial Revolution, and the Beginnings of Modern Economic Growth', *American Economic Review*, 2009, p. 349-355.

Moselle & Polak 2001
Moselle, B. & Polak, B., 'A Model of a Predatory State', *Journal of Law, Economics and Organization*, 2001, p. 1-33.

Murphy, Shleifer & Vishny 1991
Murphy, K.M., Shleifer, A. & Vishny, R., 'The Allocation of Talent: Implications for Growth', *Quarterly Journal of Economics*, 1991, p. 503-530.

Murphy, Shleifer & Vishny 1993
Murphy, K.M., Shleifer, A. & Vishny, R., 'Why is Rent-Seeking So Costly to Growth', *American Economic Review*, 1993, p. 409-414.

North 1981
North, D.C., *Structure and Change in Economic History*, New York: W.W. Norton & Company, 1981.

North & Thomas 1973
North, D.C. & Thomas, R.P., *The Rise of the Western World: A New Economic History*, New York: Cambridge University Press, 1973.

North & Weingast 1989
North, D.C. & Weingast, B.R., 'Constitutions and Commitment: The Evolution of Institutions Governing Public Choice in Seventeenth-Century England', *Journal of Economic History*, 1989, p. 803-832.

Ostrom 1990
Ostrom, E., *Governing the Commons: The Evolution of Institutions for Collective Action*, New York: Cambridge University Press, 1990.

Ostrom 1999
Ostrom, E., 'Private and Common Property Rights', in: B. Bouckaert & G. De Geest (eds.), *The Encyclopedia of Law and Economics*, Chelthenham: Edward Elgar, 1999, p. 332-379.

Ostrom 2008
Ostrom, E., 'Tragedy of the Commons', in: S.N. Durlauf and L.E. Blume (eds.), *The New Palgrave Dictionary of Economics*, New York: Palgrave Macmillan, 2008, available at: <http://www.dictionaryofeconomics.com/article?id=pde2008_T000193>.

Pande & Udry 2006
Pande, R. & Udry, C., 'Institutions and Development: A View from Below', in: R. Blundell, W.K. Newey & T. Persson (eds.), *Advances in Economics and Econometrics: Theory and Applications* (Ninth World Congress), New York: Cambridge University Press, 2006, p. 349-411.

Pattanayak & Sills 2001
Pattanayak, S.K. & Sills, E.O., 'Do Tropical Forests Provide Natural Insurance? The Microeconomics of Non-Timber Forest Product Collection in the Brazilian Amazon', *Land Economics*, 2001, p. 595-612.

Pejovich 1990
Pejovich, S., *The Economics of Property Rights: Towards a Theory of Comparative Systems*, Dordrecht: Kluwer Academic Publishers, 1990.

Pender & Kerr 1998
Pender, J.L. & Kerr, J.M., 'Determinants of Farmers' Indigenous Soil and Water Conservation Investments in Semi-Arid India', *Agricultural Economics*, 1998, p. 113-125.

Pender *et al.* 2004
Pender, J.L. *et al.*, 'Strategies to Increase Agricultural Productivity and Reduce Land Degradation: Evidence from Uganda', *Agricultural Economics*, 2004, p. 181-195.

Peters 2004
Peters, P.E., 'Inequality and Social Conflict over Land in Africa', *Journal of Agrarian Change*, 2004, p. 269-314.

Pinckney & Kimuyu 1994
Pinckney & Kimuyu, P.K., 'Land Tenure Reform in East Africa: Good, Bad, or Unimportant', *Journal of African Economics*, 1994, p. 1-28.

Pipes 1999
Pipes, R., *Property and Freedom*, London: The Harvill Press, 1999.

Place 2009
Place, F., 'Land Tenure and Agricultural Productivity in Africa: A Comparative Analysis of the Economics Literature and Recent Policy Strategies and Reforms', *World Development*, 2009, p. 1326-1336.

Place & Hazell 1993
Place, F. & Hazell, P., 'Productivity Effects of Indigenous Land Tenure Systems in Sub-Saharan Africa', *American Journal of Agricultural Economics*, 1993, p. 10-19.

Place & Otsuka 2001
Place, F. & Otsuka, K., 'Tenure, Agricultural Investment, and Productivity in the Customary Tenure Sector of Malawi', *Economic Development and Cultural Change*, 2001, p. 77-99.

Place & Otsuka 2002
Place, F. & Otsuka, K., 'Land Tenure Systems and Their impacts on Agricultural Investments and Productivity in Uganda', *Journal Development Studies*, 2002, p. 105-128.

Platteau 2000
Platteau, J., *Institutions, Social Norms, and Economic Development*, Amsterdam: Harwood Academic Publishers, 2000.

Platteau & Francois 2005
Platteau, J. & Francois, P., 'Commons as Insurance and the Welfare Impact of Privatization', *Journal of Public Economics*, 2005, p. 211-231.

Polishchuk & Savvateev 2004
Polishchuk, L. & Savvateev, A., 'Spontaneous (Non)Emergence of Property Rights', *Economics of Transition*, 2004, p. 103-127.

Posner 2002
Posner, R., *Economic Analysis of Law*, New York: Aspen Publishers, 2002.

Powell, Ford & Nowrasteh 2008
Powell, B., Ford, R. & Nowrasteh, A., 'Somalia after State Collapse: Chaos or Improvement', *Journal of Economic Behaviour and Organization*, 2008, p. 657-670.

Qian 2003
Qian, Y., 'How Reform Worked in China', in: D. Rodrik (ed.), *In Search of Prosperity: Analytical Narratives of Economic Growth*, Princeton: Princeton University Press, 2003, p. 297-333

Quinn 2001
Quinn, S., 'The Glorious Revolution's Effect on English Private Finance: A Micro-history, 1680-1705', *Journal of Economic History*, 2001, p. 593-615.

Quisumbing 2001
Quisumbing, A.R., 'Women's Land Rights in the Transition to Individualized Ownership: Implications for Tree-Resource Management in Western Ghana', *Economic Development and Cultural Change*, 2001, p. 157-182.

Rodrik 2005
Rodrik, D., 'Growth Strategies', in: P. Aghion & S.N. Durlauf (eds.), *Handbook of Economic Growth*, Volume 1A, Amsterdam: Elsevier B.V., 2005, p. 967-1014.

Rodrik 2007
Rodrik, D., *One Economics, Many Recipes: Globalization, Institutions, and Economic Growth*, Princeton, Princeton University Press, 2007.

Roland 2000
Roland, G., *Transition and Economics: Politics, Markets, and Firms*, Cambridge: MIT Press, 2000.

Rosenberg & Birdzell 1986
Rosenberg, N. & Birdzell Jr., L.E., *How the West Grew Rich: The Economic Transformation of the Industrial World*, New York: Basic Books, 1986.

Roth, Cochrane & Kisamba-Mugerwa 1994
Roth, M., Cochrane, J. & Kisamba-Mugerwa, W., 'Tenure Security, Credit Use, and Farm Investment in the Rujumbura Pilot Land Registration Scheme, Uganda', in: J. Bruce & S. Migot-Adholla (eds.), *Searching for Land Tenure Security in Africa*, Dubuque: Kendall/Hunt, 1994, p. 169-198.

Schweigert 2006
Schweigert, T., 'Land Title, Tenure Security, Investment and Farm Output: Evidence from Guatemala', *Journal of Developing Areas*, 2006, p. 115-126.

Shleifer 1998
Shleifer, A., 'State versus Private Ownership', *Journal of Economic Perspectives*, 1998, p. 133-150.

Singh 1994
Singh, K., *Managing Common Pool Resources: Principles and Case Studies*, New Delhi: Oxford University Press, 1994.

Sjaastad & Bromley 1997
Sjaastad, E. & Bromley, D.W., 'Indigenous Land Rights in Sub-Saharan Africa: Appropriation, Security, and Investment Demand', *World Development*, 1997, p. 549-562.

Skaperdas 1992
Skaperdas, S., 'Cooperation, Conflict, and Power in the Absence of Property Rights', *American Economic Review*, 1992, p. 720-739.

Smith 2000
Smith, H.E., 'Semicommon Property Rights and Scattering in the Open Fields', *Journal of Legal Studies*, 2000, p. 131-169.

Sonin 2003
Sonin, K., 'Why the Rich May Favor Poor Protection of Property Rights', *Journal of Comparative Economics*, 2003, p. 715-731.

Stasavage 2003
Stasavage, D., *Public Debt and the Birth of the Democratic State: France and Great Brittan, 1688-1789*, New York: Cambridge University Press, 2003.

Stasavage 2007
Stasavage, D., 'Partisan Politics and Public Debt: The Importance of the 'Whig Supremacy' for Britain's Financial Revolution', *European Review of Economic History*, 2007, p. 123-153.

Stokes, Schutjer & Bulatao 1986
Stokes, S., Schutjer, W.A. & Bulatao, R.A., 'Is the Relationship between Landholding and Fertility Spurious? A Response to Cain', *Population Studies*, 1986, p. 305-311.

Sussman & Yafeh 2006
Sussman, N. & Yafeh, Y., 'Institutional Reforms, Financial Development and Sovereign Debt: Britain 1690-1790', *Journal of Economic History*, 2006, p. 906-935.

Trebilcock & Veel 2008
Trebilcock, M. & Veel, P., 'Property Rights and Development: The Contingent Case for Formalization', *University of Pennsylvania Journal of International Law*, 2008, p. 397-481.

Umbeck 1981
Umbeck, J., 'Might Makes Rights: A Theory of the Formation and Initial Distribution of Property Rights', *Economic Inquiry*, 1981, p. 38-59.

Wade 1994
Wade, R., *Village Republics: Economic Conditions for Collective Action in South India*, San Francisco: ICS Press, 1994.

Wen 1995
Wen, G.J., 'The Land Tenure System and Its Saving and Investment Mechanism: The Case of Modern China', *Asian Economic Journal*, 1995, p. 223-259.

World Bank 2002
World Bank, *Building Institutions for Markets (World Development Report 2002)*, New York: Oxford University Press, 2002.

Zhang 2007
Zhang, X., 'Asymmetric Property Rights in China's Economic Growth', *William Mitchell Law Review*, 2007, p. 567-589.

Michael Faure

DOES ENVIRONMENTAL LAW MATTER?*

1. Introduction

A book addressing legal origins and the importance of institutions in economic development cannot ignore environmental policy for the simple reason that there has been a large literature dealing with the relationship between environmental pollution and economic development. At first blush economic development, increasing industrialization and economic activity seem to be the enemy of environmental quality. Many will indeed assume that with increasing industrialization also pollution levels will increase. Looking at the history of industrialization in e.g. Europe this may largely be correct. Moreover, some developing countries that have a low level of industrialization, such as e.g. in Africa, seem to have low levels of pollution as well for the simple reason that they lack industry that could pollute. However, there is an interesting body of literature showing that this story (more industrialization and economic development leading to more pollution) is only partly correct. At some point where income levels are high and pollution peaks a preference for environmental protection may emerge as a result of which increasing economic development and rising income levels may hence lead to less pollution. This development is known as the Environmental Kuznets Curve (EKC) and has been used at the policy level by the World Bank. The normative conclusion from this literature seems indeed to be (to put it rather bluntly): the best way to promote environmental protection in a country is to promote economic development. The real relationship between economic development and pollution levels seems, as often, however, to be much more nuanced and balanced.

An important question in this debate is of course also whether not only economic development, but also institutions and the regulatory structure of a country may affect pollution levels. There is increasing empirical evidence that this would indeed be the case, which would support the hypothesis that also in the

* I am grateful to Jan Smits for useful comments on an earlier draft of this chapter, to Marina Jodogne for excellent editorial assistance and to Liu Jing and Yleen Simonis for research assistance.

environmental area, institutions do play an important role, not only for economic development, but also for improving environmental quality.

A related question is to what extent the regulatory stringency in a country affects trade flows and more particularly location decisions of industry. Some hold that when a country would have a very weak environmental protection regime this may attract polluting industries. These may either *ex ante* decide to locate their polluting activity in a country with a lax environmental regime or may decide to relocate. This is in the literature referred to as the Pollution Haven Hypothesis (PHH) and is, especially in the federalism debate, often referred to as the race-to-the-bottom rationale. The question therefore arises to what extent variance in environmental stringency between legal systems will indeed affect mobility. In other words, to what extent is there proof of a Pollution Haven Hypothesis?

It is in that respect particularly interesting to look at one particular case, being Eastern Europe. Since the enlargement in 2004 a free mobility of capital, labour, persons and services provides a setting within which in Europe industry could also move to pollution havens, presumably being located in Central and Eastern Europe. The question arises to what extent this effectively occurs and what the consequences may be for European environmental law and policy in general.

Of course the question to what extent environmental law does matter has a far broader scope than the topics mentioned here. One could for example also examine the relative environmental effectiveness of various environmental instruments (liability rules, regulation, market-based instruments) or analyse to what extent various enforcement strategies affect behaviour of industry. These questions, however interesting they may be, are outside of the scope of this chapter.[1] In this chapter I will merely focus on the aspects mentioned above, which are crucial for the central question of this volume, being to what extent economic development affects environmental quality and how the relative stringency of an environmental regime may attract industry.

The remainder of this chapter is set up as follows: first the relationship between economic development and environmental quality is reviewed (2); next the empirical evidence concerning the Pollution Haven Hypothesis is examined (3) and attention is paid to the specific case of Eastern Europe (4). I end with a few concluding remarks (5).

2. Economic Development and Environmental Quality

2.1. *Environmental Kuznets Curve: Theory and Empirics*

The idea of the Environmental Kuznets Curve is named after the Nobel prize winner Simon Kuznets who wrote on the relationship between income inequality and income levels in a country.[2] Since the 1980s scholars have also applied this concept to environmental pollution, establishing an empirical relationship between

1 For an overview of the literature in this domain see Faure 2012.

2 Kuznets 1955.

measures of environmental quality and national income.[3] This literature showed an inverted u-shaped relationship, meaning that in a first phase of economic development (at low income levels) increasing economic development led to increasing environmental degradation. However, there is a certain turning point (the top of the inverted u-curve) where income levels have increased to such a point that a demand for higher environmental quality emerges and where hence increased economic welfare leads to increased environmental improvements. This work has especially become known through the World Bank which referred to it in its World Development Report 1992. The normative lesson that was drawn from this literature was obviously that developing countries would have an interest in fighting poverty and increasing income levels, since this would also lead to higher levels of environmental quality. This vision has strongly been voiced by Beckerman, who was involved in drafting the 1992 World Development Report of the World Bank.[4] He for example holds 'it is fairly clear that the best way to improve the environment of the fast mass of the world's population is to enable them to maintain economic growth' and 'the strong correlation between incomes and the extent to which environmental protection measures are adopted demonstrates that, in the longer run, the surest way to improve your environment is to become rich'.[5]

The Environmental Kuznets Curve (EKC) is at first blush surprising since the dominant view may be that more economic development (industrialization) will automatically lead to more environmental pollution. The EKC shows that in the beginning of industrialization and economic development that may indeed be the case, but that there is a point where environmental pollution peaks and subsequently increasing income levels lead to decreased pollution and higher levels of environmental quality. There is, as I will show below, empirical evidence (although debated) to support the EKC, but the difficulty is of course to identify the precise causality behind the relationship. Simply stating that increasing income levels in the end leads to less pollution is obviously too simple. Strand presents five reasons why, theoretically the EKC may work, in other words why higher income levels in a country could lead to lower pollution levels.[6]

1. When incomes grows there may be a tendency for a larger share of total demand to consist of services rather than manufactured goods. This could explain why environmental and resource burdens decrease as income grows.

2. General technological process leads to greater efficiency in the use of energy and materials. This idea is also strongly related to the work of Michael Porter, holding that environmental improvement does not necessarily come at the expense of competitiveness. Porter showed that, to the contrary increased environmental performance will also lead to an increased com-

3 See especially Grossman & Krueger 1993, and see Grossman & Krueger 1995.
4 Beckerman 1992.
5 Beckerman 1992, p. 491.
6 Strand 2002, p. 6-8.

petitiveness of nations and industries.[7] This has been known as the 'Porter hypothesis', showing that not only countries, but also companies may benefit from investments in environmental protection since it could increase their competitiveness.

3. The increase of income can also lead to changing preferences of the population: once the basic needs are satisfied the population may value a clean environment especially since it wants to enjoy free time and recreate in a clean environment. In the words of Arrow *et al.* 'People spend proportionally more on environmental quality as their income raises'.8

4. With increasing economic development an educated population may pressure for democratic reform and democratic societies tend to be more environmentally friendly.

5. Given different levels of income between countries increasing income may lead to an environmentally burdening production to move to low income countries. This environmental dumping to pollution havens[9] may reduce pollution levels in the rich countries which are able to relocate polluting activities to lower income countries.

The fact that so many different reasons could explain the interaction between income and environmental quality also points at the methodological problems in many of the EKC relationships. In fact these relationships (between income, technical progress and environmental quality) may also be determined by other underlying variables.[10] This explains that the empirical literature concerning the EKC does not provide unequivocal results. The first studies, on which the World bank study was also based, for example the one by Shafik and Bandyopadhyay[11] focused on various environmental indicators (such as clean water, urban sanitation, municipal waste etc.) related to income. Some empirical studies roughly show a relationship between per capita income and various environmental indicators and indeed suggest that (depending upon the indicator) where environmental pollution is first rising as income increases, after a turning point (referred to as the peak) pollution levels will be falling.[12] The literature on the EKC is meanwhile so abundant that one could easily fill an entire book with an overview.[13] It may be most useful to provide

7 Porter & Vanderlinde 1995.

8 Arrow *et al.* 1995, p. 92.

9 On which more in section 3 below.

10 See Strand 2002, p. 10.

11 Shafik & Bahdyopadhyay 1992.

12 See for example Selden & Song 1995. See also the contributions to the special issue on environment and development economics devoted to the environmental Kuznets curve. For a summary Barbier 1997.

13 In addition to the overview by Barbier 1997 just mentioned, see also the more recent literature overview by Dasgupta *et al.* 2002, p. 149-151 and see Stern 1998 who is very critical on the EKC literature.

a few overviews of the literature as recently summarized by Strand[14] and to point at the few recent studies on evidence of the EKC in particular developing countries.

Table 1: *Summary of EKC studies for national air pollution indicies.* All figures in USD[15]

Study	**Sulphur Dioxide**	**Smoke**	**Heavy Particles**	**NO_x**	**CO**
Grossman-Krueger (1995)	Peak at 4050, trough at 14000	Peaks at 6150	Monotonical-ly Decreasing		
Shafik and Bandyopadhyay (1992); Shafik (1994)	Peaks at 3300		Peaks at 3-3500		
Panayotou (1995)	Peaks at 3000		Peaks at 4500	Peaks at 5500	
Selden and Song (1994)	Peaks at 8700		Peaks at 10300	Peaks at 11200	Peaks at 6000
Cole *et al.* (1997)	Peaks at 6900		Peaks at 7300	Peaks at 14700	Peaks at 9900
List and Gallet (1999)	Variable, peaks at 22000 (USD only)				
Stern and Common (2001)	Peaks at 9000 (OECD), 30-100000 (world)				

Note: Figures are not always comparable; mostly in 1990-1995 USD at PPP rates.

Table 2: *Summary of EKC studies for national water pollution indicies*[16]

Study	**(Minus) dissolved oxygen**	**BOD**	**COD**	**Faecal coliform**	**Total coliform**	**Nitrates**
Grossman and Kruger (1995)	Peaks at 2700	Peaks at 7600	Peaks at 7800	Peaks at 8000	Peaks at 3100	Peaks at 10000
Shafik and Bandyopadhyay	Increases uniformly					
Cole *et al.* (1997)						Peaks at 15600

14 Strand 2002.

15 Strand 2002, p. 13.

16 Strand 2002, p. 13.

Table 3: *Summary of EKC studies for national concentration of heavy metals*[17]

Study	General	Toxicity	Lead	Cadmium	Arsenic	Mercury
Grossman and Krueger (1995)			Peaks at 1900	Peaks at 11600	Peaks at 4900	Peaks at 5100
Hettige *et al.* (1992)		Peaks at 12800				
Rock (1996)	Peaks at 10800					

If one were to summarize this literature one could hold that most studies find a tendency for particular environmental components such as e.g. water and sewage coverage to increase with income, but to the contrary municipal waste increases with income as well, which runs counter to the EKC. A particular out-layer seems to be constituted by CO_2 emissions which would either peak at a very high level of $ 35,000[18] or could not have reached a peak at all.[19] Cole *et al.* also show that meaningful EKCs only exist for local air pollutants: urban air concentrations will peak at lower income levels than per capita emissions. Global air pollutants, however, will increase monotonically with income.[20]

The problem with these studies[21] is that the studies can indicate a correlation between rising income levels and environmental quality but of course not necessarily a causality. Hence, it remains ambiguous what precisely drives this relationship.

It may be interesting, to conclude this brief overview of the available empirical literature, by having a look at some studies examining the EKC in developing countries. A similar, rather ambiguous picture is presented in a study using cross-country data on the relationship between per capita income and environmental degradation for China.[22] The paper uses cross-province penal data of seven pollutants from China and finds evidence of an EKC hypothesis in five pollutants whereas for two other pollutants an N-shaped curve was shown. Also a study addressing trends in air and water pollution in Malaysia finds that the hypothesized EKC relationship between income and particular pollutants could not be confirmed. It were rather shifting patterns of population and most important, the impacts of environmental policies that explained the variance in pollutants. The study concludes 'that policy-makers in developing countries should not assume that economic growth will automatically solve air and water pollution problems'.[23]

17 Strand 2002, p. 14.

18 Shafik 1994.

19 Holtz-Eakin & Selden 1995. See on the (complicated) case of CO_2 emissions also Moomaw & Unruh 1997.

20 Cole, Rayner & Bates 1997, p. 411-412.

21 And that particularly gives rise to much of the criticism which will be discussed in 2.3.

22 See Shen & Hashimoto 2004.

23 Vincent 1997, p. 430.

2.2. *Policy Consequences*

Irrespective of the criticism that some have on this EKC literature (see below 2.3) the question arises what normative lessons can be drawn from this literature at the policy level. Some argue that this literature, indicating that after a turning point increasing income levels lead to higher environmental quality, gives at least some room for optimism in the sense that economic development is apparently accompanied with such technological progress that environmental degradation, at least for traditional environmental quality variables such as air and water quality can be successfully reduced.[24] However, looking at the EKC literature in this simple way one could be tempted to deduce from this literature the (simplistic and therefore wrong) conclusion that the best way for a nation to promote environmental protection would be to promote economic growth.[25] Empirical evidence after all shows that higher income levels go hand in hand with increased environmental protection.[26] In the words of Dasgupta *et al.* 'In developing countries, some policy-makers have interpreted such results as conveying a message about priorities: grow first, then clean up.'[27] This would at first blush lead to the conclusion that regulatory instruments like environmental law could only to a limited extent influence environmental quality since this quality would to a large extent be dependent upon other factors, more particularly economic development and *per capita* income levels.

However, more refined empirical studies have shown that this conclusion would be too unbalanced. More particularly Panayotou has shown that as far as the case of ambient SO_2 levels are concerned, policies and institutions can significantly reduce environmental degradation at low income levels and speed up improvements at higher income levels.[28] Cole *et al.* have also shown that 'developed countries have "grown out of" some pollution problems' but 'this is by no means an automatic process. Pollution levels have fallen only in response to investment and policy initiatives'.[29] They also point at the fact that for transport generated emissions turning points in the EKC are higher than for local pollution. This points at the policy level at the need to tackle pollution in the transport sector and more particularly energy use. For global air pollutants the policy conclusion is that multilateral action is important since otherwise those will continue to increase monotonically with income.[30] Also Arrow and his co-authors conclude that 'economic liberalization and other policies that promote gross national product growth are not substitutes for environmental policy'. Indeed 'economic growth is not a panacea for environmental quality'.[31] Since 'in most cases where emissions have declined with

24 Strand 2002, p. 18.
25 This has been qualified by Ayres as 'false and pernicious nonsense' (Ayres 1995).
26 See also Esty & Porter 1998 and Esty & Porter 2000.
27 Dasgupta *et al.* 2002, p. 147.
28 Panayotou 1997. See also de Bruyn 1997 who equally argues that environmental policy, fostered by international agreements, explains why SO_2 emissions curb downward at high income levels.
29 Cole, Rayner & Bates 1997, p. 412.
30 Cole, Rayner & Bates 1997, p. 412.
31 Arrow *et al.* 1995, p. 93.

raising income, the reductions have been due to local institutional reforms such as environmental legislation and market-based incentives to reduce environmental impacts'.[32] Dasgupta *et al.* also show that the primary reason to make the Environmental Kuznets Curve lower and flatter (and hence reach quicker the turning point towards decreasing pollution with raising income levels) is related to the primary role of environmental regulation. Richer countries simply regulate pollution more strictly which is an important explanation for the EKC.[33]

This conclusion is obviously in line with much of the other legal origins literature, discussed in many other chapters of this book, holding that institutions and legal infrastructure are an important determinator of economic growth.[34]

It has more particularly been the contribution of Dan Esty and Michael Porter who examined empirically to what extent not only income levels, as suggested by the Environmental Kuznets Curve literature, but also a nation's regulatory regime influences environmental quality. The result of this powerful research, based on an examination of regulatory intensity and environmental quality in a great number of developed and developing countries, is that economic development and environmental protection go hand in hand with the improvement of a country's institutions and more particularly the environmental regulatory regime.[35] They find that not only the rigour and structure of environmental regulations have a particular impact on environmental performance, but also the enforcement. The empirical evidence hence suggests that a country can benefit environmentally not only from economic growth, but equally from developing the rule of law and strengthening its governance structures.[36] Interestingly, they also found evidence that countries that adopted a stringent environmental regime relative to their income were able to speed up economic growth rather than retarding it.[37]

An important policy conclusion from this empirical literature is hence that, even though the Environmental Kuznets Curve, indicates a relationship between economic growth and higher environmental quality, the lesson is hence not that environmental law does not matter. To the contrary, Esty and Porter could show convincingly that strengthening the regulatory structure also encourages the promotion of environmental quality.[38] Moreover, the evidence presented by Esty and Porter provides yet another confirmation of the so-called 'Porter hypothesis': countries adopting a stringent environmental regime should not be afraid that his endangers their competitive position since the evidence shows that this may speed up economic growth rather than retard it.

32 Arrow *et al.* 1995, p. 92.
33 For the reasons see Dasgupta *et al.* 2002, p. 152-153.
34 This point has repeatedly been made in the many papers of La Porta *et al.* 1998 and La Porta, Lopez de Silanes & Shleifer 2008 and builds of course further on the important research of Nobel prize winner Douglass North on the importance of institutions in economic growth. See North 1981, 1990.
35 See Esty & Porter 2005.
36 Esty & Porter 2005, p. 424.
37 Esty & Porter 2005, p. 425.
38 This is also agued by Binder & Neumayer 2005.

These studies also provide strong support for increasing effective regulatory capabilities in developing countries. The international community can hence play a valuable role in lowering and flattening the Environmental Kuznets Curve by financing appropriate training, policy reforms, information gathering and public environmental education.[39] Drafting effective environmental regulation for developing countries requires also that policy makers should pay enough attention to the legal, economic, political and social situations in which environmental regulation must function.[40]

An interesting study by Torras and Boyce has also shown that environmental quality in a (developing) country is not only affected by income levels, but also via a more equitable income distribution, wider literacy and greater political liberties and civil rights. The effects of these variables appear to be particularly strong in low income countries.[41] This is an important addition to the EKC literature which originally subordinated distributional concerns to economic growth. Their study implies that a focus on a fair distribution of power can equally have a positive effect on environmental quality in low income countries.

2.3. *Critics*

Above I already indicated that there are several methodological difficulties with the EKC, identified in the literature. One problem is that it is one thing to establish a correlation between income levels and environmental quality in the form of an inverted U-shaped curve; it is quite another to analyse the precise causality between those phenomena.[42] Moreover, the evidence concerning the EKC curve is sometimes also multi-directional.[43] As was also indicated above, the EKC may work for traditional parameters such as air and water pollution variables (local environmental indicators), but not for more complicated ones having to do with global warming and biodiversity such as carbon dioxide levels: these do not necessarily improve with higher incomes.[44] Also Arrow et al. caution the interpretation of the EKC since

> 'the relation has been shown to be valid for pollutants involving local short-term costs (for example, sulphur, particulates and faecal coliforms) not for accumulation of stocks of waste or for pollutants involving long-term and more dispersed costs (such as CO_2) which are often increasing functions of income'.[45]

Also, the evidence from developing countries does not always fully support the EKC story. For example for India there is on the one hand technological innovation which reduces environmental pollution (a technique effect), but at the same time the

39 So Dasgupta *et al*. 2002, p. 163-164.
40 So Faure, Goodwin & Weber 2010; see also McAllister, Van Rooij & Kagan 2010.
41 Torras & Boyce 1998, p. 158.
42 So Strand 2002, p. 15-16.
43 See in that respect especially List & Gallet 1999 who argue concerning the EKC that 'one size does not fit all'.
44 Cole, Rayner & Bates 1997, p. 412.
45 Arrow *et al*. 1995, p. 92.

scale of polluting activities is of such a magnitude that it outperforms the positive technique effects. The end result is that with rising income levels environmental productivity in India in fact decreases.[46] Also Brazilian research showed that it is more particularly increases education level and some other social indicators which can generate higher probabilities of changes on individual demand for environmental goods and services. There is, according to this Brazilian research, no direct relationship between poverty and environmental degradation, but rather investments on education which could lead to having a positive effect upon demand for environmental quality.[47] Also South African research concerning the EKC casts doubt on the oft stated conclusion that economic growth automatically leads to environmental improvement. This South African research argues that the observations from the EKC may also be explained by trade patterns, more particularly by the fact that the improvement in environmental quality at higher levels of per capita income can (at least partly) be explained by the tendency of developed countries to import manufactured goods from less developed countries. They would actively involve in environmental dumping and import products from developing countries which act as pollution havens. Hence, the EKC could then be explained by the relocation of pollution intensive industries from developed to developing countries.[48]

These type of criticisms are to a large part in line with the earlier mentioned point that one should be careful with drawing normative conclusions from the EKC curve in the sense that all a developing country would have to do to achieve higher levels of environmental protection would be to increase income levels. More fundamental criticisms on the EKC literature have been formulated in many publications by Stern who *inter alia* argues that the literature only looks at two variables (income and pollution emissions) which are the outcome of a production process, but which do not explain the underlying production process which converts inputs into outputs and pollutants.[49] Stern argues that 'the EKC is an essentially empirical phenomenon, but most of the EKC literature is econometrically weak'. He continues 'it is very easy to do bad econometrics and the history of the EKC exemplifies what can go wrong'. To conclude 'when we do take such statistics into account and use appropriate techniques we find that the EKC does not exist'.[50] Various criticisms are formulated both of a theoretical and of an empirical nature.[51] Stern for example also makes the point that if an EKC type relationship can be observed it is largely the result of the effects of trade on the distribution of polluting industries.[52] Over-

46 Managi & Jena 2007.

47 Granja e Barros, Mendonça & Nogueira 2002.

48 Nahman & Antrobus 2005. However, as I will show below, the empirical evidence of this race for the bottom is relatively weak (see 3.2).

49 Stern 1998.

50 Perman & Stern 2003; they show more particularly that the EKC is a problematic concept at least in the case of sulphur emissions. This builds on Stern & Commons 2001 who had shown that reductions in sulphur emissions are time-related rather than income-related.

51 See for a methodological critique also Millimet, List & Stengos 2003.

52 Stern 2001; Common & Barbier 1996.

viewing many studies Stern concludes that the main way by which emissions of pollutants can be reduced is by time-related technique effects.[53]

The result of this criticism is that it once more warns against quick and dirty conclusions concerning the relationship between economic development and improved environmental quality. It is obviously not the increase of per capita income as such which causes a reduction of pollution levels. It is rather technological innovations but also regulatory intensity that may explain the reduced pollution levels. The latter point of course underscores the importance of institutions and the environmental regulatory environment once more.

3. The Pollution Haven Hypothesis[54]

3.1. *Theory*

The race to the bottom holds that in their competition for jobs and tax revenues, jurisdictions will set inefficiently weak environmental standards. As Levinson explains,[55] the race to the bottom is basically a version of Oates' classic argument as to why redistributive taxes are impossible at the local level.[56] If a local jurisdiction were to impose a Pigouvian tax equal to the local harm from pollution on polluters so as to reduce pollution and provide the local public good of better local environmental quality, the attempt would fail, as the taxing jurisdiction would succeed only in inducing the polluters to move to a jurisdiction that did not tax away their income. The idea is that jurisdictions would engage in a race-to-the-bottom to attract foreign investments. As a result of this, prisoners' dilemmas could arise, whereby countries would fail to enact or enforce effective legislation. Jurisdictions are thus supposed to compete against each other with lenient environmental legislation to attract industry.[57] The result would be an overall reduction of environmental quality below efficient levels. This would correspond with the traditional game theoretical result that prisoners' dilemmas create inefficiencies.

Subsequent work has shown that the race to the bottom is in fact not a necessary result, but that there are conditions under which local environmental regulation will provide the efficient level of pollution control. Oates and Schwab[58] showed that if: a) all of the citizens of a jurisdiction work in the polluting industry; b) each suffers equally from pollution; c) labour is fixed in the jurisdiction; d) capital is perfectly mobile but also competitively supplied; and, finally, e) local governments choose the environmental policies that maximize the utility of the median voter, then local pollution taxes will be socially optimal. Essentially, each citizen bears both the full cost and also the full benefit of reducing pollution, and hence chooses the optimal reduction in pollution. But Oates and Schwab's result is not robust with

53 Stern 2001; Stern 2002.
54 This section of the paper is an extension of Faure & Johnston 2009.
55 Levinson 2003, p. 91 & 93.
56 Oates 1972.
57 See Revesz 1992.
58 Oates & Schwab 1988, p. 333.

respect to variations in their underlying assumptions. If a local public good must be financed with the pollution tax on mobile capital, then the local pollution tax will be too low, so as to attract capital to essentially pay for the non-environmental public good. If some citizens work in the polluting industry but others simply collect income from another source, then if the median voter works in the polluting industry, then environmental regulations will be overly lax, while if the median voter does not, then regulations will be too strict. Finally, local governments may quite obviously pursue goals other than maximizing the aggregate utility of their citizens.[59]

By varying the assumptions underlying the model of decentralized environmental regulatory competition, one can indeed generate anything from a race to the bottom - where local pollution regulations are too weak - to a race to the top - where local pollution regulations are too stringent.[60] Such a race-to-the-top could also lead to overregulation at local level which could equally create inefficiencies.[61] It has especially been David Vogel who has argued that a race-to-the-top could occur in environmental legislation as well. This would be the result of coalitions between environmental NGOs (favouring stringent environmental protection for ecological reasons) and industry groups in highly regulated countries (favouring stringent regulation to create barriers to entry).[62] Ogus argues that firms may benefit from being located in a high standard jurisdiction since this may generate technological improvements and thus competitive advantages; that may also explain a race-to-the-top.[63]

This theoretical ambiguity is somewhat unsatisfactory. The race-to-the-bottom has been an important argument used to justify federal environmental legislation both in the US and in Europe.[64] Legal scholars continue to debate whether the race to the bottom rationale justifies environmental regulatory federalization, with law and economics scholars tending to stress the benefits of competition between states or localities,[65] while other legal scholars continue tend to believe in the validity of the race-for-the-bottom rationale for centralization.[66] They also point in this context at the risk of a so-called 'regulatory chill', meaning that even if countries would not race to the bottom some country may decide not to introduce stringent environmental regulation which it otherwise would for fear that industry might otherwise move to a neighbouring pollution haven. Given the potential significance of the race to the bottom as a rationale for environmental regulatory centralization and as a normative guide for when such centralization is economically desirable, the theoretical ambiguity suggests looking to the empirical evidence on whether or not local,

59 Levinson 2003, p. 93-94.

60 See Wilson 1996; Markusen, Morey & Olewiler 1995, p. 55. See generally Wellisch 2000.

61 See Revesz 1997a, p. 1337 and see Revesz 1997b, p. 536-540.

62 See Vogel 1995. See also Vogel 2004.

63 Ogus 1999 and see Van den Bergh, Faure & Lefevere 1996, p. 141-142.

64 The argument was expressly raised by federal legislators during debate over the American Clean Air and Clean Water Acts, for example. See List & Gerking 2000, p. 453.

65 See Revesz 1992, p. 1210; Revesz 1996, p. 2341 and Revesz 2000, p. 37-79.

66 See Esty & Geradin 1997; Esty & Geradin 1998.

sub-national governments can indeed attract industry by setting lenient environmental standards.

3.2. *Empirical Evidence*

The race to the bottom is a normative story about the dangers of decentralized environmental regulation. But it is a normative story of which the key assumptions – the capital moves in response to variation in local environmental regulations, and that local regulators take such movements into account in setting regulations – demand empirical investigation.

The empirical evidence on the race to the bottom is inconclusive.[67] Jaffe *et al.* summarized the empirical literature as finding only that that the effects of environmental regulations are 'either small, statistically insignificant or not robust to tests of model specification'.[68] In their review, Jaffe et. al. suggested that the stringency of environmental regulations might have some effect on new firms in their decision to locate for the first time,[69] but would not induce existing firms to relocate.[70] They pointed out that other criteria such as tax levels, public services and the unionization of the labour force have a much more significant impact on the location decision than environmental regulation. Also many other studies have shown that pollution control costs are not major determinants of relocation[71] and that there is little evidence of a Pollution Haven Hypothesis. After all, if this pollution have hypothesis were correct one would have to see decreasing environmental quality in developing countries whereas to the contrary, major urban areas in China, Brazil and Mexico have all experienced significant improvements in air quality.[72]

Many economists remained somewhat sceptical of the empirical finding that environmental regulations were not a major determinant of industrial location,[73] and more recent empirical work shows that there is indeed an inverse relationship between the stringency of air quality regulations and the level of capital flows in pollution intensive industries.[74] The U.S. Clean Air Act distinguishes between relatively pristine 'attainment' areas and more heavily polluted non-attainment areas by imposing more stringent pollution standards on areas in non-attainment. Research found that even controlling for other observable factors that might influence capital movements, industrial plant growth is significantly higher in less

67 For an overview of the early empirical evidence see Engel 1997, p. 315-350, who argues that the empirical evidence shows a race-to-the-bottom, which is, however, denied by Revesz 1997.

68 Jaffe, Peterson, Portney & Stavins 1995, p. 157-158.

69 See Esty & Geradin 1998, p. 12-15.

70 See on the importance of distinguishing first location decisions from relocation decision List, McHone & Millimet 2003.

71 For a summary see Dasgupta *et al.* 2002, p. 159-160.

72 Dasgupta *et al.* 2002, p. 160-162.

73 For example, Xing & Kolstad 1995, argued that the laxity of environmental regulations in a host country is a significant determinant of foreign direct investment by the US chemical industry.

74 See Becker & Henderson 2000, p. 379; Greenstone 2002, p. 1175.

stringently regulated attainment areas than in non-attainment areas. Recent work (which allows for the fact that attainment status is endogenous with respect to plant location decisions, and carefully compares places that are similar in all respects except attainment status), finds an estimated cost to an area of being out of attainment with federal standards of between 0.7 and 1.3 new plants per year, a large percentage loss given that the average county in the sample studied gets only 0.4 new plants per year.[75] List, McHone and Millimet have also examined the effects of air quality regulation on the destination choice of relocating plants. Also that recent study shows that more stringent (air) pollution regulations play a critical role in the siting decision of relocating plants. Their results 'provide strong evidence that air quality regulations matter'.[76]

Levinson, however, argues that notwithstanding large differences between states in hazardous waste disposal taxes there has not been any pollution haven effect. He provides a variety of explanations, the most important one being that these state hazardous waste disposal taxes do not impose large employment losses on industries that generate waste.[77]

Other recent empirical work has tackled the problem of controlling for the full range of variables (besides just environmental regulatory stringency) that affect firm locational choice. Working with a more detailed dataset and again employing a propensity score matching estimator, Millimet and List[78] found that even at the very local (U.S. county) level, location-specific attributes such as unemployment levels and the overall level of manufacturing employment significantly impact the effect of environmental regulatory stringency. Millimet and List found that the cost of strict environmental regulations is lower both for counties with high unemployment - because they have relatively abundant, cheap labour - as well as for counties with a greater concentration of employment in manufacturing - because such counties generate agglomeration economies for manufacturing firms.

In sum, the new empirical literature on the 'race-to-the-bottom' has found that environmental regulations have statistically significant, large effects on industrial location,[79] effects that were previously either missed entirely or seriously underestimated.[80] However, it should be stressed that most of this empirical research focuses on competition between American states; the situation may be different in Europe where there is less evidence (at least as the old member states are concerned) of a 'race-to-the-bottom'.

Economists and political scientists have also investigated empirically another aspect of the race to the bottom story: whether American states do indeed compete

75 List, Millimet, Fredriksson & McHone 2003, p. 948.
76 List, McHone & Millimet 2003, p. 658.
77 Levinson 2000.
78 Millimet & List 2004, p. 239.
79 Levinson 2003, p. 96.
80 Results of a meta-analysis of literally hundreds of studies by Jeppesen, List & Folmer 2002, p. 21 show that the odd earlier results showing that the locational decisions of polluting and non-polluting industries were similarly influenced by environmental regulations may have been due to the failure of earlier studies to control for variables such as factor composition and mobility and lobbying power.

with one another in setting environmental standards. These scholars have exploited two very important features of American environmental 'cooperative federalism': 1) federal environmental statutes generally set minimum pollution standards that states are free to toughen further if they wish; and, 2) states may become 'authorized', to have the primary responsibility for implementing (in plant-specific permits), monitoring and enforcing federal environmental regulations. Thus while federalized, the American system nonetheless gives the states sufficient discretion in both standard-setting and enforcement so that sufficient state variation might be observed in these areas to permit useful empirical tests. Recent survey work does indeed indicate substantial variation in how states exercise their discretion in standard-setting as well as implementation, monitoring and enforcement.[81] While some state environmental policymakers report that they feel pressure from industry to refrain from going beyond federal standards and to be forgiving (or at least flexible) in their enforcement efforts,[82] other states have adopted more stringent air emission standards and conducted more monitoring than is federally required.[83] More systematic empirical work has found that variation in state environmental enforcement stringency reflects both political and economic factors at the state level, variation across states in what may be called the political benefits and costs of environmental regulation.[84]

As far as whether state environmental regulators are acting strategically, taking account of regulatory stringency in states with which they compete for capital and hence jobs, empirical research has found a positive relationship between environmental regulatory stringency (measured by normalized environmental abatement costs) in competitor states.[85] A recent study also finds a similarly strong positive relationship between the environmental enforcement efforts of competitor states, with a 10 per cent increase in a competitor state's enforcement efforts leading to between a 5 and 16 per cent increase in the own state's enforcement efforts.[86] Counter to the race to the bottom hypothesis, however, such interstate competition has been found to be symmetric: states respond to the regulatory behaviour of competitor states not just by lowering their enforcement efforts to match those states with weak enforcement, but also by increasing their enforcement efforts when competitor states strengthen theirs. Thus there is evidence that state environmental

81 There is also variation in whether states seek authorization to implement, monitor and enforce federal standards. Sigman 2003, p. 107 found, however, little evidence that state level variation on this dimension reflected anything systematic, other than perhaps the desire of large states (who often are not authorized) to free ride off federal enforcement efforts.

82 Davis & Davis 1999, p. 450; Engel 1997, p. 271.

83 Potoski 2001, p. 335.

84 Helland 1998a, p. 242; Helland 1998b, p. 305.

85 Fredriksson & Millimet 2002, p. 101; this finding in Fredriksson & Millimet was replicated by Levinson 2003.

86 Konisky 2008. Research by Gray & Shadbegian 2007 also found that the number of inspections at a plant, at nearby plants and at plants in the same state were associated with greater compliance, but that inspections at nearby plants in other states did not seem to increase compliance. This also seems to confirm a competition between states as far as enforcement activity is concerned.

regulators are sometimes racing to the top, and sometimes racing to the bottom. This once more underlines the importance of making a distinction between a (desirable, welfare enhancing) regulatory competition versus the (inefficient) race-for-the-bottom. The recent evidence presented here may show that states do indeed engage in regulatory competition, but are not necessarily proof of a race-for-the-bottom.[87]

Indeed, there is also evidence of races-to-the-top, aiming at strengthening the international competitiveness of domestic firms. Moreover, some other (competing) states may mimic the strict regulatory standards and the reason is that jurisdictions which have developed strict standards can force foreign producers to meet their domestic standards since otherwise market access may be denied. It would go beyond the scope of this chapter to discuss this phenomenon in detail. The best evidence probably comes from California where California used the possibility to enact stricter emission standards than the other states (thus the phenomenon is now referred to as the California Effect) whereby other states subsequently followed the California example.[88] Many more examples of this 'California Effect' exist which in fact leads to the opposite of a race-to-the-bottom, being the imposition of strict environmental standards which are subsequently exported.[89] 'California Effects' can in some cases also be found in the transatlantic relationship. These were basically situations whereby regulatory trade measures by the (then) EC have led to a strengthening of domestic regulatory standards in the US and Canada.[90] This once more shows that there is no straightforward answer on whether jurisdictions engage in a race-for-the-bottom or rather a race-for-the-top, since all depends on particular facts and circumstances.

Looking at the case of the European Union there also seems relatively little evidence that the traditional EU Member States were engaged in a race-to-the-bottom. Some high standard countries in Europe were rather involved in a race-to-the-top than in a race-to-the-bottom.[91] The case of the Directive on Integrated Pollution Prevention and Control[92] precisely proves that point: Northern European countries were strongly in favour of imposing strict emission standards (based on best available technologies) with which their industry presumably already could comply at the European level in order to create a 'level playing field'. Less developed Member States like Spain and Portugal were concerned over the potential costs to industry of having to use best available techniques as a result of the directive. The directive now clearly is to the advantage of industries in countries such as Germany, that already have strict facilities specific emission limits. They prevailed at the European level leading to a harmonization of European emission limit values. This *de facto* forces the foreign competitors in the South to follow the same strict regula-

87 See on this distinction between regulatory competition and the race-to-the-bottom also Esty 1996, p. 629-638.
88 See Vogel 2001, p. 336.
89 Vogel 2001, p. 336.
90 See on this issue extensively Princen 2002.
91 See Van den Bergh, Faure & Lefevere 1996, p. 141-142; Faure 2001, p. 272.
92 Council Directive (EC) 76/464 *OJ* 1976 L 129/23.

tion with which the industry in the North already complied.[93] This example shows that, as was indicated in the literature, a race-to-the-top can equally lead to inefficient results.

4. Eastern Europe

The enlargement of the European Union with new Member States in 2004 provides an interesting case for testing some hypothesis concerning the influence of environmental regulation on relocation of industries or trade flows. First the rather obvious point is made that by imposing very strict liabilities on purchasers of polluted land in Eastern Europe potential buyers can be deterred who will hence engage in liability avoidance techniques (4.1); next the question will be addressed whether the increased possibility to move capital to Eastern Europe after enlargement also led to an escape to pollution havens and if so, which consequences this may have for European environmental law generally (4.2).

4.1. *Increased Liability and Liability Avoidance*

An interesting effect of environmental liability was discovered in empirical research as a result of the enlargement of the European Union to Eastern Europe. Potential buyers of property in Central and Eastern Europe could be held liable, also retrospectively, for cleaning up sites that were contaminated in the past. Not surprisingly, research showed that this retrospective liability seriously limited the possibilities for privatization in those countries, since potential investors were scared away by the foresight of having to pay for the pollution of the past.[94] Other research also confirmed that limited information to investors regarding the extent of past environmental contamination (and the related clean-up costs) also reduced the investors' willingness to pay for a particular enterprise in a bid.[95]

This result is of course not surprising. It simply underlines the general point that polluting firms react to the costs imposed by regulatory measures. Imposing stricter liabilities (like in the case of Eastern Europe) upon polluters apparently comes at a price: the stricter the liability is (and hence the more costly) the more polluters may have incentives to avoid liability e.g. by not purchasing polluted sites and being held liable for pollution caused by others.

4.2. *EU Enlargement*[96]

The enlargement of the EU may provide a natural experiment testing alternative positive theories of environmental regulatory centralization. One's first thought might be that the addition of relatively less developed nations such as Slovakia and

93 See Faure 2010b.
94 Bluffstone & Panayotou 2000, p. 335-352.
95 Earnhart 2004, p. 97-122.
96 This builds further on Faure & Johnston 2009, p. 267-270.

Poland - countries with relatively cheap and abundant land, labour and other inputs to the production process - would heighten the protectionist motive for environmental regulatory centralization. But such a conjecture depends upon the implicit assumption that cheap resources would confer a competitive advantage upon firms based in countries such as Poland as they competed against firms based in wealthier, already industrialized countries such as Germany and France.

It is not yet clear whether such an assumption is correct. While it does seem as if capital is increasingly moving from older, developed EU countries into the new member states - thus threatening job loss and dislocation in the older, developed countries - it does not appear that there are actually new, competitive firms forming in the new, formerly communist nations. Capital mobility in Europe - in particular between eastern and western Europe - has increased spectacularly,[97] although the direction is certainly not always from west to east and the reason is mostly not environmental. There is, for example, the well-known phenomenon of increased labour migration from eastern European countries like Poland to western European countries like Belgium and the Netherlands[98] and there are equally some stories of western European companies moving to the east. Already before the enlargement, there were large foreign direct investments in eastern European countries.[99] After enlargement, this process has of course increased, and it takes a variety of forms, for example Dutch transport companies installing themselves in eastern Europe[100] and German chemical companies investing in eastern Europe. Indeed, western European firms (as well, of course, as American and Asian) firms are investing in new plants and facilities in the new EU nations.

The reasons as advanced by industry for this move towards eastern Europe are mostly related to lower taxes and labour costs. Average labour costs in the new member states' chemical industry are only 5 euro an hour as opposed to 27 euro in the EU 15.[101] However, it is equally reported that the run to EU membership already spurred investments in compliance technology with environmental regulations. Hence, a Deutsche Bank research report argues that the increase in environmental standards has proved a handicap for the chemical industry in eastern Europe, thus explaining the increased investments by German chemical industry in the new

97 And has very recently been further encouraged by Directive 2006/123 of 12 December 2006, which essentially establishes an individual right to provide services in any member state of the Union. See *OJ* L376/36 of 27 December 2006.

98 Workers from eastern Europe in Belgium are especially active in the building sector, which has led to concern about 'unfair competition' among trade unions in Belgium. See <http://www.eurofound.europa.eu/eiro/2005/09/feature/be0509303f.html>. Polish workers have started so many construction companies in the Netherlands that Polish officials are now complaining about a shortage on the labor market in Poland. See the remarks of the Polish Minister of Labour Migration at <http://www.elsevier.nl/nieuws/economie/artikel/asp/artnr/150315/rss/true/index.html>.

98 See Commission Staff Working Paper Document 2003.

99 Commission Staff Working Paper Document 2003.

100 <http://www.eunite.nl/main.php?lang=nl&id=1:114>.

101 < http://www.dbresearch.de/prod/dbr_internet_de-prod/prod0000000000183437.pdf>.

member states.[102] Such firms would have an incentive to favour environmental regulatory *decentralization,* so that they can take advantage of lax environmental standards in new and only recently developing member states. The question is whether enlargement has indeed lead to such a decentralized, weakening of standards. Such a weakening could occur either through formal exceptions granted by the EU Commission for the environmental acquis to new member states, or through lenient enforcement. There is however, little evidence of formal exceptions. In the Accession Treaty, there are usually some exceptions, but most of these relate to issues such as e.g. free movement, but not to environmental issues. The environmental acquis is therefore in principle applicable to new member states as well. Moreover, many new member states had a long transition period to adapt their legislation to EU norms before formal accession. Today, at least formal norms are not less stringent (as far as EU environmental law is concerned) in the east than in the west.

Leniency for new, eastern members could also arise in the field of enforcement. Work by Börzel as well as a survey on the implementation and enforcement of community environmental law in 2005 (published on 8 September 2006) shows that proceedings are equally instituted against old and new member states, both for non-communication infringements and for non-conformity infringements.[103] Remarkably, it appears to be the old member states (such as France and Italy) that lead the top as far as infringement proceedings are concerned. However, one always has to be careful with interpreting these numbers: even if there were formal implementation of EU environmental law in all new member states (which would explain why they are not confronted with more cases than against the EU 15), one has to keep in mind that the EU can merely control the formal implementation, i.e. whether national law complies with EU environmental directives. Whether in practice the legislation implementing EU environmental law is also effectively enforced is much harder for the EU Commission to control. It is also harder to measure: indeed, a crucial question is the extent to which there is actual uniformity in the national *enforcement* of EC environmental directives that have been formally implemented in national law.

A large problem for the European Union is that Member States could indeed formally meet the administrative duties corresponding with the implementation obligation, but could consequently still benefit their national industry by being weak on enforcement. Since Europe lacks a European environmental agency with enforcement powers to control actual enforcement within the Member States this has been a major source of worry. Case law of the European Court of Justice has developed in such a way that Member States are obliged not only to implement European environmental directives, but also to guarantee the enforcement of the national legislation implementing the directives. The Court for example holds that sanctions in case of a violation of implementing legislation should at least be

102 *Ibidem.*
103 See Borzel 2006, p. 1143.

'effective, dissuasive and proportional'.[104] Case law of the ECJ has also held that a lack of effective prosecution against violators of implementing legislation can be considered as a violation of European law.[105] Precisely in order to remedy this enforcement deficit a Directive 2008/99 was adopted on 19 November 2008 on the protection of the environment through criminal law.[106] This directive had to be implemented in Member States legislation before 26 December 2010.[107] This directive hence forces Member States to improve compliance with the laws for the protection of the environment by making criminal penalties available.[108] Member States are forced to punish violations of national legislation implementing European environmental law by 'effective, proportionate and dissuasive criminal penalties'.[109] The goal of these judicial and legislative actions at European level is obviously to ensure that Member States not only on paper introduce European environmental law (and hence harmonize environmental standards), but that they also enforce these obligations against violators. Even though these measures may help the problem remains that some Member States wishing to favour their own national industry may still have possibilities to do so by formally implementing European environmental law (with criminal sanctions) but by remaining weak on the enforcement side.

In sum, the enlargement of the EU brings about important changes in incentives of industry to lobby in favour of (de)centralization. The enlargement of the EU creates a situation where incentives of industry to lobby in favour of protectionist environmental standards at EU level is basically absent. Now that industrialized European nations have the possibility to export activities (and hence presumably pollution) to the new EU nations one can expect less lobbying in favour of real environmental regulatory centralization (uniform standards that are actually implemented and enforced uniformally). Western industry being active in the East may well benefit from lax environmental standards (and/or enforcement) in the new Central and Eastern European Member States.

5. Concluding Remarks

The relationship between environmental law and the legal origins literature, central to this book, is a peculiar one. The original interest of the literature was not so much whether environmental law contributes to economic growth, but rather the reverse, whether economic growth should (as one can probably presume) necessarily be the enemy of environmental protection. Economic literature found a relationship between income and environmental quality whereby increasing income per capita would first lead to increasing pollution levels, but later, after reaching a turning

104 See ECJ 21 September 1989, Case C-68/88 (Greek corn).

105 ECJ 9 December 1997, Case C-265/95 (Spanish strawberries). See further on this case law Faure 2004.

106 *OJ* L 328/28 of 6 December 2008.

107 Art. 8(1) of Directive 2008/99.

108 See for a brief summary of this directive see Faure 2011.

109 See further on the interpretation of these notions Faure 2010a.

point, lead to decreasing pollution levels. This literature, which became known as the Environmental Kuznets Curve became very popular at the policy level and led economists, but especially policy-makers to enthusiastically state that all developing countries needed to worry about was increasing income levels. The EKC showed that improved environmental quality would automatically follow.

This simplistic version of the EKC literature has given rise to much criticism. The most important one is that there may be a correlation between per capita income levels and environmental quality; the causality, explaining this relationship is still a totally different story. Later studies distinguished between scale effects (more economic development leading to more industrialization and more pollution) and technology effects (increased economic development leading to better abilities of pollution abatement). Moreover, later studies also refined the EKC by showing that the EKC relationship could be proven for particular local pollutants, but not for pollutants having a more global effect like CO_2 emissions.

The most important criticism came from empirical studies showing that environmental quality did also crucially depend upon the quality of environmental regulation, conforming the hypothesis that institutions play an important role, not only for economic growth but also for improving environmental quality. Hence, the later literature showed, with empirical support, that those low income countries that enact effective environmental policies are able to increase environmental quality in a positive way and could thus reach the turning point (where increased per capita income leads to increased environmental quality) faster than countries that don't. In other words, there is no automatism in the relationship between per capita income and environmental quality; environmental law does matter.

The literature equally indicated that an effect of increasing income levels in developed countries is that polluting activities may be exported to developing countries, thus leading to 'environmental dumping' or an escape to pollution havens. The theoretical conditions for such a Pollution Haven Hypothesis are highly debated. Some argue that industry will indeed escape to low environmental standard jurisdictions since states will engage in a race-to-the-bottom in order to attract industry with lax environmental regulations. Others, however, argue that if conditions and assumptions would change, the reverse may be the case since states could also benefit from strict environmental law, e.g. by improving their competitive position through technological innovation. Under that hypothesis a regulatory competition would rather lead to a race-to-the-top. Both hypotheses have had supporters and opponents in legal and economic scholarship since the race-to-the-bottom argument has often been used to justify centralization in federal systems such as Europe or the US. Empirical evidence of a race-to-the-bottom seems to be relatively weak. Earlier studies indicated that given high relocation costs firms will not relocate to a pollution haven also because costs of pollution abatement are only a relatively small portion of total production costs. More recent empirical evidence from the US sheds a somewhat different light and shows that differences in pollution abatement costs between states may be substantial. Moreover, even though relocation to a pollution haven may not be realistic pollution control costs could influence the *ex ante* decision of industry on choosing an appropriate location.

Regulatory competition could not only lead to a race-to-the-bottom but, under different circumstances, also to a race-to-the-top, of which also evidence exists. Hence, the evidence seems to indicate that jurisdictions do (to some extent) indeed engage in a regulatory competition, but that this is not under all circumstances inefficient and may therefore not under all circumstances justify centralization of environmental standards.

The case of Eastern Europe shows how incentives of industry can play an important role in the choice for centralization or for environmental federalism. European industry located in developed (and polluted) Member States (situated in the North) may originally have had incentives to lobby in favour of centralization of environmental standards. There is much evidence of such a race-for-the-top whereby standards with which industry in the North already had to comply were (via European directives) also forced upon Southern competitors, thus raising barriers to market entry. However, with the opening of Eastern Europe industry could move capital and benefit from lower standards or less enforcement which may thus explain their incentives to now rather lobby in favour of decentralization or at least lax enforcement in the new Member States.

Bibliography

Arrow *et al.* 1995
Arrow, K. *et al.*, 'Economic Growth, Carrying Capacity and the Environment', *Ecological Economics*, 1995, p. 91-95 (reprint from *Science*, Vol. 268, p. 520-521).

Ayres 1995
Ayres, R.U., 'Economic Growth: Politically necessary but not environmentally friendly', *Ecological Economics*, 1995, p. 97-99.

Barbier 1997
Barbier, E.B., 'Introduction to the Environmental Kuznets-curve Special Issue', *Environment and Development Economics*, 1997, p. 357-367.

Becker & Henderson 2000
Becker, R. & Henderson, J.V., 'Effects of Air Quality Regulations on Polluting Industries', *Journal of Political Economy*, 2000, p. 379-421.

Beckerman 1992
Beckerman, W., 'Economic Growth and the Environment: Whose Growth? Whose Environment?', *World Development*, 1992, p. 481-496.

Binder & Neumayer 2005
Binder, S. & Neumayer, E., 'Environmental Pressure Group Strength and Air Pollution: an Empirical Analysis', *Ecological Economics*, 2005, p. 527-538.

Bluffstone & Panayotou 2000
Bluffstone, R.A. & Panayotou, T., 'Environmental Liability and Privatisation in Central and Eastern Europe: Towards an Optimal Policy', *Environmental & Resource Economics*, 2000, p. 335-352.

Borzel 2003
Borzel, T., *Environmental Leaders and Laggards in Europe, Environmental Leaders and Laggards in Europe: Why There Is (Not) a 'Southern Problem'* (Ashgate Studies in Environmental Policy and Practice), Aldershot: Ashgate Publishers, 2003.

Cole, Rayner & Bares 2007
Cole, M.A., Rayner, A.J. & Bares, J.M., 'The Environmental Kuznets Curve: An Empirical Analysis', *Environment and Development Economics*, 2007, p. 433-450.

Commission Staff Working Document 2003
Commission Staff Working Paper, *Impact of Enlargement on Industry*, SEC (2003), 234, 24 (2003), Strasbourg: Council of Europe Publishing,

EU Commission Staff Working Document 2006
EU Commission Staff Working Document, *7th annual survey on the implementation and enforcement of community environmental law 2005*, SEC (2006), 1143, (2006), Strasbourg: Council of Europe Publishing, 2006.

Dasgupta *et al.* 2002
Dasgupta, S., Laplante, B., Wang, H. & Wheeler, D., 'Confronting the Environmental Kuznets Curve', *Journal of Economic Perspectives*, 2002, p. 147-168.

Davis & Davis 1999
Davis, CH. & Davis, S.K., 'State Enforcement of the Federal Hazardous Waste Program', *Polity*, 1999, p. 451-468.

De Bruyn 1997
De Bruyn, S.M., 'Explaining the Environmental Kuznets Curve: Structural Change and International Agreements in Reducing Sulphur Emissions', *Environment and Development Economics*, 1997, p. 485-503.

Earnhart 2004
Earnhart, D., 'Liability for Past Environmental Contamination and Privatisation', *Environmental & Resource Economics*, 2004, p. 97-122.

Engel 1997
Engel, K.H., 'State Environmental Standard Setting: Is there a "Race" and is it "to the Bottom"?', *Hastings Law Journal*, 1997, p. 271-398.

Esty 1996
Esty, D.C., 'Revitalising Environmental Federalism', *Michigan Law Review*, 1996, p. 570-653.

Esty & Geradin 1997
Esty, D.C. & Geradin, D., 'Market Access, Competitiveness and Harmonisation: Environmental Protection in Regional Trade Agreements', *Harvard Environmental Law Review*, 1997, p. 265-336.

Esty & Geradin 1998
Esty, D.C. & Geradin, D., 'Environmental Protection and International Competitiveness: A Conceptual Framework', *Journal of World Trade*, 1998, p. 5-46.

Esty & Porter 1998
Esty, D.C. & Porter, M.E., 'Industrial Ecology and Competitiveness', *Journal of Industrial Ecology*, 1998, p. 35-43.

Esty & Porter 2000
Esty, D.C. & Porter, M.E., 'Measuring National Environmental Performance and its Determinance', in: M.E. Porter & J. Sachs (eds.), *The Global Competitiveness Report 2000*, New York: Oxford University Press, 2000, p. 60-75.

Esty & Porter 2005
Esty, D.C. & Porter, M.E., 'National Environmental Performance: an Empirical Analysis of Policy Results and Determinants', *Environment and Development Economics*, 2005, p. 391-434.

Faure 2001
Faure, M., 'Regulatory Competition vs Harmonisation in EU Environmental Law', in: D.C. Esty & D. Geradin (eds.), *Regulatory Competition and Economic Integration*, Oxford: Oxford University Press, 2001, p. 263-286.

Faure 2004
Faure, M., 'A European Environmental Criminal Law: Do we really need it?', *European Environmental Law Review*, 2004, p. 18-29.

Faure 2010a
Faure, M.G., 'Effective, Proportional and Dissuasive Penalties in the Implementation of the Environmental Crime and Ship Source Pollution Directive: Questions and Challenges', *European Energy and Environmental Law Review*, 2010, p. 256-278.

Faure 2010b
Faure, M.G., 'Optimal specificity in environmental standard-setting', in: C. Dias Soares, J.E. Milne, H. Ashiabor, L. Kreiser & K. Deketelaere (eds.), *Critical Issues in Environmental Taxation. International and Comparative Perspectives*, Vol. III, Oxford: Oxford University Press, 2010, p. 730-745.

Faure 2011
Faure, M.G., 'The Environmental Crime Directive 2008/99/EC', *European Journal of Consumer Law*, 2011, p. 193-208.

Faure 2012
Faure, M., 'Effectiveness of Environmental Law: What does the Evidence tell us?', *Georgetown International Environmental Law Review*, 2012 (forthcoming).

Faure & Johnston 2009
Faure, M. & Johnston, J.S., 'The Law and Economics of Environmental Federalism: Europe and the United States Compared', *Virginia Environmental Law Journal*, 2009, p. 205-274.

Faure, Goodwin & Weber 2010
Faure, M., Goodwin, M. & Weber, F., 'Bucking the Kuznets Curve: Designing Effective Environmental Regulation in Developing Countries', *Virginia Journal of International Law*, 2010, p. 95-156.

Fredriksson & Millimet 2002
Fredriksson, P.G. & Millimet, D.L., 'Strategic Interaction and the Determinants of Environmental Policy Across U.S. States', *Journal of Urban Economics*, 2002, p. 101-122.

Granja e Barros, Mendonça & Nogueira 2002
Granja e Barros, F., Mendonça, A.F. & Nogueira, J.M., *Poverty and Environmental Degradation: The Kuznets Environmental Curve for the Brazilian Case*, Universidade de Brazilia, Departemento de Economica, Working Paper 267, December 2002.

Gray & Shadbegian 2007
Gray, W.B. & Shadbegian, R.J., 'The Environmental Performance of Polluting Plants: A Special Analysis', *Journal of Regional Science*, 2007, p. 63-84.

Greenstone 2002
Greenstone, M., 'The Impacts of Environmental Regulations on Industrial Activity: Evidence from the 1970 and 1977 Clean Air Act Amendments and the Census of Manufacturers', *Journal of Political Economy*, 2002, p. 1175-1219.

Grossman & Krueger 1993
Grossman, G.M. & Krueger, A.B., 'Environmental Impacts of a North-American Free Trade Agreement', in: P.M. Garber (ed.), *The US, Mexico Free Trade Agreement*, Cambridge: MIT Press, 1993, p. 13-56.

Grossman & Krueger 1995
Grossman, G.M. & Krueger, A.B., 'Economic Growth and the Environment', *Quarterly Journal of Economics*, 1995, p. 353-377.

Helland 1998a
Helland, E., 'The Revealed Preferences of State EPA's: Stringency, Enforcement and Substitution', *Journal of Environmental Economics and Management*, 1998, p. 242-261.

Helland 1998b
Helland, E., 'Environmental Protection in the Federalist System: The Political Economy of NPDES Inspections', *Economic Inquiry*, 1998, p. 305–319.

Hettige, Lucas & Wheeler 1992
Hettige, H., Lucas, R.E.B. & Wheeler, D., 'The Toxic Intensity of Industrial Production: Global Patterns, Trends and Trade Policy', *American Economic Review*, 1992, p. 478-481.

Holtz-Eakin & Selden 1995
Holtz-Eakin, D. & Selden, T.M., 'Stoking the Fires? CO_2 Emissions and Economic Growth', *Journal of Public Economics*, 1995, p. 85-101.

Jaffe, Peterson, Portney & Stavins 1995
Jaffe, A., Peterson, St., Portney, P. & Stavins, R., 'Environmental Regulation and the Competitiveness of US Manufacturing: What Does the Evidence Tell Us?', *Journal of Economic Literature*, 1995, p. 132-163.

Jeppesen, List & Folmer 2002
Jeppesen, T., List, J.A. & Folmer, H., 'Environmental Regulations and New Plant Location Decisions: Evidence from a Meta-Analysis', *Journal of Regional Science*, 2002, p. 19-49.

Konisky 2008
Konisky, D.M., 'Regulatory Competition and Environmental Enforcement: Is There a Race to the Bottom?', *American Journal of Political Science*, 2008, p. 853–872.

Kuznets 1995
Kuznets, S., 'Economic Growth and Income Inequality', *American Economic Review*, 1955, p. 1-28.

La Porta, Lopez de Silanes & Schleifer 2008
La Porta, R., Lopez de Silanes, F. & Schleifer, A., 'The Economic Consequences of Legal Origins', *Journal of Economic Literature*, 2008, p. 285-332.

La Porta *et al.* 1998
La Porta, R., Lopez de Silanes, F., Schleifer, A. & Visny, R., 'Law and Finance', *Journal of Political Economy*, 1998, p. 1113-1155.

Levinson 2000
Levinson, A., 'The Missing Pollution Haven Effect', *Environmental and Resource Economics*, 2000, p. 343-364.

Levinson 2003
Levinson, A., 'Environmental Regulatory Competition: A Status Report and Some New Evidence', *National Tax Journal*, 2003, p. 91-106.

List & Gallet 1999
List, J.A. & Gallet, C.A., 'The Environmental Kuznets Curve: Does one Size fit all?', *Ecological Economics*, 1999, p. 409-424.

List & Gerking 2000
List, J.A. & Gerking, S., 'Regulatory Federalism and U.S. Environmental Policies', *Journal of Regional Science*, 2000, p. 453-471.

List, McHone & Millimet 2003
List, J.A., McHone, W.W. & Millimet, D.L., 'Effects of Air Quality Regulation on the Destination Choice of Relocating Plants', *Oxford Economic Papers*, 2003, p. 657-678.

List *et al.* 2003
List, J.A., Millimet, D.L., Fredriksson, P.G. & McHone, W.W., 'Effects of Environmental Reguilations on Manufacturing Plant Births: Evidence from a Propensity Score Matching Estimator', *Review of Economics and Statistics*, 2003, p. 944-952.

Managi & Jena 2008
Managi, S. & Jena, P.R., 'Environmental Productivity and Kuznets Curve in India', *Ecological Economics*, 2008, p. 432-440.

Markusen, Morey & Olewiler 1995
Markusen, J., Morey, E. & Olewiler, N., 'Noncooperative Equilibria in Regional Environmental Policies When Plant Locations are Endogenous', *Journal of Public Economics*, 1995, p. 55-77.

McAllister, Van Rooij & Kagan 2010
McAllister, L.K., Van Rooij, B. & Kagan, R.A., 'Re-orienting Regulation: Pollution Enforcement in Industrialising Countries', *Law & Policy*, 2010, p. 1-13.

Millimet & List 2004
Millimet, D.L. & List, J.A., 'The Case of the Missing Pollution Haven Hypothesis', *Journal of Regulatory Economics*, 2004, p. 239-262.

Millimet, List & Stengos 2003
Millimet, D.L., List, J.A. & Stengos, Th., 'The Environmental Kuznets Curve: Real Progress or Misspecified Models?', *The Review of Economics and Statistics*, 2003, p. 1038-1047.

Moomaw & Unruh 1997
Moomaw, W.R. & Unruh, G.C., 'Are Environmental Kuznets Curves misleading us? The Case of CO_2 emissions', *Environment and Development Economics*, 1997, p. 451-463.

Nahman & Antrobus 2005
Nahman, A. & Antrobus, G., 'Trade and the Environmental Kuznets Curve: Is Southern Africa a Pollution Haven?', *South African Journal of Economics*, 2005, p. 803-814.

North 1981
North, D.C., *Structure and Change in Economic History*, New York: W.W. Norton and Co., 1981.

North 1990
North, D.C., *Institutions, Institutional Change and Economic Performance*, New York: Cambridge University Press, 1990.

Oates 1972
Oates, W.E., *Fiscal Federalism*, New York: Harcourt Brace Jovanovich, 1972.

Oates & Schwab 1988
Oates, W.E. & Schwab, R.M., 'Economic Competition Among Jurisdictions: Efficiency Enhancing or Distortion Inducing?', *Journal of Public Economics*, 1988, p. 333-354.

Ogus 1999
Ogus, A.I., 'Competition between National Legal Systems: A Contribution of Economic Analysis to Comparative Law', *International and Comparative Law Quarterly*, 1999, p. 405-418.

Panayotou 1995
Panayotou, T., 'Environmental Degradation at Different Stages of Economic Development', in: I. Ahmend & J.A. Doeleman (eds.), *Beyond Rio: The Environmental Crisis and Sustainable Livelihoods in the Third World*, London: MacMillan, 1995, p. 13-36.

Panayotou 1997
Panayotou, T., 'Demystifying the Environmental Kuznets Curve: Turning a Black Box into a Policy Tool', *Environment and Development Economics*, 1997, p. 465-484.

Perman & Stern 2003
Perman, R. & Stern, D.L., 'Evidence from Penal Unit Root and Co-integration Tests that the Environmental Kuznets Curve does not exist', *Australian Journal of Agriculture and Resource Economics*, 2003, p. 325-347.

Porter & Vanderlinde 1995
Porter, M.E. & Vanderlinde, C., 'Towards a New Conception of the Environment – Competitiveness, Relationship', *The Journal of Economic Perspectives*, 1995, p. 97-118.

Potoski 2001
Potoski, M., 'Clean Air Federalism: Do States Race to the Bottom?', *Public Administration Review*, 2001, p. 335–343.

Princen 2002
Princen, S.B.M., *The California Effect in the Transatlantic Relationship*, diss. University Utrecht, 2002, unpublished.

Revesz 1992
Revesz, R.L., 'Rehabilitating Interstate Competition: Rethinking the Race-for-the-bottom Rationale for Federal Environmental Regulation', *New York University Law Review*, 1992, p. 1210-1254.

Revesz 1996
Revesz, R., 'Federalism and Interstate Environmental Externalities', *University of Pennsylvania Law Review*, 1996, p. 2341-2416.

Revesz 1997a
Revesz, R.L., 'Federalism and Environmental Regulation: Lessons for the European Union and the International Community', *Virginia Law Review*, 1997, p. 1331-1346.

Revesz 1997b
Revesz, R.L., 'The Race-to-the-Bottom and Federal Environmental Regulation: A Response to Critics', *Minnesota Law Review*, 1997, p. 535-564.

Revesz 2000
Revesz, R.L., 'Federalism and Environmental Regulation: an Overview', in: R.L. Revesz, Ph. Sands & R.B. Stewart (eds.), *Environmental Law, the Economy and Sustainable Development*, Cambridge: Cambridge University Press, 2000, p. 37-79.

Rock 1996
Rock, M., 'Pollution Intensity of GDP and Trade Policy: Can the World Bank be wrong?', *World Development*, 1996, p. 471-179.

Selden & Song 1994
Selden, T.M. & Song, D., 'Environmental Quality and Development: Is there a Kuznets Curve for Air Pollution?', *Journal of Environmental Economics and Management*, 1994, p. 147-162.

Selden & Song 1995
Selden, Th.M. & Song, D., 'Neoclassical Growth, the J-curve for Abatement, and the Inverted U-curve for Pollution', *Journal of Environmental Economics and Management*, 1995, p. 162-168.

Shafik 1994
Shafik, N., 'Economic Development and Environmental Quality: An Econometric Analysis', *Oxford Economic Papers*, 1994, p. 757-773.

Shafik & Bandyopadhyay 1992
Shafik, N. & Bandyopadhyay, S., *Economic Growth and Environmental Quality: Time Series and Cross-country Evidence*, Background paper for the World Bank 1992.

Shen & Hashimoto 2004
Shen, J. & Hashimoto, Y., *Environmental Kuznets Curve on Country Level: Evidence from China*, Graduate School of Economics and Osaka School of International Public Policy, discussion papers in Economics and Business, May 2004 (paper 04-09).

Sigman 2003
Sigman, H., 'Letting States do the Dirty Work: State Responsibility for Federal Environmental Regulation', *National Tax Journal*, 2003, p. 107-122.

Stern 1998
Stern, D.L., 'Progress on the Environmental Kuznets-curve?', *Environment and Development Economics*, 1998, p. 173-196.

Stern 2002
Stern, D.L., 'Explaining Changes in Global Sulphur Emissions: An Econometric Decomposition Approach', *Ecological Economics*, 2002, p. 201-220.

Stern & Common 2001
Stern, D.L. & Common, M.S., 'Is there an Environmental Kuznets Curve for Sulfur?', *Journal of Environmental Economics and Management*, 2001, p. 162-178.

Stern, Common & Barbier 1996
Stern, D.L., Common, M.S. & Barbier, E.B., 'Economic Growth and Environmental Degradation: The Environmental Kuznets Curve and Sustainable Development', *World Development*, 1996, p. 1151-1160.

Strand 2002
Strand, J., *Environmental Kuznets Curves: Empirical Relationships between Environmental Quality and Economic Development*, March 2002, Memorandum No. 04/2002, Department of Economics, University of Oslo (<http://www.oekonomi.uio.no/memo>).

Torras & Boyce 1998
Torras, M. & Boyce, J.K., 'Income, Inequality, and Pollution: A Reassessment of the Environmental Kuznets Curve', *Ecological Economics*, 1998, p. 147-160.

Van den Bergh, Faure & Lefevere 1996
Van den Bergh, R., Faure, M. & Lefevere, J., 'The Subsidiarity Principle in European Environmental Law: An Economic Analysis', in: Eide, E. & Van den Bergh, R. (eds.), *Law and Economics of the Environment*, Oslo: Juridisk Forlag, 1996, p. 121-166.

Vincent 1997
Vincent, J.R., 'Testing for Environmental Kuznets Curve within a Developing Country', *Environment and Development Economics*, 1997, p. 417-431.

Vogel 1995
Vogel, D., *Trading up: Consumer and Environmental Regulation in a Global Economy*, Cambridge: Harvard University Press, 1995.

Vogel 2001
Vogel, D., 'Environmental Regulation and Economic Integration', in: D.C. Esty & D. Geradin (eds.), *Regulatory Competition and Economic Integration. Comparative Perspectives*, Oxford: Oxford University Press, 2001, p. 330-347.

Vogel 2004
Vogel, D., 'Trade and the Environment in the Global Economy', in: N.J. Vig & M.G. Faure (eds.), *Green Giants? Environmental Policies of the United States and the European Union*, Cambridge: MIT Press, 2004, p. 231-252.

Wellisch 2000
Wellisch, D., *Theory of Public Finance in a Federal State*, Cambridge: Cambridge University Press, 2000.

Wilson 1996
Wilson, J.D., 'Capital Mobility and Environmental Standards: Is there a Race to the Bottom?', in: J. Bhagwati & R.P. Hudec (eds.), *Fair Trade and Harmonization: Prerequisites for Free Trade*, Cambridge, Mass.: MIT Press, 1996, p. 393-427.

Xing & Kolstad 1995
Xing, Y. & Kolstad, Ch.D., 'Do Lax Environmental Regulations Attract Foreign Investment?', *Environmental and Resource Economics*, 1995, p. 1-22.

A peer-reviewed book series in which the common foundations of the legal systems of the Member States of the European Community are the central focus.

The *Ius Commune Europaeum* series includes horizontal comparative legal studies as well as studies on the effect of treaties within the national legal systems. All the classic fields of law are covered. The books are published in various European languages under the auspices of METRO, the Institute for Transnational Legal Research at the Maastricht University.

Recently published:

Volume 87: *Effective Criminal Defence in Europe,* Z. NAMORADZE, R. SMITH, T. SPRONKEN AND E. CAPE (eds.)
Volume 88: *Conflict of Laws and Laws of Conflict in Europe and Beyond. Patterns of Supranational and Transnational Juridification,* R. NICKEL (ed.)
Volume 89: *The Regulation of Architects in Belgium and the Netherlands. A Comparative Analysis,* S. SCHOENMAEKERS
Volume 90: *Evolutie van de basisbeginselen van het contractenrecht,* I. SAMOY (red.)
Volume 91: *Recidive in België en Nederland. Een analyse van 200 jaar rechtspraak en rechtsleer,* M. DAMS
Volume 92: *An EU-wide Letter of Rights. Towards Best Practice,* T. SPRONKEN (ed.)
Volume 93: *The Costanzo Obligation. The Obligations of National Administrative Authorities in the Case of Incompatibility between National Law and European Law,* M. VERHOEVEN
Volume 94: *The Effect of a Change of Circumstances on the Binding Force of Contracts. Comparative Perspectives,* R. MOMBERG URIBE
Volume 95: *The Landscape of the Legal Professions in Europe and the USA: Continuity and Change,* A. UZELAC and C.H. VAN RHEE (eds.)
Volume 96: *Constitutional Constraints on Ad Hoc Legislation. A Comparative Study of the United States, Germany and the Netherlands,* A. JASIAK
Volume 97: *The Social Security Position of Irregular Migrant Workers. New Insights from National Security Law and International Law,* K. KAPUY
Volume 98: *Educating European Lawyers,* A.W. HERINGA and B. AKKERMANS (eds.)
Volume 99: *The Draft Common Frame of Reference: A National and Comparative Perspective,* E. TERRYN, V. SAGAERT and M.E. STORME (eds.)

www.ingramcontent.com/pod-product-compliance
Ingram Content Group UK Ltd.
Pitfield, Milton Keynes, MK11 3LW, UK
UKHW051925100926
8556IPUK00022B/1376

9 789400 002173